Global Swap Markets

Global Swap Markets

Edited by
Satyajit Das

IFR Publishing Ltd

IFR Publishing Ltd, South Quay Plaza II, 183 Marsh Wall, London E14 9FU

British Library Cataloguing in Publication Data
The Global swap markets
1. Financial Markets
I. Das, Satyajit
332.1

ISBN 1 873446 10 1

Printed by Total Graphics Ltd, Edmonton, London N18

Acknowledgements

This book was assembled in the period 1990/91. As with any undertaking of this magnitude, the project involved the participation of a wide variety of people who contributed in various ways to the completed text.

First, I would like to thank the individual contributors to the book whose participation and cooperation ensured the high quality of the end product.

I am grateful to the publishers, IFR Publishing Ltd, who were supportive and enthusiastic about this project from its inception. I would like to thank Andrea Hartill (who initiated the project), Anne O'Brien, who supervised the project and Ellen Parcell, who cheerfully and dedicatedly steered the book through its various phases to completion.

I would like to thank Sharon Williams, my secretary, for her assistance in the preparation of portions of the manuscript for publication.

Last, but by no means least, my thanks go to my family for their support and encouragement throughout this project. I would like to thank my parents Sukumar and Aparna Das and my friend Jade Novakovic whose enduring support and patience made this book possible.

Satyajit Das
Sydney Australia, March 1991

Contents

Editor's notes

Satyajit Das[1]

The global swap market has established itself as one of the most significant developments in capital markets in the 1980s. In the 1990s, it promises to continue its growth both in size and market innovation.

Global Swap Markets is a successor to *Inside the Swap Market* which was originally published in 1985 to provide *practical* information on the emerging swap markets for experienced practitioners and laypersons alike. Through subsequent editions in 1986 and 1988, *Inside the Swap Market* continued to provide up-to-date information and commentary on the global swap market and its development.

In August 1989, in recognition of the maturation of the market for swaps and swap derivative products, IFR Publishing Ltd and its Australian associate, the Law Book Company Ltd jointly published *Swap Financing* which was designed to be an authoritative reference work on the global swap markets.

The positive response to the publication of *Swap Financing* and the rapid pace of financial innovation has prompted publication of *Global Swap Markets* which replaces previous editions of *Inside the Swap Market*. In recognition of the changes in the swap market, *Global Swap Markets* is significantly different from its precursors.

The book focuses upon:

(1) The provision of up-to-date information and commentary on recent developments in swap financing, including coverage of:

- ❒ developments in swap markets in individual currencies, including swap derivative markets (such as the global FRA and cap/collar markets);
- ❒ information on and analysis of swap financing product innovations and applications;
- ❒ developments in the regulatory environments impacting upon the swap markets;
- ❒ evolving legal, accounting and taxation frameworks in key jurisdictions within which swap transactions are undertaken.

(2) Essays and perspectives on various aspects of the swap market from a variety of market participants.

(3) Selected case studies.

In its new format, *Global Swap Markets* is designed to complement other IFR Publications such as *Swap Financing* and *International Financing Review*, which provides a weekly commentary on swap transactions.

Part I begins with an essay on the current state of the global swap markets (Chapter 1). Chapter 2 then provides an update of the size of the markets, based on ISDA survey data.

The remainder of Part I focuses on recent developments in individual swap markets. Chapters 3–13 provides coverage for markets in US dollars, Canadian dollars, sterling, Deutsche marks, Dutch guilders, Swiss francs, European Currency Units, Spanish pesetas, French francs, Italian lira, Swedish kronor, Danish krone, Japanese yen, Australian and New Zealand dollars and Hong Kong dollars. A special focus in this section is the inclusion of information on emerging swap markets in a variety of minor currencies such as swap markets in Hong Kong dollars, French francs, Italian lira, the Scandinavian currencies and Spanish pesetas.

Updates on recent developments in the market for swap derivatives such as caps, floors and collars, forward-rate agreements as well as the asset swap market are included in Chapters 14–16.

Part II examines developments in swap financing products and applications. The focus on applications is in two distinct areas. First, swap-driven primary issuance (Chapter 17) and secondly, the utilisation of swaps in combination with other derivative products to manage liability portfolios (Chapter 18).

A variety of new and innovative swap financing products are examined and analysed, such as arrears reset swaps (Chapter 19), spreadlocks (Chapter 20), swap/option combinations/variations on existing swaps (Chapter 21) and oil and commodity swaps (Chapter 22).

Part III sets out a series of case studies, focusing on actual transactions designed to bring together theory and practice.

In Chapter 23, the evolution of the market for new issue arbitrage to raise cheaper and more cost effective funding is analysed from the perspective of the Swedish Export Credit Agency (SEK), one of the foremost users of the swap markets. A case study of a new swap issue seen from the perspective of an investment bank involved in arranging transactions is set out in Chapter 24.

The intricacies of swapping a Nikkei indexed-linked issue and an Australian dollar/Japanese yen dual currency bond issue are analysed in

Chapters 25 and 26, respectively. The use of swap instruments from a variety of perspectives is considered in the next three chapters: swaptions (Chapter 27); forward currency swaps (Chapter 28); and commodity swaps (Chapter 29).

Part IV consists of a series of essays designed to provide an insight into a particular aspect of swap market activity.

In Chapter 30, an interesting technique for displaying and hedging the market risk of a swap within swap portfolios is analysed. The problem of hedging the floating risk component of an interest rate portfolio is considered in detail from a risk management viewpoint in Chapter 31.

Chapter 32 analyses the use of swaps from the perspective of a bank treasury, while Chapter 33 examines the valuation issues related to the purchase by one financial institution of the swap portfolios of another financial institution — likely to be an increasing part of market activity in the future.

Chapter 34 discusses the software available for swap back office systems.

Part V examines the evolving regulatory environment within which the swap markets operate. The first four chapters look at the various regulatory aspects:

- the Bank for International Settlements' (BIS) capital adequacy requirements and its impact on the swap markets (Chapter 35);
- one aspect of market reaction to the BIS capital adequacy requirements, namely the development of netting agreements and the potential development of a swap market clearing house (Chapter 36);
- counterparty risk management issues, in particular, the impact of the UK Councils' case on the operation of the global swap markets (Chapters 37 and 38).

Chapters 39–41 focus on the developments in legal and documentary issues, and in accounting and taxation treatment of swap and swap derivative transactions. The analysis in these chapters is on developments in a variety of jurisdictions within which swap transactions are undertaken.

Each chapter has been written by a practitioner with both a sound theoretical and practical knowledge of the issues affecting the global swap markets. The emphasis is on the provision of practical information of relevance to market participants and interested observers alike.

It has been put together in a manner whereby it can be read from start to finish to give the reader a current insight on the state of the global swap markets. It can equally well serve as a reference work to be read from time to time, with the reader sampling the relevant portions of the text of immediate interest to him or her.

Satyajit Das
Sydney, Australia, March 1991

Notes

1. Satyajit Das is Treasurer of TNT Group, the Australian-based international transport company. The views and opinions expressed are those of the author and do not necessarily represent the views and opinions of the company.

Part I
Recent developments in the global swap markets

Chapter 1: The current state of play in the global swap markets

Cyrus Ardalan
Paribas Capital Markets Group

The growth in recent years of a large international swap market represents a major step in the overall evolution of international capital markets. Swaps represent potentially the single most important financing development that has taken place in recent years. They provide a link between fixed and floating interest rates, assets and liabilities and bridge international capital markets. The advent of swaps has lead to increased efficiency in intermediating financial resources worldwide. In doing so, swaps have changed the way institutions view funding decisions and enabled them to manage their assets and liabilities in ways that would have been inconceivable only a few years ago.

Major changes in the markets are evident. The market has continued to experience very rapid growth. There has been a greater concentration of market-making among large commercial banks with strong balance sheets and sophisticated systems, with a number of new players, notably from insurance companies, emerging. Finally, there has been a notable growth in option products and in more complex, option-linked or sensitive swaps. Swaps are therefore increasingly becoming a part of a larger family of derivative instruments designed to manage risk.

Swaps, in many ways, represent a development of a qualitatively different nature than any other innovative technique that has emerged in the market of late. One indication of this is the prominence that swaps have achieved in the world capital markets during the last five to six years. This can be seen in several ways.

First, there is the size of the market. The market for currency and interest rate swaps and related products has grown based on figures from the International Swap Dealers Association from a negligible volume during 1980–81 to nearly US$850bn in 1987 and nearly US$2,000bn today, involving virtually every major currency. The volume of activity even in the early phase of the swap market overwhelmed the number of transactions that occurred through other innovations in the capital markets. Consider two other major innovations in the last decade, namely, the growth of the junk bond market and the mortgage-backed securities market in the US. After a decade of rapid growth, total outstandings in these two markets amounted to around US$200bn and US$800bn, respectively. Even the highly publicised and extremely successful note issuance facilities (NIFs) that are now in vogue aggregate significantly less than US$100bn.

Second, there is the commitment made by institutions to the promotion of the market. Today, virtually every major financial institution, be it a commercial or an investment bank, has established its own swap group; in may cases amounting to several dozen individuals in several financial centres. Indeed, swaps have become so popular and staffing requirements have increased to such a degree, that even though financial institutions have reduced staff levels in other trading and sales areas, swaps groups have been immune to such cutbacks.

Third, there is diversity in the types of swap techniques in use. As the market has evolved it has grown greatly in sophistication. It provides for currency swaps, using existing or prospective assets or liabilities, currency swaps synthetically created through the foreign exchange market, interest rate swaps, zero-coupon swaps, cross-currency interest rate swaps, contingent and forward swaps, swaptions and swaps involving complex customised cash flows. More recently, swap techniques are being applied for risk management for a wide range of commodities and equities.

Fourth, there is the diversity in users of swaps. Swaps are no longer a specialised art limited to a select group of practitioners. It is a technique widely used by the world's most prestigious financial institutions, corporations, investors, official institutions and indeed governments themselves. It has now become an accepted and respected technique in the funding strategy of treasurers worldwide and is beginning to make its way into the smaller middle market companies.

Finally, there is the amount of coverage that swaps have received in the international financial press, in the literature and in conferences. In recent years, there has been growing interest among regulators, as evidenced by the BIS treatment of off-balance-sheet instruments which focuses on swaps.

Unlike many new techniques which have come as specific responses to what have been rather unique market conditions, swaps have represented a fundamental development in the way in which capital markets function. For example, zero and serial zero-coupon bonds, instantly repackaged perpetuals and mini-max floaters have flourished at different times because of special tax incentives provided to certain institutions or in certain national jurisdictions. The growth of securities backed by consumer receivables, such as credit cards, have been fueled in part by an arbitrage between regulatory capital and the true economic capital required. Bonds with warrants and currency options have been a by-product of the extreme volatility in markets, stemming from the lack of a viable options market in long maturities and the existence of retail demand for options rather than representing any natural affinity between the security and the attached option. In short, many of the new techniques have emerged in response to rather specific market conditions and imperfections; their use has been, and will continue to be, sporadic and opportunistic.

The growth of the swap market, on the other hand, represents a more fundamental development.

First, swaps provide for the extension of the theory of comparative advantage from the commodity and service markets to the capital markets. It is a well known rule in international trade theory that each party should specialise in the production of those goods for which it has a relative comparative advantage. Having done so the parties can exchange these goods through trade for their desired mix of commodities and hence increase their welfare beyond that which would have been possible had they attempted to provide for all their needs directly. Swaps enable institutions, for the first time, to accomplish the same in international capital markets. Each institution can borrow where it has a relative comparative advantage. These currencies in relative comparative advantage may be a result of a number of factors. The volume of securities they issue in a market may differ. Credits of differing qualities may be valued differently between markets.

Having borrowed the funds, swaps enable institutions to restructure their borrowings into those currencies or types of liabilities, eg, fixed or floating, for which they have a preference at potentially significant cost savings. Many swaps in the past, particularly those in the Swiss market, have been precisely a result of that. Australian banks and US corporates have borrowed in Switzerland, where they have been able to achieve extremely fine terms because of the comparative advantage they have due to the scarcity of their paper, and have swapped these proceeds against US dollars to achieve substantial cost savings. Borrowings in high-coupon currencies such as Australian dollars and New Zealand dollars have provided attractive funding opportunities due to favourable tax treatment of the high coupon through structures involving swaps and forward exchange rates. Further, the deregulated swap market can provide exposure to highly regulated markets such as Italy or Spain which may be temporarily closed to foreign borrowers. Swaps are also used by asset managers to provide high yield assets taking advantage of complex cross currency tax-driven strategies complementing liability side structures. Thus, in the wake of increasing deregulation in capital markets, most recently in Japan, Germany, and the Netherlands, swaps have provided a mechanism for integrating domestic capital markets globally.

Second, swaps have led to an extension of the long-dated foreign exchange markets. Traditionally, forex markets have been limited to maturities of one, and at the most, two years. The emergence and growth of swaps have added significant liquidity to the long-dated foreign exchange market. At present, there are a number of institutions which routinely make a market in a wide variety of currencies for maturities of up to 10 years. The growth and increased liquidity of the long-dated foreign exchange market not only improves the efficiency of capital markets but also fosters the growth of trade. It enables institutions to hedge cash flows resulting from various contractual obligations, such as the purchase of aircraft, hydroelectric and nuclear plants, long into the future, providing them with greater certainty of cost in the currency in which the revenues are expected to be generated and hence reducing their risk. This development, over time, will facilitate the growth of international trade.

Third, swaps enable institutions to take a much more flexible approach towards managing their assets and liabilities in ways which would have been inconceivable a few years ago. Capital and foreign exchange markets are characterised by substantial change and volatility. The Deutsche mark, for example, fell from a high of 1.70 against the dollar in 1979 to a low of 3.45 in early 1985. Today it is once again trading below 1.70. The expectations of individuals and institutions continually undergo changes in the light of these shifting market conditions. Swaps enable institutions to act on these changed expectations in a flexible way, adjusting their portfolios in the light of current conditions and not being held hostage to past decisions. They can lock in gains or avoid higher potential losses. Swaps permit institutions to divorce the timing of borrowings from the time the rate or the spread is set on their borrowing. Alternative techniques for doing so are either expensive, eg, early retirement of their debt, or have balance sheet implications, eg, back-to-back loans. Indeed, leveraged liability (asset) portfolios where swaps are used to "overborrow" ("overlend") in particular markets while taking an opposite position in another currency are becoming a common feature for a number of institutions engaged in speculating plays through financial engineering.

Swaps, therefore, foster a more efficient global intermediation process and a more rapid growth in international trade and financial flows. Excess savings in one market can be channelled to other markets for more efficient use, a more balanced evaluation of credit spreads across markets is facilitated, and finally, institutions can manage their balance sheets more effectively. These are all fundamental changes which, in this author's view, will sustain the use of swaps in future years.

Although the swap market has grown dramatically in the past several years, the market continues to evolve. This can be seen in a number of areas. The first concerns the liquidity of the market. The swap market initially consisted of individually matched transactions, often with unique terms and non-standardised documentation. This limited the liquidity of the market and hampered unwinding and reversal of swaps.

Today the market has evolved significantly from its simple origins. A large number of institutions now run large swap "books" in a variety of different currencies which have greatly increased the liquidity of the market, particularly for interest rate swaps. There has been a move towards standardisation of swap contracts. The growing adoption of the master agreement developed by the International Swap Dealers Association (ISDA), has led to its becoming the standard of the marketplace.

In addition, significant progress has been made in the area of mitigation of the credit risks underlying swaps. ISDA's master agreement calls for netting of settlement amounts. This concept for swaps was specifically incorporated into recent changes in legislation in the US for banks and for corporates in amendments to the Bankruptcy Code. Recent studies of netting concepts by the BIS also address the area. There will hopefully emerge a consensus amongst regulators in all jurisdictions on this important concept.

Despite these developments, progress in standardisation of the credit risk underlying swaps continues to be limited. A number of new options exist, including collateralisation of swaps and the use of guarantees and even the further development of swap insurance which the World Bank has pioneered. All these techniques are designed to provide a more flexible approach to the credit issues thus making the risk management capabilities provided by swaps available to a broad range of names. Progress in this area could be particularly important for smaller middle market companies and developing countries. The bulk of Third World debt, for example, has been denominated in US dollars and has been contracted on a floating-rate basis. Swaps enable these countries to transform at least part of their debt to a fixed-rate basis, adding greater stability to their future service payments, and to adjust the currency composition of their debt to reflect their specific needs and future revenue flows. In order to facilitate this process steps will need to be taken to induce institutions to accept the potential credit exposure that would arise in such operations.

The second area concerns the widening range of swap transactions and more importantly, their contribution to the growth of the derivative securities market. The range of obligations that can be swapped has increased and will continue to do so rapidly. Beginning with Libor interest rate and currency swaps, the market has broadened to include a variety of floating-rate indices such as CP, Prime and a tax-exempt index, commodities such as oil and copper, and other types of fixed-income securities such as mortgages and high yield portfolio swaps. Simultaneously, swaps are becoming increasingly viewed as a part of a broader family of products designed to manage risk, namely, derivative securities. Derivative products include not only swaps but options as well as hybrid option-linked swaps. The scope of the market of these products will continue to grow, reflecting the broad application of the technique to a variety of situations.

The third area concerns the demand for swaps. Despite the extraordinary growth of this market, significant opportunities exist for extending their use. Companies are beginning to adopt a more sophisticated and comprehensive approach towards interest rate and currency risk management. Large corporations are becoming increasingly sensitive to factors that effect their operating margins and techniques for managing this risk using swaps and other derivative products. Smaller corporations are only now beginning to access the swap market. We are also beginning to see significant demand from new directions, in particular, sophisticated asset managers using interest rate and currency swaps to create synthetic instruments to hedge portfolios where futures markets are non-existent or to significantly alter the duration and currency exposure of the portfolio. This extension in the market will itself spur the development of new forms of swaps.

Finally, a few words about the regulatory environment for the swap market. As of this moment, the swap market faces its first significant level of regulatory oversight in the focus of capital requirements as incorporated into the BIS capital adequacy formula. Until now, it has been up to each institution to set its own credit and return standards. While the swaps market has remained clear of the credit problems facing other sectors of the financial services community, the stochastic nature of swap exposure has resulted in a variety of measures of risk and has, consequently, led to pricing anomalies. The BIS standards will have a direct impact by providing a consistent framework for allocating capital on the market price for swaps.

Chapter 2: The size of the global swap markets

Jon Macaskill
IFR Publishing Ltd

Towards the end of 1990 rumours spread among swap traders, particularly in New York, that the year would see the first decline in swaps volume since the inception of the market almost a decade before. But they were probably confusing difficulty in profitably trading the core swap product — dollar interest rate swaps — with an overall downturn in the size of the market.

When in December the International Swap Dealers Association released its figures for volume in the first six months of the year it showed that there was a 41% increase in the notional principal amount of swaps written over the same period in 1989. Even US dollar interest rate swaps recorded a 8% increase in size. Rumours of the death of the swap market appear to have been greatly exaggerated.

But there have been significant changes in the nature of the market in three main areas: the currencies traded, the requirements and sophistication of the end users, and the banks providing the products.

According to the most recent ISDA figures the first half of 1990 saw the dollar equivalent of US$656.1bn of swaps written. Of this interest rate swaps accounted for US$561.5bn and cross-currency swaps US$94.6bn. The decline in the importance of US dollar interest rate swaps was the main change over the same period the year before. In the first half of 1989 US dollar swaps accounted for 70.13% of the US$389.2bn of interest rate swaps written. In 1990 first half it was down to 52.48% of the US$561.5bn of interest rate swaps written.

The yen was up from 5.05% of total to 12.02%, taking second place from sterling which itself nevertheless rose from 7.51% of total to 10.61%. The Deutsche mark retained its fourth place position seeing a rise in its share of the interest rate swap market from 4.91% to 8.62%. The other currencies accounting for more than 2% of the market in descending order were Swiss francs, Australian dollars, Canadian dollars, Ecus and French francs.

As would be expected, the US dollar accounted for less of the cross-currency swap market: 32.95% of currency swaps in the first half of 1990 involved US dollars, down from 43.2% the year before. Yen currency swaps were virtually unchanged at 22.34% of the market. Sterling took a less important role than in the interest rate market at 4.28%. Swiss francs accounted for 8.12% of the total, Australian dollars for 8.65%, Deutsche marks for 6.44%, Ecus for 4.43% and Canadian dollars 3.82%.

In terms of the overall size of the market tremendous progress has been made since ISDA started collating figures in 1985.

In 1985 there were a total of US$170.182bn of US dollar interest rate swaps reported as written by ISDA members. At the end of 1987 (by which time ISDA had extended its ambit) the equivalent of US$682.888bn of interest rate swaps were reported outstanding in terms of notional principal in all currencies. By the end of 1989 US$1,502.6bn was the total (see Figure 1 and the accompanying table). The average size of the contracts written was essentially unchanged at US$20.35bn.

Total currency swaps were up from US$182.807bn in 1987 to US$434.849bn for 1989. Again average contract size was virtually unchanged at US$28.45m in 1989 compared with US$27.65m in 1987.

Figure 1: Total size of the interest rate and currency swap market

Total notional principal, US$ equivalent

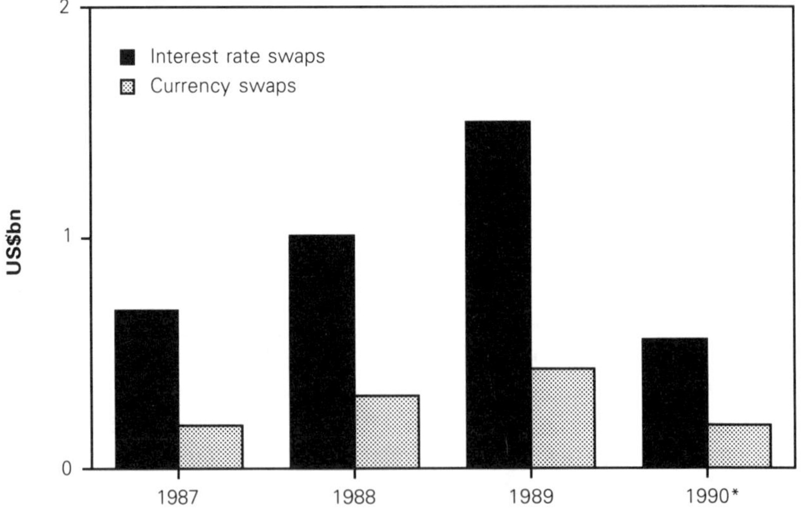

*1 January 1990 to 30 June 1990.
Represents swaps written year to date; outstandings reported at year end only.

	Interest rate swaps	Currency swaps
1987	682,888	182,807
1988	1,010,203	316,821
1989	1,502,600	434,849
1990	561,468	189,288

The unexpectedly large rise in the volume of swaps written in the first half of 1990 means that when full figures for the year are released in the middle of 1991 there is unlikely to be the feared decline in volume.

But the second half of 1990 marked a sea change in the market — both in the attitude of users of swaps and in the chief players among the banks providing the swap products.

Figure 2: Swap market composition by currency

1 January 1990–30 June 1990

(a) Interest rate swaps written

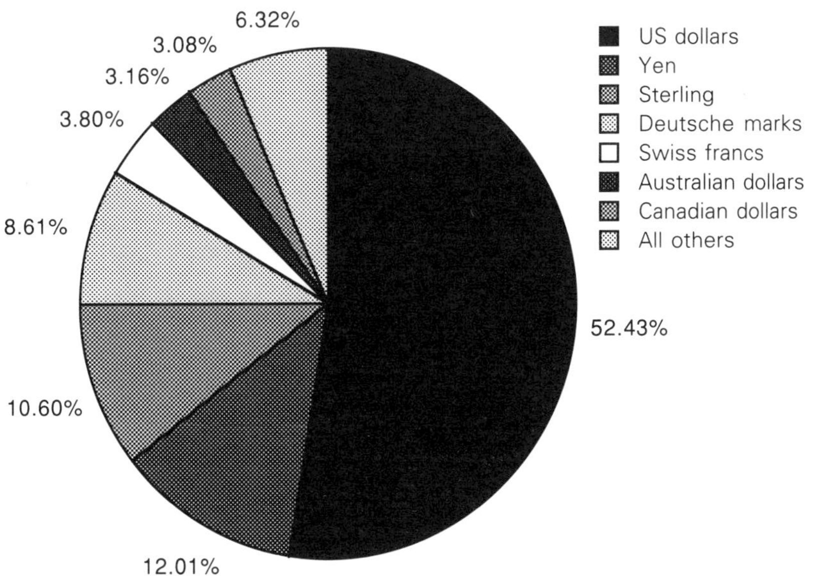

(b) Currency swaps written

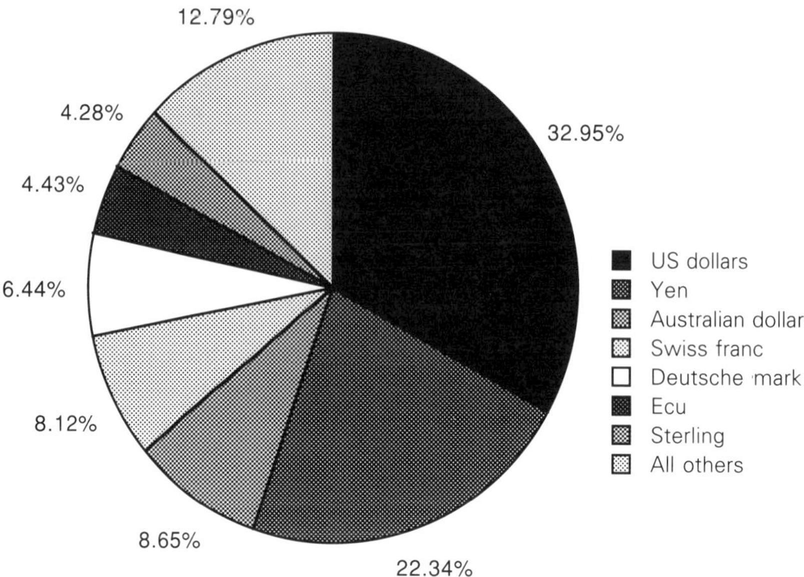

As the swap product matured and became better understood by end users the gravy train of the mid-1980's ground to a halt. Top borrowers in the international markets had for some years been able to achieve deep sub-Libor funding simply by issuing bonds and executing plain vanilla swaps, most often into floating-rate US dollars. But the wide and long lasting arbitrage opportunities prevalent in the early days of swap-driven bond issuance have disappeared. When swap windows appear today they are open for hours or days not weeks, and the spread of screen technology has made examination of basic arbitrage available to all. So use of swaps is increasingly for risk management purposes rather than fundraising-related.

Among the banks the chief change has been the decline in the influence and ability to trade of the US banks responsible for the genesis of the market. Of the 10 or so US names responsible for developing the market probably only JP Morgan has escaped the credit concerns which have effectively ended long-dated trading for the other banks. Potential counterparties — particularly in Europe and Japan — simply will not normally accept the majority of the US banks as counterparties in maturities of seven years or further out.

This has presented opportunities to the more strongly capitalised European and Japanese banks which were comparative latecomers to the market. As trading becomes more a feature of day-to-day risk management their client bases in their home markets provide a pool of business unavailable to banks which offer all products to all users. And the perception that only the strongest credits can trade all the swap maturities means that the best capitalised banks can attract the best staff. For example, when Sumitomo Bank Capital Markets set up a European currencies swap operation in London at the end of 1990 three of the staff recruited were ex-Security Pacific.

Security Pacific is a good example of the problems facing the US houses. It consistently tops polls as one of the swap operations most highly respected for professionalism by its peers, but declining credit ratings and question marks over the commitment of Los Angeles head office to the London-based swaps operation cast a pall over its ability to trade.

A look at the ratings of the US houses is instructive. At the beginning of 1985 (the year of ISDA's formation) Chase Manhattan was rated AA2 for long-term debt by Moody's. Today it is rated Baa3. Citibank had a AAA rating, today it is rated A2. Security Pacific has gone from AA2 to A3, Merrill Lynch from AA3 to A2, Chemical Bank from AA2 to Baa3, Bankers Trust from AA2 to A1 and Salomon Brothers from AA3 to A2. Even JP Morgan has gone from AAA to AA1, although its retains its AAA from Standard & Poor's.

And the credit problems in terms of ability to trade swaps increase by a multiple as the overall standing of the parent bank declines. A major reason for the ability of the European and Japanese banks to gain market share in recent years has been the fact that the US houses often have full credit lines with each other.

As well as the increasing market share of the better capitalised banks a move into the market by non-bank names has been predicted — although it has yet to materialise in practice. Insurance firms and major corporates have sophisticated treasuries and are active swap users but have to date not moved to set up active swap trading desks and compete directly with banks. An exception is US insurer AIG but it is chiefly seen in the market dealing in long-term (out to 20-year) US dollar interest rate swaps.

Away from the interest rate and cross-currency swap markets, however, non-bank names are more involved. In the burgeoning commodity swaps market, for example, oil majors such as BP and Shell compete head to head with the banks and have a major trading advantage in holding the underlying physical commodities on which futures and swap contracts are based.

The end of the dominance of the US banks in the mainstream swap markets has meant increased market share for the larger European banks.

In Germany Deutsche Bank was the first of the Big Three to wholeheartedly commit itself to the swap markets. Dresdner and Commerzbank followed. There are three main French names trading the whole array of swap products — Paribas, BNP and Credit Lyonnais. Of the

UK names Barclays and NatWest are joined by Midland as trading presences. And in Switzerland too the local Big Three, all AAA credits, have become major players in the international swap markets. Credit Suisse had been the laggard in terms of providing swap products for its clients. But at the beginning of 1990 it moved to remedy this fault by setting up London-based Credit Suisse Financial Products (CSFP), its specialist derivatives arm. Allen Wheat and 18 of his colleagues were poached from Bankers Trust in February to set up CSFP. Before its inception CSFB in London had only acted as a broker when clients required swaps, not as a provider of principal. And the only other coverage for the Credit Suisse group came from First Boston in New York. The troubled bank had a fairly large swap book (US$40bn, mainly US dollar interest rate swaps) but was suffering because of thin margins on this business and its poor creditworthiness.

CSFP took on most of First Boston's swap team but not its book. This was effectively neutered. The positions, which had an average life of four or five years, were either unwound or left to mature.

CSFP undertook a heavy recruitment drive, started trading out of London in July, and says that it had moved into profit (including start-up costs) by October. It estimates that, annualising figures from start up to November 1990, its notional volume of new business for the year would equate to US$100bn per annum.

It is a good example of how a well capitalised bank which does not have full credit lines with other banks and which is willing to spend the money needed to recruit good staff and pay for systems can take swap market share. Of the Japanese names Sumitomo, Mitsui Taiyo Kobe and Mitsubishi Finance are undertaking similar attempts to extend their share of the market.

But there need not be a move to provide the whole array of swap products. As swap markets develop in individual countries the indigenous banks are well placed to provide swap services to their relationship clients in the home currency. And they might be advised to stick to doing just that. Involvement in the alluring high risk/high reward areas of the swap market such as equity or commodity-linked swaps can prove extremely costly extremely quickly if they go wrong. Rumours in the market abound of sudden huge losses incurred in commodity swap trading by banks during the Gulf Crisis in 1990. The attractions of providing hedging tools for commodity users (mainly oil users) *via* swaps are obvious. But the futures contracts on which the swaps are based can prove unreliable or illiquid and the banks are at a serious disadvantage *vis-a-vis* commodity producers when they take out futures positions without any presence in the underlying physical market.

Similarly equity-related swaps can prove extremely risky. Equity-linked swap trading has to date mainly been linked to individual indices. Demand has been heaviest from Japan and Nikkei-linked structures the most frequently seen index-linked deals. Other indices that have proved popular include the French CAC-40, the S&P 500 in the US and the German DAX index.

The reward from equity-linked deals is higher than from normal swap business but so is the risk. More active hedging and attention to positions is required, with all the extra staff time that entails. And because of the possibility of large losses high reserves have to be put aside to cover them.

But despite the risks run by the banks the fact that these services are being offered to clients indicates the enduring flexibility of swap markets and bodes well for their continuing health.

Chapter 3: The US dollar swap market

Richard Leibovitch
JP Morgan

1990 was a year of consolidation and rationalisation in the US swap market. The exponential growth in volumes exhibited in the mid to late 1980s finally abated. Competition, along with a new focus on the underlying secondary risks of the business, forced down once attractive bid/offer spreads. The renewed attention to credit has been the single most important factor in re-shaping the composition of the US swap market. The crisis in the banking industry along with the default of several prominent swap counterparties, such as Drexel Burnham Lambert, DFC, and Hammersmith and Fulham, has brought to the forefront the importance of counterparty credit quality. Several of the less creditworthy money centre banks have been forced to shift their business strategy away from active market-making in order to focus on higher-margin trade-specific transactions. New participants, particularly non-bank financial institutions such as insurance companies, backed by a strong credit rating and clean balance sheet have been quick to try to fill the void left by the money centres.

The composition of the market players is not the only significant change to have occurred, however. The pricing and structuring of swaps has been affected as well. Stronger credits have begun to command premium pricing, particularly in longer maturity swaps. Although credit spreads vary among institutions, the differential in pricing a five-year swap between a AA and a BB counterparty ranges from 1 to 4 or more bp per annum. In the two-year sector, the pricing of that credit differential is reduced to 0 to 2bp. Interbank participants have begun to emphasise unwinds and assignments as a method of clearing lines and avoiding the "credit premium" imbedded in new swap contracts. Eurodollar futures, particularly far dated contracts, have increased in popularity as participants have been willing to take on the cash-to-futures basis risk in order to find a credit-free hedge for their open swap positions. The deterioration in the profitability of traditional market-making, due to both lower volumes as well as tighter bid/offer spreads, has forced many swap dealers to assume new types of risks in order to maintain profit levels. Asset swaps of such instruments as credit card and auto receivables, as well as CMOs in which the prepayment risks are assumed by the swap dealer, have increased in frequency. Dealers are managing other types of risks, including tax-exempt index risk, various commodity risks and equity index and equity specific risks, in the hope of capturing greater returns from these developing markets.

This chapter is divided into three segments. The first part focuses on the issue of credit — why has it become such an important issue and how has it impacted the way in which the swap business is conducted? The second section elaborates on the changes in the structure of the US swap market, particularly the impact of the long-dated Eurodollar futures contracts and the arbitrage opportunities that have derived therefrom. The final section focuses on the new structures that have arisen, namely the rise of variable principal redemption swaps, tax-exempt swaps and tax-driven structures.

The impact of credit considerations on the US swap market

The swap market originated as a credit oriented market. Many of the original market-makers in the early 1980s acted as credit intermediators, matching transactions between top-rated institutions. For example, the first interest rate swap believed to have been executed was intermediated by Salomon Brothers between IBM and the World Bank. Even as market participants began taking open swap risks, counterparties tended to be concentrated among the highly-rated *Fortune* 500 firms. In 1988, The International Swap Dealers Association (ISDA) conducted a survey of swap defaults. It found that the annual default rate was only 0.01%, involving notional principal amounts worth $33m. As competition in the swap market developed, particularly in 1988–89 when corporate debt issuance proliferated, swaps were written with increasingly weaker creditworthy counterparties.

Two of the largest users of swaps, fueled by their own growth in the mid-1980s were the thrifts and the LBO deals. They provided market-makers with large-sized, generously priced transactions which in turn injected a great deal of liquidity into the interbank market. Investment banks, such as Merrill Lynch and Drexel Burnham Lambert were particularly active, swapping many of the high-yield issues that were sold to the savings and loan institutions (S&Ls). Many of the LBOs of the mid-1980s were required by the banks to hedge a substantial portion of their debt. Generally, the hedges were provided by the lending banks themselves, again at concessionary spreads. These end user transactions had a multiplier effect on the swap market as banks offset these positions with one another. As the problems in the S&L industry grew and the economic slowdown began impacting LBO firms, swap defaults started to accelerate. Although no formal survey has been taken, it is widely believed that in the second half of 1990, the default rate had increased substantially compared to the previous years. No major bank swap counterparty has yet to default, however, the demise of Drexel as well as the well publicised decline in the general creditworthiness of US money centre banks have increased the awareness of counterparties to the credit risk of swaps.

Changes in legislation have also affected the manner in which banks look at swap credit exposure. As a result of an amendment made in June to the US Bankruptcy Code, a US corporation can now be certain that its swap exposures can be netted with a defaulting counterparty. The Financial Institutions Reform, Recovery and Enforcement Act of 1989 (FIRREA) provided the same netting ability for commercial banks and thrifts. These two changes in legislation have enabled banks to view their swap exposure to any single US counterparty as the "net" of the mark-to-market value of their total swap portfolio with that counterparty. Although considerable uncertainty remains over whether the concept of netting would be upheld with a foreign counterparty, it is likely that the changes to US law will serve as a strong precedent. These changes have resulted in lower intra-dealer credit exposure. Banks have moved from measuring swap credit exposure by notional principal amounts outstanding to counterparties within various maturity bands, to the more sophisticated approach of evaluating the "netted" expected and actual mark-to-market credit exposures. Expected exposures incorporate the potential impact due to time and interest rate volatility on the mark-to-market value.

The composition of market participants in the US swap market has clearly been impacted by the renewed emphasis on credit. US money centre banks, which have historically been very active, have seen their volumes decline over the past year. This appears to have been primarily the result of two factors: Firstly, intra-bank dealers, already close to their limits with money centre exposure, have been unwilling to increase their lines, particularly given the declining creditworthiness of the large US banks. Secondly, many end users of swaps have begun to restrict their counterparty credit quality to AA or AAA publicly-rated institutions. The longer the transaction maturity, the more restrictive the counterparty lists have become. Consequently, many of the money centres have been excluded, particularly in maturities beyond five years, and many of the less creditworthy counterparties have been forced to focus their attention on the short end of the swap curve. Apart from the ability to trade with more counterparties, the short end allows traders to use Eurodollar futures strips to hedge their portfolio. The long end of the market has been dominated over the past year by AAA or strong AA entities. This, in turn, has provided an opportunity for the strong non-US banks, particularly the Europeans, to improve their presence in the US swap market. Swap houses such as Barclays, Swiss Bank, Deutsche Bank and BNP have undoubtedly increased their market share in the long end.

The decline of the US houses has provided an opportunity for new swap groups to fill the void. These can be divided into two groups: Certain non-bank financial institutions, particularly insurance companies, have established "boutique" subsidiaries to leverage off of the parent's strong credit ratings. Mercadian Capital LP, a subsidiary of the New England Mutual Life Insurance Company, and General Re Financial Products have been the first to begin trading following the model of AIG Financial Products established in 1987. The other group of new entrants to emerge are the capital market subsidiaries of established banks. CSFB established Credit Suisse Financial Products in early 1990 to act as a swap market-maker. The Japanese have been particularly active in setting up these new groups. Sumitomo, Fuji, Sanwa and Mitsui Taiyo Kobe have all established these subsidiaries aimed at moving the banks further into the capital markets arena while taking advantage of the banks' strong credit ratings. For most of these groups, 1990 has been a year of putting the infrastructure into place. They are expected to be a significant force as we move into 1991.

Currency swaps have also been greatly de-emphasised in the markets as a result of credit concerns. Several swap houses are no longer making prices on cross-currency basis swaps. This has, in part, been due to the change in the way credit exposure is evaluated. Since the mark-to-market value of a currency swap incorporates both currency and interest rate movements, it implies that expected exposures will be much higher than those of simple interest rate swaps. In addition, the cost of managing the resulting cash positions has also increased substantially. The credit crunch of 1990 has tiered the pricing in the money markets. Fewer banks are willing to trade cash on either side of the 1/8% Libid to Libor bid/offer spread. The growing cost of managing positions in the cash market has not, however, translated itself into wider bid/offer spreads on currency swaps. Consequently, dealers have begun to re-evaluate the feasibility of making markets in currency swaps and it appears likely that spreads in that market will be forced to widen to reflect the current credit realities.

Changes in the structure of the US swap market

The increased concern over credit has not only changed the composition of market participants, but has also impacted the way in which swaps are priced. The dollar swap market originally evolved as a capital markets/corporate finance product. End users tended to be issuers of debt looking to convert their fixed liabilities into Libor. Given the liquidity of the US Treasury market and the fact that domestic and Eurobonds were priced at spreads to Treasuries, the swap market developed as a spread rather than an absolute rate market. In the past five years, the number and types of end users have increased substantially. While swapping fixed-rate liabilities continues to have a large share of total swap volume, increasingly swaps have become a popular trading instrument for bank asset and liability (ALM) managers. Although the bid/offer spread remains wider than that of the liquid US government bond market, balance sheet constraints have encouraged ALM managers to move to off-balance-sheet instruments such as swaps. Furthermore, swaps have an advantage over bonds and futures in that many institutions still account for swaps on an accrual basis, rather than on a mark-to-market basis. This has the benefit of enabling ALM managers to accrue gains and losses over the life of the swap in a net interest earnings book. Should a swap be unwound and in-the-money, the manager would of course be able to realise the mark-to-market gain at that time. This friendly accounting treatment effectively enables absolute rate players to exercise a little more predictability over their reported earnings. These two factors have been important in explaining the rapid increase in the use of swaps by ALM players. Although no formal statistics are available, an informal survey of US swap dealers indicates that the proportion of business derived from absolute rate players has increased substantially over the year, from 15% as a proportion of overall volume to 25%.

One of the consequences of this increase in absolute rate trading has been a rise in the use of Eurodollar futures as a hedge for swap dealers. Since most swap houses mark-to-market both their swap and futures positions, Eurodollar strips provide a very effective hedge for interest rate swaps. Liquidity in back-dated contracts has increased significantly over the past year. The volume in the trading of "green" contracts (third-year contracts) increased from 387,908 in 1988 to 534,436 in 1989. In response to growing swap demand, the Chicago Mercantile Exchange introduced four additional back contracts in August 1989, effectively enabling swappers to hedge out to four years. Fifth-year contracts are also under discussion. Most of the activity has been concentrated in the second and third-year contracts. Liquidity remains relatively low in the new "blue" (fourth-year) contracts.

One reason for the liquidity problems in the back contracts is that Eurodollar strips provide a less effective hedge the further out the maturity is extended. The main difference between the two instruments is that Eurodollars are non-convex whereas interest rate swaps are convex. The present value of a basis point (PVBP) for a Eurodollar contract is $25, regardless of whether absolute rates are at 3% or 13%. An equivalent swap will have its PVBP vary depending on the discount rate. When a swap is initially offset with a Eurodollar strip, the amount of contracts in the futures hedge will only be appropriate for the swap rate at the time the trade is done. As absolute yields change, the number of contracts in the hedge will need to change to reflect the change in duration of the underlying swap. As an example, if a swap dealer pays fixed on a $100m two-year swap at 8% (semi-annual bond) and hedges with a strip of Eurodollar futures at 8.03%, the true gain to the dealer is unlikely to be three basis points, because the dealer has taken on negative convexity by entering into this trade.

With a yield of 8%, one would need to buy a total of 726 contracts in order to match the duration of the swap.[1] If swap yields dropped the next day to 7%, a gain of $1,815,000 would be realised on the futures strip (assuming all the contracts moved by 100bp). At these lower yields, however, the PVBP of the swap increases to $18,581 from $18,150. Consequently, the 100bp move in yield results in a loss of $1,836,500. The net loss due to rates movement is $21,500, which equates to slightly over 1bp per annum over the life of the swap. The convexity cost of a swap versus strip position can be estimated using expected swap interest rate volatilities. The longer the maturity of the position, the greater the convexity impact will be since the impact of discounting will be felt over a greater time period. In December 1990, the convexity value of one-year swaps was estimated at 0.5bp, two-year swaps at 1bp and three-year swaps at 2bp. As a result of the liquidity provided in the futures market, swap pricing has become highly influenced by the yields implied by the Eurodollar strip. The correlation between swap and strip prices is very high for one and two-year swaps. As Figure 1 below indicates, the correlation is reduced the further out one goes along the maturity spectrum. Increased futures execution risk, interest rate volatility and liquidity concerns are all factors that result in the reduced pricing relationship.

Figure 1: Correlation between swap and strip prices

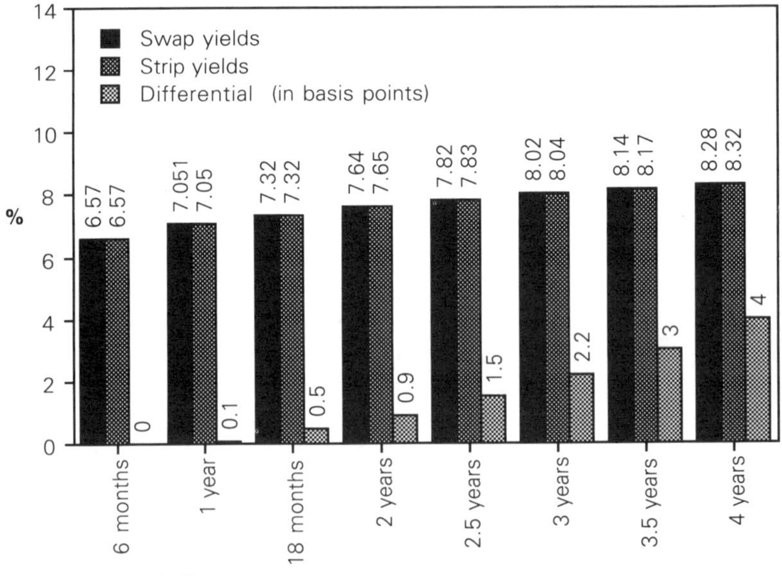

Assumes 14% volatility

Several dealers have started to use strips to price swaps beyond four years. One could price theoretical contracts out to 10 years by extending the linear relationship in the back contracts. These theoretical contracts would be hedged by back-stacking the contracts in the furthest Eurodollar contract. Although this pricing methodology and hedging strategy is only used by a small group of dealers, it is an emerging factor influencing the pricing of longer-term deals.

The success of the back-month Eurodollar contracts has drawn the attention of competing exchanges that are trying to capture the swap hedging business. In early 1990, the Simex introduced a strip contract, aimed at improving the ability to execute the various contracts by trading them simultaneously. To date, this development has had only modest success since the liquidity in Singapore hours for Eurodollars is somewhat limited. The Chicago Board of Trade (CBOT) is considering starting a three and five-year interest rate swap futures contract in early 1991. The contracts are currently designed to trade in a similar way to Eurodollars. The price would be quoted as 100 minus the implied yield, with the price converging on settlement date to the average five-year bid-side swap yields of a group of primary swap dealers. The PVBP would be, as with Eurodollars, a fixed dollar amount regardless of absolute yield levels. As with other new contracts, this product is likely to find initial resistance. It is unlikely to draw the interest of ALM players because, despite potentially smaller bid/offer spreads, the futures contract will not enable these risk takers to get favourable accounting treatment. Market-makers will be somewhat hesitant to use the contract because of the substantial convexity risks imbedded in using this product as a hedge to their swap portfolio. It appears clear, however, that the US swap market is showing signs of maturing, with increasing competition emerging from the futures exchanges attempting to make swaps more of a generic commodity.

As with many financial instruments, the majority of swap business takes place in the period of overlap between the London and New York trading days. The increase in absolute rate players, particularly out of Europe, has contributed greatly to the concentration of liquidity in the early New York hours. The reduced liquidity of the US Ttreasury market during Tokyo and London time has resulted in the postponement of launch times on larger structured transactions and bond issues in order to take advantage of the tighter bid-offer spreads available in the US Treasury and swap markets during New York hours.

Another effect of the credit squeeze has been a widening of the historical spread differential between corporate bond spreads and swap spreads. Both public and privately-placed debt issuance declined significantly in 1990. Total US dollar Eurobond volume for 1990 totalled $61bn, compared with $122bn for 1989. The decrease in liquidity, combined with such problems as the deterioration of bank credit quality, the collapse of the LBO market, event risk issues and balance sheet constraints, have widened five-year corporate spreads by 80bp, and two-year spreads by 120bp from January 1990 to its peak in January 1991 (see Figure 2). Apart from the overall decline in credit quality in the marketplace, the differential in credit qualities widened significantly. As a result, the stable relationship between AA corporate spreads and swap spreads began to break down. Essentially, other things being equal, swap spreads should reflect a basket of bond credit qualities. As the volatility in corporate spreads has increased, so has the differential between issuers, which, in turn, has impacted the performance of swap spreads as a hedge. As the spreads on corporate and bank paper began to widen, swap spreads lagged behind, influenced by the relative stability of sovereign and industrial credit spreads. Figure 3 compares the movement of corporate issuance spreads over the year by industry group.

Figure 2: Movement of two and five-year corporate spreads

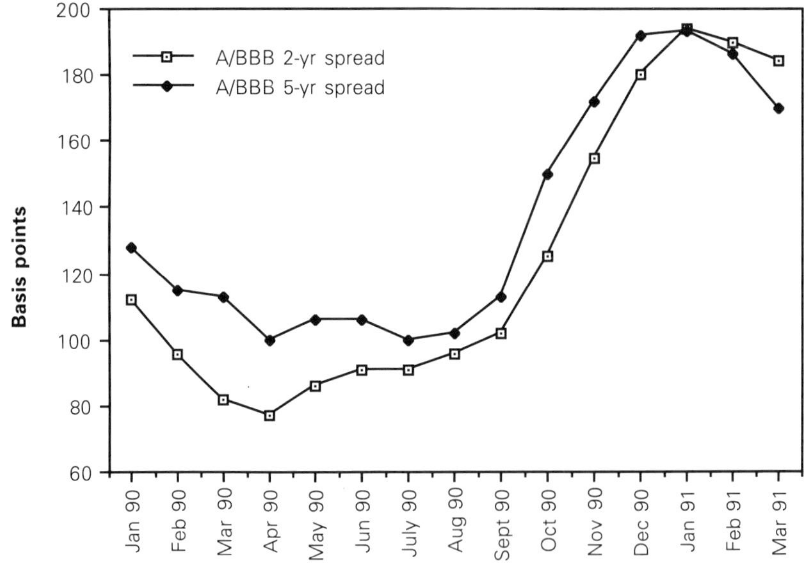

Figure 3: Movement of corporate issuance spreads
By industry group

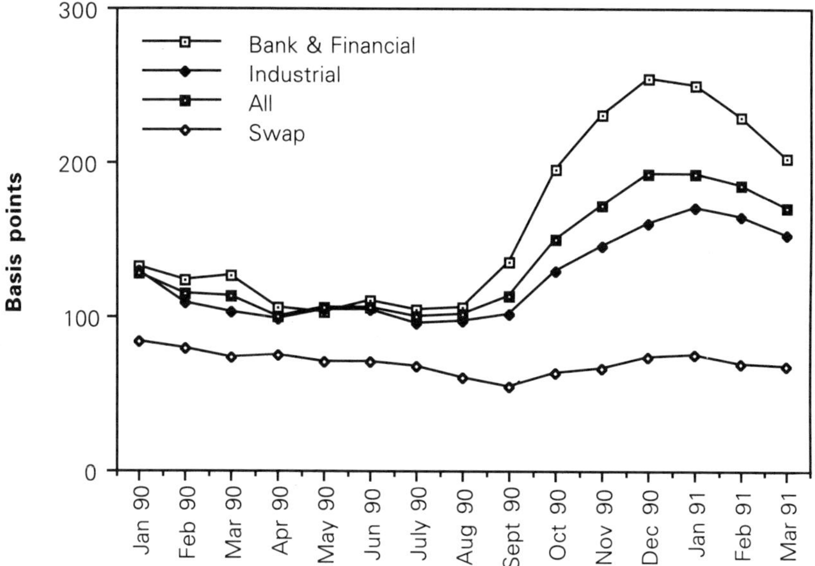

The widening in the spread differential has resulted in higher floating-rate costs of funding to corporate issuers, reflecting higher borrowing costs in all markets. Due to balance sheet and BIS constraints, the natural forces of arbitrage that tend to bring swap and corporate spreads into line did not produce the expected effects. Corporate bonds on an asset swapped basis began generating yields of Libor + 50bp where only six months earlier the same paper could be sold at Libor flat. Foreign banks, the traditional buyers of asset swapped paper, could no longer buy these products at spreads near Libor since their own funding costs began to escalate. New BIS rules allocating a 100% risk weighting to corporate bonds versus only a 20% risk weighting on other instruments such as agencies also reduced the attractiveness of asset-swapped corporate bonds. In the end, corporate and bank issuers have had to bear the cost of this widening differential. Long-term liquidity concerns have forced banks to issue longer-term liabilities despite the higher costs. The costs of term liquidity for some money centre banks skyrocketed in late 1990 as panic swept the investor community regarding the health of the US banking system. At an extreme, Chase 10-year subordinated paper could be asset swapped after the October 1990 auction at Libor + 400bp.

Despite the pressure on dealers to reduce counterparty risk exposure, mark-to-market and collateralised swaps have gained acceptance only slowly. The popularity of credit enhanced structures has improved somewhat among corporate end users, but interbank players continue to shun their use despite the credit benefits. This reluctance has, in part, been due to a desire among the highest credit qualities to keep their competitive advantage in the market. Further, no real standardisation of documentation has taken place. Market participants have been unwilling to divulge their credit enhancement techniques to the competition. The effect has been to extend the relative advantage of AAA counterparties in the market. Credit enhanced swap agreements have been most widely accepted for swaps whose maturity extends beyond 10 years. Long-term swaps arising from aircraft lease transactions and real estate driven structures have continued to be popular during 1990. These deals have impacted the term structure of swap spreads by creating an upward kink in the swap spread curve beyond 10 years. Figure 4 reflects the swap curve as it stood in December 1990 compared to 1989.

Figure 4: Comparison of swap curves

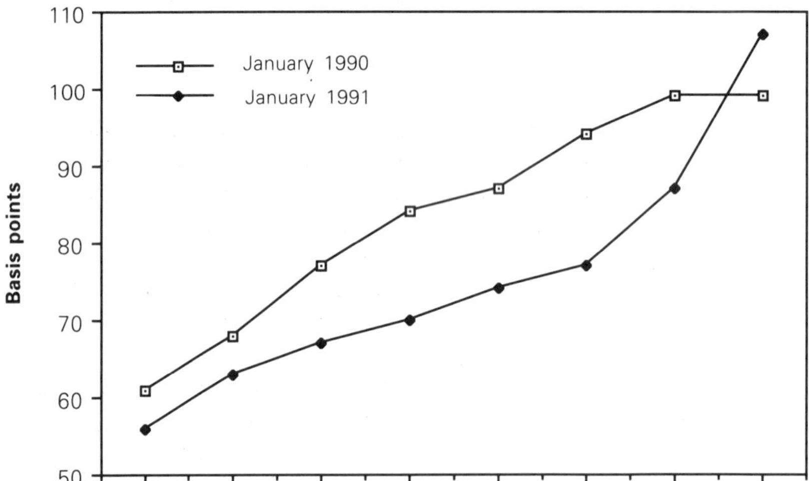

During 1990, the spread curve flattened significantly on a year-on-year basis for maturities below 10 years. The curve has remained steep beyond 10 years, however, as a result of the continued flow of lease transactions. Part of the reason for the kink stems from the lack of swapped debt issuance beyond the 10-year maturity. As a result, fixed-rate receivers for maturities beyond 10 years have remained scarce. Furthermore, because of credit considerations, interbank trading in those maturities remains very illiquid. Market-makers must sometimes hold the position for considerable periods of time before finding the offset.

The US derivatives markets have suffered similar structural changes over the past year. Plain vanilla cap and floor business volume has dropped, and the number of market-makers actively participating has also fallen. The profit margins have so suffered that dealers have sought to improve profits through complex structuring and cross-market arbitrage. Increasingly, options have been sold by re-structuring them into a variety of forms. *Compound options*, in which the buyer receives an option on an option (eg, captions); *asian options*, options on averages (for example, CP cap); *hybrid options*, an option exposure dependent on more than one variable; *knock-out options*, options that extinguish beyond a certain price level, are all different types of structures that gained popularity during 1990.

Greater cross-market risks were taken in 1990. Arbitrage houses became active spread players of cross-market volatility. Swap option volatility looked very inexpensive on a relativc basis compared to both government and mortgage-back volatility due to the selling pressure from the large number of corporate bonds whose option features were sold into the swap option market. Thus, further integration of markets also appears to be the trend in derivatives.

New swap structures

The swap market has responded to declining profit margins with increased risk-taking and cross-market integration. Markets that had traditionally been the domain of other departments, such as the tax-exempt and commodity markets, are now starting to be traded directly by swap groups. Dealers have also begun to manage new and different types of market risks. The convexity risks embedded in such products as CMOs and auto receivables are now being assumed by swap desks in conjunction with the trading desks for the underlying securities. The result has been to increase both risks and returns, but also to broaden the scope of trading for swap houses. Three of the products in which interest has increased over the past year have been variable principal redemption swaps, tax-exempt swaps, inverse floaters and structured transactions such as instantly repackaged perpetuals (IRPs).

Variable principal redemption swaps

Traditional asset swaps have been based on securities whose underlying cash flows are known. As the securitisation of receivables has increased in popularity, the desire to sell these products on a floating-rate basis has also increased. Although the securities offer an attractive yield to investors, managing the potential prepayment risks has always been a problem. These risks, particularly in the case of CMOs, result in negative price convexity to the investor. As interest rates drop, homeowners tend to accelerate their principal repayments in order to refinance at lower rates. This in turn has a negative effect on the CMO holder who finds that the duration of his high-yielding fixed-rate investment has fallen. Several swap houses are now swapping these instruments on a prepayment risk-free basis, ie, for a slight reduction in yield, investors could now buy these instruments on a floating-rate basis and be assured of the cash flows.

Different instruments have different degrees of risk associated with them. For example, longer-term instruments such as CMOs have prepayments that are more interest rate sensitive than auto receivables. The willingness of swap houses to take on the prepayment risks have produced new opportunities, particularly in swaps based on short-term receivables whose prepayment histories have tended to be reasonably random. Swaps are written based on the expected repayment schedule of the underlying security. As actual repayments take place over the life of the swap, any deviations from the expected schedule become residual swap positions for the dealer who wrote the swap. Should interest rates drop and prepayments accelerate relative to expectations, the dealer would end up with an out-of-the-money swap earlier than expected. This risk can be hedged to a certain extent by purchasing swap options with the additional yield that the swap trader was able to obtain when originally executing the transaction. The greater the amount of swap options purchased, the greater the elimination of prepayment risk.

On the liability side, an increasing amount of swaps have been written against bank investment contracts (BICs). A bank investment contract, put simply, is a bank deposit that is specifically tailored to meet the requirements of an investor such as a pension fund. The fund is obligated, under certain strict circumstances, to reduce the amount of the deposit. Swaps have been written for the deposit-taker which convert the BIC into a floating-rate deposit with certain cash flows. The likelihood of early withdrawal on most BIC transactions tends to be low. The likelihood of a variation from expected principal repayment is far higher on a receivables-based swap than on a bank investment contract. The current trend for swap dealers seems to be to take on increasing amounts of risk. In coming years, banks may be asked to take on greater risks by assuming, for example, the prepayment risks of various mortgage-backed securities such as for IOs and POs.

Tax-exempt swaps

The tax-exempt swap market emerged in late 1986 when issuers of tax-exempt debt were able to create synthetically cheaper funding through swapping their floating-rate financing into fixed-rate debt. Merrill Lynch was one of the first entrants into the market and has been the dominant player ever since. Bankers Trust, Citibank, Security Pacific and Goldman Sachs have also begun making markets in tax-exempt swaps. Other players include Morgan Stanley, JP Morgan, First Boston, and AIG. The market has exhibited tremendous growth since its inception: to date, about $18bn in swaps have been written and, over the past four years, the annual volume of the market has grown from $1bn in 1987 to $3bn in 1988, $4bn in 1989 and $10bn in 1990.

The standard tax-exempt swap is one in which one counterparty pays a fixed rate and receives a floating tax-exempt rate. The most widely used index has been the JJ Kenny index of 35 30-day municipal notes. The index measures the bid-side yield of a variety of "high grade" or "low grade" one-month tax-exempt paper evaluated on a daily basis. Other indices used include the New York Tax-Exempt Daily Interest Rate, the National TEDIR, and the Tax-Exempt Note Rate (TENOR). Since a tax-exempt swap can be decomposed into a regular interest rate swap and a tax-exempt floating rate/Libor basis swap, pricing and managing the floating-rate basis risk are critical to pricing. This spread, in turn, is dependent upon the yield differential between the taxable swap and the tax-exempt municipal yield curves. Because of the difficulty in building a forward variable tax-exempt curve, and due to the relative lack of liquidity in the market, municipal swaps trade at wide bid/offer spreads.

The original users of tax-exempt swaps were the municipal issuers, who were able to obtain a cheaper source of fixed-rate funding. In addition, arbitrageurs have been able to generate attractive asset swaps using older off-the-run bonds that are trading cheap relative to the swap curve. Other end users have proven to be fixed-rate receivers deriving attractive funding on a tax-adjusted basis. Issuers of bonds that are non-callable over a portion of the bond's life have used tax-exempt swaps as a means of fixing their debt beyond a call date or converting their liability to floating rate for the period up to the next call date. As the market matures and tax-exempt entities familiarise themselves with swaps, it is likely that end users will increasingly use swaps as a means of asset/liability management.

Market-makers can currently hedge themselves with either cash municipal bonds or with the municipal bond futures contract. Most tax-exempt swaps written to date have ranged in maturity from one to 10 years. The muni-index future is based on an underlying 20-year instrument. Consequently, the correlation between the futures and a five-year cash municipal bond is very low. In fact, the correlation between a five-year cash municipal bond and the futures is about the same as that between the municipal bond and comparable maturity US Treasury notes. It appears that hedging in this market is still an art.

As other swap markets mature, evidence suggests that an increasing number of players will begin focusing on the tax-exempt and other emerging markets as a source of new business. Another such market to exhibit tremendous growth over the past year has been the commodity swap market. Oil in particular, with the invasion of Kuwait and the consequent volatility in oil prices, has been very popular. Equity swaps, particularly those linked to indices such as the Nikkei, S&P, CAC and DAX have found success in 1990 and are expected to grow substantially over the next few years.

Inverse floaters and instantly repackaged perpetual

The bullish tone of the US credit markets in late 1990 and early 1991 have revived interest in inverse floater transactions. An inverse floater allows an investor to place funds in a leveraged instrument. The return on investment is typically based on a formula: $C - \alpha$ Libor where C is a constant number and α is the leverage factor. The formula for a one-year, three-times leveraged inverse floater with one-year swap rates at 7% qmm (assuming a flat yield curve) would be slightly under 7.00% qmm (assuming cash is deposited at Libor flat). If Libor rallies to 6%, the return multiplies to 10%. Conversely, should Libor rise to 7.5%, the return drops to 5.5%. Regardless of the movement in rates, the investor is guaranteed to receive at least his principal back at maturity.

The cash from the investment is generally placed on deposit with a bank, who issues the inverse floater note. Generally, the note is converted into a floating-rate deposit using a combination of swaps and caps or floors. The structure provides attractive funding for the note issuer and a leveraged instrument for the bullish investor.

One example of an efficient structure to raise funding and quasi capital on attractive terms is the instantly repackaged perpetual (IRP). This structure works as follows: the borrower issues a perpetual floating-rate note and enters into a contract with a special purpose vehicle (SPV) under which the SPV commits to purchase the FRN at year 15 and forego the interest thereafter against the payment of an amount equivalent to the present value of the nominal amount at year 15. The proceeds of the note are used in part to purchase a zero-coupon deposit from a high credit quality financial institution. The remainder of the money goes to the borrower. The zero-coupon deposit ensures the investor that his principal on the investment will be repaid. The borrower will pay Libor plus a spread on the par amount of the IRP note placed with the investor. Differences in accounting and tax treatments make the structure attractive to all parties. The main swaps in the structure are the ones written for the bank making the zero-coupon deposit as well as hedging the IRP issuer. Since most banks prefer floating-rate funding, a zero-coupon swap is written to convert the deposit into Libor-based funding.

Another successful structure of the past few years has been the dual-currency foreign exchange/swap arbitrage. This structure takes advantage of an asymmetric tax treatment between currency swaps and foreign exchange forwards. Swap interest is taxed as ordinary income whereas gains and losses on foreign exchange forwards are treated as capital gains and are thus taxed at a preferential rate when the forward contract matures. A variety of structures have been created to take advantage of this anomaly. The most common is one in which a borrower issues a note in a high-yield currency (such as New Zealand dollars). The note is then swapped into a low-yield currency (such as yen) using foreign exchange forwards. This generates a large capital gain. The converted yen liability is then swapped using a currency swap back into US dollars, resulting in an ordinary income loss. The tax benefits generated by going through a high and then a low-yield currency can be significant.

Conclusions

Credit considerations have clearly changed the nature of the swap business. Creditworthy players currently have a significant advantage over their competitiors. As the market matures and profitability margins dwindle, swap traders will be forced to take on new risks to maintain expected returns. The plain vanilla interest rate swap market has been somewhat affected by the new credit environment. Swap houses will be forced to focus on new and different types of risk. We have begun to see this in the market's new focus on commodity swaps, tax-exempt swaps and variable principal redemption transactions. These types of structures are likely to continue to play a more dominant role in the future as the US swap market evolves.

Notes

1. The modified duration of a two-year swap yielding 8% is 1.8149, resulting in the PVBP of $18,142 on a $100m notional value. Since Eurodollars have a PVBP of $25, it would take 726 contracts to match the PVBP of the swap.

Chapter 4: The Canadian dollar swap market

Simon Boughey
IFR Publishing Ltd

The Canadian fixed income and swap market is closely linked with the US markets and, as in other areas of its economy, largely dependent upon it. Any Canadian dollar swap trader must keep a close watch on the Canadian dollar/US dollar exchange rate, as liquidity constraints in the Canadian cash markets often force domestic banks to fund themselves in the US dollar cash market and then swap back into Canadian dollars, creating offer side interest in Canadian swaps.

Traditional reliance on US capital flows makes Canadian interest rates very sensitive to events south of the border and explains why they will nearly always be higher than US rates. This close relationship between the US and Canada, involving much cross-border corporate activity, made the development of a Canadian dollar swap market inevitable. It is worth noting that a cross-currency swap market pre-dated the development of an interest rate swap market, even though the latter now predominates. The profound significance of currency swaps has always been a marked characteristic of the Canadian dollar swap market and one that pertains to this day.

As with most innovations in the capital markets arena, the exact origin of the first Canadian dollar swap is somewhat hazy with several houses claiming the responsibility for being first on the scene. However, the consensus seems to be that the Bank of Montreal was the pioneer in the early 1980s. The first swap in Canada was contracted in August 1981 between the Bank of Montreal and a major German company. Before long, the other "Sched A banks" (so-called because of their designation "Schedule A" under the terms of the Canadian Bank Act), including Royal Bank of Canada, Canadian Imperial Bank of Commerce (CIBC), Toronto-Dominion Bank and Bank of Nova Scotia, were setting up their own swap operations. The last "Sched A bank" is the National Bank of Canada, but its market share is very small.

The Canadian dollar swap market boomed in the mid and late 1980s. According to ISDA data, between the end of 1987 and 1988 the volume of interest rate swaps outstanding grew 127% from the US dollar equivalent of \$6.49bn to \$15.771bn. Over the same year, the volume of Canadian dollar currency swaps also more than doubled; only Hong Kong dollar swaps grew more in this period. At the end of 1987, there was $13.881bn in swaps outstanding, compared to nearly $30bn at the end of 1988.

During 1989 the growth in Canadian dollar currency swaps slackened. At the end of that year, volume had increased marginally to $32.58bn, or 3.75% of the global total. Interest rate swaps continued to grow at a healthy rate, however, and volume had increased to $29.169bn at the year end. Nearly 88% of these swaps were conducted with end users, rather than ISDA counterparties, indicating the importance of the Canadian end user to the interest rate swap market.

Figures for the whole of 1990 are not yet available, but in the first half of 1990, interest rate swaps in Canadian dollars maintained progress, and volume stood at $17.275bn for the first half of the year. Currency swaps involving Canadian dollars had slumped to $7.226bn, however. Although figures for the second half of 1990 are not at hand, the Canadian dollar Eurobond market was one of the worst performers in the wake of the invasion of Kuwait, which does not bode well for the end-of-year currency swap statistics.

The Canadian dollar swap market has been described as an oligopoly, governed by CIBC, the Bank of Montreal, Toronto-Dominion Bank, the Royal Bank of Canada and the Bank of Nova Scotia. At various times, new market participants have attempted to make their mark, and some have succeeded, but these five still rule the roost. Of these five, the Royal Bank of Canada was once the most powerful, its strength derived from its huge corporate base. However, in recent years it has been rivalled by CIBC, and these two now probably account for more than 50% of the Canadian dollar swap market. More often than not it is a safe bet that one of these banks (and generally only CIBC, the Royal Bank of Canada and Bank of Nova Scotia) will have written the Canadian dollar Libor leg of any swap-driven new issue. Moreover, the incestuous nature of the Canadian market is such that a fixed-rate payer will have difficulties hiding his position from his rivals, as he will be seen buying Canadian government bonds to hedge the position.

Of the outsiders, Citibank was once a formidable participant in the Canadian market and recruited several members of the innovatory Bank of Montreal team to spearhead the onslaught. These days it is seen much less often and derives much of its business from its real estate portfolio. Bankers Trust Canada was the first house to develop the secondary derivatives products of caps, collars and floors in Canadian dollars, and initially the Sched A banks would farm out their corporate business in these instruments to Bankers Trust. Latterly, they have provided their own interest rate products. However, Bankers Trust Canada maintains a noticeable presence in the Canadian dollar swap market, and does write currency swaps off the back of new issues every so often.

Chase Manhattan once made a determined effort to launch itself in the market, but decided to bow out last year. However, UBS has recently unveiled a Canadian dollar book. JP Morgan has a significant presence in the market, and Deutsche Bank, Banque Paribas, Security Pacific, Prudential Bache and Barclays are seen from time to time. But none of these is anything more than a secondary player and they do not challenge the hegemony of the domestic Canadian banks.

In trading practice, the Canadian dollar swap market differs from the US market in few aspects. The Canadian market is still primarily a spread market, with swap prices quoted as a spread over the relevant Government of Canada bond. There is an embryonic futures market, which trades in the same way as the Eurodollar futures market in Chicago, and one-year swaps are traded by a variety of futures players, absolute-rate players and spread players, but elsewhere along the curve only spread trading exists. Difficulties arise in the buying of bonds to lock into the pay position. Not only is the Canadian bond market a physical delivery market with limited liquidity, which means the trader may not even be able to complete the bond side of the transaction, but there are no regular auctions as in the US. The trader has no idea when his on-the-run bond bought to hedge a position will be replaced by a new bond with a higher or lower yield. And given the limited liquidity of the market, a dealer will have to be prepared to warehouse a position for a longer period of time than his US counterpart, thus enhancing the chances of erratic loss or gain through changes in bond yield. It all makes pricing the roll more difficult.

Spreads are quoted out to 10 years, but the most liquid sector is up to five years. This is where the mortgage companies are most active, and credit concerns have inhibited longer-dated business latterly. The floating side of a transaction is normally set in relation to the Canadian dollar bankers' acceptance (BA) rate at 30, 60 or 90 days, or against Libor in a currency swap. Floating-rate payments are usually compounded every 90 days and payable semi-annually. Fixed-rate payments are also often semi-annual. Both fixed and floating payments are made on an actual/365 day basis, which is one of the reasons they are not fungible with European currencies.

The domestic interest rate swap market is dominated by corporations, government and quasi-government administrations and financial institutions. Corporations used to dominate the scene, but credit concerns and more recently the economic recession has curtailed their activities. The size of federal government borrowing in the shape of provincial administrations and their crown corporations has grown enormously, however. Capital spending has mushroomed, and new borrowers have emerged, like the province of Ontario, which until recently was sufficiently cash rich to eschew debt completely. The trust companies have big mortgage books to hedge and the banks have their own mortgage books. It should be noted that all these borrowers are natural fixed-rate payers. Historically, it has never been much of a problem for Canadian banks to receive fixed; laying the position off is much more tricky.

This is where the crucial significance of the EuroCanadian swap market lies; its importance to Canadian dollar swaps can hardly be overstated. The first currency swap in Canadian dollars was executed in 1982, when OKB swapped the proceeds of a Can$75m five-year Eurobond led by Morgan Stanley into Swiss francs. Since then, the market has ebbed and flowed according to the international appetite for high-yielding Canadian dollar bonds and arbitrage opportunities. Over 1990, 56 straight Canadian dollar Eurobonds were issued, worth nearly $6.5bn, making it the seventh most popular currency of issuance. Only two years ago, in 1988, the volume of issuance was $16bn, compared to a mere $500m in 1979.

The development of the Canadian dollar currency swap market gives overseas borrowers the chance to issue in Canadian dollars and swap back into their currency of choice at a reduced all-in cost and the Canadian banks the chance to pay fixed-rate Canadian dollars on the Canadian dollar Libor leg of the swap (see Figure 1). This market comes and goes, however. For example, concerns about the currency in the wake of the Meech-Lake Accord concerning the possibility of the secession of the province of Quebec, damaged the EuroCanadian market. If yields are not attractive compared to other high-yielding currencies, then investors will not be drawn to Canadian dollar bonds, and if swap arbitrage between Canadian dollars and Libor is not attractive then issuers will not be interested. In fact, the pattern of the last four months (January to April 1991), in which there has been muted corporate paying interest in a climate of recession and falling rates while there have been ample opportunities to pay into healthy Eurobond issuance, is a relatively uncommon one.

Figure 1

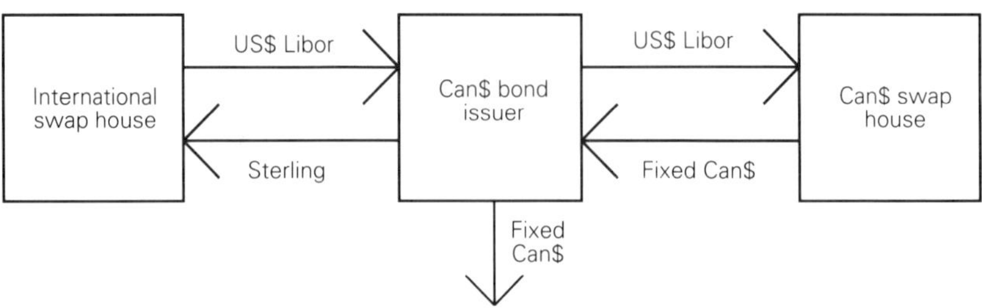

The domestic issuer also makes use of the international markets, launching bonds or private placements in foreign currencies and swapping into Canadian dollars. This, of course, puts upward rather than downward pressure on Canadian dollar swap spreads as the house in receipt of Canadian dollars from the issuer attempts to lay the position off in the market. In recent years yen private placements have been particularly popular among Canadian borrowers as a means of deriving Canadian dollar funding, and Toronto-Dominion Bank has been active in this market (see Figure 2). Aside from the new issue arena, larger borrowers in Canada have made use of the swap market to reduce foreign currency exposure in a climate of increased exchange rate volatility and relative Canadian dollar weakness. The Bank of Canada also makes use of the domestic swap market, principally to swap fixed-rate bond issues into floating rate.

Figure 2

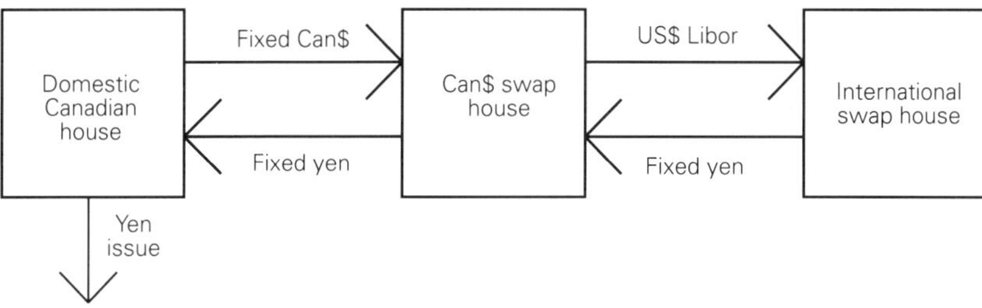

Over the last one or two years, Canadian swap market veterans mention the growth of short-end trading and increasing use of options as significant developments. In common with most markets, Canadian houses are finding enhanced profitability in highly structured transactions tailored specifically to meet client and identified investor demand. Swaps have moved closer to origination, both conceptually and sometimes physically. Inevitably, in a market that has matured with the passing years, standards of professionalism have improved and the technology at the disposal of the derivatives professionals is infinitely more powerful and comprehensive.

However, the Canadian dollar swap market could not be described as rude with health either. Its dependence on the EuroCanadian market means that it will always have to endure slow periods, but the current recession has bitten deep into the banks' other sources of swap business. And credit concerns, virtually unknown until the last one or two years, have drastically curtailed swap operations. These days, none of the big five Canadian banks is rated AAA. Toronto-Dominion Bank was recently downgraded to AA1, while CIBC and Royal Bank of Canada are rated AA2, and Bank of Nova Scotia and Bank of Montreal are both rated AA3. Two years ago, deals seemed to be crashed out with frightening speed, but so much credit was swallowed that the brakes have had to be applied. Corporates were once regularly seen swapping debt at the long end of the curve, but 10-year transactions are now much more rare. Canadian dollar swappers that have seen the market develop over a number of years attest that it is characterised by a much more conservative and risk-averse attitude than was common several years ago. The importance of the new issue market is such that when it booms, Toronto dealers will be busy and the interest rate swap market will be kept afloat by the clear domestic need for it. However, in general, the Canadian dollar swap market, relatively illiquid and dominated by five banks, may well have seen the last of its halcyon days.

Chapter 5: The sterling swap market

Tony Keane
Midland Montagu

Growth in volume

A combination of extremely volatile interest rate movements and an increase in Eurosterling issue volume, has caused a steady increase in both the size and number of swaps that have been executed in sterling during the past two years. Prior to joining the European Exchange Rate Mechanism (ERM), sterling swap volumes benefited from speculation that ERM membership was only a matter of time and that UK interest rates would fall dramatically from their relatively high levels. Indeed, entry to the system was coupled with a 1% reduction in base rates and further falls are expected in the near future despite the current level of inflation, which at the time of writing is 10.9%

It is extremely difficult to establish an accurate figure for volumes transacted. However, the International Swap Dealers Association survey for the year ending 31 December 1989 shows that sterling ranked number three when viewed in terms of the notional principal amount of swaps completed for the year. The US dollar market remains by far the largest, but it is interesting to note that swap brokers in London estimate that sterling accounts for approximately 40% (and in two cases in excess of 55%) of their business. Judging by average daily volumes, it is estimated that approximately 15,000 swaps with an average notional principal amount of £15m were written during the past year. This turnover would generate a market size of approximately £1trn depending on the maturity of the swaps.

As the market has grown, dealing spreads have become more consistent to the extent that a bid/offer spread of 5 basis points can be expected for maturities up to and including seven years and 7bp in 10 years. For longer maturities the spread becomes wider, reflecting the lack of liquidity and concerns over credit. However, it is possible to obtain prices as far out as 25 years, though deals of this duration are few and far between. The average size of swaps that these spreads will stand has increased and, depending on maturity, amounts of up to £25m can be readily transacted. For larger amounts (indeed deals with a notional principal in excess of £50m are quite common), the dealing spread will vary depending on market conditions at the time.

Pattern of participation

The pattern of participation has changed somewhat during the last year and in this regard the disappearance of the local authorities has been most noticeable. At one time the Locals were active users of the swap market as well as other derivative products. In particular, volumes in the swaptions market have reduced and there are now only a handful of banks who could be considered as market-makers.

The impact of the UK Council's case is not very clear and is the subject of much debate.[1] It cannot be denied that the latest High Court ruling was a set-back for the market and has forced many organisations to review their policies when it comes to dealing with unincorporated bodies, such as building societies. However, it is all too easy to allow this situation to dominate one's perception of how the sterling swap market has evolved over recent times and this should not be the case.

As previously mentioned, the market has continued to grow steadily and an increasing number of end users in the form of corporates (both domestic and overseas), and other financial institutions have become far more comfortable in using swaps and other derivative products for a variety of reasons. Speculation on outright interest rate movements as well as yield curve plays and swap versus gilt spread fluctuations, accounts for a major part of the business. Hedging against interest rate volatility and locking in to a fixed cost of funding makes up a large percentage of corporate activity. Restructuring asset and liability mismatches cost effectively and enhancing yields on investments also play their part. In order to meet the requirements of their customers the market-markers have increased in numbers and have become more flexible in the pricing of non-generic swaps and, despite the relative lack of liquidity in the UK gilt market, more are prepared to run sterling warehouses. Corporate clients are also sizeable users of the FRA market and are becoming more adventurous in their use of option-based products, such as caps, floors, collars and swaptions, all of which employ swaps for hedging purposes.

As with the US dollar swap market, there appear to be two distinct types of professional players. The two categories can best be described in terms of maturity; short-end arbitragers who tend to concentrate their efforts in swaps up to three years, and the capital markets-based swap houses whose underlying business requires swaps in the medium to longer-dated maturity bands. The pricing of swaps also differs depending on the period involved, with short-dated swaps being priced against strips of futures contracts and FRAs, and the longer-maturity swaps being derived from gilt yields plus a spread.

Obviously, there are overlaps and more recently the division has become less distinct for two reasons. Firstly, the Bank of England relaxed its policies with regard to sterling Eurobonds, which allowed for bonds to be issued with a maturity of less than five years. Secondly, the London International Financial Futures Exchange has introduced a third year of short sterling contracts, thereby encouraging the strip arbitragers to trade further along the curve.

The market has also benefited from speculation in sterling due to the relatively high yields available and in this regard it is becoming more common for sterling swaps to be transacted outside of London time. Most noticeable is the interest generated in both Sydney and Tokyo, especially on the back of cross-currency coupon swaps.

Another source of business which is becoming more prevalent stems from the requirements of those banks who are managing large sterling cash books. The swap has become more popular with the cash managers as they have come to realise how they can restructure their asset/liability mismatches without altering their underlying positions and with minimal impact on the balance sheet. A simple example would be for the bank to issue medium-term certificates of deposit and, by means of a swap, to convert this fixed-rate liability into cheap three-month funding.

In more recent times, the market has witnessed a limited amount of demand from institutions who have long-term liabilities, such as the insurance companies and pension funds. These organisations are natural holders of gilts to offset their liabilities, and by taking advantage of the spread differential between swaps and gilts, a synthetic, higher-yielding asset can be created. This process is very straightforward. The first step is to sell the gilt and then replace its cash flows with a swap of similar maturity. The sale proceeds are then invested in the money markets which match out against the floating side of the swap. The pick-up on the fixed side will vary depending on the swap over gilt spread. However, during early 1990, the differential was as much as 150bp in the 10-year maturity.

Two concerns are often voiced by the fund manager — credit risk and illiquidity. On the first issue, the enhancement in return on the investment far outweighs the slight increase in credit risk and on the second, there is now sufficient depth to the swap market to enable institutions to trade in and out of these instruments with ease. Despite the obvious attractions of the swap, only a handful of institutions have taken advantage of it and the reasons for this are threefold:

- the rules under which these companies have to operate do not always provide for the use of swaps;
- a lack of appreciation as to how simple the transaction can be; and

- the inability of these institutions to handle swap transactions from an administrative and accounting point of view.

Reduction in the supply of gilt stock

The main problem in managing a sterling swap warehouse, especially when compared to US dollars, is the lack of liquidity in the UK gilt market. This situation has been exacerbated by the turnaround in the fortunes of HM Treasury, which has resulted in the Public Sector Borrowing Requirement (PSBR) being transformed into the Public Sector Debt Repayment (PSDR). A combination of high tax revenues and the income generated by the Thatcher Government's privatisation programme have forced the Bank of England to become net buyers of gilt-edged stock, thus reducing the total amount of outstanding debt by approximately 23%.

This contraction in the amount of stock outstanding has pushed swap market-makers into using futures contracts to hedge their exposures, which in turn necessitates taking on extra risk in the form of basis and yield curve risk. Furthermore, it is felt that the overall decrease in the size of the gilt market has created a somewhat artificial scenario, in that gilt yields were lower than they would otherwise have been, and this in turn provides a partial explanation as to why spreads have been at such high levels during the past two years.

Pricing behaviour — spread volatility

It can be seen from Figure 1 that the spread relationship has been extremely volatile, and it is worth looking at the variety of factors that have brought this about. It is vital that any swap warehouse manager has some understanding of what drives the spread.

Prior to the transformation of the PSBR to the PSDR and the subsequent buying back of gilts by the Bank of England, the traditional relationship between spreads and absolute swap levels tended to be inversely proportional. This behaviour pattern can be readily explained — when interest rates are at relatively low levels, borrowers are prepared to lock-in to fixed-rate funding through the swap mechanism and this in turn props up the swap rate relative to the gilt yield. When rates are perceived to be at their peak the lack of demand for fixed-rate funding drags spreads down. Of course, this is a very simplistic argument and other factors, in particular the spreads between Eurosterling bonds and gilts, also play their part.

If swap spreads widen while the relationship between Eurosterling and gilts remains static, then a window of opportunity opens up which will encourage new issues to be launched. The requirement of the issuer to find a fixed-rate payer in the swap will tend to force spreads down. It is worth mentioning that the vast majority of Eurosterling issues which have a maturity of 10 years or less are swapped into floating rate. However, longer-dated issues are unlikely to be swapped to their final maturity due to the lack of liquidity in the swap market beyond 10 years.

Figure 1: Five-year par gilt yield and swap spread

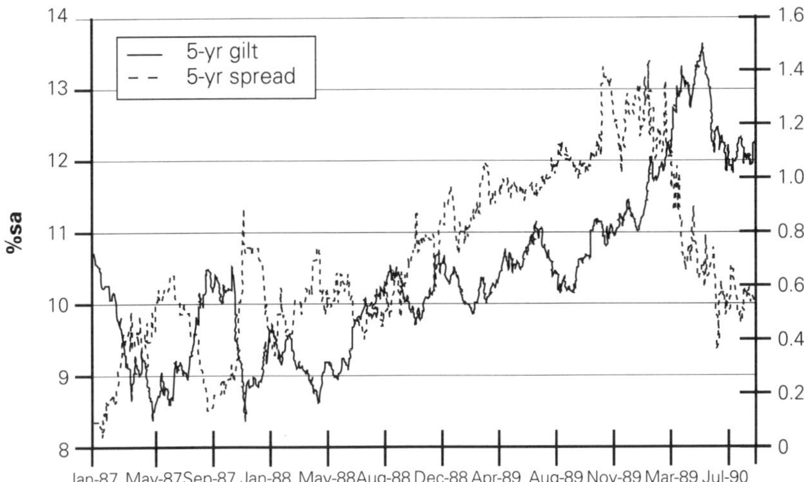

In attempting to explain the dynamics of the market, a question that often arises is, who provides the receive side when Eurosterling issues dry up? This question is particularly pertinent at the time of writing as there has been a dearth of new issues during the past few months due to the lack of demand for new paper. Despite this lack of interest there has been a range of other receivers of fixed rate.

Looking at the short end of the market, the futures/swap arbitragers will always have an interest to receive at a level relative to the futures strip. Also at the shorter end, a variety of houses which are able to issue certificates of deposit, on which they pay fixed, can swap into floating and generate funds at substantial margins below Libor. An array of corporates have chosen to unwind swaps on which they were paying fixed at lower interest rate levels and realise upfront profits, based on the view that sterling interest rates are likely to fall. Finally, swaps that were written earlier in the year against issues may still be held as part of a warehouse waiting to be placed with an end user.

Bank of England policy also plays its part in determining the spread. To be specific, only licensed gilt-edged market-makers have approval to go short of gilts and to be able to borrow them to meet their requirement. This restriction prevents swap counterparties from cleanly hedging a swap on which they would be receivers of fixed interest, unless of course they already happen to be holders of the particular stock, probably as a hedge against an existing position. As a result of this policy, swappers are reluctant to take on a swap that requires a gilt to be shorted as a hedge because the only viable alternative is the use of a long gilt futures contract with its incumbent risks. This state of affairs tends to keep spreads higher than they would otherwise be.

The use of short-dated swaps as a speculative instrument has also contributed to keeping the spread wide. During the past 18 months, in the belief that sterling base rates were unlikely to fall due to inflationary pressures, swaps have been transacted to take advantage of the steeply negative yield curve. By paying fixed to a certain maturity, say, three years, against receiving six-month Libor, there has been a massive positive cost of carry, as much as 2%, and for those in the swap community who still account for their profit and loss on an accrual basis, this type of trade appears very attractive.

Another problem for those involved in market-making, which originated from the lack of liquidity in the gilt market, is deciding which stock should be used as the pricing benchmark in each maturity. Unlike the dollar market where new bonds are issued regularly, the sterling market has not seen a new issue for a considerable time, and as a result we cannot avoid hedging with gilts that are trading at a substantial premium or discount to par. It has become standard practice to use the same gilt as a benchmark for each calendar year; for example, the five-year swap has been priced as a spread to the 12% of 1995 (which matures in January 1995) since 1 January 1990 and will continue to be priced against this stock until the year end. From this example it becomes clear that when using this particular gilt for hedging, it is necessary to adjust the amount of stock used depending on the time of year. This is one reason why virtually all swap portfolio managers hedge their exposures on a duration basis.

Furthermore, there are anomalies that crop up from time to time which cause certain stocks to trade substantially away from the par yield curve. A prime example was the introduction of gilts that are free of tax to overseas residents. It is therefore advisable to make use of the par gilt curve when reviewing the relationship between swaps and gilts over a long period of time.

Looking ahead and trying to predict the behaviour of spreads in future months is outside the scope of this discussion, though it will be interesting to see if the "traditional" relationship will return with the prospect of new gilt issuance in 1991.

Innovation and recent developments

The pace of innovation has dropped off somewhat in recent times and this does not come as any great surprise. However, swaps that were at one time looked upon as being esoteric are now dealt as part of the normal course of business. Amortising, accreting, roller-coaster, zero-coupon and just about any other customised structure can be handled relatively easily.

Other forms of swaps such as basis swaps, especially exchanges of Libor for base rate or mortgage rate linked flows, remain few and far between due to the nature of the market. For instance in the past there was reasonable demand from the UK building society sector, the bulk of whose lendings are at the mortgage rate (which in turn is base rate linked), to swap into Libor to match out their money market funding requirements. This basis swap proved virtually impossible to execute because there is no natural end user with an opposite set of needs.

More recent times have seen the use of sterling as one leg of cross-currency coupon swaps and there have been spin-offs for the sterling swap market due to the hedges that have been required. In addition, zero-coupon swaps have become more popular of late, highlighted by the issue of a 10-year £200m zero-coupon bond by British Telecom in February 1990.

It is mentioned above that as a result of the local authority situation, the swaption market had suffered rather more than the swap market itself and this view is justified by the small number of banks who are considered market-makers in this area. However, there is still a fair amount of interest in this derivative from the corporate sector as well as from interbank traders, and swaptions are all the more accessible now that virtually all deals are settled on a cash basis rather than being exercised into a swap. A further development which has been sponsored by swaptions is the cash settlement swap, for which there has been a lot of interest recently.

Of all the most recent variations, there is one that stands out and that is the forward start swap. The idea is nothing new, but during the past year the percentage of swaps commencing at a future date has increased dramatically. The inverse steepness of the sterling curve can be held responsible for this and, as can be seen from Table 1, the discounts available for forward starts can be sizeable. Naturally, the rate for the forward start swap is simply a mathematical product of the spot start swaps to the start date and maturity date of the deal in question, but for a corporate treasurer, who may have the view that sterling base rates will not fall as far as the forward/forward curve implies, this transaction is ideal. Not only have corporates been involved in the forward swaps market; interbank traders have also been active in using forward starts to arbitrage against long-dated FRAs and also against the implied futures curve out beyond two years (prior to the third year on Liffe being available). Also, those who manage large portfolios have employed the forward start mechanism to hedge against curve positions that crop up in their swap books from time to time.

Table 1: Five-year swap — forward start at 13/8/90

Start	
Spot	12.805
1 month	12.74
3 months	12.63
6 months	12.48
12 months	12.36
18 months	12.33
24 months	12.30

Prices are based on mid-market rates on a semi/semi basis

Market outlook

The outlook for the sterling swap market is difficult to predict. Competition is fierce and with the "opening up" of the European markets by 1992 the prospects look bright. On the negative side, both the implications of the final outcome of the UK Council's case and the current political situation will lead to a certain amount of nervousness.

A recent survey, carried out by IFR, demonstrated the depth of the market with a number of banks carrying out a sizeable amount of business. The UK clearing banks — Midland, Barclays, NatWest and Lloyds — are all to the fore, with the merchant banks, especially Hill Samuel, Barings, Morgan Grenfell, Hambros and Kleinwort Benson providing strong competition. From overseas there is a wide cross-section of banks running active sterling swap books, with Bankers Trust, Morgan Guaranty, Svenska Handelsbanken, Industrial Bank of Japan and Westpac being but a few. To sum up, the sterling swap market has matured considerably in recent times and is set to play a major role in the capital markets in the future.

Notes

1. For a full account of the UK Council's case see Chapters 37 and 38.

Chapter 6: The Deutsche mark and Dutch guilder swap markets

Jim Coleman
NatWest Capital Markets

Deutsche marks

Market background

The structure of the Deutsche mark swap market reflects its origins during the deregulation of the underlying debt markets. The "plain vanilla" structure is therefore an annual fixed rate on a Eurobond (12 x 30-day months in a 360-day year) basis, versus six-month Deutsche mark or US dollar Libor. The players in the swap market reflect the Deutsche mark's position as one of the three most highly-traded currencies in the world. The main players in the market include the major German banks, such as Deutsche Bank and Dresdner Bank; most US swap houses, including Bankers Trust, JP Morgan, Security Pacific and Citibank; European Banks, for example, the big three Swiss banks, Paribas and NatWest; and several Japanese banks associated with the swap market.

Although originally developing as a result of bond market deregulation, Deutsche mark swaps are also utilised by corporate treasuries and liability managers. Thus, on one side we have receivers of fixed-rate Deutsche marks in the form of highly-rated sovereign, supranational or corporate names demanded by investors, matched by corporates hedging their floating-rate borrowings and banks hedging fixed-rate loan books. This structure is illustrated in Figure 1.

As at the end of 1989, total outstandings in Deutsche marks stood at US$84.6bn for interest rate swaps, and US$53.8bn for currency swaps.

The origins of the Deutsche mark swap market date back to 1984 when the Bundesbank (the Federal Republic of Germany's central bank) deregulated the debt market, and, in particular, permitted the issue of debt intended to be swapped. This was a triumph of pragmatism as banks had already begun to ignore the prohibition on swapped issues. However, it was to be some time before full liberalisation, including the abolition of the new issue calendar, allowed the market to develop unfettered. To date, much of the activity in the swap market continues to be driven by new issues, thus a brief tour of debt instruments available in Deutsche marks is appropriate.

Figure 1: The underlying structure of the Deutsche mark swap market

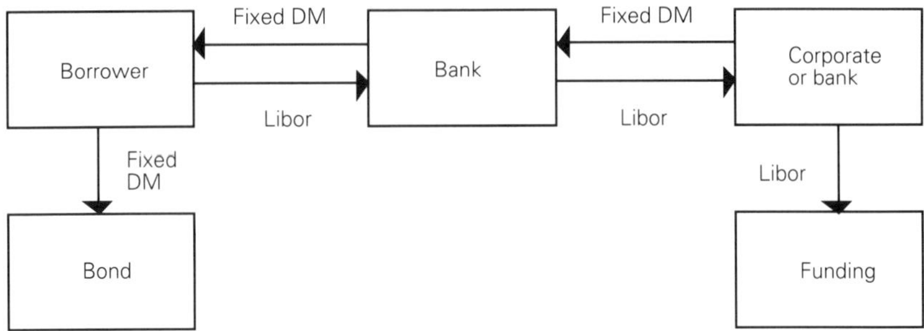

Deutsche mark debt markets

Bundesanleihen

Federal Government bonds (or Bunds) are the German equivalent of US Treasuries or UK gilts. These are medium to long-term government-guaranteed bond issues where a significant secondary market exists. Bunds are issued usually once a month, on average in eight months of the year, commonly with an original maturity of 10 years (although up to 30-year maturities have been issued). During the first half of 1990, a net DM79.2bn of Bunds were issued, almost equal to the DM80.6bn issued during 1989. Coupons are paid annually in arrears, normally on the 20th of the month to coincide with Federal Government revenues. In common with other government debt markets, liquidity is concentrated in the most recent issues.

On 29 September 1988, the London International Financial Futures Exchange (Liffe) began trading the German Government bond futures contract. This has the specifications detailed in Table 1.

Table 1: The Bund

Unit of trading	DM250,000 nominal, 6% coupon
Delivery	March, June, September and December
Minimum tick movement	DM0.01 (per DM100 nominal)
Tick size and value	DM25 per contract
Initial margin	DM1,500
Trading hours	08.10am–16.00pm London time
Contract standard	Bund with 8.5–10 years remaining on delivery date

This had the effect both of concentrating further liquidity in the 10-year maturities and of increasing the international nature of the Bund market. In fact, on many occasions, the London futures pit has led the cash market. Consequently, the German authorities are increasingly realising both the benefits and drawbacks of the international nature of their government bond market. The recent difficulties associated with the "Unity Bonds", issued by the German authorities to finance the unification of West and East, have illustrated the dichotomy. Whilst it is clear that international capital will be required during the rebuilding of the East German economy, the markets are likely to demand a price which the government is currently not prepared to pay.

Kassenobligationen

These are medium-term securities issued by the Federal Government to residents only in the primary market, but subsequently may be bought by non-residents. Kassenobligationen usually have an original maturity of three to five years, and are traded in registered form on the OTC market of the exchange. Outstandings total some one third of those of Bunds, and there is a yield premium of some five to 10 basis points over this market.

Schuldscheindarlehen

Over 50% of public sector debt is in the form of Schuldschein loan agreements documented by promissory letter. The fact that these are loans rather than bonds means that investors need not mark-to-market. Schuldschein may also be issued by banks and other borrowers, and, in conjunction with swaps, are an important source of attractive floating-rate finance for the Landesbanks. Consequently, whilst not used for hedging purposes, Schuldschein will often set the benchmark for pricing swaps, particularly at those parts of the curve where the Bund market is less liquid.

Other domestic bonds

There are several other classes of bonds available in the Deutsche mark market. Mortgage bonds (Pfandbriefe) are bearer bonds issued by mortgage banks and banks under public law; Communalobligationen are issued mainly by the larger Landesbanks; and unsecured domestic bearer bonds (Inhaderschuldvarschreibungen) are issued by most credit institutions.

These domestic bonds provide an active domestic debt market and clearly allow for significant issuing opportunities in conjunction with the swap market.

EuroDeutsche mark bonds

Together with the market for Bunds, this is probably the most familiar territory to the professional in the international capital markets, and is also the most liberal of the Deutsche mark bond markets. In May 1985, the Sub-Committee of the German Central Capital Markets Committee, which supervised EuroDeutsche mark issues, ceased to exist, so that now all that a bank planning to lead an issue need do is to notify the Bundesbank two business days prior to launch. No actual permission is required.

The EuroDeutsche mark market is open to any borrower, although in common with most Euromarkets, it is dominated by issues from sovereign or sovereign-guaranteed agencies, supranationals and large private sector borrowers. Where borrowers are rated, the range varies from AAA to as low as BB. In common with the other Deutsche mark capital markets, many issues in the EuroDeutsche mark market are swap-driven.

The swap market

The early years of the swap market coincided with the final two years of falling inflation following the tight economic policies in Germany of the late 1970s and early 1980s. Consequently, fixed rates fell during 1984 and 1985 from around 8% to 6.5% — as measured by 10-year swap rates. During 1986, inflation was zero to slightly negative in Germany, and fixed rates continued to hover around 6% at 10 years. The yield curve in swaps was consistently positive during this period, with two-year rates between 1.5% and 1.75% below 10-year rates. Throughout this first formative period for the swap market, its liquidity was very much one way, in that it was dominated at any one time by payers or receivers of fixed rate.

In 1987, a withholding tax was imposed on Bunds and caused spreads between swaps and Bunds to narrow significantly. From early 1987 to October of that year, rates started to rise as fears of fast economic growth leading to renewed inflation affected the markets. The stock market crash in October 1987, which brought fears of economic contraction, caused interest rates to be eased by the authorities, and swap rates reached an all-time low of 6.25% in the 10-year maturity in March 1988.

Rising inflation during 1988 and 1989 caused rates to rise again, and as policy was increasingly tightened the curve also began to flatten. By late 1989, 10-year rates had risen to 8.00% in the face of heightened inflationary expectations and increasing capacity constraints in the West German economy.

The collapse of communism in Eastern Europe and East Germany in particular, at the end of 1989 brought about the unification of the two Germanies. The anticipated costs of this process with its accompanying borrowing requirement of the German authorities, pushed rates higher still. As a result, by October 1990, the curve had slightly inverted, and rates across all maturities traded between 9.00% and 9.50%.

By late 1990, the Deutsche mark swap market had matured to a point where liquidity was very well developed, reflecting very active professional trading by the major market-making banks mentioned above. Underlying this professional trade are the borrowers and liability managers of sovereigns, supranationals, corporates and other institutions who use swap markets for liability management, and investors, including banks, using swaps to manage their assets. The major players of fixed-rate Deutsche marks fall into several classes:

- Corporates which borrow on a floating-rate basis from the banking sector and use interest rate swaps, firstly to fix the cost of debt when they believe that rates are low and likely to rise, and secondly to reduce the uncertainties associated with floating-rate funding costs.

- Sovereign and supranational borrowers, together with the more sophisticated corporates, often manage their liabilities on a multicurrency portfolio basis. In such cases, the borrower will have a pre-determined mix of currencies which it believes is optimal for its liability portfolio, and will aim, through its underlying borrowing and its activity in the swap market, both to achieve this particular mix, and to measure the performance of its strategic liability management decisions. For example, a sovereign borrower in a country with a currency which is managed against a weighted average of other currencies, may select a target liability portfolio reflecting this basket. The Deutsche mark, being a major world trading currency, and at the heart of the European Exchange Rate Mechanism, is almost invariably a large part of any such basket. Hence those borrowers adopting this approach to liability management will often be major fixed-rate payers in the Deutsche mark swap market.

- Banks and leasing companies will often have assets on their books which pay fixed-rate D-marks, either through straight fixed-rate lending or through leases whose payments are calculated using a fixed rate of interest. In order to hedge the mismatch of these fixed-rate assets against the floating-rate funding, swaps will be used. Here the finance house pays fixed-rate Deutsche marks to receive floating, thereby converting the fixed-rate asset into a floating-rate one.

Banks play an important role in the swap market by providing liquidity through their trading activities; either through trading outright swap rates or through positioning for other more technical movements in the market. For example, a bank may hedge a swap position where it was paying fixed rate in Deutsche marks by buying a Bund of similar maturity or through buying Bund futures contracts. Bunds, with the exception of the most recent issue which is normally a 10-year maturity, tend to be less liquid than the futures. However, cash Bunds provide a closer maturity match for swaps of less than 10 years than the futures contract, which is currently the most liquid fixed-rate D-mark hedging vehicle.

Other derivative markets in Deutsche marks are becoming more widely traded. The forward-rate agreement market is extremely liquid and interest rate and swap options are developing rapidly. The FRA market is, in essence, an extension of the swap market which provides a bridge between cash deposits and two-year swaps. Many more banks provide FRAs to their clients than are active in the swap market. They are principally used by corporates to hedge their floating-rate liabilities up to two years, in much the same way as they use the swap markets for longer-dated exposures. FRAs are often used by swap market banks to hedge structured deals, such as amortising interest rate swaps where there is a principal reduction which takes place less than two years from the trade date. The FRA market has grown very rapidly during the 1980s. In contrast, both interest rate and swap options in Deutsche marks are much more recent developments, with caps, floors and collars being used in the recent relatively high interest rate environment. Many corporates wish to hedge their floating-rate exposures but are reluctant to fix using interest rate swaps with no benefit from falling rates in the future, and so use caps or collars to allow some of this benefit to flow through to their interest rate costs.

Recently there has been a growing trend for swaps to be written against Fibor (the Frankfurt Interbank Offered Rate). There is often up to 12 basis points difference in the fixed rate quoted between a swap against Libor and one against Fibor. Indeed, the German authorities are encouraging this development primarily to increase Frankfurt's position as a financial centre, and such contracts are becoming more of the norm for interest rate swaps written within Germany.

The regulatory and documentation structure of the swap market is dependent on the centre in which transactions take place. The two major centres are Frankfurt and London, and are policed respectively by the Bundesbank and the Bank of England through its Code of Conduct. Swaps are generally written using the ISDA Interest Rate and Currency Exchange Agreement, but a significant proportion are documented through particular German agreements when transacted domestically.

Figure 2: Two-year Deutsche mark swap rate

January 1985–September 1990

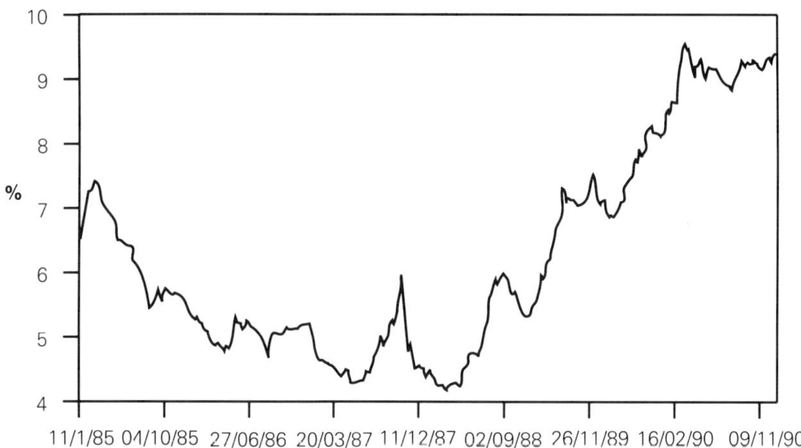

Source: NatWest Capital Markets

Figure 3: Ten-year Deutsche mark swap rate

January 1985–September 1990

Source: NatWest Capital Markets

Figure 4: Ten-year swap rate/ten-year Bund yield, 11/1/85–7/12/90

January 1985–September 1990

Source: NatWest Capital Markets

Figure 5: Deutsche mark swap volumes, 1987–89

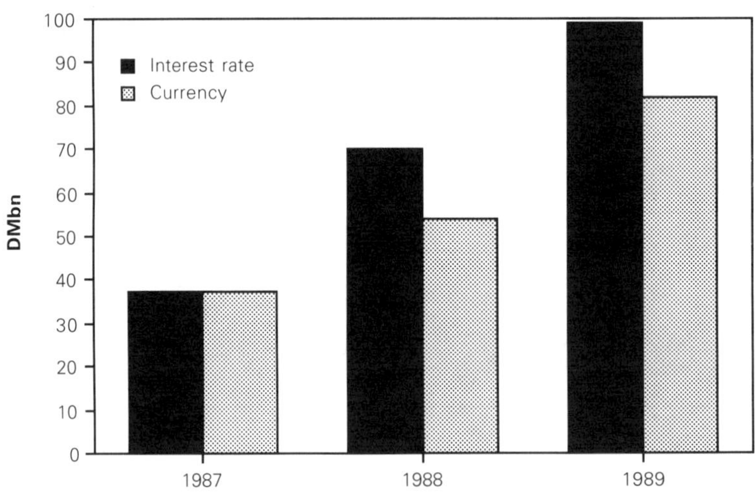

Source: NatWest Capital Markets

Market outlook

The unification of the Federal Republic and the Democratic Republic will result in a significant expansion of the Deutsche mark capital markets as investment in what was East Germany accelerates. Whilst German corporates have a number of funding alternatives (in particular tapping their substantial retained earnings, borrowing through German banks and, increasingly popular, issuing equity) the bond markets are likely to be an important source of capital. In addition, the state sector must invest significantly in the infrastructure of East Germany, especially in communications — both physical and electronic. This demand for funds is clearly discounted by the very high rates of interest across the yield curve relative to recent history. However, in the longer term, the development of the East will ease many of the capacity constraints which were both holding back the West German economy and adding to its inflationary pressures.

Simultaneously with this process of unification within the enlarged German state will come the drive towards economic and monetary union within Europe.

It is uncertain which particular currency will ultimately perform the role of European single currency, but it is clear that the Bundesbank will have a significant influence on economic and monetary policy in the future. The proposals so far put forward for monetary union in Europe are either not specific as to the final currency of union, or propose the Ecu, but are consistent in that the currency chosen should either be or mirror the hardest currency in the community. The hardest currency is without doubt the Deutsche mark and it is clear that the Deutsche mark will therefore have a major role in the future of Europe. If Europe finally integrates so that the same currency is used from Dresden to Dublin and Lisbon to Athens, then it is likely that that currency, if not actually called the Deutsche mark, will probably be its direct descendant.

Dutch guilders

After the big four European curencies (the Deutsche mark, sterling, French franc and Swiss franc) the Dutch guilder possesses the most liquid swap market. However, there is a significant difference in the level of activity between "first division" and "second division" European currencies, with outstandings in Dutch guilders at the end of 1989 of US$6.0bn in interest rate swaps, and US$10.1bn in currency swaps. Market conventions are very similar to those for the Deutsche mark, with an annual fixed rate on a Eurobond basis versus six-month Dutch guilder or US dollar Libor being the most common structure. The main players in the market include the largest Dutch banks, together with major European and US houses.

Much of the motivation for Dutch guilder swap market players is very similar to that described above when referring to Deutsche marks. Thus many of the market participants are similar in nature, although those who manage liabilities on a portfolio basis will be less active in guilders. Holland, being historically a trading nation, has a relatively open economy with major corporates such as Philips, Royal Dutch Shell and Unilever having a cost base there, and large numbers of non-Dutch companies operating in the domestic markets. Consequently, in addition to pure interest rate swap activity, there is an active market in cross-currency swaps which are transacted to hedge translation and balance sheet exposures caused by currency fluctuations. For example, a UK company operating in the Dutch markets would naturally wish to pay Dutch guilders and receive sterling to offset its revenue flows and assets denominated in the former, and its costs and liabilities denominated in the latter. This explains the higher porportion of cross-currency swaps written in Dutch guilders compared to Deutsche marks. This is illustated by Figure 6.

Figure 6: Example of UK corporate's use of Dutch guilder/sterling currency swap

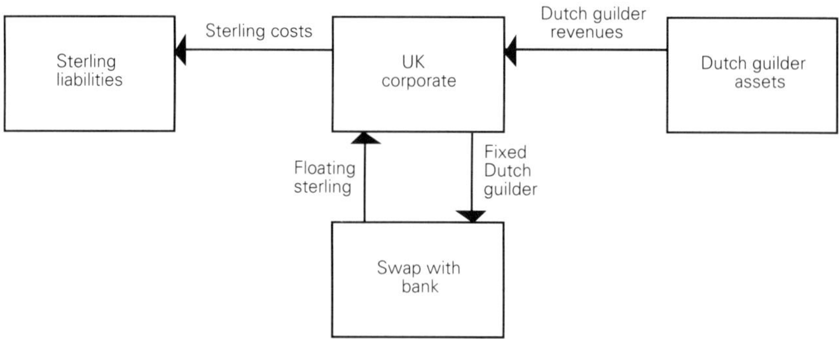

Historically, many market-makers have run their Dutch guilder swaps books in conjunction with that for Deutsche marks, using each to hedge the other. Thus, liquidity in the guilder market is often deeper than would be justified by its relatively low turnover. For example, a market-maker who was running a position in Deutsche marks, would often take an opportunity to trade in the guilder market in order partially to hedge the position. Also, a more aggressive price would be made in guilders if the market-maker felt he had an opportunity to execute an offsetting deal in Deutsche marks. This stemmed from the observed close correlation between monetary and economic forces in the two countries and therefore between market movements in the respective capital markets. Historically, Dutch guilder interest and swap rates traded at a premium of between 20 and 50 basis points over those for Deutsche marks, a relationship which had been maintained throughout the 1980s.

However, this relationship broke down at the end of 1989 as Germany moved towards unification with its resultant rise in the demand for, and therefore the price of capital. Whilst this affected the Dutch guilder markets, along with other European currencies, the impact was not as pronounced as in Germany and so by October 1990 Dutch guilder rates stood at a much reduced premium of 0.15% to Deutsche marks across the curve. This has actually had the effect of reducing liquidity in the guilder market as market-makers are now more conscious of the risks associated with a cross position between guilders and Deutsche marks. This is illustrated by Figure 7, showing the historical relationship between Dutch guilder and Deutsche mark seven-year interest rate swap rates.

Figure 7: Seven-year Dutch guilder/Deutsche mark swap rate

26/6/87–7/12/90

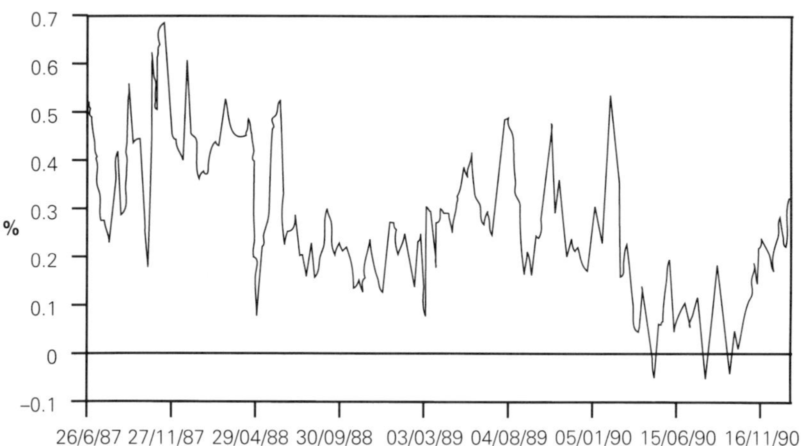

Source: NatWest Capital Markets

In common with the other Benelux currencies, the Netherlands has adopted a policy of embracing European economic and political union. Therefore, the outlook for the guilder swaps and capital markets is very much tied to that for the rest of Europe. The Netherlands, with its traditionally open trading-based economy, will probably embrace any single European currency as early and with as much enthusiasm as any other European country. Consequently, the guilder is likely to give way to the single European currency finally chosen in both a treasury management role (including invoicing and as a medium for payment) and in the capital markets.

Figure 8: Ten-year Dutch guilder swap rate

26/8/88–7/12/90

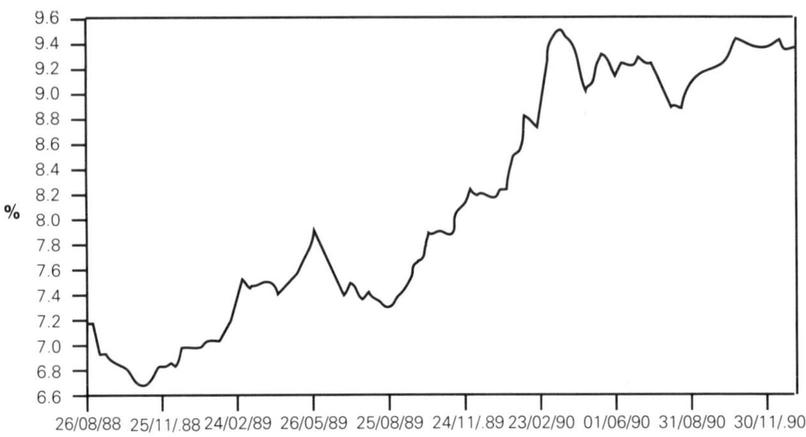

Source: NatWest Capital Markets

Figure 9: Two-year Dutch guilder swap rate

26/6/87–7/12/90

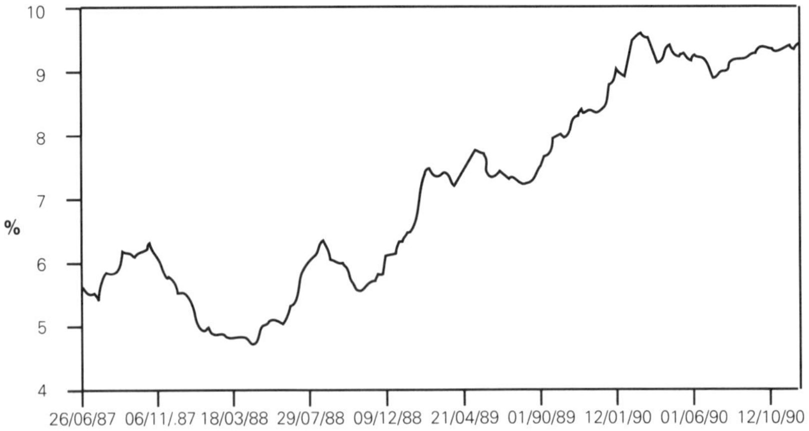

%
10
9
8
7
6
5
4
26/06/87 06/11/.87 18/03/88 29/07/88 09/12/88 21/04/89 01/90/89 12/01/90 01/06/90 12/10/90

Source: NatWest Capital Markets

Figure 10: Dutch guilder swap volumes, 1987–89

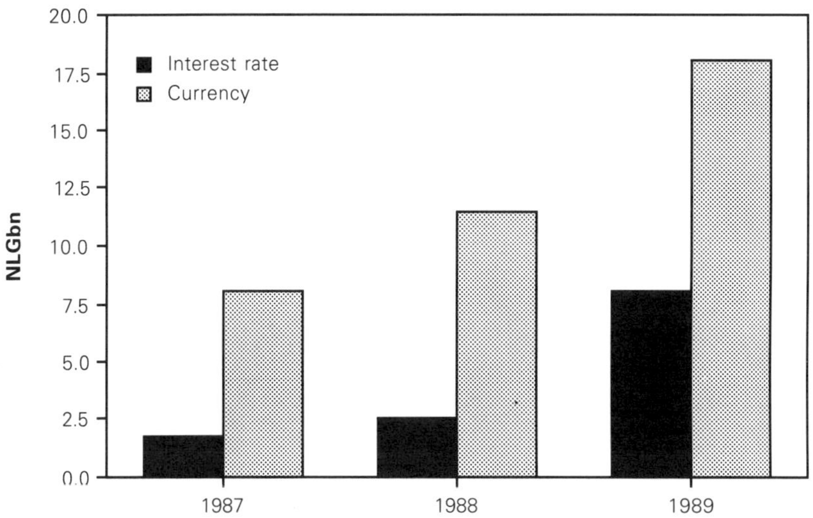

Source: NatWest Capital Markets

Figure 11: Total swap volumes, 1987–89

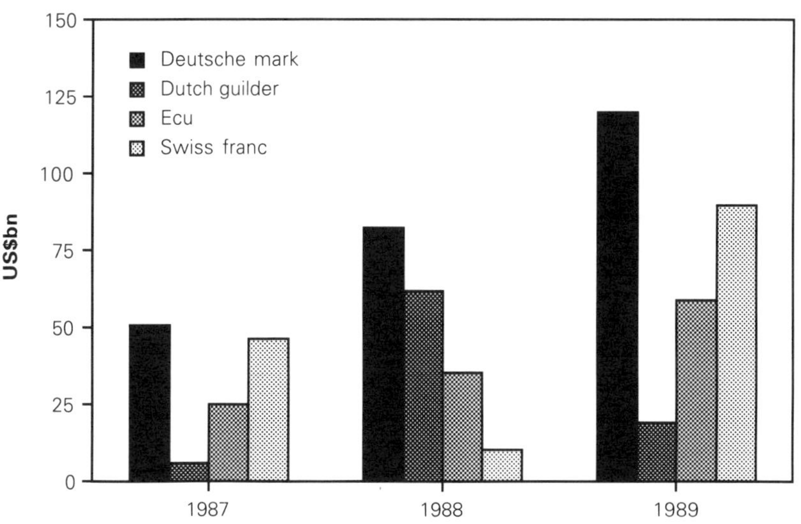

Source: NatWest Capital Markets

Chapter 7: The European Currency Unit, Spanish peseta and Swiss franc swap markets

Jim Coleman
NatWest Capital Markets

The European Currency Unit

Market background

The Ecu swap market trades with a fixed-rate benchmark quoted annually on a Eurobond basis (12 x 30-day months and a 360-day year) against six-month Ecu or US dollar Libor (actual number of days in a 360-day year). Market activity extends from maturities of two years out to 10 years, although liquidity is concentrated between two and five years. The standard contract is for spot (two business day) settlement from the trade date. The main market-makers include the large European banks, particularly the French, together with the more notable US swap houses. The major trading centre is London, although Paris is becoming a more important centre for Ecu swap activity.

At the end of June 1990, outstanding swaps in the Ecu market totalled the equivalent of US$31bn for interest rate swaps, and US$45bn for currency swaps.

Market forces

The market in Ecu swaps is still primarily capital market-driven, which explains the much greater proportion of currency swaps against US dollar Libor, where the Ecu issue is used as a vehicle to achieve sub-Libor funding. The single major issuer in the Ecu market is the Republic of Italy with other sovereigns such as Belgium, the French State agencies and the Austrian central bank (Oesterreichische Kontrollbank), being prominent. Large corporates such as IBM and British Telecom, together with many European banks have also borrowed in Ecu, although usually to take advantage of attractive sub-Libor dollar funding opportunities through the swap market. The most attractive levels achieved in 1990 have been around Libor minus 30 basis points for the highest quality borrowers. The investors in the Ecu bond markets broadly fall into two categories.

First, private investors in the Benelux countries, who are the traditional Eurobond investors, see the Ecu as a naturally stable investment currency for their private funds; secondly, institutional investors in Germany and Switzerland, together with, to a lesser extent, the French (see "outlook" below), also perceive the Ecu to be a relatively stable currency in which a yield pick-up over Deutsche mark and Swiss francs may be achieved. During 1990, a total of US$15bn in fixed-rate Ecu (including US$115m of zero-coupon bonds) and US$2.7bn of floating-rate notes were issued. It has yet to be fully accepted by corporate treasuries as an accounting currency, and so the supply and demand of fixed-rate payers and receivers is primarily driven by the bond market and tax arbitrage.

The major example of tax arbitrage stems from the Italian tax authorities' treatment of the Italian Government's *Certificate del Tresore in Ecu* (CTE's). The coupons on these fixed-rate bonds are subject to a 12.5% withholding tax. Consequently, to make CTEs attractive they must be issued at a gross yield above that of Ecu Eurobonds. However, many investors outside Italy may reclaim this withholding tax, and so may swap this Italian Government paper into an attractive floating rate. This demand to pay the fixed rate in the Ecu swap market pushes up the swap rates relative to Eurobond yields, and so provides issuing opportunities for borrowers who wish to swap their liabilities back into Libor (see Figure 1).

Figure 1: An example of an Ecu swap

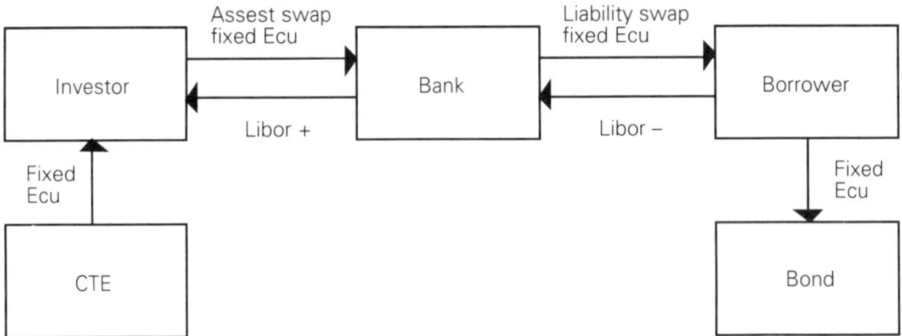

As a consequence of this arbitrage, an issue of CTEs is usually followed by issuing activity in the primary Ecu Eurobond market. However, of late the markets have become more efficient at anticipating such activity, and this has reduced the arbitrage opportunities available.

The second arbitrage stems from the nature of the Ecu as a weighted average of the component currencies. By transacting an Ecu swap, and then matching this off against a subset of the basket of currencies, a net position may be created in the other illiquid currencies. The composition of the Ecu, as at October 1990, is shown in Table 1.

Table 1: Composition of the Ecu

October 1990

0.6242	Deutsche marks	3.301	Belgian francs
0.08784	Pounds sterling	0.130	Luxembourg francs
1.332	French francs	0.1976	Danish kroner
151.80	Italian lire	0.008552	Irish punt
0.2198	Dutch guilders	1.440	Greek drachmas
6.885	Spanish pesetas	1.393	Portuguese escudos

The Ecu is also used by European and international borrowers, in particular, European Community entities such as the European Investment Bank (EIB) and the European Coal and Steel Community (ECSC), together with France, Italy and other sovereigns that both borrow and swap in Ecu. This activity supports the Ecu as a concept, and allows for cheaper funding than is domestically available. Also, for those EC countries within the ERM, substantial foreign currency reserves may be generated through Ecu borrowing to facilitate any intervention in the foreign exchange market.

Many borrowers which manage their liability portfolios on a diversified basis will use the Ecu to achieve an exposure to European currencies. As the relative weightings of the different currencies in the Ecu reflect each country's economic importance, the Ecu provides a very efficient means by which such a borrower can achieve the desired proportion of debt in each currency. Many large corporates with a Europe-wide revenue base, will use Ecu liabilities to match fund-underlying assets resulting from revenue flows from their trading activity. However, the level of this activity is relatively low compared with the swaps transacted against primary issues in the Ecu Eurobond market.

Investors and market-makers in the Ecu Eurobond market also use the swap market as a hedge of their own bond positions. Whilst this is often a less than perfect match, it does provide a degree of protection from large price movements in the Ecu capital markets.

As there is no government bond market in the Ecu, the swap market-maker has no efficient means of hedging his own positions except by using offsetting swaps. Thus the trader must either be prepared to take a view on the movement of Ecu fixed rates, or offset positions against matched business. This means that the liquidity in the Ecu market can be limited, and at any one time may be dominated by either paying or receiving interest. The London International Financial Futures Exchange (Liffe) and the Paris Marché à Terme des Instruments Financiers (Matif) both have a three-month Euro Ecu deposit contract, and Matif has an Ecu bond contract. However, all of these have very limited liquidity and unfortunately do not add to the ability of a swap market-maker to hedge a position. Many banks also use a weighted average of the constituent currencies to hedge positions, though, the illiquidity of all but the Deutsche mark, sterling and the French franc make this rather inefficient.

Other derivative markets are also developing. There is a liquid market in Ecu forward-rate agreements (FRAs) which involves most major European banks. Interest rate caps and floors and options on swaps are also increasingly being traded.

In common with wholesale markets traded out of London, the regulation of Ecu swap and other derivative markets is through the Bank of England's Code of Conduct. The standard ISDA Interest Rate and Currency Exchange Agreement is the most common basis for documentation.

Figure 2: Ecu swap volumes, 1987–89

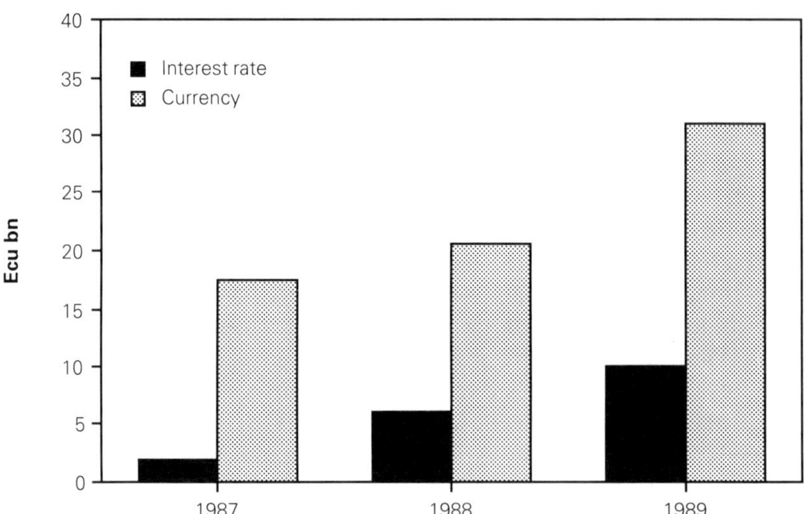

Source: NatWest Capital Markets

Figure 3: Ten-year Ecu swap rate
Weekly data, 12/1/85–7/12/90

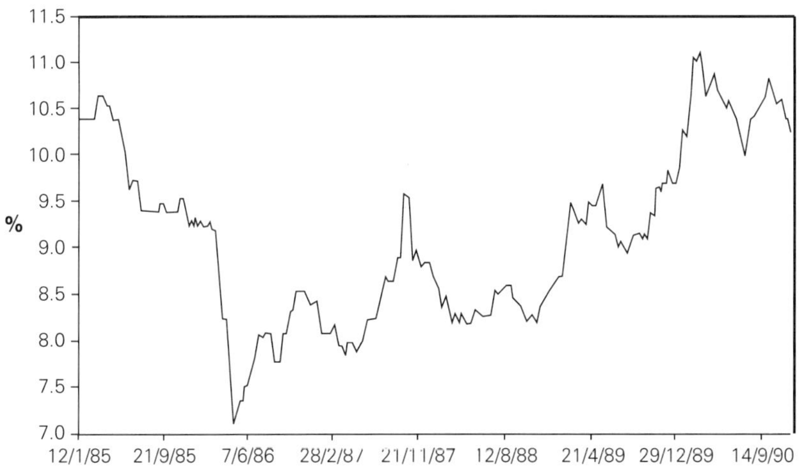

Source: NatWest Capital Markets

Outlook

The key to the development of the European Currency Unit capital market in general, and the swap market in particular, is the extent to which European monetary union is achieved, and the position of the Ecu within such a union. The Delors proposals for economic and monetary union (named after Jacques Delors, the French President of the European Community) are not specific in respect of which should be the final currency of union; all that is said is that in the final stage there should be fixed exchange rates with monetary policy for the Community set by a European central bank. It should then be a simple step for all of Europe to adopt one particular currency. Although technically it is equally possible for this to be one of the existing sovereign currencies, a political unwillingness for one country to accept the currency of another may make the use of the Ecu in this regard more likely. The alternative to Delors, UK Prime Minster John Major's recent "hard Ecu" proposal, explicitly drives towards the Ecu as the common European currency. Should this route be followed, then clearly the Ecu capital markets will develop very rapidly, and will ultimately dominate activity within Europe.

Apart from this authorities-led development of the Ecu, its future acceptance as a currency in which treasury management is widely conducted hinges on the extent to which it is used in cross-border trade. Currently, there is limited evidence of such trade and invoicing existing. A number of French, Belgian, Dutch and Italian companies do make use of the Ecu for commercial purposes, and one particular European Community initiative means that airlines which fly internationally are invoiced for over-flying sovereign EC air space in Ecu. A recent encouraging sign was the Federal Trust study group report, under the chairmanship of David Howell MP, which concluded:

> there are good reasons to suppose that there would be gains in efficiency through the wider use of the Ecu as a vehicle currency in intraEuropean trade. Its stability against a wide range of national currencies and its low transaction costs, give it natural advantages as a common medium of exchange.

Currently, the only government significantly to tap the Ecu bond market (as mentioned above) is Italy. The UK Treasury is rumoured to be well disposed towards issuing Ecu gilts, particularly as sterling has entered the Exchange Rate Mechanism of the European Monetary System. However, this will only happen if and when the UK Government has a significant borrowing requirement. There are also rumours that other European sovereign borrowers may access the Ecu market, particularly Belgium. Also, the French Ministry of Finance is discussing a change to the *Règle de Congruence*, which states that French insurance companies must cover at least 50% of their French franc-denominated liabilities with similarly-denominated assets. This may be broadened so that Ecu assets may be used as an alternative, which would clearly expand the investor base for Ecu capital market products, and so stimulate the swap market. However, the relatively conservative asset/liability management policies of the insurance companies may preclude full exploitation of this relaxation of the regulations.

Spanish pesetas

Market background

Spanish peseta swaps are most commonly quoted as fixed pesetas on an annual Eurobond (360/360) basis against six-month US dollar Libor (actual/360). The basic swap is for two-day settlement and liquidity is concentrated primarily in the two to five-year markets reflecting the underlying bond markets, but a market does exist out to 10 years.

Peseta swaps have only very recently become established, reflecting the very gradual relaxation of the rules of access for foreigners into the peseta-dominated bond markets by the Spanish authorities. The peseta swap market is dominated by the Spanish banks for both economic and regulatory reasons. Few, if any, non-Spanish banks have access to both sides of the market, and Spanish exchange contracts make it difficult for foreign banks to transact swaps.

Market forces

The Spanish peseta swap market is very capital market-oriented, with swap transactions mainly linked to new issue activity in the peseta bond market. Very few transactions are linked to corporate treasuries' liability management. New issue opportunities are created as a result of the Spanish banks lending fixed-rate pesetas to their corporate clients, and funding on a floating-rate basis. The banks will then have a significant mismatch, receiving fixed pesetas and paying floating on their underlying treasury book. Consequently, they will have an appetite to pay fixed pesetas and receive floating on swaps in support of a peseta fixed-rate bond issue. This mechanism is illustrated in Figure 4.

Figure 4: An example of a peseta swap

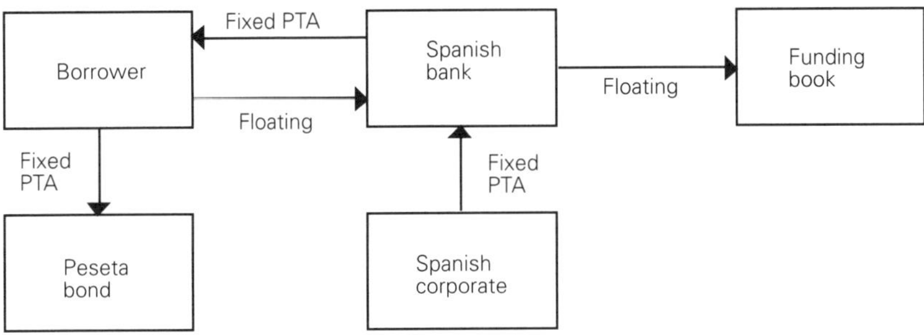

It follows then, that this market is dependent upon the desire of Spanish banks to transact this swap, and on the new issue arbitrage being effective.

Whilst there are a number of European corporates who may have a desire to pay fixed Spanish pesetas and receive Deutsche marks, sterling or dollars, particularly where the company would rather have a subsidiary in Spain and thus wishes to match its assets with its liabilities, exchange controls make it difficult to achieve this through the swap market. This is because pesetas originating in Spain (domestic pesetas) are difficult to move out of the country to pay coupons on bonds sold abroad (Euro pesetas). It is likely that these exchange controls will be relaxed in 1991 and should we see this then it is likely that corporate paying activity in Spanish pesetas will increase dramatically.

This activity has been facilitated by the deregulation of the peseta bond market by the Spanish authorities. Before 1987 there was no issuance by non-Spanish borrowers in this market. In 1987 the Spanish authorities allowed supranational borrowers to tap the market, with the first issues from Eurofima and the World Bank in August and September of that year. Both issues had a

Figure 5: Seven-year Spanish peseta/US dollar swap rate

Daily data, 8/3/89–22/5/90

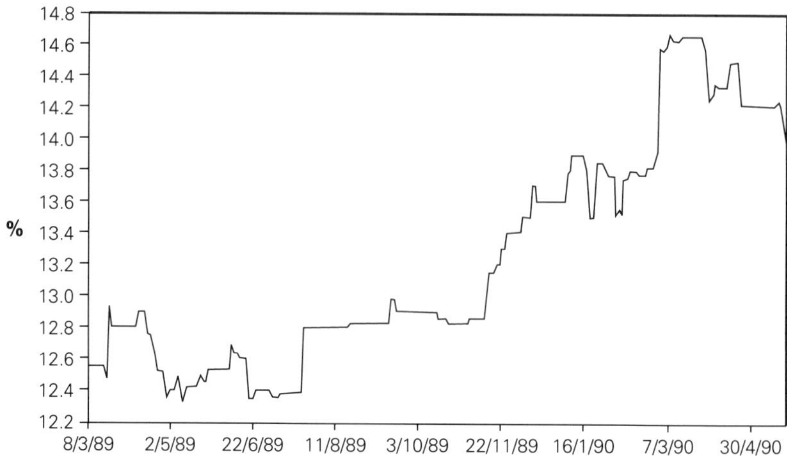

Source: NatWest Capital Markets

Figure 6: Ten-year Spanish peseta/US dollar swap rate

Daily data, 24/11/89–22/5/90

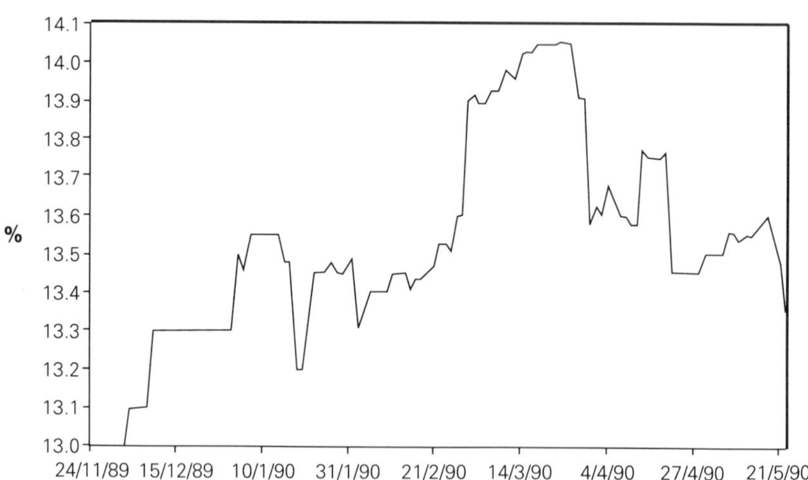

Source: NatWest Capital Markets

life of 10 years, although more recently five years has become the market norm. In addition to supranationals, the Spanish authorities have now opened the way for sovereign issuers to tap the market, with the Kingdom of Denmark being the first to take advantage of this in July 1990.

Other derivative products have yet to make any real impact in the peseta market, although as swap market liquidity increases it is likely that these will make an appearance.

Outlook

The immediate future of the peseta swap market will be determined by the continuing deregulation of the peseta bond market. The Spanish authorities maintain a very tight control over the issuers who may access this market. In particular, they are determined to ensure that only the highest quality credits may be involved whilst the market is in its early stages of development, and to maintain a very orderly market.

The expansion of swaps, and indeed other derivatives, into the area of asset and liability management is developing rapidly but may be overtaken by the drive towards European monetary union.

Swiss francs

Market background

The Swiss franc has the distinction of having one of the oldest swap markets — in particular the original World Bank/IBM swap involved this currency. Swiss franc swaps are quoted on an annual Eurobond (360/360) fixed-rate basis versus six-month Swiss franc or US dollar Libor (actual/360) with two-day settlement. Quotes may be obtained from two to 10 years, with the market being dominated by the larger Swiss banks together with major European and US banks. At the end of June 1990, outstandings in Swiss francs totalled US$39.4bn for interest rate swaps, and US$75.9bn for currency swaps.

Market forces

The market for Swiss franc swaps is divided broadly into three categories: swaps in support of fixed-rate bond issues; bond market investors who use swaps to take a view on fixed rates, which may not be possible in less liquid bond markets; and Swiss corporates and multi-currency liability managers using the swap market for treasury management. Bond issuers are receivers of fixed-rate Swiss francs against their issues. The second category are effectively traders who will look to pay the fixed rate when they feel bond yields are likely to rise, so hedging their bond investment positions, reversing the swap when they believe yields are set to fall. Treasury managers, both banks and corporates, provide the fixed-rate payers which underly the swap market.

Payers in the swap market include Swiss corporates and many supranational and sovereign borrowers who can access Swiss francs more cheaply through the swap market than by borrowing directly, or whose desire to pay is related to their active management of a liability portfolio. The Swiss banks will also have natural positions as a result of their fixed-rate lending.

The Swiss franc bond market has been attractive to borrowers for many years as a result of investors' appetite for certain issues on terms which do not reflect underlying credit ratings; providing significant credit arbitrage opportunities. For instance, the Swiss retail investor will purchase bonds issued by US corporates at risk premia well below those which would be demanded by other markets. This allows these corporates to issue in Swiss francs and swap the proceeds into US dollars for significant cost savings, up to as much as 0.5% below what would be achievable through direct borrowing or swaps from other currencies. This explains the very large relative proportion of currency swaps outstanding.

The traders' activity provides liquidity for the swap market, enabling the underlying payers and receivers to establish their required positions. Thus, Swiss francs provide a relatively liquid market. However, market-makers have no tradeable underlying government bond market with which to hedge positions, and so, from time to time, liquidity can dry up as the market is dominated by either paying or receiving interest.

The opening of the Swiss Options and Financial Futures Exchange (Soffex) may enhance liquidity in the swap market although Soffex is more renowned for its currency option contracts than interest rate hedging vehicles. Whilst there is no government bond market against which to price a long-term futures contract, a Euro Swiss Franc deposit contract could enhance liquidity in shorter-dated swaps. However, for this to be successful, the contract must prove its liquidity in a more successful way than has the similar Ecu contract on Liffe or the Matif.

There is a significant market in other derivative products, particularly caps, floors and options on swaps. The Swiss franc loan and deposit market is highly developed, and forward-rate agreements are readily available.

Although the major players in this market are the largest three Swiss banks together with the major European and US banks, most activity takes place in London. Consequently, the legal basis of the market is the standard ISDA documentation, and its activities are regulated by the Bank of England Code of Conduct.

Figure 7: Swiss franc swap volumes, 1987–89

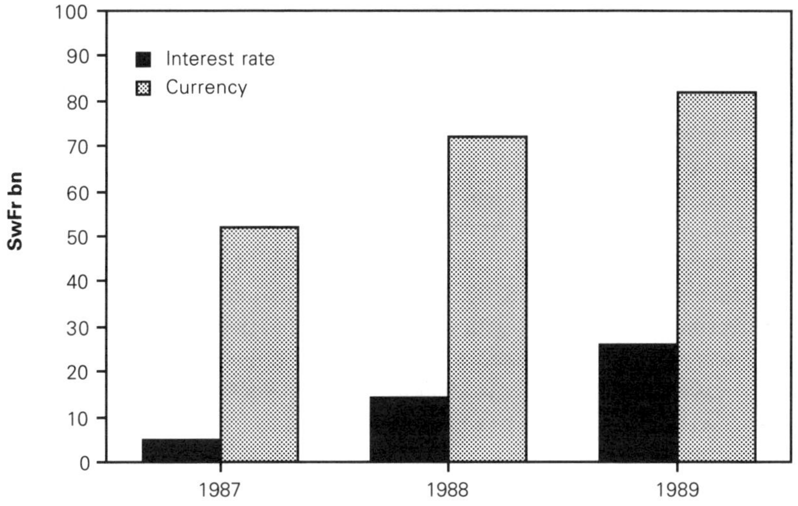

SwFr bn
100
90
80
70
60
50
40
30
20
10
0
Interest rate
Currency
1987
1988
1989

Source: NatWest Capital Markets

Figure 8: Ten-year Swiss franc swap rate

Weekly data, 29/11/85–7/12/90

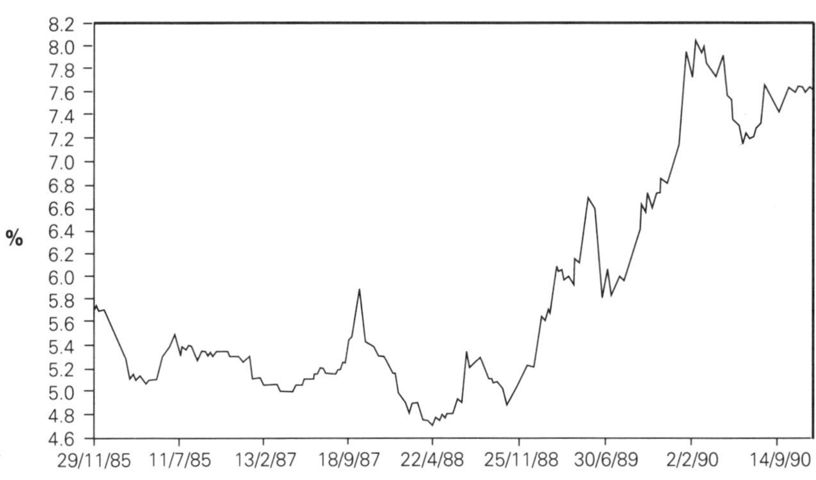

Source: NatWest Capital Markets

Outlook

The outlook for Swiss franc capital market in general and swap market in particular is by no means clear. The events in the rest of Western Europe, which is moving towards some form of economic and monetary union, will have a major part to play.

The historical attraction of the Swiss franc has been the confidential nature of investments held therein. Should these regulations be revised, this attraction to investors is likely to decline, resulting in reduced demand for Swiss franc paper. A more open financial regime will result in the Swiss economy being more influenced by the rest of Western Europe, which in turn will probably result in Swiss economic and monetary policy mirroring more closely that of its neighbours. This reduction in the attractiveness of Swiss franc investments, combined with the likelihood that potential trading profits relative to other European bond markets would be limited, will make asset markets less important to international investors. In such a scenario the Swiss swap market is also likely to be of reduced importance relative to those of the rest of Western Europe.

Should Switzerland retain its current banking practices, it is likely that it will continue in its position as a private (in all senses) banking haven. The continued operation of the current secrecy laws in the banking system will maintain the attractiveness of the asset markets to investors. This will give it an importance as a niche market and is likely to increase the dominance of the larger Swiss banks in the swap market, giving them much greater control on activity therein. In such a scenario, the Swiss market will continue to provide borrowers with funds at costs not entirely based on relative creditworthiness, and so the Swiss franc swap market will maintain its important role in the international capital markets.

Chapter 8: The French franc swap market

Jean Dominjon and Sébastien Cahen
Société Générale, Paris

Size of the market

Since its very beginning in the mid-1980s, the French franc swap market has grown steadily in terms of volume, liquidity, and number of active counterparties. The following figures, provided by the French Banking Association (Association Française des Banques (AFB)) illustrate this growth.

Table 1: Global gross outstanding*

	31/12/87	30/06/88	31/12/88	30/06/89	31/12/89
Global outstanding (FFbn)	130	228	336	466	630
Growth		+98	+108	+ 130	+164

*Calculated by adding the outstanding of the first 15 swap houses in France.

The interbank percentage of this outstanding is estimated by AFB to be stable at around 83%.

As interbank transactions typically are double-counted in the aggregate statistics, the evolution of the net outstanding can be estimated using the following formula:

$$\frac{\text{Gross outstanding x interbank \% share}}{2} + \text{swaps outstanding with non-bank institutions}$$

Applying the formula results in the following net outstanding amounts:

1 January 1988: FF76bn
31 December 1988: FF197bn
31 December 1989: FF368bn

Breaking the numbers down again, the value (and percentage share in the total outstanding) of new transactions appears as follows:[1]

Original maturity	01/88–06/88	06/88–12/88	Total 1988	01/89–06/89	06/89–12/89	Total/170 1989
2 years to less than 5 years	28	30	58 (26%)	43	72	115 (36%)
5 years to less than 7 years	26	27	53 (24%)	31	39	70 (22%)
7 years and longer	45	67	112 (50%)	65	68	133 (42%)

Several interesting features emerge from these data:

1. The new transactions are on an increasing trend.

2. The percentage of interbank transactions still is relatively high. It seems to be on a downward trend now as corporates and non-bank institutions play a steadily growing role.

3. The share of long-term (over seven years) transactions is also relatively high, although in a decreasing trend. This situation is obviously linked with the use of swaps to hedge bond issues (minimum seven years for a domestic French franc bond issue) and also to arbitrage with OATs and futures and option contracts on the Matif.

Market practice in French interest rate swaps

The French franc interest rate swap market involves a variety of different users and types of instruments. This section describes the most common features of the swaps and of market practice.

Fixed rate against TAM swaps

Value date. The standard value date for this most widely traded category is the first day of the current month if the transaction takes place between the 1st and 14th of the month, and the first of the following month if the transaction takes place between the 15th and 31st of the month (eg, the value date of a swap dealt on 5 December is 1 December, while value date of a swap dealt on 16th December is 1 January). One can still deal on the 16th or 17th based on the former (1st of the month) value date, but on special request only.

Duration. The duration is a square number of months and extends over a year or more — up to 10 or 15 years in a liquid market.

Interest periods. The first application period is from the day when the swap starts to the first date, the anniversary of which will be the final maturity of the swap; the following periods are annual, both on fixed and floating legs.

Fixed rate of the broken period, if any. The most common first fixed rate is the decompounding rate (periodic equivalent rate (PER) or daily equivalent rate (DER)) of the generic fixed rate dealt, according to the formulae:

DER = [(1 + FIR) x (1/exact) – 1)] x 360, with exact = 365 or 366.
PER = (1 + FIR) x (n days/exact)] – 1) x exact/n days)

DER is used for monthly broken period, PER for longer broken period. FIR is the annual fixed rate.

Fixed-rate basis. Period longer than one month: actual/actual. The numerator of actual/actual is the exact number of days which have run during the calculation period and the denominator which is 365, or 366 if 29 February is included in the period. Less than one month: actual/money.

Floating rate. The floating rate used is the TAM (Taux Annuel Monétaire — Annual Money Market Rate) which is the monthly compounded average of the official overnight money market rate.

The official overnight money market rate is the TMP (Taux Moyen Pondéré — Weighted Average Rate) which is published daily at 11.30am by the Banque de France on Reuter page BDFB.

Hence:

$$1 + \text{TAM} = \prod_{j=1}^{12} \left[1 + \text{T4Mj} \frac{\text{Nj}}{360} \right]$$

where Nj is the actual number of days of month j and T4Mj (= TMMMM = Taux Moyen Mensuel du Marché Monétaire) = Average Monthly Money Market Rate of the jth month.

$$\text{defined as T4M} = \frac{1}{\text{Nj}} \sum_{i=1}^{\text{Nj}} \text{TMPi (published each month on BDFB)}$$

The TAM is calculated and published ex-post on Telerate page 3205. The TAM can be used only as a floating index for 12-month period beginning and ending the first of the month. This rate is calculated every first Paris business day of the month, on the daily rates of the last 12 elapsed calendar months, allowing payment on the second Paris business day of the month.

The floating rate of a broken period, if any, can be the T4M or the accurate TAG (Taux Annuel Glissant — sliding annual rate) which is the monthly compounding of the last sliding T4M of the period (Telerate page 20050 or AFBP).

Floating rate basis. For TAM or TAG: actual/actual. For T4M: actual/360.

Fixed rate against TAG floating rate swaps

This swap is a derivative of the TAM swap, the only difference is the value date and thus the periods. TAG swaps are spot transactions, the value date is the first business day following the date of the deal. For example, a 12/01/91 to 21/01/2001 is a TAG/fixed swap.

Thus the annual or monthly periods of this swap do not coincide with calendar months. TAG is calculated daily by the French Banking Association and published on Telerate 20050 according to the TAM calculation rules.

The other characteristics of TAG swaps are similar to those of TAM swaps.

Fixed-rate swaps against Pibor (daily ex-ante)

The characteristics of the French franc Pibor swap market are highly comparable to other fixed against Libor swaps.

1. Starting date: First working day following the day the transaction takes place. Of course, it is easy to find other more specific value or maturity dates.
2. Duration: It is freely agreed between counterparties.
3. Fixed rate basis: Exact/exact.
4. Floating rate: Pibor (Telerate 20041 or PIBO) mainly three or six months.
5. Floating-rate basis: Actual/360.
6. Date for setting floating rates: The Paris business day preceding the beginning of each period (and not two days before as for Libor).

Main strategies involving swaps

Classical yield curve strategies

The swap French franc yield curve displays anomalies from time to time. Typically it is less smooth than yield curves in many other currencies.

This situation is partly due to the existence of two distinct kinds of government coupon securities that are used for swap hedging: the *Obligations Assimilables du Trésor* (OATs) are liquid bonds with maturities of seven years or more, while *Bons à Taux Annuel Normalisé* (BTANs) are for maturities of two and five years. These two instruments do not come under the same accounting and tax rules, and hence do not offer homogeneous yield rates. One can, for instance, often observe an abnormal jump between the five and seven-year swap rates, which in general does not last longer than a few weeks.

Treasury spread monitoring

Hedging swaps with BTANs and OATs naturally leads one to monitor the various Treasury spreads.

A consequence of the narrowing of this spread leads naturally to a deterioration of the conditions for new bond issues. The French franc spread (as the Deutsche mark and Ecu spreads) has reached relatively low levels in 1990: this situtation has encouraged several borrowers to issue bonds in other currencies, and to swap interests and capital into French francs; this behaviour has led to a special status for French francs, where basis swaps between French francs and other currencies, such as US dollars, are clearly unbalanced. For instance, the spread of the basis swap Pibor–French franc versus US dollar Libor, or TAM versus US dollar Libor, has significantly increased in 1990.

Monitoring TAM/Pibor curves

The two benchmarks mentioned above — TAM and Pibor (Paris interbank offered rate) — produce two distinct swap yield curves: fixed rate into TAM and fixed rate into Pibor, thereby opening up opportunities for quasi-arbitrage. The spread between the two curves typically fluctuates beween three and 20 basis points and is on the higher side of this range for short maturities.

Hedging instruments

The growth in the French franc swap market was encouraged by the emergence of a variety of liquid hedging instruments.

Cash market

Bons à Taux Annuel Normalisé (BTANs). As of the end of December 1990, FF400bn worth of these Treasury notes (with standard maturities of two and five years) was outstanding. New primary BTANs trade on a when-issued basis, thereby further enhancing liquidity. Daily turnover is about FF10bn.

Obligations Assimilables du Trésor (OATs). These are fungible government bonds with maturities of over five years. The amount outstanding as of the end of December 1990 was about FF420bn. Daily turnover is about FF10bn.

It can be noted that the aggregate notional amount traded on Matif stands at about FF60bn for all maturities, while by comparison daily turnover for swaps with maturities of over two years is only about FF1bn.

Exchange-traded futures and options (Matif)

	Notional 10 yr gov bond future	Options on notional	3-month Pibor
Average Dec 90 daily volume	63,000	31,000	13,000
Notional amount contract (FF)	500,000	500,000	5,000,000
Daily notional turnover (FFbn)	31	15	65

Caps, floors and swaptions

The size of this particular sector is difficult to gauge at this point, though it is certain to be growing.

Availability of complex structures

Like any other mature market the French franc swap sector provides a wide variety of complex structures. These have emerged gradually over time.

First came amortising and roller-coaster swaps, which typically involved annuity loans and bonds as a good many of the domestic bonds issued in 1984 and 1986, for example, were redeemable on an amortising (as opposed to a bullet) basis. Subsequently, as the market expanded on the back of improved liquidity in the cash and derivatives markets, zero-coupon and low-coupon swaps emerged with maturities of up to 15 or 20 years (the latter being driven by perpetual subordinated issues), together with all kinds of liquid spreadlock swaps (typically based on spreads over OATs and including deferred or advance rate setting whether on an optional basis or not).

With the rise in securitisation, asset-backed swaps were developed; not unexpectedly they involved private placements and such complex structures as franc-based currency swaps, resulting in a variety of single or dual-currency bull or bear indexed swaps and swaptions.

A similar range of sophistication (including amortising and roller-coaster features) is available in caps, floors, collars and, of course, swaptions where liquidity keeps growing. This contributes to turn the market for French franc swaps and other interest rate derivatives into one of the most liquid and technically advanced relative to other European and Asian markets

---

Notes

1. These statistics are based on figures provided by the following institutions:

Banque Française du Commerce Extérieur (BFCE);
Banque Indosuez;
Banque Nationale de Paris (BNP);
Banque Paribas;
Banque Régionale d'Escompte et de Dépôts (BRED);
Caisse Centrale de Réescompte (CCR);
Caisse Centrale des Banques Populaires (CCBP);
Caisse de Gestion Mobilière (CGM);
Caisse des Dépôts et Consignations;
Caisse Nationale de Crédit Agricole (CNCA);
Compagnie Parisienne de Réescompte (CPR);
Crédit Commercial de France (CCF);
Crédit Lyonnais; and
Société Générale.

AFB does not publish more detailed statistics concerning swaps. It is difficult to determine what percentage of swaps transactions are initiated following a bond issue, hedging an interest rate option or a cash operation, or anticipating a rate move.

Chapter 9: The lira swap market

Stephen Mahony and Tony Main
San Paolo Bank

The lira swap market has grown, relatively recently, from two historically separate markets: the domestic interest rate swap market and the Eurolira interest rate and currency swap market. This division had its roots in the Italian regulatory framework. As this system of regulation has been relaxed gradually so the two markets have tended to grow together.

With this process there has been a significant growth in the liquidity of the lira swap markets. However, there has not been a similar development of related instruments. Option-related transactions are relatively infrequent and there are no bond futures.

Development

The development of the lira swap market has been driven by three principal factors:

- The Italian government bond market is the third largest in the world. Gross of the 12.5% withholding tax, government bond yields are typically between 75 and 100 basis points above swap rates. The creation of synthetic assets based on government bonds has increased the number of institutions, within Italy and elsewhere, involved in the swap market. Swap business derived from such transactions has hitherto only had maturities of up to four years, but in June 1990 the first seven-year buoni del Tesoro poliennali (BTP) was issued which significantly increased volumes in the longer maturities, and a 10-year issue was launched in early 1991.

- The Eurobond market is relatively small but because of the absence of withholding tax these bonds can be sold at yields well below the gross yield on government bonds. Issuers can therefore often achieve margins below Libor, since swap levels typically trade between gross government bond yields and Eurobond yields. In recent months the pattern has changed with swap yields trading close to Euromarket yields. So long as this persists it is likely that high quality corporate issuers will be less attracted to the market than in 1989–90.

- The relaxation of the regulatory framework in Italy has encouraged Italian companies to become more active in managing risk. As expertise increases, the range of instruments used will widen.

One of the factors which inhibits the swap market is concern about the accounting treatment of swaps on the part of Italian institutions. Present Italian accounting practices differ from generally accepted accounting principles in a number of ways and institutions tend to account on an accrual basis rather than on a mark-to-market or net present value basis.

The size of the market

ISDA reported that in the first six months of 1990, US$1.94bn of Lira interest rate swaps and US$5.1bn of Lira currency swaps were transacted. This was not a complete market survey. Not only are market volumes larger, but the split between interest rate and currency swaps has changed in recent months. Lira interest rate swaps are now noticeably more liquid than Lira/dollar swaps.

The domestic swap market

There has been no systematic survey of the market to determine the volume of swaps in existence. Estimates range from ItL25–40trn existing in early 1991.

Historically, typical maturities have been in the range of 12 to 48 months, though several market participants indicate price levels out to 84 months. Liquidity is greatest between 18 and 36 months. The availability of longer maturity BTPs has begun to influence the swap market.

Fixed rates are usually paid quarterly on an ACT/360 basis. Variable rates are also usually paid quarterly on the same calculation basis. There are three variable-rate bases commonly encountered in the domestic swap market. In order of frequency of use they are: (1) Mibor — the Milan Interbank Offered Rate as quoted by the Associazione Tesorieri Istitutzioni Creditizie (ATIC) on Reuters page ATIA, or alternatively, as published in the newspaper *Il Sole 24 Ore*; (2) Rendiob — the rate at which long-term credit institutions borrow term money; and (3) Rolint — the average of Mibor and Rendiob.

These rates are precisely defined in the 1991 ISDA Definitions. The majority of swaps are transacted with the floating rate calculated as the daily average of Mibor, set in arrears. Mibor levels are typically above Eurolira Libor, which causes the fixed rate (after conversion to an annual bond basis) to be a similar amount above the Eurolira fixed rate.

There are at least two market participants who quote prices on Reuters screens (AKRM and SFNE). When the market is stable dealing spreads narrow and more institutions become active; in times of instability dealing spreads widen to as much as 40bp and liquidity may disappear.

The Eurolira swap market

The incomplete response to ISDA's lira market survey makes it difficult to estimate the volume of swaps in existence. Estimates range from ItL25–35trn existing in early 1991.

Typical maturities have been up to 10 years with most activity in the two to five-year range.

The market quotes rates on an annual bond basis. Until recently, the Eurolira swap market was driven by participants outside Italy and hence most deals were cross-currency swaps, typically lira versus US dollars. The publication in June of an official British Bankers' Association lira Libor page (Telerate 3740), the growing number of Italian participants and the capital adequacy costs of cross-currency swaps have shifted the emphasis towards interest rate swaps. Because of short-term supply and demand factors, there can be a difference of up to 15bp between lira/lira swaps and lira versus US dollar swaps.

The Eurolira swap market involves many institutions outside Italy. Several banks in London, Paris, New York and elsewhere run books and forward foreign exchange dealers from other centres also participate.

Eurobond issuers provide the single largest source of fixed-rate liabilities. Asset swappers, corporates and, at the longer maturities, domestic Italian lending institutions are structural payers of the fixed rate. The major Italian commercial banks are increasingly involved.

Most firms of swap brokers are active in lira swaps and prices are indicated on several Reuters pages (including DIMI, GAPS, ICAS, NIMI and RPMX) with varying degrees of success.

Hedging and liquidity

As the market has grown there has been an apparent increase in liquidity and indicated bid/offer spreads have narrowed.

Underlying this growth there is a difficult problem for participants in the lack of hedging instruments. There are no bond futures. Of the different bond markets, only the government bond market has sufficient depth to offer the possibility of hedging.

New issues and "on the run" bonds are usually liquid enough for trades of, say, ItL25bn to have only a small impact on market prices. Shorting bonds is often accomplished by selling bonds from a synthetic asset portfolio.

However, the relationship of swap rates to BTP yields is volatile — at least twice as volatile as the equivalent US dollar relationship. One possible reason for this lies in the trading patterns of the government bond market. During periods when there is a significant change in interest rate levels government bond prices do not move in a yield-driven way so as to bring about a parallel change in yields, but instead there tends to be a parallel price change along the range of maturities. In such circumstances, CCTs change in price in a way closely correlated to the price behaviour of BTPs. This volatile relationship between government bonds and swaps gives plenty of scope for arbitrage trading but does not represent a very reliable hedging mechanism.

Figure 1 shows the evolution of swap rates in 1990 and the relationship of the swap market to the tax-exempt (TE) and the non-tax-exempt (NTE) sectors of the Eurobond market. The convergence of swap and NTE Eurobond yields is clear.

Figure 1: Three-year swap versus NTE and TE bond indices

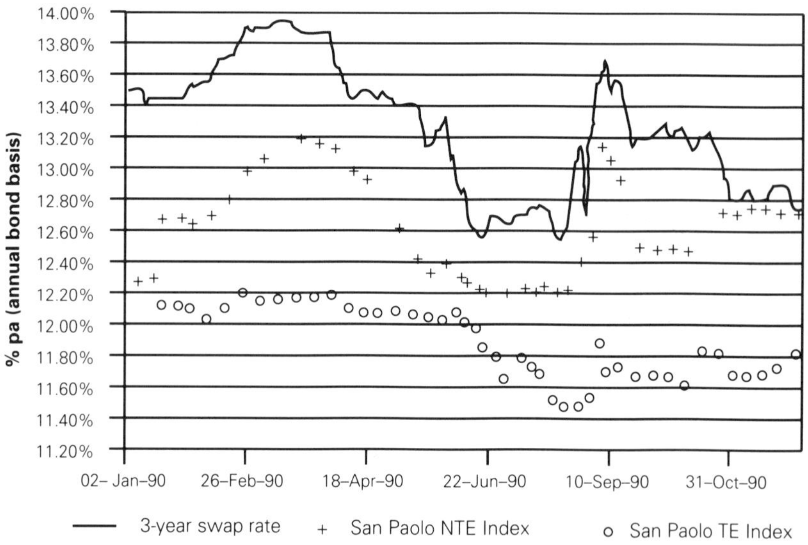

Source: Istituto Bancario San Paolo di Torino

Participants

While all the main Italian banks are active in the market, prominent participants include non-bank financial institutions and certain foreign banks.

The market has developed two tiers. The first involves a relatively small number of banks which are permitted by the Bank of Italy to lead Eurolira bond issues. These bond issue-related swaps are of sizes up to ItL600bn and generally are not taken as positions but are priced off the known interest of certain institutions. Because of the relative scarcity of such swaps and the high visibility of the related bond transactions, these swaps are not always priced in the same way as smaller swaps. These large swaps are illiquid and the theoretical bid/off spreads could be rather wide.

In the other part of the market a much larger number of institutions is active including Italian banks, and non-bank financial companies as well as foreign banks and securities houses. Typical transaction sizes are ItL15–25bn. These swaps are quite liquid and the bid/offer spreads have narrowed as liquidity has grown.

Future trends

The convergence of the domestic and Euromarkets may be expected to continue and the characterisitics of the market may change quite quickly.

There are many foreign institutions ready to apply techniques that are well known in other markets. The lira market will see more widespread use of futures and option-related products but this development is likely to be gradual.

Chapter 10: The Scandinavian swap markets

Tord Norstedt and Lars Norup
Svenska Handelsbanken and Unibank

The Swedish krona swap market[1]

Development of the market

The Swedish money and bond markets have undergone rapid development since 3 March 1980, when Svenska Handelsbanken issued the first money market instrument in Sweden — a certificate of deposit. An array of other Swedish krona instruments soon followed suit. Fuelled by large budget deficits, averaging 9% of GNP between 1975 and 1985, and the downward trend of Swedish krona interest rates in the early 1980s, market activity rose sharply. It peaked towards the mid-1980s, when for a period the Swedish market was one of the largest worldwide in terms of turnover.

The activity subsided after the 1986 bull market and was sent into a tailspin when a turnover tax was imposed on 1 January 1989 on all securities trades. The derivative securities trading was hardest hit and promptly went into hibernation. It revived only once the tax was repealed on 1 July 1990.

The transition throughout the decade paralleled the gradual shift of the lawmakers' and the *Riksbank's* (the Swedish central bank's) focus from price and quantitative regulations towards greater market orientation. The trend of deregulation and international integration of the Swedish financial system reached a climax on 1 July 1989 when the final step on the path to abolition of the core of the exchange controls (introduced as a crisis measure at the outbreak of the Second World War) was taken. Non-Swedish entities were then allowed to take part in the Swedish fixed-income market and the remaining restrictions on Swedish residents' abilities to undertake foreign investments and borrowings were lifted.

The Swedish krona interest rate swap market dates back to the 1986 bull market when the first trades were made between Swedish banks. Initially the Swedish krona interest rate swap was structured so that a party would pay an annual fixed rate against receiving the three-month Swedish Treasury bill rate fixed on IMM dates, Treasury bills being the only short-term benchmark at the time.

A Libor equivalent domestic Swedish krona deposit rate — the Stockholm interbank offered rate (Stibor) — emerged in 1988. Stibor soon came to replace the Treasury bills rate as the floating rate reference standard. For the benefit of market liquidity, floating rate payment dates are still generally set at IMM dates domestically.

In the Swedish market, the fixed interest rate is currently quoted on an effective yield basis. This means that if broken year interest periods occur, the agreed effective rate will be decompounded to the equivalent straight rate for such periods. For example, if the agreed effective rate is 12% and an interest period is 90 days the equivalent ISDA fixed rate for that period would be 11.49%. Evidently, in international dealings it is essential to clarify whether decompounding is to be applied or not.

The 1989 turnover tax on securities temporarily made interest rate swaps one of the tax-free means of redistributing interest rate risk within Sweden. By the time the tax was finally abolished in 1990 the interest rate swap had become an established instrument. Helped by the high interest rate volatility and the general rebound in fixed income activity witnessed in 1990, the market continued to enjoy increasing activity. Following a tentative start, Swedish krona interest rate swap volume has now more than doubled over the last two years.

With the abolition of exchange controls in 1989, a genuine Swedish krona fixed income Euromarket was born and the Swedish krona cross-currency swap market came into being.

The cross-currency swap market has been bolstered by several factors. First, the market has been spurred by the high degree of corporate internationalisation and the corresponding need for active foreign exchange risk management.

Secondly, since 1977 the Swedish krona has been fixed to a trade-weighted basket of 15 currencies. Following the last devaluation in October 1982 it has been pegged at an index value of 132, with a fluctuation interval of 130 to 134. The substantially lower weighted interest rates of the underlying currency basket — typically some 2–3% lower than the equivalent Swedish krona rate — has stimulated basket arbitrage. This had helped to make the case for swaps as a cost-effective means to profit from these opportunities and, more generally, as a way to adjust risk profiles.[2]

Finally, a high proportion of the spate of Eurobond issuance has been swapped. The figures below show a volume breakdown of the categories of borrowers that have issued Swedish krona Eurobonds and the types of intermediaries involved since the market's inception up to the end of November 1990.

Figure 1: Swedish krona Eurobond lead managers

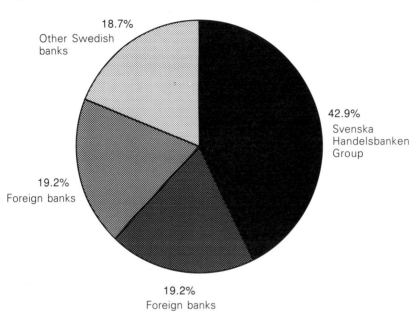

18.7%
Other Swedish banks

42.9%
Svenska Handelsbanken Group

19.2%
Foreign banks

19.2%
Foreign banks on own behalf

Figure 2: Swedish krona Eurobond borrowers

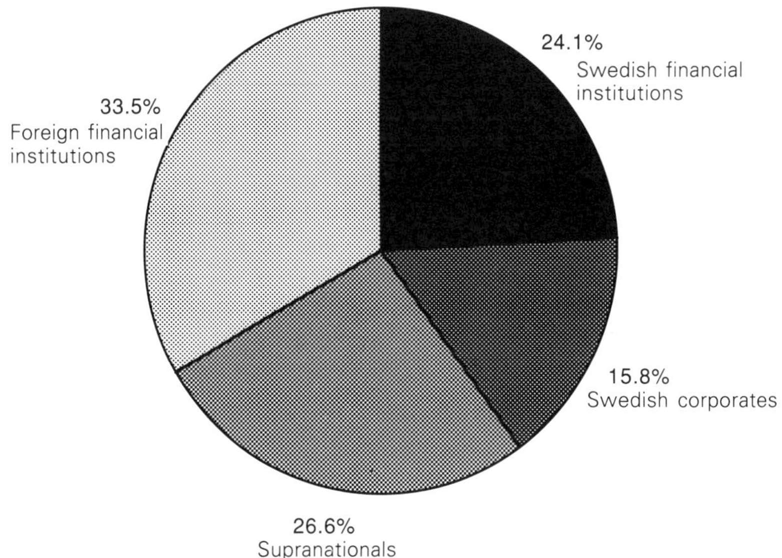

From October 1988, a total of 29 Swedish krona bond issues were launched on the Euromarket, totalling a value of SKr10.1bn. 65.5% of these issues were swapped, primarily into floating-rate US dollars. This has opened up the Swedish krona to a wide range of issuers and investors. In the previously domestic market, borrowing was almost solely the domaine of the Kingdom of Sweden and the Swedish mortgage institutions, with the insurance and pension funds and banks acting as the main buyers of bonds.

Hedging instruments

The hedging tools available in the long-dated domestic Swedish fixed income market are cash bonds, and futures and options contracts on notional cash bonds. The cash bonds traded in the market are almost exclusively government or mortgage bonds. The futures and options contracts are traded in an over-the-counter market and are cleared through the Stockholm Options Market (OM).

The most actively traded cash bonds are the benchmark Swedish government bonds ranging from two to 10-year maturities. The bonds carry a 30/360 annual coupon with denominations generally of SKr1m.

Selected Swedish banks and brokers act as market-makers for these issues. This is a telephone market, normally open between 9.30am and 3.30pm local time. Quotes of bid and offer yields (ordinarily with a 3bp spread) are made continuously, for settlement five banking days later. The standard quotes are normally good for at least SKr20m. Subsequent to dealing, the agreed yield is converted to an equivalent cash price based on a formula.

For mortgage bonds both liquidity and credit standings vary considerably. Three bank-owned mortgage institutions have launched fungible five, seven and 10-year bond issues where market-makers have committed themselves to maintaining two-way prices in the same way as for the government benchmark bonds.

The futures contracts are based on five, seven and 10-year notional government bonds. The notional maturities are five, seven and 10 years from the following IMM settlement date. Option contracts are also available based on five-year notional government bonds.

At the short end of the maturity range, FRA contracts on three-month Stibor and futures on Treasury bills are traded actively.

Relationship between swap rates and economic indicators

Reliable Swedish krona swap rate data are not available for the whole period from 1986. However, the Swedish mortgage institution yield can be used as a proxy for analytical purposes. Below is detailed the yield of the benchmark five-year government bond and for corresponding mortgage bonds and how the spread relationship has developed from July 1986.

Figure 3: Swedish five-year bond yields vs mortgage bond yields

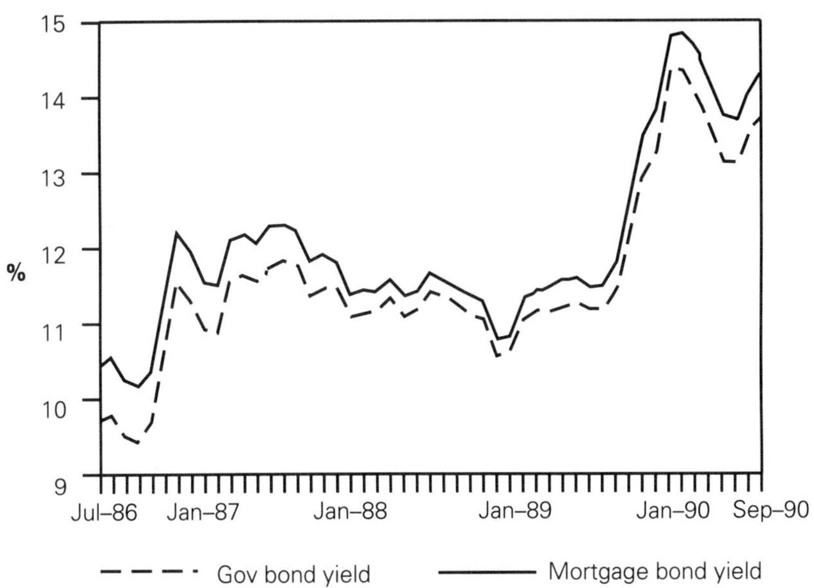

Figure 4: Spread trends

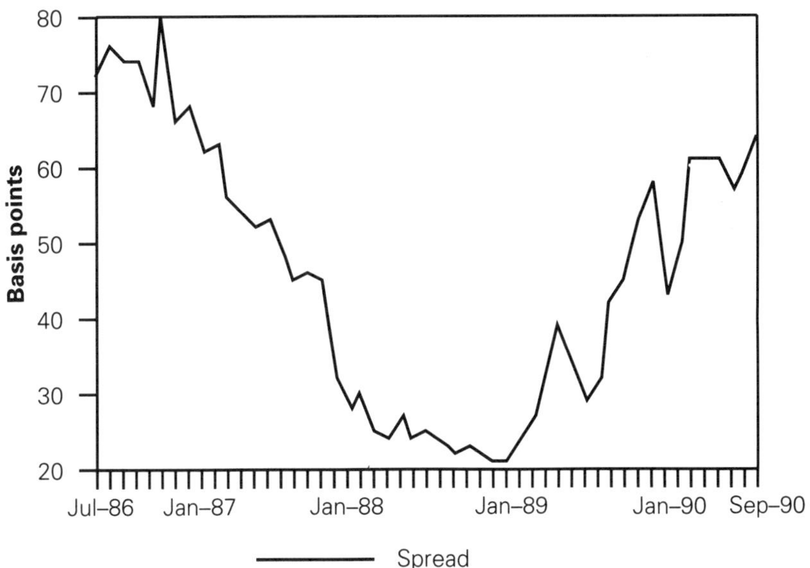

Over this period, the spread has varied quite considerably from an 80bp high in late 1986 to a 21bp low in early 1989 and up again to over 70bp in November 1990.[3]

The fall was due in part to the lower turnover in 1987 and 1988 that put a greater emphasis on long-term investment. This generated further interest in the pick-up available from investments in mortgage bonds, causing spreads to narrow steadily. Conversely, in the last two years, the high volatility and activity in the market has increased the liquidity premium required to invest in mortgage securities.

The relationship between mortgage yields and swap rates has, however, weakened over the last year. Factors particular to the mortgage companies such as the deteriorated state of the Swedish property market and tightening capital adequacy rules have probably helped to sever the relationship.

The Danish krone swap market[4]

Development of the market

Since the market's inception in 1976, the global interest rate and currency swap market has quickly grown to become one of the most important financial markets today.

The first Danish krone interest rate and currency swap was completed as late as 1985 on the back of one of the first Eurobond issues denominated in Danish krone, the World Bank issue.

Up until 1987–88 most of the very limited transactions in the Danish swap market consisted of lenders using interest rate and currency swaps to swap fixed Danish krone loans into a foreign currency, typically floating US dollars. In several cases the market participants were international, often supranational, borrowers who made use of the efficient Danish market for fixed income instruments, ie, bonds, to obtain interesting six-month US dollar or Deutsche mark Libor targets.

In 1987 the number and type of participants in the market gradually began to change. Up until this point the market consisted, with few exceptions, of financial institutions. Slowly, the municipally-owned regional Danish gas companies and the first Scandinavian corporates began to take an interest in interest rate and currency swaps. However, it should also be mentioned that, since 1985/86, the Kingdom of Denmark has made extensive use of this instrument in connection with portfolio management of its borrowings to finance its activities as well as the balance of payments deficit. Actually the Kingdom made its first non-Danish krone interest rate and currency swap in November 1983. It was in 1988 that the first banks, in Denmark and abroad, began running Danish krone interest rate and currency books and thus created the foundation of an efficient interbank market.

The Danish interest rate swap market was officially established on 1 June 1988 when Cibor, the official Danish interbank reference rate, was introduced. Danish krone interest rate swaps had been traded before using the Luxembourg fixings, but the validity of the fixing was questionable and the volume was therefore always minimal.

The Copenhagen interbank offered rate, Cibor, is fixed every banking day at 12.00 noon. The Cibor fixing procedure is modelled on the London interbank offered rate method. Eight Danish banks and savings institutions are contacted for quotes from between one and six months (the possibility of also quoting nine and 12-month periods is currently being discussed). Of the eight collected quotes, the two highest and the two lowest interest rates for each fixing period are removed from the basis of calculation, whereupon the average of the remaining four interest rates is fixed to the fifth decimal as the official reference rate Cibor.

Figure 5: Five-year Danish krone vs six-month Libor swap rate

Monthly data

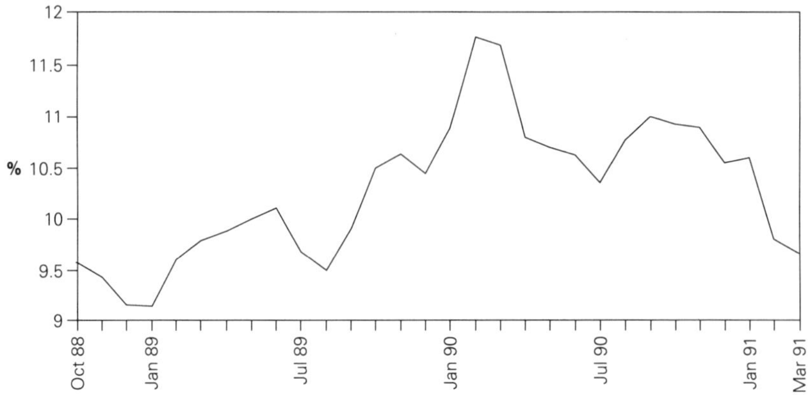

Size of the market

Although the Cibor fixing was originally established to facilitate an FRA market in Danish krone, it provided a major boost to the krone interest rate swap market.

Today the interest rate swap market in Danish krone exceeds the two currency and interest rate swap markets, fixed krone against floating six-month US dollar Libor and fixed krone against floating six-month Deutsche mark Libor.

With growth rates from around 1988 to the present day of roughly 50% pa, the bid/offer spreads have narrowed dramatically, the amounts traded have become much more flexible and the maturity dates quoted stretch out as far as 10 years. Two structured deals with maturities of 14 years have also been completed. Before 1988, the amounts traded in the market used to consist of Dkr100m only or, for obvious reasons, issue size. Over the last couple of years this has indeed changed. Today the interest rate and currency swap market in krone is quoting two-way prices for any amount between Dkr25m and Dkr1bn plus.

Although no actual empirical analyses have been conducted on the Danish interest rate and currency swap market, it is estimated that the total outstanding volume of krone swaps in 1990 amounted to Dkr120bn, which, considering the relative youth of the market, must be regarded as very satisfactory.

Although the Eurokrone bond market has been on the back burner over the past couple of years, the impressive number of issues listed on the Copenhagen Stock Exchange, both by foreign issuers and denominated in foreign currency, has fuelled the Danish krone interest rate and swap market. This trend has been aided and abetted by the abolition, on 1 October 1988, of the legislation governing listings on the Danish Exchange. Since then, several Scandinavian issuers have made their way to Denmark: 21 Swedish, eight Norwegian, and five Finnish issuers have been counted among the listings on the Copenhagen Stock Exchange during the past two years.

Two other recent Danish krone innovations, a commercial paper and a corporate bond market, have likewise contributed to the extraordinary growth in the Danish interest rate and currency swap market.

The Danish krone commercial paper market began two to three years ago and has grown rapidly. To date, 15 programmes have been established and the potential maximum outstanding value is more than Dkr10bn.

The Danish krone commercial paper market, like the emerging krone corporate bond market, is showing promise for continued future growth rates of around 30–40% pa. It would obviously be incorrect to ascribe the very impressive development in the krone swap market solely to the development in the other markets, but a certain correlation is nonetheless indisputable.

Most impressive of all is the fact that an increasing number of Danish corporates, also of the smaller to medium-sized variety, have begun to use the interest rate and currency swap market in connection with asset and liability management.

The awakening interest in the market of this group of participants and the continued participation of the Danish and foreign financial, governmental and even supranational institutions, as well as the major Scandinavian corporates, promises continued double-digit growth rates.

In conclusion, this author believes that as more and more end users discover the potential for interest rate and currency risk management *via* the swap market, this market could easily double its size in the next two years. The sophistication of the market participants is also increasing; thus a market in Danish krone interest rate instruments, namely krone caps and floors based on six-month Cibor, is beginning to take shape.

Notes

1. Written by Tord Norstedt of Svenska Handelsbanken.
2. It should be noted that Sweden's expected application for membership in the European Community is likely to prompt an alignment of the Swedish krona to the Ecu at some point in the future.
3. In 1991 the spread has widened above 100bp.
4. Written by Lars Norup of Unibank.

Chapter 11: The yen swap market

Neil Smout
IBJ International Limited, Swaps and Financial Engineering Group

Characteristics of the market

The volumes of yen swaps have grown significantly in recent years and the market can now be described as approaching maturity. Figure 1 indicates the extent of growth of both the interest rate and cross-currency swap markets since 1987 (1989 being the last full year for which statistics are available). The users of the yen swap markets may be grouped into a number of over-simplified, but useful categories:

(a) market-makers, whose principal interest is to trade both currency and interest rate markets with a view to a profit. Some of the foreign banks and more sophisticated Japanese banks would fall into this category;

(b) those yen-based entities who use the market both to hedge their natural interest rate positions and to assume trading interest rate positions. Japanese City banks are restricted to funding through short-term deposits (mainly less than one year), and the interest rate swap market allows them access to longer-term funding, improving the maturity match of their deposits to their loans (which are not restricted in maturity terms). Where these entities also "make markets" these functions may be consolidated together. The larger Japanese banks are major players in this market;

(c) the lesser Japanese players, some of the major Japanese corporates, insurance companies and others who in general can be characterised as "customers" (although a number of these are developing into leading players in their own right). In this context the rapid growth of the US dollar and Swiss franc Japanese corporate low-coupon, equity-linked debt markets, virtually all of the debt of which is swapped to fixed yen, has been a particular stimulant for the expansion of the yen swap markets;

(d) the international end users, the majority of which employ yen swaps as the link between the very well developed Euro and domestic yen capital markets, and their required funding or asset currency (in general, not the yen). In this context it is interesting to note that the Euroyen is second only to the Eurodollar capital markets in total issuance volume in the period 1987 to 1989, and although exact figures are hard to establish it is clear that the vast majority of these issues are swapped into other currencies.

Figure 1: Volumes of yen/yen and yen/US dollar swaps, 1987–89

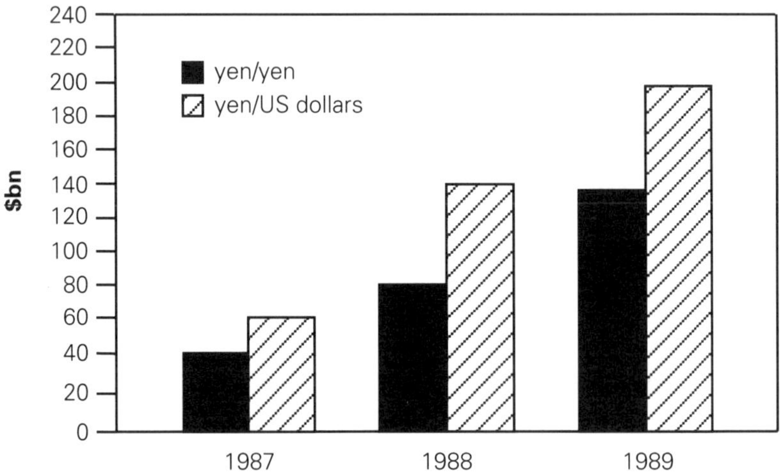

Source: International Swap Dealers Association

The "global" yen swap book is developing as a concept and yen swap prices are now available 24 hours a day, although as a general rule the market is still led by Tokyo, with London, in a convenient time zone spanning Japan and the US, the secondary centre. Analysis of the differences in volumes, average outstanding maturities and pricing of interest rate and cross-currency swaps is revealing. The yen market, with the Swiss franc and the Ecu, is one of the few where the volumes of cross-currency swaps are greater than those of interest rate swaps. The average outstanding maturity of interest rate and currency swaps is three and a half years and five years, respectively, and the average size of interest rate and currency swaps are Y3.3bn and Y4.4bn, respectively.[1] Although it is difficult to draw hard and fast conclusions from these facts, we can observe that the relatively high volumes of currency swaps reflect both extensive use of the yen capital markets by foreign borrowers (very few of whom have demand for pure yen liabilities) and of foreign capital markets by Japanese borrowers, who almost invariably swap back into fixed yen. The longer maturity and greater average size of currency swaps would also testify to this, reflecting the preference for longer maturities of the international capital markets.

Recent development of the market

In qualitative terms it is clear that in the three years since 1987 the Japanese banks have increased their sophistication markedly, and while some still lag behind American and certain other foreign banks in this area, others compete on a more or less equal technical footing. The large profits that were available to the foreign banks two or three years ago, due to their large lead in expertise, are drying up as the Japanese banks maintain their traditional hold on end-customer business. It is also true that increasing end user awareness has reduced the total profit available in the market, a fact witnessed by the general decline in bid/offer spreads in both yen/yen and yen/US dollar markets, and by the dramatic upsurge in interest in yen derivative products (we take the term here to refer specifically to option-based products), viewed as a potentially more lucrative sector of the market. Good evidence for this trend is provided by the fall in bid/offer spreads in the swap market — whereas two or three years ago spreads of 10 basis points in yen/yen and higher in yen/US dollars were not uncommon, markets tighter than 5bp in both interest rate and currency swaps are now commonplace.

Pricing techniques for yen swaps within the market are now broadly uniform (although see below in this section). The technical lead of the more sophisticated banks now manifests itself in areas previously thought more peripheral, such as interest rate risk management, asset/liability management, systems coordination and the globalisation of yen swap books. Two important trends which will reduce this lead are highlighted here.

First, the requirement that Japanese banks meet the BIS regulations for capital exposure by March 1993, and specifically that their capital adequacy ratio is at least 8% by this date, is becoming an increasingly important business consideration for them. Previously, the availability of cheap core capital from the booming equity market led many Japanese banks to be relatively insensitive towards considerations of capital, and this insensitivity undoubtedly contributed to the aforementioned surprising prevalence of currency swaps in the yen swap market. With the greater stress upon capital adequacy this developmental lag in the measurement and monitoring of swap capital and exposure is likely to erode.

Secondly, the Japanese, unlike virtually all of the other participants in the yen swap market, are not allowed to use the present value accounting method for profit and loss calculations. This limitation also applies to the hedging of swap books with cash bonds, futures or other instruments, where the possibility of upfront loss on the hedge instrument, without being able to realise compensating mark-to-market profit on the swap being hedged, effectively precludes such hedging. The lack of exposure to the present value method of accounting for or (in the early days of the market) valuing swaps has been a major factor contributing to the relative lack of sophistication of some Japanese banks compared to their foreign counterparts. While this has been a disadvantage for them in the market as a whole, it has probably promoted the growth of the overall yen swap markets due to the arbitrage opportunities that exist betweeen banks using different types of accounting concepts.

Swap pricing

Both yen/yen and yen/US dollar swaps are still almost exclusively traded on an absolute basis, that is, not as a spread to the underlying Japanese Government bond (JGB). There are a number of reasons for this:

(a) The JGB market itself is dominated by one bond ("the benchmark") which is of 10-year maturity. Bonds of other maturities are far less liquid and, additionally, the process by which the market chooses a particular benchmark is not simple or predictable. The corollary to this is that the yen/yen swap is now the main instrument for defining the bank yield curve in its own right, due to the liquidity and range of maturities available.

(b) Cash JGBs are in general subject to withholding tax for foreign entities. Of the alternatives, the extremely liquid JGB future traded in Tokyo is subject to a transaction tax, and although the JGB future traded on Liffe in London is not, the liquidity is poor. In any case, since the bonds deliverable into these contracts (although differing slightly in specification) are basically 10 years in maturity, the trader would run a substantial yield curve risk position if attempting to hedge anything other than 10-year swaps with either cash JGBs or futures.

(c) As mentioned previously, Japanese banks have difficulty using hedging instruments for accounting reasons.

(d) Although it is a chicken-and-egg argument the basis between 10-year swaps and 10-year JGB yields (using the on-the-run benchmark) is highly volatile (see Figure 2) and the correlation with other swap maturities is worse.

For these reasons, few traders hedge swap risk with JGBs, and this situation has changed little as the market has matured. Most have taken to hedging the short end (Libor) risk of their books with Euroyen futures since the advent of this contract in 1989, while relying on "curve hedging" (that is, short one maturity swap against long another on a delta-weighted basis) to reduce the risks of the term part of their books, only occasionally hedging the overall total exposure with JGBs if they feel the volatility of the market warrants it.

Figure 2: Spread of 10-year yen/yen swap to on-the-run JGB

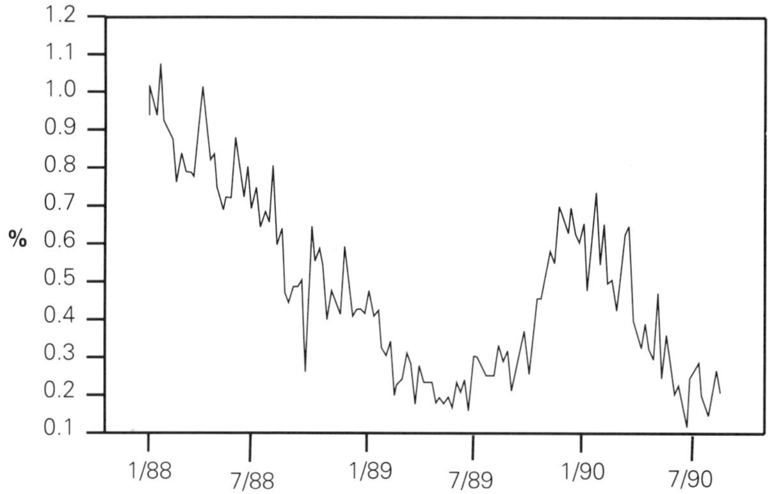

Source: IBJ International Limited

This is not to say that the spread between 10-year JGBs and yen/yen swaps is not closely watched in the market. In common with the similar spread play between Euroyen bonds and JGBs, the spread trade has become very popular with a number of more speculative accounts, although of course it is difficult to say whether this strategy has generally proved profitable. As shown by Figures 2 and 3, the swap market anticipated the dramatic rise in yen interest

Figure 3: 10-year yen/yen swap rate

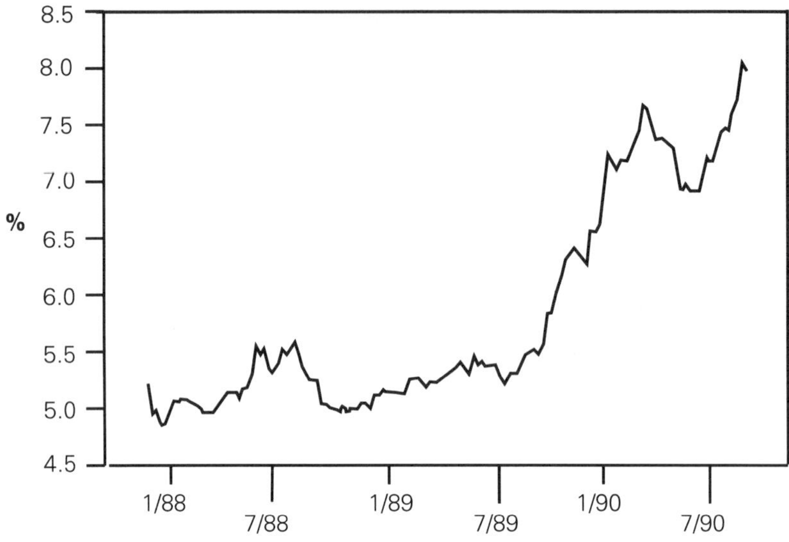

Source: IBJ International Limited

Figure 4: Five-year yen/yen swap rate versus LTPR

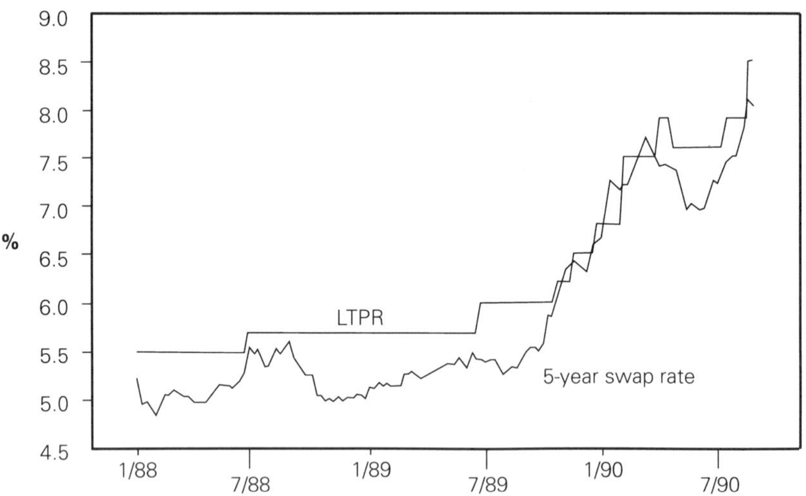

Source: IBJ International Limited

rates from July 1989 to January 1990, but at other times there seems to have been little correlation between the spread and rates. Interestingly, the spread of swaps to Euroyen bond yields, rather than their government bond counterparts, has been far more reliable (Figures 5 and 6). Figure 6 shows, for example, that except in the periods of sharply rising rates beginning in January 1990 and then again in July 1990, when the Euroyen bond market was temporarily closed to new issues, the spread between top credit Euroyen bonds and 10-year swaps has traded consistently between 20 and 50 basis points.

Figure 5: AAA Euroyen 10-year yields versus 10-year swap rate

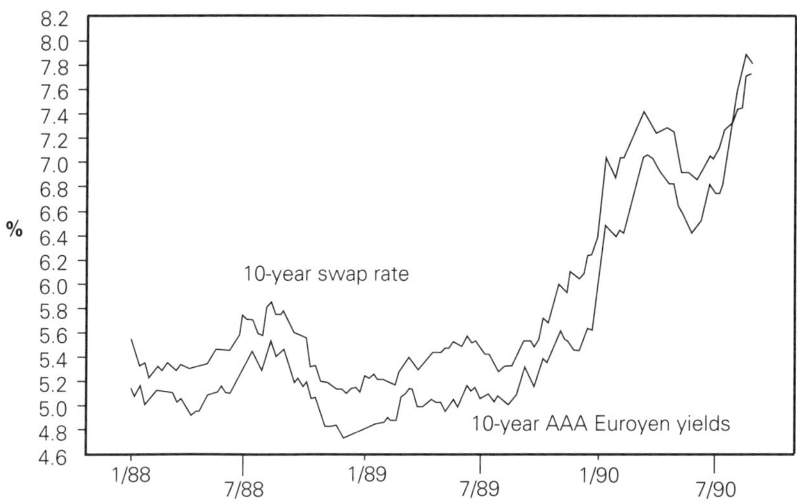

Source: IBJ International Limited

For a variety of reasons the five-year swap has become the benchmark for the market. As highlighted above, the city banks, because of restrictions upon the maturity of their funding, have natural demand for medium-term swaps. On the other hand, the five-year maturity has also been the historically favoured lending maturity for the long-term credit banks, where the benchmark fixed loan rate is termed LTPR ("long-term Prime rate"), which rate also governs where these banks issue their prime funding source, five-year debentures, to the retail market. The five-year swap represents a key link between these markets and undoubtedly the opportunity for arbitrage between these markets *via* the swap is monitored very closely by all Japanese banks. Figure 4, which

Figure 6: Spread between 10-year swap rate and AAA Euroyen 10-year yields

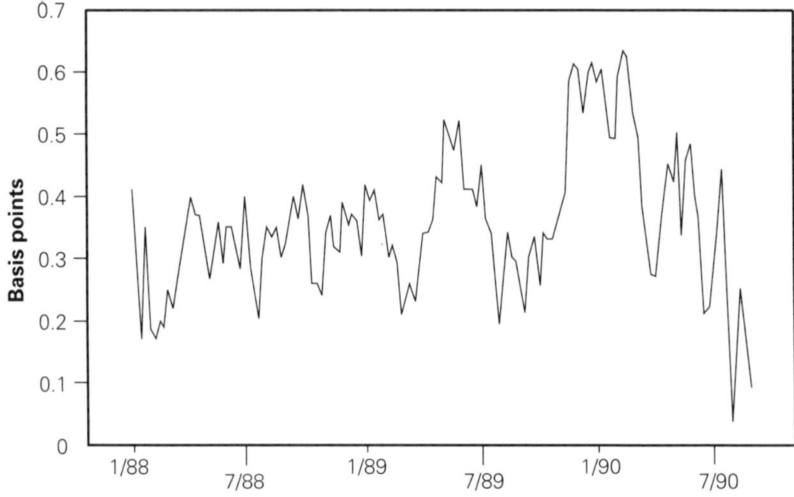

Source: IBJ International Limited

Figure 7: Spread between five-year yen/yen and yen/US dollar swap rate

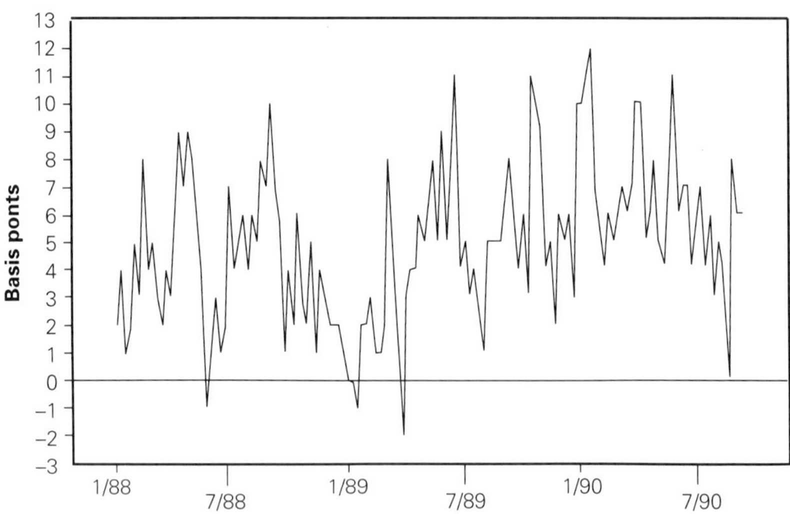

Source: IBJ International Limited

shows the historical relationship between LTPR and the five-year yen/yen swap rate, demonstrates some degree of correlation between the two rates, but it is clear that this arbitrage has not yet fully developed. The lack of existence of a LTPR/yen Libor basis swap market in any real sense of the word would also support this conclusion.

The yen Libor/US dollar Libor basis swap as implied by the difference between yen/yen and yen/US dollar swap rates has as a rule remained between 0 and 10 basis points in favour of yen Libor (that is, the market pays more to receive yen Libor) (see Figure 7). As the basis swap should theoretically have no value, this trend may reflect imperfect access to and arbitrage between swap and interbank lending markets in the two currencies, although it is difficult to be more specific than this.

Innovations in the market

While the simple yen interest rate swap is still the preferred hedging instrument for most users in the market, a number of innovatory structures have caught on to greater or lesser extents. Structured deals such as amortising, zero coupon, forward forex arbitrage and others are commonplace. Of the various options available on interest rates, swaptions, although relatively recently developed, seem to be the most popular and have been repackaged in a number of bond and loan structures, while the traditional Japanese appetite for taking unhedged currency risk (either on the asset or liability side) has been manifested in strong growth in (particularly) the yen/Australian dollar swap market.

The success of the swaption is due to the preference of Japanese customers for fixed-rate funding and the aforementiond prevalence of the swap as the major instrument defining the yen interest rate yield curve. Any call or put in bonds or loans thus naturally leads to the use of the swaption, while the demand for caps and floors, natural corollaries to floating-rate funding, has been less strong. The callable yen Eurobond proved extremely popular with investors in late 1988 to early 1989, while loan structures have included callable fixed rate, floating or fixed-rate convertible loans (into fixed or floating, respectively) and other variants on the theme. Each of these structures involves a one-time call or conversion and is hedged with the corresponding payers' or receivers' swaption (depending upon the particular structure); the arbitrage has simply been to induce the investor or borrower to "misprice" the relevant option relative to the market. In fact it is fair to say that in the above-mentioned deals investors were selling the calls substantially cheaper than market levels, but as investors have gained experience of the structure this pricing mismatch has narrowed substantially. One common thread is that Japanese customers are almost completely averse to buying interest rate protection, preferring to write options for premium income, and this has historically resulted in a situation where the swaptions market has been consistently one way round. As a result, implied volatilities have generally traded lower than the historical volatilities of the underlying swaps.

Another popular loan structure has been the reverse floater type, where the borrower pays a coupon of X (a fixed rate, of the order of twice the swap rate) minus yen Libor, with the total interest payable usually capped at a level below X to prevent the coupon going too high (thus the borrower is effectively buying a floor from the lender). This is one of the few structures where the customer is willing to buy options.

The strong growth of the yen/Australian dollar currency swap sector has resulted in the Australian dollar being the second most popular currency after the US dollar for currency swaps against yen in 1989.[2] On the asset side, Japanese customers' predilection for high yielding currencies and their familiarity with the Australian dollar in particular, fuelled the expansion of the reverse dual currency bond (payment and redemption in yen, coupon in Australian dollars), virtually all of which required yen/Australian dollar coupon-only swaps to "normalise" the borrower's cash flows before another swap into floating US dollars. On the debt side, Japanese borrowers have been willing to take the same risk by taking yen funding where the coupon payable is two times a normal yen fixed rate minus a fixed coupon in Australian dollars, or variants thereof. For banks running either swap or forward forex books in both yen and Australian dollars on a present value basis these coupon-only swaps are relatively easy to hedge, but again the relative novelty of this swap structure yielded good profits at the inception of the market.

The future

There is no reason to believe that trends already established in the yen swap markets will not continue. Greater concern over capital usage should lead those Japanese banks still lagging in this area to increase their systems efforts to monitor capital effectively, and boost the prevalence of yen/yen swaps at the expense of yen/US dollars. This may be mitigated by the continued requirement of international borrowers for US dollars as end funding currency, although there are signs of increasing readiness on their part to take yen as a final liability (boosted not least by the higher bid rates available in the interest rate swap markets). The sharp rise in yen interest rates beginning in the autumn of 1989 will stimulate the development of more effective ALM methods and risk management systems, especially in those banks used as a matter of course to running substantial asset/liability maturity mismatches. Greater familiarity on the part of the Japanese with the present value concept, and the possibility of a change in accounting methods, will reduce the profit available in even the most sophisticated swap structures, and there is no reason to think that the options/derivatives market will not face a similar profitability squeeze, albeit from a higher base. Substantial repatriation of Japanese capital, attracted by the higher yen rates, should provide a boost for market volumes. The yen swap will continue to be the major instrument for defining the yield curve.

Although competitive pressures on the foreign banks in the market should therefore intensify, especially given the cheaper cost base and dominance of retail custom of their Japanese counterparts, there are some trends which should give them cause to be sanguine about their future prospects. There is increasing evidence that Japanese customers are losing their reluctance to deal with foreign banks, and the pressure on Japanese banks to reduce their balance sheets should assist this trend. Meanwhile, some of the more technically advanced of foreign banks have already reduced their dependence upon the bottom-end, low-margin swap business where profitability is most likely to suffer, while managing to maintain a strong grip in the highly sophisticated option/derivatives areas.

In short, the yen swap markets will follow others down the road to reduced profitability, increasing transparency and greater capital and risk management awareness. As in any other market, those banks which can retain and expand retail business will emerge the strongest.

Notes

1. Source: International Swap Dealers Association.
2. Source: International Swap Dealers Association.

Chapter 12: The Australian and New Zealand dollar swap markets

Maxwell G W Morley[1]

The Australian dollar swap market

Recent developments

The Australian dollar swap market, despite the geographic isolation of its domestic base, remains one of the most internationally flavoured of the world's swap markets.

There are two "official" measures of Australian dollar swap activity — the bi-annual surveys conducted by the International Swap Dealers Association (ISDA) and, since 1988, annual surveys under the auspices of the Australian Financial Markets Association (AFMA). While the results of these two sources are not directly comparable (ISDA surveys just its members, of which only a handful are Australian-based; AFMA surveys approximately 30 institutions which are widely agreed to be the most active Australian dollar swap market participants), a joint examination of their results provides an insight into the international contribution of the Australian dollar swap market.

The growth in new Australian dollar swap business since January 1987 as recorded by ISDA's semi-annual surveys is shown in Figure 1.

The ISDA survey of new swap business for the first half of calendar year 1990 placed the Australian dollar sector as the sixth most active interest rate swap market in the world, with a notional volume of US$17.8bn equivalent and the third most active currency swap sector, with US$16.4bn equivalent transacted.

The ISDA results show that the total volume of world swap markets expanded by 41% year on year to the first half of 1990. The AFMA survey for the year ended 30 June 1990, puts new Australian dollar swap business at A$134bn, a 42% increase over the previous year. In an overall sense, therefore, the Australian dollar swap market is keeping pace with the continuing growth of global swap activity.

Figure 1: Australian dollar swap volumes

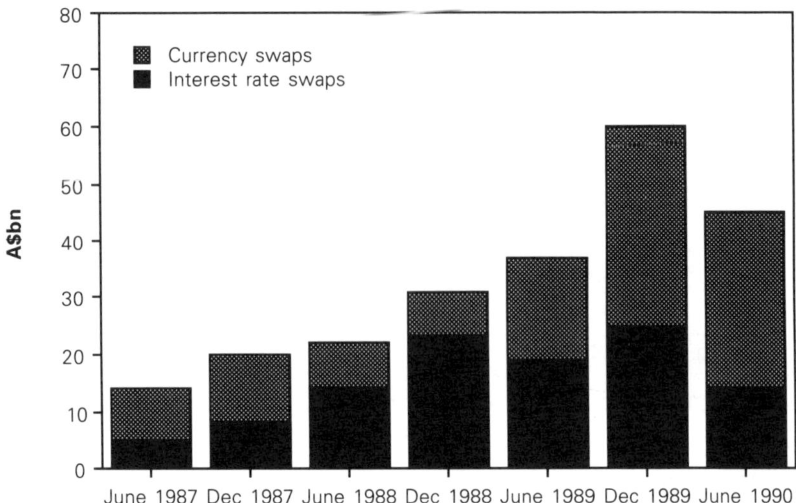

Source: International Swap Dealers Association

According to the AFMA surveys, the government/semi-government sector represents about 10% of total Australian dollar swap volume, while interbank/professional activity accounted for 22% in 1989/90, having fallen from 28% in 1988/89. A partial explanation for this reduction may be the departure from the market of several institutions, although growing credit exposure difficulties would also have constrained professional dealing. Not surprisingly in these capital cost conscious days, the proportion of total Australian dollar swap activity accounted for by currency swaps fell from 27% to 21% from 1988/89 to 1989/90.

The profile of swaps outstanding as at 30 June 1990 shows maturities heavily weighted to shorter dates — 73% of interest rate swaps having less than three years to run and 94% having less than five years — reflecting significantly lower market liquidity for terms longer than five years.

Although the AFMA surveys record the responses of approximately 30 active professional swap houses, the market is very concentrated as the top five players conducted 49% of the interest rate swap business and 72% of currency swap volume for the year ended 30 June 1990.

Quite apart from continuing to grow in volume, over the late 1980s the Australian dollar swap market has increased in sophistication and generally matured. Virtually any non-vanilla or innovative structure developed in other swap markets has been, or could be, priced, executed and hedged in the Australian dollar market. Forward starts, off-market coupons, zero coupons, amortising and accreting, basis swaps and other customised structures have all been transacted; however, some techniques seen offshore such as "Libor-in-arrears rate setting" have found neither acceptance nor application in the Australian dollar environment. Similarly, swaptions, despite the existence of considerable price-making capability, enjoy very limited levels of activity, with A$1.5bn transacted in the year to 30 September 1990 according to the AFMA survey of the Australian dollar options market.

In 1990, the Australian dollar swap market took an important step forward in the documentation of swap transactions, with the presentation of an ISDA master agreement specifically adapted to operate under Australian laws and conditions. Taking the form of amendments to the 1987 ISDA Interest Rate and Currency Exchange Agreement, the document was developed under the direction of AFMA and endorsed by ISDA for use in Australia between Australian counterparties. It is now becoming widely accepted among the professional market and will eventually completely displace the ageing "AIRS terms" and a multitude of variations thereon, moving Australia into line with international trends in documenting swaps.

Market structure

The structure of the Australian dollar swap market changed significantly during the late 1980s, with the main influences tending to be related to the capital markets:

- declining Australian dollar Eurobond new issuance;
- the emergence of large volumes of swapped Australian dollar/yen reverse dual currency debt issues;
- the establishment and subsequent heavy issuance of term domestic debt by State semi-government central borrowing authorities (State treasury corporations) coincident with the decline in Commonwealth government borrowing;
- the re-opening of the Australian dollar corporate bond market.

The impact of each of these developments is discussed below and Figure 2 illustrates the demand and supply (of fixed-rate funds) effects of each factor on the Australian dollar swap market.

Figure 2: The structure of the Australian dollar swap market

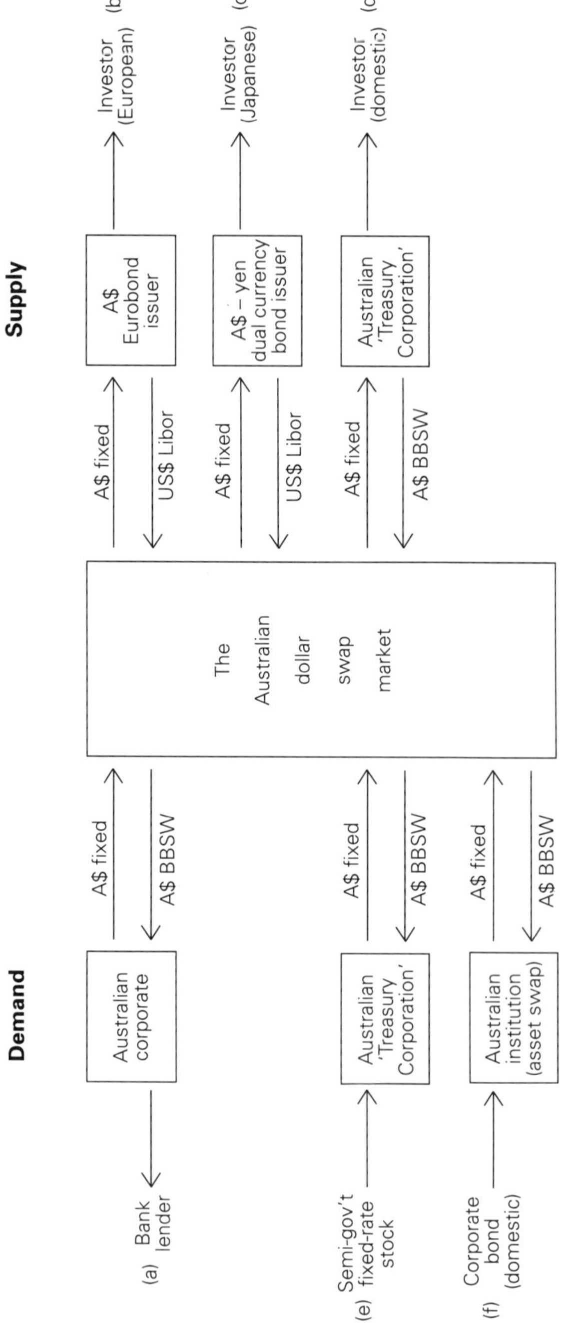

Until the late 1980s, the fundamental demand and supply factors in the Australian dollar swap market could have been explained by flows (a) and (b) in Figure 2. Australian corporates (with the exception of a few very highly-rated credits) had no direct access to fixed-rate funds, either domestically or offshore, and were heavy users (payers) of two to five-year swaps to hedge the cost of their floating-rate bank finance. The Australian dollar Eurobond market thrived during the mid-1980s as wide interest differentials to central European currencies attracted a pool of German, Belgian and Dutch retail investors. This allowed borrowers, typically European banks, multinational corporations and supranational entities, to issue three to five-year Australian dollar paper swapped to provide the issuer with cheap US dollar (or Deutsche mark) funding — frequently at margins of more than 0.50% below Libor. In addition to this European retail investor base, a significant volume of one to five-year Australian dollar paper was placed into the Yankee institutional market over a short period in 1987/88.

The matching of onshore fixed-rate payers (borrowers) and offshore fixed-rate receivers (issuers) in maturities up to five years was altered in the late 1980s by the factors listed earlier; Australian dollar Eurobond issuance declined as European retail investors became preoccupied with continental political developments and interest rate differentials between the Australian dollar and continental currencies began to narrow. As European investors became less aggressive in their buying of Australian dollar paper, the funding arbitrage available to issuers tightened and Eurobond-related Australian dollar swap activity declined. Of itself, this change in the onshore/offshore borrower/investor balance would have put pressure on Australian dollar swap spreads to widen were it not for developments in the domestic fixed interest market and the opening up of a new source of offshore investor interest in Tokyo.

During 1987 and 1988, the bulk of the fixed-rate debt of State and semi-government authorities was consolidated into "hot stocks" (a few large liquid lines of inscribed stock) issued by State treasury corporations with the stated aim of undertaking more active and efficient management of liabilities. These entities quickly became the most active issuers of high-quality fixed-rate debt in Australia as the Federal government transferred financing responsibilities to the States, moved towards running the Federal budget in surplus, and actively started to remove Commonwealth bonds from the market. To manage the large liability (and asset) portfolios for which they were now responsible the State treasury corporations became heavy users of the swap market (both as fixed-rate payers and receivers in line with the new emphasis on active portfolio management). As a result, the State treasury corporations became active managers of the spread between the swap curve and their own fixed-rate debt on issue — liability swapping (issuing stock and receiving fixed rate) at margins up to 0.30/0.40% below BBSW and asset swapping (buying back their stock and paying fixed rate) at margins up to 0.20/0.30% over BBSW. This swap-to-stock-spread management activity is probably unique in the world financial markets and has contributed to the major role played by the State treasury corporations in the Australian dollar swap market.

The second major change to the structure of the swap market occurred during late 1988 as Australian dollar/Japanese yen reverse dual currency bond issues (and several private placement variants) found favour with Japanese investors in the light of wide Australian dollar/yen interest rate differentials and Australian dollar/yen exchange rate stability. The importance of this activity cannot be overstated: the 1990 ISDA survey reports more than 60% of Australian dollar currency swap business as being Australian dollar/yen! This type of debt generally carried maturities of seven to 10 years and was usually swapped into low cost US dollars or yen funding at similar margins to those achieved in the Australian dollar Eurobond market earlier in the decade (see flow (c) in Figure 2). A detailed description of the mechanics of swapping this debt appears elsewhere in this book; suffice to say that the long maturities and large volumes issued significantly altered the balance of activity in the least liquid maturities of the Australian dollar swap curve. As a direct result of this business, the 10-year swap rate traded below most semi-government yields for a large part of 1990 (an apparently anomalous relationship) despite heavy asset swapping activity (flow (e)). Following heavy transaction volumes in 1989 and most of 1990, narrowing interest rate differentials (as monetary policy was eased in Australia) and foreign exchange movements combined to stall this activity — at least temporarily — by the end of 1990.

While the Australian dollar/yen dual currency swap business was booming, Australian dollar Eurobond swap activity was in decline. Although a burst of short-dated issues with embedded Australian dollar/US dollar or Australian dollar/Deutsche mark currency options maintained new issuance volumes in 1989, 1990 saw new Australian dollar Eurobond issuance fall to below A$7bn — the first time that new issuance did not cover redemptions (almost A$10bn for 1990). Narrowing Australian dollar/Deutsche mark interest rate differentials and a more introspective focus from investors on central European developments has dramatically reduced the impact of this sector on the Australian dollar swap market.

The final development in the structure of the Australian dollar swap market was the re-opening of the domestic corporate bond market in the late 1980s. Most recent issuance has tended to be in the form of term bank certificates of deposit (about A$5bn on issue), mortgage-backed securities (A$5.5bn approximately) and government backed/guaranteed bonds (for example, Civil Aviation Authority and Australian Wool Corporation). So while the swap flow (Figure 2 (a)) from companies seeking to fix the cost of their borrowings has not been replaced by direct issuance (since virtually no true industrial corporation has been able to tap the corporate bond market recently), the renewal of this market has opened up further asset swapping opportunities (see Figure 2 (f)) and highlighted a re-pricing of term bank debt to levels well above the swap curve.

Pricing

With the Commonwealth government running budget surpluses and conducting reverse tenders to remove Commonwealth government bonds from circulation, and the State treasury corporations actively issuing and establishing hot stocks, the swap-to-bond spread had given way to the swap-to-TCorp spread (New South Wales Treasury Corporation having been established as the market benchmark) as the main method of pricing longer-dated swaps by the late 1980s. Each of the changes to the structure of the market already mentioned has impacted the absolute and relative levels of these spreads:

- The weight of semi-government debt issuance and liability swapping (possibly at relatively too expensive swapped funding costs) has held swap spreads since 1987.

- Declining Australian dollar Eurobond swap activity in 1990 (historically for three to five-year terms) has been offset by a reduction in corporate paying interest (historically two to five years) due to falling interest rates and the onset of recession.

- The large volume of seven to 10-year reverse dual currency bond issues swapped during 1989–90 forced long-dated swap spreads to narrow dramatically to levels below TCorp yields until issuance levels dropped late in 1990.

- The spreads of most other semi-government issuers widened significantly to TCorp benchmarks in December 1990 and pushed swap-to-TCorp spreads wider through asset swap activity (as dual currency swap activity stalled).

- Term (non-government) bank paper spreads widened to TCorp benchmarks and virtually all this debt is trading at least 30–40 basis points over the swap curve — a phenomenon which can be explained by lack of investor appetite for term bank risk and the historically heavy liability swapping activities of semi-government authorities.

Figure 3: New South Wales Treasury Corporation asset swap margins
1993, 1995 and 1999 maturities

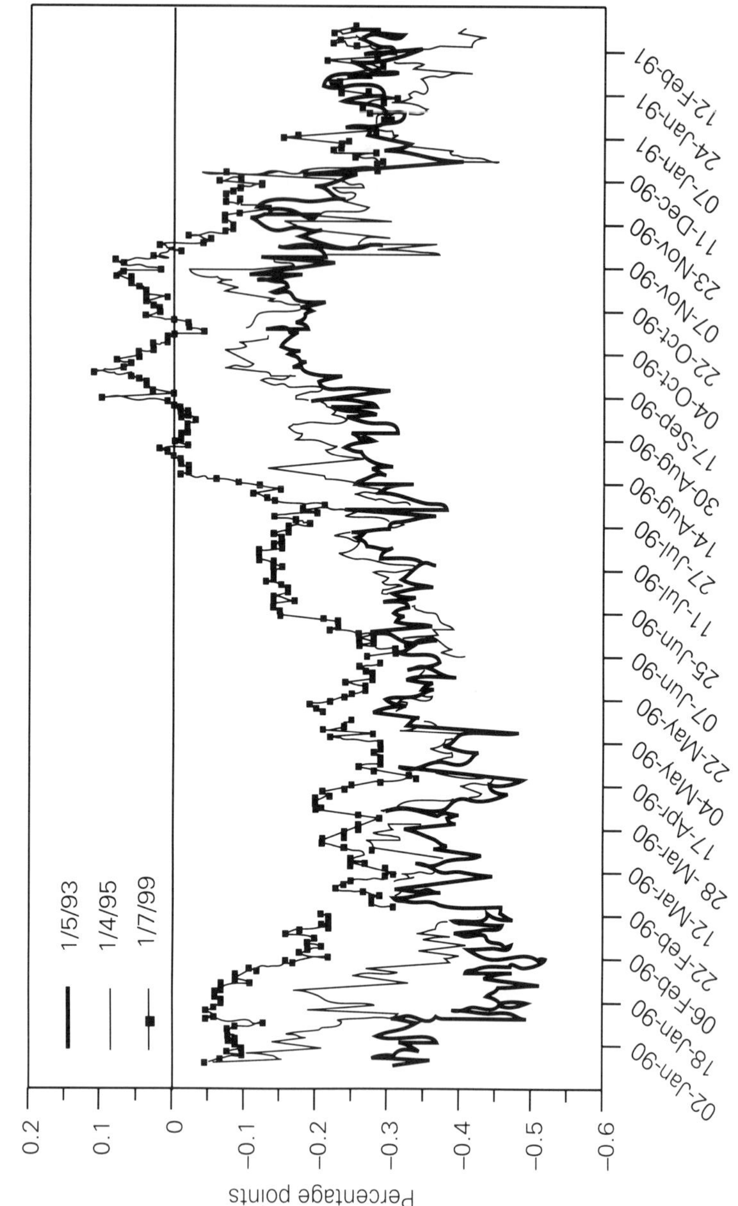

The progression of swap spreads to benchmark TCorp stocks under the influence of the above factors is illustrated in Figure 3.

Another factor impacting swap pricing recently is the dramatic shift from a steeply inverse yield curve (November 1989) to a positive/flat curve as monetary policy was progressively eased during 1990. The expectation of falling rates enforced a strongly bullish tone in the bank bill futures strip; hence short-dated swaps tended to trade at very tight spreads to (or even below) short-dated semi-government stocks for most of 1990.

Hedging developments

In spite of the move to pricing longer-dated swaps on a spread-to-TCorp basis, swap players continue to use a cocktail of hedging instruments including three and 10-year Commonwealth bond futures contracts, a variety of the State treasury corporations' hot stocks and, of course, strips of bank bill futures and FRAs for shorter-dated transactions. Although the strip is traded out to three years, lower liquidity in the back months and the existence of the three-year Commonwealth bond futures contract have created two schools of hedging/pricing two to four-year swaps — "bill strippers" and "stock spreaders". The result is that there is often activity driven by the overlap of the bill and bond markets around the three-year maturity (where the swap curve often changes slope or has a "blip") and the quarterly (standard market practice for one to three-year swaps) to semi-annual (four to 10-year swaps) "gross-up" has become much more efficiently priced in the two to four-year maturities.

Although swap warehouses definitely use the three-year bond futures contract and it is generally accepted that a five-year semi-government futures contract should be an attractive hedging tool, attempts to introduce such a contract have failed. The overriding requirements for a good swap hedge are liquidity and good spread stability. The five-year semi-government contracts proposed to date have failed to provide these characteristics partly due to deliverability issues, but also because the State treasury corporations have established very active stock lending programmes to enhance the liquidity-providing capabilities of market-makers (in their stocks) through the facilitation of short selling. These stock lending programmes are not "repo" arrangements and are fee-based rather than market price driven. As such they are a unique element of the Australian dollar swap market, allowing swap warehouses to short-sell physical stocks — generally cheaper than the theoretical cost of running the short position!

The consolidation into hot stocks, the active stock lending programmes and the use of swaps in the asset/liability management of State treasury corporations has greatly increased the use of semi-government stock as a hedging instrument in swap warehouses over the last few years.

Outlook

Although Australian dollar Eurobond, Japanese dual currency and even domestic corporate swap activities were all at low levels at the end of 1990, the future of the Australian dollar swap market looks quite good. Corporate borrowers will return to the market as the interest rate cycle bottoms and economic activity increases. In addition, the ongoing requirement for the State and treasury corporations to manage substantial liability and asset portfolios will continue to contribute to swap market activity.

The future impact of offshore Australian dollar capital market activity is very difficult to predict. However, although minor activity will no doubt continue, a major resurgence is dependent upon such factors as changing interest rate differentials and perceived stability of exchange rates. For the time being the "high coupon" attraction of the Australian dollar has diminished.

It should be noted that the Australian legal environment is one of the most favourable in the world for the introduction of widespread netting for credit purposes; a factor supporting the long-term liquidity of the Australian dollar swap market.

The next structural development of the Australian dollar swap market is likely to come from a restructuring of the Australian financial sector itself. The Federal government's current retirement policy implies a major alteration to the flow of funds within the financial sector — away from deposits with banks and other non-bank financial institutions towards superannuation funds. It is extremely unlikely that managers of such (ultimately) large asset portfolios will not become significant users of the Australian dollar swap market.

The New Zealand dollar swap market

New Zealand dollar interest rate swap business for the six months ended 30 June 1990 was reported by ISDA members at US$1bn (equivalent) and currency swap business at US$1.5bn (equivalent). While this is the only actual survey of swap activity, other estimates suggest that current total annual New Zealand dollar swap turnover is slightly higher at NZ$8–9bn.

The New Zealand dollar swap market, having boomed during Eurobond-related activity in the mid-1980s, contracted in the late 1980s as Figure 4 shows. Sharp falls in interest rates and the flattening from a very steeply inverse yield curve have removed the "high coupon" currency status which once attracted Eurobond investors. In addition, the severity of the prolonged economic recession and doubts about the resilience of the economy have generally caused offshore investors to ignore New Zealand recently. The exception has been direct acquisition-based investment by Australasian entities seeking a strategic foothold in the region. With this acquisition finance usually sourced from offshore, investors have used New Zealand dollar currency swaps to hedge their New Zealand dollar-denominated investment, thereby providing the only offshore "growth" influence for the swap market.

Figure 4: New Zealand dollar swap volumes

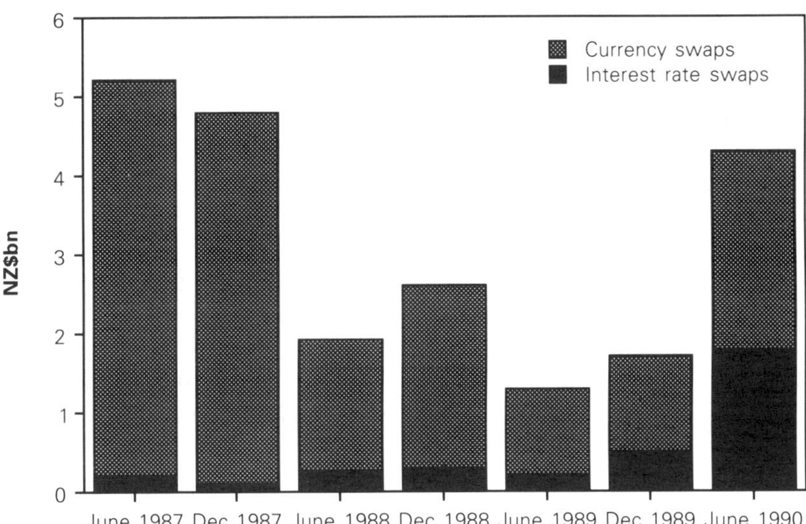

Source: International Swap Dealers Association

Low levels of economic activity have dampened corporate interest in the swap market leaving new swap volumes to be supported by the hedging requirements of project or infrastructural financings and the liability management activities of fixed-rate issuers such as utility corporations and local authorities.

The contraction of the market has left four major market-making houses active together with a handful of fringe professional players. Interestingly, only one of the original "Eurobond swap providers" is still a major participant in the market. As liquidity is therefore inhibited, bid/offer spreads of 20/25bp are common.

Pricing and hedging New Zealand dollar swaps pose further liquidity problems. The underlying lines of government bonds are generally quite small and stock is usually scarce. There is virtually no liquidity in the three-year government bond futures contract (that is, it does not trade) so most long-term swaps are hedged against the five-year government bond contract. The July 1997 government bond is the longest maturity stock useful for hedging; other liquid stocks being November 1993 and July 1992. Swaps of maturity longer than seven years rarely trade and liquidity past five years is extremely poor (interbank credit being a major constraint).

The longer maturities (five to seven years) have tended to trade 75–90bp above government yields, while spreads in the shorter maturities (two to three years) are generally narrower at 20 35bp. A lot of one to two-year swap business is produced by arbitraging exporters' foreign exchange hedging activity and has, on occasion, forced the two-year swap down to flat on government bond yields. A relatively active bill futures market facilitates strip hedging out to one-year terms.

The outlook for the New Zealand dollar swap market hinges on three factors:

- how quickly any upturn in economic activity will lead to corporate expansion requiring new finance and therefore swap hedging;
- how offshore investors perceive New Zealand risk in the future given that the New Zealand dollar has lost its "high coupon" status;
- whether liquidity and the ability to lay off and spread market risk through the professional swap market remains stymied by credit exposure constraints.

Although the economy may recover and investors may reassess their investment parameters, interbank liquidity will remain a limitation while the market can only support a small number of players and netting for credit purposes is not widely accepted.

Notes

1. Max Morley is currently Manager, Risk Management Products in the Australian Financial Markets Group of Westpac Banking Corporation, Sydney.

Chapter 13: The Hong Kong dollar swap market

Stephen F Myers
Hongkong and Shanghai Banking Corporation

The origins and evolution of the Hong Kong dollar swap market

The epidemic which swept through the Eurobond market in 1982 in the guise of the swap product and its uses in reducing borrowers' funding costs took a further 12 months to reach Hong Kong in any substantial form. This was largely due to the undeveloped nature of the domestic capital market, at that time the vital ingredient in any swap transaction. In those early days, virtually all swap transactions took place using the arbitrage that existed between the various currency bond markets and credit perceptions. It is therefore not surprising that it took a little while for the full potential of the swap product to filter down to those markets with little or no capital market presence as the salesmen devoted their attentions to the most obvious, not to say profitable, applications.

In those early days, that is, pre-market-making of swaps in any currency, all swaps were concluded on a matched basis. That is to say, the major swap arrangers were exactly that, persons operating on behalf of investment and commercial banks seeking out counterparties with equal and opposite requirements in terms of amount, maturity and structure. If the payer of the fixed was prepared to pay more than the receiver by a sufficiently large margin (25 to 40 basis points per annum on the principal was felt to be a reasonable return in those days, together with an upfront arrangement fee) then the arranger was able to put a deal together, usually placing itself as intermediary bank between the two counterparties.

The development of the swap market in Hong Kong arose out of a different use of swaps where the initial transactions were mainly currency swaps or cross-currency interest rate swaps, and they were usually structured between fixed or floating-rate Hong Kong dollars and fixed or floating-rate US dollars. The users of the first swaps were normally domestic corporations, banks and multinationals with offices in Hong Kong. The main motivations were similar to those that existed in the original days of the parallel loan market, namely a means of accessing markets to which little or no direct access existed.

For example, a typical arrangement might be, on the one hand, a Hong Kong exporter looking to match its domestic Hong Kong dollar financing base to its revenues in the currency of the country to which its products are being exported and, on the other hand, a non-domestic company exporting goods to Hong Kong looking to match its US dollar Libor-based funding with its Hong Kong dollar revenues.

Figure 1: A typical cross-currency interest rate swap

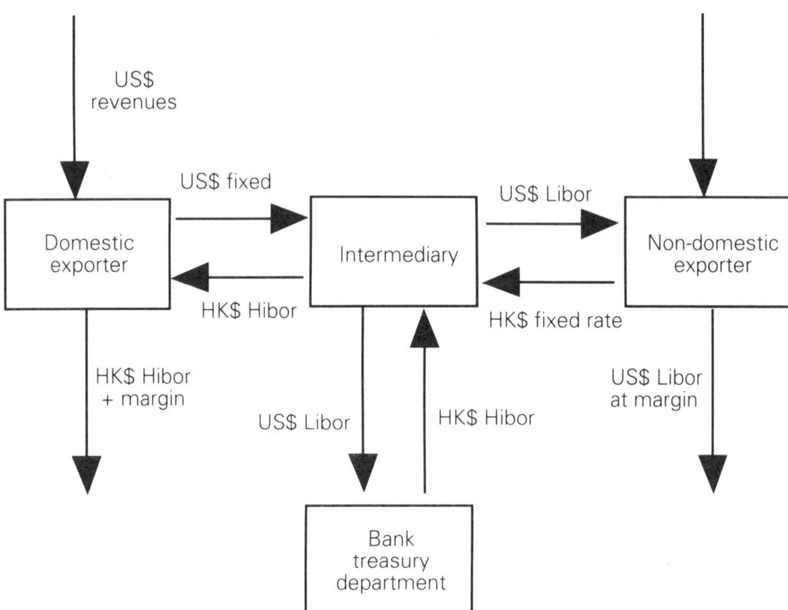

Figure 1 illustrates a fairly standard usage of the cross-currency interest rate swap. The intermediary, usually a bank, is able to create a Hong Kong dollar/US dollar Hibor/Libor swap using its Hong Kong dollar and US dollar loans and deposit base and thereby effectively obtains sub-Libor/Hibor funding.

The birth of a fixed-rate short and medium-term CD market in Hong Kong dollars in 1984 led to a significant rise in the volume of both interest rate and currency swaps in Hong Kong dollars. Banks and other financial institutions found they were able to issue fixed-rate CD's on favourable terms and use the relatively cheap funding base to provide the supply side of the fixed-rate Hong Kong dollar swap market, the side which was always in demand. A bank would issue a fixed-rate CD for say three years and swap it into floating-rate US dollars or Hong Kong dollars at a sub-Libor or Hibor margin.

The rapid rise of the domestic fixed-rate CD market and a burgeoning capital market resulted in a corresponding increase in the volume of Hong Kong dollar-based swaps from 1984 to 1988. However, the Hong Kong dollar swap market's dependence on the CD and other capital market instruments was so strong that any contraction in the fixed-rate issuance market was immediately reflected in a substantial reduction in the volume of Hong Kong dollar swaps. It is of academic debate as to whether the fall in the issuance of fixed-rate Hong Kong dollar paper was as a result of the fall in demand for swaps or whether the decline in fixed-rate paper issuance through a lack of investor interest then led to the reduction in swap volumes. If one looks back to 1988, however, one discovers that at that time investors were reluctant to place funds in the domestic medium-term market, preferring to keep funds on short-term deposits or placed offshore, which would account for at least part of the decline in the investor base.

The development of market-making in Hong Kong dollar swaps

If one examines the most liquid swap market, namely the US dollar interest rate swap market, and compares the availability of instruments which assist the market-maker to temporarily hedge one side of a swap position, it becomes clear why the Hong Kong dollar market has been unable to develop much beyond its current capacity. The following characteristics apply to the US dollar market:

- An active two-way business between fixed payers and fixed receivers across a wide maturity spectrum. The preponderance of US corporates unable to tap the fixed-rate domestic market on reasonable terms and the continued dominance of US dollars in the fixed-rate Eurobond market provide just two of the many elements of the US dollar market which compose the demand and supply side of the swap.

- An active US government bond market in which it is possible to buy or sell virtually any quantity of bonds at minimal bid/offer prices in the actively-traded maturities of two, three, four, five, seven and 10 years and at any time of the day or night.

- An active government bond lending and borrowing market (repo and reverse repo).

- An active and liquid Eurodollar futures market based on three-month Eurodollars, with the front contracts actively traded on Simex and Liffe as well as contracts currently extending to maturities of four years in Chicago.

These components, *inter alia*, facilitate the making of markets in US dollar swaps and the whole range of interest rate derivative products in all maturities out to 10 years and any structure. Using these instruments the professional market-maker is able to substantially control the risks of entering into one side of a US dollar interest rate swap.

Unfortunately, the Hong Kong dollar market does not satisfy any of the above requirements, if one is able to regard the above as perquisites of a successful and dynamic market. The Hong Kong dollar has very little active two-way business. As previously stated, the activity in the CD market, or rather the recent lack of it, has more or less resulted in a drying up of the supply side of the the market. On the other hand, there remains an over-abundance of fixed-rate payers looking to lock in fixed-rate funding. This imbalance can result in a distortion of medium-term rates as the demand pushes swap rates up until they find a level which attracts the potential receivers.

Similarly, the lack of an active domestic government bond market means that there is no base index for medium-term swaps and no ability to hedge medium-term positions. Most swap markets are directly or indirectly related to the underlying bond market, directly, for example, in the case of the US dollar market where medium-term swaps are priced as a spread over the yield of the government bond of similar maturity, or indirectly, for example, in the case of the Deutsche mark swap market where swaps are quoted as an absolute rate but trade within a narrow range to the underlying domestic Bund market.

The one potentially saving grace of the Hong Kong dollar market was the introduction of a short-term interest Hibor contract on the Hong Kong Futures Exchange (Reuter's page HKFR). However, since its introduction in February 1990 the combined daily volume of the front two contracts has rarely risen much over 1,000 contracts, reflecting a distinct lack of liquidity. However, it does provide the professional market-maker with the ability to hedge the variable side of a swap, and to a limited degree, short-term swaps. It is, however, the movements in the medium-term rates which give rise to the greatest exposure and for which no real hedge currently exists.

One can point to the pegging of the Hong Kong dollar to the US dollar in 1983 and ask why there should be any demand at all for swaps in the Hong Kong dollar, as one could take on a US dollar swap as a proxy hedge without running any currency exposure. However, that is to totally misunderstand the relationship of the Hong Kong dollar to the US dollar. If one pegs the value of

Figure 2: Hong Kong dollar versus US dollar

Three-year interest rate swaps

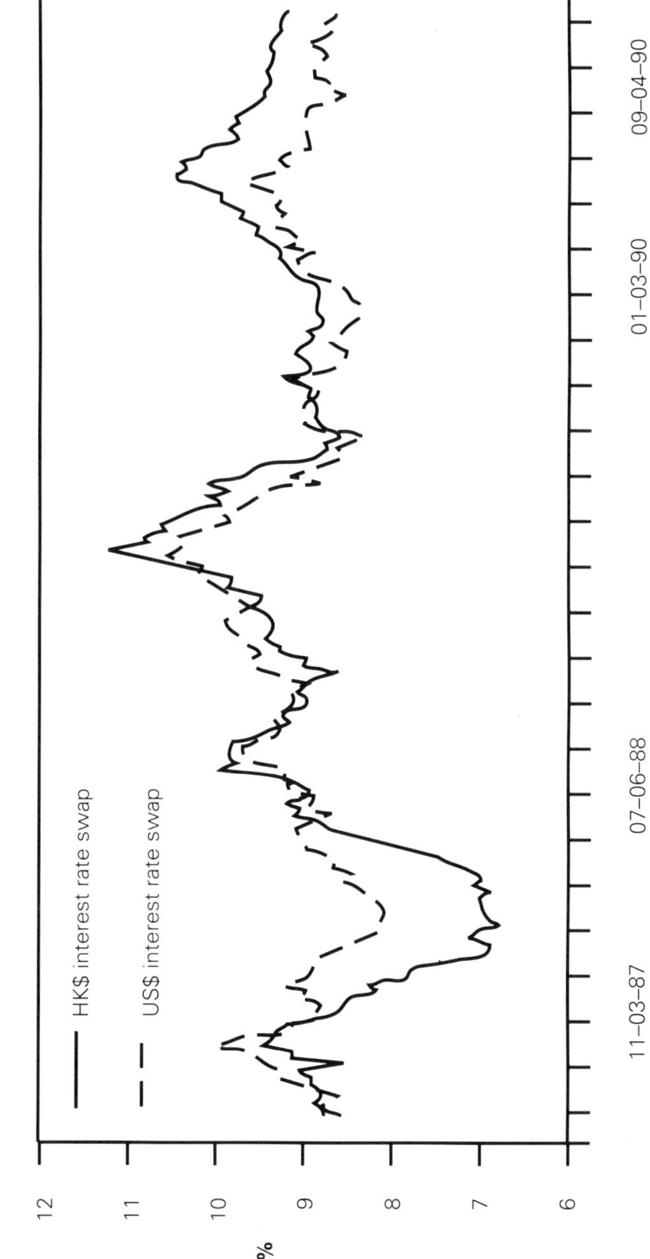

Data supplied by Wardley Limited, Hong Kong and Hongkong and Shanghai Banking Corporation Limited

one currency to another then it is effectively reducing the number of variables that can be changed to reflect movements in the underlying strength or weakness of the relative economies. The most obvious variation that one can make to bring the relative values of the currencies back into a stable balance is to push interest rates up or down. (See Figure 2 for the relative volatility of Hong Kong dollars and US dollars.)

Thus, for example, one might believe that to hedge an interest rate swap in Hong Kong dollars, one could simply put the transaction against an opposite swap in US dollars whereby the fixed cash flows would offset each other leaving a Hibor/Libor swap. Ignoring the different calculation basis (see below) the short-term interbank rates do not move in parallel. Indeed, it is not unusual for six-month Hong Kong dollar Hibor to trade at a differential of 1%+ to US dollar Libor. Such reliance on the pegging of the currency to the US dollar while ignoring the interest rate risk has resulted in more than one instance of substantial loss.

Characteristics of the Hong Kong dollar swap market

Hibor is the floating-rate index used in Hong Kong dollar swaps and is fixed daily using the HIBO screens on Reuters and Telerate 9898. Hong Kong dollar interest accruals, both fixed and variable, are calculated, like sterling, on the basis of the actual number of days in a year of 365 days. The similarity to sterling interest calculations extends to the fact that the variable rate is fixed on the first day of the calculation period, that is, not two business days in advance as with most other currencies. Currently, the fixed rate is conventionally quoted on a quarterly money market basis, "money market" in this instance being actual/365.

Liquidity, if one can call the Hong Kong dollar swap market liquid in the conventional sense, is restricted to five years, ie, 1995, with very little activity beyond that maturity. This reflects to some degree the current concerns over the future of the Hong Kong market beyond the extinction of the lease in 1997 as well as the lack of adequate medium-term fixed-rate hedging instruments. It should be stated, however, that the continuation of its own currency forms part of the agreement with China and therefore swaps denominated in Hong Kong dollars should be possible beyond this maturity.

The major players in the Hong Kong dollar market include the "local" banks, Hongkong Bank, Wardleys and Standard Chartered, together with the usual major swap players such as Chase, Citibank and Manufacturers Hanover. Unlike most other swap markets very few of the players are willing to give two-way prices, and if they do the bid/offer spread tends to be extremely wide, with 20 basis points being the norm. This wider bid/offer spread is, however, required to cover the higher than average risks in temporarily warehousing such a transaction. Given the stability of the exchange rates *vis-à-vis* the US dollar it is possible to "hedge" the fixed side of the swap through the purchase or sale of US government bonds. This is similar to the US dollar swap positioning in that a spread position is assumed between the Hong Kong dollar swap rates and US government bonds. The floating side can be hedged using the new Hibor futures contract. The lack of liquidity in the Hibor futures market combined with the volatility between Hong Kong dollar and US dollar interest rates leads to higher transactional costs and increased risk

The standard transaction size is HK$50m with the occasional deal of HK$100m. The average deal size of some US$6m equivalent compares to an average of US$20m in US dollar swaps. There is very little in the way of interbank trading, with most of the deals being transacted on the back of corporate and other end-user demand. Actual swap volumes are difficult to estimate but based on figures supplied to ISDA, which show an annualised volume by reporting members of some HK$8–10bn, one would guess that total market volume would be of the order of HK$20–30bn.

Other than the market-makers and issuers of CDs, the users tend to be mainly corporate, both domestic, looking at floating-rate funding, and international exporters looking to hedge receivables into their normal funding base.

The lack of adequate hedge instruments and general liquidity in the swap market has rendered it difficult to introduce the other derivative products seen in the major currencies, such as caps, floors and swaptions.

Hong Kong dollar swap documentation

Some three years ago, the Hong Kong Capital Markets Association introduced a Master Agreement for the Hong Kong dollar interbank interest rate swap market. The document also carries the approval of the Hong Kong Association of Banks but has been specifically designed for use by banks and deposit-taking companies. The Agreement may also be used for transactions with corporate counterparties but it is suggested that the document be amended to reflect the nature and credit-standing of the counterparty. Similar to the ISDA *Master Agreement* in concept, once the Master Agreement has been entered into by both counterparties to a transaction further transactions are evidenced by a mutual exchange of short form contract confirmations.

One aim in the drafting of the Master Agreement was to ensure that individual swap transactions between counterparties could be regarded on a net basis. The intention was two-fold, firstly, to reduce the capital requirements following the introduction of capital adequacy by the BIS and, secondly, to enable banks to look at their swap exposure against individual counterparties on a net basis in the event of bankruptcy. It is a mute point as to whether these intentions have been fulfilled. In the US it was necessary for a Bill to be passed by the Senate before netting could be fully and legally recognised by the authorities. This has left the question of netting in other jurisdictions far less clear as authorities are now able to point to the precedent of the US and claim that without specific laws netting may not be permissable.

Recent developments

The political events of 4 June 1989 had a dramatic impact on the domestic swap market, driving fixed interest rates up as the supply side of the market disappeared. Interest rates fell back to normal levels as the political situation became more relaxed. However, while the future of Hong Kong beyond 1997 remains an issue of concern to the Western world the Hong Kong dollar swap market is likely to suffer violent swings as emotions change. As and when confidence is restored and the future becomes more easily discernable then one can see the continuation of the Hong Kong dollar swap market for many years to come.

The issuance of fixed-rate paper has fallen substantially over the last couple of years removing with it a major source of fixed-rate receivers. On the other hand, the demand for fixed medium-term funding has remained unchanged. In theory, at least, if one were able to place fixed-rate debt then sub-Hibor funding would still be possible. Recently, the Hong Kong government has relaxed certain tax disincentives on the issuance of paper by non-bank borrowers giving the investor a greater choice of issuers. Whether this will have the desired effect of bringing the investor back to the Hong Kong dollar market remains to be seen.

Finally, it is interesting to note that ISDA statistics show that Hong Kong dollar swaps outstanding have maturities beyond 1997, although the author is given to understand that the counterparties to such transactions have been usually driven by Chinese-based corporations.

Chapter 14: The global FRA market

Tim Frost
JP Morgan

Forward-rate agreements (FRAs) as a product are still relatively new and exhibit many characteristics of immaturity. The market is experiencing rapid growth and many organisations have chosen to become involved, however, there is still a large measure of ignorance amongst some participants. This growth in FRA markets has been stimulated by the need for many banks to increase their capacity to manage interest rate risk off balance sheet. The Bank for International Settlements' capital adequacy requirements now mean that hedging a deposit with a re-deposit and developing a bloated balance sheet, is expensive in terms of capital.

When two parties enter into an FRA there is no exchange of principal. The parties agree to exchange the interest differential between a mutually-agreed contract level and a mutually-agreed interest rate (eg, six-month US dollar Libor), at a particular date in the future. Thus the buyer of a US$10m six-month Libor FRA at 8.00% fixing on 15 September will receive US$10m x 182/360 x 0.1 for every basis point six-month US dollar Libor fixes over 8.00% on 15 September.

It will be appreciated that an FRA can be thought of as an over-the-counter futures contract. Indeed, in some currency markets, FRAs are traded as substitute futures contracts by trading a three-month FRA fixing on the future's expiry date. The further development of the FRA market is crucially dependent on the relationship between the FRA and futures markets. Each market has its advantages and disadvantages but it seems clear that the global FRA markets will only continue to develop if they complement futures markets, providing extra flexibility in terms of hedging and risk taking. As a simple speculative instrument, a futures contract will always have the edge because there is greater liquidity and no counterparty risk. So what are the characteristics of the FRA which differentiate it from futures contracts and which will ensure its continued development?

In the more sophisticated FRA markets — dollars, sterling and Deutsche marks — it is possible to secure quotes for FRAs fixing for three, six, nine or 12 months on any day as far out as one-year forward. This flexibility enables precise hedging of an exposure, precision which futures contracts cannot provide. Thus in the sterling markets, swap market-makers use the FRA market to hedge the floating side of their swap book. In the Deutsche mark market, organisations with outstanding floating-rate notes fixing off Deutsche mark Libor may buy a Deutsche mark FRA to lock in an attractive refixing, or a series of refixings.

FRAs differ from futures in not involving margin payments. This represents a significant advantage in terms of a reduced requirement for support staff to arrange payment/receipt of margin; it also influences the basis between FRAs and futures. Margin payments ensure that futures contracts exhibit greater convexity than FRAs and consequently futures will trade at slightly higher yields than the equivalent FRA.

Market participants

Bank treasuries have been the first to develop knowledge of the FRA product in all currencies, stimulated by the banks' increased desire to manage risk off balance sheet. Systems, techniques and people successfully operating in one currency market are readily transferable into others.

Once FRA trading expertise has been developed within a bank, it should only be a short time before knowledge of how to use FRAs percolates through to the bank's interest rate swap group. FRAs are ideally suited to manage the floating side of a swap portfolio. The use of three-month futures contracts to hedge floating risk leaves the swap trader exposed to the risk between three and six-month rates. The use of a six-month FRA, fixing on the same day as the floating side of the swap, and fixing off the same benchmark rate, eliminates all risk; whilst the more imaginative use of FRAs provides ample opportunity to take risk. All this can be achieved at little or no extra cost as compared to the use of futures.

FRAs can also be used with positions in the forward foreign exchange market to isolate one side of the interest rate exposure on an outstanding deal. Thus a trader who is happy with his over-lent yen position, but no longer sees any value in his over-borrowed dollar position, can isolate the yen exposure and neutralise the dollar exposure by selling an appropriate dollar FRA.

Forwards and FRAs are very similar products and there are many obvious advantages of using these products together. Whilst many banks have not as yet exploited the potential for synergies, more advanced institutions are beginning to exploit arbitrage opportunities between the two markets, and to make prices to corporate customers in the FRA market on the basis of axes generated in the forward market and *vice versa*.

The use of back-to-back FRAs (eg, long 6V12 Dm FRA, short 6V12 $ FRA) to create synthetic forward foreign exchange positions has stimulated the development of a hybrid FRA or foreign exchange agreement "FXA" market. Whilst still in its early stages of development this market promises to provide greater liquidity, and arbitrage opportunities in all FRA markets.

More sophisticated corporate treasurers, particularly those active in the swap markets have also become active in the FRA market. Much of the recent growth has come from the corporate sector, where treasurers are increasingly happy to use FRAs, rather than the cash or futures market, to manage their short-term interest rate risk exposure. The benefit of being able to match exactly a rate refix day is of particular benefit to corporates, and, where the corporate intends to hold the FRA through to the fixing date, reduces the disadvantage of the lower liquidity of the FRA market as compared to the futures market. The corporate pays no bid/offer spread to close a position held through to the fixing date.

Corporates also benefit from the more favourable treatment of FRAs from a credit standpoint. Banks commonly debit their counterparty credit lines with 0.5%–2% of the face value of the FRA, so, in FRAs, corporates have found an instrument with which it is possible to manage more actively their interest exposure, without rapidly filling precious credit lines. The corporate need to hedge specific refixings has ensured a steady level of core customer business in all the major FRA trading centres.

Corporations with a particularly heavy exposure to fluctuations in short-term interest rates have, unsurprisingly, been quick to develop FRA trading expertise. Thus, in the sterling markets, the building societies and specialist mortgage lenders are increasingly using the market to hedge their short-term liabilities — often floating-rate notes.

FRA trading centres

The historic deposit trading centres tend to have enhanced their previous dominant positions by developing FRA trading expertise. Thus, within European trading hours, London is probably the dominant trading centre not only for sterling, dollar and yen FRAs but also for most other currency FRAs. Frankfurt leads in Deutsche mark FRA trading, and Paris in French franc trading. In the US, New York dominates. It is usually possible to obtain competitive prices in yen, Deutsche marks, sterling and Swiss FRAs within American trading hours. Within the Asia/Pacific time zone, Tokyo shares pre-eminence with Singapore, but there is an important local centre in Sydney.

Once again the relative under-development of the FRA market is demonstrated in the trading patterns within and between centres. Where particular bank branches within a particular trading centre have embraced the FRA trading market wholeheartedly, they have ensured a prominent role for their bank within that centre. But the same bank may have little or no involvement in another trading centre, where management is less keen, or trading expertise has not been developed. This is to say, there is weak linkage between trading centres, and even between branches of the same bank within different trading centres. Banks which have succeeded in realising some of the potential advantages of trading FRAs against forward foreign exchange positions in-house are obviously at a competitive advantage when quoting to corporate customers.

Liquidity

Liquidity varies from currency to currency and from centre to centre. The US dollar FRA market is traded 24 hours a day, and it is always possible to get a tight spread of three or four basis points on FRAs out as far as 12 v 24 (ie, one-year Libor in one-year's time). The dollar market also quotes FRAs fixing off non-standard Libors such as one month, two month etc. Most large banks are involved in the market as traders, hedgers, and to service corporate interest. There is also a lively market in interest rate guarantees or "options on FRAs".

The recent introduction of the one-month Eurodollar contract has assisted liquidity in the ultra-short end of the dollar FRA market. Traders who have had little interest in making prices in short-dollar FRAs are happy to quote spreads around the futures contract to satisfy corporate interest. Thus it can be seen that the FRA market has drained liquidity from the new one-month contract.

The Deutsche mark FRA market exhibits good liquidity out as far as 12 v 24s, but there is significantly less interest in the Deutsche mark market in Asian and American trading times. The introduction of the Euromark futures contract on Liffe has significantly enhanced liquidity in the Deutsche mark FRA market, and the introduction of a three-month Deutsche mark interest rate contract on Simex should further enhance liquidity in Asian trading time.

The introduction of Swiss franc futures on Liffe has had surprisingly little impact on the Swiss franc FRA market, which is liquid and actively traded. The futures have served to make the FRA market more transparent and consequently have helped to attract corporate interest. Before the futures opened, the FRA market could trade significantly out of line with the forward forwards implied by the Swiss franc deposit market, and larger players could squeeze particular FRAs by aggressive position taking.

The Ecu FRA market has probably grown at the most rapid rate over the past year, but remains thin relative to other markets.

Chapter 15: The global cap and collar market

Michael S Rulle, Jr
Lehman Brothers

Less than five years ago, the interest rate cap market was in its infancy. To cap the rate on the Libor index, institutions could buy a series of put options on Eurodollar futures, which had started to trade on the International Monetary Market (IMM) in the early 1980s. The resulting product was bound by the underlying options market in terms of maturity (initially, it was no longer than one year), strike level, index, reset dates and size.

Today, caps can be created on a variety of indices, including the Fed AA composite commercial paper index, the Prime rate, and indices in currencies such as Deutsche marks, sterling, yen and Australian dollars. Products are readily tailored to purchasers' requirements for customised strike rates, reset dates, maturities and sizes. The current market for caps and related products approaches US$500bn, with over half of the amount transacted in 1989 alone. Non-US dollar-denominated transactions comprise approximately one-third of the total market.

The proliferation of cap-related products and applications, such as captions, collars and corridors, has enabled borrowers to hedge their floating interest expense to their own specifications. Since the first rudimentary use of caps in the early 1980s, however, a number of developments pertaining to both the product's supply and demand have shaped the characteristics of the current market.

Cap supply developed quickly

As a precursor to the more customised and longer-dated interest rate cap product available today, options on straight Eurodollar futures met with limited demand from liability managers. Starting in the mid-1980s, however, alternative sources for cap supply began to develop relatively quickly.

The stripped cap market

In 1985, Lehman Brothers introduced a novel technique for creating longer-dated caps through capped floating-rate note issues. After identifying investor demand for long-dated FRNs in the Euromarket, the firm determined that investors would be willing to buy capped floaters in return for receiving a wider spread over Libor. For an issuer of these capped FRNs, the cap feature could essentially be "stripped" off and resold to other institutions for an upfront premium.

Lehman Brothers launched the first stripped cap transaction in June 1985, with a 12-year Libor-based FRN issued by a French bank in the Euromarket. The floater yielded Libor plus 5/16%, with a maximum yield of 13-1/6%. The issuer, which could have issued a straight floater at Libor plus 1/16%, paid 25 basis points as a spread premium for the cap feature. Lehman Brothers then arranged for the French bank to sell contingent payments above the maximum rate to a US financial institution, which paid an upfront price for the cap.

If Libor exceeded 12-3/4%, the issuer would pay the FRN holders the maximum rate of 13-1/16%, and the difference to the cap purchaser. The sale of these contingent payments created, in effect, a synthetic uncapped FRN for the issuer. The upfront proceeds it received from the sale of the cap, when amortised, exceeded the 25bp incentive premium it paid to investors for the cap feature. This difference resulted in a saving of approximately 12.5bp per annum over the conventional FRN it could have issued.

Stripping embedded caps from capped FRNs quickly became the primary vehicle for creating long-term caps. Issuers were eager to take advantage of the arbitrage to lower their all-in cost of financing, and purchasers, which included thrifts, banks and industrials, provided ample demand for the cap product. Over the following year and a half, more than $7bn of caps were generated through capped FRNs in the European and US domestic markets before investor appetite weakened and the arbitrage disappeared.

The professional market

Companies, however, had come to rely on the cap product to manage their interest rate exposure and began to seek more tailored structures. In response to this demand, financial intermediaries started to create "synthetic" caps in 1986 by taking positions in interest rate futures, options on Eurodollar futures, and interest rate swaps and swaptions. These synthetic caps could be created at almost any ceiling level, for a wide range of maturities, and on a variety of interest rate indices. Also, they could be designed with amortising notional amounts, ceiling rates which vary with time, flexible reset dates and other twists.

Creating these caps, however, requires fairly complex hedging strategies. When a dealer sells a cap, its portfolio becomes subject to volatility risk, which is the *degree* of change, as opposed to the *direction* of change, in the price of the underlying instrument (such as Eurodollar rates in the case of Libor caps). To illustrate volatility, let us assume a rather unrealistic scenario in which Libor increases directly from 8% to 16% in one year's time, with absolutely no intermittent decreases along the way. Although the directional change in interest rates is significant, volatility would be zero, since there has been no fluctuation around that change.

To hedge the risk of directional change, dealers take offsetting positions in Eurodollar futures and forwards, interest rate swaps or US Treasuries. Hedging the volatility risk, however, is best achieved by buying other options, which do not need to have the identical strike, maturity or index of the cap sold. Options on Eurodollar futures traded on the IMM are excellent hedges for the volatility risk of caps.

The limitations of these options as hedging instruments, however, are their relatively short maturities. Consequently, dealers began to create a longer-term options market on their own by running long or short positions on volatility. To the extent that the degree of volatility of options sold exceeds or is less than that of options purchased, a dealer's options portfolio is "net short" or "net long" volatility — a short volatility position suffers from high realised interest rate volatility, while a long volatility position benefits from it. Many dealers began to act on their market views to try to increase their profits. Although most managed this process successfully, a few did not and have either scaled back or exited the cap market altogether.

Nonetheless, the development of this market-making activity gave a much-needed injection of liquidity into the cap market. Knowing that they could offset longer-term volatility risk in the market, dealers became more comfortable with writing longer-dated caps. Investment and commercial banks established themselves as cap dealers and began making markets for cap products, playing the important role of bridging mismatches between maturities, indices, strikes and amounts. Mirroring the swap market a few years earlier, the cap market began to grow dramatically.

Swaptions, superfloaters and other sources

The swaptions market, which started to develop in 1987, provided dealers with a new technique for hedging caps. Corporate borrowers that sold swaptions in conjunction with issuing callable or puttable bonds, a frequently-used swaption application during the late 1980s, provided dealers with an attractive opportunity to buy long-dated options embedded in swaps. As a capital-raising technique, these transactions enabled issuers to take advantage of an arbitrage between differing option values in the bond and swap markets. For example, a borrower could issue a bond with a call feature and, by entering into a callable swap, effectively sell the call option in the swap market at a higher price. Swap dealers could essentially "buy" long-term volatility through these callable swaps, which gave them the right to terminate the swap on the call date.

Buying swaptions enabled dealers to reduce the degree to which their cap portfolios were net short volatility. Initially, dealers were able to buy these swaptions at substantially lower implied volatilities than those of the caps they were selling. Over time, however, this gap narrowed as dealers began to sell the caps at significantly lower implied volatilities. This has been a beneficial development for cap end users, since lower implied volatilities result in lower cap prices. Until 1987, implied volatilities for Libor caps and floors averaged an annualised rate of 20% or more for most maturities. In the current market, caps and floors of most maturities are quoted at implied volatilities of 13–14%, with higher implied volatilities for the shorter maturities and lower figures for the longer maturities.

For a brief period in 1988, the "superfloater" swap, which was actively used by US thrift institutions, emerged as another source of cap supply. Thrifts purchased fixed-rate mortgage assets which they typically funded with floating-rate liabilities. In order to eliminate the fixed-floating mismatch, they entered into swaps in which they paid fixed and received floating, and effectively sold out-of-the-money caps (which were embedded in the swaps) to increase their returns. These thrifts were essentially taking a view on the future level of short-term interest rates in order to enhance their income. Although superfloater swaps were in vogue for only a brief period, they generated a substantial amount of cap supply for dealers.

From time to time, end users have demonstrated a willingness to sell caps or floors to generate income, and to lower the cost of their liabilities. For example, in late 1988 and early 1989, Japanese financial institutions emerged as substantial sellers of caps in order to generate current income. In addition, financial institutions or sovereigns that swap fixed-rate liabilities into floating rate occasionally sell floors to lower their floating-rate cost of funds. Thus they replicate the traditional Eurodollar floater with its "minimum" rate of interest paid to investors.

Who buys caps?

As with most option-based products, caps are often perceived as "expensive" hedging instruments when compared to forward-based products such as swaps. However, cap products have found demand from a broad range of end users. Unlike swaps, caps enable floating-rate borrowers to benefit from low short-term rates. Perhaps more importantly, caps are credit-blind — borrowers of any credit quality can purchase caps by making an upfront payment. For these and other reasons, borrowers from most industry sectors have used caps at various points in time.

US borrowers

Thrift institutions have traditionally used cap products to hedge the inherent risk in funding long-term assets with short-term liabilities. Thrifts were active purchasers of the initial long-dated caps (that is, five to 12 years) stripped from capped FRNs. In recent years, thrifts have sought caps with shorter maturities and lower upfront costs. In general, however, thrifts have become less active cap purchasers as they focus more on shrinking their balance sheets than growing them.

In 1988 and 1989, demand for caps was fueled by companies that assumed large amounts of floating-rate bank debt for leveraged buy-out or acquisition purposes. These borrowers were often required by their lenders to implement risk protection in the form of swaps or caps, but were excluded from the swap market for credit reasons. Caps were, in most cases, the only hedging vehicle available to them. Many of these entities instituted large cap programmes, purchasing several billion dollars worth of caps over a short period of time.

Investment-grade industrial borrowers in the US were infrequent buyers of caps until the creation of products using the commercial paper rate, a more prevalent index for corporate borrowers than Libor. Two factors buoyed the demand from this sector in the late 1980s. After the RJR Nabisco leveraged buy-out was announced in the autumn of 1988, investment-grade companies with similar perceived event risk found their access to the bond market severely limited. As a result, many relied on the commercial paper market for funding, and, thus, the swap and cap market for hedging this sudden increase in their exposure to floating interest rates. In 1989, an inversion in the short end of the yield curve led to a decrease in cap prices and an increase in floor values. Thus, "free" collars became attractive transactions for industrials seeking to hedge their short-term interest expense over a six-month to two-year period.

European and Japanese borrowers

Perhaps the greatest area of growth in caps has been outside of the US dollar market. Several of the larger and more sophisticated dealers have parlayed their hedging, trading and marketing expertise developed in the US dollar cap market, to offer caps denominated in Deutsche marks, sterling and yen to clients in Europe and Japan. The volatility of interest rates in these currencies in the last 12 to 18 months has heightened activity in these markets, with the largest degree of growth in the Deutsche mark cap market. The non-dollar market for caps and related products was estimated at year-end 1989 to be approximately $150bn, or one-third of the total market.

Investors

A variety of hedging and income enhancement strategies for investors are possible with the use of cap products. For example, an investor can sell an out-of-the-money cap to enhance the coupon on a floating-rate asset, if it believes that rates will not climb as high as the strike of the cap. Alternatively, it can buy a floor on the floating-rate index to ensure that its income does not fall below the floor rate should rates fall. To date, investors have not been active market participants. However, over the next few years, it is likely that many will increase their use of caps and swaps in connection with their investing activities. Fixed income asset managers, in particular, are natural candidates.

Product development innovations

In recent years, the spectrum of tools to manage floating interest rate exposure has broadened to include a multitude of cap-related products.

Interest rate floor

The purchaser of an interest rate floor receives payments from the floor seller if the floating-rate index is below the specified floor rate on a reset date. Payments are equal to the difference between the floor rate and the floating-rate index, based upon the notional amount of the contract for that period. Floating-rate investors can purchase floors to secure a minimum yield on their assets. Floating-rate borrowers occasionally sell interest rate floors to reduce their costs of funds, knowing that at worst their floating interest expense will be at an acceptable minimum rate.

Interest rate collar

A floating-rate borrower can lower the cost of purchasing an interest rate cap by simultaneously selling a floor at a lower strike rate. The proceeds from the sale of the floor help to offset the purchase price of the cap. If rates increase above the cap level, the company would receive payments from its collar counterparty; conversely, if rates decreased below the floor level, it would have to make payments to the counterparty. The net result is that the company's floating-rate liability is "collared" within a band of interest rates.

"Free" interest rate collar

A company can enter into a collar that requires no upfront amount by selling a floor at a strike high enough to produce proceeds that fully offset the cost of purchasing the cap. Free collars are most attractive in inverted yield curve environments.

Participating cap

A variation on the collar, the participating cap structure allows a company to purchase a cap at a reduced cost, or in extremely inverted yield curve environments, at no cost. The company buys a cap and sells a floor at the same strike, but on a smaller notional amount. Effectively, the company is protected against rates moving above the cap rate, and it participates in a percentage of downward movement in interest rates (see Figure 1). From Figure 1 it can be seen that the company can be completely hedged against increases in Libor over 9%, but if Libor decreases below 9%, it receives only 50% of the benefit.

Figure 1: A participating cap

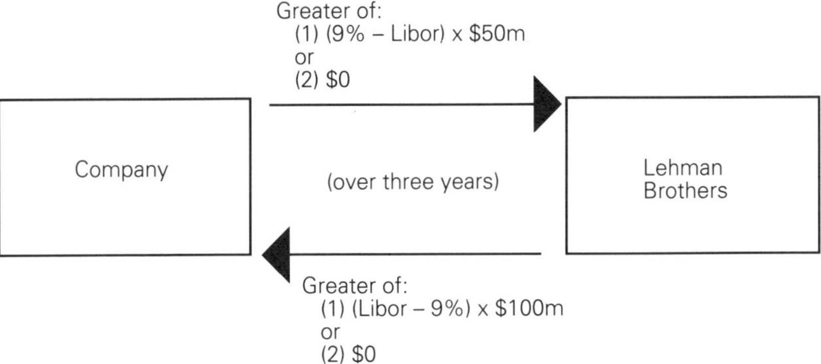

Weighted collar

A weighted collar is similar to a participating cap but with a floor level that is *lower* than the cap level, thus creating a collar or "band" around rates. The company maintains full protection in the event of a rise in interest rates, but sacrifices only partial opportunity cost in a low interest rate environment.

Corridor

A company can lower the upfront cost of purchasing a cap by simultaneously selling another cap at a higher strike rate. For example, it can buy a cap at a strike rate of 9%, and sacrifice some of the "upside" by selling a cap at 11%. Thus, it is fully protected if interest rates increase up to 11% (see Figure 2). In Figure 2, assume that a straight three-year cap on Libor at 9% would cost 100bp upfront. A company can reduce this cost to 75bp by selling the protection over 11%. Thus, the company is completely hedged against Libor increases between 9% and 11%, but is not hedged against increases greater than 11%. A corridor can also be constructed using interest rate floors — a buyer of a floor can reduce its upfront cost by selling another floor at a lower rate.

Figure 2: A corridor

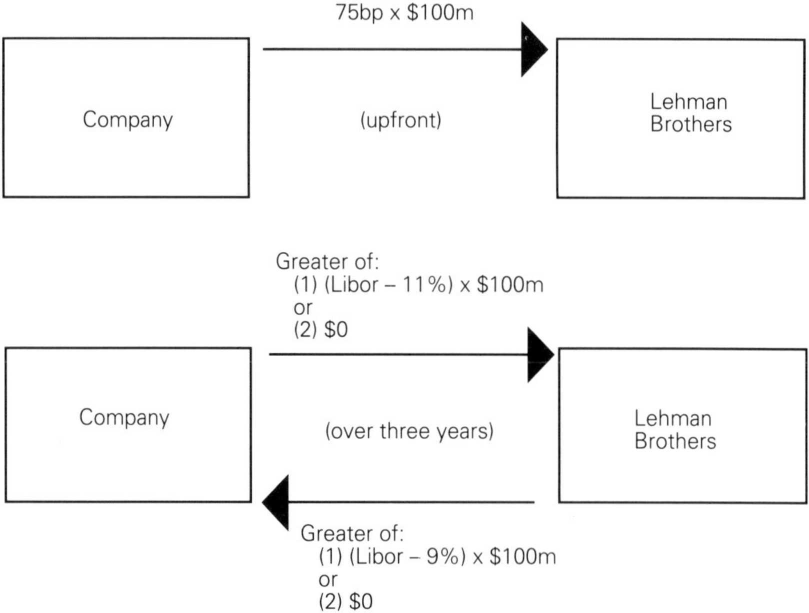

Delayed cap
A delayed cap can be purchased at a lower cost to obtain interest rate protection that becomes effective at some point after the date of purchase. Relative to a straight cap of the same maturity, the upfront premium is reduced by the value of selling the cap for the initial delay period. Delayed caps are appropriate for companies that expect short-term rates to remain low in the near term, but which want future protection.

Caption
For a smaller upfront premium, a company can buy an option to purchase a cap at a specified price. If cap prices increase, the company can exercise its option to buy the cap at a "below-market" price. Or, if cap prices have declined, the purchaser can let the caption expire. Although captions are

usually expensive, they offer a more leveraged way to protect against interest rate increases (see Figure 3). From Figure 3 it can be seen that, by making an upfront payment of 30bp, a company can buy the right to purchase a 9% cap in one year at a set price of 100bp. If cap prices are lower one year from now, it can let its option to buy the cap expire.

Figure 3: A caption

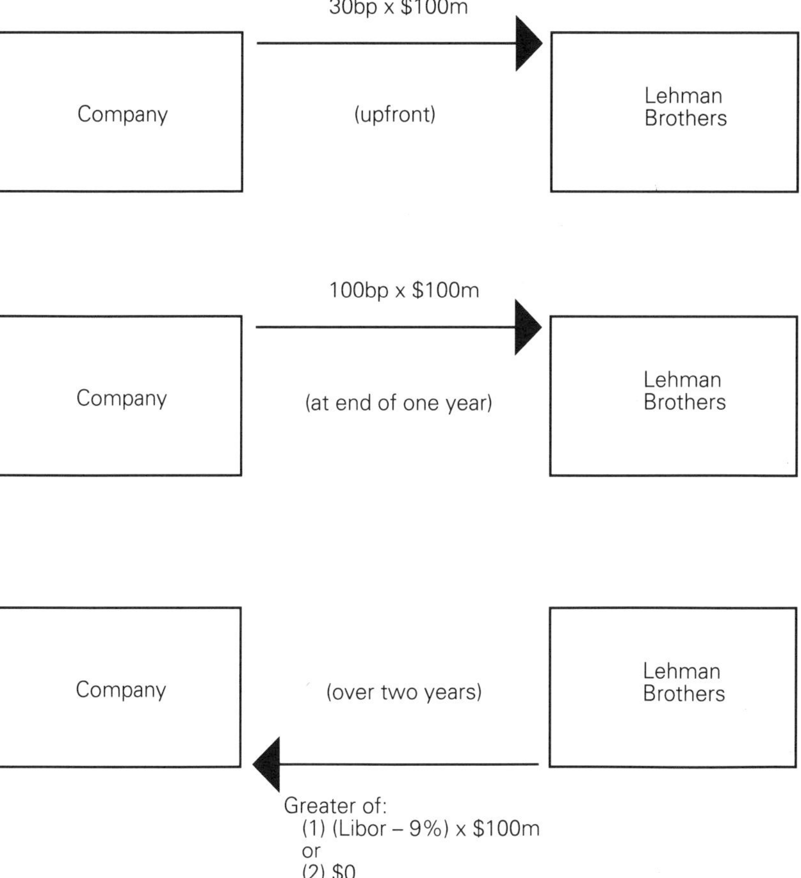

Step-up coupon cap

A company can reduce its upfront cost by purchasing a cap that has a strike rate that increases over time. By providing greater interest rate protection in the initial years, a step-up coupon cap is appropriate for a company that is more concerned about its cash flow in the near term than in the long term. Similarly, a cap can be structured with a coupon that steps down over time.

Cash flow variations

The notional amount of cap, collar and floor contracts can be tailored to a company's specific hedging needs. For example, contracts can be structured on revolving notional amounts to accommodate seasonal borrowing requirements, or on declining notional amounts to match the funding for amortising assets. Nearly all cash flow structures can be accommodated.

Where does the market go from here?

In the past few years, the increasing number of cap dealers has resulted in a liquid, deep cap market offering a wide variety of products to end users. However, activity has undergone a slowdown in the past year, particularly in the US dollar market — in the second half of 1989, volume for US dollar cap products dropped by over 40% compared to the first half of 1989, and continued to drop in the first half of 1990. The shrinking number of natural end users in the overall market, such as thrifts and newly-leveraged companies, is the primary cause for this drop in demand. Without the entry of a new or revived source of demand or a resurgence in the volatility of interest rates, the immediate prospects for this market are less buoyant than they appeared three years ago.

End users could, in fact, emerge or re-emerge. For example, Latin American countries and institutions which have large amounts of interest rate exposure are natural candidates for cap products. However, to date, these borrowers have been unwilling to make large upfront payments for rate protection. A change in the industry environment for thrifts could generate a revival of demand from these institutions, which are natural users of caps. In fact, as of late 1990, we have begun to see signs that thrift demand for caps is starting to revive. In the meantime, it appears that markets outside of the US are the only substantial source of growth. While the US dollar cap market declined in late 1989, the non-dollar cap market more than doubled. Given this kind of growth, it is conceivable that the markets in the European and Japanese currencies will mirror that of the US dollar, and continue to expand into the 1990s.

Of course, a change in the US economic environment could provide a boost to the US dollar cap market. If the economy begins to experience sharply higher inflation and interest rates return to the double digit levels of the early 1980s, many industry sectors are likely to return to the cap market.

Chapter 16: Asset swaps — bringing technology to investors

Piers Hartland-Swann
UBS Phillips & Drew Securities Limited

For many investors asset swaps represent their first and sometimes only point of contact with the swap market. This has only happened because over the course of the 1980s swaps themselves have changed from being an exotic product, little understood by most finance professionals, into an indispensable tool for interest rate and currency risk management. Alone this was not enough to make swaps accessible to investors. The crucial factor was the application of computer technology to swap market making which allowed the development of trading strategies previously too complex to contemplate. In particular, swap warehousing, where a market-maker manages a pool of unmatched swap positions on a portfolio basis, has allowed the minimum deal size in a swap to shrink rapidly from levels associated with Eurobond issues (US$100m) to that of a typical institutional investor's holding (US$1–10m). Previously, swap traders had to find matching counterparties in order to effect a trade. Warehousing allowed traders simply to add a new swap to an existing pool and manage risk on an aggregate basis. This significantly reduced the unit cost of dealing in swaps and thus made smaller transactions economic. These developments in swap technology made it possible to apply swaps to investment instruments as a risk management tool, thus creating asset swaps. The latter half of the 1980s saw an increasing number of investors executing swaps in this guise, and these techniques have thus achieved respectability within the investment community. Development continues in the 1990s, with investors increasingly taking a leaf out of swap traders' books and managing their own risk on a portfolio basis using swaps and other risk management techniques pioneered by the swap market.

Development of the asset swap market

As discussed above, developments in technology provided the means for the creation of the asset swap market. But the forces stimulating the growth of this market from almost nothing in 1985 to its present size of US$125–250bn derive from broader events in the capital markets.

Banks and securitisation

The process of securitisation in the 1980s meant that commercial banks lost their main source of high quality assets. High quality borrowers increasingly found it easier to issue bonds in the securities markets than to borrow from their relationship banks. Bond covenants were usually less onerous and frequently borrowers could borrow on substantially cheaper terms than many banks. Concerns about bank asset quality and profitability, expressed by regulators in the form of higher capital ratios and by investors in the form of higher return requirements, caused banks to concentrate much more on maximising return on assets (while keeping loan losses to acceptable levels) and less on absolute balance sheet size. This provided a ready-made source of demand for floating-rate assets that were both high quality and high yielding. In the mid-1980s banks gave the asset swap market its initial impetus and since then have been its mainstay on the demand side.

Secondary Eurobond liquidity

On the supply side of the equation, there was a large outstanding population of high quality but illiquid fixed-rate Eurobonds. This lack of liquidity meant that such bonds often traded with very high yields since investors were reluctant to take on positions without some compensation for the risk that if interest rates rose (reducing the value of their portfolio) they would have difficulty finding a buyer for the bonds. In many cases this illiquidity premium led to yields higher than the swap rate for the equivalent maturity, making it possible to create assets with a higher yield than commercial banks' floating-rate cost of funds. Banks were not concerned about the lack of liquidity, being long-term holders of floating-rate assets, and therefore took to this new instrument with enthusiasm as a substitute for conventional loan assets. For this reason the most popular type of asset swap uses a swap to convert a fixed-rate instrument such as a Eurobond into a high yielding floating-rate asset, usually with a return in excess of Libor, usually for a bank investor.

Ex-warrant Eurobonds

Since the supply of illiquid high quality Eurobonds is at any time finite and increases only slowly, paper suitable for asset swapping rapidly became scarce as a result of all this activity. The next main source of supply came from Japanese equity warrant bonds, which became a significant force in 1987. Around US$15bn of issues were launched in 1986, and by early 1987 there was acute oversupply of the ex-warrant bonds in the Eurobond market. Investors were mainly interested in the equity warrants, which gave a highly geared exposure to an ever-rising Japanese equity market, but few could find a use for the ex-warrant rump. The discovery that there was a ready home for such paper in asset-swapped form with commercial bank investors rapidly eased this problem, so much so that issues of equity warrant bonds grew dramatically, peaking in 1989 with nearly US$70bn issued in that year alone. Since the vast majority of the issues were guaranteed by high quality Japanese banks, even concerns about capital adequacy initially had little effect since the bank guarantee resulted in a capital requirement one fifth of that for corporate loans. Only in 1990 has the pace slackened, caused by falling prices in the Japanese equity markets and the problems this caused for Japanese banks' BIS capital ratios. Nevertheless, it is safe to say that the vast majority of outstanding asset swaps are backed by ex-warrant bonds, and will continue to be so for a number of years to come, even with the significantly lower issuance volumes now prevailing.

Figure 1: Equity warrant bond issues
US$ equivalent

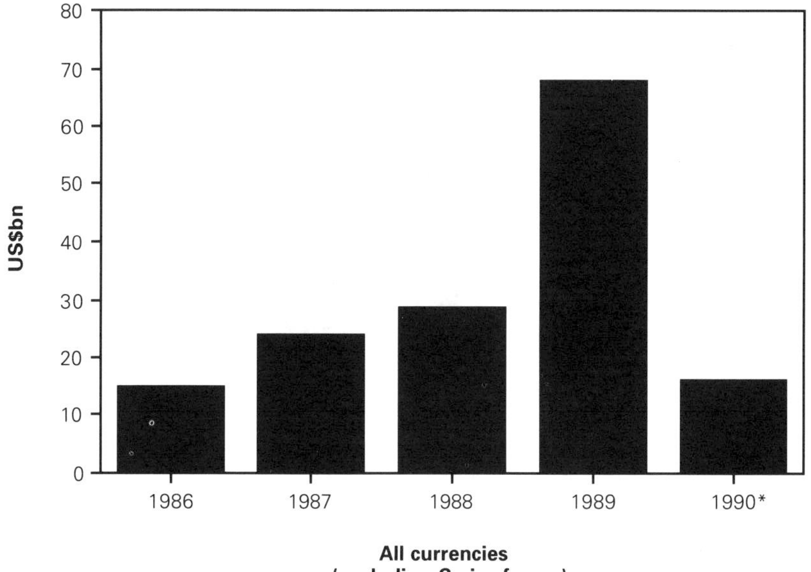

*First three quarters
Source: Euromoney Bondware

Repackaged bond issues

Although a number of repackaged bond issues have just involved pass-through structures, the vast majority are effectively securitised asset swaps. In what is essentially a private market, these issues are often the only public source of information as to what is happening in the asset swap market. The first repackaged bond issues almost pre-dated the first asset swaps, being executed in 1985 (repackaging the United Kingdom 1992 FRNs into fixed-rate bonds), but the real stimulus for repackaging came from the growth of the equity warrant bond market. This was principally driven by the fact that the investment banks that had the largest ex-warrant bond holdings were Japanese investment banks that had lead managed such issues.

Figure 2: Repackaged ex-warrant issues
US$ equivalent

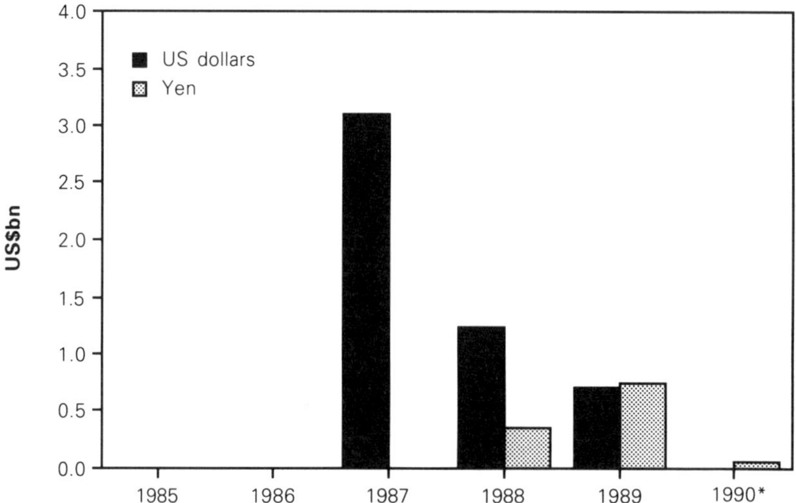

*First three quarters
Source: Euromoney Bondware

From around 1987 onwards, while other investment banks tended to sell ex-warrant bonds in asset swap form, Japanese banks had sufficiently large positions to make it worthwhile to repackage whole issues of ex-warrant bonds into FRNs. It is notable that, with few exceptions, the vast majority of such issues were repackaged by Japanese banks. Even in the peak year, 1987, with US$3bn repackaged, this still accounted for only 13% of the US$23bn ex-warrant bonds issued, and in subsequent years this proportion declined significantly. Out of US$141bn of ex-warrant bonds issued since 1984, some US$6bn have been repackaged. It is reasonable to assume that since around 90% or US$127bn of ex-warrant bonds outstanding have been repackaged or asset swapped, the asset swap proportion is a very large component of that figure. Estimates of the total size of the asset swap market are tentative at best, but extrapolating from the proportions of repackaged issues to asset swapped issues in the equity warrant bond market gives a total asset swap market size of US$250bn based on US$12bn total of all repackaged issues since 1985. This estimate is probably on the high side, since it ignores maturing bonds, but even US$125bn would be a very conservative estimate.

Figure 3: All repackaged issues
US$ equivalent

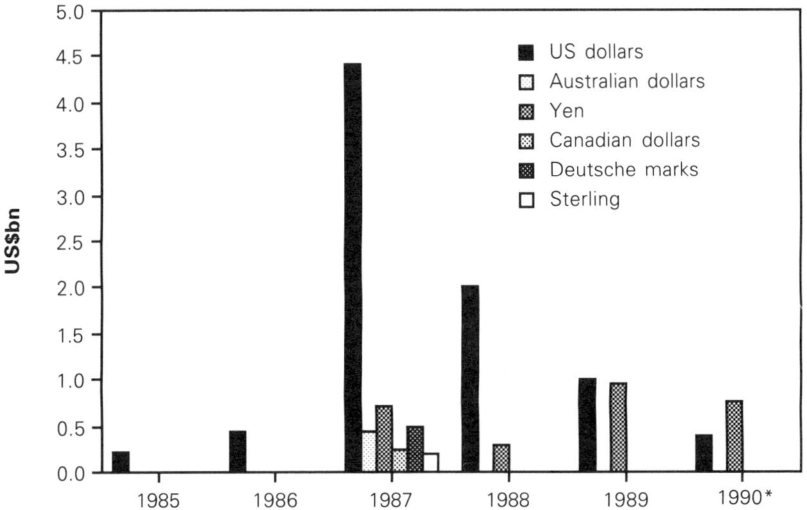

*First three quarters
Source: Euromoney Bondware

Perpetual FRNs

The total collapse of the perpetual FRN market in 1987 heralded a new type of asset swap structure. After the collapse, perpetuals frequently traded at sufficiently low levels that it became economic to combine them with dated zero-coupon bonds or high quality securities in such a way that the maturing proceeds of the zeros were sufficient to repay the principal of the perpetual and still give a significant yield over Libor. As an added bonus, investors could realise a further profit from any residual value left in the perpetual when the zeros matured. Because of the complexity of these deals, the majority of them occurred in repackaged rather than pure asset swap form (a swap was required to adjust the cash flows from the perpetual), and they account for most of the repackaged issues backed by floating-rate assets. This type of transaction has now become rather rare, mainly because the subordinated status of most perpetuals has made them less attractive to banks facing ever greater capital constraints.

Figure 4: Repackaged issues by floating-rate source bond
US$ equivalent

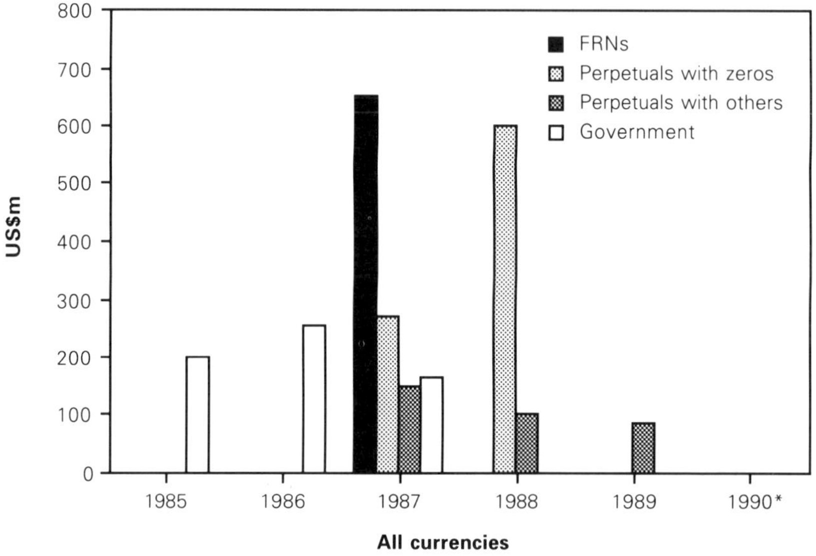

*First three quarters
Source: Euromoney Bondware

Tax-driven asset swaps

Because of the offshore nature of the Eurobond market there are few inconsistencies in tax treatments that investors can take advantage of. However, the opening up of many European domestic bond markets as a result of deregulation has sometimes presented profitable opportunities for investors. A notable example of this is the case of Italian domestic government securities denominated in Ecu, *Certificati del Tesoro in Ecu* (CTEs). Originally CTEs were free of withholding tax to foreign investors (and a number of repackagings took place in 1986 and 1987). However, in September 1986 the Italian government imposed a withholding tax on all new CTE issues of first 6.25% and then later 12.5%. Since then, certain overseas investors have been able to benefit from double taxation treaties between Italy and their country of residence by reclaiming the withholding tax against their domestic tax liability. Net of withholding tax, CTEs yield less than equivalent tax-free Ecu Eurobonds, but the pre-tax yield can be significantly higher. As a result these investors have been able to achieve yield pick-ups of 0.30%–0.40% on asset-swapped five-year CTEs over returns available in the public FRN market from the same risk. The scale of this activity (which still continues) has been sufficient to generate substantial growth in the Ecu swap market and coincidentally give a boost to the Ecu bond market by providing more frequent opportunities for swap-driven new issuance.

Figure 5: Repackaged issues by fixed-rate source bond
US$ equivalent

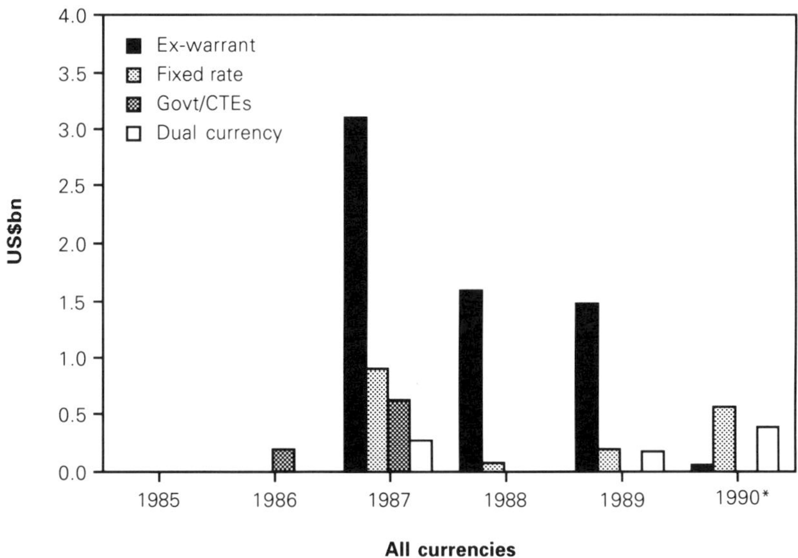

*First three quarters
Source: Euromoney Bondware

Structured bond issues and asset swappable new issues

Other sources of supply of asset-swappable paper, although less significant in terms of volume, are nevertheless worthy of note. The Eurobond market has always been noted for its innovation, and some of the more complex instruments created to meet specific investor requirements surface from time to time in the secondary market. Often the only way to generate any liquidity for the holder is to reverse-engineer the original structure by means of an asset swap, converting the securities back into something with broad investor appeal. The most notable sector for this type of activity has been with dual currency and reverse dual currency bonds, usually originally sold to Japanese investors.

Another important source has been bond issues specifically designed to be placed in asset-swapped form. This area is particularly difficult to quantify, as few borrowers or lead managers will admit to this activity, but there has been a steady flow of such issues, usually from less creditworthy borrowers. Such borrowers often prefer the less restrictive covenants and greater publicity of bond issues, or they may have highly structured borrowing requirements. The paper gets placed in asset swap form with those best able to analyse the credit risks, the banks.

Figure 6: Repackaged issues by type

US$ equivalent

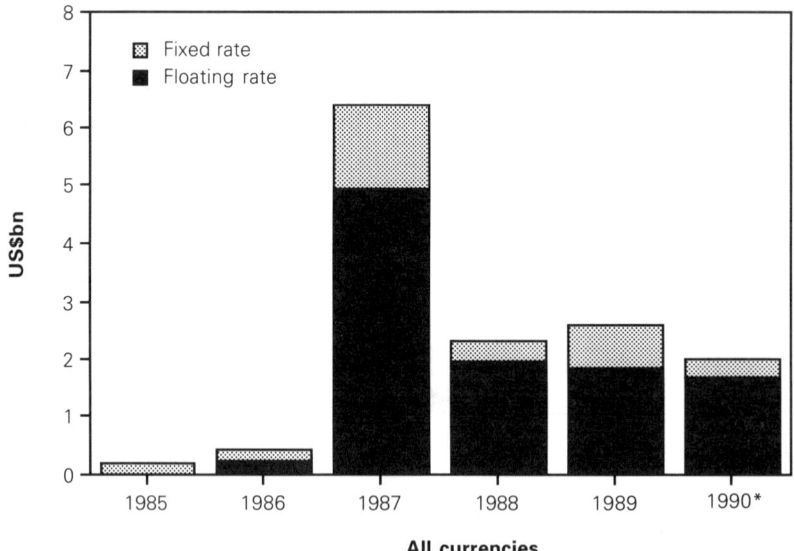

*First three quarters

Source: Euromoney Bondware

Non-bank investors

The market for asset swaps is not confined to floating-rate investors such as banks. Japanese non-bank investors, such as life assurance companies and corporates, have been attracted to the high fixed-rate yields obtainable from yen-denominated asset swaps. Also, there is significant demand from large corporations and investment funds, driven not so much by high returns (in either fixed or floating rate), as by flexibility. Asset swaps allow these investors to create portfolios without regard for the availability of assets in the underlying markets since they can use swaps to generate the cash flows they need, both in terms of timing and currency. Any investor seeking to optimise portfolio characteristics should consider using asset swaps as a means of achieving this goal.

Asset swap yields

Although the asset swap market is far from homogeneous, clear pricing trends have emerged over the course of the 1980s, especially in the sector that comes closest to being the benchmark for pricing, bank-guaranteed ex-warrant bonds asset swapped into floating-rate form. In the early days of the market, when investors were unfamiliar with the product, there were very generous spreads over Libor to be had from floating-rate asset swaps, for example Libor + 0.40% on AAA-rated sovereign risk. As the supply of illiquid bonds declined and ex-warrant bonds became more common, spreads on ex-warrants settled around Libor + 0.25% and on better quality bond issues around Libor + 0.125%. Over the course of 1986 and early 1987 these spreads tightened, to Libor + 0.10% (and occasionally tighter) on ex-warrants. Following the 1987 crash, spreads widened to around Libor + 0.15%, mainly because of greater concerns about credit, and remained stable through 1987 and 1988. In 1989, and more dramatically in 1990, spreads widened significantly, first to Libor + 0.25% and more recently Libor + 0.50%. This was precipitated by a "credit crunch" in the global banking system, brought on by a combination of higher capital requirements, closely followed by the onset of a worldwide recession. The question for the 1990s is whether spreads are likely to continue at these or wider levels, or whether once recessionary fears abate they will tighten again back to historical levels. Arguably, since credit is in short supply, the latter scenario seems more likely once banks face less pressure on their balance sheets.

The effect of asset swaps on the capital markets

The widespread acceptance of asset swaps by investors has had a significant effect on the way in which professionals operate in the primary and secondary Eurobond markets.

In the primary market, asset swaps are mainly used in two ways. First, they assist in the placement of lower credit quality fixed-rate paper by broadening the investor base; bonds can be placed as asset swaps with banks in floating-rate form in addition to placement with traditional fixed-rate investors. Secondly, asset swaps provide a floor price for new issues that, for one reason or another, have not performed well and whose price might otherwise fall to unrealistic levels.

In the secondary market, the impact of asset swaps has been less visible although no less significant. Since asset swaps use swap technology to arbitrage between different markets, the result, as with all arbitrage techniques, is an improvement in market efficiency. As more and more participants take advantage of an imperfection, markets naturally adjust until eventually the imperfection disappears (fortunately for asset swap investors, not permanently). A few years ago most bond traders would not even have known where to look for swap rates let alone calculate whether the bonds they traded were suitable for asset swapping. Today, it is rare to find a trader who does not keep an eye on swap rates, if only to see where his bonds are trading relative to them and thus assess the likelihood either of swap-driven new issuance or of asset swap activity. As a result it is rare to find an illiquid high quality bond trading much cheaper than where it can be asset swapped.

The effect on market liquidity is a more contentious subject. It has been argued by some that asset swaps take bonds permanently out of the market and therefore impair liquidity, to the detriment of investors in general. However, this begs the question as to why in the first place bonds become cheap enough to asset swap since generally any liquid bond of good credit quality will never be worth asset swapping. Logically it is clear that bonds must *already* have become illiquid in order to be asset swappable. The existence of a firm bid in large size to create asset swaps is the only thing preventing the price of such a bond falling even further, as used to happen before asset swaps were common. It is therefore safe to say that these techniques provide much-needed liquidity to the international bond markets.

Who should use asset swaps?

There are several groups of investors who, if they are not already doing so, should consider investing in asset swaps:

Investors seeking higher yield

Any investor looking for high yielding instruments and who is prepared to sacrifice some liquidity should strongly consider asset swaps. In the floating-rate market, pick-ups of 0.10%–0.20% on AAA-rated sovereign issues over equivalent public floating-rate assets (such as FRNs or syndicated loans) are not unknown, with even bigger margins achievable on investment-grade (ie, BBB rating or better) paper. Similar yield pick-ups may be achieved in the fixed-rate market. Given that most investors have a core weighting in a particular market there are strong arguments for them to take advantage of the higher yield available from asset swaps since liquidity will be less of a concern for that core component.

Investors looking to diversify risk

In any particular market, there is only a limited number of issuers who have used it. For example, the FRN market has a strong concentration of bank issues and comparatively few corporate issues. Asset swaps allow an investor concentrating on one or a group of markets to look to issuers who are not present in that grouping by bringing in issues from other markets. For example, an investor with a Deutsche mark portfolio can use an asset swap to create a Deutsche mark asset from an issuer who has only ever issued securities in the US dollar market.

Investors wanting to modify portfolio performance

The Euromarkets have in the past responded to pockets of investor demand by bringing new issues with special features, usually priced heavily in favour of the issuer. Investors have justifiably become cautious about some of the features attached to such new issues, particularly those featuring some form of embedded option, such as an issuer's option to redeem a bond in a different currency. Usually, when such an issue is analysed in terms of its components it becomes apparent that the value of the parts is considerably less than the cost of the whole; the difference has gone to subsidise the issuers' cost of funds and provide a healthy profit to the bank which thought up the structure. It is impossible therefore for investors to avoid a substantial loss from such investments, whether in terms of realised or opportunity costs. With asset swaps they have the means to achieve their portfolio goals by having asset swaps tailor-made to fit, often on significantly better terms since there is no hidden subsidy to the issuer. Additionally it is possible to buy an asset swap with the coupon dates set so as to match an investor's underlying funding periods, or to have a portfolio of asset swaps created with all coupons paid on specific dates.

Taking portfolio management a stage further, it is easy for investors to modify the rate basis and/or currency of an entire portfolio without changing the credit composition. Rather than restructure the whole portfolio, with all the attendant dealing costs, applying a swap can achieve the same goals of modifying portfolio duration, currency weighting or interest rate exposure, with the advantages of greater simplicity and competitive cost. In many ways this is the most exciting new development in the asset swap market and is clearly the next major area for growth.

Conclusion

In the financial markets the first users of a new product do not always understand precisely how it works and therefore need guidance from their financial advisors. As time goes by and as these users become more sophisticated so they can begin to play a more active part in the trading of that product, effectively disintermediating the original providers. This is a good indicator of the maturity of a financial product. On this basis it is clear that asset swaps are now in the mature stage of the product lifecycle. An increasing number of sophisticated investors now have the capacity to identify and structure asset swaps for their own account as they have become more active users of the swap market, at least for those transactions of a standard type. However, one of the reasons why this maturity does not necessarily imply a slackening in the growth rate of the market is that new derivative products are continually being developed, and with each new product new asset swap opportunities appear. Also, the investor base for asset swaps is still considerably smaller than for securities in general, suggesting that there is still room for considerable growth as new applications are developed.

As is borne out by the size of the market, asset swaps offer many tangible benefits to investors. Although they may sometimes be complex to create, thereafter they are straightforward for investors to handle. In today's fast-moving markets, where the arbitrage opportunities to create asset swaps are fleeting, few investors have the resources to monitor markets all the time to take advantage of imperfections or even to keep up with the latest developments in financial technology. Therefore, they must look to financial institutions to provide them with supply and expertise in this market. Only the largest and most creditworthy investment banks, with a presence in all the major bond and swap markets around the world, and the balance sheet capacity to trade these instruments in substantial size, have the power to intermediate in the creation of asset swaps and provide real value-added solutions for investors.

We are now in a period where the means for investors to realise portfolio strategic goals have never been so comprehensive or readily available. The major limiting factor has been investor awareness of the vast range of techniques that can be used and what is really achievable with them. Asset swaps give straightforward access to these techniques and have therefore been a significant addition to an investor's choice of instruments.

Part II
New developments in swap financing products and applications

Chapter 17: A survey of swap-driven primary issuance in the international bond market

Rosario Benavides and John Lipsky
Salomon Brothers, Inc

Cross currency interest rate swaps — or currency swaps, as they are commonly called — emerged during the 1980s as an important instrument in international capital markets. In its most basic form, a currency swap agreement entails an initial (optional) exchange of principal, an exchange of interest payments throughout the duration of the transaction, and a final exchange of principal at an exchange rate determined at the outset. In many ways, currency swaps are similar to long-dated currency forward contracts, and as such, can be used to arbitrage longer yield curve maturities in most major Eurobond markets.

Use and purpose of the market

Initially, the use of currency swaps was spurred by arbitrage opportunities created by capital market liberalisation. As the swap market matured in the 1980s, it became a standard tool for asset/liability management. However, this chapter will focus on the use of currency swaps in creating synthetic liabilities, by combining a swap agreement with the issuance of a debt instrument. In many cases, a synthetic liability has provided financing at a cost less than that available through the issuance of traditional forms of debt. This is possible because a given borrower may be able to obtain funds on terms that are better relative to a benchmark in one market than in another. Use of a currency swap in these circumstances allows the borrower to arbitrage across differing relative credit perceptions in two markets. In addition, such arrangements may be useful in taking advantage of different regulatory or tax treatments. However, as international capital markets have become increasingly deregulated and efficient, the incentives for swap-driven primary issuance have waned somewhat.

By providing an instrument that can be used to control interest rate and currency exposure, the currency swap market aids risk management. However, the currency swap itself carries a number of risks, including counterparty credit risks. In part, these risks are absorbed by swap market-makers, whose activities have been an important element in opening the market to smaller and less well-known participants. Even with the participation of market-makers, however, the liquidity of swap markets — and hence the opportunities for swap-driven primary bond issuance — varies between currencies. However, most swap-driven primary issuance has been accounted for by high-quality international organisations and multinational corporations.

The analysis of swap-driven primary issuance in international bond markets is hampered by the lack of reliable, comprehensive data. Even though the terms of primary Eurobond issues are usually publicised, details of the associated swap agreements are usually not. Nonetheless, Salomon Brothers has constructed a database that includes swap-driven primary issues from 1981 to the third quarter of 1990. While the data probably are not complete, the database contains sufficient information to draw reasonably reliable conclusions regarding the size and nature of the market.

- The currency swap market grew explosively through 1989. In the last five years, the size of the market increased sixfold. In 1989 alone, new issue currency swaps more than doubled to almost $121bn, from about $53bn in 1988 (Figure 1). However, the market slowed significantly in 1990, in response to a number of factors. At the same time, the asset swap market also slowed, in part because of the weakening demand from traditional investors in this market, such as leasing companies.

- The primary currency of issuance of swap-driven instruments has become the US dollar, trailed by the yen and the Canadian dollar (Figure 2). In 1985, in contrast, the yen was the principal currency for swap-driven primary issuance.

- New Eurobond issuance denominated in Canadian, New Zealand and Australian dollars, and in Spanish pesetas, has in the past primarily been swap-driven. However, in 1990 and so far this year we are seeing more Canadian and Australian dollar issuers who are not swapping.

- In 1989, almost 60% of swap-driven issuance in international bond markets was by Japanese entities. French and Italian issuers followed the Japanese in terms of new issue volume, although they comprised only one-seventh of the volume of Japanese issues. Much of the swap-driven new issuance by Japanese entities comprised Eurodollar bonds with equity warrants attached, with the proceeds swapped back into yen. Such activity virtually halted in 1990, following the sharp fall in the Japanese equity market, and such issuance is not expected to reach the rate of 1988–89 any time soon.

- In recent years, growing concern over event risk and over the credit quality of US corporations led to a drop in issuance by US corporations in non-dollar bond markets. Non-dollar issuance by US entities has fallen by almost half since it peaked in 1986. At the same time, the proportion swapped declined from almost 66% in 1986, to 43% in 1989. Rather, US corporations seeking to raise non-dollar funds increasingly have issued dollar-denominated debt, and have swapped the proceeds. At the same time, sovereign entities have become more prominent borrowers in non-dollar markets.

- In general, issuance in the traditional Euro-Ecu bond market has been substantially swap-driven. However, the rapidly growing volume of large, liquid Ecu-denominated bonds issued outside the Eurobond market by sovereign borrowers has not been swapped.

- The majority of swap-driven new issues are straight bonds with bullet maturities. During 1988–89, many of these issues had equity warrants attached. The 1990 drop in equity markets significantly reduced the volume of swap-driven new issues, and activity does not appear to have recovered so far in 1991.

Figure 1: New issue currency swaps, 1981–1989

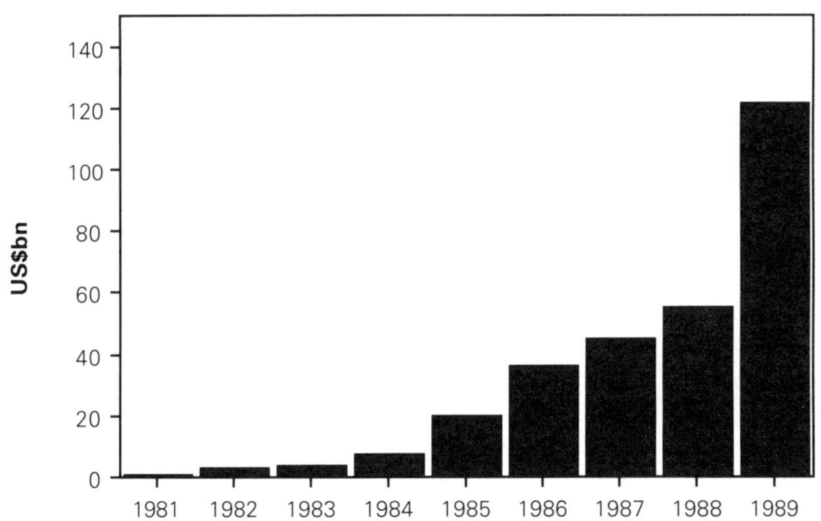

Figure 2: New issue swap transactions in 1989

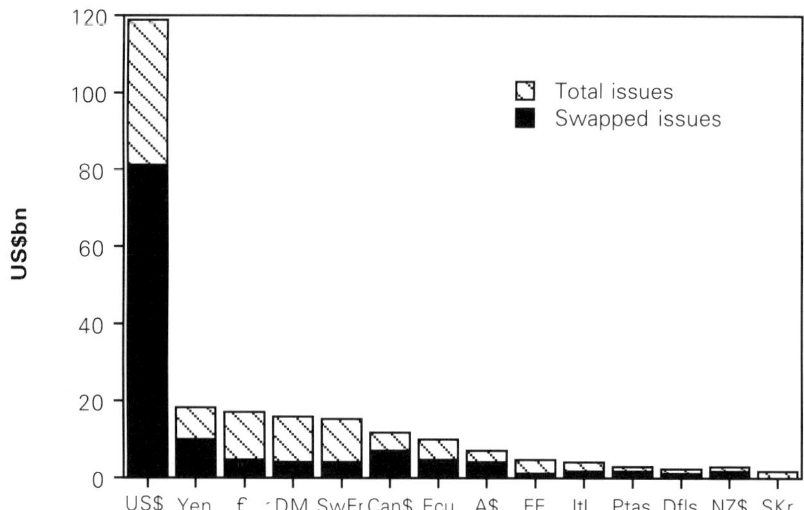

Anatomy of the market

Size of the market

Since the inception of the market in 1981, the volume of swap-driven primary issuance has exploded: in 1989 such issuance increased by over 120 times in US dollar terms compared with 1981. The largest year-to-year increase took place from 1988 to 1989, when the value of new issue currency swaps more than doubled. Compared with 1985, the number of swap-driven issues increased by 153%, from about 330 issues in 1985 to at least 851 in 1989 (see Tables 1 and 2). The rate of growth of swap-driven primary issuance far exceeded that for all international bonds, which was a modest 5%.

Previously, changes in the regulatory environment were major forces in shaping the market. In the mid-1980s, the enforcement of withholding taxes on domestic issuance in a number of countries created opportunities for arbitrage through the Eurobond markets. Moreover, the liberalisation of currency markets opened up opportunities. The 1984 dismantling of West German rules prohibiting currency swaps also generated new possibilities.

In addition, the currency swap market has helped boost the development of new Eurobond markets. Prior to 1986, Eurobond issuance in currencies such as the Belgian franc, the Dutch guilder, the Italian lira and even the Hong Kong dollar was virtually non-existent. More recently, the Spanish peseta, the Finnish markka and the Swedish krona markets have expanded, in some cases substantially, aided in part by swaps.

Table 1: Number of swap-driven primary issues by currency of issue, 1981–1989

	1981	1982	1983	1984	1985	1986	1987	1988	1989
Australian dollars	0	0	0	4	52	77	150	63	63
Austrian schillings	0	0	0	1	2	0	2	0	0
Belgian francs	0	0	0	0	0	1	0	0	0
Canadian dollars	1	2	3	6	12	19	47	69	64
Dutch guilders	0	0	0	1	0	1	1	2	8
Danish krone	0	0	0	0	5	1	5	1	1
Deutsche marks	0	0	4	3	14	14	13	12	34
Ecu	0	0	10	20	63	33	31	19	45
Finnish markka	0	0	0	0	0	0	1	0	0
French francs	1	0	0	0	2	5	3	3	7
Hong Kong dollars	0	0	0	0	0	0	1	0	1
Italian lire	0	0	0	0	0	1	3	2	14
Luxembourg francs	0	0	0	0	6	7	11	1	18
New Zealand dollars	0	0	1	0	35	18	40	13	12
Spanish pesetas	0	0	0	0	0	0	2	0	14
Swedish kronor	0	0	0	0	0	1	0	0	5
Swiss francs	2	17	25	30	40	68	37	43	37
UK sterling	0	0	2	5	6	7	29	14	32
US dollars	10	17	19	31	36	71	78	187	328
Japanese yen	0	2	0	4	57	98	87	127	168
Total	**14**	**38**	**64**	**105**	**330**	**422**	**541**	**556**	**851**

Table 2: Number of swap-driven primary issues by nationality of issuer, 1981–1989

	1981	1982	1983	1984	1985	1986	1987	1988	1989
Supranational	5	4	6	5	16	25	32	15	51
Multinational	1	1	0	1	3	3	3	1	4
Argentina	1	0	0	0	0	0	0	0	0
Australia	0	0	4	17	19	14	20	24	36
Austria	1	6	5	10	10	11	20	17	23
Belgium	0	0	2	2	8	12	13	5	16
Bulgaria	0	0	0	0	0	0	0	0	1
Canada	2	7	12	8	13	27	36	22	53
Cayman Islands	0	0	0	0	0	0	0	0	1
China	0	0	0	0	0	0	0	1	0
Denmark	0	0	1	5	13	11	12	8	27
Finland	0	0	0	1	8	18	8	17	49
France	0	3	4	2	22	19	48	46	62
Greece	0	0	0	0	0	0	0	0	1
West Germany	0	0	2	6	19	43	80	38	34
Hong Kong	0	0	0	0	1	1	2	0	0
India	0	0	0	0	0	0	0	1	0
Ireland	0	0	0	0	0	1	1	0	1
Italy	0	0	0	0	7	17	15	18	30
Japan	2	4	6	26	48	45	48	211	296
Korea	0	0	0	0	0	0	0	0	1
Luxembourg	0	0	0	0	0	2	3	2	2
Netherlands	0	2	1	2	13	13	19	8	10
Norway	0	0	3	1	10	9	29	21	21
New Zealand	0	0	0	1	2	1	7	3	2
Portugal	0	0	0	0	0	0	1	0	1
Soviet Union	0	0	0	0	0	0	0	0	2
Spain	0	0	1	0	1	0	1	1	3
Sweden	0	0	2	4	11	11	25	30	44
Switzerland	0	0	1	0	0	0	5	5	9
Thailand	0	0	0	0	0	0	0	1	0
United Kingdom	1	1	5	4	10	14	21	25	36
United States	1	10	9	10	96	125	92	36	35
Total	**14**	**38**	**64**	**105**	**330**	**422**	**541**	**556**	**851**

Currency distribution of swap-driven new issues

In 1987–88, non-dollar issuance dominated Eurobond markets. However, such issuance peaked in 1988, declining in 1989 to 1987 levels. Out of more than $110bn of non-dollar bonds issued in 1989, nearly 35% was swap-driven. Primarily denominated by equity-linked borrowing, 1989 witnessed the resurgence of US dollar-denominated issuance. Out of 1989 Eurodollar bond issuance totalling $120bn, almost $82bn — or close to 70% — was swapped (see Figure 3 and Table 3).

Aside from the US dollar and the yen — which have together dominated the swap-driven primary issuance market — the Canadian dollar, the Ecu, the Australian dollar, the Italian lira, the New Zealand dollar and the Spanish peseta Eurobond markets are primarily swap-driven, as almost 50% or more of the issuance in these markets is currency-swapped (see Table 4).

Figure 3: Non-dollar and straight US dollar issues swapped in international markets

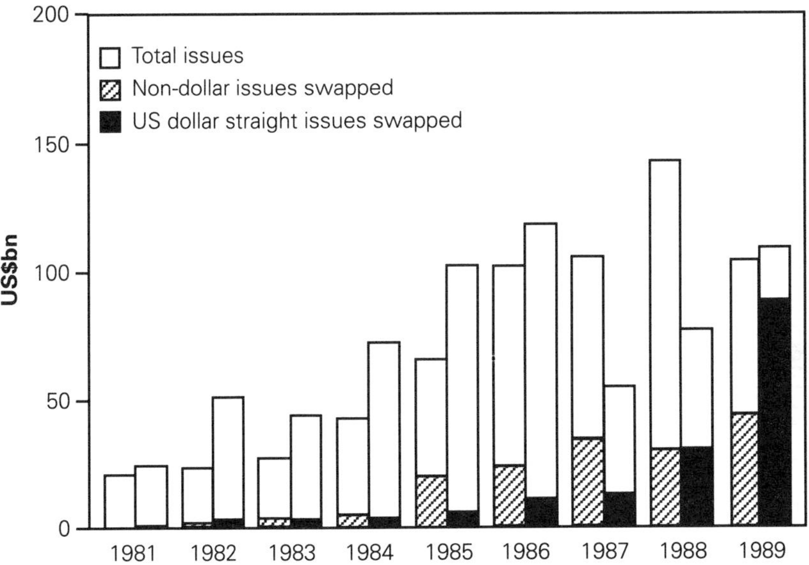

Table 3: Swap-driven primary issuance by currency of issue, 1981–1989

US dollars in millions or equivalent

	1981	1982	1983	1984	1985	1986	1987	1988	1989
Australian dollars									
Austrian schillings	0	0	0	132	1,850	3,822	6,866	3,036	3,555
Belgian francs	0	0	0	0	0	117	0	0	0
Canadian dollars	61	71	174	330	722	1,444	2,978	5,385	6,507
Dutch guilders	0	0	0	33	0	91	50	146	831
Danish krone	0	0	0	0	105	61	205	50	39
Deutsche marks	0	0	197	132	1,034	1,244	1,179	834	2,689
Ecu	0	0	432	839	2,971	2,638	2,926	1,987	3,794
Finnish markka	0	0	0	0	0	0	67	0	0
French francs	86	0	0	0	167	334	265	248	633
Hong Kong dollars	0	0	0	0	0	0	64	0	64
Italian lire	0	0	0	0	0	35	132	202	1,399
Luxembourg francs	0	0	0	0	36	45	88	8	168
New Zealand dollars	0	0	7	0	889	736	1,933	659	1.203
Spanish pesetas	0	0	0	0	0	0	158	0	1.256
Swedish kronor	0	0	0	0	0	43	0	0	282
Swiss francs	70	514	1,047	1,296	2,226	4,874	2,788	3,774	2.361
UK sterling	0	0	77	355	422	438	2,703	1,979	4.481
US dollars	790	1,511	1,526	2,460	3,563	8,703	12,270	27,165	82.505
Japanese yen	0	144	0	282	5,594	10,481	10,712	7,893	10.109
Total	**$1,007**	**$2,240**	**$3,460**	**$5,900**	**$19,632**	**$35,106**	**$45,482**	**$53,366**	**$121.876**

Table 4: Relative share of swap-driven primary issuance by currency of issue, 1981–1989
Based on percentage of total volume

	1981	1982	1983	1984	1985	1986	1987	1988	1989
Australian dollars									
Austrian schillings	0	0	0	2.2	9.4	10.9	15.1	5.6	2.9
Belgian francs	0	0	0	0	0	0.3	0	0	0
Canadian dollars	6.1	3.2	5.0	5.6	3.7	4.1	6.5	10.1	5.3
Dutch guilders	0	0	0	0.6	0	0.3	0.1	0.3	0.7
Danish krone	0	0	0	0	0.5	0.2	0.5	0.1	0
Deutsche marks	0	0	5.7	2.2	5.3	3.5	2.6	1.6	2.2
Ecu	0	0	12.5	14.2	15.1	7.5	6.4	3.7	3.1
Finnish markka	0	0	0	0	0	0	0.1	0	0
French francs	8.5	0	0	0	0.9	1.0	0.6	0.5	0.5
Hong Kong dollar	0	0	0	0	0	0	0.1	0	0.1
Italian lire	0	0	0	0	0	0.1	0.3	0.4	1.1
Luxembourg francs	0	0	0	0	0.2	0.1	0.2	0	0.1
New Zealand dollars	0	0	0.2	0	4.5	2.1	4.3	1.0	1.0
Spanish pesetas	0	0	0	0	0	0	0.3	0	1.0
Swedish kronor	0	0	0	0	0	0.1	0	0	0.2
Swiss francs	7.0	22.9	30.2	22.0	11.3	13.9	6.1	7.1	1.9
UK sterling	0	0	2.2	6.0	2.2	1.2	5.9	3.7	3.7
US dollars	78.5	67.5	44.1	41.7	18.1	24.8	27.0	51.2	67.7
Japanese yen	0	6.4	0	4.7	28.5	29.9	23.6	14.7	8.3
Total	**100.0%**	**100.0%**	**100.0%**	**100.0%**	**100.0%**	**100.0%**	**100.0%**	**100.0%**	**100.0%**

Major borrowers

At the market's inception, supranational issuers comprised the bulk of the borrowers. In 1981, such borrowers accounted for nearly 36% of all issues, and 56% of the total value. Since 1981, the profile of the typical borrower in the currency swap market has changed. By 1989, a mere 3.7% of the volume of swap-driven issuance was accounted for by supranationals. In part this reflects the drop in borrowing by these institutions. Rather, Japanese corporations by far were the most prominent issuers. Moreover, equity-linked issuance accounted for about 33% of total 1989 Eurobond issuance. Most of this issuance was in the form of Eurodollar bonds with equity warrants attached. Similarly, equity-linked issuance played a major role in the Swiss franc foreign market. In both cases, Japanese borrowers were the principal major participants, accounting for almost 60% of 1989 currency swap volume in the market. British, Italian and French borrowers each comprised between 4.0%–4.6% of the market (see Tables 5 and 6).

In the mid-1980s, the dominant issuers were the US and the Japanese, with the volume of US borrowing twice that of the Japanese. Furthermore, over 65% of non-dollar issuance by US entities — which peaked in 1986 — was swapped into another currency. In 1989, the volume of non-dollar issuance declined by more than half, and the percentage swapped had dropped to 43%.

1990 developments

Preliminary estimates of swap-driven issuance in the first three quarters of 1990, depict a substantially different picture: Japanese entities remained the largest issuers, accounting for 30% of the market. At the same time, however, West German borrowers emerged as the second-largest issuer, accounting for about 11% of swap-driven issuance. US issuers fell to sixth place, behind British, French and supranational borrowers.

Despite the drop in swap-driven new issuance involving Eurodollar bonds with equity warrants attached, US dollar-denominated issuance continued to dominate the market, with over 26% of the total, while the yen-denominated issuance has followed closely behind. The Deutsche mark, the Swiss franc and the Ecu together comprise one-third of the market, with almost equal shares.

In general, the relative importance of swap-driven primary issuance has varied from year to year in individual Eurobond markets. The most extreme example is that of the Eurodollar market, where swap-driven issuance accounted for nearly 70% of the total in 1989, but only for about 3% of the total as recently as 1985.

Table 5: Swap-driven issuance by nationality of issuer, 1981–1989

	1981	1982	1983	1984	1985	1986	1987	1988	1989
Supranational	560	705	399	273	1,048	2,613	3,339	1,491	4,462
Multinational	50	50	0	43	150	195	255	40	435
Argentina	50	0	0	0	0	0	0	0	0
Australia	0	0	126	709	1,170	1,245	1,456	1,672	2,863
Austria	86	333	379	655	878	828	1,469	1,221	2,953
Belgium	0	0	100	132	581	2,188	1,441	371	1,239
Bulgaria	0	0	0	0	0	0	0	0	75
Canada	107	234	590	525	603	2,668	2,828	1,361	3,430
Cayman Islands	0	0	0	0	0	0	0	0	103
China	0	0	0	0	0	0	0	118	0
Denmark	0	0	100	422	733	982	1,495	481	2,189
Finland	0	0	0	30	322	1,319	710	757	2,783
France	0	168	222	96	1,247	2,158	4,557	3,122	5,496
Greece	0	0	0	0	0	0	0	0	150
West Germany	0	0	96	194	819	1,913	3,982	2,221	2,907
Hong Kong	0	0	0	0	40	60	264	0	0
India	0	0	0	0	0	0	0	106	0
Ireland	0	0	0	0	0	94	142	0	137
Italy	0	0	0	0	251	1,206	2,004	1,470	5,531
Japan	100	213	325	1,614	2,953	3,440	5,431	28,090	70,936
Korea	0	0	0	0	0	0	0	0	50
Luxembourg	0	0	0	0	0	62	110	116	153
Netherlands	0	22	75	147	406	612	1,129	410	749
Norway	0	0	93	20	496	944	2,263	1,318	1,610
New Zealand	0	0	0	47	96	90	901	397	167
Portugal	0	0	0	0	0	0	82	0	53
Soviet Union	0	0	0	0	0	0	0	0	171
Spain	0	0	100	0	100	0	101	36	483
Sweden	0	0	81	195	547	819	2,292	2,014	3,146
Switzerland	0	0	79	0	0	0	350	403	851
Thailand	0	0	0	0	0	0	0	137	0
United Kingdom	30	50	306	216	477	1,219	2,019	2,888	4,909
United States	24	465	389	582	6,715	10,451	6,862	3,126	3,846
Total	**$1,007**	**$2,240**	**$3,460**	**$5,900**	**$19,632**	**$35,106**	**$45,482**	**$53,366**	**$121,876**

Table 6: Relative share of swap-driven issues by nationality of issuer, 1981–1989

	1981	1982	1983	1984	1985	1986	1987	1988	1989
Supranational Multinational	55.6	31.5	11.5	4.6	5.3	7.4	7.3	2.8	3.7
Argentina	5.0	0	0	0	0	0	0	0	0
Australia	0	0	3.6	12.0	6.0	3.5	3.2	3.1	2.3
Austria	8.5	14.9	11.0	11.1	4.5	2.4	3.2	2.3	2.4
Belgium	0	0	2.9	2.2	3.0	6.2	3.2	0.7	1.0
Bulgaria	0	0	0	0	0	0	0	0	0.1
Canada	10.6	10.4	17.1	8.9	3.1	7.6	6.2	2.6	2.8
Cayman Islands	0	0	0	0	0	0	0	0	0.1
China	0	0	0	0	0	0	0	0.2	0
Denmark	0	0	2.9	7.2	3.7	2.8	3.3	0.9	1.8
Finland	0	0	0	0.5	1.6	3.8	1.6	1.4	2.3
France	0	7.5	6.4	1.6	6.4	6.1	10.0	5.9	4.5
Greece	0	0	0	0	0	0	0	0	0.1
West Germany	0	0	2.8	3.3	4.2	5.4	8.8	4.2	2.4
Hong Kong	0	0	0	0	0.2	0.2	0.6	0	0
India	0	0	0	0	0	0	0	0.2	0
Ireland	0	0	0	0	0	0.3	0.3	0	0.1
Italy	0	0	0	0	1.3	3.4	4.4	2.8	4.5
Japan	9.9	9.5	9.4	27.4	15.0	9.8	11.9	52.6	58.2
Korea	0	0	0	0	0	0	0	0	0
Luxembourg	0	0	0	0	0	0.2	0.2	0.2	0.1
Netherlands	0	1.0	2.2	2.5	2.1	1.7	2.5	0.8	0.6
Norway	0	0	2.7	0.3	2.5	2.7	5.0	2.5	1.3
New Zealand	0	0	0	0.8	0.5	0.3	2.0	0.7	0.1
Portugal	0	0	0	0	0	0	0.2	0	0
Soviet Union	0	0	0	0	0	0	0	0	0.1
Spain	0	0	2.9	0	0.5	0	0.2	0.1	0.4
Sweden	0	0	2.3	3.3	2.8	2.3	5.0	3.8	2.6
Switzerland	0	0	2.3	0	0	0	0.8	0.8	0.7
Thailand	0	0	0	0	0	0	0	0.3	0
United Kingdom	3.0	2.2	8.8	3.7	2.4	3.5	4.4	5.4	4.0
United States	3.0	0.4	11.2	9.9	34.2	29.8	0.2	5.9	3.2
Total	**100%**	**100%**	**100%**	**100%**	**100%**	**100%**	**100%**	**100%**	**100%**

Chapter 18: Corporate liability portfolio management — using swaps and swap derivatives

Satyajit Das and John Martin
TNT Group

The development of swaps and swap derivatives instruments has been a central feature of global capital markets over the last decade.[1] This development of the market has been characterised by the following:

- A growth in the volume of swaps transacted and increased liquidity in the markets for these instruments.
- The establishment of swap markets in an increasingly wide variety of currencies.
- The development of a variety of products based on extensions and variations of the basic concepts of swaps, including combinations of swaps with a variety of interest rate and currency option elements.

The technical or "product" evolution of the swap market has been paralleled by a corresponding focus on "applications", ie, the use of these products in corporate financial management.

This applications focus is often referred to as "financial engineering", a term used to describe the construction of innovative asset and liability structures featuring combinations of traditional instruments (such as fixed-interest bonds, floating-rate notes and other funding instruments) and derivative products (such as interest rate and currency swaps, caps, floors, collars, FRAs etc).

The primary objective of this chapter is to develop an analytical framework for the use of swaps in the management of corporate liability portfolios.[2] *Section 1* outlines the basic applications of swaps in corporate liability portfolio management, including the rationale underlying these applications and the evolution of these practices under current market conditions. *Section 2* examines alternative analytical frameworks within which portfolios of swap transactions entered into by corporations can be analysed. The theoretical/pricing technologies available to assess the value of these transactions and to analyse restructuring opportunities are also considered. *Section 3* sets out a number of examples of swap portfolio management strategies under a variety of market conditions. Finally, *Section 4* provides a brief summary.

In this chapter there is no attempt to create a comprehensive catalogue of possible swap strategies. Instead, we have chosen to consider a number of possible strategies under selected market environments, reflecting the fact that the development and execution of specific transaction strategies are, to a large extent, unique and situation specific.

(1) Corporate use of swaps and swap derivatives

Swap applications

Corporate use of swaps focuses, primarily, on two major types of application:

- *New issue arbitrage*: whereby an issuer combines an issuance of debt with concurrent entry into a swap transaction, thereby creating a synthetic liability that, in the specific circumstances, provides financing at a cost less than that available through conventional direct access to the relevant funding market.

- *Asset/liability management*: whereby an organisation enters into a swap transaction in order to alter the cash flow characteristics (typically, the currency and/or the relevant rate basis — fixed, floating — and/or the relevant interest rate index) of an underlying debt portfolio.

The use of swaps in new issue arbitrage is motivated by the entity's desire to access funding and minimise its borrowing costs. Other factors which may be relevant are the diversification of funding sources, the flexibility of liability management, and specific factors which may prevent direct access to particular currencies and/or capital markets.[3]

The use of swaps in asset/liability management applications is predicated on using these instruments to convert fixed-rate exposures to floating rate and *vice versa*, and/or to convert assets and liabilities from one currency to another.[4]

The underlying decision to alter the interest rate basis and/or the currency of the liability is dictated first by changes in fundamental business circumstances, such as the purchase and sale of assets denominated in particular currencies, and secondly, by interest rate and/or currency exposure management considerations whereby the swap is used to convert the underlying portfolio to a basis more consistent with interest and currency rate expectations.

The evolution of swap applications

The role of swaps in new issue arbitrage and asset/liability management has undergone significant changes in recent years in response to changes in the market environment.

The practice of new issue arbitrage is firmly based in a historical period covering the early to middle 1980s, when highly-rated borrowers could, almost as a matter of course, undertake capital market transactions which were then swapped into the borrower's desired form of funding at substantial margins below their alternative cost of funding in the relevant currencies.

However, new issue arbitrage transactions resulted, predictably, in erosion of the arbitrage gain, as the process of exploiting the arbitrage opportunity forced the market towards its equilibrium state. For example, in the US dollar market, whereas the first swap transactions routinely generated floating-rate funding for banks and prime sovereign borrowers at Libor less 0.625%–0.75% pa, those same institutions would now be struggling to achieve funding at Libor less 0.125%–0.25% pa through a straight Eurodollar bond issue combined with an interest rate swap.

The reduced arbitrage opportunities are the result of an elimination or narrowing of arbitrage gains through the process of active exploitation,[5] a change in market environment and an increased understanding of the process of new issue arbitrage with a greater number of borrowers now seeking to avail themselves of more limited arbitrage opportunities.[6]

The shift in market environment is especially noteworthy. The process of new issue arbitrage thrived in the market environment which prevailed in the mid to late-1980s. During this period, intense competition between financial institutions seeking to increase market share in the highly competitive fund-raising business (particularly in international securities), as well as unprecedented growth in capital market activity and generally favourable market conditions, created an environment ideally suited to new issue arbitrage activities.

The market downturn, which commenced with the collapse of global equity markets in 1987, has resulted in a changed market environment characterised by a reduction in the level of competition in the financial services industry, with a number of major participants withdrawing, as well as a marked shift in investor attitudes signalling a subtle shift from a borrower's market to a lender's market. These factors have all combined to significantly reduce opportunities for new issue arbitrage transactions.

The changed market environment has not eliminated the opportunistic basis of arbitrage borrowing which continues to exist as a legitimate part of borrowers' funding strategies. However, it has led to fundamental differences in the way these transactions are now undertaken. The market has evolved in two complementary directions.

The first development involved the search for "new" arbitrage opportunities and the development of transaction structures designed to exploit the identified market discrepancies to provide net economic gains to the parties involved. This led to the emergence of a series of "exotic" securities structures designed to appeal to niche investors seeking to achieve specific investment objectives. These issues were then swapped using highly specialised swap structures usually designed to securitise one or more option or derivative elements embedded in these transactions.[7]

The second development (which was related to the first) was the increasing need for borrowers to accept, as part of the new issue arbitrage process, some risk elements of these transactions. These risk elements included:

- *Amount uncertainty*: whereby the borrower would not be certain of the amount of funding generated by the transaction although its cost would be predetermined.
- *Maturity uncertainty*: whereby the borrower was certain of the amount of funding and its cost, but not of its precise maturity, although the possible range of maturities would be known.
- *Interest basis uncertainty*: that is, whether the borrowing was on a fixed or floating-rate basis.
- *Currency uncertainty*: whereby the borrower was subject to uncertainty about the currency in which the borrowing was denominated.

The presence of these risk elements dictated that new issue arbitrage borrowers were increasingly forced into risk/reward trade-offs in undertaking these particular transactions. Sophisticated borrowers were usually prepared to accept some of these risks: Most large borrowers were prepared to accept uncertainty in respect of the amount and/or maturity which could be absorbed into their overall liability portfolios; a number of large borrowers, particularly sovereign entities, were prepared to accept uncertainty as to the fixed or floating nature of the underlying funding generated; and a limited number of borrowers were willing to accept the currency uncertainty of certain types of transactions.

The use of swaps for asset/liability management also evolved during this period, but for different reasons. The major influences included an increased volatility of interest and exchange rates, a growing acceptance of the concept of *zaitech*, and a shift in corporate philosophies whereby the minimisation of financing costs came increasingly to be viewed as a component of the competitive positioning of an entity.

The unprecedented volatility of interest and exchange rates through the 1980s forced most organisations to focus closely on their exposure management practices. Initially, this focus encouraged the use of swaps and other derivative instruments to protect corporate profitability and cash flow from substantial fluctuations caused by movements in interest and exchange rates. The shift to increasingly active management of asset/liability portfolios also resulted in an increased understanding of the profit opportunities created by financial market volatility.

The trend to more active management was allied to an increasing acceptance by a wide variety of corporations of the concept of *zaitech*.[8] The concept, at least, in its most common form, was seen to legitimise the active management of an organisation's financial flows in a manner designed to generate profits *in its own right*. This included, in its most extreme form, corporations entering into transactions for purely speculative reasons, totally unconnected to their underlying business activities or, in more modest forms, to organisations actively trading specific exposures generated by their core business activities in an effort to generate profits as a by-product to the actual minimisation of exposures that was the primary motivating factor in such activity.

The increasing globalisation of industry and increased competition across a variety of industries also forced, at or about the same time, an increased focus on the minimisation of financing costs, as well as, in its most extreme form, the generation of *zaitech* profits, as a component of the competitive positioning of particular organisations.

Implications for the management of corporate swap portfolios

These developments had significant implications for the management of corporate swap portfolios. The coalescence of these complex and inter-related factors created an environment within which organisations came to view their underlying liability and derivative portfolios as streams of cash flows capable and demanding of active management on an ongoing basis.

Traditionally, corporate users undertook swap transactions which were matched to the characteristics of their underlying debt portfolio. The swap was completed and maintained until maturity. The only exception to this pattern of activity was where changes in the underlying business or debt portfolio necessitated the termination or restructuring of the swap.

However, corporations increasingly came to view their swap transactions as a coherent portfolio of cash flows that must be managed separately or in conjunction with the corporation's underlying asset or liability portfolio. The major impetus for this change in approach to corporate swap portfolio management was the changing nature of new issue arbitrage and asset/liability management applications to which swap transactions were being put.

For example, as new issue arbitrage transactions became more complex, each transaction increasingly embodied a variety of option and/or other derivative products with specific value characteristics. Moreover, since the value characteristics of these components evolve specifically in response to movements in financial market rates, the fact that the value of each of these elements could change depending on the particular direction and quantum of movements in interest and/or exchange rates — creating specific profit opportunities or potential opportunity gains or losses — forced corporations to view these swap transactions on an individual basis, requiring separate and active management.

Similarly, the increased trend towards active asset/liability management, as described above, forced organisations to see their swap portfolios as potential sources of value. The increasingly complex dictates of asset/liability management necessitated the use of a wide variety of swap derivatives. The increasing complexity of the underlying instruments and the various component elements generated value creation opportunities (as with new issue arbitrage transactions, as discussed above) which could not be ignored.

Additional impetus to this "new" approach to swap portfolio management came from a number of additional factors:

- Growth in the number of transactions undertaken by large corporations meant that these entities had swap portfolios totalling hundreds of millions, and in a few cases, billions, of dollars.

- Increased liquidity of the swap market and the availability of market makers capable of structuring swaps based on customised cash flow requirements allowed new and more flexible transaction structures to be generated.

(2) An analytical framework

There are two fundamental issues in the management of corporate swap portfolios. First, it is important to develop a framework within which the swap/swap derivatives portfolio can be considered in relationship to the underlying liability portfolio. Secondly, any analysis must include the theoretical pricing techniques used to assess the value of these transactions and to examine restructuring opportunities. There are two potential approaches to corporate swap portfolio management: the integrated portfolio approach and the separate portfolio approach.

Figure 1: Corporate liability portfolio management analytical frameworks

Integrated portfolio approach

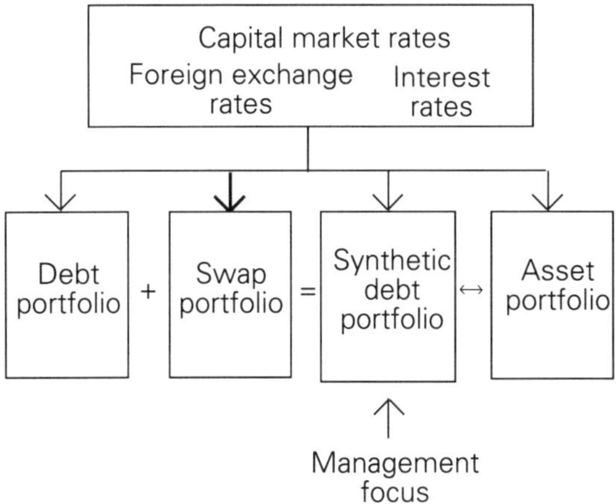

Separate portfolio approach

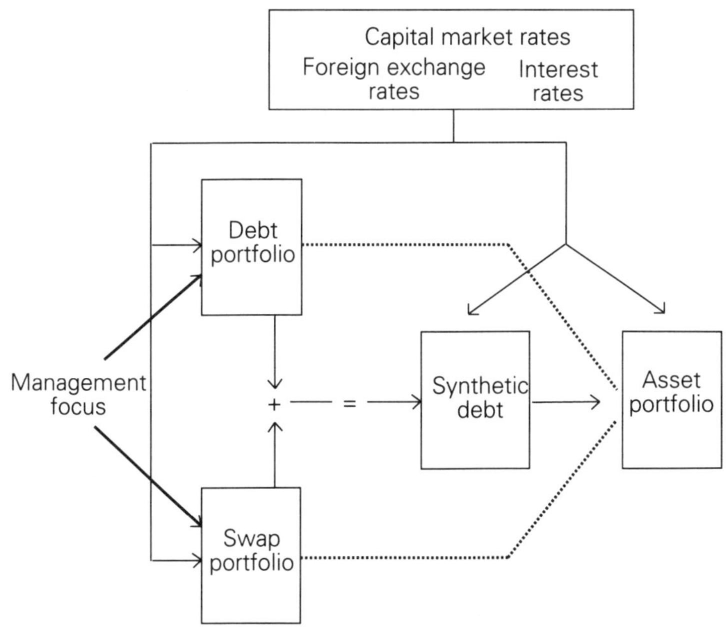

The integrated portfolio approach. The swap/swap derivatives portfolio is regarded as an integral part of the liability portfolio, that is, the underlying debt in conjunction with the swaps equate to a synthetic debt portfolio. Under this approach, the focus of portfolio management is on the end cash flows to be managed. The separate debt and swap cash flows are ignored except insofar as they constitute the unified synthetic debt portfolio.

The separate portfolio approach. The underlying debt and swap portfolios are treated as two separate portfolios, each having different cash flow characteristics and different value characteristics which are totally time specific. The transient values (eg, gains or losses, including opportunity gains or losses) are a function of movements in interest and exchange rates. These values are capable of being captured or released by specific action being taken in respect of the debt and/or swap portfolios.

Figure 1 sets out a schematic overview of the two potential approaches. It highlights a number of key differences between the two approaches:

- The impact of changes in interest and exchange rates is different under the two approaches. Under the integrated portfolio approach, the changes in value of the synthetic liability portfolio and its relationship to changes in the value of the asset portfolio are the primary focus. In the separate portfolio approach, the changes in value of three portfolios — the asset, debt and swap portfolio — and their inter-relationships are the primary focus.

- Under the separate portfolio approach, it is probable that for a given moment in interest or exchange rates the value of the debt and swap portfolios will change in opposite directions. This is because, by definition, the cash flows in the swap will be designed to offset the debt cash flow to effect a transformation of the interest rate basis and/or currency denomination.

- Under the separate portfolio approach, the quantum of the change in the value of the debt and swap portfolios will often vary. This is because different factors will invariably impact upon the respective markets at a given point in time.[9]

- Under the separate portfolio approach, the relationship between the asset portfolio and the various components of the liability portfolio is more complex. This relationship is capable of being affected by external action taken to alter: (1) the debt portfolio; (2) the swap portfolio; or, (3) the synthetic debt portfolio.

- In the case of the integrated portfolio approach, the risk dimensions of the relationship between the asset and the "total" liability portfolios are clearly defined.

- In the case of the separate portfolio approach, the risk inter-relationships between the asset and the "total" liability portfolios are extremely complex. Any change in the debt, swap or synthetic debt portfolios will alter the total risk profile and also its evolutionary path over time in response to changes in interest and exchange rates.

The two approaches to corporate swap portfolio management are environment or organisation specific.

The integrated portfolio approach is more suitable for *passive* asset/liability portfolio management. Under this approach, the organisation practices a high degree of asset/liability matching in terms of interest and exchange rate sensitivity. The liability portfolio is then created either through direct debt issuance or debt issuance combined with swap transactions to generate a preferred liability profile. The ultimate synthetic liability portfolio is then managed in response to changes in the characteristics of the asset portfolio it supports.

The separate portfolio approach is more suitable for *active* asset/liability management. This type of asset/liability manager will specifically manage his portfolio on a risk/reward trade-off basis. The liability portfolio constructed will match the corresponding asset portfolio but will explicitly take into account interest rate and/or exchange rate expectations. The active risk manager will then manage the underlying debt and swap portfolios separately, seeking to optimise the value of both sets of cash flows within its evolving interest rate and exchange rate expectations to preserve and maximise the value of each portfolio.

The objective of maximising the value of the debt and swap portfolios independently will often necessitate the deliberate creation of exposures relative to the asset portfolio being funded. For example, the closing out of an interest rate swap in order to lock in an unrealised gain may increase the overall risk of the asset/liability portfolio. This is because, unless rates move in the anticipated manner allowing the swap to be re-established at rates equivalent to or better than the close-out levels, the overall portfolio will have an increased level of interest rate risk.

The separate portfolio management approach is significantly different from the integrated portfolio management method because it is inherently a higher-risk approach, trading off an increased risk profile for higher earnings possibilities and it also more truly realises the potential of swaps and derivative products, as it allows the maximum benefit to be derived from the separation of liquidity from currency and interest rate selection. This chapter focuses primarily on the separate portfolio management approach.

The separate portfolio approach

The separate portfolio approach to the management of corporate swap portfolios is characterised by: (1) The separation of the debt portfolio (which provides the base funding/liquidity) from the swap/swap derivatives portfolio (which is used to structure the portfolio's currency and interest rate basis), and (2) the debt and swap portfolios are valued and managed separately to maximise the value of the debt and swap portfolio as independent sets of transactions. Under this approach, the management objectives applied to the two portfolios are different.

Debt portfolio management is predicated upon the following principles:

- The debt portfolio, ideally, is on a floating-rate basis in one or more currencies of the borrower's choice. Typically, this would be in floating-rate US dollars (priced off Libor) and/or in the base currency of the borrower.

- The major objective of debt portfolio management is to provide assured liquidity through the maintenance of an appropriate maturity structure and an appropriate diversification of funding sources.

- Minimisation of the after-tax borrowing cost of the debt portfolio, requiring minimisation of the credit margin payable on the borrowings and appropriate tax planning.

- Maximisation of portfolio flexibility in terms of repayment and prepayment rights etc.

Management of the swap portfolio, however, is guided by a different set of principles:

- The swap transactions are used to restructure the currency and interest rate basis of the debt portfolio in order to achieve the desired currency/interest rate basis to match the characteristics of the assets to be funded.

- The value of the swap portfolio will be sensitive to currency/interest rate movements (its value may change quite differently to that of the underlying debt portfolio for a given change in market rates).[10]

- Ongoing management of the swap portfolio will be dictated by (i) expectations of interest and current exchange rate movements over the relevant time horizon, (ii) the organisation's asset/liability interrelationship and, in particular, the evolving characteristics of the asset portfolio, and (iii) the risk/reward attitude of the organisation.

Valuation issues

The separate portfolio approach requires the capacity to construct innovative liability structures by combining various swap derivative products to create desired risk return configurations. This process, often referred to as "financial engineering" relies on the capacity to decompose the various debt instruments, swaps and swap derivative products into basic financial instruments whose value and pricing characteristics are well understood.

The separate portfolio approach requires the independent valuation of the debt instruments and the swap/swap derivatives.

The valuation of debt instruments is relatively straightforward and involves the use of conventional present value and internal rate of return concepts as embodied in standard bond pricing techniques. Gains and losses are measured as the present value of the differential between the original issuance rate and current market rates.

The valuation of debt instruments for the purposes of portfolio management requires two additional factors to be taken into consideration:

- Currency gains and losses resulting from changes in currency parities between the reporting (or home) currency of the borrower and the currency denomination of the debt. In addition, there may be cross-rate currency gains and losses resulting from the movements in the values of the asset/liability portfolios relative to each other and to the borrower's reporting currency.

- Changes in the value of derivative elements embedded in the structure of the debt instrument. This may take the form of option components such as the right to prepay or call the debt (an implicit call option on the underlying debt granted by the investor to the borrower) or other specifically tailored elements of the transaction.[11]

Swap/swap derivative instruments can typically be decomposed into forward contracts, option contracts and combinations of the two.[12] Decomposition of swap instruments into their basic elements and analysis of the interrelationships is vital in understanding both the structural and economic aspects of such transactions. In this regard, it is essential to deal with currency and interest rates swaps, LTFX, FRAs, caps, floors and collars, and variations based on these instruments, not as separate instruments but as a highly integrated set of financial transactions.

The relationship between interest rate swap contracts and forward contracts derives from the fact that, in effect, the swap contract is a series of forward contracts. An interest rate swap entails the exchange of specified cash flows determined by reference to two different interest rates. The interest rate swap can be represented by a series of cash inflows in return for a series of cash outflows. This contractual arrangement can be decomposed into a portfolio of simpler, single payment contracts, which can in turn be divided into a series of forward contracts. Using this approach, it is possible to restate an interest rate swap as a series of implicit forward contracts on interest rates. An FRA contract is essentially a market in forward interest rates — in effect, forward contracts on interest rates. Consequently, FRAs are logically linked to

Figure 2: Swap, forward and option market inter-relationships

In the same currency (US$)

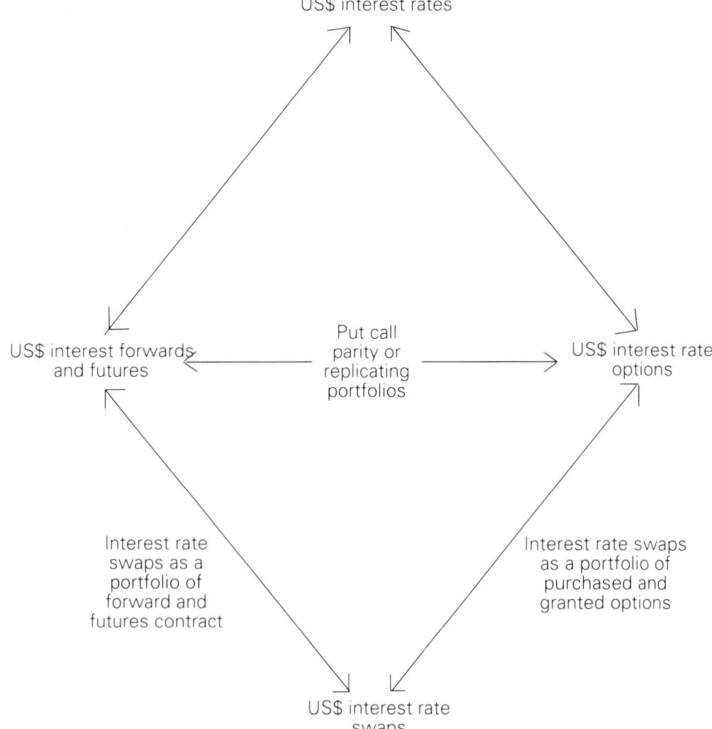

interest rate swaps in a manner identical to the linkage between forward contracts and interest rate swaps.

Between two currencies (A$ and US$)

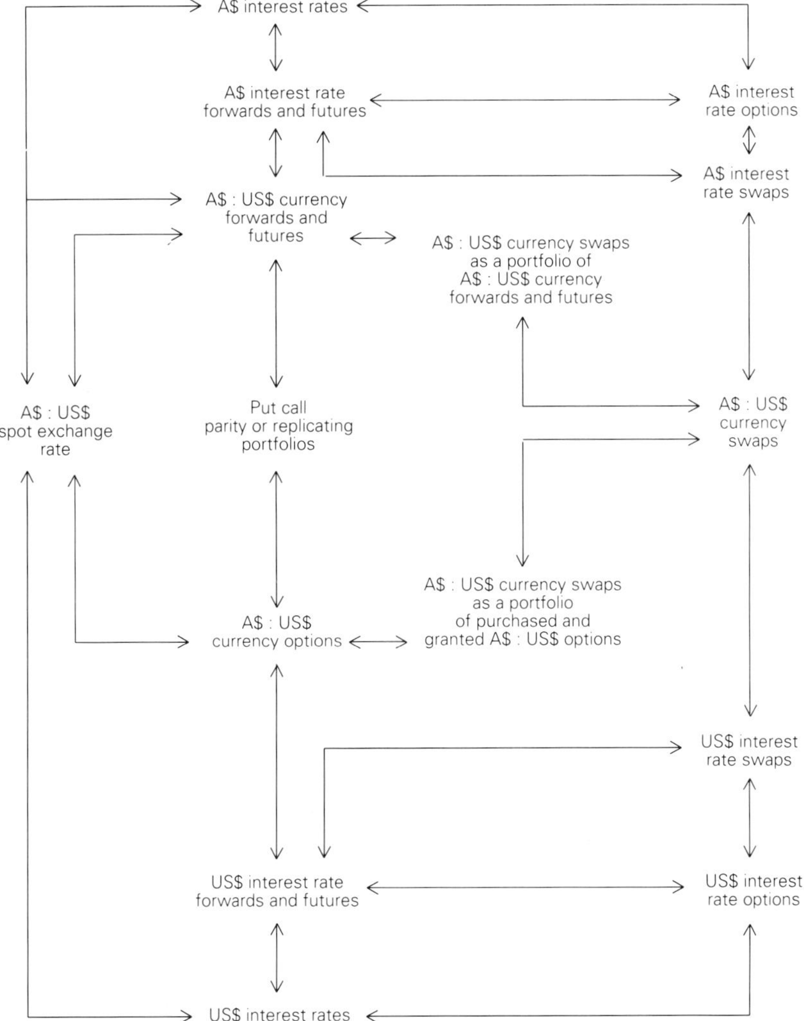

Source: Das, Satyajit (1989), Swap Financing, Sydney: Law Book Company, London: IFR Publishing Ltd at p 23.

The relationship between option contracts and swap transactions operates on two levels since the relationship between option contracts and forward contracts differs from that between option contracts and interest rate swaps. It can thus be demonstrated that there are at least two inter-related linkages between options and forward contracts.

- A call option can be replicated by continuously adjusting or managing a portfolio of securities or forward contracts on the underlying asset (for example, securities or foreign exchange) and riskless securities or cash. As the price of the asset rises, the call option equivalent portfolio would contain an increasing proportion of the assets or forward contracts. As the financial price of the asset decreases, the call option equivalent portfolio would reduce its holding of the assets or forward contracts.

- Option contracts can be used to replicate forward contracts through a relationship known as put/call parity. In terms of this relationship, the simultaneous purchase of a call option and the sale of a put option is equivalent to a forward purchase while the sale of a call option simultaneously combined with the purchase of a put option is equivalent to a forward sale.

These two levels of linkage between options and forward contracts imply a natural structural and economic relationship between the two instruments. In turn, option contracts impose a similar influence on interest rate swaps indirectly through their relationship with forward or futures contracts.

More directly, as noted above, options may have a direct relationship to interest rate swaps insofar as an interest rate swap can be characterised as a portfolio of purchased and sold options. This, of course, reflects the fact that an interest rate swap can be characterised as a series of forward contracts while forward contracts can be replicated through option contracts.

Swap instruments, such as caps, floors and collars are, in effect, a series of option contracts. This means that they are directly equivalent to underlying option contracts and, consequently, would enjoy a similar relationship to both forward and futures contracts or their customised equivalent FRAs, as well as to interest rate swaps.

The discussion to date has confined itself to instruments in a single currency. However, the analysis is capable of extension to a multi-currency situation. A currency swap is equivalent to a portfolio of currency forwards and futures or, alternatively, a portfolio of purchased and sold currency options. The currency forwards and currency options themselves are linked first to each other through option put/call parity and replicating portfolio relationships, and second, to the interest rate swap, forward and/or futures and option markets in their respective currencies.

This complex inter-relationship between swap, forward and option markets is illustrated in Figure 2.

This basic ability to dismember swap transactions into the basic constituent forward and option contracts is the basis for valuation and structuring of more complex asset/liability applications of these types of transactions.

As is evident from the examples set out in Section 3, these structural relationships allow the specific elements of individual transactions to be separated and revalued. Values contained in particular segments of the transaction can be released by reconfiguring the transaction to create new instruments. This process (often described as the "additivity aspect of swap transactions") facilitates the trading and hedging of swap transactions for more complex asset/liability management applications.

(3) Examples of swap portfolio management strategies

In this section, several examples of the use of swaps and swap derivatives in corporate liability portfolio management are discussed. As well as illustrating the theoretical principles outlined above, these examples cover both new issue arbitrage and asset/liability applications of swaps.

Example 1: Balance sheet management

Initial position

Company B (a United States-based corporation) has acquired a German company for a total sum of DM200m. Company B finances this acquisition by (1) issuing a 10-year Swiss franc bond in the Swiss capital market and (2) by entering into a 10-year currency swap under which it receives fixed-rate Swiss francs (matching the Swiss franc outflows under the bond issue) and, in exchange, makes Deutsche mark payments.

The combination of the two transactions generates attractive Deutsche mark funding for Company B to finance its acquisition. The details of the transaction are set out in Figure 3. The funding structure adopted by Company B reflects a number of important considerations:

- *Currency exposure.* The use of a synthetic Deutsche mark liability to match fund the Deutsche mark asset minimises any currency exposure. Company B operates an active approach to those currency exposure management policies which allow the company to "match" or "proxy hedge" by funding assets within a particular currency bloc with other currencies within the same currency bloc.

In the past, Company B has funded Deutsche mark assets with Swiss franc liabilities on the basis of (1) a strong correlation between the two currencies, and (2) a lower interest cost in Swiss francs relative to Deutsche marks (which provides a "cushion" against adverse movement in the Deutsche mark/Swiss franc exchange rate).

On this occasion, Company B prefers to minimise its exposure by financing in Deutsche marks on the basis that the Deutsche mark is expected to weaken against the Swiss franc and that the interest advantage of borrowing Swiss francs relative to Deutsche marks is minimal.

- *Funding*. The funding structure reflects the fact that Company B has good access to the Swiss capital market, based on a series of successful transactions undertaken over a number of years. In contrast, the company is not well known in the German capital market. These factors are reflected in the fact that the transaction structure has allowed Company B to generate Deutsche mark funding at a rate of approximately 0.30% pa below the funding cost achievable through a direct Deutsche mark funding transaction (see Figure 3).

Current position

Assume that over the next six months, the Swiss franc appreciates against the Deutsche mark (from DM1 = SwFr0.833 to DM1 = SwFr0.7692). During this period the Deutsche mark and Swiss franc interest rates remain unchanged. Company B's position is set out in Figure 4 at the new exchange rates. Its position can be summarised as follows:

- The net position remains unchanged, although the specific components of its asset/liability position have changed significantly.

- The Deutsche mark investment has appreciated by approximately US$7.2m (reflecting the weaker US dollar against the European currencies). However, this gain in the asset is offset by an equivalent but opposite change in the value of its Deutsche mark liabilities.

- The specific components within the liability portfolio have, predictably, moved in equal but opposite directions. The Swiss franc borrowing shows an unrealised loss equivalent to US$17.1m. This unrealised loss on the Swiss franc borrowings is offset by a gain on the Deutsche mark/Swiss franc swap equivalent to US$9.9m (SwF12.9m).

- The *net* change in the liability position (the Swiss franc/borrowing combined with the Deutsche mark/Swiss franc currency swap) shows a net unrealised loss of US$7.2m which exactly matches the gain on Company B's Deutsche mark asset.

Figure 3: Detailed structure

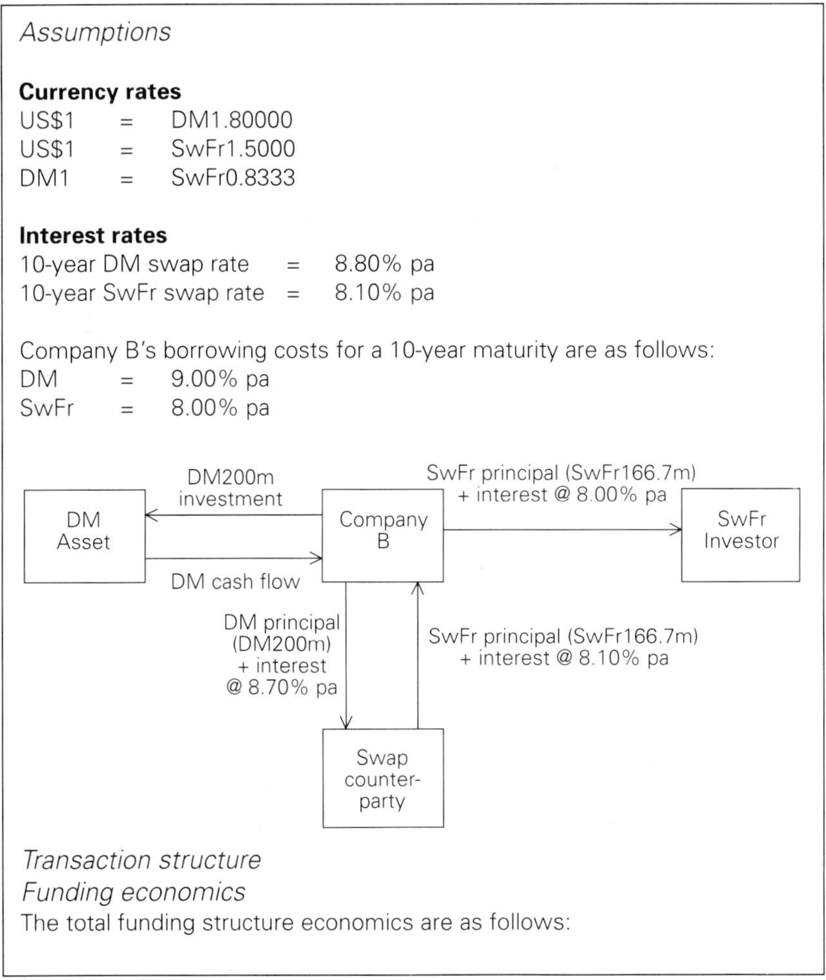

Assumptions

Currency rates

US$1 = DM1.80000
US$1 = SwFr1.5000
DM1 = SwFr0.8333

Interest rates

10-year DM swap rate = 8.80% pa
10-year SwFr swap rate = 8.10% pa

Company B's borrowing costs for a 10-year maturity are as follows:

DM = 9.00% pa
SwFr = 8.00% pa

Transaction structure

Funding economics

The total funding structure economics are as follows:

continued:

	SwFr (% pa)	DM (% pa)
Bond issue		
Payment to SwFr lenders	(8.00)*	
Currency swap		
SwFr receipts	8.10	
DM payments		(8.80)
	+0.10	**(8.80)**

*Figures in brackets represent payments.

The net Deutsche mark borrowing cost is approximately 8.70% pa (8.80% pa–0.10% pa).

The funding cost saving to Company B is 0.30% pa (calculated as Deutsche mark borrowing cost of 9.00% pa less the actual Deutsche mark borrowing cost generated by the swap of 8.70%).

Currency exposure — initial position

The translation exposure position for Company B is summarised in the table below.

Item	Foreign currency amount (m)	Exchange rate (US$1 =)	US$ equivalent (US$m)
Assets			
DM investment	DM200	DM1.80	111.1
Liabilities			
SwFr borrowing	SwFr(166.70)	SwFr1.50	(111.1)
DM/SwFr swap			
— DM payments	DM(200)	DM1.80	(111.1)
— SwFr receipts	SwFr166.7	SwFr1.50	111.1
Net			**0**

Portfolio management alternatives

Company B can, if it chooses, realise the gain on the currency swap or, alternatively, protect this gain from being eroded by using one of a number of methods, such as cancelling the swap, purchasing a Swiss franc put/Deutsche mark call option, or selling a Swiss franc call/Deutsche mark put option.

Some of these above techniques can be combined, for example, by writing a swaption whereby Company B agrees to receive fixed-rate Swiss francs and pay fixed-rate Deutsche marks with an agreement to take the prevailing Swiss franc/Deutsche mark spot rate as the exchange rate. Each of these methods is analysed in detail below.

Figure 4: Impact of currency fluctuations

Currency rates
US$1 = DM1.6905
US$1 = SwFr1.300
DM1 = SwFr0.7692

Interest rates
As before

Currency exposure — current position
The translation exposure position for Company B at a current market rates is summarised in the table below.

Item	Foreign currency amount (m)	Exchange rate (US$1 =)	US$ equiv (US$m)
Assets			
DM investment	DM200	DM1.6905	118.3
Liabilities			
SwFr borrowing	SwFr(166.70)	SwFr1.30	(128.2)
DM/SwFr swap			
— DM payments	DM(200)	DM1.6905	(118.3)
— SwFr receipts	SwFr166.7	SwFr1.30	128.2
Net			**0**

Swap cancellation
Under this alternative, Company B would cancel the existing Deutsche mark/Swiss franc currency swap, but maintain the Swiss franc borrowing, which provides the underlying liquidity to fund the Deutsche mark investment.

Cancellation of the currency swap would result in Company B realising a gain of US$9.9m (SwFr12.9m). This realised gain and the resulting cash asset would offset the *net* unrealised loss of the same amount in the books of Company B on its Deutsche mark investments and the Swiss franc liabilities funding the investment. Company B's balance sheet is summarised in Figure 5.

Figure 5: Impact of swap cancellation

Following cancellation of the Deutsche mark/Swiss franc currency swap, the translation exposure position for Company B is summarised in the table below.

Item	Foreign currency amount (m)	Exchange rate (US$1 =)	US dollar equivalent (US$m)
Assets			
DM investment	DM200	1.6905	118.3
Gain from swap cancellation	US$9.9		9.9
			128.2
Liabilities			
SwFr borrowing	SwFr(166.7)	1.30	(128.2)
Net			**0**

Purchase of a Swiss franc put/Deutsche mark call option

As discussed above, a currency swap transaction can be decomposed into its currency option components. In this case, the position under the Deutsche mark/Swiss franc currency swap equates to Company B purchasing a Swiss franc call/Deutsche mark put option and granting a Swiss franc put/Deutsche mark call (both with a strike price of DM1 = SwFr0.8333).

Company B can protect the unrealised gain under the currency swap by purchasing a Swiss franc put/Deutsche mark call option with the strike price being equal to the current spot exchange rate DM1 = SwFr0.7692.

The purchased Swiss franc put/Deutsche mark call option protects Company B's unrealised gain in the currency swap because if the Swiss franc continues to appreciate against the Deutsche mark, the option would expire unexercised, thereby allowing it to enjoy the continuing appreciation in the value of the swap corresponding to the increase in the value of the Swiss franc against the Deutsche mark. Also, if the Swiss franc weakens against the Deutsche mark, then Company B can exercise its option to preserve a portion of its previously unrealised gain on the swap.

Company B can either purchase the option until the maturity of the swap (that is, 9.5 years) or, alternatively, purchase short-term insurance via the purchase of a Swiss franc put/Deutsche mark call option for a period shorter than the final maturity of the swap. Figure 6 sets out a detailed analysis of this strategy.

Figure 6: Hedging swap currency gain via purchase of a Swiss franc put/Deutsche mark call

By purchasing a Swiss franc put/Deutsche mark call, Company B is ensuring that it will at least realise the current foreign exchange gain in its existing Swiss franc/Deutsche mark currency swap. If the Swiss franc should depreciate against the Deutsche mark, then Company B is able to exercise the option and the gain realised will go towards offsetting the opportunity loss in the swap. Whereas, if the Swiss franc should continue to appreciate, then the option is left to expire worthless while the currency gain within the swap increases. The option premium represents the cost of this insurance and has considerable influence on the economics of the transaction.

Company B could purchase a Swiss franc put/Deutsche mark call for the remaining term of the swap (9.5 years) or it could purchase insurance from short-term fluctuations (say a six-month term). The current market prices for these options are as follows:

Type	Term	Strike (DM1 =)	Premium (% of face value)	(DMm)
Buy SwFr put/DM call	6 months	SwFr0.7692	1.6%	3.2
Buy SwFr put/DM call	9.5 years	SwFr0.7692	9.0%	18.0

By purchasing the option, a substantial portion of the current FX gain within the swap is given away. In fact, the premium for the 9.5 year option exceeds the value of the current gain. However, the options provide different terms of insurance and in fact if the premium is expressed as an increase in borrowing cost over the term of the transaction, then it will have the following result:

Effective Deutsche mark borrowing cost (before currency effect)

Term	Deutsche mark funding cost (% pa)	Deutsche mark funding cost with premium (% pa)
6 months	8.8	9.01
9.5 years	8.8	10.21

The increase in Deutsche mark borrowing cost reflects the cash outflow of the option purchased. The increase in the overall borrowing cost is lower where the maturity of the option is short. However, this lower total borrowing cost is at the cost of a shorter period of protection against a decline in the Swiss franc relative to the Deutsche mark. Such a decline, without the protection of the option, would result in an erosion in the unrealised value within the original currency swap.

The combined impact of the underlying borrowing, currency swap and currency option is demonstrated in the table below which calculates the profit and loss impact of purchasing the 9.5-year option over a range of exchange rates at the maturity of the Swiss franc put/Deutsche mark call option:

Figure 6 continued:

*Payoff table: currency gain and loss (US$m)**

Exchange rate at option maturity (DM1 =)	SwFr borrowing	Swap	Option	Combined Total
SwFr0.6667	(27.7)	27.7	(10)	(10)
SwFr0.7143	(18.5)	18.5	(10)	(10)
SwFr0.7692	(9.3)	9.3	(10)	(10)
SwFr0.8333	0	0	(0.7)	(0.7)
SwFr0.9091	9.3	(9.3)	8.6	8.6
SwFr1.00	18.5	(18.5)	17.8	17.8

* Assumed exchange rate US$1 = DM1.8

This payoff table demonstrates the three possible outcomes of this strategy.

- If the Swiss franc continues to appreciate against the Deutsche mark, then the swap continues to offset the loss on the Swiss franc borrowing hedging the Deutsche mark asset. However, as the option expires worthless, the premium represents a cost.
- If the Swiss franc depreciates against the Deutsche mark, then the loss on the Swiss franc liability is reduced and the swap gain is reduced while the option value increases.
- If the Swiss franc remains steady, then the only impact is the loss of income due to premium paid.

Sale of a Swiss franc call/Deutsche mark put option

Using the same decomposition analysis outlined above as an alternative to the purchase of a Swiss franc put/Deutsche mark call option, Company B could securitise the purchased Swiss franc call/Deutsche mark put component of the original currency swap by granting a Swiss franc call/Deutsche mark put with the strike equivalent to the Deutsche mark/Swiss franc exchange rate at the time these transactions were initiated (DM1 = SwFr0.8333). Company B receives a premium for writing a deeply in-the-money option.

This strategy has the following impact:

- The premium received (together with interest earnings on the premium) has the effect of (i) reducing the cost of the Deutsche mark funding generated by Company B and (ii) providing a cushion against adverse currency movements (that is, further appreciation of the Swiss franc against the Deutsche mark).

- If the Swiss franc continues to appreciate against the Deutsche mark, then the Swiss franc call/Deutsche mark put option will be exercised against Company B. This would effectively close out the foreign exchange component of the currency swap. In fact, Company B could, where the option is exercised, simultaneously cancel the currency swap.

- If the Swiss franc weakened against the Deutsche mark, then the option would not be exercised. Under these circumstances Company B would be entitled to retain the premium, although the unrealised gain under the swap would be diminished.

  As in the case of the Swiss franc put/Deutsche mark call option, the option could be sold for a maturity coinciding with the maturity of the swap (9.5 years) or for a shorter maturity. Figure 7 analyses the detailed economics of this alternative.

Figure 7: Hedging swap currency swap with sale of a Swiss franc call/Deutsche mark put

In this case, Company B is willing to give up any further currency gains in the swap for the receipt of an upfront premium. If the Swiss franc continues to appreciate until maturity of the option, then the option will be exercised against Company B. If the exchange rate remains stable or the Swiss franc depreciates, then the option expires unexercised and Company B earns the premium.

As in the previous scenario, Company B can write short-term options against the underlying borrowing and swap or it can match up to the 9.5-year term of the underlying structure.

Type	Term	Strike (DM1 =)	Premium % of face value	(DMm)
SwFr call/DM put	6 months	0.8333	9%	18
SwFr call/DM put	9.5 years	0.8333	19%	38

Both options are substantially "in-the-money" and have a high delta (particularly the six-month option).

The premium earned provides some protection against this eventuality and provides a cushion against further Swiss franc appreciation. The extent of this cushion is calculated below and is referred to as the strategy's "breakeven".

Term	SwFr appreciation breakeven (DM1)
6 months	0.7645
9.5 years	0.6874

Figure 7 continued:

Further, if the exchange rate should remain steady then the premium provides a substantial reduction in Deutsche mark interest cost.

Term	DM borrowing cost (%pa)	Effective DM borrowing cost incl'g premium (%pa)	Interest saving (%pa)
6 months	8.80	8.10	0.70
9.5 years	8.80	7.32	1.48

The payoff of this strategy if 9.5-year options are granted is demonstrated in the table below.

*Payoff table: FX gain and loss (US$m)**

Exchange rate at option maturing (1DM =)	SwFr borrowing	Swap	Option	Combined total
0.6667	(27.7)	27.7	(6.7)	(6.7)
0.7143	(18.5)	18.5	2.6	2.6
0.7692	(9.3)	9.3	11.9	11.9
0.8333	0	0	21.1	21.1
0.9091	9.3	(9.3)		
1.00	18.5	(18.5)	21.1	21.1

* Assume US$1 = DM1.8

As opposed to the bought option strategy (Figure 6) the preferred outcome is that the Swiss franc/Deutsche mark rate remains steady or declines.

Comparing the alternatives

Each of the alternative methods of crystallising the unrealised gain in the currency swap is predicated on the willingness of Company B to accept a currency exposure. This exposure entails the funding of a Deutsche mark asset with a Swiss franc liability.

If Company B believes that the Swiss franc provides a sound long-term hedge for its Deutsche mark assets, ie, there is a strong correlation between the two currency units, and if it is also willing to accept the risk of fluctuations in the Deutsche mark/Swiss franc exchange rate on the basis of the lower interest cost in Swiss francs which provides a "cushion" against adverse movements in the Deutsche mark/Swiss franc exchange rate, then the company may be willing to accept this exposure.

While each of the strategies discussed is predicated on this willingness to accept a Deutsche mark/Swiss franc currency mismatch, the individual alternatives have different risk profiles. The optimal strategy is contingent upon Company B's expectation of future movements in the Deutsche mark/Swiss franc exchange rate over the remaining life of the transaction. Figure 8 sets out a comparison of the economic impact of the three alternatives discussed above.

Figure 8: Payoff diagram of reversal strategy

Swap structure: swap and reversal

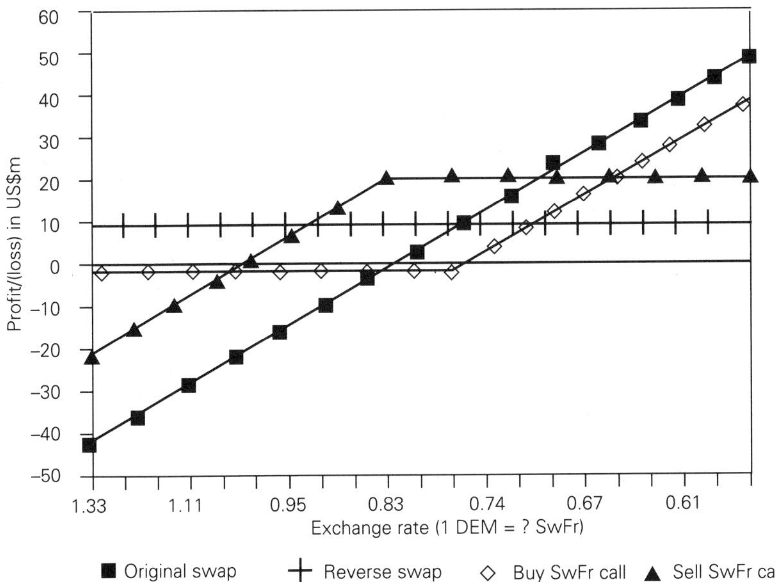

In summary, the analysis indicates the following:

- *Swap cancellation.* The swap cancellation is the optimal strategy if the Swiss franc depreciates against the Deutsche mark over the remaining life of the transaction. If the swap is cancelled and, contrary to expectations, the Swiss franc continues to appreciate against the Deutsche mark, Company B will be exposed to foreign exchange losses under the Swiss franc borrowings which are not offset by corresponding gains under the currency swap. This will result in a net total unrealised loss to the company as the increase in value of its Deutsche mark investment is more than offset by unrealised losses on its Swiss franc borrowings.

- *Purchase of a Swiss franc put/Deutsche mark call option.* The purchase of the option is the preferred strategy where the Swiss franc is expected to continue appreciating against the Deutsche mark but protection is sought against a sudden and unexpected reversal in this application. This strategy is the most risk adverse of the alternatives. It locks in a gain at maturity of the currency swap but as the swap is not cancelled, Company B is not exposed to potential currency losses on the mismatch on its Deutsche mark investment and the supporting Swiss franc borrowing.

- *Sale of a Swiss franc call/Deutsche mark put option.* The option granting strategy is the preferred alternative if the Swiss franc/Deutsche mark exchange rate remains relatively constant and oscillates within a tight band around its current level (DM1 = SwFr0.7692). However, if the Swiss franc continues to appreciate, then the option would be exercised, forcing Company B to terminate the currency swap and open a currency exposure. In contrast, if the Swiss franc depreciates against the Deutsche mark from its current levels, then although Company B retains the premium received for the granting of the option, it suffers a loss as the value of the currency swap deteriorates over time, potentially eliminating all the present unrealised gain.

Example 2: Floating-rate liability management

Initial position

Company A has an existing US dollar interest rate swap for a notional principal amount of US$100m within its portfolio. Under this swap, Company A pays 9% per annum semi-annually and receives six-month Libor. The swap has a maturity of five years and was entered into to convert part of its floating-rate borrowings into a fixed-rate liability.

At the time of entry into this swap, the interest rate structure for US dollars was as follows:

Six-month Libor:	8% per annum
Five-year swap rate:	9% per annum (semi-annually)

Current position

Over the next six months, US dollar interest rates rise rapidly across the maturity spectrum to the following levels:

Six-month Libor: 13% per annum
4.5-year swap rate: 11% per annum (semi-annually)

As a result of the increase in interest rates, the existing swap position is currently showing an unrealised gain. This gain (in present value terms) is approximately US$7.0m.[13]

Portfolio management alternatives

Company A may choose to manage its swap position to preserve its *unrealised* gain, by either cancelling the swap or by purchasing or selling caps and floors.

Swap cancellation

Company A could choose to reverse or cancel any existing swap. This reversal would generate an upfront gain equivalent to US$7.0m (or 7% of the principal value of the transaction), which is equivalent to 2% pa over the remaining 4.5 years of the transaction.

However, reversal of the swap has the following impact on Company A's position:

- Company A's interest cost rises immediately to the level of current six-month Libor, 13% pa (an increase of 4% pa from its existing fixed level of 9%). The upfront gain (together with interest earnings thereon) provides a degree of protection against the immediate rise in interest cost, equivalent to 2% pa over the remaining life of the transaction.

- Company A, as a result of unwinding its swap, has no protection against interest rate increases above current market levels or an inversion of the yield curve. However, it benefits where six-month Libor averages lower than 11% pa over the next 4.5 years.

Cap/floor strategies

These strategies are based on Company A's swap transaction being bundled into a series of option transactions.

Paying fixed rates and receiving floating rates under an interest rate swap can be characterised as buying a cap and simultaneously selling a floor with a strike price equivalent to the fixed rate under the swap, ie, 9% pa.

Using this theoretical construct, Company A can manage its existing position by entering into a series of option transactions, eg, writing caps, buying floors or both (selling collars) or, alternatively, purchasing or granting options on the fixed-rate portion of the swap.

These strategies revolve around the contingent nature of options. They allow the benefit of the original swap to be maintained while protection against unfavourable movements can be purchased or additional income generated through the sale of options.

Purchasing options

Company A could implement the following strategies:

- *Purchase a swaption* whereby Company A can elect to receive fixed rate (at 11% pa) against payment of six-month Libor. The swaption purchased by Company A expires in six months' time and affords Company A protection from a decline in swap rates over the six-month period. If swap rates decline, then the value of the swaption increases, offsetting the loss of value in the underlying swap position.

- *Purchase floors* whereby Company A would benefit if six-month Libor declined below the strike level (say 11% pa) over the term of the floor. Using this strategy, Company A, in return for the payment of an upfront premium, repurchases the sold floor or call option component of the swap. The purchase allows Company A to switch back to floating-rate funding if six-month Libor falls below the strike yield level.

Assume the current market rates are as follows:

Swaption

Type:	Purchase of option on swap (swaption) to receive fixed rate and pay floating rate under an interest rate
Strike rate:	11% pa (semi-annually)
Floating-rate index:	Six-month Libor
Option expiry:	Six months
Premium:	0.87% (flat)

Interest rate floor

Type:	Interest rate floor agreement (call options)
Floating-rate index:	Six-month Libor
Strike level:	11% pa
Term:	4.5 years
Settlement:	Six-monthly in arrears against spot six-month Libor
Premium:	2%

The swaption allows Company A to reverse its swap in six-months' time if swap rates decline. Exercise of the swaption will reverse the original swap for an upfront gain of US$5.5m. This upfront gain is lower than the amount which would be gained by an immediate cancellation of the swap because the present value of interest flows has declined with the lapse of six months, and a premium of US$0.87m was paid for the swaption. For this strategy to be the preferred alternative, the decline in swap rates has to occur during the term of the swaption.

The floor also hedges Company A from an interest rate decline. However, the payoff profile differs to that under the swaption. Under the floor, Company A receives a net payment should six-month Libor fall below 11% pa over the remaining term of the swap (4.5 years). Under this arrangement, Company A continues to pay fixed rates under the swap and maintain its protection against interest rate increases. The cost of the floor has the effect of increasing the effective swap rate by 0.58% pa (the amortised premium) to 9.58% pa.

The use of floors and swaptions to manage the existing swap position entails an element of yield curve risk.

It may be possible for swap rates to decline back to 9% pa while Libor does not fall below 12% (the strike level of the floor). In this case, the swap gain is extinguished but is not offset by a gain on the floor transaction. On the other hand, while a swap reversal through the exercise of the swaption exposes Company A to any future increase in interest rates, the combination of the swap and floor affords protection from any upward movement in interest rates, while still allowing it to benefit from any fall in short-term rates.

In essence, the combined position is a type of "cross-yield-curve" cap. Put/call parity suggests that a bought call (the floor) and a "short" underlying position (the swap) equates to a bought put (an interest rate cap). It is a cross-yield-curve cap because Company A is protected from an upward movement in both swap rates and Libor while it only benefits when rates fall if Libor declines.

The effectiveness of realising the gain in this manner depends on the shape of the yield curve. The maximum gain is achieved if short-term rates fall further than swap rates (ie, the yield curve moves to a positive shape). A lesser gain is realised on the swap reversal if swap rates decline more than Libor (ie, the yield curve becomes more inverted).

Another interesting aspect to the strategy entailing a floor is that it could be purchased over a shorter period, say one year, effectively purchasing back the call option component of the original swap for only a portion of the remaining term.

Selling options

Instead of purchasing options to manage its existing swap position, Company B can sell options (interest rate caps or swaptions) to manage its existing swap portfolio. The sale of options has a radically different risk profile as they leave Company A exposed to any upward movement in interest rates and provide a small benefit from a fall in rates.

The impact of selling options on the six-month Libor and fixed-rate element of the swap is set out below. Assume the following market rates:

Swaption

Type:	Sale of option on swap (swaption) to receive fixed rate and pay floating rate under an interest rate
Strike rate:	11% pa (semi-annually)
Floating-rate index:	Six-month Libor
Option expiry:	Six months
Premium:	0.60% (flat)

Interest rate cap

Type:	Interest rate cap agreement (put options)
Floating-rate index:	Six-month Libor
Strike level:	11% pa
Term:	4.5 years
Settlement:	Six-monthly in arrears against spot six-month Libor
Premium:	1.5% (flat)

The sale of the swaption has the following impact:

- Company B receives the premium equivalent to 0.60% which is equivalent to 0.17% pa and subsidises Company A's borrowing costs.

- If swap rates continue to increase, then the swaption will be exercised. Exercise of the swaption will result in cancellation of the swap realising a gain of US$6.3m to Company A (US$6.9m inclusive of the swaption premium). However, there is an opportunity loss as Company A could have closed down the swap at a higher gain. Also, upon cancellation of the swap, Company A has no further protection from increases in interest rates as it has effectively reverted to a floating-rate borrowing.

- If swap rates decline, the swaption will not be exercised. However, the fall in swap rates will result in an erosion of value in the existing swap position which will only be partially offset by the premium received.

The securitisation of the fixed-rate component of the swap through the sale of the cap has the following impact:

- Company A receives the premium equivalent to 1.5% of the contract value at the commencement of the transaction. This is equivalent to an annualised amount of 0.43% pa which has the effect of subsidising Company A's borrowing costs.

- If six-month Libor rates fall, then the cap is not exercised. The premium received lowers the effective fixed rate under the swap but there is, however, an opportunity loss to Company A if rates average less than 8.57% pa for the remainder of the life of the swap transaction (that is, 4.5 years).

- If rates increase above the strike level, 11% pa, then the cap is exercised and Company A is required to make payments to the cap purchaser which effectively transforms its borrowing into a floating-rate liability at a rate equivalent to six-month Libor less 0.43% pa (the amortised premium). Consequently, Company A has no protection against increases in six-month Libor rates if they average more than 11.43% pa for the next 4.5 years.

The sale of option strategies seeks to exploit the potential for further gains within the swap instead of "locking in" the existing gain resulting from market interest rate movements to date.

The sale of these interest rate options effectively prevents Company B from benefiting from any further rises in interest rates. Company A forgoes its protection in return for the receipt of a premium.

In these cases, Company A's maximum benefit is realised if interest rates remain at or about the current level for the term of the option as it continues to receive the interest cost saving generated by the original swap and benefit from the premium received from the sale of options.

Comparing the alternatives

The alternatives for managing the interest rate swap portfolio considered above relate to the situation where an increase in interest rates creates an unrealised gain in the existing swap portfolio.

Similar management techniques are applicable to where, due to a fall in interest rates, the existing swap position shows an opportunity loss.[14]

As discussed above in Example 1, each of the alternatives available to manage an existing swap position implies an inherently different risk/reward profile. The basic management alternatives are all based on the following assumptions:

- The willingness and/or capacity of Company A to convert part of its portfolio from fixed to floating rate. This presumes that (i) Company A has a sufficiently large portfolio of fixed and floating-rate borrowings where a change from fixed to floating of US$100m has no significant strategic impact on the competitive position of the company, and (ii) that the Company's assets and revenue flows are sensitive to and correlated with interest rate movements.

- The willingness to actively manage the fixed/floating mix of the portfolio within pre-established risk/reward parameters in order to minimise the group's interest costs.

As will be evident from a consideration of the above, the choice between alternatives is complex. Figure 9 sets out a comparison of the various strategies outlined under different interest rate scenarios. The selection between alternatives is driven substantially by Company A's expectation of future interest rate movements, including the expected shape of the yield curve.

Figure 9: Reversal strategies' payoff

Total structure at maturity

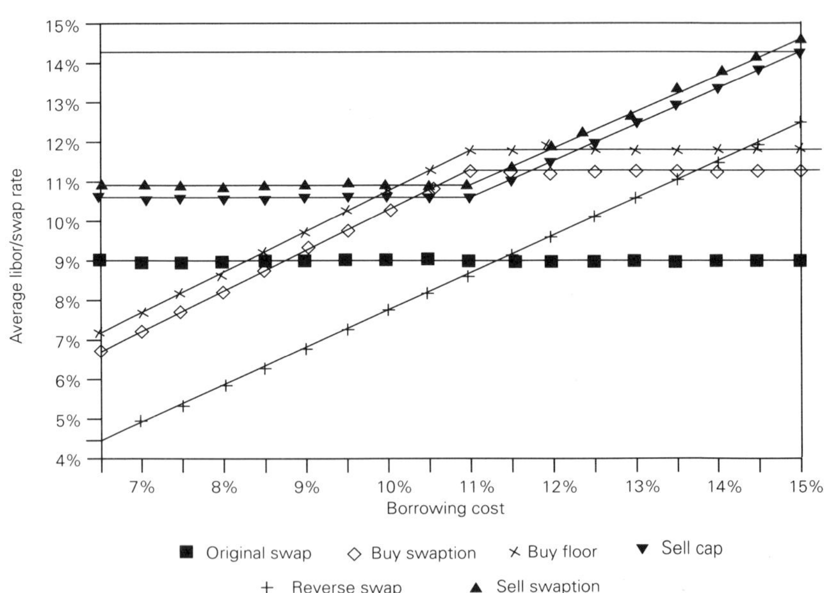

In summary, Company A's selection between the alternatives would be influenced by the following factors:

- If interest rates are expected to decline across the yield curve, then the maximum benefit is realised by reversing the existing interest rate swap today.

- If, however, the interest rate decline is expected to take some time, an alternative may be to reverse part of the swap by entering into a forward swap to reverse, say, the last two or three years of the existing five-year swap. This would leave Company A protected for the first two to three years but would convert it into a floating-rate borrower for future periods when interest rates are expected to be lower.

- If interest rates are expected to decline but there is considerable uncertainty as to the timing or degree of the decline, then the preferred alternative is the purchase of either the floor or swaption. The selection between the floor and swaption will be dictated by expectations of the anticipated shape of the yield curve of the future.

- If rates are expected to increase, then no action needs to be taken although a floor or swaption may be purchased to protect against a failure of these expectations being realised.

- If rates are expected to remain relatively static at or around current levels, then the sale of caps/swaptions is the economically superior alternative.

Example 3: Floating-rate liability management

Initial position

Company C purchases a US$100m interest rate cap to hedge its portfolio of floating-rate US dollar borrowings. The terms of the cap are as follows:

Type:	Purchase of interest cap (put options) on US dollar six-month Libor
Floating-rate index:	Three-month Libor
Strike level:	9% pa
Option term:	Two years (spot start)
Premium:	0.44% (flat)

The market rate structure at the time of entry into the transaction was as follows:

Three-month Libor: 8% pa
Two-year swap: 8.5% pa

The interest rate cap purchased is 0.5% pa out-of-the-money (being 0.5% pa above the two-year swap rate or implied forward rate on three-month Libor).

The purchased interest rate cap provides protection for Company C against interest rate increases above 9.24% pa (implied by the strike rate together with the amortised premium paid). If at each settlement date, three-month Libor averages over 9.24% pa, then Company C benefits from a cost of funds which is lower than that which would have been applicable in the case when Company C did not purchase its protection. Table 1 summarises the payoff profile of the interest rate cap and contrasts it with that of an interest rate swap for the same maturity.

Table 1: Interest rate cap payoffs

Average 3-month Libor (% pa)	Gain/loss under: 2-year interest rate swap (%pa)	2-year interest rate swap (%pa)	Company C interest cost: 2-year interest rate swap (%pa)	2-year interest rate cap (%pa)
6	(2.5)	(0.24)	8.50	6.24
7	(1.50)	(0.24)	8.50	7.24
8	(0.50)	(0.24)	8.50	8.24
9	0.50	(0.24)	8.50	9.24
10	1.5	0.75	8.50	9.24
11	2.5	1.76	8.50	9.24

Current position

Over the next three months, US interest rates rise to the following level:

Three-month Libor: 11% pa
1.75-year swap: 10% pa

As a result of the increase in interest rates, the interest rate cap position is currently showing an unrealised gain.

Portfolio management alternatives

Company C can choose to manage its existing interest cap position to preserve its unrealised gain either by purchasing or selling caps and floors, or by entering into interest rate swaps. The strategies outlined are based on similar inter-relationships between interest rate swaps and interest rate caps and floors as those identified in Example 2.

Sale of the cap

Company C could choose to liquidate its interest rate cap by selling the position. Under current market conditions, the cap (now for a term of 1.75 years) can be sold for 2.31% pa (flat). This represents a gain of 1.87% or US$1.87m on the transaction.

When the cap is sold, Company C reverts to a floating-rate US dollar borrowing. This borrowing is at a cost of three-month Libor less 1.18% pa. This margin under Libor represents the gain on the sale of the cap amortised over the remaining life of the original transaction.

The company benefits if three-month Libor averages less than 10.18% pa over the remaining 1.75 years of transaction.

Entry into an interest rate swap

As an alternative to selling the cap, Company C could lock in the gain on its cap position by entering into an interest rate swap for a notional principal amount of US$100m whereby it receives fixed rates (at 10% pa the current market rate) and pays three-month Libor.

This transaction has the following impact:

- The swap locks in a gain of 1% pa (the difference between the swap rate and the cap rate) on each of the remaining seven quarterly periods. This equates to a present value benefit of 1.59% flat which, adjusted for the premium paid for the cap, is equivalent to 1.15%.

- Company C will have no protection if interest rates increase from current levels.

- Where interest rates decline, entry into this interest swap has the effect of leveraging the returns to the company. This is because receiving fixed rate under an interest rate swap is the equivalent of selling a series of interest rate put options and simultaneously purchasing a series of interest rate call options. This transaction, the sold put embedded in the swap, is offset by the previously purchased interest rate cap. This leaves Company C with a purchased call option or interest rate floor which increases in value if interest rates decline. The payoffs from this particular strategy are summarised in Table 2.

The use of the swap to reverse the interest rate cap position is a particularly useful alternative where sale of the interest rate cap cannot be affected at or about its true economic value.

Table 2: Reversal of cap with interest rate swap

Average 3-month Libor Libor (%pa)	Gain/loss under Interest rate cap (%pa)	Interest rate swap (%pa)	Total (%pa)	Company C total interest rate cost (%pa)]
7	(0.24)	3.0	2.76	4.24
8	(0.24)	2.0	1.76	5.24
9	(0.24)	1.0	0.76	8.24
10	0.76	0.0	0.76	9.24
11	1.76	(1.0)	0.76	10.24
12	2.76	(2.0)	0.76	11.24

Buying a floor

Company C could seek to lock in its gain, without sacrificing protection against further interest rate increases, by purchasing a floor for a maturity of 1.75 years at a strike price of 10.0% pa for a premium of 0.51% (flat) or 0.32% pa.

Table 3 sets out the return from the strategy. The table indicates that Company C remains protected against further increases in interest rates, albeit at a slightly higher level, but continues to benefit from future falls in interest rates.

Selling a floor

Company C could protect its gain under the cap by writing a floor. This written floor combined with the bought put (interest rate cap) equates to an interest rate swap whereby Company C pays fixed rate and receives three-month Libor.

If rates were anticipated to remain steady or increase, then the premium resulting from the sold floor would decrease the cost of borrowing for Company C, partially offsetting the previously incurred cost of purchasing the interest rate cap. Table 4 sets out the payoff of the strategy.

Table 3: Hedging cap with purchased floor

Average 3-month Libor (%pa)	Gain/loss under: Interest rate cap (%pa)	Interest rate floor (%pa)	Total (%pa)	Company C total interest rate cost (%pa)
8	(0.24)	1.68	1.44	6.56
9	(0.24)	0.68	0.44	8.56
10	0.76	(0.32)	0.44	9.56
11	1.76	(0.32)	1.44	9.56
12	2.76	(0.32)	2.44	9.56

Table 4: Hedging cap with sold floor

Average 3-month Libor (%pa)	Gain/loss under: Purchased interest rate cap @ 9% (%pa)	Sold interest rate floor @ 9% (%pa)	Total (%pa)	Company C total interest rate cost (%pa)
7	(0.24)	(1.87)	(2.11)	9.11
8	(0.24)	(0.87)	(1.11)	9.11
9	(0.24)	0.13	(0.11)	9.11
10	0.76	0.13	0.89	9.11
11	1.76	0.13	1.89	9.11
12	2.76	0.13	2.89	9.11

As in the case of Examples 1 and 2, the management alternatives identified are all predicated on the willingness of Company C to switch between fixed and floating-rate borrowings. Each individual strategy, however, has a different risk profile. For example, if interest rates are expected to continue to increase, the purchased or sold floor alternative would be the preferred method of management of this portfolio. However, if interest rates are expected to decline, then the sale of the cap, entry into an interest rate swap where Company C received fixed and paid floating rates, or the purchase of the floor would represent the optimal economic mechanism by which the portfolio's value would be maximised.

(4) Summary

Increasing attention has focused on the use of swaps and swap derivatives in the management of corporate liability portfolios. This process, often referred to as "financial engineering", has resulted from increased attention by corporate financial officers on the active management of corporate debt portfolios to minimise the borrowing costs of the entity within specified risk/reward guidelines.

The inter-relationships between interest rate swaps and other swap derivatives and the capacity to compose and decompose synthetic liability and asset structures by complex combinations of these instruments are increasingly being used to exploit value creation opportunities within existing portfolios of debt and derivative instruments maintained by large corporations.

Continuing high levels of volatility in financial market rates — both currency and interest rates — together with increased focus on the use of corporate financial management expertise to generate value seems likely to ensure that these developments will continue to increase in importance.

Notes

Satyajit Das is the Treasuruer and John Martin is Manager, Treasury Planning of the TNT Group. The views and opinions expressed herein are those of the authors and do not necessarily reflect the views of TNT. Earlier versions of this chapter have been presented at the Third Australasian Finance and Banking Conference at the University of New South Wales on 29–30 November 1990.

The authors would like to thank Sharon Williams and Judy Payne for thier assistanace in the preparation of this chapter for publication.

1. The term "swaps" and "swap derivatives" is used to cover the following types of transaction structures: interest rate swaps; currency swaps; long-term foreign exchange contracts (LTFX); forward-rate agreements (FRAs); interest rate caps, floors and collars; and non-generic transaction structures based on these instruments. For an overview of these instruments and their inter-relationships, see Das (1989), Ch 2–6.

2. The chapter assumes familiarity with basic structural and pricing aspects of swap transactions.

3. For a detailed analysis of new issue arbitrage, see Das (1989), Ch 13.

4. For a detailed discussion of the use of swaps for asset liability management, see Das (1989), Ch 14; Das (1987).

5. It is important to differentiate between various sources of swap arbitrages. Some sources of swap arbitrage derive from tax and regulatory frameworks which because of their structural nature are not eroded/eliminated through the process of exploitation. For a detailed discussion of swap arbitrages, see Das (1989), Ch 7.

6. See Das (1989), Ch 12.

7. For example, see some of the transactions analysed in Das (1989), Ch 17.

8. For a discussion of the concept of *zaitech*, see Yokoi, Kumiko and Hubbard, Philip M., "Zaitech: The Japanese Perspective on Financial Engineering" *Journal of International Securities Markets*, Spring 1988, vol 2, pp 67–72.

9. This represents a temporary or permanent disequilibrium condition arising from a failure of market efficiency. This market inefficiency may result from a number of factors including: restrictions on free capital flows, institutional deficiencies in market structure, the presence of taxes, the imperfect flow of information and/or short-term market frictions, such as supply/demand imbalances.

10. Analytically, the delta and gamma of the debt portfolio with respect to interest rate and currency movements is different to the delta and gamma of the swap portfolio reflecting inherent structural differences between the instruments, in particular their cash flow characteristics.

11. See Das (1989), Ch 17.

12. See Smithson (1987) and Smith (1989).

13. The gain on the swap results from the fact that Company A can enter into a swap whereby it receives 11.0% (the current swap rate) thereby locking in a margin of 2.0% relative to the existing swap where it pays 9.0% pa the floating-rate (six-month Libor) legs under the swap would offset. Typically, the original swap would be cancelled or "bought out" with the counterparty making a payment to Company A representing the present value equivalent of the margin of 2.00% pa.

14. See Das (August 1989).

References

"Corporate Speculators' Loophole or Noose?" *Corporate Finance*, November 1987 pp 17–18.

Das, Satyajit "Utilising Swaps As An Instrument For Dynamic Asset Liability Management " *The Australian Banker*, April 1987, vol 101, no 2, pp 63–68; June 1987, vol 101, no 3, pp 108–114.

Das, Satyajit (1989) *Swap Financing*, Law Book Company Ltd, Sydney; IFR Publishing Ltd, London.

Das, Satyajit "Swap Strategies in the New Climate" *Corporate Finance*, August 1989, pp 12–13.

Goodman, Laurie S, "The Use of Interest Rate Swaps in Managing Corporate Liabilities" *Journal of Applied Corporate Finance*, Winter 1990, pp 35–47.

Ireland, Louise "Getting a Fix with Swaps" *Corporate Finance*, October 1988, pp 39–42

Lee, Peter "Why Investors Are Missing Profits" *Euromoney*, April 1989, pp 56–57.

Smith, Donald J, "The Arithmetic of Financial Engineering" *Journal of Applied Corporate Finance*, Winter 1989, pp 49–58.

Smithson, Charles W, "A Lego Approach to Financial Engineering. An Introduction to Forwards, Futures, Swaps and Options" *Midland Corporate Finance Journal*, Winter 1987, pp 16–28.

Chapter 19: Arrears reset swaps

Gregory E Marposon
Prudential Global Funding, Inc

Libor reset in arrears interest rate swaps were developed by Prudential Global Funding, Inc in the autumn of 1987 to take advantage of the combination of a steep US Treasury yield curve, relatively low short-term US dollar Libor rates and relatively high swap spreads to Treasury's in the aftermath of the US stock market's rapid decline of October 1987. Liability managers could pay six-month Libor minus a significant spread for 1.5 to 10 years by electing to set Libor to be paid for each respective given period at the end of the period rather than the conventional reset two banking days before the start of the floating-rate interest calculation period. For example, interest paid for a February 15 to August 15 calculation period would be set on August 13 and paid August 15 for the preceding period at the prevailing six-month Libor rate. The application of arrears reset swaps extended from domestic US commercial banks to Euromarket issuers during the first quarter of 1988, enabling high quality credits to achieve significant sub-Libor funding when the new issue spreads were too high relative to the swap markets for conventional Libor swaps to achieve aggressive sub-Libor funding targets. The steeper the slope of the yield curve and the shorter the maturity, the greater the Libor-minus spread (roughly 15–20 basis points from two to 10 years).

Arrears swaps caught on quickly in the first quarter of 1988. Swap dealers replicated arrears reset swaps and extended the concept to other forward-rate structures. Prestigious and sophisticated issuers employed arrears asset swaps to borrow several billions of Eurodollar and domestic US dollar funding, including combinations with currency swaps for issuers whose home currency was not US dollars. The standard size of each transaction ranged from $100m to $250m of notional principal. Initially, their reaction was cautious as issuers' exposure to shifts in the shape of the yield curve and the direction of short-term rates was uncertain.[1] In fact, the implicit value of the arrears reset swap is a function of the slope of the yield curve and regarded by critics as a "sleight of hand".[2] However, short-term rates remained relatively low for the remainder of 1988, allowing beneficial first settings in arrears for most payers of the reset. By the first quarter of 1989, 1% monthly increases in US price indices inverted the US dollar yield curve dramatically, enabling Prudential Global Funding to convert these arrears reset swaps profitably to conventional Libor swaps reset in advance of the interest rate payment period and lock-in, or realise, significant gains of 10 to 50 basis points per annum for issuers funding themselves for a range of maturities out to 1998 (10 years). Prudential Global Funding hedged these arrears swaps in conjunction with its aggregate swap portfolio and was consequently indifferent to the inversion.

The success of this structure depended upon liability managers flexible enough to accept the arrears reset for the maturity of the swap and to accept the potential for the yield curve to steepen further against them, although the swaps were conceived at relative maximum positive slopes of the yield curve. Furthermore, funding decision makers able to trade the yield curve and capitalise on the inversion of the yield curve of 1989 and 1990 were able to take their profit from the arrears structure and go back into conventional Libor settings for the remainder of the swap, satisfied with the innovation. We will look at some transactions very similar to those carried out in the first quarter of 1988 and analyse the structures. However, first let us build up a conceptual step-by-step approach to arrears reset swaps by looking at their components: FRAs, forward swap rates, the relationship between arrears and conventional Libor swaps, and the corresponding relationships between par coupon, forward and zero-coupon swap rates. (We will leave out some steps in the derivation, but identify the important steps with numerical examples.)

Eurobond: new issue swap application

Assume the following standard Eurobond issue terms:

Issuer:	AAA European agency
Principal:	$200,000,000
Annual coupon:	9% or $18,000,000 per annum
Maturity:	10 years
Underwriting fees:	1% or $2,000,000
Par swap rate = 9.08% sa =	9.286% annual
Normal cost of borrowing (IRR basis):	9.157%
Add reset in arrears benefit:	0.181%
All-in cost of borrowing:	6-month Libor – 31bp (sub-Libor basis)

Under the terms of a conventional new issue swap the swap dealer agrees to pay the issuer's coupon and underwriting fees (effectively funding the fees at the swap rate) in exchange for the issuer paying a floating rate of Libor reset every six months. To evaluate this numerically, let us use the derived yield curve from 11 February 1988 (see Table 1).

Table 1: Yield curve derivation, 11 February 1988

US$

Maturity	Libor	Treasury yield or equiv	Swap spread	Par coupon swap rate	Zero coupon swap rate	Derived 6-month forward rates
6 months	6.8125	6.91				
1 year	7.1250	7.10				
1.5 years				7.475	7.44	
2 years		7.135	62.5	7.750	7.78	
3 years		7.320	78.0	8.100	8.15	
4 years		7.500	85.0	8.350	8.43	
5 years		7.650	90.0	8.550	8.65	
6 years				8.710	8.83	
7 years		7.950	91.0	8.860	9.02	
8 years				8.930	9.11	
9 years				9.010	9.20	
10 years		8.160	92.0	9.080	9.29	
10.5 years				9.090	9.31	9.54

Accepting the convention that the par fixed swap rate for any maturity is equal to floating Libor flat, we can subtract the cost of borrowing (IRR basis) to the issuer over 10 years, including fees, from the swap rate (9.286% – 9.157% = 0.129%). Use this as an approximate measure of the borrowing cost relative to six-month Libor, excluding compounding and day count adjustments, on an IRR basis. Six-month Libor –12.9bp would not ordinarily be sufficient to achieve the sub-Libor borrowing objective of such a prestigious borrower. However, by combining the Libor reset in arrears structure with the floating rate paid by the issuer and adding the full benefit of the arrears reset (18.1bp), the issuer would pay six-month Libor reset in arrears – 31bp (assuming no profit to the swap dealer).

Alternatively, including the NPV benefit of the arrears reset ($2,419,813) with the Eurobond cash flows (including fees) gives an all-in cost of borrowing of 8.967% annually (IRR basis). Subtracting from the 9.286%, corresponding to Libor flat, gives an approximate all-in cost of borrowing of six-month Libor – 31.9bp. The difference in the approximations (31.9bp vs 31bp) reflects the difference between amortising the NPV of the arrears reset at the IRR to measure the benefit in basis points per annum; rather than correctly amortising over the derived zero-coupon yield curve which gives an accurate value of 18.1bp running for 10 years to the arrears reset structure. (The difference is relatively small owing to the magnitude of the NPV of the arrears benefit relative to the principal.)

Again, this structure was attractive because there was a demand for high credit quality Eurodollar issues while the yield curve was steeply positive and absolute rates relatively high and spreads relatively wide. Furthermore, conventional swap-driven issues were insufficient to achieve the sub-Libor borrowing levels required by prestigious borrowers, hence the innovation's application.

Compound interest

Assume six-month Libor is 8%, giving a semi-annual periodic rate of 4%. Compounded at the same rate for another six-month period would give an annual periodic rate of 8.16% (rather than 8%). (In rate terms, this can be expressed numerically by (1.04 x 0.04 = 1.0816–1.) In fact, 8.16% for one year, paid at the end of the year, would be a zero-coupon rate. Furthermore, the rate we compounded at for the second six months (8%) is the forward rate implied by six-month Libor at 8% and the annual zero-coupon rate for one year at 8.16%.

$$(1 + c)/(1 + a/2) = 1 + b/2$$
$$1.0816/1.04 = 1.04$$

a = spot six-month rate = 8%
b = forward rate = 8%
c = zero-coupon rate = 8.16%

We could not achieve 8.16% if the reinvestment opportunity were not 8% six months forward, unless the one-year Libor or swap rate is traded at 8.16% annually and we choose that over 8% for six months and take our chances for the forward six months.

Spot Libor swaps translate fixed par coupons at positive spreads to US Treasury yields to Libor reset periodically. Zero-coupon curves relate par coupons or periodic floating rates to final interest payments at maturity, reflecting the difference between the present value of a series of fixed interest payments on a given notional principal compounded (ie, reinvested) at six-month Libor. Forward rates correspond to forward Libor payments derived from six-month Libor and a par coupon yield curve and the associated zero-coupon yield curve. The trick is to realise that compounding, whether reinvesting or borrowing, using the zero-coupon yield curve to find forward rates and future values and discounting using the zero-coupon yield curve to find present values can equate par coupon fixed payments, forward Libor payments reset periodically and zero-coupon interest payments at maturity to par, represented numerically in rate terms as 1. We will look at the equation later with zero-coupon rates.

Zero-coupon rates are used in the calculations to eliminate assumptions of funding and reinvestment rate risk in the future. Libor reset in arrears swaps are compared to spot Libor reset swaps to measure their benefit, or cost, depending on the shape of the yield curve. When the yield curve is steeply positive, the Libor reset in arrears is paid minus a spread relative to spot Libor. As the yield curve flattens and inverts, this negative spread can actually be realised and Libor reset in arrears can be converted to conventional Libor resets, and *vice versa*. Libor reset in arrears is a latent yield curve trade on the liability side of the reset payer's balance sheet.

Returning to our numerical example, if we change the annual rate, or zero rate, to 8.5% (steepening the yield curve), the implied forward rate (IFR) would increase to 8.654% (1.0850/1.04 = (1.04327–1) x 2).

Now imagine that we discount this forward rate by the spot rate, or calculate the difference for six months between 8.654% and 8% for an assumed notional principal, let us say $200m. The difference is 663,083.33/1.04 = $637,580 or 63.75bp amortised over one year. This is the source of the benefit of an arrears reset in a Libor reset in arrears swap. Saving 25bp for 10 years on $200m would equal a present value (PV) of $3.375m or 1 + 3/16% of the notional principal — providing the yield curve flattens or inverts sufficiently to actually realise this benefit. This illustrates the attraction of taking the yield curve risk implicit in an arrears reset swap.

Forward rates

A six-month Libor reset in arrears swap for one year looks like two forward FRAs and longer maturities resemble a similar series of combined forward rates. The swap warehouse's portfolio receiving the reset would be long a 6 x 12 FRA and a 12 x 18 FRA in the one-year case. The interest rate swap would normally have an annual fixed-rate payment flowing in the opposite direction.

Reset 1	**Reset 2**	**Fixed rate**
– 6-month rate	– 12-month rate	– 12-month rate
+ 12-month rate	+ 18-month rate	

– indicates a short position
+ indicates a long position

Let us isolate the Libor reset in arrears (floating side) which we will compare to spot Libor resets. In effect we will consider a basis (floating/floating) interest rate swap Libor reset in arrears versus spot Libor. For risk measurement purposes, the 12-month positions cancel and we are left with short six months and long 18 months rate risk. The effective risk profile of the swap is lengthened to 18 months. If the arrears swap is against a fixed rate, the warehouse portfolio also takes on a short 12-month rate position.

Compare a 10-year fixed versus six-month Libor reset in arrears swap with a fixed semi-annual coupon versus six-month (spot reset) Libor for 10 years.

Arrears	**versus**	**Libor swap**
– Fixed-coupon rate (10 years)		– Fixed-coupon rate (10 years)
– 6-month rate at spot date		+ 6 million
+ 12-month rate		
– 10-year rate risk	final period	
+ 10.5-year rate risk	arrears reset	

The combined 10-year and 10.5-year rate risk is equivalent to a forward rate for 10.5 years 10 years forward and represents the final Libor in arrears reset.

Zero-coupon yield curves

Assuming the following yield curve, let us derive the 18-month and 24-month zero rates and generalise this concept to calculate zero rates for 10 years and 10.5 years. Then we can use these rates to find the value and interest rate risk of a 10-year arrears reset swap relative to a normal Libor swap for 10 years. The forward rate for the Libor in arrears payments to be made at maturity in year 10 is given by: (((1 + (Z 10.5)/2) / (1 + (Z 10)/2)) – 1) x 2. In our $200m 10-year case, this six-month forward rate equals 9.54% corresponding to the period from year 10 to 10.5.

PV [(first spot Libor rate – last forward Libor rate reset in arrears) x notional principal] gives an approximation of the PV difference between the arrears reset and conventional spot Libor swaps. Amortising this difference along the full maturity at par swap rates gives the Libor minus spread to be paid versus spot Libor. In this example, it is 18.1bp. This can be used as an effective trading rule. However, the intermediate forward rates (ie, between the first and last payment dates) do not exactly cancel each other out.

Assume that you are receiving the arrears side of a two-year swap. The value of the swap will be:

PV (arrears payments) – PV (normal reset payments)

PV (arrears payments) equals:

$$\frac{6f12}{Z6} + \frac{12f18}{Z12} + \frac{18f24}{Z18} + \frac{24f30}{Z24}$$

where:
xfy = a forward rate determined at the trade date multiplied by the notional principal reset two days before x months and having a term of y–x months; and Zn = a zero rate determined on the trade date for a period of n months.

PV (normal reset payments) equals:

$$\frac{0f6}{Z6} + \frac{6f12}{Z12} + \frac{12f18}{Z18} + \frac{18f24}{Z24}$$

Therefore the value of the swap equals:

$$\frac{6f12}{Z6} + \frac{12f18}{Z12} + \frac{18f24}{Z18} + \frac{24f30}{Z24}$$

minus

$$\frac{0f6}{Z6} + \frac{6f12}{Z12} + \frac{12f18}{Z18} + \frac{18f24}{Z24}$$

simplifying, we get:

$$\frac{6f12-0f6}{Z6} + \frac{12f18-6f12}{Z12} + \frac{18f24-12f18}{Z18} + \frac{24f30-18f24}{Z24}$$

Intuitively, this formula says that the present value of an arrears swap equals the present value of the expected net payments discounted.

Changing each *par swap* coupon rate (or, implied Libor rate) by 1bp, while holding all other *par swap* coupon rates constant at their current market levels and observing the change in present value of the swap will indicate the risk per basis point for a given point along the *swap curve*. To hedge the swap, this calculation should be done for each risk point along the swap curve. An equivalent portfolio of securities would be sold to offset each long risk position and *vice versa* (ie, if a 1bp upward change in the 10-year rate causes a PV loss of $13,000, you would short an amount of 10-year Treasuries that would create a PV gain of $13,000 for a 1bp upward change in the 10-year rate).

Again, the majority of these forward Libor cash flows mitigate each other versus a conventional swap Libor except for the first and last Libor cash flows (we will represent this algebraically in the next section).

To be precise, an actual rate set in the future will most probably be different than a forward rate computed on the trade date. Furthermore, there is no real reason to believe that actual periodic rate settings will continually increase due to the fact that the yield curve was positively sloped on the trade date. But, therein lies the beauty of the arrears swap. The dealer that receives the arrears payment is indifferent to movements in spot, zero and forward rates because he is hedged, and he will continue to adjust his hedges as market conditions warrant. The risk manager who pays the reset receives a hefty payment from the swap dealer, and he has no reason to believe that he will have to give it back at an appropriate zero-coupon rate.

Assume six-month Libor = 6.91% bond equivalent yield (beq), ie, 6.8125% in Libor terms.

Semi-annual (SA) one-year rate:

[(1 + R1) ^ (1/2) – 1] x 2
= [1 + (0.07125 x 365/360)] ^ (1/2) – 1] x 2 = 7.10% (ie, 7.125% in annual Libor terms).

Annual money market rate (actual/360) converted to SA beq basis:

R1.5 = (R1 + R2)/2 = 7.425 SA(beq) interpolated rate for 1.5 years.
(Note: C = R1.5/2 = 0.37125.)

Assume the present value of a market rate swap = par

PV (C + C + 1+C) = 1		
6mth	12mth	18mth
0.5	1.0	1.5

To solve for zero-coupon rate at 18 months (Z1.5):

0.037125/(1 + 6m x ACT/360) + 0.037125/(1 + 12m x ACT/360) + 1.037125/(1 + Z1.5/2) ^ 3 = 1
0.03589 + 0.03462 + 1.037125/(1 + Z1.5/2) ^ 3 = 1

Simplifying and solving for Z1.5 gives 7.44%.

To find the two-year zero-coupon rate, let C = 0.0775/2 = R2.0/2 = 0.03875. Substitute 7.44% for Z1.5 and extend the derivation to find the zero rate for two years (Z2.0).

PV (C + C + C + 1+C) = 1			
6mth	12mth	18mth	24mth
0.5	1.0	1.5	2.0

0.03875/(1 + 6m x ACT/360) + 0.03875/(1 + 12m x ACT/360) + 1.03875/(1 + 0.0744/2) ^ 3 + (1+ 1.03875)/(1 + (Z2.0/2)) ^ 4 = 1
0.03589 + 0.03462 + 1.037125/(1 + Z1.5/2) ^ 3 = 1
0.037456 = 0.036139 + 0.03346 + 1.03875/(1 + Z2.0/2) ^ 4 = 1

Simplifying and solving for Z2.0 gives 7.78%, the two-year zero rate.

Now we will use a computer program to calculate the zero-coupon discount rates for 10 years and 10.5 years in Table 1. With this yield curve, let us go back to comparing Libor reset in arrears swaps to spot Libor resets and calculate the negative spread to Libor and the risk profile of the arrears reset swap.

Comparing the value of a Libor reset in arrears swap with a spot Libor swap

Generalising from our simple reset in arrears example at 8.50% in one year and 8% in six months, we can use the IFR rate given by the zero-coupon discount rates in 10.5 years and 10 years to get a six-month Libor rate 10 years forward. Using our yield curve table, that rate is 9.537%. Again, from the zero-coupon yield curve section:

(((1 + (Z10.5)/2/(1 + (Z10/2) – 1) x 2 =
(((1 + 0.0931/2)/(1 + (0.0929/2)) – 1) x 2 = 9.537%

We can use a short cut approximation to calculate the PV of receiving the arrears payments in an arrears swap relative to a spot Libor swap.

PV (last six-month forward (reset in arrears) rate – six-month spot Libor)/2 x notional principal.

In our example: (9.537% – 6.91%)/200,000,000 = $2,627,000.

Amortising at the 10-year spot fixed Libor spot rate of 9.08% gives roughly 20bp using HP 12C solution. At the start, we said the value was 18bp. The difference results from mismatches in the timing of the forward rates. Since the implied forward cash flows will be discounted using different zero rates (in all but totally flat swap curve environments), the intermediate flows would not cancel out. The more severe the positive or negative slope of the curve, the worse of an approximation this $2,627,000 will provide. Let us look at the cash flows of this reset in arrears swap relative to spot Libor flows to understand this intuitively.

Assume a swap portfolio receives the arrears reset and pays spot Libor (floating) for 10 years:

L = Libor payments	– means pay the cash flow
N = semi-annual period	+ means receive the cash flow

– L0 – L1 – L2 – L3 ... – Ln
+ L1 + L2 + L3 + ... Ln + L(n + 1)

Adding down; Libor resets L1 ... Ln cancel leaving:

– L0 + L(n + 1)

Where: L0 = spot Libor rate or corresponding first spot floating payment; and L(n + 1) = last six-month forward rate reset in arrears cash flows and paid at maturity in (N) years.

This approach only works in a precise manner in flat yield curve environments when all zero-coupon discount rates are equal; otherwise it is a relative approximation.

The corresponding risk profile for receiving the reset would be:

Maturity	Risk ($ per bp increase in rates)	
6 months	(10,008)	Long the spot Libor CF
10.5 years	11,524	Short the implied forward Libor CF
Yield curve risk	21,532	(Absolute value of the sum of six-month and 10.5-year rate risk)

For example, we never pay the first spot Libor setting, leaving us long conceptually, and we never really receive the last Libor reset at year 10.5 which would be similar to a 6 x 12 FRA 10-years forward. The idea is to give this benefit to the reset payer (the customer in this transaction) by hedging these interest rate exposures with Eurodollar futures, 10-year Treasuries or 10-year interest rate swaps. Hedging this risk would be done by selling roughly 400 of some combination of the first and second nearby Eurodollar futures contracts and buying $17.7m 10-year US Treasury notes, assuming a modified duration of 6.5 years given the actual coupon, yield, and maturity of the 10-year notes.

Inversion of the yield curve

By inverting the yield curve from the levels taken from February 1988 to the yield curve actually observed on 15 March 1989, we can go through the exercise of converting the reset in arrears to a spot Libor structure and measure the change in present value or the corresponding spread to a spot Libor swap and evaluate the risk measures.

Table 2: Yield curve change

Maturity	11 Feb 1988	15 March 1989	Change
6-month Libor	6.8125%	10.5625%	+3.7500%
1-year Libor fixed	7.125%	10.9375%	+3.8125%
10.5 year Libor swap rate	9.093%	10.01%	+0.917%
Spread 6 month to 10.5 years	+2.28%	+0.5525%	
Yield curve change			−1.7275%

This inversion of the yield curve by 172.75bp changes the value from Libor –18.1bp reset in arrears to Libor +5.9bp, making the 2,419,813 PV benefit to the receiver of the reset into a benefit to the payer of the reset equal to 746,557. Adding these together gives a positive PV result of $3.2m to the payer of the reset on $200m of notional principal. This illustrates the PV volatility of the reset in arrears structure.

Hedging the yield curve risk to the swap portfolio receiving the reset is necessary to offset the PV change and preserve the risk-free benefit. The combined position of $21,500bp of risk on $200m to the yield curve inverting between six months and 10.5-year swap rates multiplied by 172.75bp equals approximately $3.7m. The difference between the PV change predicted by the risk measures and the actual change in value reflects the sensitivity of the Libor reset in arrears yield curve risk to changes in both the level of rates and shape of the yield curve. The ability to measure accurately, hedge effectively and monitor consistently the yield curve risk and value of the Libor reset in arrears structure are priorities for the swap dealer's warehouse portfolio and to the end user's balance sheet liability management.

Present and future applications of arrears reset swaps

For the arrears reset to work, the curve must be positive and bank liability managers and Eurobond users must be flexible. Flat yield curve environments make arrears resets less appealing to the arrears payer. However, this structure could work in an inverted yield curve environment if the liability manager *received* the reset. The evolution of forward-rate structures, that have come to include six-month Libor reset monthly, have made swap portfolios more flexible and given the investment and liability managers the ability to match the resets of their assets and investments to their funding advantage or existing liability structures. The arrears reset will probably not become a vehicle for speculative trading of the yield curve. However, the complexity of the product's risk combined with its apparent intuitive appeal make it a relatively efficient structure and demonstrate the flexibility swaps and derivative products afford. Arrears swaps were most popular among Korean banks in 1990. Users of the arrears reset will need to be more sophisticated to make more frequent use of the few over-the-counter off-balance-sheet means of trading views on the yield curve. The extension of the Eurodollar futures market to 48 contract months covering four years gives a yield curve hedge with a continuous set of implied forward rates (with limited liquidity). However, beyond four years, only yield curve swaps and forward-rate structures like the arrears reset swap can be used in large size with the efficiency of pricing and hedging afforded by a swap portfolio.

Notes

1. See "Set Libor In Arrears For Cheaper Funding", *Corporate Finance*, April 1988.
2. See "The Merely Cosmetic Value Of Reset Swaps", *Corporate Finance*, September 1988.

Chapter 20: Using spreadlocks

Krishnan Chandrasekhar
World Bank

Swap rates in several currencies are quoted as a spread over the underlying government bond yield for the appropriate maturity. The classic example is US dollars, where the swap rate is made up of two distinct components — a base Treasury yield level and an add-on swap spread. In a normal interest rate swap transaction, the counterparties to the trade agree upon and establish each of the two components of the swap rate at a single point in time, that is, at the time of execution of the swap. A spreadlock is a simple variant of a conventional interest rate swap that enables an end user (or a professional market participant, for that matter) to lock in the two components of the swap rate at different points in time.[1] Specifically, it allows the end user to initially lock in a swap spread and defer setting the base Treasury yield on the fixed-rate side of the swap to a future point in time. The underlying Treasury yield on the swap will have to be established subsequently on or before a specified future date at the election of this counterparty.

It should be noted that a spreadlock is a binding commitment on each of the two counterparties to the transaction, just as an interest rate swap is; the only difference with a spreadlock is that one of the counterparties has the option of determining the time at which the underlying Treasury yield level is set on the swap. Typically, the period over which the spread is locked in can vary from two weeks to three months. Since spreadlocks are most common in US dollars, much of the discussion here will focus on the US dollar interest rate swap market. This should not, however, detract from the general nature of the topic or its applicability to other currencies where swap rates are quoted on a spread basis.

Demand and supply considerations

Demand for spreadlocks

The demand for spreadlocks arises from the fact that the two components of the swap rate do not generally move in tandem. In fact, movements in the swap spread are often negatively correlated with those in the underlying Treasury yield level, as illustrated in Figure 1.

Figure 1: Five-year US Treasury yield and swap rate

5/11/87–29/6/90

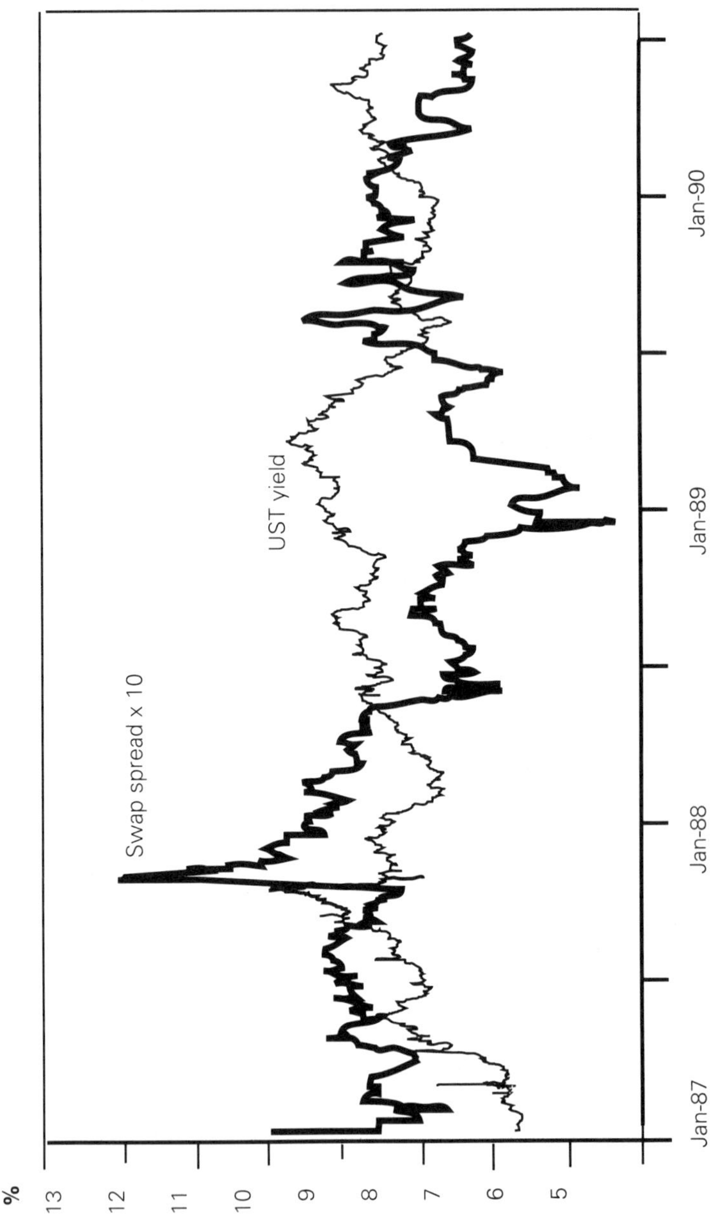

%
13
12
11
10
9
8
7
6
5

Swap spread x 10

UST yield

Jan-87
Jan-88
Jan-89
Jan-90

More often that not, finer swap spreads tend to materialise when the underlying Treasury yield levels are relatively high, and *vice versa*. The level of swap spreads, much like the price of any traded commodity, is determined by demand and supply forces — the demand of "fixed-rate payers" versus the supply of "fixed-rate receivers" in this instance. Swap spreads tend to widen out when there is a strong paying interest in the market as during times of declining Treasury yields, and tend to shrink with any slackening in the demand to pay fixed rate.

A swap counterparty may therefore find it advantageous on occasion to lock in the swap spread and the underlying Treasury yield at different points in time through a spreadlock mechanism. The spreadlock would allow the counterparty to enjoy enhanced timing flexibility with regard to the fixing of the two components of the swap rate in response to specific interest rate and/or spread views. A typical example could be that of a fixed-rate payer which wants to lock in a relatively low swap spread while retaining the flexibility to benefit from an expected future decline in overall yield levels.

To the extent that swap spreads at the medium and long maturities are correlated with new issue spreads of A and AA-rated entities, spreadlocks can also be used by such issuers as a device to lock in attractive spreads in advance of the launch of new issues.

Supply considerations

Whether or not spreadlocks can be made available by market-makers to end users, and the ease with which this can be done depends essentially on the characteristics of the underlying swap and Treasury markets. Firstly, as the name implies, spreadlocks are generally feasible only in markets where swaps are quoted on a spread basis relative to an underlying reference yield level. Spread markets are those where there is a clearly established and well-defined yield curve for government bonds, and where swap market-makers can and do actually buy or sell benchmark government bonds to hedge away the absolute-rate component of the composite swap rate. Only then is it possible to identify and isolate a specific spread component from the underlying yield level. The US dollar and Canadian dollar swap markets are typical spread markets, while the Swiss franc and Deutsche mark swap markets — where there are either no or few clearly discernible benchmark government bonds that can be used for hedging purposes — are absolute-rate markets. For this reason, spreadlocks are not prevalent in currencies such as the Deutsche mark and the Swiss franc. In fact, it is only in US dollars that there is a reasonably well-developed market for spreadlocks. This in turn can be attributed not only to the enormously liquid market for US Treasury securities, but also to the existence of a well-developed repurchase (or, repo) market that can be used for financing short-term purchases of US Treasury securities used to hedge swaps.

Transaction mechanics

Let us now work through a simple numerical example that will help to illustrate the concept of spreadlocks. A corporate end user XYZ is interested in paying fixed and receiving six-month Libor on a five-year interest rate swap for a notional principal amount of US$100m. The market conditions at the time — as of 12 September 1990 — are as follows:

Five–year Treasury note yield*:	8.45%
Five-year bid/offer swap spread:	50/55 basis points

* Yield of current on-the-run five-year Treasury security, the 8-1/2s of 11/95.

In particular, let us assume that XYZ regards the prevailing level of swap spreads — as of 12 September 1990 — to be quite attractive, but is somewhat less sure about the Treasury market where it expects to see a rally over the next four weeks. In this case, XYZ could negotiate a four-week spreadlock on a five-year US dollar interest rate swap transaction where it locks in the prevailing swap spread but retains the flexibility to have the underlying Treasury yield level on the swap established anytime before the close of business on 10 October 1990. Let us say the swap spread that is locked in by XYZ is at the offer level of 55 basis points — we ignore, for the time being, any additional costs that XYZ may be charged for the spreadlock arrangement.

Apart from the fact that the base Treasury rate is left open to be fixed subsequently, the spreadlock is identical in all other respects to a regular spot-start interest rate swap negotiated on the trade date. In particular, it should be noted that XYZ only has the flexibility to choose the time at which the base Treasury yield level is set on the swap; it cannot turn away from the interest rate swap transaction itself. Failure to establish the base Treasury yield level before the expiration of the spreadlock period would cause the five-year Treasury rate prevailing as at the close of business on 10 October 1990 to be set as the default Treasury rate for the interest rate swap transaction under the spreadlock arrangement.

Let us now assume the Treasury market does rally and XYZ decides to have the Treasury rate set on the swap on 26 September 1990 at the then prevailing bid-side yield level of 8.25%. In this case, the fixed rate that XYZ would have to pay over the life of the swap would be 8.80% (that is, 8.25 + 0.55). The effective date and the termination date on the swap would normally be 14 September 1990 and 14 September 1995, respectively, as with any conventional interest rate swap that is executed on 12 September 1990. Depending on the requirements of the end user, coupon payments on the swap could also be structured instead to begin accruing from the day on which the base Treasury yield level is established.

The example cited above is an illustration of an arrangement where the end user XYZ locks in the paying spread on an interest rate swap. The converse arrangement would be one where the end user locks in the receiving spread on an interest rate swap.

Hedge details

The main difference between a spreadlock and an otherwise similar interest rate swap to a swap trader or market-maker is in terms of their slightly different hedging requirements. In the case of conventional interest rate swaps, swap traders hedge away the Treasury component of the swap rate through an offsetting Treasury trade that they undertake at the same time as they price the swap, pending execution of an offsetting swap in the opposite direction. The appropriate benchmark Treasury security would be bought in the case where the trader pays fixed on the swap, and it would be sold in the case where the trader receives fixed on the swap. In the case of spreadlocks, the offsetting Treasury trade would only be undertaken at the time that the underlying Treasury yield level is established on the transaction rather than at the time that the spread is agreed to. In the example described above, XYZ's counterparty would sell the benchmark five-year Treasury security on 26 September 1990 rather than on 12 September 1990 which is what it would have done with a regular interest rate swap.

Pricing of spreadlocks

The cost of a spreadlock, if any, is typically reflected in the form of an incremental spread that is added to the spread for a comparable plain vanilla swap, and can be traced to the costs and risks that arise from the slightly different hedge requirements on the spreadlock as described above.

Figure 2 provides a schematic illustration of the market-maker's cash flows for a conventional interest rate swap transaction, where it receives fixed against paying six-month Libor (Step 1), and also for the subsequent hedging/offsetting transactions. The Treasury hedge in this case is one in which the market-maker sells short, and borrows the appropriate benchmark Treasury security against cash collateral in the repo market (Step 2), pending execution of an offsetting floating-to-fixed swap (Step 3). At the time the offsetting floating-to-fixed swap is executed, the market-maker would lift off the Treasury hedge (Step 4), leaving itself with a net cash flow equal to $(s_1 - s_2)$, being just the difference between the receiving and paying swap spreads.

Figure 3 provides a similar illustration of the market-maker's cash flows in the case of a spreadlock, including that for the subsequent offsetting/hedging transactions. It is assumed that the spreadlock (Step 1) is followed by an offsetting floating-to-fixed swap as in the previous instance

(Step 2), which in turn is hedged through a purchase of Treasury securities financed in the repo market (Step 3). The net cash flow position on the hedged spreadlock *until the time the base Treasury rate is established on the transaction* is then $(s_1 - s_2) + (T_0 - R)$, where the second term in parenthesis is the carry on the Treasury security, being the difference between T_0 (the base Treasury yield that is yet to be determined) and R (the overnight repo rate). When the base rate is established on the spreadlock, the market-maker would close out the Treasury hedge (Step 4), leaving itself with a final net cash flow position equal to $(s_1 - s_2)$ which is the same as that for the conventional interest rate swap considered above.

Figure 2: Cash flows for a conventional interest rate swap*

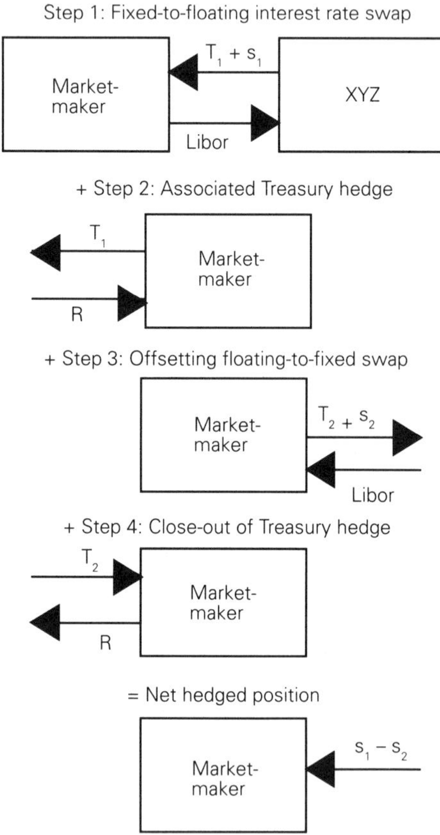

*T_1, T_2 : respective base Treasury yield levels on receiving and paying swaps; s_1, s_2 : respective spreads on receiving and paying swaps; R : overnight repo rate (this is assumed to remain unchanged between Steps 2 and 4).

Figure 3: Cash flows for a spreadlock*

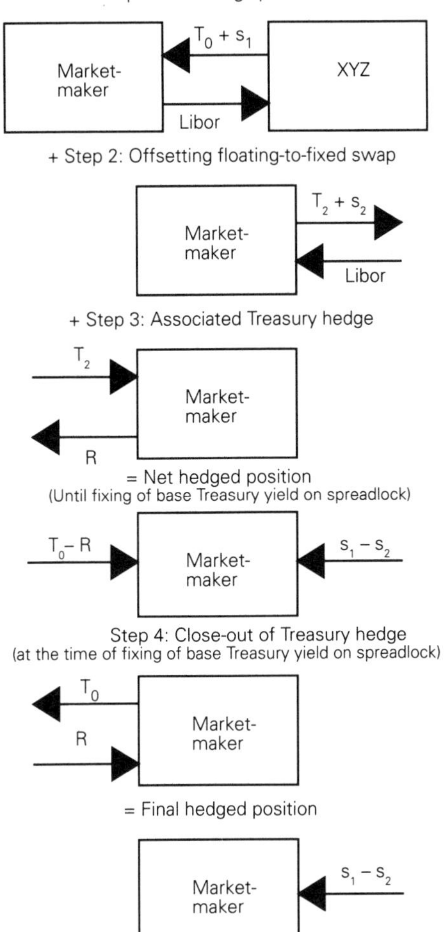

*T_0 : base Treasury yield level on receiving spreadlock determined in Step 4; T_2 : base Treasury yield level on paying swap.

As far as the market-maker is concerned, the effective difference in the value of cash flows between a spreadlock and a conventional interest rate swap is then the cumulative carry on the Treasury security until the time that the base rate is fixed on the transaction. In a positively-sloped yield curve environment in which the repo rate is lower than the yield on the Treasury security, the carry would be positive and would work in the market-maker's favour.

However, the precise value of the carry benefit will only be known ex-post. The market-maker is exposed to changes in the repo rate until the time the spreadlock is activated, and an increase in repo rates resulting from an inversion in the yield curve could still result in a cumulative negative carry for the spreadlock period. Also, the market-maker faces uncertainty as to the time at which the spreadlock will be exercised (from which point the carry will cease to accrue), since this will be at the discretion of the end user. Given these financial risks that the market-maker is subject to, it is not common for any of the carry benefit to be passed on to the end user even in a positively-sloped yield curve environment. At best, pay-side spreadlocks that have relatively short exercise periods may cost the end user nothing extra compared to a conventional swap. Spreadlocks with longer exercise periods may actually cost the end user a few basis points depending on the market-maker's views for repo rates during the spreadlock period.

If the yield curve is inverted and the repo rate exceeds the Treasury yield, the carry would be negative and the market-maker would charge the difference to the end user as a spreadlock fee in addition to any other charge that may be necessary to cover the risk of a further inversion in the yield curve. Again, the actual carry cost would only be known ex-post. The longer the time interval before the base Treasury yield is established on the transaction, the higher the carry cost. The market-maker would normally be inclined to price the transaction conservatively on the basis of an assumption that the spreadlock may only be exercised at the end of the spreadlock period. Alternatively, the cost for the spreadlock can be negotiated as a progressive incremental cost for each week that the Treasury rate fixing is deferred under the spreadlock arrangement. The advantage with this alternative is that the end user will only have to pay for the actual length of the deferred period rather than for the entire spreadlock period.

The incremental cost of a spreadlock where the market-maker agrees to pay fixed at a pre-determined spread would be the mirror image of the cost in the above case where the market-maker agrees to receive fixed. An end user may not have to pay anything extra for a receive-side spreadlock (with a relatively short exercise period) in an inverted yield curve environment; on the other hand, such a spreadlock may entail significant costs when the yield curve is positively sloped and the carry is positive. The exact level at which the facility is priced would depend again on the market-maker's views for repo rates during the spreadlock period, including, in particular, the potential for the underlying Treasury security to "go on special" during the spreadlock period, as would happen often before an auction of a new security at the particular maturity.[2]

Treasury rollover

The underlying Treasury security for determination of the base rate in respect of a spreadlock is the prevailing on-the-run Treasury security as at the time the spread is locked in. A Treasury auction prior to the date of exercise of the spreadlock would result in the emergence of a new on-the-run or benchmark security. New interest rate swaps executed after the auction date would all generally be priced off this new benchmark. In contrast, interest rate swaps resulting from the exercise of spreadlocks entered into before the auction date will be priced off the old security, unless specifically provided for otherwise.

Forfeiture of benchmark status by the old security after the auction date will generally cause it to be traded at an increasing price discount (or yield premium) to the new benchmark with the passage of time. An end user who has locked in a paying spread under a spreadlock may consequently find itself exposed to an adverse widening yield differential between the old and new benchmark securities, if the spreadlock is still outstanding long after the auction date. The fixed-rate payer can protect itself against this risk by requiring that the reference security for all rate fixings done after an auction date be the new benchmark. This rollover provision in the spreadlock contract can cost anywhere between an extra 2–4bp for the end user. A fixed-rate receiver can expect to have a similar rebate in cost if a rollover provision is included in the spreadlock contract.

Variation on a theme

It has become increasingly common in the past few years for capital market issuers to use deferred-rate setting arrangements in connection with new issues, which are sometimes referred to as spreadlocks as well. These arrangements allow issuers to lock in the new issuance spread on a borrowing, while permitting them to have an effective all-in cost on the borrowing that is based on the Treasury yield prevailing at one or more subsequent points in time.

Conclusion

A spreadlock is a convenient mechanism that allows end users of interest rate swaps to lock in the two components of the swap rate — the base Treasury yield level and the swap spread — at different points in time. This flexibility can be valuable since swap spreads generally tend to widen during Treasury rallies and narrow during setbacks in the Treasury market. The market for spreadlocks is well established in US dollars. Transactions in non-dollar currencies are, however, few and far between since many of these are not true "spread" markets. The incremental cost of a spreadlock as compared to a conventional interest rate swap would depend on the expected carry on the

Treasury security for the spreadlock period. Depending on the shape of the yield curve at the time as well as the market-maker's expectations for the future, this cost can vary significantly.

Notes

The opinions and conclusions expressed in this chapter are entirely those of the author and should not be attributed in any manner to the World Bank, to its affiliated organisations, or to members of its board of executive directors or the countries they represent.

1. Spreadlocks are not particularly common in the professional market though. They are used mainly by end users.

2. It is also possible to visualise the incremental cost of a spreadlock as the cost of writing a complex financial option on the repo rate or the carry on the relevant Treasury security. The option is complex because the timing of the exercise would be a function of movements in the underlying Treasury yield level, while the pay-off itself would be a function of the carry on the underlying security. At any rate, since it would be extremely difficult to hedge such an option in practice, spreadlocks are rarely ever priced on this basis.

Chapter 21: Variations on conventional swap structures — swap/option combinations

Colin McKeith and Jim L'Estrange[1]
Citibank Limited, Sydney

The long-dated derivatives business in the four primary markets (foreign exchange, interest rate, commodity and equity) began in the early 1980s and has since developed into a mature business. A key feature of more recent times is the linking up of derivative products with the financing and investment needs of borrowers and investors. Principally it has been the demand for solutions and flexibility that has lead the market to provide a greater variety of option products and applications.

This chapter focuses on one area of derivatives, the interest rate swap/option combinations, and will specifically examine the product, the commercial rationale behind it, pricing dynamics and variations on the basic concept.

The combination of the two product ranges of swaps and options has created a whole new set of terms and jargon. Effectively, they link together three plain vanilla products to provide the flexibility of cover that has been demanded by the market and in some cases to satisfy the need for innovation that is both market driven and bank originated.

The concertina swap

During the second part of the 1980s, especially after the crash of 1987, rapid changes in Australian interest rates were prevalent. Governments were continuing to use monetary policy to achieve their economic objectives. One of the results was that Australian interest rates were dominated by high short-term rates and lower long-term rates, commonly called an inverse yield curve. One of the consequences of this inverse curve was that Australian companies found that their floating cost of funds was well above budget expectations and that they needed to be flexible in their liability management.

The concertina swap was developed to enable the active interest rate exposure manager to exchange the value of one swap transaction for another swap transaction. Effectively, and most practically, the treasurer can adjust exposures to match changes in expectations by using the value of swaps currently on the corporation's books. If the value of swap A equals the value of swap B then the cash flow can be exchanged — a net present value swap — which will entail the adjustment of one or more of the variables of the swap deal. The variables of each transaction are simply the rate, the maturity and the volume.

The concertina swap proved to be a most effective risk management tool in the inverse yield curve environment. It effectively allowed the liability manager to change an existing swap to protect his funding cost.

Commercial rationale

Company XYZ has covered $50m of its $500m debt for six years at a time when interest rates were historically low and the yield curve flat. Over time, interest rates rose and the existing yield curve became inverse. Although the swap was in-the-money, XYZ was now funding at a higher rate on the majority of its debt.

Current position (Position A)

Total borrowings:	$500,000,000
Floating:	$450,000,000
Fixed (interest rate swap)	$50,000,000
(12% sa, six years remaining)	
Current six-month bills:	17%
Average cost of funds:	16.50% pa

The underlying rationale for the initial use of the concertina was the rapid movement in the Australian interest rate structure in which the yield curve moved up in yield by approximately 4%–6%. While this meant that any swap where the customer paid fixed was in-the-money, it created the major problem that, in many cases, too small a proportion of debt had been covered. The problem was thus to "create" the extra cover but not at the currently high prevailing interest rate.

The concertina swap solved this problem by challenging the initial premise of the interest rate swap, that is, that a swap is an agreement to exchange a nominated cash flow, on a nominated date at a nominated rate for a nominated maturity.

The current scenario is that six-month rates have soared to 17%, the six-year swap rate has also risen but at a reduced rate. XYZ has budgeted for a rate (see Figure 1) of 15% and has many alternative strategies to achieve its 15% hurdle: it could simply swap the balance of $450m floating debt to fixed at the current swap rate of 14% and achieve the targeted level.The company's opinion, however, is that tight monetary policy will be temporary and that locking its total debt away at historically high levels for a long period would not be prudent and thus not a genuine alternative.

The company decides to do a concertina swap and use the value available in its six-year swap, now 2% in-the-money. By using the net present value (NPV) on its existing swap, XYZ can increase the volume swapped to reduce its current borrowing cost for, say, one or two years. The net result is that the overall cost of funds of Company XYZ has been covered due to the higher volume covered at an aggressive rate albeit for a shorter maturity.

Table 1 shows what volume and maturity the company can achieve by doing a concertina swap and using its six-year swap position and the rates currently available.

Figure 1: Current yield curve

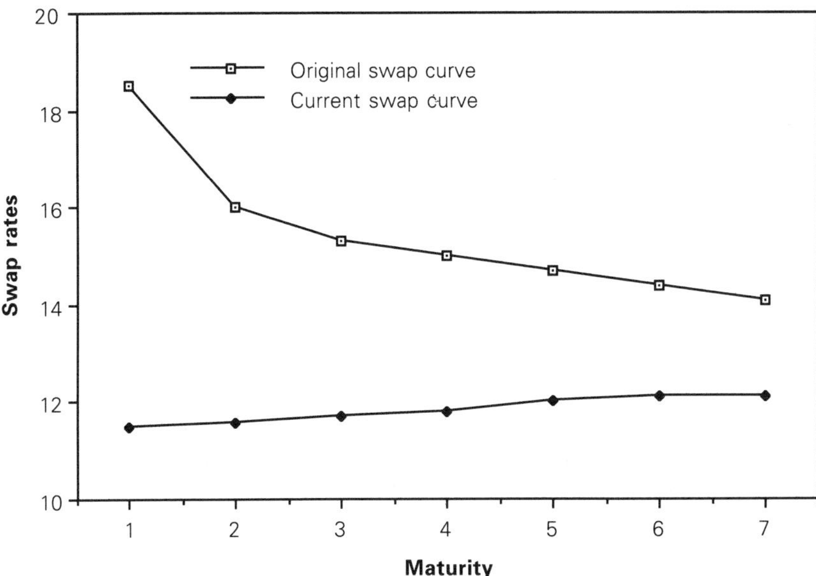

As can be seen from the matrix, by shortening the six-year swap Company XYZ has a variety of options available to reduce its current borrowing cost. The company's decision is based upon its own priorities of its budget and expectations of future changes in interest rates.

Table 1: Swap matrix

Semi-annual rate	1 year	2 years
15%	445,401,408	
14%	222,700,704	237,142,806
13%	148,467,136	118,571,403
12%	111,350,352	79,047,602

New position (Position B)
(A six-year swap becoming a two-year swap)

Total borrowings:	$500,000,000
Volume floating:	$381,428,597
Volume fixed:	$118,571,403
Current bills:	17%
Current cost of funds:	16.05%
New maturity:	2 years

This creates a benefit of 0.45% on Company XYZ's original position.

Variations

It is also possible to "stretch" a transaction, that is, to extend the maturity of a deal and either adjust the rate or the volume so that the two deals are of equal value.

In relation to the example, if rates were to fall then Company XYZ could concertina the other way by pushing the maturity out and re-adjusting the volume/rate to suit its view and exposure management strategy.

Summary

The major users of the concertina are liability managers who usually have a higher proportion of floating debt than fixed debt and who, due to market conditions (such as an inverse yield curve environment) have a rising cost of funds.

The concertina family of products heightens the awareness that the major components of the plain variable swap, the volume, the maturity and the rate, are adjustable and adds a totally new dimension to the interest rate swap transaction.

Superfloater swaps

The superfloater is a swap where the customer pays fixed and receives floating and at the same time sets upper and lower strike rates whereby they can leverage their cover.

For example, it is possible to set the upper strike so that the floating yield on the roll dates will move at a predetermined ratio. That is, for each point that the bank bill increases above the upper strike the counterparty will receive the benefit of the ratio, effectively lowering the overall cost of funds.

Alternatively, in the event that the bank bill falls below the lower strike, the floating rate will fall at a predetermined ratio, effectively raising the cost of funds compared to the floating rate.

The superfloater provides the necessary fixed-rate protection plus the ability to significantly benefit from any increases in short-term floating rates. For those who are bearish on short-term rates, it provides a no-cost opportunity to maximise their opportunities.

Commercial rationale

Maturity:	2 years
Swap rate:	16% quarterly, XYZ pays fixed

Company XYZ is an active manager of its interest rate exposure and has taken the view that short-term interest rates are on the increase. It decides to hedge its total floating borrowing with a superfloater swap, enhancing its view on an increase in short-term rates.

The company enters into the following superfloater transaction, for two years at 16.00% with predetermined rates of:

Upper strike:	18.35%
Multiplier:	2
Lower strike:	14%
Multiplier:	1.7

The multiplier is the number of times the difference between the strike rate and the floating rate is multiplied above and below the levels of the strikes.

Three scenarios are shown below:

(i)	Bank bill rate	=	19.35%
	Floating payment to customer		
	18.35% + 2 x (18.35% – 19.35%)	=	2.00%
	Cost of funds (16.00% – 2.00%)	=	14.00%
(ii)	Bank bill rate between 18.35% and 14.00%		
	Floating payment to customer is the bank bill rate		
(iii)	Bank bill rate	=	13.00%
	Payment by customer		
	1.7 x (14.00% – 13.00%)	=	1.7%
	Cost of funds (16.00% + 1.70%)	=	17.70%

The super floater rate and the bank bill rates and the effective fixed rates are compared in Figure 2.

Figure 2: Super floater — pay-off diagram

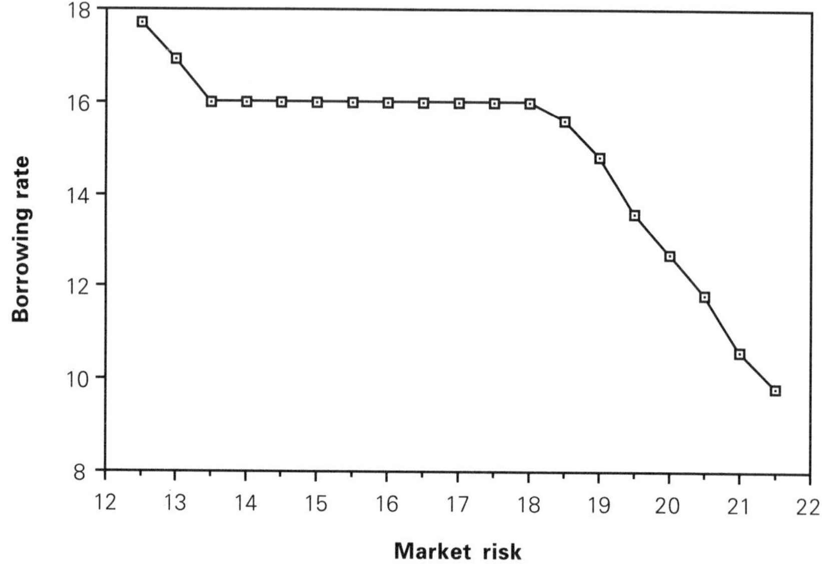

Summary

The superfloater is a combination of a plain vanilla swap and an interest rate option where the client both buys and sells the relevant option.

It is generally used by liability managers who are prepared to see it as consistent with their original decision and a method of being "more correct" whilst creating little downside. More recently investors have begun to use the strategy along the same basis.

Dual coupon swap

The development of products is a direct correlation to the sophistication of the market and the end user or, simply stated, if the product is too complicated, irrespective of the benefits, it will not be used. The dual coupon swap provides the simplicity and sophistication that highlights the combination of swap and option strategies.

Product description

The dual coupon swap is an interest rate swap where the coupon on each coupon date is reduced in consideration for interest being paid either in US dollars or Australian dollars at a predetermined exchange rate. (The exchange rate can be any two currencies.) The product levers of the strength of FX options by embedding an option for the coupon value on the coupon date and adjusts the swap rates to allow for the benefit of the premium. The dual coupon swap is the combination of a plain vanilla swap and a flat rate option (par option) over the complete coupon dates of the swap.

The dual coupon swap is a most effective management tool for those companies which have debt and foreign currency exposures and which can take advantage of the high interest rate differential. For example,, Australian companies with Australian dollar debt and US dollar receivables have been prolific users of this strategy.

Figure 3: A dual coupon swap

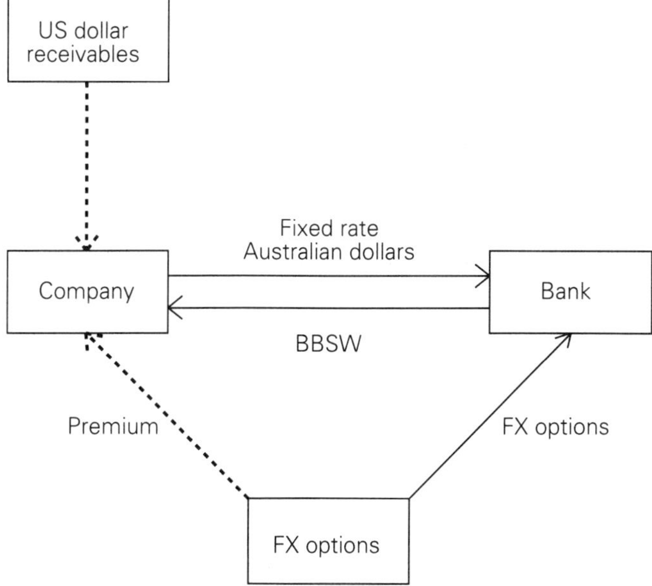

Commercial rationale

The dual coupon swap is effective as an interest rate management tool as it reduces the cost of fixing debt as well as providing a foreign exchange option for receivables on the coupon dates for the amount of the coupon only, ie, the Australian exporter is a natural buyer of Australian dollars.

Embedded Australian dollar put option/US dollar call options

Company ABC has floating Australian dollar debt which it intends to swap into fixed for two years. It does an Australian dollar interest rate swap in which it embeds an Australian dollar put/US dollar call option.

Volume:	A$50,000,000
Start date:	March 1990
Maturity date:	March 1992
Coupon:	13.20% (quarterly) (market swap 14.00%)
FX index:	0.7200 – (current spot 0.7650)

If, two business days before the settlement date, the spot Australian dollar/US dollar exchange rate is:

(i) > 0.7200 A$50,000,000 $\times \frac{13.20}{100} \times \frac{90}{365}$

Under the swap, ABC pays: A$1,627,397.26

The settlement is paid in Australian dollars as normal. The option that ABC has granted is not exercised as the exchange rate is above the predetermined trigger of 0.7200. Any US dollar receivable would need to be sold at the governing exchange rate.

(ii) < 0.79001 A$50,000,000 $\times \frac{13.20}{100} \times \frac{70}{365}$

ABC is committed to pay A$1,627,397.26. However, the option is exercised so that this fixed amount is to be settled in US dollars, ie, 0.7200, thus, $1,171,726.03. This amount is serviced by the US dollar receivables. Company ABC has locked into the purchase of Australian dollars at 0.7200 on the amount of the coupon and thus has an opportunity loss to the level of the

Australian dollar if it is under 0.7200. It is important to remember that in this example the option was originally written 450 basis points out-of-the-money.

Company ABC receives: 90-day BBSW

The settlement of BBSW continues irrespective of the changing currency settlement on the fixed leg. It is always paid in Australian dollars and settlement is as for a normal interest rate swap.

The dual coupon swap is particularly attractive in Australian dollars as it uses the high interest rate differential which allows the writer of the put option to set an aggressive strike level and earn an excellent premium which can be used to adjust the interest coupon.

Variations

It is possible to use the dual coupon swap on non-Australian dollar debt such as US dollar debt where the company has no receivable to service the debt and has a currency exposure on the coupon amount due and on the principal at maturity. On the coupon dates, therefore, the company is a seller of Australian dollars.

If Company XYZ decides to fix the US dollar debt for two years, it can do a dual coupon swap in which it embeds an Australian dollar call/US dollar put option.

Volume:	US$50,000,000
Start date:	March 1990
Maturity date:	March 1992
Coupon:	7.99% (market rate 8.12)
FX index:	0.7600 (market rate 0.7600)

If two business days before the settlement date, the spot Australian dollar/US dollar rate is:

(i) $> 0.7600 \text{ US\$}50{,}000{,}000 \times \frac{7.99}{100} \times \frac{180}{360}$

XYZ is due to pay US$1,997,500. However, the option is exercised so that this settlement is due in the equivalent Australian dollars at the predetermined index — A$2,628,289.47. This would be serviced by underlying Australian dollars and would not create a new exposure.

(ii) $< 0.7600\ \text{US\$}50{,}000{,}000 \times \frac{7.99}{100} \times \frac{180}{360}$

XYZ would pay $1,997,500 as per a usual swap settlement for the option to settle in Australian dollars would not be exercised. XYZ continues to receive the settlement of Libor irrespective of the changing settlement on the fixed rate, eg, it is always paid in US dollars as per a normal interest rate swap.

Generally, this deal is not as prevalent as the original dual coupon swap since the premium earned on the embedded option and thus the discount given on the interest rate swap to the market rate is not attractive.

The user of the dual coupon generally continues to be the Australian exporter with Australian dollar-denominated debt.

Notes

1. Colin McKeith and Jim L'Estrange are Deputy Treasurers at Citibank (Aust) Ltd. The views and opinions expressed are those of the authors and do not necessarily reflect the view of Citibank.

2. Pricing

Finding this present value of an annuity, eg, PV of 14%–12% for the six years.

Formula $\frac{(R_2 - R_1)}{2} \times P \frac{(1 - V^n)}{i}$

where

$V = \frac{1}{1 + i}$

$i = 14.00\%$ sa

$n = 12$

$P = 50{,}000{,}000$

$R_1 = 12\%$ sa

$R_2 = 14\%$ sa

$$PV = \frac{(14 - 12) \times 50{,}000{,}000}{200} \times \frac{(1 - V^{12})}{14/200} = \$3{,}971{,}343.15$$

$$V = \frac{1}{1 + 14/200} = 0.934579$$

To structure a new deal for, say, one year at 14% semi-annually, when the market rate for one year is 16.00% semi-annually, on a principal sufficient to generate a PV of \$3.97m, we proceed as follows:

Let

r_m = the market rate for the new maturity

r_d = the desired rate for the new maturity

i = rm/2 is the *effective* market rate for each semi-annual period

$$v = \frac{1}{1+i}$$

n = number of semi periods in the new maturity = 2

PV = present value of original deal = \$3.971m

x = volume of new deal required at rate r_d

Then, each semi-annual period the new deal is in the money by

$$X \times (r_m - r_d) / 2$$

and thus using the annuity formula:

$$PV = X \times \frac{(r_m - r_d)}{2} \times \frac{(1 - v^n)}{i}$$

$$SO = \frac{2 \times (PV) \times i}{(r_m - r_d) \times (1 - v^n)}$$

Putting

PV = 3,971,343.15, r_m = 0.16, r_d = 0.14, i = 0.08

n = 2, v = 1/1 + 0.08

gives

x = \$222,700,704.30

Chapter 22: Oil and commodity swaps

Satyajit Das[1]
TNT Group

The market for commodity swaps has grown significantly since its emergence in 1986. The advantages to both commodity users and producers have allowed the market to grow and to extend its coverage to a wide variety of both hard and soft commodities, although activity has been concentrated on oil, oil products and base metals.

The term "commodity swap" refers to a special class of financial exchange transactions in which counterparties agree to exchange cash flows related to commodity prices with the objective of managing commodity price risks. The term typically designates a wide range of transaction structures, including fixed-for-floating commodity price swaps, commodity price-for-interest swaps, and extensions thereof.

The development of commodity swaps reflects increasing focus on the management of commodity price risk. Major commodity markets have, over recent times, experienced considerable price volatility. Price stabilisation attempts have generally been unsuccessful at least in bringing long-term price stability to commodity markets. A wide range of products have evolved in response to the requirements of commodity producers and users to transfer and manage the risks inherent in commodity price movements.

This chapter provides an introduction to commodity swaps as a special class of financial exchange transactions. *Section 1* outlines the basic concept and structure/mechanics of commodity swaps. *Section 2* examines the pricing of commodity swaps from both a theoretical and market perspective. *Section 3* examines the institutional structure of the commodity swap market including an examination of its history, rationale, market participants, regulatory considerations and future outlook.[2]

(1) Commodity swaps — structure and mechanics

There are two basic types of commodity swaps: (1) fixed-for-floating commodity price swaps; and (2) commodity price-for-interest swaps.

The majority of activity relates to fixed-for-floating commodity price swaps. There are also a number of variations on these generic structures, in addition to a substantial market in over-the-counter (OTC) options on commodities, including commodity price caps, floors and other derivative products.[3]

Fixed-for-floating commodity price swaps

A fixed-for-floating commodity price swap is an agreement whereby an end user (producer) fixes the purchase (sale) price of its commodity relative to an agreed established market pricing benchmark for the commodity for an agreed (usually extended) period of time.

This type of agreement enables both producer and user to fix the price of the commodity.

Figure 1 sets out in diagrammatic form the basic structure of a fixed-for-floating commodity price swap. In the example the commodity used is oil. Table 1 sets out the underlying transaction cash flows.

Figure 1: Fixed-for-floating oil price swap — cash flows

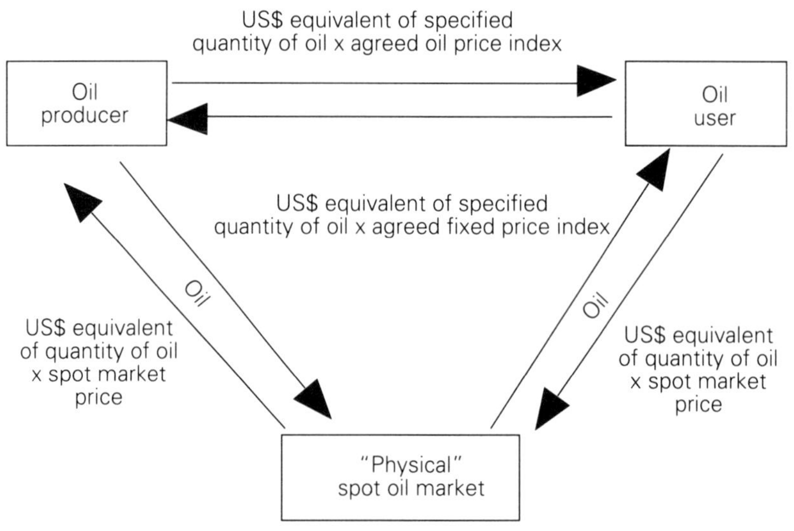

"Hypothetical" terms

The terms of the above swap are:

Specified quantity of oil	—	2,000m
Agreed fixed-price index	—	US$25/barrel
Agreed oil price index	—	West Texas Intermediate (WTI) crude oil
Maturity	—	three years
Settlement basis	—	cash settlement based on spot WTI price semi-annually

Table 1: Fixed-for-floating oil price swap — cash flows

Year	WTI price (US$1/barrel)	Amount received from spot oil transaction (US$)	Commodity swap Receipts (US$)	Payments (US$)	Net cash flow (US$)
Oil producer					
0.5	WTI	+(1m x WTI)	+ (1m x US$25)	– (1m x WTI)	+ (1m x US$25m)
1.0	WTI	+(1m x WTI)	+ (1m x US$25)	– (1m x WTI)	+ (1m x US$25m)
1.5	WTI	+(1m x WTI)	+ (1m x US$25)	– (1m x WTI)	+ (1m x US$25m)
2.0	WTI	+(1m x WTI)	+ (1m x US$25)	– (1m x WTI)	+ (1m x US$25m)
2.5	WTI	+(1m x WTI)	+ (1m x US$25)	– (1m x WTI)	+ (1m x US$25m)
3.0	WTI	+(1m x WTI)	+ (1m x US$25)	– (1m x WTI)	+ (1m x US$25m)
Oil user					
0.5	WTI	– (1m x WTI)	+ (1m x US$25)	– (1m x WTI)	– (1m x US$25m)
1.0	WTI	– (1m x WTI)	+ (1m x US$25)	– (1m x WTI)	– (1m x US$25m)
1.5	WTI	– (1m x WTI)	+ (1m x US$25)	– (1m x WTI)	– (1m x US$25m)
2.0	WTI	– (1m x WTI)	+ (1m x US$25)	– (1m x WTI)	– (1m x US$25m)
2.5	WTI	– (1m x WTI)	+ (1m x US$25)	– (1m x WTI)	– (1m x US$25m)
3.0	WTI	– (1m x WTI)	+ (1m x US$25)	– (1m x WTI)	– (1m x US$25m)

1. Positive signs refer to cash inflows; negative signs refer to cash outflows.
2. WTI is the spot price (US$/barrel) for WTI crude at the specific point in time, ie, WTI price at year 0.5 etc (typically, an average of the price over the period would be used).
3. The oil producer is assumed to undertake a spot transaction selling 1m barrels of oil at six monthly intervals at the prevailing WTI spot market price.
4. The oil user is assumed to purchase 1m barrels of oil at six monthly intervals at the prevailing WTI spot market price.
5. The commodity swap flows are calculated with reference to the terms specified in Figure 1 whereby: the oil producer (user) pays (receives) the US dollar equivalent of 1m barrels at the WTI crude price (the agreed price index) against receipt (payment) of the US dollar equivalent of 1m barrels at US$25/barrel (the agreed fixed price).
6. The net cash flows are the accumulation of the various cash flows incurred at that specific point in time.

In the example of Figure 1, in order to manage its exposure to oil price fluctuations, an oil producer enters into an oil price swap to "lock-in" a fixed price for West Texas Intermediate (WTI) crude oil. The opposite side of this oil price swap is taken by an oil user which seeks, similarly, to lock in a fixed price for its oil purchases over an identical period.

Under the terms of the oil price swap, the oil producer and oil user agree to exchange cash flows (typically denominated in US dollars) whereby the oil producer receives US$25 per barrel on one million barrels and agrees to pay to its counterparty the floating oil price index (agreed to be the WTI Price Index) on an identical number of barrels. The counterparties agree on cash settlement based on spot WTI prices on a semi-annual basis.

As set out in Table 1, the transaction effectively allows both the oil producer and oil user to lock in a price of US$25 per barrel on one million barrels of oil priced off the WTI Index every six months (or two million annual production or purchase).

Under the terms of the swap, however, both the oil producer and the oil user continue to operate normally in the spot oil market. For example, the oil producer continues to produce oil normally and sell it into the spot oil physical market at *current market prices*. In this example, it is assumed these sales take place at six monthly intervals (a swap can be tailored to cover staggered sales over the six-month period by using an average settlement mechanism — see below). Similarly, the oil user continues to purchase its oil requirement from the spot market at prevailing market prices. However, the US dollar receipts and payments under the oil price swap have the effect of fixing the purchase or sale of oil to allow both producer and user to achieve guaranteed prices.

Figure 2 shows the actual settlement mechanics on one specific settlement date. The settlement mechanism allows both producer and user to achieve a guaranteed price, as agreed, of US$25/barrel. The final price achieved by producer and user is subject to basis risk (see discussion below) depending on the degree of correlation between the hedge or commodity swap index used and the pricing basis of the physical market transaction.

A numbre of essential features of the fixed-for-floating commodity price swap structure should be noted. Firstly, the commodity price swap is purely financial, that is, there is no physical exchange of commodities between the counterparties. The transaction assumes that both parties continue normally to operate in the spot market for the commodity, to purchase or sell the required amount of oil or other commodity being swapped. The commodity price swap itself is totally independent of these underlying physical transactions and the purchaser or seller in the spot transaction does not enter into contractual relationships with the commodity swap counterparty and, in fact, would not necessarily be aware that the commodity swap had been undertaken.

Next, it should be noted that the financial nature of the transaction allows the "decoupling" of the acquisition of the commodity with the setting of the effective price at which the transaction is undertaken (at least, after the commodity swap payments are factored into the overall transaction). This unbundling of the price setting and the physical transaction holds benefits and drawbacks. A major advantage is the ability to time pricing decision to exploit market cycles in a manner which is both flexible and retains confidentiality from physical suppliers. The major disadvantage is that the price at which the physical transaction is undertaken is assumed to be identical to the level of the agreed commodity price index against which settlement is determined (this problem of basis risk is discussed below).

Thirdly, the financial settlement undertaken is on a net basis only. The amounts owed to and by each counterparty are netted as at each settlement date with the party owing the greater amount paying the difference to the other. There are no intermediate cash flows and the commodity price swap would not generally be subject to any margin or mark-to-market requirement.

Moreover, the commodity price swap structure requires the counterparties to agree *precisely* on several aspects of the transaction, including the essential features described below.

Figure 2: Fixed-for-floating oil price swap

Settlement mechanics

Assume that on the first settlement date of the transaction set out in Figure 1 and Table 1, the agreed oil price index (WTI crude) is above (US$26.55) or below (US$17.37) the fixed price agreed. The net settlement amount would be calculated as follows:

Case (in US$)	**(1)**	**(2)**
WTI price (US$/barrel)	26.55	17.37
US$ equivalent of 1m barrels at US$25/barrel	25;000,000	25,000,000
US$ equivalent of 1m barrels at current WTI price	26,550,000	17,370,000
Net settlement amount	(1,550,000)	7,630,000

In case (1) (the WTI index is above the agreed fixed price), the oil producer pays the net settlement sum of US$1,550,000 to the oil user. In case (2) (the WTI index is below the agreed fixed price), the oil producer receives from the oil user the net settlement sum of US$7,630,000.

Continued:

The impact of the settlement payments on the total overall position of the counterparties is summarised below:

Case (in US$)	**(1)**	**(2)**
WTI price (US$/barrel)	26.55	17.37
Oil producer	**US$**	**US$**
Physical transaction (US$ proceeds of sale of 1m barrels at *current* WTI price)	26,550,000	17,370,000
Oil price swap settlement	(1,550,000)	7,630,000
Net receipt	25,000,000	25,000,000
Net effect: oil producer receives	US$25/barrel	US$25/barrel
Oil user		
Physical transaction (US$ cost of purchase of 1m barrels at *current* WTI price)	(26,550,000)	(17,370,000)
Oil price swap settlement	1,550,000	7,630,000
Net payment	(25,000,000)	(25,000,000)
Net effect: oil user pays	US$25/barrel	US$25/barrel

Quantity/quality

A specified quantity of the relevant commodity would be agreed to by the counterparties. For example, in the case above, the oil user wishes to hedge against price fluctuations on one million barrels every six months for three years (a total of six million barrels over the period). This requirement could be structured in a number of ways such as a two million barrel oil price swap settling *annually*; an oil price swap for one million barrels settling semi-annually (the actual transaction described); or, an oil price swap for 500,000 barrels settling quarterly. The commodity will also need to be defined with great precision (for example, the closing price of the WTI near-month contract on the New York Mercantile Exchange (NYMEX)). This is important as the value/price of the product may vary significantly depending on its specifications.

Maturity

The maturity of the transaction needs to be agreed between the counterparties.

Commodity price index

The settlement payment associated with the commodity price swap is typically based on an agreed price index. This can be a futures price, an actual physical selling price, or an established price index.

For example, for a typical oil swap, a suitable index might be the NYMEX light sweet WTI crude oil price, the Brent price (for North Sea oil), or other product price indices such as heating oil, jet fuel, naptha, etc, for which there is no established futures market but which are routinely traded and reported in industry journals such as *Platts Oilgram*.

Major considerations in designating the index include: it should be readily available; it should reflect a fair basis (that is, it correlates closely to actual physical commodity transactions to be undertaken by the producer or user); and it is fair/impartial and not readily capable of artificial manipulation.

This agreed price index is used to calculate the "floating" price under a fixed-for-floating commodity price swap.

Settlement methods

Settlement can be effected against the agreed commodity price index on a specific day or, alternatively, against an average of the index for each trading day during the settlement period (in the above example, the six-month period). Under the averaging process, at the end of the period, the floating price for the settlement calculation would be derived from the simple arithmetic average of all the closing prices for each business day during the period.

The averaging method is used for a number of reasons, including:

- Producers and users particularly seek to match the swap with the underlying physical transactions which are likely to be undertaken *over the settlement period*, rather than at a spot date. This means that the average settlement price method would provide a better hedge that a one-day settlement price.

- The averaging method is more likely to reflect actual movements in crude oil prices during the period than taking the spot price at the end of the period as it reduces the impact of short-term "spikes" in commodity prices and also lessens the impact of any temporary market distortions which may occur.

Miscellaneous requirements

In a number of jurisdictions, regulatory requirements may necessitate a maximum and/or minimum level of the agreed commodity price index to be specified to place a maximum on the size of the settlement amount which might be payable under the transaction. In practice, these "cap" and "floor" prices are set some distance away from the agreed fixed prices and, while legally necessary, are rarely economically significant.

The structure depicted above details a commodity producer and user directly contracting with each other to guarantee the commodity price for the purchase and sale transaction. Such a structure would require each party to accept its counterparty's credit exposure on the transaction.

In practice, most transactions use an intermediary, usually a bank or other financial institution such as a commodity trading house, with each counterparty separately contracting with the intermediary.

This contractual structure, as with other derivative products, is designed to ensure confidentiality, insulation of the counterparties from counterparty credit risk as well as eliminating, where the intermediary agrees, the need for exact matching of the two legs of the commodity price swap. The separation of the contractual obligations enables transactions involving different amounts and a number of parties with different needs to be matched. The insertion of the intermediary also allows economies of scale and price advantages to be generated, as well as allowing additional flexibility in respect of early termination.[4]

Commodity price-for-interest swaps

The commodity price-for-interest swap is a variation on the commodity price swap structure. Under a commodity price-for-interest swap, a commodity producer and a user agree to exchange a fixed amount of the specified commodity for floating-rate (usually related to US dollar Libor) payments.

The rationale for commodity price-for-interest swaps is as follows:

- The commodity producer obtains protection from increases in its financing cost relative to current prices for its product; that is, the structure directly hedges its natural position of being "long" the commodity and "short" interest expense/rates.

- The commodity user locks in the price of its commodity purchases on a longer-term basis.

Figure 3 depicts the structure of a typical commodity price-for-interest swap and Figure 4 sets out the detailed cash flows of such a transaction.

Figure 3: Commodity price-for-interest swaps

Structure

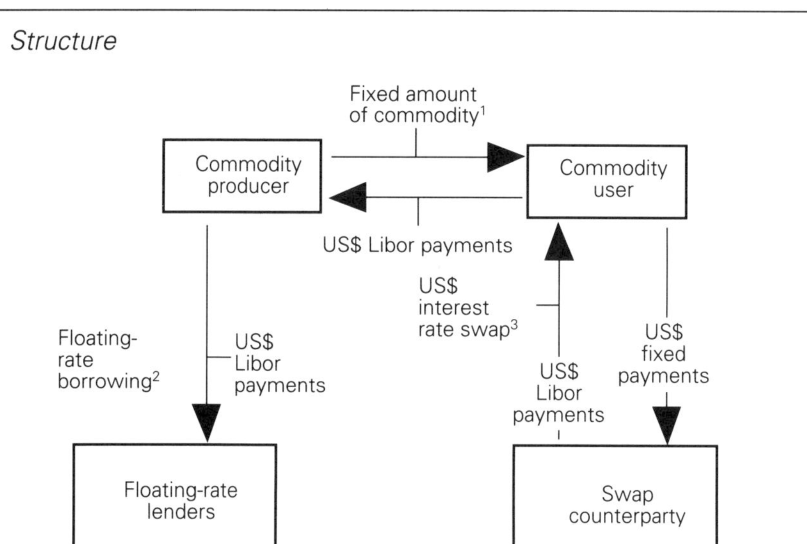

The transaction is made up of three distinct components:

(1) A commodity price-for-interest swap — whereby the commodity producer agrees to pay to the commodity user a fixed amount of a specified commodity in exchange for receiving US dollar Libor payments on an agreed notional principal amount

(2) A floating-rate borrowing — whereby the commodity producer undertakes a US dollar Libor floating-rate borrowing to finance its production of the commodity.

(3) A US dollar-denominated interest rate swap — whereby the commodity user enters into a US dollar interest rate swap to lock in the fixed US dollar cost of its commodity forward purchase.

Commodity price-for-interest swap using notional commodity flows

It is common to structure commodity swaps in terms of notional flows rather than actual physical commodity flows. Under this structure (set out below), the specified fixed amount of the commodity is substituted with a notional amount calculated as the US dollar equivalent of agreed commodity volume at the agreed price index for the commodity. In addition, both parties are required to undertake physical transactions.

Continued:

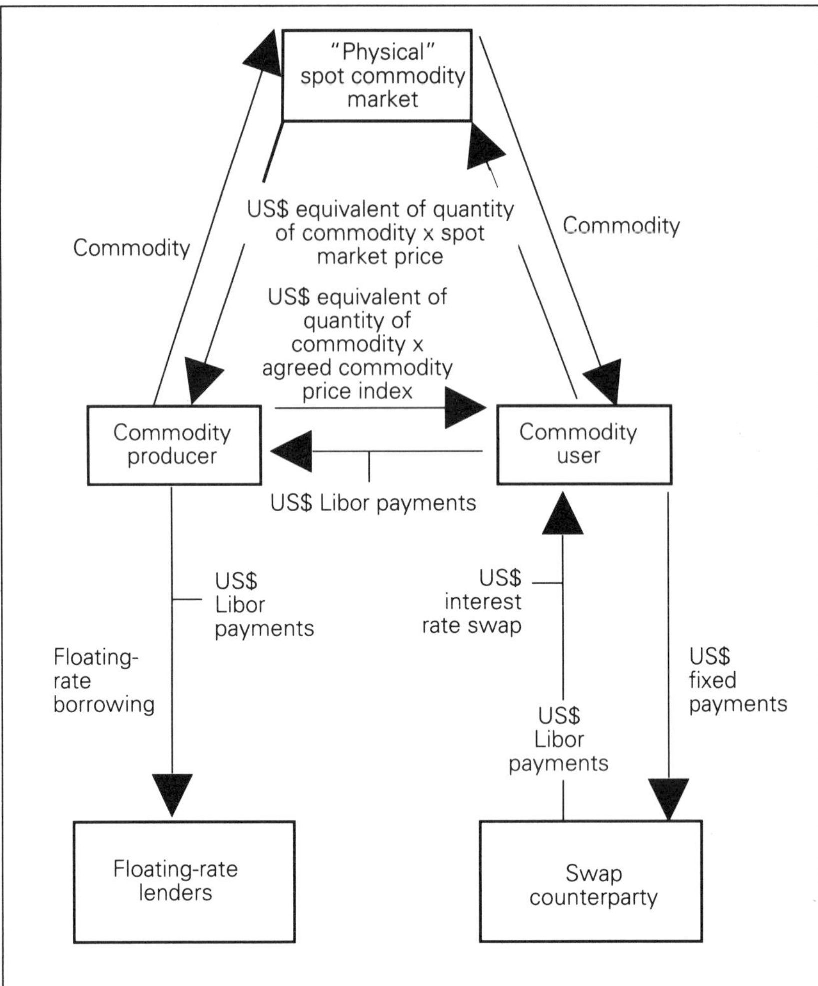

Commodity price-for-interest swap — intermediated structure

In practice, the commodity price-for-interest rate swap would be unbundled into a series of separate transactions (see below). A primary factor dictating such unbundling is the fact that from the viewpoint of the commodity user, the transaction is identical to a fixed-for-floating commodity swap price.

Continued:

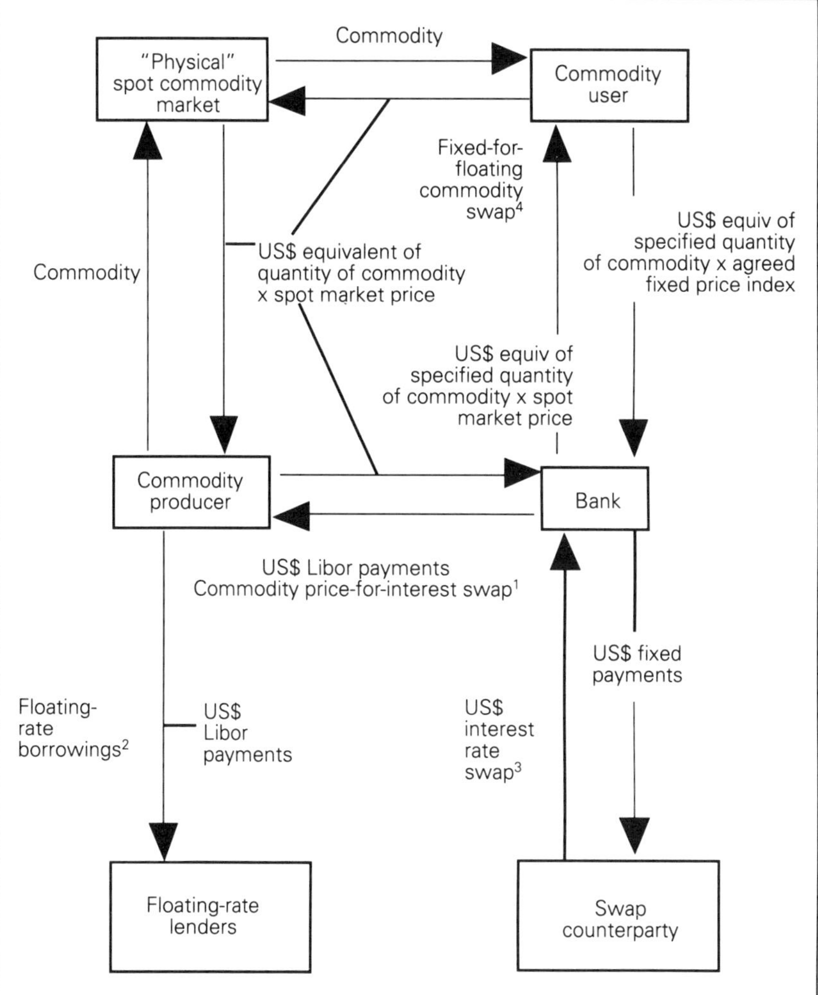

1. The semi-annual equivalent of the 1m barrels per annum agreed to be delivered; that is, 1m barrels x floating-price index.
2. Calculated as US$294,117,647 (the notional principal amount) at 8.25% (six-month Libor) for six months.
3. Calculation is the same as 2. and assumed to be the Libor payments on debt incurred by the oil producers. (Please note that is a notional calculation and does not in any way imply that the oil producer borrowed the notional principal amount to finance the production of the agreed amount of oil.)
4. Calculated as US$294,117,647 (the notional principal amount) at 8.50% per annum (the two-year fixed rate) for six months.

Figure 4: Commodity price-for-interest swaps — example

1. The transaction

Assume the following parameters for an oil/interest rate commodity price-for-interest swap:

Annual fixed amount of oil	·1,000,000 barrels
Fixed price of oil	US$25/barrel
Maturity	2 years
Settlement	Semi-annual settlement
Fixed US$ interest rate swap rate (for 2-year maturity)	8.5% pa (semi-annual)
Current 6-month Libor	8.25% pa
Notional principal amount for transaction	(Fixed amount of oil x fixed price) divided by 2-year swap rate = (1m x US$25)/0.0850 = US$294,117,647

2. Implied cash flows at commencement

This implied initial semi-annual (the selected settlement period) cash flows as at the date the transaction is entered into as follows:

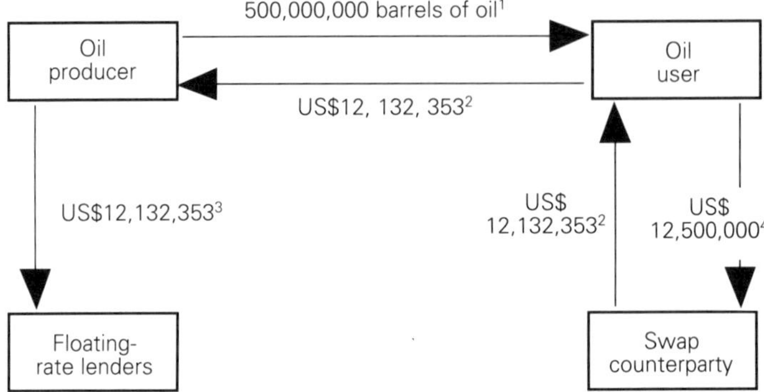

1. The semi-annual equivalent of the 1m barrels per annum agreed to be delivered.
(2. Calculated as US$294,117,647 (the notional principa amount) at 8.25% (six-month Libor) for six months.
3. Calculation is same as 2. and assumed to be the Libor payments on debt incurred by the oil producers. (Please note that is a notional calculation and does not in any way imply that the oil producer borrowed the notional principal amount to finance the production of the agreed amount of oil.)
4. Calculated as US$294,117,647 (the notional principal amount) at 8.50% per annum (the two-year fixed rate) for six months.

Figure 4 continued

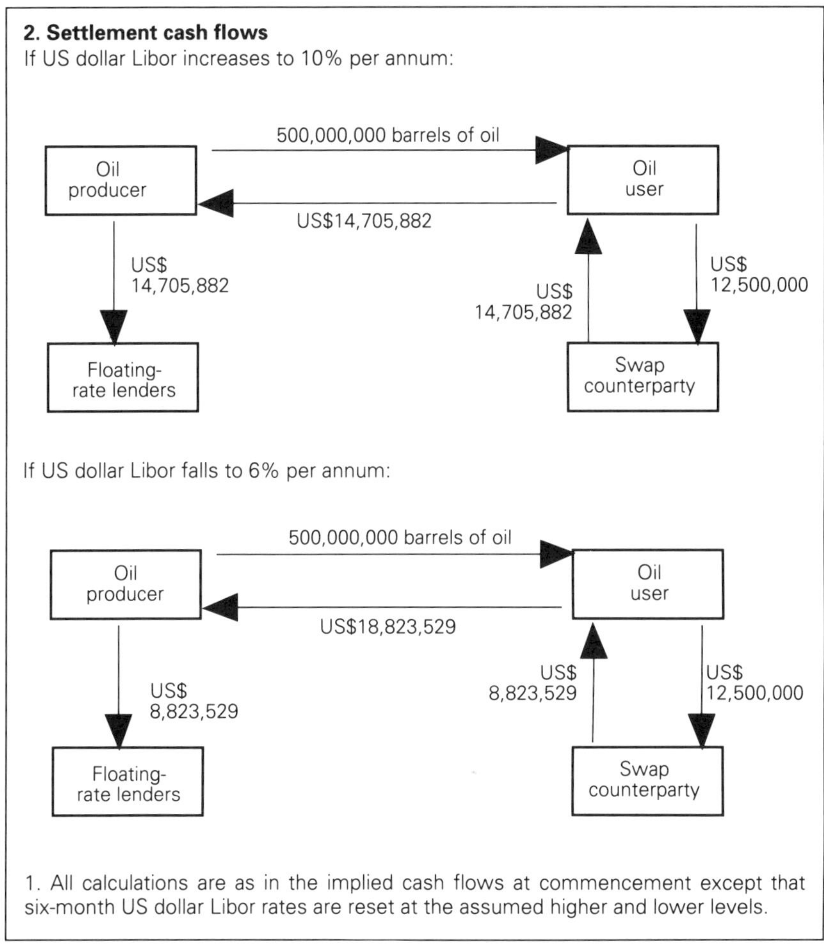

1. All calculations are as in the implied cash flows at commencement except that six-month US dollar Libor rates are reset at the assumed higher and lower levels.

The analysis of the commodity price-for-interest swap is complex, as outlined beow.

(a) From the user's point of view

In the example (refer to Figure 4), the commodity user has effectively locked-in a price for one million barrels of oil per annum for a period of two years. The agreed, guaranteed price of US$25 per barrel is achieved as shown in Table 2. Under the structure, irrespective of the level of US dollar Libor, the oil user is guaranteed a price of US$25 per barrel.

Table 2: Commodity price-for-interest swap

	Physical commodity*	US dollar flows
1. Oil price-for-interest swap	+ 0.5m barrels	– Libor (US$12,132,353)**
2. Interest rate swap		
Fixed rate —		– 8.50% (US$12,500,000)
Floating rate —		+ Libor (US$12,132,353)
	+ 0.5m barrels	–US$12,500,000
Net effect: oil user pays US$25/barrel		

*Likely to be a dollar amount based on 0.5m barrels x prevailing commodity price.
**Based on implied cash flows at commencement.

(b) From the oil producer's point of view
From the producer's perspective, the commodity price-for-interest swap is more complex. The producer has converted its floating-rate US dollar-denominated debt into, effectively, *commodity-denominated borrowings*. It has synthesised a commodity loan, notionally selling forward its production to service its debt. A structure entailing the amortisation of principal is also feasible.

The payments received by the commodity producer under the swap go towards servicing its US dollar-denominated floating-rate borrowings. If interest rates rise, then payments received under the price-for-interest swap increase and would presumably offset the higher interest payments incurred by the commodity producer on its floating-rate borrowings. The converse would occur if interest rates fell.

The commodity producer's revenue stream is now variable, being a function of interest rates (as it is related to US dollar Libor). The producer effectively makes debt payments using a commodity rather than US dollars. The commodity producer is now immunised against variations in US dollar interest rates but risks opportunity losses if commodity prices exceed those implied in the swap. The difficulty lies in relating the amount/payments under the swap to the underlying level of borrowings, production costs, etc which would determine the producer's total profitability.

The structure may have additional benefits in that where actual physical delivery of the commodity is required, the commodity user may be attracted to the transaction as it can gain assurance of obtaining fixed amounts of raw material on a long-term basis at guaranteed prices. Conversely, the commodity producer may be attracted to this particular structure because of the capacity to link its debt servicing to the production and delivery of its own commodity, allowing it to benefit from increased certainty in terms of management of currency exposures, management of its debt portfolio, and particularly its debt repayment schedule and planning of production. However, where physical delivery is not of special interest to the counterparties, these benefits can be retained in a notional swap structure, together with flexibility of supply.

Despite their intellectual elegance and practical utility, commodity price-for-interest swaps are not as common as fixed-for-floating commodity swaps.

(2) Commodity swaps — pricing methods

The pricing of derivative instruments is based on the ability to decompose all such products into a number of basic instruments (forwards or futures contracts and/or option contracts) for which well-developed pricing methodologies exist. As far as commodity swaps are concerned, the essential insight is that this type of transaction (particularly, a fixed-for-floating swap) can be decomposed into a portfolio of forward contracts on the commodity.[5]

For example, in the case referred to in Figure 1, the oil producer (user) enters into a *series* of forward contracts to sell (buy) an agreed quantity of oil at a fixed price. The oil producer agrees to sell one million barrels of oil every six months at an agreed price of US$25 per barrel. Conversely, the oil user agrees to purchase one million barrels of oil every six months at a price of US$25 per barrel. Essentially, the oil producer and user have entered into six forward contracts with maturities of between six months and three years to undertake forward purchases and sales of oil.

The basic concept of a commodity swap as a forward purchase or sale contract may require some minor variations depending upon the terms of the transaction itself. For instance, where the settlement mechanism under the swap requires the floating oil price to be the average for the preceding six months, the commodity swap must be decomposed into a series of *daily* forward contracts (not six monthly forward contracts) to derive the appropriate pricing.

Based on the intuition that a commodity swap consists of a portfolio of forward purchase or sale contracts, a pricing model for this type of transaction can be developed. Figure 5 sets out a conceptual model for the pricing of fixed-for-floating commodity swaps.

Figure 5: Commodity swaps — pricing model

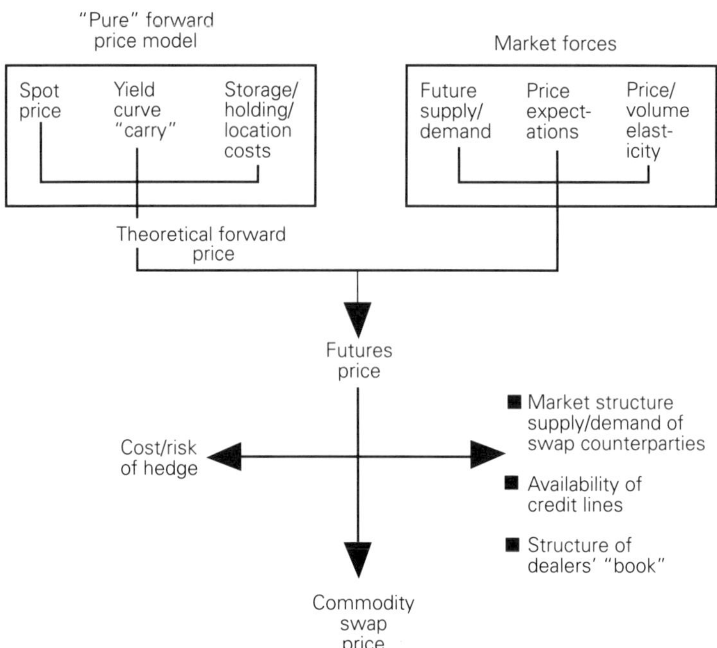

The starting point in pricing commodity swaps is the determination of the "pure" forward price of the commodity. The forward price of a commodity is a price set today to be paid in the future for the purchase or sale of the identified commodity.

This price depends in part on an assessment of the future price of the underlying commodity at delivery, based on information available in the market at the time the forward contract is entered into.[6] The major factors determining the "pure" forward price are:

- the spot price of the commodity;
- current interest rates as built into in the yield curve or the "carry" cost; and
- storage, holding and "location" or transportation costs, including any special factors relevant to the commodity such as perishability, seasonality etc.

This information, which is freely available in the market, goes into the calculation of the forward price, based on the essential condition that a forward contract can be replicated by entering into a series of transactions which would have the same economic effects as the forward contract.

Figure 6: Forward price of a commodity*

Assumptions
Assume that the spot price of WTI crude oil is US$18/barrel. The yield curve for US dollar securities is as follows:

Year	Interest rates (%pa)
0.5	8.000
1.0	8.375
1.5	8.625
2.0	8.875
2.5	9.000
3.0	9.125

Storage/holding costs of oil are (approximately) 0.5% per annum (a hypothetical estimate).

Forward price
Based on the above date, the following forward prices of WTI crude can be derived:

Year	Forward price excl storage costs (US$/barrel)	Forward price incl storage costs (US$/barrel)
Spot	18.00	18.00
0.5	18.72	18.77
1.0	19.51	19.60
1.5	20.40	20.54
2.0	21.34	21.53
2.5	22.35	22.61
3.0	23.39	23.71

Note: the forward price is calculated using the following relationship:
Forward price = spot price + carrying cost
FP = SP x [1 + (i + h)] ^t

where:
FP = the forward price in t period
SP = spot price
i = the annualised interest rate
1 = the annualised holding cost of the commodity
t = period

For example, a forward seller of a commodity could arrange to purchase the required quantity of the commodity *today* at the current market price, fund and store it until the delivery date, and deliver the commodity to the forward purchaser on the agreed forward date. A forward purchaser could replicate a forward sale by selling the commodity on the spot market and investing the proceeds until the forward purchase date, when the maturing investment could be used to fund the purchase of the agreed amount of the commodity. The cost associated with the immediate purchase, funding and storage until delivery therefore forms a basis of the pricing for the forward contract.

Figure 6 offers a simple example where the forward price of a commodity is calculated using the pure forward price model. As can be seen in Figure 6, the forward price of a commodity should always be above the spot price. This reflects the fact that the process of replication of the forward position will normally incur holding costs.

The major component of the holding cost is the interest expense of funding the holding of the spot commodity. In addition, the holding of a position in the physical commodity will result in expenditure on storage costs. These costs will include not only the physical storage and (possibly) the physical loss of the commodity through wastage and deterioration of the *quality* but also location costs. Location costs occur because the consummation of a physical purchase or sale may require the commodity to be transported to a specific location. This may be in the form of actual physical transportation of the relevant commodity or, more probably, a "location swap" whereby specific amounts of a commodity *in different locations* are exchanged between two counterparties. These location swaps may incur costs, which must be factored into the forward price.

However, actual forward market prices for commodities are often lower than the theoretical forward price implied from the pure carry-cost model described above. That is, the market is said to be in backwardation (spot price is lower than the forward prices) rather than in contango (forward price is higher than the spot price) as implied by theoretical forward price models. For example, in early 1990 the forward prices of oil implied from the NYMEX futures contract on WTI crude oil was as set out in Table 3.

The forward prices of oil as expressed in terms of the NYMEX contracts on WTI crude imply a market in backwardation. For example, the June 1991 contract implies that the forward price of oil is at a 10.3% per annum discount to the current spot price.

As noted above, the pure forward price model would imply that the price for oil in forward months would be at a *premium* to the spot price. The arbitrage process underlying the derivation of the theoretical forward price of the commodity would, in the circumstances, prove attractive and force the forward price to its theoretical equilibrium.

Table 3: WTI crude oil prices on NYMEX

Delivery month	Price (US$/barrel)
March 1990	21.59
June 1990	20.10
September 1990	19.22
March 1991	18.67
June 1991	18.52

All prices are based on the forward price implied from the Nymex futures contracts on WTI crude in January 1990.

Where the forward price is at a discount to the theoretical forward price, this arbitrage process would be as follows: the arbitraguer would sell the commodity in the spot market, and, simultaneously, repurchase an identical amount of the commodity *in the forward market*. The proceeds of the sale would be invested in an interest bearing investment until the maturity of the forward contract. Interest payments on this placement would be used to fund the forward purchase. This process, in the circumstances described, would yield the arbitrageur a clear risk-free profit.

A number of factors dictate that the actual forward price deviates significantly from that derived using the pure forward price model. These factors include the difficulty of undertaking arbitrage transactions of the type described, and the presence of certain market forces or factors which are not properly integrated in the pure forward price model.

The process of arbitrage to force forward prices to their equilibrium levels assumes:

- free purchase and sale of securities, including short sales;
- availability of storage and holding facilities for commodities; and
- absence of market frictions such as trading costs and taxes.

Many of these conditions are not satisfied in the traded market for commodities. A major violation is the inability of arbitrageurs (with the possible exception of large commodity producers and a few large trading companies) to enter into short sales of securities. Where short sales are possible, the cost of financing or borrowing a commodity to be sold short is extremely high — at times, prohibitively so. In essence, it is only possible to be "long" or "flat" commodities, a fact which effectively eliminates certain types of arbitrage activities. The only economic means of creating a short position in a commodity is in the futures market for the commodity, if one exists.

These inadequacies in the institutional structure of commodity markets dictate that the arbitrage process, which would otherwise be expected to force prices to their theoretical equilibrium forward levels, does not function in accordance with the dictates of theory.

The deviation of actual forward prices from the theoretical forward price reflects the influence of a number of other market forces:

- future supply/demand expectations;
- price expectations;
- price/volume elasticity of the commodity.

The actual forward price of commodities often reflects *anticipated* changes in the *future* supply and demand of a particular commodity.

For example, increases in production in most commodities cannot be effected instantaneously. Where supply falls short of demand, the price in the spot market will increase to market clearing levels. However, simultaneously, production levels of the commodity may also increase, though this very process, together with the resulting increase in supply in the spot market may be subject to considerable time lags. The backwardation in the forward market may reflect this lag whereby the increased supply of the commodity is *expected* to more accurately balance demand and eventually result in lower prices.

In addition, a number of commodities are subject to seasonal pricing cycles which may also impact upon the actual levels of forward prices and the premium or discount to the spot price.

A major factor influencing the level of forward prices will be the price/volume elasticity of the commodity. For example, the *absolute* level of prices for a particular commodity will reflect the nature of the demand for it.

Following the oil shocks of the 1970s, for instance, consumers of energy products have made considerable advances in structuring their energy consumption in a manner which allows them to switch between different energy products. A price rise in oil products may result in switching behaviour whereby major consumers of oil increase their purchases of coal or natural gas products in preference to oil-based energy sources. Similarly, a fall in oil prices may induce a reverse switching behaviour. The forward price must take into account expectations as to these types of changes in the supply and demand for commodities.

The expectations of producers and users, which will reflect many of the factors discussed above, will also be built into in the actual forward price.

The complexity of the elements which need to be factored in the forward price mean that the theoretical price forecasts of the pure forward price model are likely to be only one of a number of factors which will determine the physical forward price. In practice, the market consensus forward price is best reflected in the futures contract prices for a variety of commodities which are traded on organised futures and options exchanges.

These forward prices derived from traded futures contracts form the basis of commodity swap pricing.

The relationship of commodity swap prices to futures prices is based on:

- the fact that the futures price reflects a consensus between market participants of the current expected forward price (given that such participants are the primary users of commodity swaps); and

- the use of commodity futures by financial institutions in hedging commodity swap positions.

As noted above, the majority of commodity swaps are transacted *via* a financial intermediary who assumes both the credit risk in, and responsibility for, the matching of counterparties in each particular transaction. Where a commodity swap trader is approached to provide a price for a particular transaction, he will have two options in offsetting the risk of undertaking a commodity swap:

- locate and transact the offsetting component of the swap with a counterparty; or

- if a counterparty is not readily available, enter into the commodity swap with the risk being assumed in one of two ways:
  (i) assume the price risk and leave the position unhedged until a counterparty can be located;
  (ii) hedge the risk of fluctuations in the price of the commodity by entering into a series of transactions in the physical or forward/futures market for the commodity to provide a temporary hedge until a counterparty can be located.

This behaviour of the trader necessarily means that the commodity swap price will reflect the market structure at that particular point in time as well as the cost and risk of a temporary hedge. Important market structure factors which may influence the commodity swap provider's price include: the perceived supply/demand of swap counterparties; the availability of credit lines to enter into transactions with counterparties; and the structure of the dealer's book.

In practice, few dealers take pure price risks when entering into commodity swap transactions. Typically, the dealer will hedge the *absolute* price risk with the help of the best available hedge instrument. In this way he will carry the risk *on the hedge* in preference to *the risk of short-term movements in the price of the commodity.*

The cost or risk of the hedge will be calculated as the cost of setting up the hedge involving the physical commodity or the forward/future, the basis risk of the hedge, the liquidity of the hedging instrument used, and the time period for which the hedge has to be held.

To summarise, the pricing of a commodity swap is far from an exact science. It reflects the influence of a number of factors. The principal of these is the prevailing forward/futures price of the commodity, which reflects the fact that a commodity swap can be decomposed into a portfolio of forward contracts. The forward/futures price itself reflects both the theoretical forward price as generated by the arbitrage-based pure forward pricing model and the influence of market forces on the forward price of the underlying commodity.

The methodology discussed above relates primarily to fixed-for-floating commodity swaps. The pricing of a commodity price-for-interest swap in intrinsically more complex.

Pricing a commodity price-for-interest swap can be separated into a number of distinct steps:

(1) pricing the fixed purchase price for the commodity from the perspective of the commodity user;

(2) pricing the interest rate swap;

(3) pricing the amount of commodity to be exchanged for the US dollar Libor payments.

Pricing of steps (1) and (2) can be readily generated. The fixed forward purchase price for the commodity user will conform closely to the price of a fixed-for-floating commodity swap. This is because from the perspective of the commodity user the two transactions are direct substitutes.

The interest rate swap price is freely available given the presence of a substantial, liquid and freely traded market in the instrument.[7]

The final pricing step — step (3) — can be forced out once steps (1) and (2) are known.

In practice, from the perspective of the commodity user there is no difference between a straight fixed-for-floating commodity price swap and a commodity price-for-interest swap (except for possible assurance of supply) and the commodity user may in fact prefer to structure the transaction as a straight fixed-for-floating commodity price swap.

However, the complex impact of the commodity price-for-interest swap on the commodity producer and, in particular, the asymmetric profile of the transaction (the impact on the producer will not necessarily mirror that on the user because of differences between producers in terms of capital structure, debt availability, debt structure, production costs etc) dictates that the actual transaction price will deviate, often significantly, from the theoretical price. In this respect, the pricing of commodity price-for-interest swaps entails a greater "barter" element whereby the exact supply and demand of counterparties may significantly influence pricing at any point in time.

(3) Institutional structure of the commodity swap market

Evolution of the commodity swap market

The earliest commodity swap apparently was transacted in 1986. The technique is thought to have been pioneered by Chase Manhattan, among others. The market has evolved relatively rapidly with current annual volumes of around US$10bn of notional principal amount in petroleum and oil products *alone*.

The major commodity involved has been oil and related energy products. Commodity swaps are available in a variety of energy products, including WTI, Brent, heating oil, jet fuel, naptha and bunker fuel (to name just a few). More recently, commodity swap products in natural gas have also been introduced.

Commodity swap transactions in a variety of metals are also available. The major material here is copper but deals involving zinc, aluminium and nickel are also available. Commodity swaps involving precious metals such as gold, silver, platinum etc have also been available.[8] The fungibility of precious metals, which approximates the characteristics of currency markets, has allowed this market to evolve more rapidly. Products involving soft commodities such as sugar, coffee, cocoa and paper pulp are also likely to bcome increasingly available to market participants.

A number of factors determine whether commodity swaps or related transactions in a particular commodity are feasible. These include:

- prices fixed by market forces with reliable transparent reporting mechanisms;
- a liquid spot market; the presence of a liquid futures market in the commodity is helpful although not essential;
- opposing price expectations for consumers and producers of the commodity and sufficient numbers of both; and
- price volatility.

Some commodities, such as diamonds or wool where the supply and price are tightly controlled, are not suitable for commodity swap transactions.

The growth in the commodity swap market, both in terms of the size and variety of materials used, reflects the influence of a number of factors, such as:

- increasing sophistication of corporate financial management and focus on corporate risk management;
- improvements in financial engineering technology; and
- increased commodity price volatility.

The level of financial risk in the environment in which companies operate has increased dramatically in the last two decades. Unanticipated changes in financial market rates for foreign currencies, interest rates and commodity prices rapidly impact upon corporate profitability. The increased focus on commodity price risk management is part of the increased focus on financial risk management within corporations. This more widespread awareness of commodity price risk management also coincides with increasing volatility in commodity markets.

Figures 7a–d plot the history of prices for major commodities. The graphs indicate that the prices of major commodities, including petroleum products, metals etc, have been increasingly volatile.[9]

For example, basic commodity prices in the 1970s rose sharply, reflecting high rates of inflation in the global economy. The declining purchasing power of monetary assets increased the demand for commodities, resulting in an increase in the prices of real goods, including commodities, relative to financial assets. The major impact of this period was the massive transfer of wealth from commodity users to commodity producers, particularly oil-producing countries.

Figure 7a: US Commodity Research Bureau index

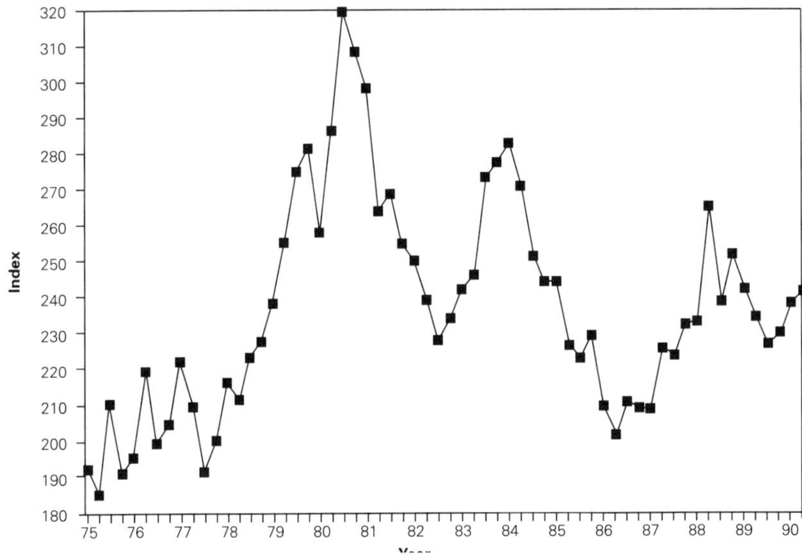

Figure 7b: Crude oils

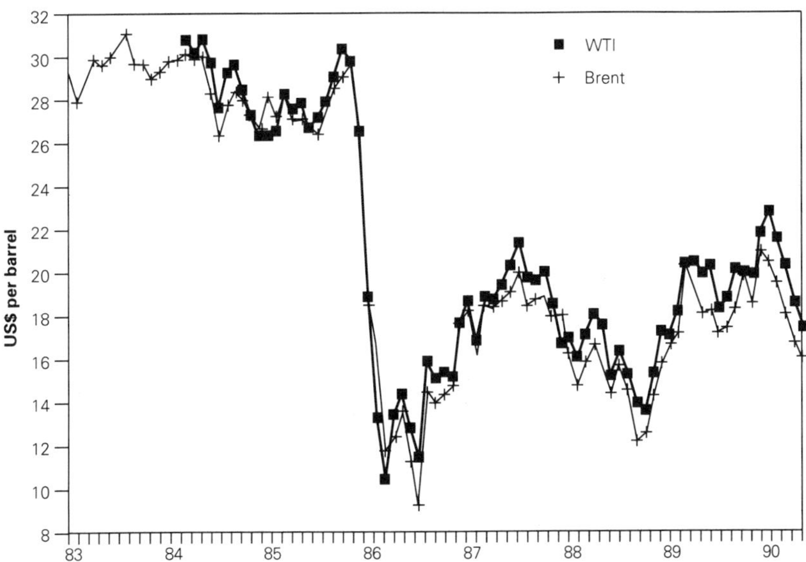

Figure 7c: Metal prices

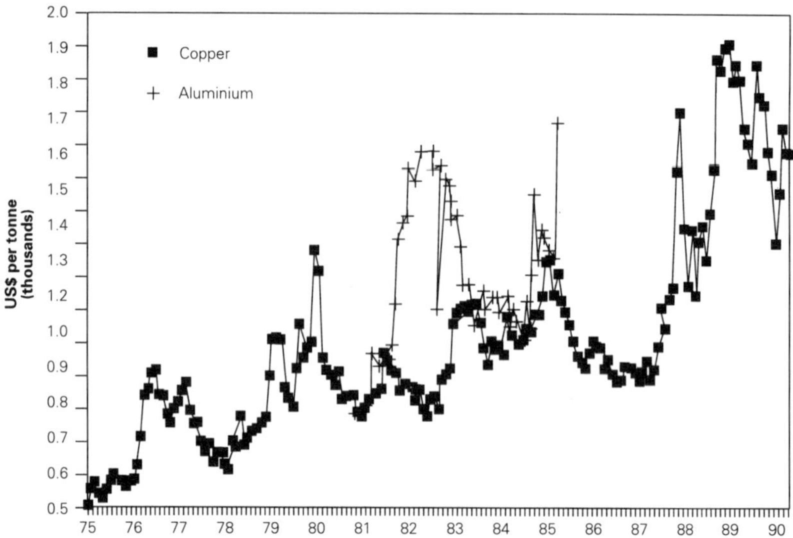

Figure 7d: Food commodity prices

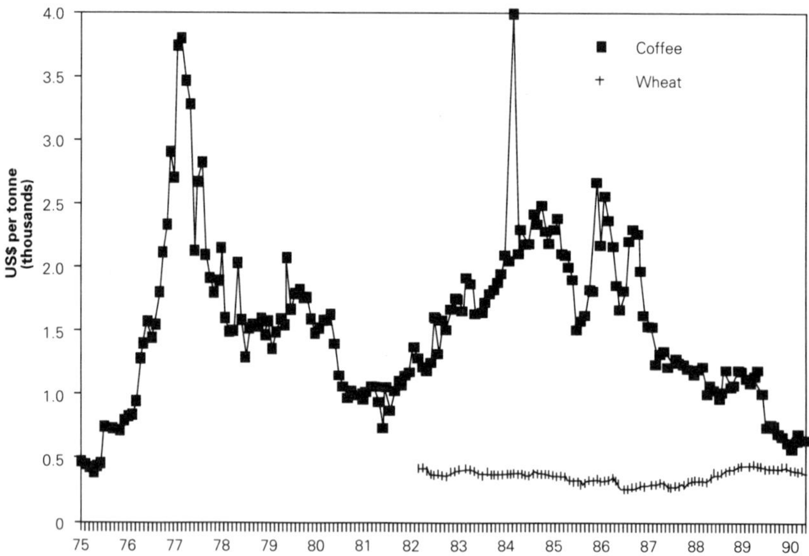

However, high real interest rates in the late 1970s and throughout much of the 1980s meant that the relationship between commodity prices and financial assets changed dramatically. As real interest rates rose, the opportunity cost of holding inventories of commodities increased, resulting in a shift out of commodities and into financial assets.

This increased volatility in commodity prices prompted the development of a number of commodity risk management products. These included, initially, forward/futures markets in many commodities. However, the market also evolved a variety of highly customised commodity risk management products including commodity-indexed securities, commodity warrants and commodity swaps.

However, in marked contrast to the market for foreign exchange and interest rate derivatives, the development of commodity swaps has been impeded by the action of regulators, particularly the US Commodities Futures Trading Commission (CFTC)

In 1987, following Chase Manhattan's advertisement of their services in the *Wall Street Journal* and the publication of a brochure on commodity swaps by the Bank, the CFTC subpoenaed the manager of Chase Manhattan's commodity index swaps and financing group as part of its investigative action to consider whether it should regulate the market. The agency also released an advance notice of proposed rule making on hybrid instruments which viewed commodity swaps as a form of futures contract which could only be traded on a recognised exchange. The impact of the decision was that the commodity swap market essentially moved overseas and US banks were only allowed to participate in this market through overseas subsidiaries.

The CFTC position led to a number of transactions, including a gold-linked certificate of deposit issue by Wells Fargo Bank, having to be withdrawn.

However, in 1989, the CFTC reversed its stance and accepted the position that commodity swaps do not fall under its jurisdiction; consequently it discontinued its investigative actions. In a policy statement (dated 14 July 1989) the Commission set out the features which characterised the swap market and accepted that, provided the transaction meets a number of conditions, they are in a "safe harbour" and outside the CFTC's regulatory ambit. These conditions (which largely reflect existing market practice) include:

- transactions must be individually tailored;
- transactions are terminable in the absence of default only with the consent of the counterparty;

- transactions do not have the credit support of a clearing organisation nor are they marked-to-market or use a variation settlement system which eliminates individual credit risk;

- transactions are undertaken as part of the participant's general line of business; and

- transactions are not offered to the retail public.

The only criteria which creates difficulty is the third. Increasingly, swap transactions (both in the commodity swap market and in similar products such as interest rate and currency swaps) resort to mark-to-market and/or collateralisation provisions as a means of reducing counterparty credit exposures for capital adequacy purposes. However, there are significant differences between the daily mark-to-market mechanisms of a futures contract and those employed in connection with commodity and related swaps. These differences are expected to allow most transactions to satisfy the "safe harbour" provisions specified by the CFTC.

The CFTC's decision will assist the development of the commodity swap business significantly.

Market participants/product application

Predictably, the major participants in the commodity swap market have been commodity producers and users. Others include financial institutions and, to a lesser extent, major commodity trading houses who have been active in facilitating transactions between producers and users.

The major motivations for using commodity swaps (for both commodity producers and users) have included:

- *Seeking protection against commodity price volatility.* Commodity swaps have offered both producers and users the ability to lock-in the price of a regular stream of commodity purchases or sales.

  For the producer, it has the benefit of fixing revenue for a given maturity, often allowing it to use the "locked-in" receipts to ensure the viability of an operation. This is of particular importance to high cost producers who, by sacrificing the potential windfall gains of higher production prices, have gained protection against a price fall that could, in the extreme, result in pressure to close production of a high-cost pit or field.

  For the user, these transactions have guaranteed prices for the purchases of essential raw materials, often allowing profit margins on end products to be determined.

- In the case of commodity price-for-interest swaps in particular, the transaction *may* also assure both producer and user of a guaranteed market or availability of an essential commodity.

- *Additional financing flexibility.* The availability of commodity swaps ensures that producers can increase the certainty of cash flows, thereby allowing the organisation to raise funds against guaranteed revenues. This is particularly important in the case of commodity producers in less developed countries (LDCs) seeking financing for resource and other (typically non-recourse) projects (see discussion below).

The market for commodity swaps has grown as more producers have become attracted to these financing instruments.

Traditionally, companies avoided hedging on the basis that commodity price movements are, first, a common competitive position of each participant in the industry; secondly, can be passed on to customers; and, thirdly, producers in particular often argued that the investors in their equity securities sought an exposure to the underlying commodity price volatility. However, as market structures have changed, companies have had to rethink their strategies.

A number of aggressive commodity producers and users have tried to use commodity swaps and related techniques to generate competitive advantage by, for example, guaranteeing revenue flows for projects that are extremely sensitive to price fluctuations and might have otherwise been foregone. Commodity users and producers may also use these instruments to take views upon and position themselves for the long-term price cycles by buying or selling forward production at what is believed to be attractive prices (relative to what is expected to prevail).

As participants within an industry begin to use instruments to generate potential competitive advantages, competitors are increasingly forced to focus on the desirability of similar strategies as commodity price fluctuations do not affect all competitors equally and impede the possibility of transferring the risk to consumers.

An example of this type of industry behaviour is to be found in the airline industry where a number of airlines have used commodity swaps on crude oil or jet fuel to lock-in cost structures allowing them to price airline fares in advance without assuming exposure to fuel price changes.

Commodity swaps have evolved as a preferred method of managing commodity price risk for both producers and users because of certain structural inadequacies of commodity futures markets in the relevant commodities.

As noted above, futures markets in a wide variety of commodities have been available for some time. However, the use of futures, while well suited to hedging individual transactions, is not as useful in hedging typical corporate cash flows underlying commodity transactions. The major advantages of commodity swaps over futures transactions include those outlined below.

Maturity

Commodity futures are typically traded for periods up to two years. However, only the near-month contracts (up to three and, at most, six months out) are sufficiently traded and liquid to provide a basis for hedging exposures.

In contrast, commodity swap transactions can be structured over a longer horizon for periods up to 10 years (most commodity swaps are for maturities around six months to three years).

Futures contracts can cover longer-dated exposures but require that the hedge be rolled over periodically (eg, monthly or quarterly). This rollover process is administratively clumsy as it requires cash settlements to be made at the time of rollover, as well as exposing the hedger to the risk of the changing basis between the relevant futures contracts.

Administrative simplicity

Commodity swap transactions, unlike futures contracts, do not require initial deposits and, in most cases (subject to the credit standing of the counterparty), margin calls, as the contracts are not marked-to-market periodically.

Basis risk

Hedging with commodity futures involves the hedger assuming basis risk.[10] This risk arises from the fact that the commodity futures contract design must be specified precisely and the contract months are preset with no flexibility to depart from these contract standards.

Wherever the hedger uses the traded futures contract to hedge a product related but not identical to, the commodity specified in the contract *and/or* seeks to cover an exposure in a month not coinciding exactly with the futures delivery month, the hedger must assume basis risk. These risks can be classified as follows:

(1) *Product basis risk.* That is, the hedging of one commodity with a related but different commodity, for example, covering an exposure to jet fuel using WTI crude oil futures.

(2) *Timing risk.* That is, hedging an exposure in a month in which the commodity futures contract is not traded or, alternatively, is not

sufficiently liquid to allow its use, requiring the hedger to structure the hedge by trading in a contract expiring in a different time period from his actual exposure.

(3) *Commodity location risk.* Where the subject of the futures contract is deliverable at a different location from the delivery requirements of the actual physical commodity transaction being hedged. For example, hedging WTI crude on a CIF (cost, insurance, freight) New York basis with a Brent crude FOB (free on board) product delivered in Rotterdam.

(4) *Commodity futures currency risk.* The difference between the currency denomination of the commodity futures contracts (typically in US dollars) and the actual currency in which the hedge is required, which may be in the producer's or the user's local currency (other than US dollars).

A major advantage of commodity swaps is that they can be tailored to overcome such basis risks. For example, each commodity swap can be tailored precisely to the requirements of the producer or user to overcome each of the basis risks identified. This would allow the hedger to secure a better performance for its hedge relative to its underlying physical transaction, by comparison with a situation where it was forced to use a commodity futures contract which did not quite meet its physical transaction requirements.[11]

Design flexibility

As is evident from the above, a major benefit of commodity swaps is that they can be tailor-made to suit the specific cash flow, commodity product type and time-frame requirements of producers and users.

The features of commodity swaps which make them particularly attractive are similar to the features of interest rate and currency swap transactions which differentiate them from interest rate and/or currency futures. Essentially, commodity swaps function as an over-the-counter forward contract on specific commodities just as interest rate and currency swaps function as over-the-counter forward contracts on interest rates and currencie, respectively.

These similarities extend to the mechanical/settlement features of the two types of transactions, particularly in the case of fixed-for-floating commodity price swaps.

However, despite these similarities, the relationship between the two types of transactions should *not* be overstated. The market for commodity swaps does not (at least currently) involve the more complex integrative and financial arbitrage functions of currency and interest rate swaps.[12]

Currency and interest rate swaps operate in a highly distinctive way. They link together not just capital markets in various currencies but also segments within individual capital markets. This is because, through swaps, comparative advantage theory is extended from the market for goods and services to the market for financial assets and liabilities.

In contrast, commodity swaps, as they are structured currently, function purely as a mechanism for the transfer of risk between producers and users of commodities as well as speculators. In this regard, the market for commodity swaps is regarded more accurately as an extension of the forward/futures markets in the respective commodities.

The role of financial institutions

Financial institutions as well as, to a lesser extent, a number of commodity trading houses, have acted as facilitators of commodity swap transactions. Moreover, a number of producers (for example, British Petroleum) have set up units to market commodity swap transactions.

The role played by these institutions in the commodity swap market is quite similar to that played by institutions in the market for other derivative products (including interest rate and currency swap transactions and other derivative products).[13]

These institutions provide:

- credit enhancement to the transaction by acting as a counterparty to both end users; and

- speed and flexibility in execution by allowing each party to:
  (i) structure the transaction to suit its specific requirements; and
  (ii) enter into the transaction at its option in terms of timing, irrespective of the availability of a counterparty.

The number of entities willing to price and enter into commodity swap transactions on a principal basis are relatively few. Institutions active in running books in, or warehousing commodity swaps include Chase Manhattan, Banque Paribas and Bankers Trust, as well as commodity trading houses such as Phibro and oil companies such as BP.

These institutions will enter into commodity swaps without necessarily having an opposite and exactly matching counterparty. The risk assumed as a result of an individual transaction is absorbed into their overall commodity swap book with the residual price risk being hedged by transactions in the physical or forward/futures market in the commodity — a practice referred to as *warehousing*.

For example, a commodity swap provider entering into a swap with an oil user whereby the swap provider guarantees a series of forward purchase prices to the oil user, would require it to enter the spot or futures market for oil to purchase an appropriate amount of the commodity to hedge its exposure as a result of the transaction. Conversely, where a transaction guarantees an oil producer a forward sale price, the commodity swap provider would need to create a short position in the physical or futures market to hedge its exposure.

However, as discussed above, the fact that the commodity swap entails a series of forward contracts would require a provider to enter into a series of futures contracts to precisely match up the actual forward contracts embedded in the commodity swap. In practice, such exact matching of the hedge to the transaction may not be feasible because of the parameters of the swap transaction. The residual risk must then be carried by the entity until such time as an opposite swap can be entered into in order to offset its position.

The operation of a commodity swap warehouse is essentially very similar to the function of operating an interest rate and currency swap warehouse. Both function as a risk management mechanism whereby temporary risk positions are managed through a series of surrogate hedges until the opposite side to a swap transaction can be arranged. However, there are important differences between the two types of warehouses:

- Banks do not typically carry commodity price risks on their balance sheets in the same way as they face inherent interest rate and currency risks as a result of normal banking transactions, and this reduces the capacity of a bank to benefit from economies of scope and scale in the operation of a commodity swap warehouse.

- The significant differences in the structure of commodity markets relative to foreign exchange and securities markets restrict hedging practices.

These factors may necessarily restrict participation in commodity swaps to a greater extent than, for example, in interest rate and currency swaps. In addition, for commodity trading houses that are active participants in the physical market for the commodity, operating commodity swap warehouses may bring significant advantages.

The presence of institutions willing to make markets in commodity swaps in a variety of currencies is an extremely important development in the evolution of the commodity swap market. An absence of market-makers would severely impede the growth of this market as seasonal, geographical and other discrepancies are such that that offsetting counterparties may not necessarily be available, particularly *at the required point in time,* to facilitate a liquid and highly traded market in commodity swaps.

(4) Conclusion

A major area of potential growth in commodity swaps is the integration of such transactions in natural resource project financings, particularly for the LDC resource producers. Commercial bank financing for economically self-sufficient projects has been extremely difficult. A recent transaction completed by Banque Paribas for the Mexican copper producer, Mexicana de Cobre, may well form the basis of other transactions where commodity price management instruments are used as part of corporate financing packages to fund projects.

Figure 8: Case study — Mexicana De Cobre copper indexed pre-export financings

Mexicana De Cobre (MDC) is the owner and operator of Mexico's largest open-pit mining and metallurgical copper complex.

In July 1989, MDC entered into an innovative commodity swap related pre-export financing, arranged by Banque Paribas (Paribas).

The transaction (set out in the diagram below) had three components:

(1) A syndicated loan (arranged by Paribas and provided by European and Mexican banks) for US$210m for a maturity of 38 months. The loan carried interest at a rate of 11.48% per annum (based on interbank rates for three years and a margin of 3%). The loan is to be repaid through 12 equal quarterly payments.

(2) MDC entered into a forward-rate arrangement for its production with SOGEM SA, a subsidiary of Societe de Belgique. Under the terms of the contract, SOGEM committed to purchase 4,000 tonnes of copper from MDC per month for 38 months at the average London Metal Exchange (LME) price.

(3) MDC entered into a fixed-for-floating commodity swap with Paribas whereby it paid floating rate linked to the average LME price (matching its receipts under the sale contract with SOGEM) and received an agreed fixed price for copper.

The combined result of the series of transactions is that: MDC achieves guaranteed sales of its copper production at a known fixed price with the proceeds of the sale being used to effect repayment of the loan.

Continued:

The structure of the financing effectively protects lenders against the project risks:

- the risks of sale of the copper production is covered by the SOGEM purchase contract;
- the price risk on future sales of copper is hedged *via* the commodity swap;
- the major risk borne by the lenders is that of the failure of MDC to produce the required amount of copper.*

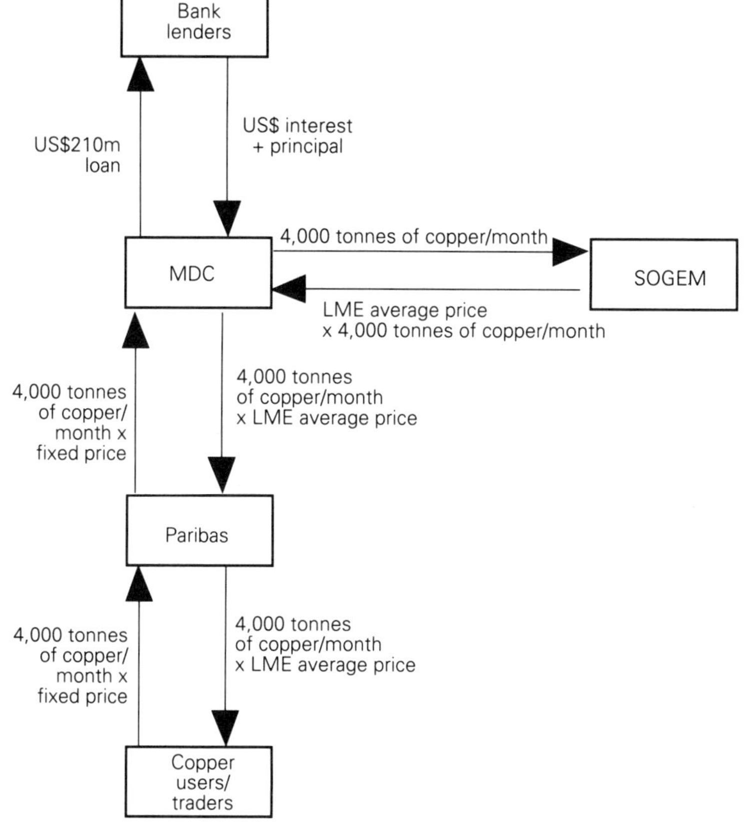

**Source: Simon Brady, "Commodity financiers sharpen up", Euromoney, August 1989, pp 38–44*

Notes

1. Satyajit Das is the Treasurer of the TNT Group, the international transport company. The views and opinions expressed are those of the author and do not necessarily reflect the views of TNT.

An earlier version of this chapter was published as "Oil and commodity swaps", *Journal of International Securities Markets*, Vol 4, Autumn 1990, IFR Publishing Ltd.

The author would like to thank: Nigel Harvey (Chase Manhattan) and Bruce Lafranchi (Salomon Brothers) for their comments on an earlier draft of the chapter; and John Martin (TNT) for his comments and for his assistance in the preparation of the graphs on commodity price movements. The author would like to thank Sharon Williams and Judy Payne for their assistance in the preparation of this chapter for publication.

2. This chapter assumes a reasonable level of familiarity with interest rate and currency swap and derivative transactions — refer Das (1989).

3. The OTC options market on commodities is very similar in structure and instrument design to OTC interest rate options (interest rate floors, caps and collars). For example, in August 1989, one US bank announced the introduction of a natural gas price collar product whereby natural gas suppliers are guaranteed receipt of their desired minimum floor price for sale of their product and are reimbursed when their sale price falls below that level in return for foregoing the benefit of higher gas prices above an agreed maximum cap price level. See *International Financing Review*, No 788, 12 August 1989, p 57 (IFR Publishing Ltd).

4. For a discussion of the impact of financial institution intermediation in financial swap transactions see Das (1989), pp 34, 35 and 449–453.

5. The discussion in this section focuses primarily on the pricing of fixed-for-floating commodity swaps. The pricing of commodity price-for-interest swaps is discussed at the end of the section.

6. For a discussion of the pricing of forward contracts see Peter Ritchen, *Options: Theory, Strategy and Applications*, (1987), (Glenview, Illinois: Scott, Foresman and Company), Chpt 11.

7. For a discussion of the pricing of US dollar interest rate swaps see Das (1989), Chpts 6, 7 and 20.

8. It is worth noting that a substantial market for commodity hedging and commodity linked funding transactions has existed for precious metals, particularly gold, for a long time.

9. See Rawls III and Smithson (1989).

10. For a good discussion of basis risk in financial futures transactions see Edward Schwarz, Joanne M Hill and Thomas Schneeweis, *Financial Futures: Fundamentals, Strategies and Applications*, (1986), (Homewood, Illinois: Richard D Irwin, Inc), Chpt 7.

11. The transference of basis risk is not costless. The counterparty assuming the basis risk from the end user will presumably include the cost of managing the risk in the price quoted to the client. However, it is unlikely that the cost of managing this basis risk is *lower* in the context of a large commodity swap book than on an individual transaction. This would reflect the benefits of scale economies as well as the diversification gains within a large book entailing transactions involving a wide variety of indices.

12. See Das (1989), Chpt 7. It may ultimately be helpful to characterise the forward/futures commodities market (particularly its pricing aspects) as a forward *loan* market in the commodity — paralleling the forward market in currencies and securities. The pricing features of this market then become a function of the implied *commodity interest rates* which may be different to normal interest yields. This approach has an inherent difficulty as it is not clear how the forward loan market in commodities would determine its price level *particularly in the first instance*.

13. See Das (1989), Chpts 25–27.

References

"CFTC stages volte-face over commodity swap", *International Financing Review*, No 785, 22 July 1989, pp 67–69.

Chew, Lillian, "The bespoke approach", *RISK*, Vol 2/No 5, May 1989, pp 12–14.

Das, Satyajit, *Swap Financing*, 1989, Sydney: Law Book Company, London: IFR Publishing Ltd.

"The grey dawn of commodity swaps", *Euromoney*, December 1986, pp 9–11.

Krzyuzak, Krystyna, "From basis points to barrels", *RISK*, Vol 2/No 5, May 1989, pp 8–12.

Kryuzak, Krystyna, "Copper bottomed hedge", *RISK*, Vol 2/No 8, September 1989, pp 35–39.

Rawls, III, S Waite, and Charles W Smithson, "The evaluation of risk management products", *Journal of Applied Corporate Finance*, Vol 1 & 4, Winter 1989, pp 18–26.

Part III
Case studies

Chapter 23: New issue arbitrage — designing bond/ swap packages at SEK

Bernt Ljunggren
AB Svensk Exportkredit (SEK)

Ever since becoming active in the international capital markets in 1979, SEK has striven to achieve and maintain the lowest cost of funding *vis-à-vis* its borrowing competitors. The basis on which this competitive position rests is constantly at the forefront of planning and policy formulation at SEK. It also provides an interesting angle for analysing the recent history of the international capital markets.

Using this approach and borrowing the methods of the paleontologists who classify primitive societies by their use of tools, we can divide the history of the market into clearly distinguishable stages according to its use of swaps. In this way we can distinguish:

- *pre-swap age*, where the basis for competition was complex and diverse;
- *new swap age*, where the basis for competition was the ability to understand swaps;
- *middle swap age*, where the basis for competition was innovation and reaction time;
- *late swap age*, where the basis for competition was credit versus sub-Libor target; and
- *the post-swap age*, where competition is based on ability to manage the risk/return relationship.

The pre-swap age: complex and diverse basis for competition

At this stage in the development of the market, the tone, even in international bond markets, tended to be set by domestic bond market practices. In many cases it was necessary to notify the relevant authorities well in advance of a planned issue. The catch about this was that it was often necessary for a borrower to ask a potential lead manager to make the notification on his behalf, and this easily turned into a commitment to confirm the appointment of the same house as lead manager. The lead manager of a bond issue could therefore be securely appointed even many months before the launch of a deal. This in turn focused negotiations with the lead manager (after his appointment) on the timing of the issue and, finally, terms and conditions and pricing of the issue. For the intermediary banks this was the age of the mandate.

For the borrower there were many inputs into each one of these matters. Even to identify, for example, his own ideal target timing was a complex decision. Some view had to be formed of currency and interest rate trends and likely market conditions. The (official and unofficial) regulations of the market had to be understood. Consideration had to be given to the degree of exposure of the borrower's own name and assessing the potential impact of the other borrowers lined up for issue. Internal funding requirements and staff availability had to be determined and clarified.

These were just some of the factors which had to be determined and weighed in the balance in the process of targeting the timing of a particular issue. That was before the negotiations with the potential lead manager, with his competing demands from other borrowers, got under way!

Whilst this picture was most obviously true of the domestic bond markets, other markets, even the non-regulated Eurobond markets in the early days, tended to follow a similar pattern.

The scope of the background work necessary to prepare for a bond issue was therefore potentially immense. It would be misleading to pretend that SEK, or any other borrower for that matter, had ever completely covered the necessary work in sufficient depth. Clearly great demands were made on the analytical and decision making (not to mention negotiating) skills of the borrower. The ideal borrower needed to be an economist, a lawyer, a manager, a psychologist and perhaps even an artist. It was, however, possible to gain a competitive advantage over other borrowers by more thoroughly analysing and more rationally balancing these matters.

The "buzz words" at this time tended to spin off from the central concept of securitisation (sometimes thought to be a recent invention but actually an apparently "evergreen" market innovation). Words like "liquidity" and "placement power", often seemed to refer to things which all banks claimed to provide but which few, in reality, knew anything about. They also represented goals for the borrower, the achievement of which would enhance the borrower's name and consequent funding cost.

The positive attempt to promote liquidity and good distribution of securities had to be a major determinant of the policies pursued by SEK in launching new issues. In addition, SEK developed at this time and continues actively to pursue, a programme of trading in its own bonds.

For the highly rated borrower this was one "golden age". Even if he was required to work hard, the balance of power in the market was securely tipped in the borrower's favour. Borrowers were, after all, the only big players at that time. Borrowers dealt in hundreds of millions of dollars while investors dealt in hundreds of thousands of dollars. The intermediary "syndicated the risk". The day of the massive Japanese institutional investor and the bought deal where the intermediary also started dealing in hundreds of millions of dollars, had not yet arrived.

Borrowers who combined two normally incompatible qualities — a high credit standing and a high borrowing requirement, cornered the market in its most desirable commodity — the mandate for a top name. For SEK this was a great period, partly, we believe because we managed to keep up with, if not ahead of, the borrowing competition in respect of our analysis and decision making around these factors.

While none of these concepts has actually fallen into total disuse, it is true to say that they have, on the whole, been slowly upstaged by subsequent developments and are, by now, well and truly relegated to a back seat.

The new swap age: ability to understand swaps

This takes us back to the beginning of the 1980s when swaps were too new and strange to be fashionable.

At this stage the borrower was rewarded with lower borrowing costs for his acceptance of what was, at that time, a complicated story involving unfamiliar calculations, cash flows and credit risks to name but a few considerations.

A swap-related transaction in those days seemed to be a veritable minefield of potential sources of exposure and misunderstanding, made more dangerous by having to be negotiated simultaneously with the issue of bonds. Even matters trivial by today's standards, such as daycount and business day conventions, had not been standardised and required to be negotiated on a case-by-case basis.

Since sensible borrowers would only accept a structure they could understand, the borrower's ability to understand and his further ability to obtain necessary internal and external permissions for swap-related packages, became the critical factor in allowing a borrower to access the lower funding costs achievable only through swap-related issues.

SEK had early identified the potential in swap-related financing and sought to develop and apply expertise in it. Very few borrowers felt happy with the use of swaps at this stage, many making explicit policy statements to avoid it, others simply hoped that it would go away and that they would be able to avoid the trouble of getting to understand it.

SEK, on the other hand, succeeded early on in establishing a reputation for this expertise in swap technology which contributed greatly to a strong competitive position during this period.

The middle swap age: innovation and reaction time

By this stage the swap was perceived to be driving the bond rather than *vice versa*. The general pattern had emerged whereby banks bringing bond/swap packages were asked to compete on the sub-Libor but not to squeeze the pricing of the bond. The borrower saw a "golden age" in which it seemed possible both to bring a well priced bond to the market and to achieve an exceptional cost of funds.

At this stage the analytical and administrative skills of borrowers in relation to swaps were still not so widespread. Skill in swaps was still regarded as a speciality — the rightful domain of the "rocket scientist". In the traditionally conservative field of borrowing, some major players even continued to keep up a disdainful attitude towards swap-related borrowing.

The combination of these factors limited the competition and allowed borrowers, advanced in swap analysis and administration skills, to maintain very favourable trading conditions. The borrower's reaction time became the crucial factor in enabling him to reach a market window before it slammed shut. Arranging banks, eager to avoid missing market windows, therefore focused primarily on the turnaround speed of borrowers in seeking potential targets for proposals. Hence a borrower who could more quickly analyse, absorb and react to a swap-related financing proposal, could afford to set more aggressive sub-Libor borrowing target levels and gain a competitive advantage over other borrowers.

Particularly at this point in the history of the market, SEK actively courted innovation as well as the reputation for innovation. The first was instrumental in ensuring that new, value creating, ideas were both conceived and developed by SEK and the second, that the new ideas of others were brought to SEK as potential first issuer. Since very often even transactions looking superficially like transactions already done had some new wrinkle which would require a positive approach to innovation, the reality and the image of innovation contributed substantially to SEK's achievement of exceptional borrowing costs during this period.

Unfortunately for SEK these conditions were not destined to continue forever and another "golden age" drew slowly but surely to a close.

Late swap age: credit versus sub-Libor target

Now everyone was doing it. At least every borrower with even a half decent credit rating and even a basic grasp of financial concepts had jumped on the swaps bandwagon. Like fishermen going to sleep by their rods, borrowers baited their lines with sub-Libor targets and waited to be woken up by the fish pulling on the line. The bond/swap package had developed into a true commodity product.

The phenomenon fed through to the investor's side of the market as sophisticated institutional investors learned also to look at sub-Libor levels being achieved by borrowers to gauge the value in a transaction for them. Finally, through the development of the asset swaps market, investors learned to look through the packages of bond options and swaps to the floating rate equivalent return of any package deal.

To the intermediary banks this bought both increasing competition and increased freedom to structure any kind of instrument into a package. As long as he could see his sub-Libor cost of funds secured at the other end, the borrower was often indifferent to the contents of the package. Diversification of both fundamental financial instruments, and derivatives of those instruments, progressed rapidly to the point where it became difficult to think of any financial instrument or derivative which had not been structured, in some shape or form, into a swapped financing package. Government bonds, commodities, currencies, equity, equity indices and futures and options on any of these, all found their way into swapped financing packages.

Competition squeezed profits on both the bond and the swap, forcing banks to focus attention on devising ways of making money in the "middle" through deal structuring. Not unnaturally many banks leading this field tried to keep the internal mechanisms well hidden in a black box.

Bond pricing was no longer the main focus of attention in price negotiations, partly because it was now only one factor, and, compared with structuring, embedded derivative and swap pricing, probably the least controversial factor in determining final cost of funds to the borrower. The controversy had been drawn out of the bond pricing partly as bonds, even when presented publicly as underwritten offers, were often, in fact, completely preplaced with one or two investors. And partly because, when bonds were genuinely being underwritten and offered publicly, a consensus would normally emerge on appropriate pricing of the bonds in competitive offers received.

By now the borrower's role had deteriorated into a mind numbing process of establishing borrowing targets and checking through proposals to see whether they met the targets and, if so, to ensure there were no hidden snags. Gone was the pre-swap age need for a financial "renaissance man" and the early/middle swap age need for a "rocket scientist". Sub-Libor borrowing had become almost a purely administrative routine capable of being carried out even by a reasonably able secretary. No wonder that any investment demand, particularly from Japanese institutional investors routed through a bank's capital markets network, would now instantly be met by a list of borrowers complete with credit rating and estimated borrowing targets, all reputedly "ready to move".

Unfortunately for SEK, investors were not always eager to pay a high premium for the highest credit standing and, as the lists of borrowers with their targets became ever longer, so the hungrier borrowers became ever more ready to drop their targets. For the intermediary banks, the day of the pre-eminence of the mandate had well and truly passed and, with it for the time being at least, the dominant position of the borrower in the market. Credit, in the good old days, had been traded in select boutiques where no prices were displayed and where "if you had to ask the price you couldn't afford it." Now credit was being sold like fruit in a street market with each variety price labelled and displayed ignominiously for public scrutiny.

In this situation, as a seemingly endless supply of new "triple A-rated" sub-Libor borrowers streamed into the market with ever more modest targets, it became increasingly difficult for SEK to gain competitive advantage by levering off its swaps-related skills in the mainstream borrowing business. As a result, this was probably the least satisfying period for SEK in the recent history of the capital markets. At best it can be regarded as a period of consolidation where the skills acquired in the main long-term funding business were honed and polished and spread into the other sectors of the business, particularly the treasury, lending and administration areas.

Against this background, SEK in common with many other borrowers looked hard for new ways of creating value within the context of structured transactions with a locked-in sub-Libor cost of funds. This search brought SEK finally to the conclusion that the way to win back some of its competitive edge was to access some of the value previously retained by the arrangers who managed the risk in structured transactions, and use this to reduce cost.

The post-swap age: active risk management

The commoditisation of the swaps-related financing business was, on the whole, detrimental to SEK's competitive borrowing position. It did, however, produce some useful by-products. One such by-product was overcapacity in SEK's technical and analytical resources. It was a natural next step for SEK to apply some of this overcapacity to taking apart some of the black boxes of the banks to see whether their mechanisms could be applied to reduce its borrowing cost.

Being very aware of venturing into largely uncharted territory, the decision was made to hire a knowledgeable local guide. Hence SEK teamed up with Westminster Equity Limited, a specialist risk management consultancy firm, initially to analyse, and subsequently to design and manage, suitable risk positions. Together we have developed a programme of controlled risk management centred on the dynamic hedging of option-related positions.

The eroding competitive position in simple sub-Libor funding was the initial spur to this process and the corresponding technical overcapacity was a helpful contributory factor. The well established SEK tradition for innovation was the deciding factor.

Having just lived through the entire life cycle of the swap from its development as an arbitrage instrument to commodity product and basic widely used financial technique, SEK felt it could see the potential for similar development with options. Clearly the lion's share of the value in this process would go, as it had in the swaps market, to those at the forefront of this process.

Even if this vision turned out to be wrong, it was clear that a sound grounding in option-related financial concepts could be instrumental in allowing more penetrating analyses and a deeper understanding of a wide range of our activities. Concepts once learned can be forgotten but not unlearned. Even if future developments are not centred on option-related products, it is clear that markets will not fail to reflect fundamental concepts and techniques of option theory. By building up this expertise now, SEK expects to achieve optimal flexibility in both reacting to and playing a leading role in developing, the next generation of financial products.

It is not uncommon in financial circles to hear this type of commitment to innovation being criticised. Often it is dismissed as a kind of vain need always to be fashionable. This we believe to be a fundamental confusion. Fashion, particularly in clothing, may be fickle. Today's fashions are tomorrow's charity donations and may or may not be the high fashion of the year 2000. There is no fundamental logic to the dynamic of fashion.

The difference between this and the kind of innovation we are talking about here is that financial innovation is cumulative. There is progress in the evolution of financial technology. Those who fail to keep to the forefront of it are doomed to being allowed to extract only limited value from it. At SEK therefore we are not prioritising innovation for the sake of a love of novelty but because it is essential to retain a leading position and continue to support the Swedish exporting industries in ever competitive markets.

Chapter 24: Case study of a new issue swap

Ayesha Shah and Michael Bass
Nomura International Plc

The capital markets' arena serves to match the needs of borrowers of capital (issuers) with those of lenders of capital (investors). The development of the Euromarkets opened up a number of potential new markets for issuers to tap. This has predicated the question of which investor market is the most appropriate for a particular borrower, and what cross-market arbitrage opportunities are available. The cross-currency swap market developed in response to these possibilities, allowing issuers to borrow at the cheapest rate in their desired currency, whilst satisfying investor demand in what may be another currency or combination of currencies.

Recent trends in the new issue swap market have been characterised by increasing sophistication of all parties, an erosion of the funding opportunities available, greatly increased credit awareness and major shifts in the factors driving new issuance.

The development in awareness of the arbitrage opportunities of new issue swaps has inevitably reduced the differentials in borrowing costs between markets. However, the capacity of borrowers to react quickly to opportunities has led to swap-driven issues appearing whenever swap "windows" (ie, an abnormally wide secondary-bond/swap yield spread) facilitate particularly attractive funding levels. The pattern of issuance has consequently become less homogeneous and more concentrated on specific currencies and maturities at any one time. Increasingly, the desire of swap houses to offset or create positions (ie, by paying fixed in particular currencies/maturities) has also driven new issues.

Concerns over credit and the introduction of BIS capital adequacy requirements have caused swap houses to examine the profitability of the more capital intensive areas of business, and have increasingly excluded lesser quality credits from the market. The preoccupation with event risk has also undoubtedly raised, *ceteris paribus*, the cost of funds for a significant proportion of Euromarket borrowers. The net effect is that the scope for cross-market arbitrage has been significantly narrowed for all but top-quality credits.

The erosion of attractive funding levels from vanilla deals has prompted borrowers to adopt a variety of structures, such as embedded options, caps, floors and swaptions to reduce their overall cost of funds. A typical example would be the inclusion of a put option on the bond which, if exercised by the investor, would reduce the maturity of an issue. The premium payable for such an option by the investor is reflected in a reduced all-in cost of funds to the issuer. However, in the case of a swapped new issue, the issuer would need to purchase a put swaption to cancel the swap should the investor's put be exercised. Another common strategy for an issuer willing to set a minimum absolute level on the floating interest rate payable, would be the sale of a floor. Again, the option premium is annuitised over the life of the deal, and serves to enhance the floating rate achieved from the swap. Clearly, there is an opportunity cost to the issuer should short-term rates fall below the strike level of the floor.

A further innovation, for borrowers who do not wish to set the fixed cost of funds of a bond issue at the time of launch is the delayed rate set (DRS) facility. This is in effect the equivalent of a borrower swapping into floating rate at the time of issue, and then reverting to fixed rate as required (for example, when funds are on-lent at a fixed rate). Should an issuer wish to set the fixed rate in this way for a large number of tranches, executing and unwinding swaps becomes unwieldy, and hence DRS is the preferable option.

The private placement market has also been a fertile ground for innovation. Investor demand, derived from either tax or accounting requirements or an unusual risk-return profile, has also led to a wide variety of new structures. In the majority of cases, the asymmetry between investor demand and borrowers' needs is resolved *via* swaps. Typical products involve the investor receiving some enhanced investment characteristics (for example, capital appreciation, coupon income or option type redemption) in return for some increased risk (perhaps currency or commodity price sensitive) which is deemed acceptable by that investor. Products include deep discount bonds, reverse dual currency bonds, notes whose redemption value is currency, commodity or stock index linked and so on.

The concurrent development of swap techniques has been vital for swap houses to manage the irregular risk profiles involved. It is frequently the case that the borrower wishes to offload the specific risk inherent in the instrument, usually to an institution with a more natural business exposure in that area. This is often achieved *via* the swap market, and hence the swap house is often required to warehouse highly irregular cash flows. An integrated approach to the management of all types of risk has clearly become a prerequisite for any successful swap operation. One manifestation of this has been the move by swap banks towards pricing long-term forex within their currency swap book. In addition, most houses now attempt to manage the risk of all their fixed-income exposures within a unified framework.

The final major trend we must consider is the emergence of the Ecu sector. The Ecu bond market has a number of peculiarities which are of relevance here. The first point is that the nature of the investor base (ie, those investors wanting the relatively high yield/low currency risk balance of the Ecu — the so called "high yield Deutsche mark") has tended to result in relative illiquidity of all but the largest issues. At the same time, the lack of adequate hedging instruments and one-sided nature of the Ecu swap market (since the majority of end-user demand is to receive fixed-rate Ecu against bond issues) has meant that a reasonable size for an Ecu bond issue (perhaps Ecu300m) is an extremely large size by Ecu swap market standards.

At the time of writing it remains the case that the only significant end-user source of fixed-rate Ecu is the tax-driven arbitrage of Italian CTE asset swaps. Another anomaly of the sector is that at the present time the majority of outstanding Ecu swaps are cross-currency; a reflection of the fact that the greatest demand for funds, raised *via* Ecu bonds, has in fact been for floating US dollars.

For institutions exploiting potential arbitrages, an understanding of all inherent risk factors is vital. Whereas in the case of a Eurodollar straight swapped into floating dollars, only three variables need to be assessed in order to calculate the cost of funds to the issuer, more complex structures will hinge upon both interest and currency swap levels, as well as spot and forward forex and option prices. Each of these variables will independently impact the profitability of the deal, and although they may be interrelated, there is often a time lag between the movement of a more volatile index and the mirror movement of a related index.

Typically, for all but the simplest structures, there will be a number of possible routes open to the issuer to achieve the desired funding from a particular bond issue. These may involve some combination of interest rate and currency swaps, and spot and forward forex, as well as other interest rate options (floors, swaptions etc). The choice of structure will depend on economic viability; that is, it will be a function of sourceable customer/counterparty demand, liquidity and so on. The increased sophistication of market players has resulted in many of the potential arbitrages, such as those between currency swaps and forward forex, being quickly closed, and hence far more difficult to exploit than previously.

If we take the example of a five-year Euroyen bond issue swapped into floating-rate Deutsche marks, we essentially have the choice between forward forex and an interest rate or currency swap or a single currency swap, to produce the desired funding.

We will assume in this case that preliminary evaluations indicate the lowest funding cost will be achieved *via* yen/US dollar forward forex and a US dollar/Deutsche mark currency swap.

We may now take the following issue terms:

Amount:	Y25bn
Re-offer price:	100.00%
Coupon:	6.875%
Maturity:	five years
Fees:	25bp

Assumed market rates are as follows:

Five-year Treasury yield:		7.485%
Swap spread:		65bp
US dollar/Deutsche mark spot fx:		1.4800
Yen/US dollar spot fx:		131.40
Yen/US dollar	one-year forward fx:	–0.36
	two-year forward fx:	–1.60
	three-year forward fx:	–3.30
	four-year forward fx:	–6.30
	five-year forward fx:	–9.10

The spot and future annual yen cash flows are converted into fixed US dollar cash flows at the forex rates indicated above, and the annual US dollar flows are then swapped into semi-annual Deutsche mark Libor, with initial and final exchange of principal at the current Deutsche mark/US dollar rate.

Figure 1: Spot cash flows

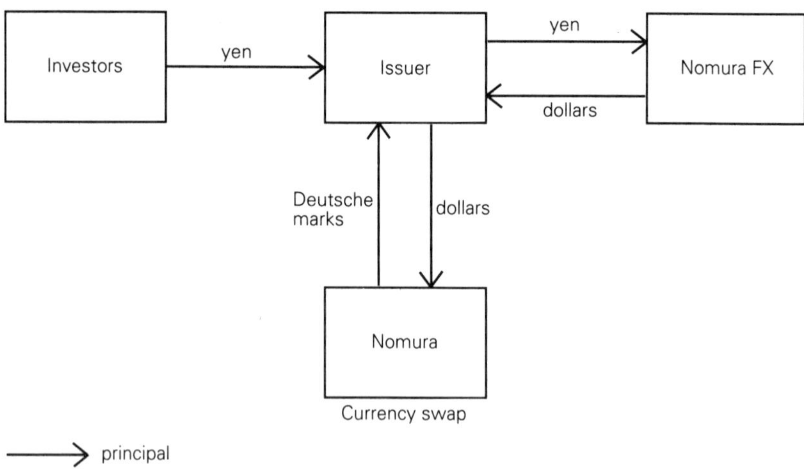

Table 1: Issuer cash flows

Years	Fixed yen cash flow (Yen annual)	Fixed US dollar cash flow (US dollar annual)
0	(24,937,500,000)	(189,783,105.02)
1	1,718,750,000	13,116,224.05
2	1,718,750,000	13,241,525.42
3	1,718,750,000	13,417,252.15
4	1,718,750,000	13,739,008.79
5	26,718,750,000	218,468,928.86
	IRR* = 6.936%	IRR* = 8.404%

Years	Floating Deutsche mark cash flow (DM semi-annual)
0	(280,878,995.43)
1	Libor - 0.1035%
2	Libor - 0.1035%
3	Libor - 0.1035%
4	Libor - 0.1035%
5	Libor - 0.1035%
	280,878,995.43

*IRR = Internal rate of return.
(We assume that the US dollar/Deutsche mark basis swap is transacted at zero cost.)

The impact of changes in the variables on the profit/loss of the deal is as follows:

	Yen/US dollar spot 1 yen	**Yen/US dollar 5-yr forward** 1 yen	**5-yr Treasury yield** 1bp	**5-yr swap spread** 1bp
Estimated impact on p/l (US dollar)	82,000	1,100,000	71,000	71,000

Figure 2: Future cash flows

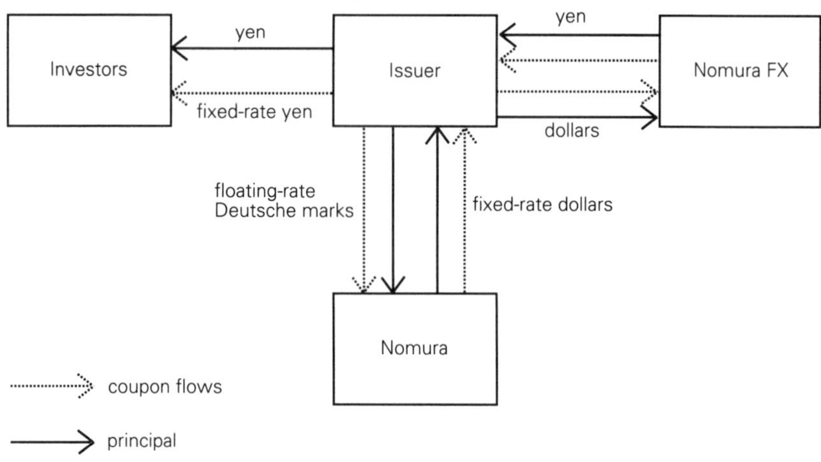

Consider now the case of an issuer who is willing to take some view on future forex movements, in order to achieve a substantially enhanced sub-Libor margin relative to the vanilla structure we considered in the previous example.

In this case, the issue is a three-year Ecu straight, with the proceeds swapped into floating Deutsche mark coupons and US dollar principal; the issuer pays the coupon in the higher yielding currency, and is prepared to repay principal in the lower yielding currency. In the example considered here the issuer is taking the view that the appreciation of the US dollar against the Deutsche mark to the redemption date will be less than the current forward forex market implies. The issuer's obligation to repay the US dollar principal at the current spot rate allows him to take full advantage of a possible depreciation of the US dollar. This structure can be neatly combined with the issuer writing a European currency option, in this case a US dollar put/Deutsche mark call (at-the-money spot). In times of high volatility, such an option will yield a substantial premium, which if annuitised over the life of the deal will greatly enhance the issuer's sub-Libor funding. In the scheme above, the option will only be exercised at maturity if the US dollar has depreciated from the spot at issue. Recall that the issuer gained on the currency play on redemption under such a circumstance. The issuer is merely trading off the opportunity loss against the substantial reduction in funding costs. Of course, should the US dollar appreciate, the option will expire unexercised.

Taking the following issue terms and assumed market rates:

Amount:	Ecu150m	Maturity:	3-year
Re-offer price:	99.85%	Fees:	20bp
Coupon:	9.875%		

Ecu/US dollar spot:	1.3828	Ecu/US dollar swap:	10.00%
DM/US dollar spot:	1.4905	DM/US dollar swap:	9.31%
DM/US dollar volatility:	10.95%	US dollar/US dollar swap:	8.01%

In this case, the issuer's Deutsche mark cost of funds, excluding the option premium, would be around Libor – 102 basis points. This contrasts with a funding rate of Libor + 7bp had the issuer swapped the proceeds directly into Deutsche marks. The option premium would reduce the cost of funds by a further 188bp. Clearly, this represents a substantial enhancement. It must be stressed that the issuer also incurs some currency exposure in this structure.

One possible interpretation of the (theoretical) component parts of this structure is as follows:

Figure 3: Spot cash flows

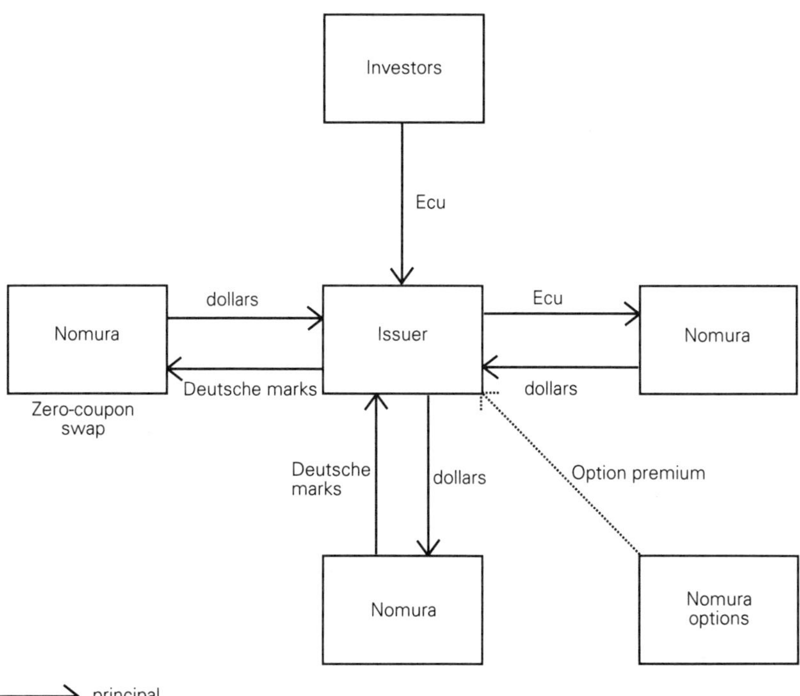

Figure 4: Future cash flows

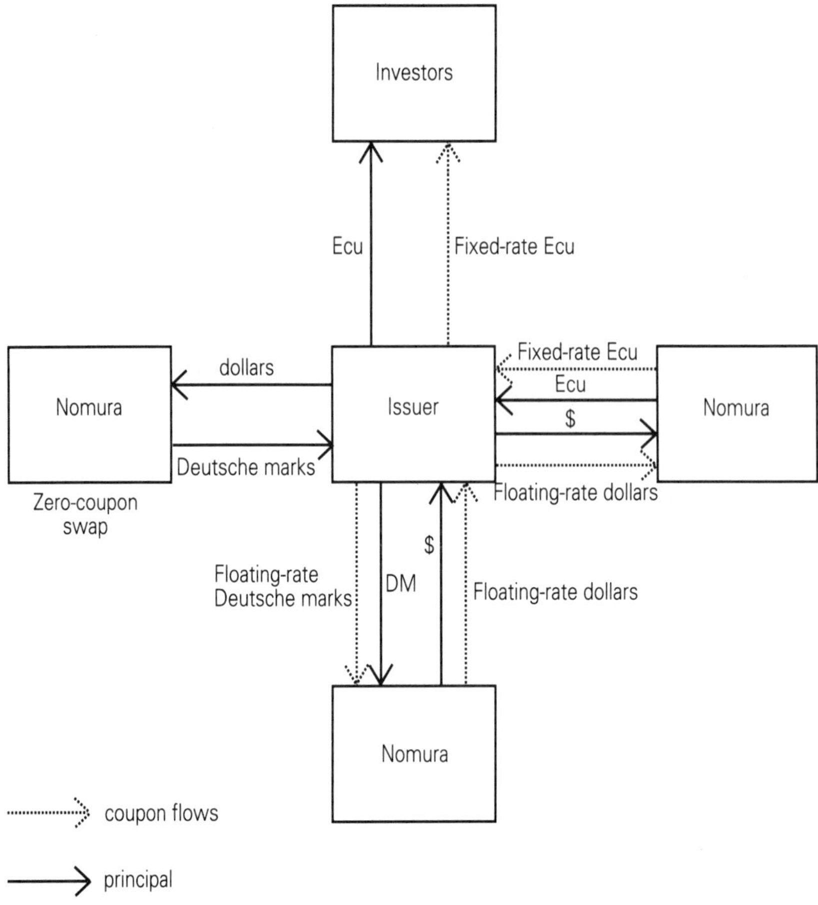

It is clear from our first example that timely execution of the separate parts of a new issue swap transaction, when combined with a view of likely market movements, can add considerable value to the arbitrage obtained by the issuer. Any risk assessment and deal execution strategy must therefore combine a thorough knowledge of the relationship between relevant variables and their respective volatilities, combined with some expectation of market movement.

It should be equally clear that successful exploitation of potential arbitrages must be based on an awareness of an increasing range of disparate markets, as well as the ability to identify those issuers best placed to exploit them.

Chapter 25: Swapping a Nikkei index-linked issue

Damian Kissane
Mitsubishi Finance International plc

In 1988 and 1989, there were in excess of 300 Nikkei 225 index-linked issues in the public markets. The number of private transactions can only be estimated. In 1990, the number of transactions declined considerably as the fall in the index discouraged investors from entering the market. Nikkei 225-linked issues are placements of debt where the coupon the investor enjoys or the principal repaid at maturity is linked to the performance of the Nikkei 225 Index in some way. The recent growth of this essentially Japanese phenomenon can be attributed to a number of reasons:

- the relatively low yields available from conventional debt instruments such as Eurobonds and the government debt markets since the October 1987 crash;
- the requirement of Japanese insurance companies to post higher and higher current yields on their portfolios;
- the superior returns available in equity markets;
- the rapid rise of the Nikkei 225 Index prior to 1990 (see Figure 1);
- the belief on the part of many investors that the Nikkei 225 Index would continue to exhibit the growth pattern witnessed prior to 1990;
- the need on the part of many investment funds invested long-term in Japanese equities to produce current or dividend income. The dividend yield on the Nikkei 225 Index in 1989 was less than 0.5%, compared with a yield of 4.75% from the FTSE 100 in the UK;
- restrictions on the investment criteria of many funds which prohibit investment in over-the-counter or exchange-traded options. Nikkei 225

index-linked issues can be viewed as security investments rather than investments in options or equity forwards.

Figure 1: The Nikkei Stock Index, 01/01/86 to 20/03/91

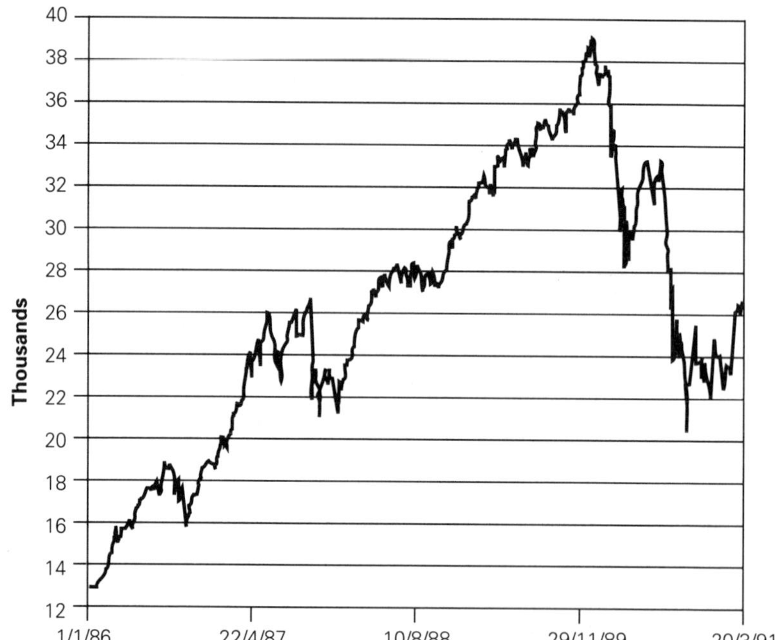

Types of Nikkei 225 index-linked structures

The growth of particular types of structures has probably been more a function of the requirements to circumvent various strictures on the investment of funds by fund managers than of the evolution of any particularly efficient structure, although in the latter part of 1989 interest rates did play a part in influencing the structures coming to the market.

There are two broad groups of structures:

- futures or forward-linked; and
- option-linked.

Futures or forward-linked structures require the investor to hold a forward position in the Nikkei 225 Index at a level fixed at the outset, thereby creating an exposure to the upward and downward movements of the index. Option-linked structures generally expose the investor to a single-direction movement of the index, ie, up or down, although bi-directional structures are possible (straddles). The exposures created can be favourable or unfavourable. The remainder of this chapter will concentrate on swapping an option-linked structure.

Types of Nikkei 225 option-linked structures

There are two basic option-linked structures:

- *High coupon (capital at risk) structures.* These offer a high coupon to the investor from the writing of a call or put option on the index, but place the investor's capital at risk. The investor earns a high coupon, but his principal redeemed at maturity is reduced if the index rises (falls) about the strike rate of the transaction.

- *Low coupon (capital gain) structures.* These offer a low coupon where the investor effectively purchases a call or put option on the index. The investor's return is then enhanced by a rise (fall) in the index about the strike rate set at the outset which can alter the coupons or the principal redeemed at maturity.

Variations on these basic structures are unlimited. The structure chosen is a matter of the risk the investor is willing to take relative to the size of market movement he expects. Thus, if the investor expects that the Nikkei will only fall by 20% he can cap his potential upside from that fall at 20%, thereby reducing the cost of the structure at the outset. In 1989, vanishing option structures were very popular whereby investors typically wrote puts on the Nikkei 225 Index in the expectation that it would not fall, with a vanish so that if it rose by say 5% or 10% the put option would vanish. This effectively reduced the investor's market risk decision, in his own eyes, to one of whether he believed that the index would rise by a further 5% or 10%. In return for writing the option, the investor received a higher coupon. The example below analyses two simple Nikkei-linked structures aimed at investors who believed at the time of launch that the Nikkei 225 Index would continue to fall and either required protection from that fall or wished to take advantage of it.

Example 1: High coupon structure, one-year call

An investor writes a call on the Nikkei 225 Index to the issuer in return for a higher coupon. If the Nikkei 225 rises from the strike rate set on the structure at the outset the principal redeemed at maturity is reduced.

Typical issue terms are:

Issuer:	European AA-rated financial institution
Principal:	Y2bn
Coupon (Annual (30/360)):	16.50%
Issue price:	100.875%
Fees:	0.875%
Maturity:	One year from payment
Payment date:	One month from launch
Redemption formula:	In yen at maturity

With maximum = 100%, and a minimum redemption amount of 0%, then:

$$100 - \left[\frac{(\text{Nikkei at maturity} - \text{Nikkei at launch})}{\text{Nikkei at launch}} \right] \times 100$$

Table 1: Pay-off of a high coupon structure

Nikkei at maturity (% of current level)			Bond redemption	Coupon	Total repaid
			(Percentage of principal, 100%)		
50	(14,490.23)		100	16.50	116.50
60	(17,388.27)		100	16.50	116.50
70	(20,286.32)		100	16.50	116.50
80	(23,184.36)		100	16.50	116.50
90	(26,082.41)		100	16.50	116.50
100	**(28,980.45)**	**Launch**	**100**	**16.50**	**116.50**
110	(31,878.50)		90	16.50	106.50
115	(33,327.52)		85	16.50	101.50
120	(34,776.54)		80	16.50	96.50
130	(37,674.59)		70	16.50	86.50

Typically, in the structure outlined above, the investor's return would be enhanced further by additional gearing. For example:

$$100 - \left\{ \text{gearing} \times \left[\frac{(\text{Nikkei at launch} - \text{Nikkei at maturity})}{\text{Nikkei at launch}} \right] \times 100 \right\}$$

Gearing	Coupon
2x	27.00%
3x	36.625%

In a geared structure the investor effectively writes an option based on a larger principal amount than the issue size. At a gearing of 2x (3x), the investor writes an option based on a principal of Y4bn (Y6bn) to the issuer. The issue size remains at Y2bn. The reader will recognise that in a structure where the investor's principal is at risk, the most he can lose is his original investment, ie, 100%. At a gearing of 2x (3x), each one yen rise in the Nikkei 225 Index (from Y28,980 to Y28,981) has the effect of reducing the investor's principal redeemed at maturity by two yen (three yen). The attraction of geared structures is that they offer the confident or aggressive investor even higher returns, although they put more of the investor's capital at risk, ie, they have higher exposure. They do not involve a higher market risk than the non-geared structures. The market risk in the above example is that the Nikkei 225 Index will be above the strike rate at maturity.

Example 2: Low coupon structure, one-year put

An investor purchases a put on the Nikkei 225 Index from the issuer in return for receiving a lower coupon. The investor has the opportunity to profit from a fall in the Nikkei 225. In all cases the investor is assured of his interest and principal at maturity.

The issue terms are:

Issuer:	European AA-rated financial institution
Principal:	Y2bn
Coupon (Annual (30/360)):	0%
Issue price:	101.50%
Fees:	0.875%
Maturity:	One year from launch
Payment date:	One month from launch
Redemption formula:	In yen at maturity,

With maximum = 200% and a minimum redemption amount of 100%, then:

$$100 + \left[\frac{(\text{Nikkei at launch} - \text{Nikkei at maturity})}{\text{Nikkei at launch}}\right] \times 100$$

In the above structure the investor is guaranteed redemption of 100% at maturity. In addition, he has the opportunity to further profit from a fall in the Nikkei 225 Index.

Table 2: Pay-off of a low coupon structure

Nikkei at maturity (% of current level)			Bond redemption	Coupon	Total repaid
			(Percentage of principal, 100%)		
50	(14,490.23)		150	0.00	150
60	(17,388.27)		140	0.00	140
70	(20,286.32)		130	0.00	130
80	(23,184.36)		120	0.00	120
90	(26,082.41)		110	0.00	110
100	**(28,980.45)**	**Launch**	**100**	**0.00**	**100**
110	(31,878.50)		100	0.00	100
120	(34,776.54)		100	0.00	100
130	(37,674.59)		100	0.00	100
140	(40,572.63)		100	0.00	100

The advantage to the issuer of Nikkei 225 index-linked issues

The attraction of a Nikkei 225 index-linked structure to the issuer is that he is protected from the effects, favourable or unfavourable, of the option and is left in a position of raising funds at an attractive level. The Japanese investors these issues are targeted at are typically required to hold investments listed on exchanges such as London or Luxembourg and issued by companies which have received formal credit ratings from agencies such as Moody's or Standard & Poor's. Alternatively, a credit rating from a Japanese rating agency is often acceptable. Name recognition is also an important factor. The result of this, when combined with the sub-Libor target generally achieved from these issues, is that the issuers tend to be European financial institutions, particularly Scandinavian and German. These institutions have a large and continuous appetite for US dollar sub-Libor funding which necessitates a quick response to funding opportunities which meet their requirements, unlike corporates which are typically more contemplative in their funding decisions, linking the raising of funds to a defined requirement rather than an attractive opportunity. Additionally, BIS capital requirements mean that for investors which are also financial institutions, these issuers are 20% capital weighted versus 100% for corporates.

Elements of pricing

The mechanics of pricing Nikkei 225 index-linked issues are relatively simple. It is possible to net out the component elements and analyse them individually. The components of pricing are:

- the issuer's sub-Libor target and the currency required;
- fixed fees;
- the currency swap rate; and
- the option price.

These elements of pricing are examined individually below.

The issuer's sub-Libor target and the currency required

Issuers of Nikkei 225 index-linked bonds typically require sub-Libor funding in US dollars at six-month Libor less 0.25% per annum or better. Nikkei-linked issues are generally smaller than normal Eurobond issues, the most typical size being Y2–3bn (approximately US$13.8–20.7m). Issues of only Y1bn in size are unusual while Y5bn is reasonably common. The factors determining issue size are purely investor demand and pricing.

Fixed fees

The fees involved in issuing Eurobonds are generally a fixed cost in the region of US$75,000, and in Nikkei 225-linked issues they often represent a significant part of the cost. On an issue of Y2bn, US$75,000 is approximately 0.54% of the issue at the outset, and this has to be recovered.

The currency swap rate

Because the issues are swapped from yen to US dollars, the currency swap rate is very important. The appropriate rate is the currency swap rate at which the swap markets pay fixed yen for one year on an annual bond basis, to coincide with the timing of the bond cash flows against receipt of six-month US dollar Libor, payable semi-annually on a money market basis. The first cash flow is typically one-month forward from launch to coincide with the normal timing of the payment date on a Eurobond issue. There is an exchange of the cash flows at the payment date when the proceeds of the bond paid in yen by the investors are exchanged by the issuer for US dollars with the swap counterparty. At the maturity of the transaction the cash flows are re-exchanged. The issuer repays the US dollar principal amount and receives yen, equivalent to the principal amount of the issue, Y2bn above, from the swap counterparty plus any yen interest payments due.

At the time of the above issue's launch, the currency swap market was willing to pay 8.09% for a start date one-month forward on an annual bond basis (30/360), against receipt of US dollar six-month Libor less 0.25% per annum payable semi-annually, with an initial exchange at the spot rate prevailing at the time of issue (US$/Y145.00).

A characteristic of Nikkei 225 index-linked issues is that they are generally issued with the proceeds of the issue, net of fees, corresponding to 100%. The issue price less full fees is never more than 100% because of the adverse impact this can have on the reported yield under Japanese accounting practices. Where investments are held on an original cost basis, payment of above par at launch gives rise to a loss at maturity representing the difference between the price paid at issue and 100%. For instance, if the issue price in the above examples were 101% of the face amount of the bond, the investor, net of fees, would pay 100.125%. At maturity he would realise an accounting loss of 0.125% representing the difference between the price paid for the bond (100.125%) and the principal amount of the bond (100%). In addition, if he is evaluated on current yield representing the coupon on his investments divided by the price paid it is easy to calculate that issues with par issue prices (ie, 100%) maximise the all important current yield measure used by Japanese financial institutions. Current yield is equivalent to coupon divided by price paid.

The option price

The option price is the most important component of a Nikkei-linked issue. In the high coupon (capital risk) structure above, the principal amount repaid to the investor at maturity is reduced if the Nikkei 225 Index is above the strike rate of 28,980. The investor has effectively written a 13-month, European style (only exercisable on one day) call option to the issuer; 13 months because the option is effectively bought and sold at the time of launch, not on the payment date. Launch date to maturity date is 13 months. These targeted transactions never appear on brokers' screens at launch with indicative bid-offer spreads. The issue size corresponds to the sum total of investor demand.

The size of the option the investor writes is Y2bn. At launch, each one yen movement in the Nikkei corresponds to a movement of Y69,013 in the redemption proceeds of the issue, ie:

$$\frac{2{,}000{,}000{,}000}{28{,}980} = 69{,}013$$

At the time of launch a call option of the above type could be sold for 8.25%.

In the low coupon (capital gain) structure the investor purchases a European style, 13-month put option on the Nikkei 225. The investor gains from a fall in the Nikkei below the strike. In return for owning this option the investor effectively gives up the coupon on the bond at maturity, that is, the investor gives up a one-year coupon for a 13-month put option. At the time of launch this put option could be purchased for 6.88% of the principal amount.

Mechanics of pricing

With the component parts analysed it is now possible to combine them together.

Example steps in a high coupon issue

Currency swap agreement between the lead manager (swap and option counterparty) and the issuer

The issuer and lead manager agree the following:

- The proceeds of the issue in US dollars, ie, the amount of funding raised in US dollars on the payment date when the issue proceeds of Y2bn are exchanged for US dollars (the "US dollar principal amount").

- The semi-annual interest payment date and maturity date when interest is due and repayment of the US dollar principal amount.

- The all-in rate achieved by the issuer from the issue in US dollars, ie, the cost of funding payable on each interest payment date, here six-month US dollar Libor — 0.25% per annum, payable semi-annually.

The lead manager agrees to service the yen obligations of the bond in return for the above US dollar cash flows, ie, to pay at the maturity date of the bond a coupon in yen of 16.5% and to repay the principal amount of the bond according to the formula outlined above.

Currency swap agreement between the lead manager and the swap market

The lead manager receives 8.09% annual bond basis (30/360) at the bond's maturity date, starting from the payment date of the bond, ie, one-month forward start. In return he pays to the swap market six-month US dollar Libor – 0.25% per annum — corresponding to the interest payment dates above on the US dollar principal amount. In addition, there are two exchanges of principal as per a usual currency swap:

- on the payment date the swap market receives Y2bn from the lead manager and pays to the lead manager the US dollar principal amount of US$13.79m (exchange rate agreed US$/Yen 145);

- on the maturity date (final exchange) the swap market pays Y2bn to the lead manager and receives from the lead manager the US dollar principal amount of US$13.79m.

Option agreement between the issuer, lead manager and the option market

The lead manager sells a call option to the market for 8.25%, (Y166m). The lead manager covers the expenses of the issue immediately, representing US$75,000 (Y10.875m). The remainder, Y154m, is invested to the final maturity date of the bond 13-months hence. Typically this would be done *via* the above currency swap. Proceeds at bond maturity date, assuming the lead manager can reinvest at the swap rate, are Y168.2m, or 8.41% of the bond issue. When combined with the yen interest payment from the swap market shown above (8.09%) the coupon is 16.50% of the issue. In return for this higher coupon the investor has written a call option to the issuer who sells directly to the lead manager *via* the swap agreement. In 1989 and 1990 a number of issuers, in particular SEK (the Swedish Export Credit Agency), chose to hedge the underlying option risk themselves using traditional option hedging techniques whilst being advised by independent consultants. The objective has been to increase the resulting sub-Libor achieved from these transactions by the issuer as part of the fund-raising exercise.

Position of the option at maturity date

The option will either expire with some value or it will expire worthless. If it expires worthless the option counterparty will not exercise the option and the investor will receive back his initial principal amount, ie, 100%. If the option does have value the option counterparty will exercise the option he has purchased from the lead manager.

For example, at maturity the Nikkei 225 Index has risen to 33,327 so exercise of the option by the option counterparty will generate:

$$\text{Y2bn} \times \frac{(33{,}327 - 28{,}980)}{28{,}980} = \text{Y0.3bn}$$

(Y0.3bn = 15% of Y2bn)

The investor's position at maturity date

If the option expires with some value (ie, is in-the-money) the issuer repays to the investor:

$$\text{Y2bn} \times \left[1 - \frac{(33{,}327 - 28{,}980)}{28{,}980} \right] = \text{Y1.7bn (85\%), plus the coupon of 16.5\%}$$

Total amount paid to investor at maturity = Y2.03bn (101.5%).

The issuer and the lead manager are thus protected from movements in the Nikkei 225 Index. Any loss is directly passed on to the investor at the maturity date of the bond *via* the redemption formula.

A criticism of the structures is their lack of liquidity since an issue will typically be sold to a small group of investors. This has prompted interest in "one touch" or "vanishing" structures where the investor's return is guaranteed if the market achieves a given target level, for example, if the market were to fall by 5% in the above example the call option written by the investors would automatically expire worthless.

Example steps in a low coupon issue

In the low coupon structure the investor purchases a put option from the issuer.

Currency swap agreement between the lead manager (swap and option counterparty) and the issuer

The issuer and lead manager agree that the issuer's all-in cost of funds, ie, including all expenses, is six-month US dollar Libor – 0.25% per annum, based on the agreed US dollar principal amount of the currency swap.

The lead manager agrees to service the yen principal obligations of the bond — there are no coupon obligations — in return for the above US dollar cash flows, ie, to pay at the maturity date of the bond a coupon in yen of 0% and to repay the principal amount of the bond according to the formula set out above.

Currency swap agreement between the lead manager and the swap market

The lead manager receives 8.09% in yen annual bond basis (30/360) in the currency swap market at the bond's maturity date starting from the payment date of the bond, ie, one-month forward start. In return he pays to the swap market six-month US dollar Libor – 0.25% per annum, corresponding to the interest payment dates shown above on the US dollar principal amount from the issuer. In addition, there are two exchanges of principal as per a usual currency swap. This is identical to the high coupon (capital risk) structure.

- on the payment date the swap market receives Y2bn from the lead manager and pays to the lead manager the US dollar principal amount of US$13.79m (exchange rate agreed = US$/Yen 145);

- on the maturity date (final exchange) the swap market pays Y2bn to the lead manager and receives from the lead manager the US dollar principal amount, US$13.79m.

Option agreement between the lead manager and the option market
The lead manager purchases a put option from the market for 6.88%, (Y137.6m). The lead manager covers the expenses of the issue immediately, representing US$75,000 (Y10.9m), leaving a total deficit of Y148.5m. This amount is effectively borrowed until the final maturity date of the bond 13-months hence *via* the currency swap market. The deficit, including interest at the maturity date, coincides with the yen payment on the swap at maturity of 8.09%.

Position of the option at maturity date
The option will either expire with some value or it will expire worthless. If it expires worthless the investor receives at maturity his original principal amount. If the option does have value the lead manager exercises the option on the investor's behalf and passes that benefit through the swap to the issuer and on to the investors *via* the bond proceeds at maturity. For example, at maturity, the Nikkei 225 Index has fallen to 25,000 so exercise of the option by the lead manager and issuer on the investors' behalf will generate:

$$\text{Y2bn} \times \left[\frac{(28{,}980 - 25{,}000)}{28{,}980}\right] = \text{Y0.27bn}$$

to add to the principal amount of the issue. Total repaid is Y2.27bn. An effective yen coupon of 13.7% over one year for the investor.

Future developments

In 1990 the number of Nikkei-linked issues declined dramatically as the index fell, leaving investors uncertain as to the direction of the market and traditional debt investors unwilling to risk their capital. Additionally, higher interest rates around the world made straight debt structures relatively more attractive to those investors. Holders of Nikkei-linked structures already issued suffered considerable market-to-market losses which prompted a reconsideration of their merits. The renewed rise of the market in 1991 and the demand by end investors for the highest return possible may yet tempt many investment managers back to these hybrids in 1991.

Chapter 26: Swapping an Australian dollar/yen dual currency bond issue

Maxwell G W Morley[1]

The transaction

The fundamentals of the issuance and swapping of an Australian dollar/Japanese yen dual currency bond issue are exactly the same as for swapping any other debt issuance, with the exception that the fixed coupons and the redemption of the principal of the bond are in different currencies.

The currencies of the cash flows of the bond are structured to appeal to a particular group of investors. The issuer of the instrument, not having funding requirements complementary to those of the targeted group of investors, swaps the proceeds and cash flows of the issue to achieve a more suitable funding result. In this way, Australian dollar/Japanese yen dual currency bonds have much in common with most other offshore Australian dollar capital market transactions — the issuer is simply taking advantage of a credit or structural arbitrage based on investors' preferences to obtain low-cost funding through the swap market.

The swap house manages the risk associated with the highly structured interest rate and currency swap required to marry up to the coupon and principal flows of the bond, thereby leaving the issuer with no residual or unwanted interest rate or foreign exchange exposure.

For ease of exposition, we will consider a hypothetical 10-year Y20bn face value dual currency bond issue carrying 8.50% Australian dollar annual coupons (these bonds have been issued with both Eurobond and Samurai structures). As will become apparent further into the example, the yen/Australian dollar exchange rate implicit in the calculation of the Australian dollar coupons is of critical importance to the economics of the issue and swap. We will assume a yen/Australian dollar exchange rate of 110. If the bond is issued at par, then its cash flows are as set out in Table 1 (from an investor's perspective):

Table 1: The cash flows of a Y20bn dual currency bond issued at par with annual 8.50% A$ coupons at an exchange rate of yen/A$ 110

Period	Principal	Coupons
0	Y(20,000,000,000)	
1		A$15,454,545
2		A$15,454,545
3		A$15,454,545
4		A$15,454,545
5		A$15,454,545
6		A$15,454,545
7		A$15,454,545
8		A$15,454,545
9		A$15,454,545
10	Y20,000,000,000	A$15,454,545

Economic rationale

For a dual currency bond to be successfully issued and swapped, the transactions involved must make economic sense to three parties — the investors in the bond (taken as a whole), the issuer and the swap provider. Figure 1 shows the flows of principal and coupon among these parties diagrammatically. The commercial considerations relevant to each party are discussed below.

The investor

As is usually the case for highly structured capital issues, it is the requirements or aims of the investor which lead to the creation of the structure and drive the transaction. This is clearly the case with dual currency bonds. Simplistically, the investor is willing to give something away to obtain some other benefit. In the case of Australian dollar/yen dual currency bonds, yen-based investors take exchange rate risk on the Australian dollar coupons (that is, give up the certainty of yield offered by a conventional yen bond) in the expectation of obtaining a higher running yield (A$8.50%) than that which would be available "at market" if the instrument was a conventional yen bond. In short, the investor obtains a higher running yield to the extent that his perception of future yen/Australian dollar exchange rate movements is more or less correct. Table 2 indicates how the investor's breakeven might be reached (or breached) assuming the alternate yield for a conventional yen bond issue of similar standing is 6.00% (AIBD basis).

Figure 1: Flows of principal and coupon among the parties to the swap transaction

(a) Initial principal exchange

(b) Periodic coupon flows

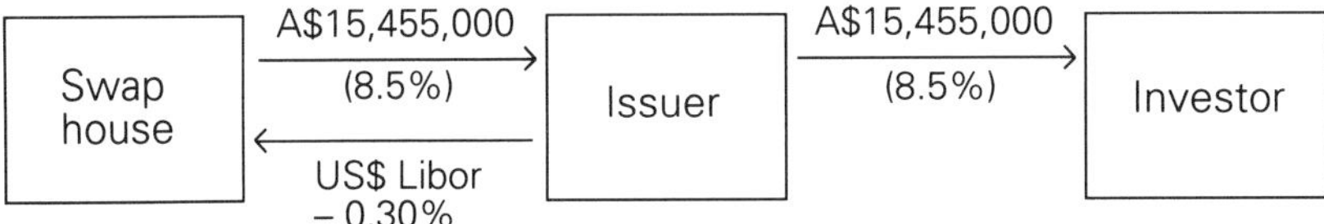

(c) Final principal exchange

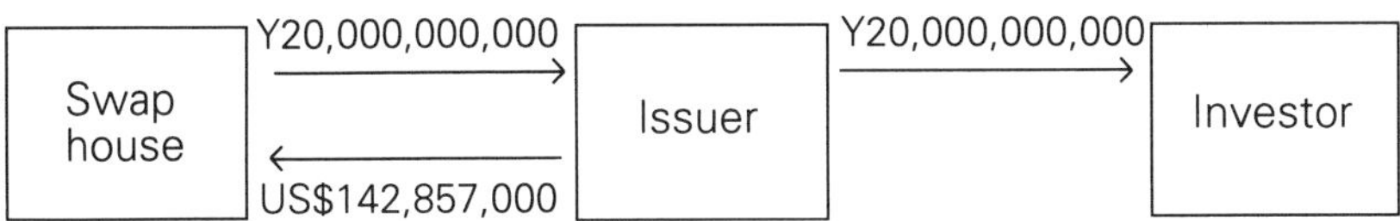

If the investor is able to realise all the Australian dollar coupons back into yen at the exchange rate (of 110) locked into the bond cash flows (scenario A in Table 2), then his realised yen yield will be 8.50%; 2.50% greater than his breakeven yield level for a similar straight yen issue. However, scenario B shows that a steady 7% per annum depreciation of the Australian dollar against the yen will push the realised yen return from the dual currency bond below the investor's breakeven level. Similarly, a large, sharp depreciation of the Australian dollar early in the life of the bond, even if followed by a stable exchange rate environment, will eat into the investor's return. In scenario C, a 30% depreciation of the Australian dollar prior to the payment of the first coupon followed by stable exchange rates is sufficient to bring the realised yen yield from the dual currency bond down to the breakeven level. The investor's implied "average" exchange rate (to break even) is yen/A$ 77 — well below historical lows. In addition, the dual currency investment, unlike a traditional "high coupon" Australian dollar security, does not expose a yen-based investor to foreign exchange risk on the principal redemption at maturity.

Table 2: Performance of an Australian dollar/yen dual currency bond issue under various exchange rate scenarios

		Scenario A		Scenario B		Scenario C	
Period	A$ coupons ('ooos)	Yen/A$ future spot rate	Realised yen cash flows (m)	Yen/A$ future spot rate	Realised yen cash flows (m)	Yen/A$ future spot rate	Realised yen cash flows (m)
0		110.0	(20,000)	110.0	(20,000)	110.0	(20,000)
1	15,455	110.0	1,700	102.3	1,581	77.0	1,190
2	15,455	110.0	1,700	95.1	1,470	77.0	1,190
3	15,455	110.0	1,700	88.5	1,367	77.0	1,190
4	15,455	110.0	1,700	82.3	1,272	77.0	1,190
5	15,455	110.0	1,700	76.5	1,183	77.0	1,190
6	15,455	110.0	1,700	71.2	1,100	77.0	1,190
7	15,455	110.0	1,700	66.2	1,023	77.0	1,190
8	15,455	110.0	1,700	61.6	951	77.0	1,190
9	15,455	110.0	1,700	57.2	885	77.0	1,190
10	15,455	110.0	21,700	53.2	20,823	77.0	21,190
Realised yen yield:			8.50%		6.03%		5.95%

Conversely, any appreciation of the Australian dollar against the yen will benefit the dual currency bondholder and it should be noted that the investor always has the ability to "lock in" such favourable movements (which might take the form of either Australian dollar appreciation or a narrowing of Australian dollar/yen interest rate differentials) by hedging forward the future receipt of coupons.

Australian dollar/yen dual currency issues are largely targeted at Japanese life insurance companies, giving these investors the opportunity to earn higher running yields (allowing the maintenance of higher current dividend payments) available from foreign "high coupon" currency investments without exposing the capital value (the yen principal) of the investment to foreign exchange risk. Dual currency bonds are therefore an acceptable compromise for the investor, providing access to higher yielding investments with lower foreign exchange exposure than conventional foreign currency investments.

The issuer

For the issuer, the dual currency bond issue offers an alternative low-cost funding source (on a swapped basis) more akin to a private placement of debt since these issues rarely trade in the secondary market. Just as numerous

German banks tapped the Australian dollar Eurobond market simply to generate cheap US dollar or Deutsche mark funding using the credit arbitrage available *via* the swap, so a variety of issuers have issued Australian dollar/yen dual currency bonds. In this case it is not so much a credit advantage that the issuer is able to realise *via* the swap, but a structural one. The attraction of the dual currency structure to the investor has enabled opportunistic issuers to raise low-cost swapped funding and at the same time diversify away from their traditional investor base.

Table 3 shows how the issuer's obligations under the dual currency bond are completely immunised against interest and exchange rate risks by the customised nature of the swap hedging into (in this case) a floating US dollar cost of funding.

Table 3: Swapped Australian dollar/yen dual currency bond to generate US dollar floating rate funding — issuer's perspective

All amounts in thousands

Period	Bond cash flows	Swap cash flows: receipts	payments	Issuer's net cash flow
0	Y20,000,000	US$142,857	Y(20,000,000)	US$142,857
1	A$(15,455)	A$15,455	US$ (Libor – 0.30%)	US$ (Libor – 0.30%)
2	A$(15,455)	A$15,455	US$ (Libor – 0.30%)	US$ (Libor – 0.30%)
3	A$(15,455)	A$15,455	US$ (Libor – 0.30%)	US$ (Libor – 0.30%)
4	A$(15,455)	A$15,455	US$ (Libor – 0.30%)	US$ (Libor – 0.30%)
5	A$(15,455)	A$15,455	US$ (Libor – 0.30%)	US$ (Libor – 0.30%)
6	A$(15,455)	A$15,455	US$ (Libor – 0.30%)	US$ (Libor – 0.30%)
7	A$(15,455)	A$15,455	US$ (Libor – 0.30%)	US$ (Libor – 0.30%)
8	A$(15,455)	A$15,455	US$ (Liobr – 0.30%)	US$ (Libor – 0.30%)
9	A$(15,455)	A$15,455	US$ (Libor – 0.30%)	US$ (Libor – 0.30%)
10	A$(15,455)	A$15,455	US$ (Libor – 0.30%)	US$ (Libor – 0.30%)
10	Y(20,000,000)	Y20,000,000	US$(142,857)	US$(142,857)

Through the issuance of a Y20bn dual currency bond with A$ 8.50% annual coupons based on a yen/Australian dollar exchange rate of 110, the issuer has raised almost US$143m in funding (assumed yen/US dollar exchange rate of 140) at a margin of 30 basis points below US dollar Libor *via* the swap mechanism without carrying any yen or Australian dollar exposure on the borrowings.

The swap provider

Given the investors' parameters (high yield/foreign exchange risk trade-off) and the issuer's requirements (all-in funding rate or margin), it is up to the swap provider to price, execute and hedge the structured interest rate and currency swap detailed in Table 3.

The construction of the swap can be broken down into vanilla or base products in several ways; for example:

- a fixed yen/floating US dollar swap with an initial and final exchange of principal, but where the fixed yen coupons have been switched into fixed Australian dollar coupons using a strip of forward foreign exchange contracts written at a flat rate; or
- a fixed Australian dollar/floating US dollar swap with initial and final principal exchanges, but with a long-dated foreign exchange swap (or zero-coupon Australian dollar/zero-coupon yen swap) superimposed on the principal exchanges.

Regardless of the view taken of the transaction, the theoretical pricing will not vary, although in practice the finest achievable price will depend on choice of the "vanilla" products against which market risk is to be priced and laid off (for example, the extent to which the long-dated foreign exchange market may be trading "favourably" slightly away from theoretical arbitrage levels).

For the purpose of illustrating the pricing of the dual currency swap shown in Table 3, the current coupon Australian dollar and yen swap curves (and zero-coupon curves derived therefrom) shown in Table 4 will be used. All rates are annual or annually compounding and bid/offer spreads are ignored for simplicity.

Table 4: Australian dollar, US dollar, and yen spot FX rates and interest rate and currency swap curves

All rates are annual or annually compounding

Period	Australian dollar swap rates: current coupon	zero coupon	Yen swap rates: current coupon	zero coupon
1	14.80%	14.80%	6.51%	6.51%
2	14.64%	14.63%	6.41%	6.41%
3	14.55%	14.53%	6.32%	6.31%
4	14.50%	14.47%	6.25%	6.24%
5	14.50%	14.48%	6.19%	6.17%
6	14.35%	14.27%	6.13%	6.11%
7	14.20%	14.05%	6.08%	6.05%
8	14.15%	13.99%	6.04%	6.00%
9	14.10%	13.92%	6.02%	5.98%
10	14.05%	13.84%	6.00%	5.96%

Spot FX rates:		
	yen/A$:	110.00
	yen/US$:	140.00
	US$/A$:	0.7857

Using these curves (which are not dissimilar to actual rates prevailing for part of 1990) and basic zero-coupon pricing and valuation techniques, the key exposures created by the execution of such a swap and related pricing considerations may be deduced from Table 5.

Table 5: Construction and pricing of the Australian dollar/yen dual currency swap — swap provider's perspective

All amounts in thousands

Period	Australian dollar/yen dual currency swap with issuer	Swap flows required to match bond cash flows	Swap flows generating issuer's funding	Present value of fixed flows is Y8,789,775 A$(79,907) ie, zero at yen/A$ 110	Zero-coupon discount rates
0	Yen principal	20,000,000		Y20,000,000	NA
0	US dollar principal		(142,857)		
1	8.5% A$ coupon	(15,455)	US$ Libor – 0.30%	A$(13,463)	14.80%
2	8.5% A$ coupon	(15,455)	US$ Libor – 0.30%	A$(11,762)	14.63%
3	8.5% A$ coupon	(15,455)	US$ Libor – 0.30%	A$(10,288)	14.53%
4	8.5% A$ coupon	(15,455)	US$ Libor – 0.30%	A$(9,000)	14.47%
5	8.5% A$ coupon	(15,455)	US$ Libor – 0.30%	A$(7,861)	14.48%
6	8.5% A$ coupon	(15,455)	US$ Libor – 0.30%	A$(6,943)	14.27%
7	8.5% A$ coupon	(15,455)	US$ Libor – 0.30%	A$ (6,157)	14.05%
8	8.5% A$ coupon	(15,455)	US$ Libor – 0.30%	A$ (5,423)	13.99%
9	8.5% A$ coupon	(15,455)	US$ Libor – 0.30%	A$ (4,784)	13.92%
10	8.5% A$ coupon	(15,455)	US$ Libor – 0.30%	A$ (4,228)	13.84%
10	US dollar principal		142,857		
10	Yen principal	(20,000,000)		Y(11,210,225)	5.96%
A		B	C	D	E

To generate the stream of A$ 8.50% coupons (Table 5, column B), the swap provider may price these flows as an annuity (in which case an initial period 0 investment of A$79,907,000 is required, that being the sum of the present values of each Australian dollar coupon discounted at the appropriate rate (columns D and E)). If the period 10 Y20bn payment is treated in a similar fashion the period 0 investment (that is, the present value of Y20bn flow in period 10) required is Y11,210,225,000 (see columns D and E). However, the initial principal exchange (US dollar/yen) of the swap will generate Y20bn for the swap provider in period 0 — a net positive flow of Y8,789,775,000 in period 0. The same initial US dollar/Japanese yen principal exchange also generates a short US$142,857,000 position on which US dollar Libor is received for the life of the transaction and the final yen/US dollar principal exchange "covers" that short US dollar position exactly.

The swap provider's net position in period 0 is short A$79,907,000 (required to generate the A$ 8.50% 10-period "annuity" stream) and long Y8,789,775,000 (the surplus from the initial yen principal flow after investing Y11,210,225,000 to generate the Y20bn payment necessary in period 10), a position which can be hedged out exactly in the spot foreign exchange market (buy Australian dollars/sell yen) at the prevailing exchange rate of 110. At this point the swap provider is exposed to both Australian dollar and yen re-investment risk and the instruments used to "hedge" those risks are likely to be a combination of swaps and long-dated foreign exchange. Alternatively, these risks could be warehoused and carried in a swap portfolio as spread or yield curve positions.

In addition, the existence of a sub-Libor margin of 0.30% must not be ignored and this shortfall in each period should be hedged or managed accordingly (these US dollar shortfalls generate an additional foreign exchange position which is not shown in Table 5 for the sake of clarity). Also, the above swap, because it is bond issue-related, would normally have to be priced and executed with a two to six-week forward start.

From the above example, it should be clear that the shape and absolute levels of the Australian dollar and yen (and US dollar) yield curves as well as the levels of spot foreign exchange rates are all critical factors in the pricing and hedging of an Australian dollar/yen dual currency swap. Ignoring any of these elements will immediately introduce pricing inaccuracies or unmanaged exposures.

Other issues

The swapped dual currency bond is very much a foreign exchange dependent product. The exchange rate implicit in the cash flows of the bond determines the breakeven level for the investor and, as a corollary, is of critical importance to the pricing and hedging of the swap. The whole packaged deal is extremely sensitive to changing spot foreign exchange rates and interest rate differentials. Specific attention needs to be paid to the spot foreign exchange positions created by the execution of the dual currency swap.

Another difficulty is one of market valuation. The dual currency cash flows and implicit exchange rate of the bond make conventional bond yield to maturity calculations meaningless. In addition, the targeted (often virtually private placement nature) of these issues means trading in the public market is rare — hence there is almost never an observable "market" price for these issues.

Such valuation problems do not exist in the case of the swap. It is reasonable to assume that any swap provider in a position to price, construct, execute and hedge a dual currency swap accurately should obviously be in a position to mark such a swap to market. However, most dual currency swaps are documented using fairly standard ISDA master agreements under which the primary early termination/default calculations are based on market quotations. As is the case with all highly structured swaps (particularly where pricing expertise is required in at least two currencies, one of which is not US dollars), there is a risk of considerable variation in quoted close-out amounts.

In summary, the essence of swapped Australian dollar/yen dual currency issues is the combination of a high coupon currency and a low coupon currency. As investors have thus far tended to be exclusively Japanese, the low coupon currency has almost always been yen. Although the Australian dollar has been a favoured high coupon currency, swapped yen dual currency bonds have also been issued with US dollars, sterling, Canadian dollars, New Zealand dollars, Ecu and pesetas — the latter having become a more acceptable foreign exchange risk after having joined the European Monetary System.

Notes

1. Max Morley is currently Manager, Risk Management Products in the Australian Financial Markets Group of Westpac Banking Corporation, Sydney.

Chapter 27: Swaptions — extracting value from callable financings

Per A Sekse
Manufacturers Hanover Trust

The explosive development of interest rate and currency swaps since 1980 has provided many sophisticated borrowers with the tools necessary for identifying attractive funding opportunities in the international capital markets. The appearance of interest rate option products just a few years later (caps, floors, collars and swap options) offered these same borrowers new opportunities to lower the cost of their financing activities.

In this chapter, we look at how swaptions have been used by a AAA-rated bank to extract value from the interest rate swap options embedded in callable financings.

Case study: A callable Eurobond issue

A European bank was considering several alternatives for raising medium-term floating-rate debt. Their funding objective was to lock-in long-term liabilities at an average cost of 20 basis points (1bp = 1/100 of 1%) below six-month Libor. The actual maturity of the liability did not matter to them because the bank expected to use the proceeds for funding their short-term lending activities.

As a frequent visitor to the Eurobond markets, they were familiar with the funding opportunities offered by swapping fixed-rate issues into floating. Unfortunately, the swap arbitrage was not generating enough to meet their funding objectives. Two examples of deals they had recently been shown highlighted the problem:

Two-year bond issue	**Seven-year bond issue**
US$100m	US$100m
7-7/8% annual coupon	8-3/4% annual coupon
101-3/8 issue price	101-7/8 issue price
1-3/8% fees	1-7/8% fees
7.875% all-in-cost	8.75% all-in-cost

Two-year swap	**Seven-year swap**
Swap counterparty pays 7.91%	Swap counterparty pays 8.78%
Issuer pays Libor	Issuer pays Libor

or

Counterparty pays 7-7/8 coupon	Counterparty pays 8-3/4 coupon
Issuer pays Libor –0.035%	Issuer pays Libor –0.03%

Given the spread to US Treasuries the bank's bonds were trading at at the time and the corresponding swap spreads for each maturity, it was obvious that a simple interest rate swap would not meet their requirements, regardless of the maturity they selected for an issue. Additional value had to be created which would help them reach a better sub-Libor margin.

Manufacturers Hanover identified such an opportunity. It was based on the European bank's indifference to the maturity of its floating-rate debt profile. They suggested including a call feature in the seven-year issue, arguing that investors were currently buying longer-dated issues not only for yield, but because they expected interest rates to decline for a 12 to 18-month period, followed by a rising rate environment in subsequent years. This interest rate view implied that the investors were not expecting the bonds to be called by the call date and therefore, lead them to undervalue the call options in outstanding issues.

This was borne out in the secondary market where comparable seven-year issues with calls after two years were trading at yields only marginally higher than non-callable issues. The terms of the seven-year callable issue Manuafacturers Hanover was suggesting were nearly identical to the non-callable issue described above, the only change necessary was to add the call option after two years.

Structuring the transaction

Two questions remained for the European bank (the issuer) to answer before proceeding. First, how should the swap be structured to maximise the value of the call option? Secondly, did the callable bond plus swap plus swaption package satisfy the funding target of Libor – 20bp? Manufacturers Hanover suggested structuring the deal in one of two ways:

(1) The European bank (as issuer) could enter into a two-year swap, receiving the 8.75% coupon from the swap counterparty and selling the counterparty the right to extend the swap by a further five years on the two-year call date of the seven-year bond issue.

(2) The issuer could enter into a seven-year swap, receiving the 8.75% coupon from the swap counterparty and selling the counterparty the right to cancel the swap on the two-year call date of the seven-year bond issue.

Assuming the swaption market was pricing efficiently, the issuer should be indifferent as to whether they sell a call (receiver's) option or a put (payer's) option to the swap counterparty. Although the upfront payments would be quite different, the actual cash flows on a net present value basis would be the same.

To convince them of this, Manufacturers Hanover helped the European bank to evaluate these alternatives by creating a spread sheet which compared the discounted cash flows generated by the two swap transactions plus the respective upfront payments quoted for the swaptions (see Figures 1 and 2). This also served to prove to the bank that it was meeting its minimum funding target of Libor – 20bp.

Swap structure 1

In this structure, the issuer enters into a swap transaction where it receives the 8-3/4% coupon on the bond issue for two years and pays six-month Libor flat. At the same time, it sells to Manufacturers Hanover a payer's option giving it the right to extend the swap on the same terms after two years for a further five years, making the total tenure of the swap transaction seven years if the payer's option is exercised.

At this point the issuer has a couple of options. It could elect to receive an upfront payment of $2,515,000 (Figure 1, column I) for the swaption less the difference between the two-year market swap rate of 7.91% and the 8.75% coupon (column F – net present valued or US$1,494,347) for a net upfront payment of US$1,020,653. Alternatively, it could accept a sub-Libor margin equivalent to this of Libor – 55bp (column G) for two years. In both cases, if the option is exercised it would then continue to pay Libor flat for five more years.

To determine whether this package meets its funding target, the issuer has to consider what happens to their cost of funding if the option expires unexercised as well as if it is exercised. This can be done by spreading the upfront benefit of the swaption payment over both scenarios (the net interest flow columns).

If the option is not exercised, the issuer calls the bond and refinances in the interbank market at Libor. This either leaves them with funding at Libor – 55bp for two years or, Libor – 20bp if the benefit is amortised over the full seven years. The seven-year analysis assumes that they can continue funding on a short-term basis after the call period for five years at Libor. If the option is exercised, the issuer does not call the bond issue, continues to receive fixed rate under the swap at 8.75%, and pays Libor flat.

The spread sheet in Figure 1 takes this approach by allowing the issuer to solve for the Libor subsidy level which creates a net present value of all cash flows equal to zero for the swap counterparty and swaption buyer. Columns D, E and F lay out the fixed-rate cash flows which occur during the first two years, as well as the potential remaining fixed-rate cash flows if the option is exercised. Columns G and H present the benefit to the issuer of paying Libor minus a spread compared to receiving the upfront swaption payment, a cost to the swap counterparty. These flows are summed and then net present valued (columns M and N).

This leaves the issuer with the decision of whether to take the upfront payment and pay Libor flat on the swap for two or seven years, or, pay Libor – 55bp for two years followed by Libor flat. Either way, the analysis proves that the European bank will pay no more than its target level of Libor – 20bp for its funding.

Swap structure 2

In this structure, the issuer enters into a swap transaction where it receives the 8-3/4% coupon on the bond issue for seven years and pays six-month Libor flat. At the same time, it sells to Manufacturers Hanover a receiver's option in the form of the right to cancel the swap after two years on the call date. Thus, although the swap tenure is seven years, it could be reduced to two years if the option is exercised.

As with the first alternative, the issuer has a couple of options. It can elect to receive an upfront payment of $970,000 for the swaption it has sold (column I) plus the difference between the current seven-year market swap rate of 8.78% and the 8.75% coupon of the bond for two years (column F – net present valued or $53,370) for a net upfront payment of $1,023,370. Alternatively, it could receive the same benefit by paying a sub-Libor margin of Libor – 55bp for the first two years of the swap (column G). If the option is not exercised, it would then pay Libor flat for five more years.

To determine whether this alternative also meets its funding objectives, the issuer again looks at what happens if the option is exercised or allowed to expire. If the option is not exercised, the issuer does not call the bond issue, continues to receive fixed rate at the 8.75% coupon, and pays Libor flat for five more years. If the option is exercised, the swap is cancelled and the issuer reverts to funding on a short-term basis (Libor) for the remaining five years.

The spread sheet in Figure 2 repeats the same procedures used in Figure 1. The issuer solves for the Libor subsidy by plugging for the margin which brings all cash flows on a net present value basis to zero. The analysis again proves that the European bank will achieve its target funding level of Libor – 20bp.

Summary

As this case demonstrates, the European bank was able to achieve its funding target by successfully combining the use of swaps and swaptions with its access to the Eurobond market. By taking advantage of the fact that investors were underpricing the value of bond calls in general, the issuer effectively purchased a call option cheaply, in the form of a callable issue, and sold it for a higher price to its swap counterparty in the form of a payer's or receiver's swaption.

In conclusion, it is worth noting that although the swaption techniques described here were first applied to the public bond markets, they are now an integral part of many financing packages. For example, the Japanese private placement market frequently builds call options into the yen debt placement, taking advantage of an investor's preference for asset quality and indifference to asset maturity. The yen swaptions are stripped out as part of a complete swap package which swaps the borrower into their desired currency at highly attractive rates.

Ship owners have also taken advantage of the swaption market by selling the free embedded call options they receive when ordering new vessels under subsidised export finance schemes. These free options come in the form of the right to prepay the fixed-rate financing at any time during the life of the loan.

Finally, it is worth stressing that the European bank was able to maximise the value it extracted from its callable issue by breaking the package down into its individual parts: bond pricing, swap pricing and swaption pricing. This not only allowed it to accurately analyse the value of each component, but also ensured that its funding target was not compromised in any way.

Figure 1: Swap structure 1

Issuer:	European bank	2-yr swap rate:	7.91%	(Swap rate Manufacturers Hanover would pay for 2 years)
Amount:	$100,000,000	Swaption proceeds:	$2,515,000	(If issuer sells put option/payer's option to MH for upfront payment)
Coupon:	8.75%	*or*		
Issue price:	101.875%	Libor margin of:	–0.55%	(If issuer takes put option sale benefit over first 2 years of bond issue, option expires unexercised)
Fees:	1.875%	NPV over 2 years:	($0)	(Solve for Libor margin which creates $0 NPV) (G)
Final maturity:	7 years			
Call option:	2 years	*or*		
All-in-cost of issue:	8.75%	Libor margin of:	–0.20%	(If issuer takes put option sale benefit over 7 years of bond issue, option expires unexercised)
		NPV over 7 years:	$0	(Solve for Libor margin which creates $0 NPV) (H)

	Cash flows of bond issue (issuer's perspective)		**Cash flows of swap (Manufacturers Hanover's perspective)**			**Issuer's sub-Libor margin**	
A	**B**	**C**	**D**	**E**	**F**	**G**	**H**
Date	**Issue proceeds**	**Coupon payments @ 8.75%**	**2-yr swap rate would pay @ 7.91%**	**Issuer receives cpn payments @ 8.75%**	**Swap surplus (deficit)**	**Pay Libor + or – 2 yrs –0.55%**	**Pay Libor + or – 7 yrs –0.20%**
11.12.90	$100,000,000						
11.06.91						($280,495)	($98,881)
11.12.91		($8,750,000)	$7,910,000	($8,750,000)	($840,000)	($280,495)	($98,881)
11.06.92						($281,264)	($99,152)
11.12.92		($8,750,000)	$7,910,000	($8,750,000)	($840,000)	($281,264)	($99,152)
11.06.93							($98,881)
11.12.93		($8,750,000)	Remaining payable only if option ex'cised	($8,750,000)			($98,881)
11.06.94							($98,881)
11.12.94		($8,750,000)		($8,750,000)			($98,881)
11.06.95							($98,881)
11.12.95		($8,750,000)		($8,750,000)			($98,881)
11.06.96							($99,152)
11.12.96		($8,750,000)		($8,750,000)			($99,152)
11.06.97							($98,881)
11.12.97	($100,000,000)	($8,750,000)		($8,750,000)			($98,881)

Cash flows of swaption – creates sub-Libor margin (Manufacturers Hanover's perspective)

Date	I Receive swaption proceeds	(+ F + G + I) Net interest flows over 2 years	(+ F + H + I) Net interest flows over 7 years	Zero coupon discount rates	M Net present value over 2 years	N Net present value over 7 years
11.12.90	$2,515,000	$2,515,000	$2,515,000		$2,515,000	$2,515,000
11.06.91		($280,495)	($98,881)	7.35%	($270,735)	($95,440)
11.12.91		($1,120,495)	($938,881)	7.68%	($1,040,602)	($871,937)
11.06.92		($281,264)	($99,152)	8.09%	($250,268)	($88,225)
11.12.92		($1,121,264)	($939,152)	8.44%	($953,394)	($798,547)
11.06.93			($98,881)	8.61%		($80,423)
11.12.93			($98,881)	8.79%		($76,803)
11.06.94			($98,881)	9.02%		($73,092)
11.12.94			($98,881)	8.62%		($71,048)
11.06.95			($98,881)	8.70%		($67,926)
11.12.95			($98,881)	9.13%		($63,888)
11.06.96			($99,152)	9.29%		($60,839)
11.12.96			($99,152)	9.44%		($57,708)
11.06.97			($98,881)	9.59%		($54,517)
11.12.97			($98,881)	8.85%		($54,605)
					($0)	**$0**

Figure 2: Swap structure 2

		7-yr swap rate:	8.78%	(Swap rate Manufacturers Hanover would pay for 7 years)
Issuer:	European bank	Swaption proceeds:	$970,000	(If issuer sells call option/receiver's option to MH for upfront payment)
Amount:	$100,000,000	*or*		
Coupon:	8.75%	Libor margin of:	–0.55%	(If issuer takes call option sale benefit over first 2 years of bond issue, option expires unexercised)
Issue price:	101.875%	NPV over 2 years:	$0	(Solve for Libor margin which creates $0 NPV) (G)
Fees:	1.875%			
Final maturity:	7 years	*or*		
Call option:	2 years	Libor margin of:	–0.20%	(If issuer takes call option sale benefit over 7 years of bond issue, option expires unexercised)
All-in-cost of issue:	8.75%	NPV over 7 years:	($0)	(Solve for Libor margin which creates $0 NPV)

	Cash flows of bond issue (issuer's perspective)		Cash flows of swap (Manufacturers Hanover's perspective)			Issuer's sub-Libor margin	
A	B	C	D	E	F	G	H
Date	Issue proceeds	Coupon payments @ 8.75%	7-yr swap rate would pay @ 8.78%	Issuer receives cpn payments @ 8.75%	Swap surplus (deficit)	Pay Libor + or – 2 yrs –0.55%	Pay Libor + or – 7 yrs –0.20%
11.12.90	$100,000,000						
11.06.91						($281,242)	($99,144)
11.12.91		($8,750,000)	$8,780,000	($8,750,000)	$30,000	($281,242)	($99,144)
11.06.92						($282,012)	($99,416)
11.12.92		($8,750,000)	$8,780,000	($8,750,000)	$30,000	($282,012)	($99,416)
11.06.93							($99,144)
11.12.93		($8,750,000)	Remaining payable	($8,750,000)			($99,144)
11.06.94			only if option ex'cised				($99,144)
11.12.94		($8,750,000)		($8,750,000)			($99,144)
11.06.95							($99,144)
11.12.95		($8,750,000)		($8,750,000)			($99,144)
11.06.96							($99,416)
11.12.96		($8,750,000)		($8,750,000)			($99,416)
11.06.97							($99,144)
11.12.97	($100,000,000)	($8,750,000)		($8,750,000)			($99,144)

Cash flows of swaption – creates sub-Libor margin (Manufacturers Hanover's perspective)

Date	I Receive swaption proceeds	(+ F + G + I) Net interest flows over 2 years	(+ F + H + I) Net interest flows over 7 years	Zero coupon discount rates	M Net present value over 2 years	N Net present value over 7 years
11.12.90	$970,000	$970,000	$970,000		$970,000	$970,000
11.06.91		($281,242)	($99,144)	7.35%	($271,456)	($95,694)
11.12.91		($251,242)	($69,144)	7.68%	($233,328)	($64,214)
11.06.92		($282,012)	($99,416)	8.09%	($250,934)	($88,460)
11.12.92		($252,012)	($69,416)	8.44%	($214,282)	($59,023)
11.06.93			($99,144)	8.61%		($80,637)
11.12.93			($99,144)	8.79%		($77,008)
11.06.94			($99,144)	9.02%		($73,286)
11.12.94			($99,144)	8.62%		($71,237)
11.06.95			($99,144)	8.70%		($68,107)
11.12.95			($99,144)	9.13%		($64,058)
11.06.96			($99,416)	9.29%		($61,001)
11.12.96			($99,416)	9.44%		($57,862)
11.06.97			($99,144)	9.59%		($54,662)
11.12.97			($99,144)	8.85%		($54,750)
					$0	**($0)**

Chapter 28: A case study of cross-currency forward interest rate swaps

Security Pacific Merchant Bank

For years global capital markets have assisted institutions and corporations in managing their short and long-term interest rate and currency exposures. New products have evolved to cater for the increasing sophistication required by market participants. Of note has been the gradual expansion of the swap market into areas previously considered the domain of other specialists. A case in point has been the use of the cross-currency swap market to manage longer-dated currency exposures previously handled by dealers of forward-dated foreign exchange.

One particular case occurred in 1987, when Security Pacific, through its multi-currency swap warehouses, arranged a transaction for Credit National in which unrealised interest and exchange rate profits embedded in an existing currency swap were crystallised and made payable to Credit National in the form of US dollars. Covering three currencies, the transaction synergised the swap, currency and securities markets to create value consistent with the business requirements and forecasts of Credit National.

As Credit National, like other French borrowers, was constrained by the French authorities from issuing French francs, it issued Japanese yen-denominated bonds in November 1982 and converted the borrowings to fixed-rate Ecu *via* the currency swap market. Ecu was chosen because of its close correlation to the French franc. Credit National issued Y20bn 8.50% semi-annual bonds with a maturity date of November 1992 and swapped into Ecu128.74m at 8.86%. The Samurais were callable in November 1988 and were structured on an amortising basis, with principal repaid at the rate of Y3bn in each of the four years spanning 1988 to 1991, inclusive, and a final Y8bn in 1992. The yen-raising and currency swap cash flows are shown in Figure 1.

The years following November 1982 saw considerable movements both in yen interest rates and the yen/Ecu exchange rate. Yen interest rates decreased while the yen strengthened against the Ecu. Both of these factors provided an increased value in the original swap. The decline in yen interest rates provided a benefit each period because Credit National derived an advantage from receiving yen fixed in the original swap and by paying yen fixed at a lower coupon in a current market swap. The gain in the currency was reflected in the initial currency transfer that occurred at the commencement of a new offsetting swap.

Figure 1: Original Credit National currency swap

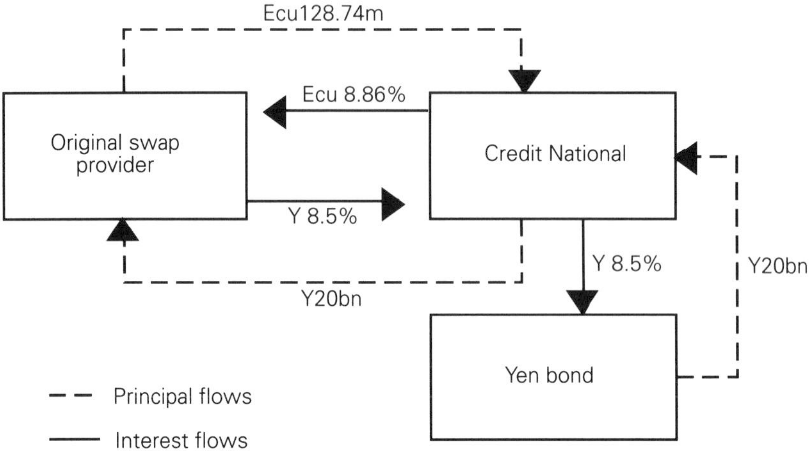

Credit National approached Security Pacific with a view to crystallising the benefit brought on by the favourable interest and exchange rate movements and the opportunity provided by the bond call option. The amount derived could be taken upfront by Credit National and used to offset any future borrowing costs.

Security Pacific structured the transaction in mid-1987. Under the arrangement:

- Credit National would enter an offsetting swap with Security Pacific that would match its obligations under only Y8bn of the original currency swap. This Y8bn represented the final repayment of principal under the Samurai scheduled to occur in November 1992;
- the offsetting swap would commence in November 1988, when the Samurai issue would be called, and mature in November 1992;
- at the bond call date, Credit National would receive yen principal from Security Pacific equal to Y8bn. In return, Security Pacific would receive Ecu51.496m;

- Security Pacific would also pay to Credit National an amount in mid-1987 which would represent the then current value of the currency and interest flows to be swapped.

Figure 2 shows the arrangement. The swap between Security Pacific and Credit National within the diagram will be referred to as Swap 0.

Figure 2: Swap arrangement between Security Pacific and Credit National — Swap 0

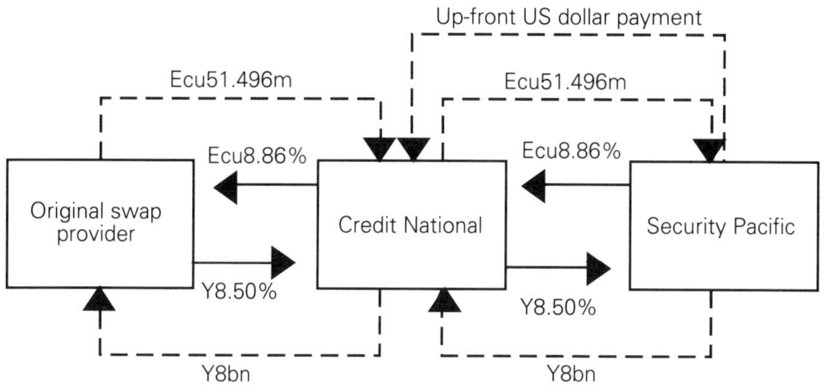

Mechanics

What follows is a description of two methods available to Security Pacific in structuring the hedge for the transaction with Credit National. Briefly these are:

(1) To transact forward currency swaps with principal amounts equal to Y8bn and Ecu51.496m (these being the principal flows between Security Pacific and Credit National in November 1988) and to convert the residual unmatched foreign currency flows to US dollars *via* the forward foreign exchange market.

(2) To transact two series of currency swaps to exactly match the cash flows between Security Pacific and Credit National after November 1988. It will be seen that this method removes the requirement for forward foreign exchange present in the first method.

For commercial reasons the structure of the transaction is described in general terms. The calculation shown uses interest and exchange rates (mid rates) which approximate those at the time the transactions were completed.

Interest and exchange rate data

The reader is referred to Appendix 1 at the end of this chapter for a full listing of the data used in the calculations of Methods 1 and 2 hereunder.

Method 1: Utilising cross-currency interest rate swaps and forward foreign exchange contracts

Security Pacific could transact forward currency swaps to mirror the yen and Ecu principal amounts of Swap 0. These currency swaps would be transacted in mid-1987, start in November 1988 and mature in November 1992. The two swaps transacted would be a yen/US dollar currency swap (which will be termed Swap 1) and an Ecu/US dollar currency swap (Swap 2).

Figure 3: Yen/US dollar currency swap — Swap 1

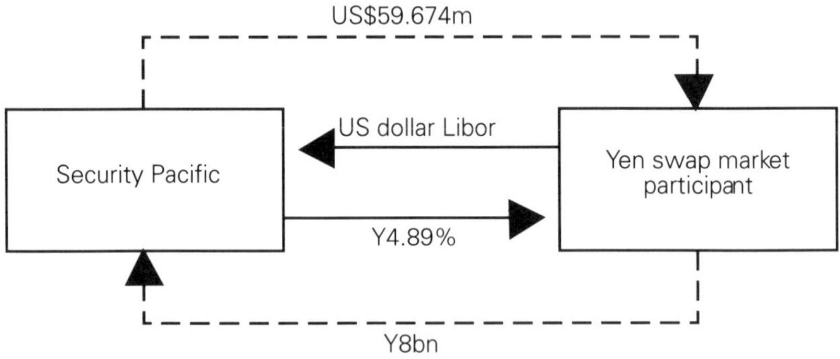

Figure 4: Ecu/US dollar currency swap — Swap 2

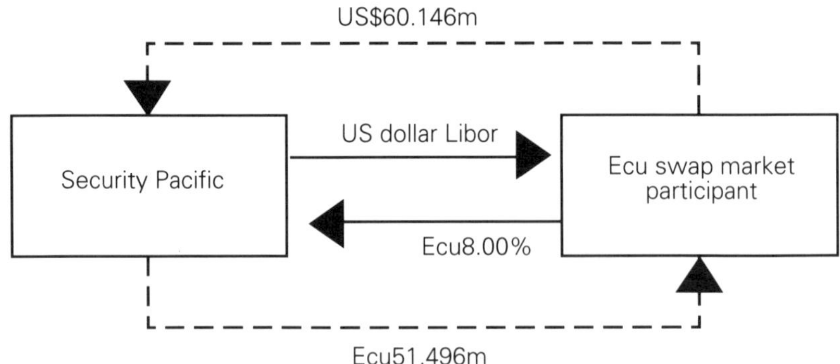

Figure 5: Removing exposure to movements in US dollar Libor rates — Swap 3

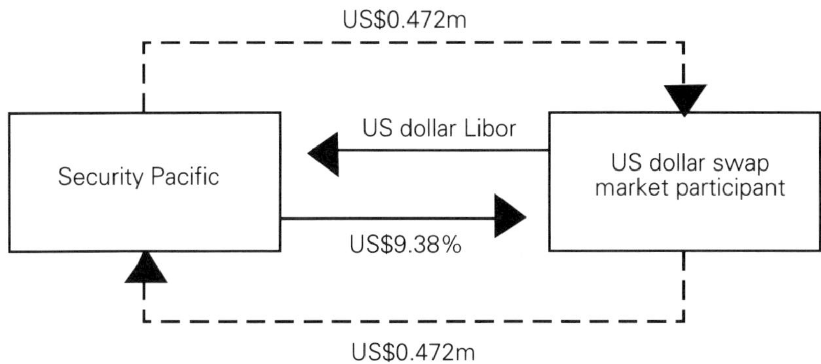

Figure 6: Summary of Security Pacific's position so far

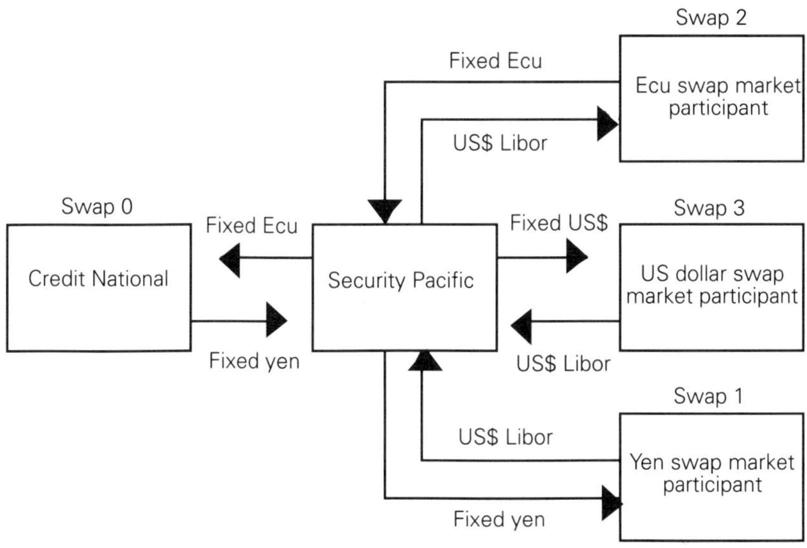

The yen and Ecu interest rates applicable to Swaps 1 and 2 would reflect the forward starting nature of the swaps. The calculation of the foward interest rates and derivation of the related forward foreign exchange levels is left to the reader; however, for guidance, Appendices 2 and 3 provide worked examples of each to demonstrate the methods used.

Since the US dollar principal amounts within Swaps 1 and 2 differ, there exists residual exposure to US dollar Libor. This may be removed by transacting a forward-starting US dollar interest rate swap with notional principal equal to US$0.472m (ie, the difference in US dollar principal amounts). In this way, exposure to movements in US dollar Libor rates is removed. The details of this swap, Swap 3, are as shown in Figure 5.

Figure 6 summarises the position of Security Pacific to this stage of Method 1. For clarity we have excluded principal flows from the diagram.

Table 1 details the cash flows into and out of Security Pacific under Swaps 0, 1, 2 and 3.

It can be seen from Table 1 that the structure depicted in Figure 5 contains foreign exchange risks. The risks relate to the unmatched currency flows found when comparing those passed between Security Pacific and Credit National (Swap 0) and those between Security Pacific and its counterparties under Swaps 1 and 2. As an example, under Swap 0 Security Pacific would receive from Credit National yen interest at the rate of 8.50% on principal of Y8bn and yet, in turn, pay to its counterparty under Swap 1 yen interest at the rate of 4.89% on the same principal amount. To remove this risk, forward foreign exchange contracts may be used. Contracts entered into would be to sell yen forward (and buy US dollars) and to buy Ecu forward (and sell US dollars). In this way, all cash flows are converted to a common US dollar basis as shown below. The reader will note the forward foreign exchange rates used in the conversion are those listed in Appendix 3.

Summarising the position to this stage, we see that the transaction has been converted to one containing only US dollar cash flows. To determine the amount to be received by Credit National in May 1987 we need only to perform a present-value calculation of the US dollar cash flows generated by the forward foreign exchange contract and the US dollar interest rate swap. In other words, we need simply to calculate the present value of the US dollar total column in Table 2. This calculation, which is also shown in Table 2, is completed by multiplying the amounts of this column by the US dollar zero-coupon discount factors listed within Appendix 2. This calculation yields a result of US$5,342,349. It is this amount that would be payable to Credit National in mid-1987.

Table 1: Cash flows into and out of Security Pacific under Swaps 0, 1, 2 and 3

	Swap 0			Swap 1
Date	Fixed yen	Fixed Ecu	Floating US$	Fixed yen
Nov 88	(8,000,000,000)	51,496,000	(59,674,262)	8,000,000,000
May 89	340,000,000	0	2,685,342	(195,681,677)
Nov 89	340,000,000	(4,562,546)	2,685,342	(195,681,677)
May 90	340,000,000	0	2,685,342	(195,681,677)
Nov 90	340,000,000	(4,562,546)	2,685,342	(195,681,677)
May 91	340,000,000	0	2,685,342	(195,681,677)
Nov 91	340,000,000	(4,562,546)	2,685,342	(195,681,677)
May 92	340,000,000	0	2,685,342	(195,681,677)
Nov 92	8,340,000,000	(56,058,546)	62,359,604	(8,195,681,677)

	Swap 2			Swap 3
Date	Floating US$	Fixed Ecu	Fixed US$	Floating US$
Nov 88	60,146,056	(51,496,000)	0	0
May 89	(2,706,573)	0	(22,132)	21,231
Nov 89	(2,706,573)	4,120,737	(22,132)	21,231
May 90	(2,706,573)	0	(22,132)	21,231
Nov 90	(2,706,573)	4,120,737	(22,132)	21,231
May 91	(2,706,573)	0	(22,132)	21,231
Nov 91	(2,706,573)	4,120,737	(22,132)	21,231
May 92	(2,706,573)	0	(22,132)	21,231
Nov 92	(62,852,628)	55,616,737	(22,132)	21,231

	Totals		
Date	Yen	Ecu	US dollars
Nov 88	0	0	471,794
May 89	144,318,323	0	(22,132)
Nov 89	144,318,323	(441,808)	(22,132)
May 90	144,318,323	0	(22,132)
Nov 90	144,318,323	(441,808)	(22,132)
May 91	144,318,323	0	(22,132)
Nov 91	144,318,323	(441,808)	(22,132)
May 92	144,318,323	0	(22,132)
Nov 92	144,318,323	(441,808)	(493,925)

The calculations assume equal half-yearly periods and US dollar Libor to be 9% semi-annual.

Table 2: Calculating US dollar cash flows

Date	Yen	Ecu	US$	Yen in US$	Ecu in US$
Nov 88	0	0	471,794	0	0
May 89	144,318,323	0	(22,132)	1,099,603	0
Nov 89	144,318,323	(441,808)	(22,132)	1,121,459	(521,820)
May 90	144,318,323	0	(22,132)	1,143,790	0
Nov 90	144,318,323	(441,808)	(22,132)	1,171,025	(529,582)
May 91	144,318,323	0	(22,132)	1,200,332	0
Nov 91	144,318,323	(441,808)	(22,132)	1,225,477	(539,854)
May 92	144,318,323	0	(22,132)	1,254,637	0
Nov 92	144,318,323	(441,808)	(493,925)	1,280,993	(547,599)

Date	US$ total	ZCDF[1]	PV
Nov 88	471,794	0.886331	418,165
May 89	1,077,471	0.847944	913,635
Nov 89	577,507	0.811640	468,728
May 90	1,121,658	0.776053	870,467
Nov 90	619,311	0.739782	458,155
May 91	1,178,200	0.703993	829,445
Nov 91	663,491	0.672247	446,030
May 92	1,232,506	0.641547	790,710
Nov 92	239,468	0.613920	147,014
			5,342,349

1. Zero-coupon discount factors.

Method 2: Utilising a series of cross-currency interest rate swaps

The first method at Security Pacific's disposal involved the transacting of forward currency swaps with yen and Ecu principal amounts equalling a portion of Credit National's original swap. In this case, the resulting interest amounts differed from the original transaction. The second method involved the transacting of currency swaps to exactly match the currency flows passing between Credit National and Security Pacific. It will be seen that this removes the need for forward foreign exchange contracts and the reinvestment assumption inherent in the calculation of the upfront US dollar amount.

Under the second method, two series of currency swaps are transacted to replicate the yen and Ecu cash flows of Swap 0. If we consider the yen cash flows only of Swap 0 then the objective becomes to transact a series of yen/US dollar currency swaps of correct principal, term and interest rate to ensure that the amount and timing of the yen cash flows received by Security

Pacific from Swap 1 exactly equal the total yen to be paid by Security Pacific under the series of yen/US dollar currency swaps. The strip of swaps would all commence in May 1987 and mature on the coupon dates of Swap 0. At the commencement of the swaps an initial exchange of principal would occur which would provide Security Pacific with a net yen exposure which would be translated through the spot FX market to provide a US dollar amount. We have listed below the series of currency swaps required to replicate the yen cash flows of Swap 0. The reader should note that the yen swap rates are taken directly from Appendix 1.

As shown in Table 3, the original cash flow in column A is totally offset by the strip of swaps shown in columns B to L (or totalled in column M). Swap rates are derived from the yield to maturity rates as demonstrated in Appendix 1 for the relevant maturities as shown.

For example: to offset the final cash flow in column A of Y8,340,000,000 we require a cash flow in column B of Y(8,340,000,000). This amount includes principal and interest and represents the final payment of the November 1992 swap. The principal portion in the November 1992 swap can be determined as follows:

Principal = Final cash flow/(1 + swap rate/2)
= Y8,340,000,000/(1 + 0.0470/2)
= Y8,148,510,015

This procedure is repeated to calculate the principal for the May 1992 swap in column C. In the calculation of this particular principal amount it should be noted that cash flows occurring on this date generated by swaps maturing subsequent to that date (that is, the interest flow on the November 1992 swap) should be used to offset the total yen requirement for the same date. In other words, the interest flow on the November 1992 swap occurring in May 1992 reduces the principal amount required to match the original Swap 0 cash flow.

For example:

May 1992 flow (col C) + Nov 1992 interest (col B) + May 1992 flow (Swap 0) = 0
May 1992 flow (col C) + (Y191,489,985) + Y340,000,000 = 0

ie, May 1992 flow (col C) = Y(148,510,015)

and:

Principal of swap in column C = Y148,510,015/(1 + 0.0470/2)
= Y145,100,161

This process is repeated until a full strip of swaps is produced as shown in columns B to L which, when added, equate to a reversal of the original swap in column A.

Table 3: Zero-coupon strip of swaps, yen leg

Maturity date	A Swap 0	B 4.70%	C 4.70%	D 4.70%	E 4.65%	F 4.60%	G 4.55%
May 87		8,148,510,015	145,100,161	141,768,599	138,547,372	135,432,427	132,419,874
Nov 87		(191,489,985)	(3,409,854)	(3,331,562)	(3,221,226)	(3,114,946)	(3,012,552)
May 88		(191,489,985)	(3,409,854)	(3,331,562)	(3,221,226)	(3,114,946)	(3,012,552)
Nov 88	(8,000,000,000)	(191,489,985)	(3,409,854)	(3,331,562)	(3,221,226)	(3,114,946)	(3,012,552)
May 89	340,000,000	(191,489,985)	(3,409,854)	(3,331,562)	(3,221,226)	(3,114,946)	(3,012,552)
Nov 89	340,000,000	(191,489,985)	(3,409,854)	(3,331,562)	(3,221,226)	(3,114,946)	(3,012,552)
May 90	340,000,000	(191,489,985)	(3,409,854)	(3,331,562)	(3,221,226)	(3,114,946)	(135,432,427)
Nov 90	340,000,000	(191,489,985)	(3,409,854)	(3,331,562)	(3,221,226)	(138,547,372)	
May 91	340,000,000	(191,489,985)	(3,409,854)	(3,331,562)	(141,768,599)		
Nov 91	340,000,000	(191,489,985)	(3,409,854)	(145,100,161)			
May 92	340,000,000	(191,489,985)	(148,510,015)				
Nov 92	8,340,000,000	(8,340,000,000)					

Maturity date	H 4.45%	I 4.35%	J 4.25%	K 4.25%	L 3.75%	M
May 87	129,537,661	126,780,192	(8,042,320,497)	(41,439,899)	(40,677,202)	973,658,703
Nov 87	(2,882,213)	(2,757,469)	170,899,311	880,598	41,439,899	0
May 88	(2,882,213)	(2,757,469)	170,899,311	42,320,497		0
Nov 88	(2,882,213)	(2,757,469)	8,213,219,808			8,000,000,000
May 89	(2,882,213)	(129,537,661)				(340,000,000)
Nov 89	(132,419,874)					(340,000,000)
May 90						(340,000,000)
Nov 90						(340,000,000)
May 91						(340,000,000)
Nov 91						(340,000,000)
May 92						(340,000,000)
Nov 92						(8,340,000,000)

Table 4: Zero-coupon strip of swaps, Ecu leg

Maturity date	A Swap 0	B 7.94%	C 7.94%	D 7.94%	E 7.88%	F 7.82%	G 6.85%	H Total
May 87		(51,933,075)	(404,915)	(375,129)	(347,720)	51,670,809	84,510	(1,305,520)
Nov 87		2,062,736	16,080	14,893	13,705	(2,020,008)	(87,405)	0
May 88								0
Nov 88	51,496,000	4,125,471	32,160	29,785	27,409	(55,710,826)		(51,496,000)
May 89								0
Nov 89	(4,562,546)	4,125,471	32,160	29,785	375,129			4,562,546
May 90								0
Nov 90	(4,562,546)	4,125,471	32,160	404,915				4,562,546
May 91								0
Nov 91	(4,562,546)	4,125,471	437,075					4,562,546
May 92								0
Nov 92	(56,058,546)	56,058,546						56,058,546

Similarly, the Ecu cash flows may be replicated by a series of Ecu/US dollar currency swaps. The required swaps and the related cash flows are shown in Table 4.

Clearly, under this second method there exists no requirement for forward foreign exchange transactions as the yen and Ecu cash flows of Swap 0 are exactly offset by the obligations of Security Pacific under the series of yen/US dollar and Ecu/US dollar currency swaps listed in Tables 3 and 4.

As noted, the yen and Ecu cash flows generated by the process shown can be seen to offset the cash flows in Swap 0. However, there remain residual cash flows in May 1987. These cash flows are the surplus of yen and deficiency of Ecu produced by the two strips of swaps transacted to match out the post-May 1987 cash flows. These are removed by selling yen spot (and buying US dollars) and buying Ecu spot (and selling US dollars). In practice, part of the yen surplus would probably be converted to Ecu to repay the Ecu deficiency whilst the remaining yen would be converted to US dollars. These conversions produce an amount of US$5,342,349 which is the amount to be given to Credit National in May 1987.

The reader should note that this amount equates to the amount derived under Method 1. In theory, both methods should produce the same result. However, in practice, different results are likely as they are subject to varying liquidity, pricing and bid/offer spreads in the underlying markets used.

Table 5: Principal amounts associated with the two swap series in Tables 3 and 4

	Yen/US$ swaps		US$/Ecu swaps		
	Yen principal	US$ principal	Ecu principal	US$ principal	Net US$ principal
May 87	973,658,703	(6,856,751)	(1,305,520)	1,514,403	(5,342,348)
Nov 87	40,677,202	(286,459)	(84,510)	98,032	(188,427)
May 88	41,439,899	(291,830)		0	(291,830)
Nov 88	8,042,320,497	(56,636,060)	(51,670,809)	59,938,138	3,302,078
May 89	(126,780,192)	892,818		0	892,818
Nov 89	(129,537,661)	912,237	347,720	(403,355)	508,882
May 90	(132,419,874)	932,534		0	932,534
Nov 90	(135,432,427)	953,749	375,129	(435,150)	518,599
May 91	(138,547,372)	975,686		0	975,686
Nov 91	(141,768,599)	998,370	404,915	(469,701)	528,669
May 92	(145,100,161)	1,021,832		0	1,021,832
Nov 92	(8,148,510,015)	57,383,873	51,933,075	(60,242,367)	(2,858,494)

Table 5 shows the principal amounts associated with the two swap series shown previously in Tables 3 and 4. The amounts shown as May 1987 principal represent the total principal exchanges to occur on this date. Since the yen surplus and Ecu deficiency are converted to US dollars to make the upfront payment to Credit National we see that Security Pacific will have a shortfall of US dollars which it will need to borrow.

The shortfall is equal to US$5,342,349 as shown in the last column of Table 5. This amount is repaid by the series of US dollar principal flows occurring from November 1987 onwards (ie, the US dollar amounts of the last column). An exposure which may arise is that since Security Pacific has borrowed from the market on a US dollar Libor basis and receives and pays US dollar Libor under the swap series, any change in the cost of funds of Security Pacific from Libor will cause fluctuations in the earnings of the transaction. If this situation has been anticipated a margin would be required to compensate for the reduced earnings.

The second method involves a larger number of swap transactions than the first method. These can be dealt directly into the market, enabling Security Pacific to provide an effective hedge for the transaction. This contrasts with Method 1 which requires Security Pacific to approach two different markets and to accept the risks arising from any anomolies which may exist.

Conclusion

The two methods discussed provide a similar hedge and in the analysis certain assumptions have been employed to illustrate this. The risks involved are similar, though several key differences do exist.

The first difference is the use of two different markets to hedge the transaction in Method 1 in contrast to Method 2. This involves coordinating deals between the two markets and therefore utilises two different types of credit exposures, "back office" management and documentation. The spreads in the two markets could also differ, especially in the forward foreign exchange market where spreads tend to widen significantly in the longer-dated contracts because of a lack of liquidity in contrast to the swap markets.

The second difference is the reinvestment assumption made on the US dollar cash flow in the first method in contrast to the second method. The first method assumes that the US dollars to be paid to Credit National will be borrowed over the life of the deal at the various swap rates used to generate the zero-coupon rates. The second method assumes that the US dollars borrowed at the commencement of the deal to fund the payment (or to cover the initial exchange of principal on the cross-currency swap if the yen and Ecu principal amounts received/borrowed are used for the upfront payment) will be borrowed at Libor, as the surplus cash is required only for the re-exchange of principals at maturity of all the cross-currency swaps. The resulting interest receipts from the swaps will then be used to cover the borrowing cost of the US dollar funds required. The risk here is that these funds cannot be raised at Libor and if this is the case an appropriate margin should be included in pricing the cross-currency swaps. This position can also be managed by transacting basis swaps that result in the swap warehouses' cash balances being close to zero.

The difference in the two hedging methods would have provided Security Pacific with appropriate cover; however, for the reasons described above, the second method would provide a more efficient hedge and thus allow Security Pacific to manage the transaction with a more acceptable level of risk in one market, not two.

Appendix 1: Interest and exchange rate data

Spot foreign exchange rates are:

US dollar/yen: 142.0
Ecu/US dollar: 1.16

Swap rates

	Yen (sa)	Ecu (a)	US$ (sa)
6 months	3.75	6.85	8.00
1 year	4.25		8.00
1.5 years	4.25	7.82	8.20
2 years	4.35		8.40
2.5 years	4.45	7.88	8.50
3 years	4.55		8.60
3.5 years	4.60	7.94	8.75
4 years	4.65		8.90
4.5 years	4.70	7.94	8.95
5 years	4.70		9.00
5.5 years	4.70	7.94	9.00

Appendix 2

The calculation of the parameters of the yen/US dollar currency swap entered into by Security Pacific under Method 1 (shown in Figure 3) is described below.

The following series of zero-coupon discount factors may be derived from the interest rate data of Appendix 1.

	Z_i	Yen	Ecu (a)	US$
6 months	Z1	0.9816	0.9669	0.9615
1 year	Z2	0.9588		0.9246
1.5 years	Z3	0.9388	0.8924	0.8863
2 years	Z4	0.9174		0.8479
2.5 years	Z5	0.8956	0.8264	0.8116
3 years	Z6	0.8734		0.7761
3.5 years	Z7	0.8524	0.7644	0.7398
4 years	Z8	0.8315		0.7040
4.5 years	Z9	0.8106	0.7081	0.6722
5 years	Z10	0.7920		0.6415
5.5 years	Z11	0.7738	0.6560	0.6139

To illustrate the iterative method employed in their derivation consider that, if from the list of yen zero-coupon discount factors Z1 = 0.9816 and Z2 = 0.9588, then Z3 is the solution to the equation:

$$1 = 0.0425/2 \times (Z1 + Z2 + Z3) + Z3$$

where 4.25% is the semi-annual rate for a swap maturing in November 1988 (ie, three half years from May 1987).

Similarly, Z4 is found by using the results for Z1, Z2 and Z3 and the two-year yen swap rate; Z5 is found by using the results for Z1, Z2, Z3 and Z4 and the two and a half-year swap rate, and so on.

It should be noted that to commence the iterative process we find Z1 as follows:

$$Z1 = 1/(1 + \text{6-month rate}/2) = 1/(1 + 0.0375/2)$$

and by successive substitution we find Z2 from the formula:

$$1 = \text{1-year swap rate}/2 \times (Z1 + Z2) + Z2$$
$$= 0.0425/2 \times (Z1 + Z2) + Z2$$

Z3, Z4 etc then follow from the above.

The forward yen semi-annual swap rate commencing in November 1988 and maturing in November 1992 becomes R, the solution to:

$$Z3 = R \times (Z4 + Z5 + Z6 + \ldots + Z11) + Z11$$

It can be found by substitution that R = 4.8920%.

Appendix 3

The calculated forward foreign exchange rates, given the interest and exchange rate data of Appendix 1, are tabled below:

	US$/Yen	US$/Ecu
6 months	139.10	1.166
1 year	136.93	1.173
1.5 years	134.06	1.168
2 years	131.25	1.176
2.5 years	128.69	1.181
3 years	126.18	1.189
3.5 years	123.24	1.199
4 years	120.23	1.212
4.5 years	117.77	1.222
5 years	115.03	1.232
5.5 years	112.66	1.239

As an example the theoretical US dollar/yen forward foreign exchange rates may be formed *via* the formula:

$$\text{US dollar/yen } (i \text{ periods}) = \frac{1/Zi\text{ (yen)}}{1/Zi\text{ (US\$)}} \times \text{spot US dollar/yen}$$

The computed forward US dollar/yen exchange rate for November 1988 is one US dollar = 134.06 yen, or:

$$\frac{1/0.9388}{1/0.8863} \times 142$$

where i = 3, Z3 (yen) = 0.9388 and Z3 (US dollars) = 0.8863

Using this exchange rate, we can verify, for example, that the US dollar principal amount of Swap 1 of Method 1 above is US$59,674,262 (approximately 8bn/134.06).

Chapter 29: Airlines — managing jet fuel price risk

Zahid J Ullah
Chemical Bank

The trend over the last decade has been for a consolidation in the airline industry. These airlines have routes that are no longer confined to particular geographical regions and so extend to all parts of the globe. Fuel is purchased from points all along these routes. This has the effect of increasing risk as fuel prices are affected by local supply and demand that causes differentials in fuel prices from one location to another.

Fuel costs typically are an airline's second highest expense, accounting for roughly 10%–20% of total operating expenses. Given the size of this expense and the extreme volatility of fuel prices, the airlines' operating results are highly unpredictable. A small change in the price of fuel greatly affects the airlines already depressed earnings. It would be prudent, therefore, for an airline to manage its fuel price risk. The idea of risk management is not new to airlines; they already manage interest rate and currency risks that represent a much smaller percentage of total costs. Airlines are not alone in being exposed to jet fuel price risks. Air forwarders have very similar risks, and travel operators are exposed to fuel price risks by locking in prices for holiday packages three to six months ahead of the season.

Figure 1 shows the magnitude of fuel price volatility. Prices can fluctuate by 50% or more in a period as short as three months. Historically, annual fuel price volatility has been in the range of 35% to 42%. In the last 15 months, fuel prices have doubled with the Middle East crisis pushing prices to record highs. Airlines are facing large operating losses. The larger airlines purchase several hundred million gallons of fuel each year; a one cent increase in prices adds several million dollars to their operating expenses. This highlights the need for price risk management.

When a corporation formulates any risk management policy it goes through a number of critical steps. First is the measurement of risk. For an airline it is fairly clear as to what its exposures are. An airline needs to determine its fuel purchases by location. The next step is to choose between exchange-traded or over-the-counter (OTC) hedging instruments. This involves correlation analyses of the limited number of exchange-traded energy products against the types and location of jet fuels that the airline buys. Other factors that have to be considered are the liquidity and terms available between OTC and exchange-traded instruments. Lastly, the airline will need to develop a strategy to implement the risk management policy.

Figure 1: Fuel price volatility on NYMEX

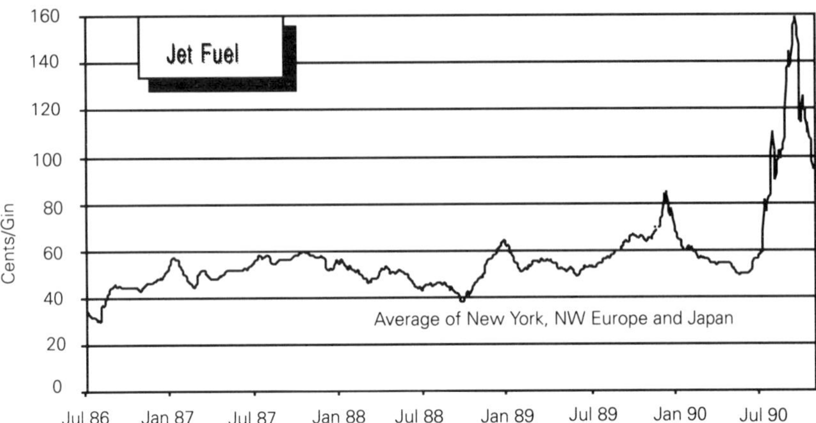

The exchange traded energy products that are most similar to jet fuels in physical content are the No. 2 heating oil contract on the New York Mercantile Exchange (NYMEX) and the Gasoil contract on the International Petroleum Exchange (IPE) in London. As a starting base, we can assume that No. 2 heating oil will correlate to jet fuels from the US East coast and that Gasoil will correlate to European jet fuel. As no exchange in the Far East trades a clean product there is no ready answer for Far Eastern jet fuel.

However as Figure 2 shows, the Jet/No. 2 price basis can become very exaggerated. This basis typically trades between 3 and 7 cents per gallon. However, during the current Middle-East crisis, the basis jumped to a high of 39 cents. During last winters extreme cold spell the basis reached a high of 27 cents. An airline using the NYMEX No. 2 contract to hedge its jet fuel risk would find itself paying some 25 cents per gallon more for physical jet purchases than it would be receiving on the hedge. Similar results would occur if the airline used either gasoil or No. 2 to hedge jet fuel from any other location (see Figure 3). The correlation between these fuels follow:

- Jet NYHB vs No. 2: 76%
- Jet NYHB vs WTI: 64%
- Jet NWE vs Gasoil: 69%

Figure 2: Jet fuel price basis

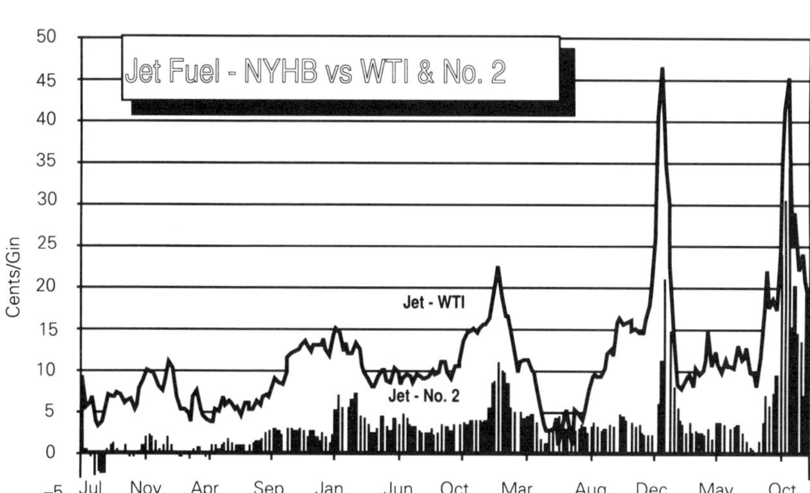

Jet fuel — NYBH is the cash price for jet fuel A — New York Harbour;
WTI is the NYMEX contract for West Texas Intermediate light sweet crude oil;
No. 2 is the NYMEX contract for No. 2 heating oil — New York Harbour.

Figure 3: Hedging with jet fuel and gasoil

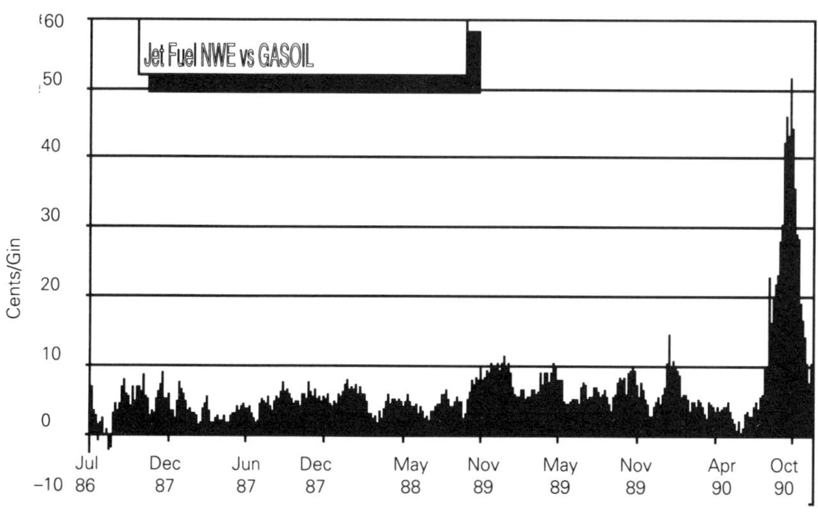

This basis risk is not the only argument against using futures to hedge jet fuel. The No. 2 and Gasoil contracts are quoted out to 13 months and nine months respectively; however, most activity takes place in the near months. Therefore, it is not feasible to use futures contracts to hedge risks beyond six to nine months. Although the NYMEX West Texas Intermediate (WTI) crude oil contract is now quoted as far out as three years, WTI is less precise a hedge then No. 2 heating oil.

An airline can perfectly hedge its jet fuel risk in the OTC market. Today, jet fuel fixed for floating price swaps and jet fuel price caps are available in the same manner as swaps and caps are available for currency and interest rate management. OTC commodity swaps and caps can be indexed to jet fuel prices from any number of major cities. Commodity swaps and options are available for maturities anywhere from a few months to several years. Commodity swaps and options offer much flexibility as to notional volumes, amortisation schedules, price references, and strike prices. Typically the swaps and caps are indexed to jet fuel prices from the *Platts's Oilgram* Price Report. These are financial instruments calling for settlement by way of cash only.

In going to the OTC market an airline has three alternatives for hedging its jet fuel price risks — swaps, caps and collars. In selecting one these instruments, an airline must consider the level of price protection it requires, price expectations, and the relative costs of hedging alternatives. If an airline strongly feels that prices will rise, then a swap will provide full protection at the lowest cost. If instead prices are expected to fall, and the airline wants a ceiling, then a cap will be the appropriate hedge. Finally, if the airline is uncertain about price movements, then the best hedge may be a collar, which protects against extreme price movements at little or no cost. Figure 4 highlights the different level of price protection provided by swaps, caps and collars.

A swap would enable an airline to lock in a fixed price for its jet fuel consumption. In the swap, an airline would pay a fixed price for jet fuel and in return receive the spot price. At the end of each settlement period, if the spot price is greater than the fixed price, then the airline receives the difference between the spot price and the fixed price, multiplied by the notional quantity of the commodity. If the fixed price is less than the spot price, then the airline pays the difference in prices, multiplied by the notional quantity to the counterparty. When spot jet fuel prices rise relative to the fixed price, the airline receives a payment that offsets increased jet fuel costs. When spot prices fall, the airline foregoes its cost savings. The swap effectively stabilises the operating costs of the airline (see Figure 5).

Figure 4: Levels of price protection provided by swaps, caps and collars

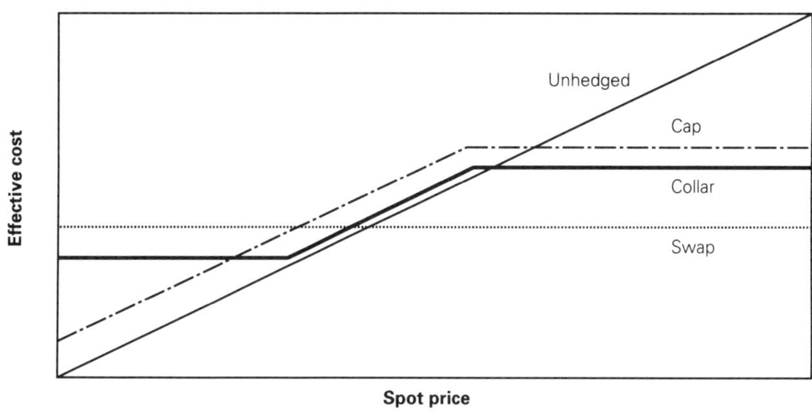

Figure 5: A swap transaction

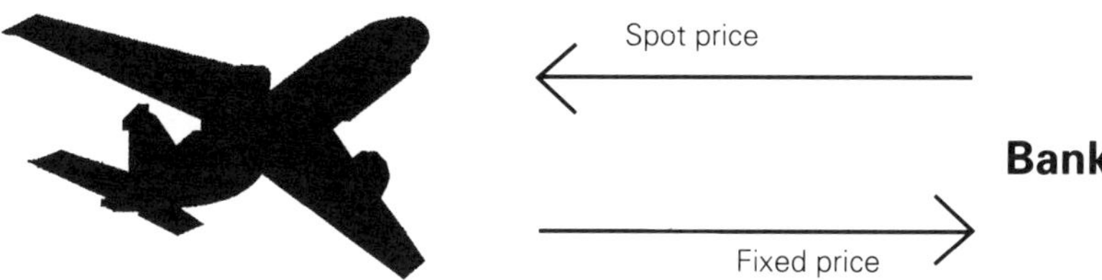

In a commodity cap, the airline pays an upfront premium to the cap seller in return for a payment when the spot price for jet fuel rises above a fixed strike price. At the end of each settlement period, the strike price is compared to the spot price. If the spot price exceeds the strike price, the airline receives the difference between the spot price and the strike price, multiplied by the notional quantity of the commodity. If the spot price is less than or equal to the strike price, then there is no payment. The strike price is set at the outset of the transaction. Although the strike price can be set at any level, the upfront premium will increase as the strike price is lowered.

Figure 6: A cap transaction

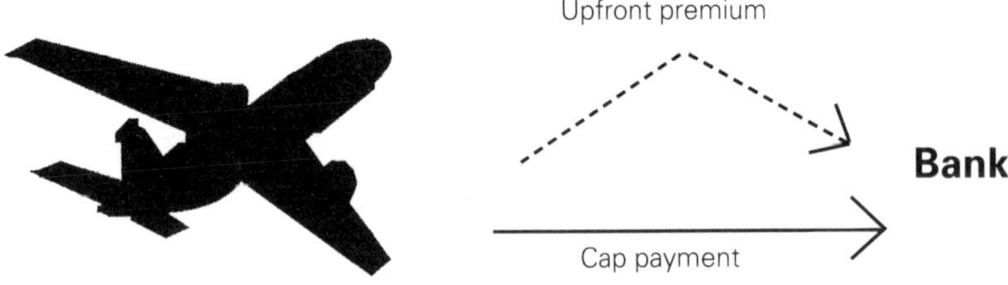

When spot price > cap strike price,
Airline receives (spot – strike) x quantity

In a collar, the airline sells a floor at a lower strike price than that of the cap it buys. The upfront premium will be reduced or eliminated, depending upon the individual premiums of the floor and the cap. In a collar, the airline retains the benefits of having a cap in place. If the spot price is above the cap strike price, the airline receives a payment for the difference between the spot price and the cap strike price, multiplied by the notional quantity of the commodity. However, if the spot price is below the floor strike price, the airline makes a payment for the difference between the floor strike price and the spot price, multiplied by the notional quantity. If the spot price lies between the strike prices, then there is no payment.

Figure 7: A collar transaction

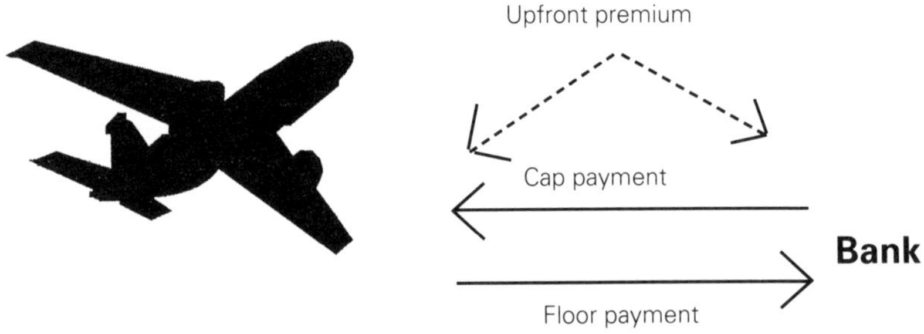

When spot price > cap strike price airline receives (spot – strike) x quantity

Whe spot price < floor strike price, bank receives (strike – spot) x quantity

An example of a jet fuel swap

Skyline Air operates out of the New York region and it estimates that its jet fuel purchases will be 8 million gallons per quarter for the next two years. Anticipating rising prices, Skyline would like to hedge 50% of its exposure. Skyline has to decide the hedging product that will best fit its exposure, risk appetite, and market view. Its alternatives are as follows:

- Futures: No. 2 heating oil, unleaded gasoline, WTI
- OTC: Jet fuel NYHB, No. 2 heating oil, unleaded gasoline, WTI, swaps, options

Since Skyline is an US-based airline it would not make sense for it to use the European-based futures contracts. The NYMEX WTI contract is traded out to three years. However, WTI prices do not follow jet prices terribly well (correlation is 64%). No. 2 heating oil and jet fuel prices correlate reasonably well (76%). However, the NYMEX contract trades out to one year; this does not cover the two-year exposure that Skyline wants to hedge. Skyline would have to stack the hedge in the last No. 2 contract. This exposes the airline to significant calender risk as well as the basis risk between jet fuel and No. 2. Futures contracts require a great deal of daily management. Each day the number of contracts in the hedge have to be adjusted to create an averaging effect (the airline buys fuel on a daily basis). Additionally, margin has to be posted to the exchange. This margin is subject to day to day changes in the mark-to-market value of the contracts (variation margin).

Skyline can access the OTC market for a more effective hedge. Skylines' interest is for swaps indexed to jet fuel, thereby eliminating all basis risk, or for No. 2 heating oil swaps for the full two years of its exposure horizon. The decisions here depend upon the basis between the fixed prices on the two swaps. Historically, the basis has been around 4 cents per gallon. A jet fuel swap makes sense if Skyline can arrange a jet fuel swap at a premium of between 4–6 cents over No. 2 heating oil. If the jet fuel basis is quoted higher than this, the No. 2 swap should be chosen.

The OTC market also offers options (caps, floors, and collars) on all the above fuels. The decision between swaps and options (caps) is driven by the cost of the cap. The cap premium is a function of maturity, strike price, and most importantly, volatility. The recent increase in volatility, due to the Middle East crisis, has made all options very costly. Skyline could enter into a collar to reduce the premium payments. This entails Skyline buying a cap and selling a floor. The strike prices on the cap and floor can be set such that the option premium is reduced or eliminated.

Given that Skyline is primarily concerned with higher prices, a jet fuel swap makes the most sense.

By entering into a swap, Skyline will establish a fixed price for jet fuel of $0.56 per gallon. Skyline will receive the quarterly average of settlement prices for the *Platt's* Jet Fuel FOB Barge quotation for New York. This reference price best reflects the cost of Skyline's purchases of jet fuel in the New York region.

Figure 8: Jet fuel price swap

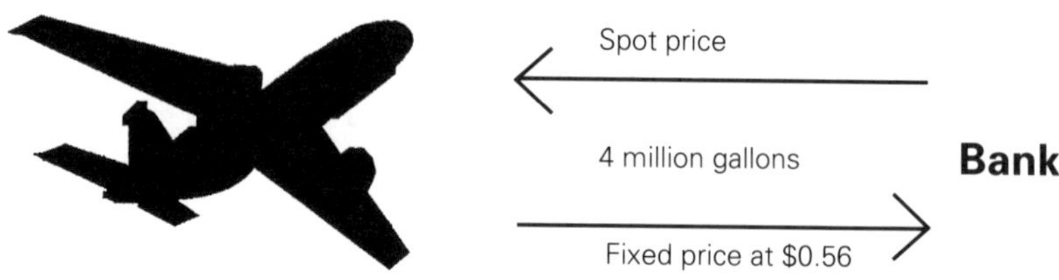

If jet fuel prices rise as expected, Skyline will receive a payment that will offset the higher cost of purchasing jet fuel. If prices fall, contrary to expectations, the firm will not benefit from a lower cost of jet fuel. However, a $0.56 per gallon cost will provide Skyline with a comfortable margin.

In the first quarter, jet fuel settlement prices average $0.59 per gallon. Skyline therefore receives [($0.59-$0.56) x 4 million gallons] or $120,000 from the counterparty. This sum offsets the higher price paid for jet fuel in the cash market, providing Skyline with an effective cost of $0.56 per gallon. In the second quarter, settlement prices average $0.55 per gallon. Thus, Skyline pays $0.55 for its jet fuel in the cash market. It then pays the counterparty [($0.56-$0.55) x 4 million gallons] or $40,000, for an effective jet fuel cost of $0.56. Irrespective of jet fuel price movements, Skyline has locked in a fixed cost of $0.56 per gallon.

Skyline could arrange swaps that are indexed to jet fuel prices from other cities. The most common indices are the Platt's quotations for New York Harbour, US Gulf Coast, North West Europe, NWE basis ARA[1], Rotterdam, Mediterranean basis Italy, and Kerosene quotes for Singapore and Japan.

At this time, airlines are increasing their risk management activities. They have suffered through the Middle East crisis and resulting devastation of airline profitability. This was due to sharply higher fuel prices and a drop in passenger traffic because of concern over terrorism. Airlines are choosing different ways to manage their price risks. A few of the US and European airlines are using futures to hedge short-term risks. Some hedged with WTI while others hedged with No. 2. Most of the airline involvement with OTC contracts has been by a small number of Canadian, European and Far Eastern airlines. It is clear that all airlines are now looking to both the futures and OTC markets to manage their price risks.

Table 1: Outcome of the jet fuel price swap

Quarter	Settlement price	Receipt	Effective cost
1	$0.59	$120,000	$0.56
2	$0.55	($40,000)	$0.56
3	$0.55	($40,000)	$0.56
4	$0.57	$40,000	$0.56
5	$0.55	($40,000)	$0.56
6	$0.57	$40,000	$0.56
7	$0.60	$160,000	$0.56
8	$0.58	$80,000	$0.56

In summary, OTC commodity swaps, caps and collars provide airlines with hedges that almost perfectly match their actual price exposures. An airline has to closely evaluate both its competitive position and risk profile when deciding between swaps, caps and collars. These risk management instruments are a new and exciting addition to the range of tools' corporations can use in managing their economic risks. Airlines now have the capability to remove many of the uncertainties from their operating results.

Notes

1 Amsterdam, Rotterdam and Antwerp

Part IV
Market perspectives

Chapter 30: Measuring, displaying and hedging the market risk on a swap[1]

Bernd P Luedecke
Merrill Lynch (Australia) Pty. Limited

The aim of this chapter is to outline a methodology and describe an approach to the measurement, display, monitoring and hedging of the market risk of an interest rate swap portfolio. A further aim is to describe a regression-based minimum-variance hedging methodology which addresses the problem of basis risk.[2]

The scenario is that of a risk manager overseeing a couple of dealers who are working positions around the same swap portfolio. The problem being addressed is that of keeping in touch at all times with the shifting risk position. A good solution to this problem also solves, at the same time, the "hedging problem", *viz*, if the swap position changes, what should the appropriate change in the hedges be in order to keep the overall book (swaps plus hedges) inside certain prescribed limits?

Most of the ideas presented here will be familiar to many readers. The aim is to bring familiar concepts to bear on a practical solution to the portfolio risk management problem. I hasten to add that no new swap theory will be revealed here. The underlying level of mathematical sophistication is no more than is required to present-value a future cash flow. Nothing is differentiated or integrated. The only calculus-like concept required is the notion of partial derivative.

The author has implemented the methodology described here with considerable success in controlling the risk on a portfolio comprising a large number of disparate swaps and more general "cash flow structures". The implementation came very close to being an example of continuous, dynamic hedging in real time. The only thing missing, due to limitations of the then available computer technology, was live digital feeds from the various electronic data services (Reuters, Telerate, *etc*). The hardware platform consisted of fast, IBM-compatible, networked personal computers.

Value functions for financial instruments

Before one can discuss risk management, hedging and such for any financial instrument one has to know precisely what that instrument is worth. The question "What's it worth?" is answered by the instrument's value function.

The value function for a financial instrument is the formula (algorithm, procedure or whatever) which gives the dollars and cents value of the instrument. This function shows the fair value or price which would be paid/received for this instrument if it were bought/sold under current market conditions.

Once the value function for a particular instrument has been identified, the value function for a portfolio of those instruments is simply the sum of the individual value functions.

Consider, for example, a bank bill.[3] Its value function is the familiar bill discounting formula: divide the face value by (1 + (the yield x the number of days to maturity ÷ by 365)).

In the case of a government, semi-government or corporate bond the value function is the Reserve Bank of Australia (RBA) bond formula,[4] replete with all its finicky little details about when to round to three decimals and what to do with fractions of inter-coupon periods. The RBA also provides the value functions for Treasury notes and other discount instruments.

The value function for an interest rate swap is a little more nebulous. While there may be a consensus among market participants about how a swap should be valued in principle, there is no agreed standardised value function with implementation details as explicit as that for bills and bonds. In effect, every market participant has their own.

While the form of the value function is different for every different instrument, they all have some things in common. Their inputs fall into three broad categories:

(1) interest rates;

(2) time; and

(3) contractual features of the instrument. These include such things as the face value, the coupon rate, coupon/interest settlement dates, whether it is a bought or sold position, *etc*.

In the case of more complicated instruments, such as options, there are other types of inputs. The price of the underlying instrument and the volatility of this price would each be in a category of their own while strike price would fall into the third category.

Notice that only some of these inputs are market determined. Examples are interest rates, volatilities, the price of the underlying instrument and the like. Time is a peculiar sort of input in that it only ever moves one way. But time *is* very important. Those inputs which are contractual features of the instrument — category (3) — are singled out here only because they do not change much, if at all, after the instrument has been dealt. Interestingly, interest rate swaps have a contractual feature (the current floating rate) which changes regularly.

Whatever the value function may be for an interest rate swap (and it varies from institution to institution), it can be thought of as a function of several inputs. A typical swap value function might depend on the 15 interest rates listed below.

(1)	Onight	overnight cash rate
(2)	1Week	one-week cash rate
(3)	$Bill_1$	one-month bill rate
(4)	$Bill_2$	two-month bill rate
(5)	$Bill_3$	three-month bill rate
(6)	$Bill_4$	four-month bill rate
(7)	$Bill_5$	five-month bill rate
(8)	$Bill_6$	six-month bill rate
(9)	$Swap_1$	one-year swap rate
(10)	$Swap_2$	two-year swap rate
(11)	$Swap_3$	three-year swap rate
(12)	$Swap_4$	four-year swap rate
(13)	$Swap_5$	five-year swap rate
(14)	$Swap_7$	seven-year swap rate
(15)	$Swap_{10}$	10-year swap rate

This set of 15 interest rates comprises a typical swap yield curve. Whenever any one of these 15 interest rates moves, the value of the swap portfolio changes. Also, as each day passes the value of the portfolio changes. Whenever a swap has a new floating-rate setting, the value of the portfolio changes. If a swap has one of its settlement dates altered, say because of a public holiday, the value of the portfolio changes. Recognition and monitoring of all these sources of changing value (that is, profit and loss) *is* the risk management function.

Delta

Delta is used to monitor the dollars and cents effect of changes in the various interest rates. Delta is defined as the change in the value function due to a one basis point rise in an interest rate at a specific point on the yield curve. Thus there is an overnight delta, a one-week delta, a one-month delta, a one-year delta and so on out to a 10-year delta. There is a delta corresponding to each of the 15 interest rates which are inputs into the swap value function.

The reader may recognise that delta is analogous to the partial derivative of the value function with respect to each of the 15 interest rates. It is not exactly the partial derivative since the change in each interest rate is one basis point, which is not infinitesimal. But delta is indeed a practical implementation of the notion of partial derivative.

The usefulness of the delta is that it answers a very pertinent question for each of the inputs into the swap value function, namely: "What does it cost us or profit us if this particular rate rises/falls by one basis point?" If a particular delta is zero, then that swap is completely immune to movements in that particular interest rate.

To illustrate how delta is calculated, consider a long position in a 91-day bank bill with a face value of $5m. Suppose this bill is currently selling at a rate of 17.80%. Then its present value (price) is $4,787,538.23, obtained by dividing the face value by (1 + 0.1780 x 91/365). If the yield rose by one basis point to 17.81% the present value (price) of the bill would be $4,787,423.95, obtained by dividing the face value by (1 + 0.1781 x 91/365). The delta of this bill is thus $4,787,423.95 – $4,787,538.23 = –$114.28. If this was a short position in the same bill the delta would be +$114.28.

This also serves to illustrate a fundamental property of deltas: future cash inflows have negative deltas while future cash outflows have positive deltas. This is just another way of saying that long positions lose value as yields rise (prices fall) while short positions gain value as yields rise (prices fall).

Theta

Just as changes in interest rates affect the value of a portfolio of swaps, the passage of time also changes the portfolio's value. This dollars and cents effect of the passage of time is called theta. It is defined as the change in the value function due to another day passing, assuming no change whatsoever in interest rates. Just like delta, theta is a practical implementation of the notion of partial derivative, this time with respect to time.

To illustrate how theta is calculated, consider again the bank bill with a face value of $5m. With 91 days left to run at a yield of 17.80%, this bill has a present value of $4,787,538.23. Tomorrow this bill will have 90 days left to run. Then its present value will be $4,789,774.82, obtained by dividing the face value by (1 + 0.1780 x 90/365). The theta of this bill is thus $4,789,774.82 – $4,787,538.23 = $2,236.59. If this was a short position in the same bill the theta would be –$2,236.59.

This illustrates a fundamental property of theta. Future cash inflows have a positive theta while future cash outflows have a negative theta. This is quite intuitive — as we move closer in time to an asset or a liability it looms larger in a present value sense, ie, the (positive) present value of a cash inflow becomes more positive while the (negative) present value of a cash outflow becomes more negative.

Theta can be interpreted as a type of cost or profit of carry, or a daily accrual amount.

Delta graphs and risk management

Once all the deltas for each swap have been computed, they may be summed to produce a global delta profile for the entire portfolio. Figure 1 is an example of a global delta profile. Past experience has shown the global portfolio delta profile is arguably the most useful risk management tool at a dealer's disposal. It is easily displayed as a picture — bar graphs will do. This picture is easily carried around in one's head. The picture shows precisely where the portfolio will be "hit" by interest rate movements. It very clearly exposes the implicit view embedded in the portfolio — a view which may have come about in a more or less unplanned way through a series of individually profitable deals by different dealers.

Figure 1: Global delta profile — swaps plus GCFA

Dollars per basis point rise

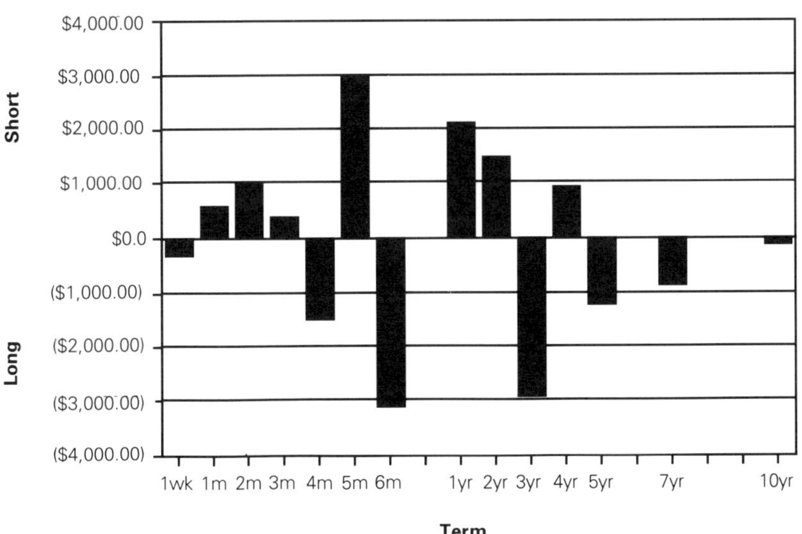

The beauty of computing each delta individually is that this does not assume that all rates move together by a point, ie, that yield curve movements take the form of parallel shifts. In fact, it highlights precisely what will happen when the yield curve flexes — the most usual type of movement in the curve. A quick glance at the global delta profile focuses one on the dominant exposures. And displaying each delta individually facilitates analysis of all manner of yield curve movements (eg, steepenings, flattenings, rotations, humps at particular points, *etc*).

It should be borne in mind here that the risk manager knows exactly how to shut down all the exposures — by dealing appropriate swaps whose deltas have the opposite sign to the deltas on display. This cannot always be done profitably, but that is precisely the decision that a risk manager has to make. If a portfolio is haemorrhaging present value it is because of the interaction between one or more of the deltas and adverse movements in those particular interest rates. That is, the portfolio's implicit view is wrong, at least in the short run. It is the risk manager who faces the ugly trade-off between having to put on losing deals (ie, negative present value deals) now, in order to stem the flow, versus possibly losing more present value if the yield curve continues to flex against the position. The usefulness of the global delta profile in this decision-making process is that it pinpoints where things are going right and where they are going wrong; it tells one what to concentrate on first.

The global delta profile is also an aid in the (difficult) process of managing the exposures at the floating end of a swap portfolio. By "floating" is meant out to, say, one year. Suppose we agree that forward-rate agreements (FRAs) are an appropriate instrument with which to hedge these shorter-term exposures. Then with a little practice one can easily see from the global delta profile the appropriate mixture of FRAs required to close down, shrink or grow the exposures.

For example, looking at the global delta profile in Figure 1, one can see that the following new positions would negate deltas at the short-term end of the yield curve:

- paying on a one-month by four-month FRA;
- paying on a two-month by four-month FRA;
- paying on a five-month by six-month FRA;
- buying a three-month bank bill one week forward.

At the longer-term end of the yield curve, Figure 1 clearly exposes the following delta-negating positions:

- paying on a three-year swap one year forward;
- paying on a three-year swap two years forward;
- paying on a five-year swap;
- paying on a seven-year swap four years forward.

One must add a final word on the usefulness of the global delta profile in the context of a swap portfolio which is not matched on dates. (A date-matched portfolio is one in which every paying/receiving swap has a receiving/paying swap put on against it which settles on exactly the same dates. While this locks in a positive or negative spread for the matched deals it does not lock in the present value — the locked-in spread is still subject to market risk.) Where swaps are not date-matched a different sort of "portfolio" or "diversification" effect is at work, ie, bits of some swaps are hedging bits of other swaps in the one portfolio. But it may be quite impossible to identify exactly which swaps are hedging (ie, negating the deltas of) which other swaps. The point to be made here is that it does not matter. The global delta profile identifies what are appropriate hedging swaps against the current exposure of the overall portfolio. It identifies which new swaps would be delta-opposite to some combination of existing swaps. And delta-oppositeness can be achieved without date-matching.

The global delta profile depicted in Figure 1 is itself a dynamic, changing thing. If one were to simply let the portfolio sit, without adding any new deals, the pattern of risky exposures would change (albeit fairly slowly) in the following way: The deltas would move to the left and simultaneously shrink in absolute value. This phenomenon is best explained with reference to an example. Consider a four-year receiving swap with six-monthly floating-rate re-settings which has just had its first floating-rate setting. This swap has two primary exposures: large negative delta at the four-year point and smaller positive delta at the six-month point. The longer-term delta will be larger (in absolute value) than the shorter-term delta because time acts rather like a "moment arm" effect on the magnitude of a delta — the further away in time is a future cash flow the larger will be its delta, *ceteris paribus*. The swap would also have deltas at all the six-monthly points in between but their magnitudes are negligible relative to the major exposures — one to the fixed, long-term rate and another to the floating, short-term rate. In three months time this same swap will have smaller (and shrinking) negative delta at the four-year point, increased (and increasing) negative delta at the three-year point, essentially zero delta at the six-month point and large positive delta at the three-month point. All these delta shifts arise because the swap under consideration is now a 3-3/4-year swap with three months until its next floating-rate setting. The shrinkage in its four-year delta and concomitant growth in its three-year delta is a sort of "interpolation effect" reflecting the fact that the swap yield curve is only observed in annual increments. The market interest rate now being used for marking the swap to market (present-valuing it) is a 3-3/4-year rate. The disappearance of the six-month delta and concomitant appearance of the three-month delta reflects the fact that this swap is now only three months away from its next floating-rate setting. The market interest rate now being used to present value the next cash settlement is a three-month rate. The delta profile thus reflects the ageing of each deal and hence the maturing of the entire portfolio. As will be expounded below, this gradual changing of the deltas has ramifications for the unwinding of the hedge(s) when a swap which offsets the existing swap is dealt.

Delta, basis risk and hedging

Description of the methodology

The detailed identification and measurement of the dollars and cents value of a basis point at various points along the yield curve suggests an approach to hedging a swap portfolio.

The present value of a swap portfolio depends on the interest rates defined in the swap yield curve defined above. So one can construct a perfect hedge, devoid of basis risk, by holding some mixture of overnight cash, one-week cash, one-month bank bills, two-month bank bills, six-month bank bills and, of course, one-year, two-year, three-year out to 10-year swaps. That is, one holds some appropriate amount of those money market instruments which themselves value off the same set of interest rates. This is possible because the short end of the swap yield curve is a derived yield curve. It feeds off other markets.

But doing this requires the swap desk to become rather like a mini-treasury, dealing in all manner of instruments in order to hedge itself. It also chews up a certain amount of balance sheet. This is fine if the swap portfolio has access to significant amounts of balance sheet and can hedge itself using any appropriate mix of on-balance-sheet instruments (as is typically the case if the swap desk is under the umbrella of the treasury). In this context various bonds (corporate, semi-government and government) are available to hedge the swap portfolio, thus reducing, but not eliminating, basis risk. If, on the other hand, one's mandate is to run a basically off-balance-sheet operation, then the futures market is an obvious place to look for hedging instruments. The interest rate contracts traded on the Sydney Futures Exchange (SFE) have the following features which make them ideal as hedging instruments:

- they are very liquid, usually trading at one point bid/offer spreads. The TRB (three-year bond futures) contract is an exception here, as is the five-year semi-government bond futures contract. All too often these markets are rather thin and "lumpy" and bid/offer spreads blow out;
- their prices/rates move more or less in line with those of other financial instruments;
- one can easily go short;
- transaction costs are relatively low.

Many swap warehouses use the SFE TRB contract as well as the BAB (90-day bank bill futures) contract and the XYB (10-year bond futures) contract to hedge their swap portfolios.

The practical hedging question to be answered is: "What is the right number/mixture of BABs, TRBs and XYBs to hold as a hedge against the swap portfolio?"

Notice that these futures contracts are hedging the *residual* delta, ie, that exposure which is not negated by swaps hedging swaps. And since a contract other than a swap has now entered the picture, the issue of basis risk raises its ugly head. A practical definition of basis risk is the lack of perfect correlation (either positive or negative) between changes in the interest rate of the thing to be hedged and changes in the interest rate of the hedging instrument. That is, basis risk is the absence of a perfect linear relationship between movements in rates.

While the correlations between the 15 interest rates in the swap yield curve and the three futures contracts are not perfect, nor are they zero. One should be able to exploit what correlation there is in order to derive the correct number of hedging contracts. What follows is a recipe for doing this:

- Gather historical data, on a daily basis, on every rate used to value the swap portfolio. In this case it will comprise 15 time series of observations on the variables defined in the swap yield curve above.
- Gather historical data, on a daily basis, on the three futures contracts (BABs, TRBs and XYBs) to be used as hedges.

- Compute daily changes for everything in sight. Let Δ represent the daily change operator. Then ΔOnight is the daily change (today's value minus yesterday's value) in the Onight time series. Likewise, compute Δ1Week, $\Delta Bill_1$, $\Delta Bill_2$, *etc*, $\Delta Bill_6$, $\Delta Swap_1$, $\Delta Swap_2$,..., $\Delta Swap_{10}$. Likewise construct ΔBAB, ΔTRB and ΔXYB.

- Compute the simple regression of each of the variables constructed in the section above on the variables ΔBAB, ΔTRB and ΔXYB. Perform not only the simple (single explanatory variable) regressions, but also all possible combinations of two explanatory variables as well as the three explanatory variable regressions. There is no constant term (intercept) in any of these regressions.

- Re-do all this daily. This is necessary because the relationship(s) between the swap yield curve rates and the hedging rate(s) is not stationary (stable). This instability is another dimension to basis risk. One way to handle this is to re-estimate the relationship(s) whenever a new observation is available.

At this stage, one has constructed several linear basis relationships (models, equations) relating changes in the hedging instruments (the BABs, TRBs and XYBs) to changes in each of the rates to be hedged (Onight, 1Week, *etc*, through to $Swap_{10}$). Now exercise some model/user interaction. That is, choose, for each of the 15 rates to be hedged, the model you like best (a more detailed explanation of this process is outlined below).

For example, one regression might yield the result $\Delta Swap_1 = 0.638966 \Delta BAB$. The hedging coefficient 0.638966 comes from the regression procedure. Then the number of BABs to hold against the swap portfolio's one-year exposure is the current one-year delta of the portfolio divided by (0.638966 times the current delta of a BAB). Notice that the more sensitive is the one-year swap rate to movements in the BAB, the fewer the BABs required to hedge the one-year exposure. The delta on a BAB is simply the value of one SFE BAB contract at (one point less than the current market price) minus its value at the current market price. At current BAB prices this is roughly $11.54.

Likewise, another regression might yield the result $\Delta Swap_5 = 0.2404 \Delta TRB + 0.2027 \Delta XYB$. In this case the portfolio's exposure to the five-year swap rate is being hedged with a mixture of TRB and XYB contracts. There are two hedging coefficients. Then the number of TRBs is the portfolio's five-year delta divided by (0.2404 times the current delta of a TRB) and the number of XYBs is the portfolio's five-year delta divided by (0.2027 times the current delta of an XYB). Again notice how increased sensitivity of movements in the five-year swap rate to movements in the two futures contracts implies that fewer futures contracts are required to hedge the exposure. At current prices the delta of a TRB is about $23.59 and that of an XYB about $50.63.

Table 1 shows some hedging coefficients recently computed from daily data.

Table 1: Hedging coefficients

	BAB	TRB	XYB
1Week	0.264412	0.000000	0.000000
$Bill_1$	0.508153	0.000000	0.000000
$Bill_2$	0.524454	0.000000	0.000000
$Bill_3$	0.633201	0.000000	0.000000
$Bill_4$	0.524256	0.000000	0.000000
$Bill_5$	0.611929	0.000000	0.000000
$Bill_6$	0.675544	0.000000	0.000000
$Swap_1$	0.638966	0.000000	0.000000
$Swap_2$	0.336910	0.188810	0.000000
$Swap_3$	0.000000	0.278600	0.225200
$Swap_4$	0.000000	0.221400	0.239900
$Swap_5$	0.000000	0.240400	0.202700
$Swap_7$	0.000000	0.200600	0.243000
$Swap_{10}$	0.000000	0.000000	0.510020

An inspection of Table 1 exposes the flexibility of the regression-based methodology for quantifying basis risk. It provides a consistent framework for a "mix-and-match" approach for using different futures contracts to hedge different rates. In this table, the 1Week, $Bill_1$,..., $Swap_1$ exposures are being hedged purely with BABs. The $Swap_2$ exposure is being hedged with a mixture of BABs and TRBs. The $Swap_3$, $Swap_4$, $Swap_5$ and $Swap_7$ exposures are being hedged with a mixture of TRBs and XYBs. The $Swap_{10}$ exposure is being hedged purely with XYBs.

An example

At this stage an example should help to explain the dynamic interactions between the delta profile and the hedging coefficients.

Consider the following sequence of dealing and hedging which frequently arises in the portfolio risk mangement context: (1) a new swap is dealt and (2) hedged using futures contracts. The deal is warehoused for a while in the swap portfolio until, some time later, (3) an "offsetting" swap is dealt (hopefully at a positive spread) and (4) the futures hedge is unwound. As has been explained in a previous section, the delta profile of the original deal will have changed (shifted and shrunk) slightly over the warehousing period. The magnitude of this change depends on the length of time the swap was warehoused. But since the present methodology does *not* rely on matching up particular swaps with other swaps (in fact, this is explicitly eschewed), the exact delta profile of the original swap is no longer important. What is important is how the original swap contributes to the overall exposure of the entire portfolio, and this contribution is already measured in (has been summed into) the portfolio's global delta profile. Hence the "offsetting" swap should be judged not according to whether it exactly matches, date for date, the original swap but rather according to its impact on the portfolio's then global delta profile.

What is arguably even more important is that the basis relationship between movements in the swap rate(s) and movements in the futures yield(s) will most likely have changed. If, on the day the "offsetting" swap is dealt, movements in the swap rate(s) are now more (less) sensitive to movements in the futures yield(s) then the number of futures contracts to be unwound is less (more) than were put in place when the original swap was dealt. For swaps with large face values this difference can be significant.

This example serves to highlight the importance of frequent re-estimation of the basis relationship(s) in order to implement frequent re-balancing of the swap portfolio's futures hedge(s). In this way the minimum-variance optimality of the entire position (swap portfolio plus futures hedge(s)) will be preserved. This author's experience is that daily re-estimation suffices

Rationale and comments

To some readers the procedure described above may seem unnecessarily complicated. Why perform all those time series regressions? Why not just use simple delta hedging to determine the number of futures contracts to hold? That is, why not divide every one of the computed deltas by the delta of an appropriate futures contract?

The most compelling reason is a technical one. The linear relationships derived by the regression procedure have a certain minimum-residual-variance property. That is, if tomorrow's basis experience is accurately reflected in the sample period over which the regressions have been computed (a necessary assumption, common to all technical methodology) then using any other set of coefficients would add more variability to the value of the combined position (swaps plus hedges).

Recognition of the minimum-variance optimality of the hedging coefficients has some practical ramifications. It says, among other things, that "trading the hedge" will surely add variance to the bottom line. This does not mean that trading the hedge will not also add more profit to the bottom line. It simply highlights the fact that this potential extra profit comes about by taking on more risk. Most traders don't like this sort of thing being made explicit. It smacks too much of "dog and pilot" and frustrates the risk-taker. It also confronts the risk manager squarely with the risk/return trade-off: How does he (or his organisation) decide whether or not the extra risk is worth the extra potential return?

A second reason is that simple delta hedging implicitly makes the assumption that the futures rates and the 1Week, $Bill_t$ and $Swap_t$ rates move in a point-for-point way. But the most casual observation of the markets denies this. If futures and 1Week, $Bill_t$ and $Swap_t$ rates moved point for point, then the spreads between them would remain constant. It is well known that sometimes spreads come in and at other times they blow out. The hedging coefficients derived from the regressions described above provide a quantitative handle on this phenomenon. The regression result $\Delta Swap_1 = 0.638966 \Delta BAB$ has the following interpretation: When the BAB contract moves by a point, the one-year swap rate moves by 0.638966 of a point. The regression result $\Delta Swap_5 = 0.2404 \Delta TRB + 0.2027 \Delta XYB$ is interpreted as: When the TRB contract moves by a point and the XYB contract moves by a point the five-year swap rate moves by 0.4431 of a point. Simple delta hedging does not address this dimension of basis risk. Simple delta hedging would reduce Table 1 to zeros and ones (where would *you* put the zeros, and where would *you* put the ones?).

A useful feature of the regression-based delta hedging methodology is that it provides a consistent and accurate method for "pricing off the hedge". Once the hedging coefficients have been determined, the mid-market $Swap_1$,..., $Swap_{10}$ rates can be predicted to within three or four points of where the swap brokers put them. This is an affirmation of the methodology. It also serves as a reminder that the hedging coefficients' predictions need to be frequently tested against the touchstone of truth, *viz*, where the market actually is right now. This frequent re-calibration over the course of a day also helps to keep things from getting too far out of whack.

Probably the nastiest dimension to basis risk is that, whatever the relationships that do exist between futures rates and the 1Week, $Bill_t$ and $Swap_t$ rates, these relationships are not stable over time. This forces one onto the treadmill of constantly re-examining the relationships as another day's basis moves are revealed. Without going overboard in the basis risk modelling department, experience demonstrates that the discipline of re-estimating the regressions at the end of each day (it is best done virtually automatically as part of the daily close of business bean counting), followed by an informed and critical scanning of the new relationships, provides a good handle on the changing nature of basis risk. "Informed and critical" is to be emphasised here. The choice of hedging coefficients for tomorrow's delta hedging is indeed where experience, "market feel" and view-taking meet the science/art of econometrics.

Extensions

The notion of a global delta profile lends itself to some creative uses. It allows different portfolios valuing off the same yield curve to be immediately linked and used as delta-offsetting tools. In a previous job this author has had experience of a portfolio of "vanilla" swaps (Australian dollar fixed/floating swaps and FRAs whose fixed and floating sides settled on the same dates). There was also a separate portfolio of swaps with bells and whistles attached. These included swaps where the fixed/floating sides did not settle on the same dates (eg, quarterly BBSW versus semi-annual BBSW basis swaps, quarterly BBSW[5] versus fixed annual swaps off the back of Euro issues, longer-dated zero-coupon structures versus BBSW, *etc*). These we called Generalised Cash Flow (GCF) structures and they lived in the GCF portfolio. Most of these GCF structures valued off the swap yield curve. That is, their value functions used as inputs the *same* set of interest rates as the vanilla swaps and FRAs. This meant that any delta computed for the GCF portfolio was the same type of animal as a delta computed for a vanilla swap. Hence one could add them up. In fact, the global delta profile for the GCF portfolio and the global delta profile for the swap/FRA portfolio were rather like two pieces in a large jigsaw puzzle. Through judicious selection of newly dealt swaps and newly dealt GCF structures, the two global delta profiles would cancel each other out to a large extent. Thus portfolios can, and did, hedge other portfolios.[6]

Where two portfolios do not value off the same yield curve one is back in the realm of basis risk analysis. Consider, for example, a portfolio of government bonds, a portfolio of semi-government bonds and a portfolio of corporate bonds. While these instruments have virtually identical value functions, they value off different yield curves. This means that their deltas may not be added unless one makes the (strong) assumption that spreads are constant. If the relationships between the various yield curves were known then the various deltas could be adjusted so as to all be related to the same yield curve. So in calculus terms, $\partial \text{Value}/\partial x$ cannot be added to $\partial \text{Value}/\partial y$ — one needs to know $\partial x/\partial y$. After this adjustment the global delta profiles of different portfolios could be used to offset each other.

At the risk of indulging in a bit of megalomaniac fantasy here, the global risk offsetting idea can be carried further. Could one not, by intensively analysing basis relationships, relate nearly every financial instrument to a single, highly-liquid reference instrument? Then the global delta profiles for all portfolios could be used to offset each other and any residual delta left after that could be hedged with an appropriate position in the reference instrument.

Integrating theoretical constructs into the day-to-day risk management function

The material presented in this chapter and the methodology just expounded will leave many readers with a two-fold impression — (1) the approach builds on simple but powerful "theoretical" underpinnings (eg, the notion of risk-aversion/tolerance as something that a risk manager, or the institution, should focus on along with the use of minimum-variance as a hedging criterion) and (2) the implementation is highly data-intensive.

That the implementation should be data-intensive should not be surprising. Data is, after all, a manifestation of "information", and "information" in one form or another is widely acknowledged to be the engine which drives financial markets.

But, just like any other form of information, data needs to be interpreted. And it is this process of interpretation which leads one to well-known ways of summarising and condensing huge volumes of data, and, inevitably, to the modelling of (conjectured) relationships. The various technical analysts and chartists upon whom some traders rely so heavily are well versed in a wide array of models for representing a single time series. Examples are: trading strategies based on the recognition of patterns such as head-and-shoulders and double-bottom formations, the use of Koppock, momentum and relative strength indicators, and the application of Elliott's wave theory.

As has already been mentioned, the validity of such techniques rests on an article of faith, *viz*, that the experience of the recent past is a reasonable pointer to what is likely to happen tomorrow. The basis relationship modelling approach being advocated here rests on the same article of faith. The fundamental difference is one of focus: basis modelling involves estimation of the relationships between several time series whereas most commonly available technical analysis concentrates on recognition of patterns within a single time series. Putting it in technical jargon, the difference in approach is one of multivariate time series analysis versus univariate time series analysis.

For example, the time series regressions outlined in "Description of the methodology" above evolved from a thought process that ran as follows: Simple delta hedging (that is, determining the number of futures hedge contracts by dividing the portfolio's overall delta by the delta of a futures hedge contract) assumes point-for-point movement of the futures yield with the swap rate. If these rates indeed move point for point, then spreads between them must be constant. Casual observation denies this. So the relationship between futures yields and swap rates must be something other than point-for-point movement. Perhaps the relationship is one of simple proportionality between changes, but with the coefficient of proportionality being something other than unity. Perhaps one could estimate the proportionality coefficient. If the proportionality coefficient is less than (greater than) unity this means that as rates rise spreads narrow (widen) and as rates fall spreads widen (narrow).

It is but a small step from such thoughts to implementation in the form of data-gathering and time series-based estimation procedures. Then, suddenly, the huge body of time series estimation theory becomes useful, not as a theoretical irrelevancy, but as a way of protecting and preserving the botttom line.

The exposition in this chapter should help put to rest the "It's too hard!" objection to implementing a data-based modelling approach. The hedging regression recipe set out in "Description of the methodology" above describes something that was actually being done as a matter of routine on a day-by-day basis, just like counting the beans at the close of each day's business.

The point to be made here is that the requisite information distribution, storage and retrieval technology is already available. Financial markets are already well supplied with a number of highly reliable electronic data services (Reuters, Telerate, Pont, to name but three). And there is a constant avalanche of numbers being distributed electronically by the various futures, stock and commodities exchanges all around the world. It is now fairly common to have live, real-time data fed into the cells of a spreadsheet, allowing immediate revaluation of positions and, in principle, immediate re-estimation of shifting basis relationships. Complementing this, we have access to a wide range of conceptual frameworks ("models" and "theory") to assist in interpreting this information. This brings us very close to being able to implement the ideal of continuous, dynamic, real-time hedging.

The race is on to implement. And the institution which first puts in place an integrated risk management strategy along the lines described here must be well placed to out-perform its competitors in the 1990s.

Notes

1. The opinions expressed in this chapter are those of the author. They do not necessarily reflect the opinions, views or policy of, nor should they be construed to bind, Merrill Lynch, Pierce, Fenner & Smith Incorporated nor any of its affiliates or subsidiaries

2. While this chapter is written in the context of Australia and its financial institutions, regulations and conventions, the application to capital markets in other countries is quite straightforward.

3. In Australia, a bank bill is a short-term (rarely longer than six months to maturity) zero-coupon discount instrument, akin to a banker's acceptance.

4. The methodology behind the RBA's bond formula is the familiar way of pricing coupon-bearing instruments: discount every coupon as well as the face value to be repaid at maturity at the same rate (the yield to maturity).

5. BBSW is the bank bill reference rate used in Australia for resetting the floating rates on interest rate swaps. It plays the same role as Libor in the US dollar swap market. It is displayed daily at 10.30am on Reuters page BBSW.

6. From a risk management perspective there is no reason for the deals described here to reside in distinct portfolios. Their separation arose for administrative convenience — the plain vanilla swaps were confirmed, settled, *etc via* a nearly automated system while the GCF portfolio required much more manual intervention by the back office. The point to be made here is that the global delta profile provides the risk management link for offsetting one portfolio's exposures with those of another.

Chapter 31: Managing the floating-rate component of a swap portfolio

Satyajit Das and Colin McKeith
TNT Group and Citibank Limited

Financial intermediaries active in the swap market operate swap portfolios (also referred to as "books" or "warehouses") which allow entry into one leg of a swap transaction without the necessity of simultaneously arranging an exactly offsetting transaction.

Swap portfolios are operated on the basis that the exposure underlying unmatched swaps is directly analogous to cash market positions, whereby transactions involving physical cash market instruments or financial futures on the relevant cash market instrument can be used to offset the market risk assumed until the swap is matched with an offsetting transaction.

Traditionally, in managing such portfolios, institutions have decoupled the management of the fixed-rate flows from the floating-rate flows under a swap transaction. This is because, in general, these flows belong to different markets/market segments and must be managed separately, and because of differences in the perceived risk level of the different flows.

The initial assumption made by swap portfolio managers was that the longer maturity of the fixed-rate flows made this component of the book more risky and, predictably, most research was directed to valuing the term cash flows and enhancing the methods available to hedge these risks. Management of the floating-rate component of the swap portfolio attracted limited attention because of the implicit assumption that the floating rate resets periodically at the new market rate implying relative stability at or about par value, even where there are substantial movements in rates.

However, experience with the operation of swap portfolios has highlighted the fact that substantial mismatches on floating-rate reset dates expose portfolios to the risk of large potential losses or gains. A particularly important feature of this risk is that it is extremely volatile and dynamic. The fact that each transaction in the floating-rate portfolio is reset at least six monthly, coupled with the speed at which the short end of the yield curve can move and change shape, exacerbates the risk profile. Management of the floating-rate component of a swap portfolio under these circumstances becomes a daily positioning function with the objective of maximising the difference between cash receipts and cash payments on floating-rate payments under transactions within the swap portfolio.

The objective of this chapter is to examine a number of aspects of the management of the floating-rate component of swap portfolios. It identifies the risk elements of managing floating-rate cash flows and considers the methodologies designed to value the portfolio. A number of risk management approaches are then examined.

Risk components within the floating-rate portfolio

There are two basic categories of risk associated with the floating-rate swap portfolio:

Timing mismatches

This refers to the exposure resulting from differences in repricing dates; for example, a swap portfolio could be receiving/repricing three-month Libor on 15/5/X1 and paying/repricing three-month Libor on 19/5/X1.

A swap portfolio always has a timing mismatch unless each floating-rate swap *receipt* within the portfolio is precisely matched by a floating-rate swap *payment* under a different transaction, the payment being exactly equal (in amount and maturities) and opposite to the first. In order to provide an "exact" hedge, the second transaction must be the same as the first in the following respects:

- *Repricing date*: the transactions must reprice on the same day at the same time, using identical rate setting mechanisms (including the same side of the bid/offer spread).

- *Face value amounts*: the exact face value amounts must be equivalent.

- *Index/interest rate period*: the two transactions must reprice "off" the same index for the same interest rate period or frequency (that is, three or six months, etc).

The maturity dates of the two transactions can vary. However, this creates an inherent problem within the portfolio because when one of the matching paired swaps terminates, a replacement swap will be required to be entered into in order to neutralise the floating-rate exposure.

Index mismatches

There are two levels of index mismatch:

- Receiving six monthly and paying three monthly will, of course, result in "mismatches" or portfolio "gaps" even if both fixed legs are completely matched. If the second three-month rate set is hedged through a forward contract (like a future or FRA contract), then the compounded cash flow payment on the six-month date may vary significantly from the receipt under the six-month reset.

  In certain markets, such as the Australian market, the compounded three-month rate plus the forward may consistently differ from the prevailing six-month rate set. On large transactions, a 0.1 basis point per annum cost caused by a mismatch can be very expensive. As the only known cash flows are those that can be present valued now, there is no way to value these mismatches, at least exactly.

- Different indices in the same currency will, of course, trade at *variable* margins relative to each other, ie, Libor versus commercial paper (CP). An added complication may be differences in the methods by which rates are calculated. Commercial paper swaps are generally quoted as an average of 30-day CP compounded each month and paid semi-annually. As most CP borowers would issue 30-day paper on one day in each month there are potential discrepancies caused by yield curve movements between the average and the day they issue and reprice their CP borrowings.

The existence of these "mismatches" or "gaps" within the floating-rate component of the swap portfolio exposes the portfolio to the risk of economic gain or loss from two sources:

- *Absolute rate changes*; for example, if the portfolio systematically reprices its receipts prior to payments, the portfolio will gain (lose) if interests fall (rise).

- *Changes in the shape of the yield curve*; for example, if the portfolio structure is such that the majority of receipts are priced off three-month Libor while its payments are priced off six-month Libor, the portfolio will gain (lose) under an inverse (positive) yield curve (provided certain conditions regarding movements in the absolute rate levels hold).

A typical floating-rate portfolio is generally complex, with a mixture of timing and index mismatches. Portfolios may not demonstrate a *systematic* pattern of risk. Under those circumstances, the exact impact of a change in either the absolute rate or yield curve shape may be difficult to separate.

The risk components inherent within the floating-rate component of a swap portfolio are generated by a number of institutional and market factors:

- customer demand for transaction structures;
- the institutional structure of the market which may dictate a particular pattern of transactional flow which creates these portfolio mismatches;
- the process of rebalancing hedges and the availability and the attendant cost of offsetting transactions may necessitate the absorption of some of these risks into the portfolio;
- the hedge efficiency between the fixed-rate and the floating-rate component of the swap portfolio must be balanced.

This last factor is particularly interesting. Management of a swap portfolio necessitates a continual and dynamic series of choices whereby hedge efficiency in respect of the fixed-rate component of the portfolio must be balanced continually against the risk profile of the floating-rate component within the same portfolio. The portfolio manager is constantly confronted with the choice of reducing the exposure on one component of the portfolio at the risk of increasing the exposure in the other.

For example, a portfolio manager may have a substantial position whereby the portfolio has paid fixed rates against receipt of floating-rate payments. The position is hedged with a long position in underlying government bonds. However, the volatility of the swap spread prompts the portfolio manager to liquidate the hedge position simultaneously with entry into a hedging swap where it receives fixed and pays floating rates. However, the floating rate it receives reprices on three-month resets, while the rate it pays under the offsetting swap reprices at six-monthly intervals. In this case, the swap portfolio manager must assume either the spread exposure on the fixed-rate side or the index timing mismatch on the floating-rate portion of the portfolio at the most favourable hedge.

Approaches to floating-rate portfolio risk management

Exposure identification

The information required to allow evaluation of portfolio risk is as follows:

- The floating cash flows must be separated from the fixed cash flows. These can be hedged later as an integrated portfolio but must be segregated to enable exposures to be identified and analysed in a manageable format.

- The portfolio must be separated further into the different indices, ie, three-month rate set in one portfolio, six-month in another, etc.

When the portfolio exposures have been appropriately segregated, the overall portfolio position is valued and analysed.

Valuation issues

The valuation of the floating-rate portion of the swap portfolio uses standard present value techniques to discount receipts and payments within the portfolio structure.

The valuation of the floating-rate portfolio typically entails the following:

- *Cash flows to be discounted.* At any one point in time, only known cash flows can be valued. Within the floating-rate portfolio, these cash flows are a combination of the interest payable on the next repricing date plus the principal amount of the transaction. The actual principal is included at this point, rather than at the actual maturity date of the transaction because, at this point, the future floating rates that will occur cannot be determined. However, it is possible to apply forward rates from the existing yield curve but the present value determined by the forward rates will match that at the present value of the principal at the next repricing date.

  Margins on floating coupons should be treated and valued on a similar basis, that is, if you are paying Libor plus 10bp then the 10bp per period should be present valued. The margins are included and valued in the fixed-rate portfolio rather than in the floating-rate portfolio by some institutions. This is especially true when valuing floating-rate margins in different currencies.

- *Time vectors.* While it is theoretically possible to value the floating-rate cash flows on a *daily* basis, in practice, cash flows are segregated into a number of convenient weekly or monthly vectors (often referred to as "buckets") which are then managed.

- *Discount rates.* Each component of the floating-rate portfolio is discounted using the yield curve of the relevant floating-rate index. The relevant yield curve can be derived from physical or cash market securities or alternatively, in certain cases, by combining futures with physical transactions to determine the yield curve. It is also often necessary to interpolate between reference rates for the dates that lie between months quoted on the cash and/or futures curve.

An interesting issue arises in respect of bid/offer spreads (which could be relevant where positions must be hedged). A number of practitioners use mid-points to cover this contingency.

Valuation and risk

The identified cash flows are discounted using the yield curve for the relevant floating-rate index. The economic value of the floating-rate portfolio is the present value of receipts less the present value of payments. The portfolio management objective is to ensure that receipts are greater than payments.

The discounting process provides the basis for the analysis of how the portfolio will react to changes in yield curve structures. An essential element of this valuation process is the sensitivity of the portfolio to changes in interest rates and time decay.

The floating-rate portfolio is volatile and dynamic with the nature of the exposures being highly sensitive to new transactions being added and old transactions being rolled over and repriced at current market rates. In addition, the portfolio present values are effected by changes in interest rates and yield curve shapes, the slope of the yield curve becoming relevant as the payment pattern alters, time decay becoming a factor as payment days approach.

Risk management approaches

The approach to floating-rate portfolio management is dictated to an extent by the objective of the institution. A number of institutions manage the floating-rate portfolio on a "breakeven" or loss minimisation basis with the portfolio profit being sought to be generated from the fixed-rate portfolio. Other institutions actively manage the floating-rate portfolios, seeking to generate earnings from this component of the portfolio.

Approaches currently available for the management of the floating-rate flows within a swap portfolio include:

- positioning approaches;
- diversification strategies;
- hedging techniques.

A number of portfolio managers use positioning strategies whereby floating-rate mismatches are managed aggressively to take advantage of anticipated movements in the yield curve. The portfolio is managed in a manner analogous to a short-term securities trading portfolio with the portfolio manager either seeking to engineer transaction flow which creates the optimal portfolio position consistent with interest rate expectations or, more commonly, overlaying physical and/or futures contracts in the relevant short-term interest rates on the existing portfolio to optimise the portfolio structure.

Positioning strategies can be designed to take advantage of absolute rate and yield curve movements as well as spread movements between indices. For example, under the latter type of strategy, a portfolio manager could receive six-month Libor while paying commercial paper rates on the basis that six-month Libor rates are expected to average a level greater than one-month CP rates.

An alternative strategy is to diversify the floating-rate swap portfolio. This can be conceptualised in one of two ways:

(1) Management of the fixed and floating-rate components of the swap portfolios can be integrated with both being valued using the same yield curve to ensure that the exposure in the fixed portfolio offsets at least part of the exposure in the floating-rate component of the portfolio. The combined "net" exposure is then managed. This type of strategy would usually entail a high degree of exposure to changes in the shape of the yield curve.

(2) An alternative might be to diversify portfolio risk through the size and structure of the portfolio. This approach seeks to diversify and thereby reduce the significance of small reset date mismatches on the basis that gains and losses on individual transactions will be mutually offsetting. A number of intermediaries use the term "date insensitive portfolio" to such diversified floating-rate portfolios. Such diversification practices are often accompanied by elaborate simulation models which sample the portfolio to determine risk estimates associated with date

mismatches, with hedging transactions being undertaken at the margin to avoid excessive mismatches within such large portfolios.

The majority of swap portfolio managers seek to manage mismatches within the floating-rate portfolio. The hedges required are effected through a variety of mechanisms:

- The floating-rate component of the swap portfolio may be integrated with the institution's cash/short-term securities trading portfolio as exposures within these two operations may be offsetting.

- Basis swaps may be used to match or eliminate mismatches within the portfolio. The use of basis swaps can be costly unless the market structure facilitates the basis swap itself. A further disadvantage is the use of additional credit lines.

- The gaps within the floating-rate portfolio can be hedged using short-term interest rate futures contracts, forward-rate agreements or short-dated securities transactions. Identified mismatches are then offset by equal and opposing positions taken in these forward contracts.

Hedging requires slight adjustments to be made to hedge equivalents to overcome problems associated with different dollar value movements for basis point changes in various instruments. Large exposures or significant concentrations of transactions on particular repricing dates (the "lumpy" exposures) are often segregated and hedged individually under this approach. As an alternative to the use of forwards, options may be used. The decision to use symmetric instruments (ie, forwards) as against asymmetric instruments (options) is purely a trading decision based on the portfolio manager's expectations of interest rate movements.

The risks and benefits of individual portfolio management strategies are largely related to the structure of a portfolio and the currency of the swap portfolio itself. An additional factor is the organisation's tolerance for risk.

Increasingly, swap portfolio managers are combining approaches in the management of these floating-rate exposures. Two approaches are becoming common:

(1) Portfolio simulation, whereby statistical methods (such as Monte Carlo simulation techniques) are used to quantify the risk profile of the portfolio and to determine the minimal number and structure of hedge transactions designed to optimise the portfolio's exposure profile.

(2) The layered approach, whereby the manager focuses on the net portfolio mismatch which is then managed using the following "layers" of transactions:

Layer 1
Actual swap transactions, priced attractively to induce participants to transact under particular structures, are used to reduced portfolio exposures.

Layer 2
Basis swaps are used, where possible, to smooth out major timing or index mismatches.

Layer 3
Forward or option-based hedges are used to minimise residual exposures. Alternatively, the residual portfolio exposures are positioned as "acceptable" risks.

Examples

The following examples are based on the hypothetical portfolio in Table 1. The portfolio is based on the following assumptions: (1) the currency is in Australian dollars and the floating index is bank bills (with interest being calculated on actual/365 days); and (2) 90-day bank bill futures (traded on the Sydney Futures Exchange) are used to hedge the portfolio.

The following series of examples examine the impact on the portfolio of interest rate movements, including absolute rate movements and changes in yield curve shape, and the effect of time on the portfolio.

Table 1: Initial portfolio (as at 1/1/X1)

Position	Pricing amount ($)	Floating rate (%)	Settlement date	Days until settlement	Settlement ($)
Receive	20,000,000	11	01/04/X1	90	20,542,466
Pay	(50,000,000)	10.25	01/05/X1	120	(51,684,932)
Pay	(70,000,000)	9.85	01/06/X1	151	(72,852,452)

Example 1: Parallel shift in yield curves

By valuing the portfolio at the current market rates, the net present value (NPV) of the portfolio can be determined.

Table 2: Determining the NPV of the portfolio

	Settlement amount ($)	Discount rate (%)	Number of days	Present value ($)
01/01/X1	0	10		0
01/02/X1	0	10		0
01/03/X1	0	10		0
01/04/X1	20,542,466	10	90	20,048,128
01/05/X1	(51,684,932)	10	120	(50,039,788)
01/06/X1	(72,852,452)	10	151	(69,958,287)
01/07/X1	0	10		0
NPV				**(99,949,947)**

To determine the sensitivity of the portfolio to parallel shifts in the yield curve the same dates are used with an adjustment in the yield curve by 1bp.

Table 3: Determining the sensitivity of the portfolio

	Settlement amount ($)	Discount rate (%)	Number of days	Present value ($)
01/01/X1	0	10.01		0
01/02/X1	0	10.01		0
01/03/X1	0	10.01		0
01/04/X1	20,542,466	10.01	90	20,047,646
01/05/X1	(51,684,932)	10.01	120	(50,038,195)
01/06/X1	(72,852,452)	10.01	151	(69,955,508)
01/07/X1	0	10.01		0
NPV				**(99,946,057)**

The value of the portfolio has fallen from (US$99,949,947) when discounted at 10% to (US$99,946,057) when discounted at 10.01%. Therefore, the portfolio sensitivity to interest rate movements is US$3,833 per basis point in yield.

As previously discussed, various methods are available for eliminating any changes in value for yield curve movements. The most common would be the use of futures contracts to counteract the effects of changes in the yield curve. In this example, March futures contracts are used as the hedge because this is the next deliverable contract.

As the yield curve is flat at 10%, it is assumed that the futures contract is trading at 90.16 level or 9.84%, assuming the cash curve is arbitraged correctly.[1]

On the basis that for each movement in interest rates, up or down, the value of the portfolio will gain or lose US$3,890, the number of futures contracts required to eliminate this sensitivity is calculated as US$3,890/US$11.75 = 331 contracts (on the basis that the price sensitivity of the futures contract is A$11.75 per basis point).

As the value of the portfolio changed in value from ($99,949,947) to ($99,946,057) when interest rates rose by 1bp, to counteract this loss of value to a rise in interest rates it is necessary to sell the 331 $0.5m face value contracts.

Example 2: Shifts in the shape of yield curves

This example examines the effect on the portfolio of a change in the shape of the yield curve.

Valuing the original portfolio at the same date as Example 1 and moving the yield curve into a positive shape it is possible to analyse the change in value.

Table 4: Determining the NPV of the portfolio

	Settlement amount ($)	Discount rate (%)	Number of days	Present value ($)
01/01/X1	0	9.4		0
01/02/X1	0	9.5		0
01/03/X1	0	9.6		0
01/04/X1	20,542,466	9.7	90	20,062,612
01/05/X1	(51,684,932)	9.8	120	(50,071,664)
01/06/X1	(72,852,452)	9.9	151	(69,986,090)
01/07/X1	0	10.0		0
NPV				**(99,995,142)**

The value of the portfolio is now ($99,995,142) a change of $45,192 from ($99,949,947). The effect of the positive change in shape is a loss to the portfolio.

Using the same yield curve, it is possible to determine a theoretical yield for the March futures contract.[2] Therefore, the March futures should be at a level of 9.94% given the new level of interest rates. The futures position shows a gain of $38,892 on the 331 futures contracts. The net effect is a loss of $6,302 by combining the floating book portfolio and the futures used to hedge the portfolio.

Other methods of hedging the portfolio may counteract the movement in the shape of the yield curve more efficiently. In this example, the futures delivery date does not correspond with the portfolio exposure. The use of FRAs with a risk profile opposite to the portfolio, would cover the portfolio position more accurately avoiding the problems of a change in the convexity.

Example 3: Effect of time on the portfolio

The NPV of the portfolio will gradually increase to the value due on the settlement date. The effect of changes in interest rates or sensitivity on the portfolio will also change as the time period to the settlement date diminishes. In contrast, the hedges taken (futures contracts) have a fixed value to changes in yield and time.

Moving the original portfolio forward one month while keeping the curve flat at 10% allows the effect of time on the value of the portfolio to be understood.

Table 5: Determining the NPV of the portfolio

	Settlement amount ($)	Discount rate (%)	Number of days	Present value ($)
01/02/X1	0	10		0
01/03/X1	0	10		0
01/04/X1	20,542,466	10	60	20,210,243
01/05/X1	(51,684,932)	10	90	(50,441,176)
01/06/X1	(72,852,452)	10	121	(70,514,836)
01/07/X1	0	10		0
NPV				**(100,745,770)**

The value of the portfolio has moved to ($100,745,770) from the original value of ($99,949,947). As the yield has remained constant, the portfolio exposure has grown as a result of the fluxion of time rather than the result of any adverse movement in interest rates.

The portfolio's sensitivity to movements in interest rates is altered. Determining the sensitivity as in Example 1 allows the effect of time on sensitivity to be examined.

The portfolio sensitivity can be determined by a comparison of the two NPV amounts ($100,745,770 – $100,742,621 = $3,148). This indicates that one month on the portfolio sensitivity is $3,148 per 1bp increase in interest rates versus $3,890 per 1bp currently. Consequently, as the maturity of the portfolio decreases, the effect of interest rate changes also decreases. This has a significant impact on the efficiency of the hedge. It requires that the number of contracts used in the hedge will need to be adjusted to match the changing duration and, therefore, interest rate volatility of the portfolio. In the example, as the sensitivity of the portfolio reduces to $3,148 per basis point, the number of hedge contracts will need to be adjusted from the original 331 contracts to 268. Ideally, the adjustment to the hedge should be undertaken gradually as the portfolio maturity alters.

Table 6: Determining the sensitivity of the portfolio

	Settlement amount ($)	Discount rate (%)	Number of days	Present value ($)
01/02/X1	0	10.01		0
01/03/X1	0	10.01		0
01/04/X1	20,542,466	10.01	60	20,209,916
01/05/X1	(51,684,932)	10.01	90	(50,439,963)
01/06/X1	(72,852,452)	10.01	121	(70,512,574)
01/07/X1	0	10.01		0
NPV				**(100,742,621)**

Summary

Swap portfolio managers have increasingly become aware of the significant degree of risk within the floating-rate component of swap portfolios. The volatility of short-term interest rates and the periodic resets of floating rates within the portfolio combine to make management of three exposures complex. This chapter outlines a framework for the identification of risk and a variety of techniques for the management of this risk. A combination of portfolio diversification and hedging techniques, primarily derivative products such as basis swaps, futures/FRAs and options, provide the fundamental basis for portfolio risk neutralisation.

Notes

1. The breakeven yield formula is as follows:

$$1 + \left(R5 \times \frac{D5}{365}\right) = \left(1 \times R2 \times \frac{D2}{365}\right) \times \left(1 + \frac{RF}{100} \times \frac{90}{365}\right)$$

$$RF = \frac{(1 + R5 \times D5/365)}{(1 + R2 \times D2/365) - 1} \quad \frac{365}{90 \times 100}$$

Example 1, where:

R2 = 10%   D2 = 59
R5 = 10%   D5 = 149

$$RF = \frac{(1 + 10\% \text{ x } 149/365)}{(1 + 10\% \text{ x } 59/365) - 1} \quad \frac{365}{90 \text{ x } 100}$$

RF = 9.84%

2. Example 2, where:

R2 = 9.6   D2 = 59
R5 = 9.9   D5 = 149

$$RF = \frac{(1 + 9.9\% \text{ x } 149/365)}{(1 + 9.6\% \text{ x } 59/365) - 1} \quad \frac{365}{90 \text{ x } 100}$$

RF = 9.94%

The authors are Treasurer, TNT Group and Deputy Treasurer, Citibank Limited. The views and opinions of the authors do not necessarily reflect those of their respective employers.

References

Das, Satyajit *Swap Financing* (1989) Law Book Company Ltd, Sydney; IFR Publishing Ltd, London.

Chapter 32: Swaps from a bank treasury and trading perspective

David Gelber
Hongkong and Shanghai Banking Corporation

During the early 1970s the banks were increasing the size of their balance sheet footings with abandon. The critical ratio was "return on risk assets" and, in the case of American banks, interbank placements were excluded from risk assets. The collapse of the Herstalt Bank with the resultant realisation of the credit risks associated with interbank business was the beginning of the end for massive balance sheet footings. Coupled with this, bank analysts began focusing on the "return on total assets" ratio which, with the smaller margins available in the interbank market, was not looking too healthy.

This had a particularly adverse effect on medium-term interbank lending (two to five years), with the market contracting sharply. The advent of the swap market was thus a welcome development for bank treasurers who are now able once again to run a medium-term book. The reasons the swap permits this are primarily twofold. Firstly, since an interest rate swap does not involve movements of principal, the risk associates a factor of some 2% to 3% per annum of the notional principal amount as the risk. Thus, a three-year swap for $50m would only be considered to have a risk of $3.0–$4.5m. Secondly, all swap activity is accounted for off-balance sheet and therefore has no impact on footings or ratios but, albeit that it has a small impact on capital as will be explained below. This capital impact is heavily reduced by the "reduction" of up to 80% in capital required for dealing between OECD incorporated banks. The bank treasurer can thus use the swap technique to create medium-term, short-funded and long-funded positions where the potential profits are substantial.

Further, because of the off-balance-sheet maturity of swaps and lesser received credit risks, the market has become quite liquid, enabling positions to be closed rapidly to minimise losses or realise profits, something which was never the case with the medium-term interbank market which even at its heyday was fairly illiquid. The swap technique is superior to medium-term interbank lending and/or positioning securities since at no time is the balance sheet being utilised. No assets are created when a position is opened or closed.

The days of the "off-balance-sheet" nature of swaps are now over. Recently implemented proposals by the Bank for International Settlements embracing all major central banks will mean that swaps will be given a balance sheet treatment by including them, subject to various scaling factors, in the calculation of assets for capital ratio purposes. However, when compared with traditional lending, swaps will be much less capital intensive.

The capital required is arrived at by marking-to-market the swap and adding a figure of 0.5% of the notional principal to cover future exposure. The result is the on-balance-sheet "asset equivalent". However, for interbank transactions with OECD incorporated banks (the vast majority of interbank counterparties) the result is reduced by 80%, with non-OECD banks and non-banks receiving a 50% reduction.

Of course, it is not possible to know how much a swap will move in/out of the money during its life but the International Swap Dealers Association (ISDA) has come up with a series of "expected values" which represent the average expected replacement cost of a swap. To illustrate, a three-year US dollar swap has an expected value of 0.63%. The average amount of risk against which capital has to be provided per $1m of swaps with an OECD bank is:

$$1{,}000{,}000 \times (\underbrace{0.0063}_{\text{expected value}} + \underbrace{0.005}_{\text{future exposure factor}}) \times \underbrace{0.20}_{\text{80\% reduction}} = \$2{,}260$$

It can be seen that this is a de-minimus amount. If one compares this with the risk amount for a $1m loan to the same bank, the figure here is a straight 20% of the loan principal, ie, $200,000, which is not far off a 100-fold differential.

Conventional bank treasury use

The volume of fixed-rate medium-term lending to corporate clients has declined sharply as this sector has been able to access capital markets directly and cheaply, but the swap technique can be used to generate fixed-rate funding cheaply and rapidly in order to match such lending if this is required. This is particularly true for non-US dollar fixed-rate lending where many banks do not have access to matching deposits. The vast majority of swaps are against floating-rate US dollars at Libor and such funds are generally available. Using a swap the bank can readily convert these short-term funds obtained through deposits or CD issuing into a fixed-rate funding at attractive rates. Consider for example, a situation prevailing at the time of writing. Let us assume that a bank requires to fund a three-year fixed-rate US dollar loan. Three-year Libor is 9.125% in a fairly illiquid market. Three-year fixed-rate US dollars versus six-month Libor can be obtained, however, through the swap at 8.95%. Under such an arrangement the bank would pay 8.95% annually and receive six-month Libor for three years. If, however, its average cost of deposits is Libor – 0.125 it would be generating the fixed-rate funding at 8.825, a full 0.30% cheaper than three-year Libor. The bank must, however, have a fairly high degree of confidence in its ability to raise short-term deposits at attractive rates relative to prevailing Libor.

From time to time, the arbitrage works the other way whereby the bank can issue a fixed-rate CD for, say, three years and using a swap convert this into floating-rate funding at a small margin under Libor. Japanese banks, who find it difficult to secure a ready source of floating-rate deposits at attractive rates are heavy users of this technique when the "window" appears in the market.

A similar technique can be used to generate fixed Deutsche marks for five years, for example. This can be used to facilitate the growing desire to reduce balance sheet assets, with banks often trying to sell off their assets. However, the asset in question may be denominated in a currency for which there are no buyers, or the buyers of a particular asset may want exposure in their local currency or at a fixed rate. An example of such a situation is South African assets which are not easily saleable. There does, however, exist from time to time an appetite in Germany for South African risk, provided it is "denominated" in fixed-rate Deutsche marks.

Assuming the original asset is in floating-rate US dollars at, say, Libor + 0.50 for five years, the bank can arrange a swap into fixed-rate Deutsche marks and sell off the asset as a Deutsche mark one. Figure 1 illustrates how such a transaction might work.

Figure 1

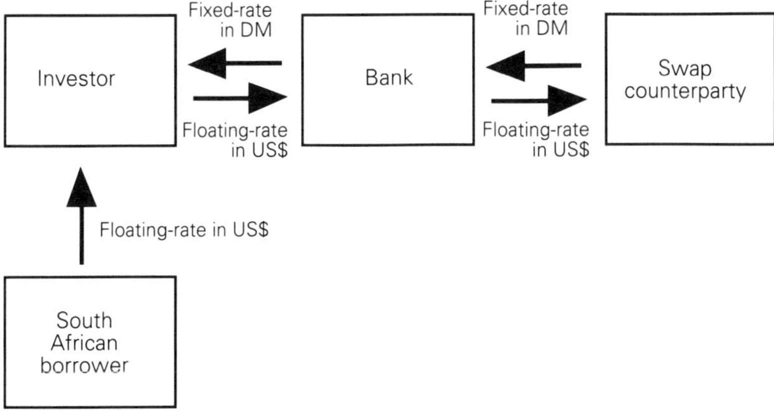

At the start of the transaction the investor pays the bank an amount of Deutsche marks determined by the prevailing spot rate and the size of the asset. The bank pays the Deutsche mark to the swap counterparty and receives US dollars, thus effectively having "sold" the asset. At maturity the reverse occurs, using the original spot rate.

In the event of default by the borrower the bank looks to the investor to carry on with the payments. Thus the credit risk is transferred from the bank to the investor.

A further example of the use of swaps in the typical bank's treasury department is for the raising of long-term funding/capital using the international capital markets. It is probably true to say that the vast majority of all fixed-rate bond issues done by banks, regardless of the currency of issue, are then swapped into floating-rate US dollars. The results achievable by this technique generally provide funds at Libor, or sometimes well below, which compares very favourably with the only other alternative for raising long-term floating-rate funds, ie, the floating-rate note market.

A final example is the use of a swap to lock-in a differential between two different interest rate bases. Consider a New York branch of a relatively small European bank with a portfolio of Prime rate-based assets. The bank may not have ready access to domestic-based funding, whereas it can secure Libor based funds with relative ease. It thus runs the risk that the relationship between Prime and Libor will narrow or, as has happened in the past, invert with Libor exceeding Prime. Using a swap, not only can the bank protect itself against such an inversion but it can lock-in a permanent positive spread. A typical five-year Prime/Libor swap might be done at Prime – 0.80 versus Libor so that the bank's position is as demonstrated in Figure 2. Other

Figure 2

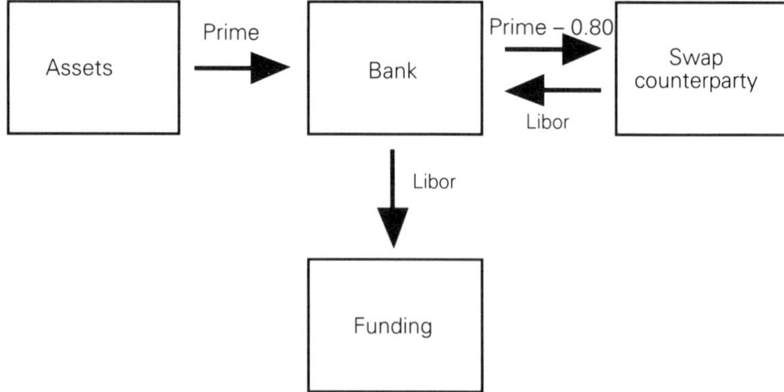

examples of "basis" swaps used by banks are commercial paper versus Libor (used when the bank has a commercial paper programme in operation but requires Libor-based funds to match its assets), and Libor/Libor swaps (for example, three month versus six month) to better match the maturity of its assets and liabilities.

Arbitrage opportunities

The term arbitrage is commonly understood to imply the use of more than one market to execute opposite transactions on a fully-hedged basis at a profit. In other words, a discussion of arbitrage in the swap market is not meant to cover the basic use of swaps to obtain a benefit since this is implicit in the whole swap technique and has been briefly discussed above. Rather, I refer to the execution of a swap trade and one in a different market, as an end in itself.

Arbitrage opportunities do exist from time to time using swaps and some examples will be discussed below.

Cash versus swaps

From time to time the cash interbank market and the swap rates diverge to such an extent that an arbitrage exists. The reasons for this are varied but one cause is the fact that US dollar interest rate swaps are generally based on the yield of US government securities at a given moment in time. Eurodollar deposit rates tend to move more slowly than US government security yields and can diverge significantly at times such as during a perceived banking crisis, with a "flight to quality" occurring. Thus a bank may be able to borrow or lend in the cash market and do the reverse with the fixed-rate component

Figure 3

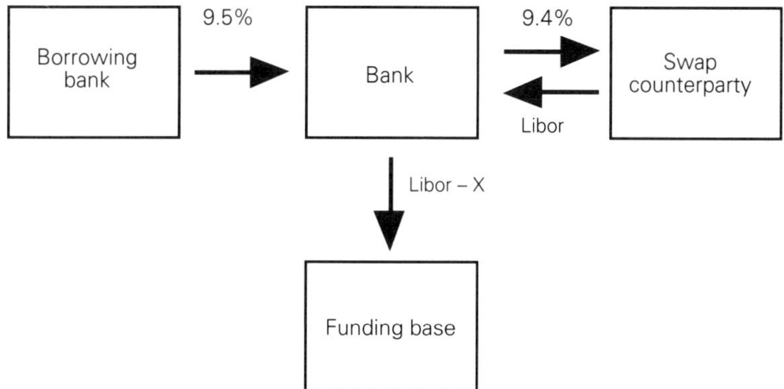

through a swap. Consider a situation when two-year Eurodollars can be lent at 9.5% whereas a fixed/floating-rate two-year swap can be obtained at 9.4%. The resulting transactions would be as shown in Figure 3.

To the extent that during the term of the swap the bank can fund at less than Libor this will increase the arbitrage profit.

The problem with such an arbitrage is that it will cause both a balance sheet impact and a credit exposure, and for the potential returns available is probably not worthwhile.

FRA versus swaps

The forward-rate agreement can be used from time to time to guarantee the future floating-rate levels payable or receivable under a swap and thus effectively convert the floating-rate side into a fixed-rate one. If the FRAs executed can be arranged so that the difference between the actual rate and the FRA rate is settled at maturity, instead of on a discounted basis as is usual, the exercise becomes far simpler.

To illustrate, assume that a one-year versus six-month Libor swap, for a receiver of the fixed-rate annually and payer of the floating-rate semi-annually, can be done at 8.7%. Current six-month Libor in six months' time can be obtained at 8.75%. The bank would, by executing the swap and FRA, have the following cash flows (assuming 182 days in first six months and 183 days in the second six months and a principal of $10m):

6 months
–(10m x 0.0825 x 182/360) = –410,763

12 months
–(10m x 0.0825 x 183/360) = –444,791
+(10m x 0.0870 x 365/360) = +882,083

+432,222

It can be seen that, provided the cost of funding the initial shortfall of $410,763 for the second six months does not exceed $432,222 – $410,763 = $21,459, the transaction will be profitable. In interest rate terms this is equivalent to 10.28% which is a risk the bank may be willing to accept or indeed include as part of its other exposure which it hedges from time to time.

Futures versus swaps

This is almost identical to the FRA arbitrage described above, except that the futures market is used to hedge the future floating-rate levels. It is beyond the scope of this brief chapter to describe the uses of the futures market, the risks, imperfections, etc. An arbitrage such as this should only be undertaken by a relatively sophisticated bank treasury, fully conversant with the use of financial futures. However, it should be noted that the activity in short-term US dollar swaps (up to three years) has seen explosive growth and is entirely driven by the futures markets. The operation is by no means risk-free as practitioners often resort to techniques such as "stacking" whereby due to unavailability of instant access to large quantities of far-dated futures contracts the bank purchases or sells all the required futures in the nearest time period and later tries to "unstack" these into the required "strips".

The returns on this type of swap operation are miniscule (often as low as two to three basis points) and thus require huge volume to justify it.

Foreign exchange forwards versus swaps

This is one of the most complex but profitable arbitrage opportunities that arise from time to time. The following is only a very brief description of the technique.

As mentioned previously, almost all currency swaps are based on fixed rate in the currency against a floating rate in US dollars. The first step is therefore to combine a typical currency swap with an interest rate swap in US dollars which results in known flows in both US dollars and currency. To illustrate, assume a bank can "borrow" five-year fixed-rate Deutsche marks through a swap at 5.5% annually versus six-month Libor. A five-year interest rate swap with the bank receiving fixed rate and paying six-month Libor can be done at 9.4%. By entering into both transactions for an amount of $10m and DM16.5m the bank will have annual cash flows as shown in Table 1.

Table 1

Year	$ cash flow	DM cash flow
1	940,000	–907,500
2	940,000	–907,500
3	940,000	–907,500
4	940,000	–17,407,500

Note that the floating-rate Libor payments net to zero each six months.

The resulting flows can now be covered using the long-dated foreign exchange market whereby the Deutsche mark outflow is purchased against US dollars.

Assume the foreign exchange rates outlined in Table 2 are obtainable. The difficult problem is to evaluate properly the resulting net US dollar position since its value is highly dependent on the reinvestment rates available for the surpluses in the first four years, which will be required to offset the shortfall of $1,629,592 in year five. This is a matter for the individual bank treasury. The net present value of the flows using a discount rate of 6% is positive.

Table 2

Year	DM rate	DM bought	$ sold	Net $ position
1	1,5900	907,500	–570,755	+369,245
2	1,5300	907,500	–593,137	+346,803
3	1,4725	907,500	–616,299	+313,701
4	1,4170	907,500	–640,438	+299,562
5	1,3850	17,407,500	–12,568,592	–1,629,592

Trading

The origins of the swap market were firmly based on matching the equal but opposite requirements of two counterparties. In recent years more and more swaps are undertaken on a one-sided basis, being eventually matched to a greater or lesser degree when a suitable counterparty is found. During the time the position is held it is generally hedged with fixed-rate securities. This activity is now termed "warehousing".

The advent of the warehouse has resulted in a reasonable two-way market developing with bid/offer prices available in most maturities and currencies.

As a result, it is now much easier for a bank to "trade" the swap product. Nevertheless, with the one exception discussed below, the swap is inherently a very poor instrument for trading. The reason is that even when a position is closed out, exposure remains and payments, rate settings, etc continue for the remaining life of the swap. So although a bank may have "borrowed" fixed rate at 10% and "lent" it at 10.05% through two offsetting swaps for five years done in the space of a day, the swap obligations and risk of default will remain for the full five years. Whilst it is always possible to close out swap positions by approaching the counterparty and agreeing an upfront payment or receipt for cancellation of the deal, or indeed attempting to assign the swap contract to another bank, these techniques are both time consuming and used very infrequently.

Further, each swap will require documentation, often lengthy, to be negotiated. The ability of a bank to continue high volume trading is likely to be diminished over time as the exposure to the various swap counterparties mounts and clogs the available credit limits. In order to overcome these problems the market participants are working towards standardising documentation, using telex confirmations as acceptable documentation, and the possible netting of swap exposures between two banks.

The only exception to the unsuitability of swaps as a trading tool concerns the short end of the market, trading for the same days as financial futures. These one and two-year swaps are highly liquid and market practice has evolved which eliminates the need for complex documentation. These swaps move exactly in line with the financial futures prices and thus offer liquidity and possible arbitrage opportunities against the cash market.

Swapper versus money market traders

The trend in the banking industry has been to integrate the swap department into the traditional treasury as opposed to having the former resident in a separate "capital markets" or "investment banking" department. However, this integration leads to potential conflicts between the two units. Some of the issues worthy of comment are mentioned below.

- Swap books (or "warehouses") operate on very fine spreads although they perceive that the risk they take is much less than outright interest rate traders, due to their hedging policy. Traditional interest rate trading involves a higher risk/reward and these two philosophies can come into conflict.

- Money market traders use the swap technique extensively as discussed above and in a situation where two distinct teams (and, more importantly, profit centres) are dealing in the same product conflicts are bound to arise. Thus, while most banks try to impose a rule that only the "swap group" should deal with the outside world this gives rise to inevitable clashes when the swap group is not providing the money market with competitive pricing.

- Where, as in most banks, credit lines are a scarce resource, the perception often arises with the money market traders that the swap group is "churning" vast volumes of swaps and thus using up scarce lines for what they view as very little return.

- Many banks operate an "investment" book for the purpose of taking long-term interest rate positions which do not have to be marked-to-market on a daily basis. Swaps have become a common feature of such investment books as they provide higher returns than, for example, government bonds. This gives rise to a serious accounting issue whereby one unit of the bank can transact a swap with another yet the swap book is being revalued daily whereas the investment book is not. Thus a completely non-existant transaction from an accounting consolidation point of view is being treated differently by two units. A further concern often expressed by auditors is that such an approach could lead to poor trading positions being transferred to the investment book. Tight controls must therefore be in place governing transfer pricing between the units.

The above issues can only be properly addressed through good management and clear definition and demarcation of each group's objectives. There can be little doubt that there is room for both types of activity in a trading room.

Chapter 33: Purchasing an interest rate portfolio

Malcolm Coleman
Macquarie Bank Ltd

As we head into the 1990s, one notable feature of financial markets is the partial retracement of the globalisation trend which was so prevalent throughout the 1980s. Some financial institutions are reassessing their strategies and are now concentrating on core businesses in core currencies. One common outcome of this shift in strategy is the selling off or liquidation of unwanted asset portfolios which may include assets such as equities, property, loans and interest-bearing securities. One secondary effect of this asset sell-off is the requirement, in some cases, to unwind the derivative financial instruments which are tied to the primary assets and would include products such as interest rate and currency swaps, foreign exchange forwards, forward-rate agreements (FRAs) and the myriad of option products which are now offered on these financial instruments.

Macquarie Bank has had first hand experience of this retracement process in that the Bank has purchased five derivative interest rate portfolios in the last two years and has tendered on others. This chapter discusses the steps that have typically taken place when buying an interest rate swap portfolio as well as attempting to identify some of the benefits to both the buyer and seller. This discussion could equally apply to other financial portfolios such as foreign exchange, bonds, short-term securities, bullion and equities as well as options on these asset classes. To cover the various issues on this subject the chapter has been classified into the following categories:

- reasons for buying and selling swap portfolios;
- valuation of portfolios;
- selecting potential buyers;
- negotiation and the sale;
- documentation; and
- future trends.

Buying and selling swap portfolios

Selling swap portfolios

The major benefits in selling a portfolio are to alleviate one or all of the following:

(1) ongoing costs;

(2) market risk;

(3) basis risk;

(4) credit risk.

Ongoing costs can be split into three areas: bookrunning costs, systems costs and settlement and administration costs. If the profit/loss of a swap portfolio is taken into account on a net present value (NPV) basis then the above costs can be significant in allowing the portfolio to roll off, particularly if some of the transactions have maturities of five to 10 years. An "ongoing cost" budget needs to be calculated for the swap portfolio so that it can be compared to the cost of selling the portfolio today.

Market risk refers to a swap portfolio which has other instruments such as bonds, bank bills or futures acting as hedges against the swaps. Over time the relationship or margin between the hedges and the swaps will almost certainly change, creating future uncertain benefits or costs.

Basis risk can either occur within a swap portfolio or a portfolio which is matched against an asset portfolio such as loans and leases. In the former case, basis risk most commonly arises with swaps that are offsetting on a portfolio basis but have slight date mismatches. Basis risk is normally crystallised when the rate of the floating leg of one swap is set on one day and for the "matching swap" on a following or later date. Cash discrepancies can occur if there is volatility in rates over this rate-setting period.

If swaps are matched against other asset portfolios, basis risk can also occur due to date mismatches. However, more commonly basis risk occurs over time if there are slight changes in the asset portfolio such as early repayments. This can cause a divergence of the duration between the two "matching" portfolios.

The last factor mentioned, "credit risk", is the benefit such that when a swap portfolio is sold, the swaps are novated to the purchaser and hence all ongoing credit risk on the swap counterparties is passed on.

Advantages of buying a portfolio

In addition to the obvious reason of commercial or economic value, the reasons for buying a swap portfolio depends to some degree on the current status and future business direction the financial institution has planned for its swap operation. For example, if the existing swap operation is relatively small and the strategy is to expand book size (ie, gain market share), buying a portfolio can be a convenient way to quickly achieve this goal. One of the benefits of achieving a portfolio "critical mass" is that it may be possible to price future transactions more aggressively against the increased number of positions the portfolio now has. A small swap operation could pay a higher price for a swap portfolio compared to other potential buyers and this premium could reflect their willingness to achieve "critical mass".

Another benefit of buying a portfolio is to gain exposure to a client base which is different to the current one. This potentially allows future sales opportunities with these clients. This advantage applies equally to large or small portfolios.

For swap portfolios which are relatively large in size, purchasing a portfolio may help to reinforce the high profile or dominant position in the market. In addition, the purchase of a portfolio may provide an inexpensive mechanism for offsetting existing market exposures or positions.

Valuation of portfolios

The value that buyers place on a swap portfolio may vary depending on how much emphasis each buyer places on the different risks the swap portfolio has, that is, credit risk, basis risk, market risk and the ongoing cost of running the portfolio (as mentioned above).

Before this final value can be determined, there first has to be a mathematical evaluation of the economic worth of the swap cash flows (and hedging instruments) within the portfolio. Obviously, the worth of any one swap transaction is its replacement or "mark-to-market" value. On a portfolio basis individual swaps would not be revalued at the bid or offer price of each swap but would be typically revalued at the mid-rate price between the bid and offer. Once a mid-rate swap curve has been determined the portfolio can be revalued. The dollar value that different financial institutions place on the portfolio would typically vary due to the following:

- The mid-rate swap curve used for revaluation could be marginally different.

- The mathematical method for discounting the future swap cash flows could be different. Common methods of discounting include, the zero-coupon method, discounting at each swap rate (similar to a bond calculation) and using a discount rate from the swap mid-rate curve which is halfway between today and the maturity of the swap. The former and latter methods attempt to overcome the problem of swap curves which are non-linear in shape.

The swap revaluation should also include the "stub" period at the start of each swap so that it can be revalued and discounted against the previous rate setting which is due at the next rollover date. Once this "objective" revaluation is calculated then the subjective assessments mentioned above can be made.

- If there are interest rate hedges included in the portfolio (such as bonds and futures contracts) then their value also has to be calculated. This process is usually fairly simple as the hedges are normally liquid market instruments and their value is easy to calculate.

In the case where the hedges are over-the-counter products, the method for change of ownership of these assets is typically by market convention. Where the interest rate hedges are exchange-traded such as futures contracts, advice should be sought from a futures broker and the appropriate exchange so that the rules of the exchange can be followed. It has been Macquarie Bank's experience that the interest rate hedges are sold in conjunction with the swap portfolio. The main benefit for doing this is that outright interest rate risk is minimised during the "change-over" stage. Once the deal is agreed and completed then rehedging (if needed) can take place so as to fine tune the risk of the combined portfolios.

It is envisaged that there would be no real competitive disadvantage to the buyer of a swap portfolio who did not require the hedges, as they can be easily liquidated in the market by the vendor. The only issue would be one of price, for example, a buyer of the swap portfolio, including the hedges, may value the hedges at a mid-rate price and hence the overall price may be more attractive.

Selecting potential buyers

Listed below are some criteria that may act as a helpful guide to choosing potential buyers of a swap portfolio:

(1) Strong existing relationship(s).

(2) An acceptable credit rating. If the purchaser has a sound credit rating there is a greater chance that the existing swap counterparties will be satisfied with the swap novation.

(3) Strong systems and back-up. If the purchaser has the systems ability to monitor the portfolio over the negotiation and sale period, it allows for consistent checking of the portfolio value.

(4) A counterparty with whom there are a large number of existing transactions. Such a counterparty may be willing to purchase the portfolio at a finer price as their credit exposure would be lower due to the fact that they would be effectively "unwinding" a portion of the "new" swap portfolio.

(5) Well regarded in the market place as professional and having a commitment to that market.

Once a list of potential buyers has been established, there is normally a tender process to create a short list of two or three potential buyers. Typically, the vendor of the portfolio would give the details of the swap transactions (as well as any hedging instruments such as bonds and bank bills which are included in the portfolio) to prospective buyers and set a time for the buyers to submit their valuation of the portfolio. At this stage, the names of the swap counterparties are normally not disclosed. Using these valuations the vendor would choose a short list of candidates.

If there is a specific reason (such as point (4) above) for the vendor to choose one counterparty as the buyer for the portfolio, then the following discussion on negotiation and sale still applies, except for the tender process itself.

Negotiation and sale

At this stage the vendor of the portfolio would give the names of the swap counterparties in the portfolio to the short list of potential purchasers so that credit checking can take place. In addition, a time would be set for the final quote. There is no best time to ask for the final quotes as it really depends on the structure of the portfolio. For example, if there are large duration mismatches in the portfolio, the buyers would prefer to quote, and be informed of the outcome, during market trading hours so that the appropriate interest rate cover can be taken. Alternatively, if the book is reasonably matched on a duration basis then the close of a business trading day may be suitable. If the book is very large then the close of business on a Friday may be the best time so that there is a weekend available if extensive systems work is required.

If there is a significant discrepancy in the portfolio valuation between the portfolio buyer(s) and the portfolio vendor, it may be appropriate for the parties involved to go through the portfolio and check each individual swap revaluation so that differences can be explained.

During the time between the short list being decided and the final tender date for the portfolio, it is common practice for the vendor to contact the swap counterparties and inform them of the impending novation and to ascertain if there are any problems in novating the swaps to the potential buyers. This contact normally takes the form of an initial telephone call followed up by a letter or fax to the counterparty showing the swaps to be novated and the potential buyers involved. At this stage, it is helpful if the existing swap counterparty can give an "in principle" agreement to the novation of the swaps.

If the situation arises where the swap credits are not acceptable to either the new buyer or the existing counterparty these issues normally have to be addressed on a case-by-case basis. Some common outcomes are that the swaps are unwound with the existing counterparty or that the vendor intermediates between the buyer and the current counterparty.

In the case where the vendor is no longer incorporated in Australia then the intermediary may be the offshore parent.

If the above issues have all been addressed then once the quotes have been received on the tender day, the last decision for the vendor is the choice of the portfolio buyer. Once the choice has been made, the novation documents should be drawn up and circulated as quickly as possible.

Documentation

The sale of a swap book is usually effected by a novation of contracts from the vendor to the purchaser. Novation is the process whereby the old contract between the counterparty and the vendor is terminated and a new contract between the counterparty and the purchaser is created. It is not sufficient for the vendor to assign the swaps to the purchaser because swap contracts consist of two-way obligations and it is therefore necessary for the purchaser to assume the obligations of the vendor.

The purchaser of a swap book inherits any defects in the documentation of the vendor. It is therefore necessary for the purchaser to either establish that all swaps are properly documented or take steps to ensure that documentation is put in place with its new counterparty. The purchaser should receive from the vendor all original documents as these may be needed in a dispute. If the swaps novated are subject to AIRS terms[1] this problem will not arise.

It is usual for the vendor to give some warranties regarding the swap book such as:

- That all details are correct.
- That no events of default have occurred.

- That no swaps have been amended.
- That it will assist the purchaser if there is a dispute regarding a swap.

Although the vendor gives a warranty that the details provided for each swap are correct, it is also usual for the counterparty to confirm the details in the novation agreement.

Other issues include:

- Will the vendor indemnify the purchaser for counterparty credit risk?
- As the counterparty does not have to agree to the sale, the vendor and purchaser should agree on an adjustment to the swap price if a counterparty refuses to novate.
- Obtain legal advice to ensure the sale is not subject to stamp duty on conveyance.

Future trends

As evidenced by the boom in derivative financial products over the last decade, the sky is the limit in terms of new products. This remark, however, should be tempered by the fact that a period of rationalisation is taking place in financial markets and that one could expect product growth, albeit at a slower pace. If a revolutionary product or idea was introduced (as was the case with options theory), then one would expect product growth to accelerate once again.

One noticeable trend of the derivative products boom is the huge increase in the turnover and velocity of transactions. If this trend continues, there will be increasing emphasis on counterparties to minimise the credit usage and capital adequacy usage of transactions. In the US swap market, this pressure has been addressed by the legal acceptance of netting of swap exposures. Over time one would expect netting to be adopted in other countries as well. Also in the future we could see a greater divergence in pricing (or price tiers) to distinguish between the credit and capital adequacy usage of the different types of entities which use derivative products.

One of the secondary effects of purchasing derivative portfolios is the concentration of larger portfolios to a smaller group of financial institutions, ie, the market may increase in total turnover of volume, but the number of bookrunners will contract. This effect will exacerbate the problem of credit lines between participating financial institutions.

As a result, financial institutions which are large bookrunners in derivative instruments, may sell sub-sets of their portfolio which consists of deals with one or a number of other counterparties to a third counterparty who is looking to increase book size or is looking to increase their market exposure to the counterparties within that sub-set. This could be one method used in the future to realign absolute credit and capital adequacy exposures within the marketplace.

Finally, wc could one day see all derivative instruments classified as cash flows under one generic legal agreement so that netting across product boundaries can take place. The impetus for this type of arrangement will almost certainly come from credit and capital adequacy constraints.

Notes

1. AIRS terms stands for Australian dollar fixed and floating interest rate swap terms.

Chapter 34: Swap back office systems

Brady PLC, Cambridge Science Park, Milton Road, Cambridge CB4 4WE, UK

System	Part of integrated system
Types of swap handled	Interest rate, irregular cashflow, amortising, accreting
User interface	Pop down menus
Valuation method	Zero coupon
Interpolate intermediate swap points?	Splining on zero coupons
Sensitivity analysis	Non-parallel yield curve, gap analysis
Automatic confirmations	Yes
Source code language	Compiled Basic
Hardware and operating system	PC running DOS
Ability to input own algorithms	No
Relational database availability	Planned
Types of reports available	Cash, swap, Euro$ futures, bond equivalent, mark to market, sensitivity, P/L; sophisticated report writer using SQL-style interface allows users to define own reports
Number of swaps and currencies handled	Limited only by disk space
Speed with which portfolio can be valued	About 120 trades every 30 seconds (on 386 PC with co-processor, running across Novell network
Integration with mainframe	ASCII file output; format conversion on request
Integration with other instruments	Fully integrated with other interest rate instruments, including options
Hedging facilities	Extensive
Integration with other databases	ASCII file output
Accounting capabilities	Mark to market, accounting model with general ledger interface
Frequency of P/L reporting	Real time
Audit trails	Yes
Customisation policies	Languages, no; regulatory requirements, by negotiation
Planned enhancements	Can be upgraded to handle wide range of interest rate trades, including derivatives. Planned enhancements include windowing interface, relational database capability; others on request

Cats Software, 1800 Embarcadero Road, Palo Alto, CA 94303, US

System	Swapware, Risk Manager
Types of swap handled	Currency, interest rate, foreign exchange, deposits, basis, coupon, forward starting, amortising, accreting, irregular cashflow, rollercoaster and stub periods
User interface	Menu/parameter, with flexible frameworks for creation, manipulation, cashflow generation, revaluation; multiple windows currently available
Valuation method	Par yield, zero coupon, synthetic, blended, user-defined
Interpolate intermediate swap points?	Linear interpolation of selected yield curves
Sensitivity analysis	Parallel and non-parallel, two types of duration analysis, gap analysis, payments analysis, principal stripping, convexity analysis, IRR, cash analysis, accrual analysis, reinvestment analysis, cash-flow gridding, average life, future value, partial differential sensitivity
Automatic confirmations	Through telex facility
Source code language	C
Hardware and operating system	PC with MS-DOS; Sun with Unix; DEC with Ultrix or VMS planned
Ability to input own algorithms	Integration with other external models
Relational database availability	Yes
Types of reports available	BIS reporting, counterparty exposure, risk management reports, hedging recommendations, etc
Number of swaps and currencies handled	Unlimited number of swaps, 25 currencies, with 8 user-definable
Speed with which portfolio can be valued	350 a minute (386 PC); 3,000 a minute (Sun Sparc 1)
Integration with mainframe	Via ASCII files, packetised transaction, market data files
Integration with other instruments	Fully integrated with caps, floors, FRAs, bonds, money markets, futures, T-bond futures and swaptions
Hedging facilities	Delta, partial differential, pyramid hedging with cashflow gridding with variety of hedge instruments, including user-defined instruments
Integration with other databases	Lotus, Paradox, dBase, etc
Accounting capabilities	Mark to market, P/L on user-defined portfolios, daily accruals, rate refixing with averaging and compounding, notifications, institution/personnel databases, payments generation
Frequency of P/L reporting	Daily, weekly, monthly, yearly
Audit trails	Discount factor by cashflow reporting for any transaction
Customisation policies	Consulting and systems integration services available
Planned enhancements	Extensive

Digital Equipment Service Industries Solutions Company Limited, Harefield Place, The Drive, Uxbridge, Middlesex UB10 8AG

System	Trader Workbench
Types of swap handled	Currency, interest rate
User interface	Menu-driven; windowing
Valuation method	–
Interpolate intermediate swap points?	Linear
Sensitivity analysis	No
Automatic confirmations	No
Source code language	Microsoft Excel, C
Hardware and operating system	PC, MS-DOS and MS Windows
Ability to input own algorithms	Yes
Relational database availability	No
Types of reports available	No
Number of swaps and currencies handled	–
Speed with which portfolio can be valued	–
Integration with mainframe	Integrates with Data Logic Digital Distribution System
Integration with other instruments	FRAs
Hedging facilities	No
Integration with other databases	Integrates with most digital feed suppliers
Accounting capabilities	No
Frequency of P/L reporting	None
Audit trails	–
Customisation policies	Supplied as Excel compatible, therefore readily modifiable
Planned enhancements	–

Devon Systems International, 10 Devonshire Square, London EC2M 4PY, UK

System	The Devon System
Types of swap handled	Single/cross-currency interest rate swaps: fixed/floating, floating/floating, fixed/fixed; amortising, accreting and rollercoaster notionals, compounding, averages, discount indices, delayed starts, irregular interest periods, bullet cashflows, varying margin, yield curve, zero and asset swaps, commodity and domestic specific
User interface	Multi-language menus and parameters
Valuation method	Zero coupon
Interpolate intermediate swap points?	Other
Sensitivity analysis	Gap (equivalent, actual and notional), value of .01, parallel and non-parallel yield curve sensitivity for value of .01 and gamma, exchange rate sensitivity, time decay analysis, multi-currency correlated standard deviation analysis, equivalent risk profile in cashflow, money market futures, cash bonds, generic swaps, debt futures
Automatic confirmations	Multi-language automatic confirmation/advice for opening, payments, fixings, principal exchange, maturity; SWIFT supported
Source code language	APL, C, Fortran, Assembler
Hardware and operating system	VAX 8550, 86xx, 88xx, 89xx, 6320-6360; MicroVax 3xxx; DECstation 3100, DECsystem 3100; IBM RT/PC; SUN series 3-4; IBM 43xx, 308x, 309x; IBM PS2 70-80; Compaq 386/20, 25, 33; MS-DOS, UNIX, VMS
Ability to input own algorithms	Proprietary models supported
Relational database availability	Yes
Types of reports available	Multi or consolidated currency; P/L, gap, position and risk; equivalent risk profile in cashflow, money-market futures, cash bonds, generic swaps, debt futures; limit, capital adequacy, regulatory, administrative, cashiering, accounting/general ledger, interest accrual, etc
Number of swaps and currencies handled	All currencies: number of trades is hardware dependent
Speed with which portfolio can be valued	Deal and hardware dependent
Integration with mainframe	Fully compatible; can be mainframe resident or export interface files
Integration with other instruments	Swaptions, caps, floors, FRAs, cash bonds, loans and deposits, OTC options, currency spot, forwards and options; exchange-traded instruments
Hedging facilities	By user designation, for accounting or performance tracking
Integration with other databases	Standard and user-defined interfaces to external systems; ad hoc query/extract facility
Accounting capabilities	Mark to market and/or accrual-based accounting; alternative methods for currency translation to accounting currency available
Frequency of P/L reporting	Real time
Audit trails	Report with pricing parameters: yields, day counts, zero coupon yield equivalent, discount factors
Customisation policies	On request
Planned enhancements	Market-driven; released semi-annually

Investment Support Systems UK, 1 Norton Folgate, London E1 6DA, UK

System	Futrak Swaps System
Types of swap handled	Currency, interest rate, irregular cashflows, amortising, accreting, arrears, up-front settlement, FRA style (amortised or recognised), asset-based, compounding weighted/unweighted average, etc; swap types can be entirely defined by the user
User interface	Menu and parameter-driven; point-and-shoot windows
Valuation method	Zero coupon and par yield, selected by user
Interpolate intermediate swap points?	Linear
Sensitivity analysis	Ability to define linear and non-linear yield curve shifts; P/L, gap and periodic interest rate exposure analysis
Automatic confirmations	Yes; template-based, can be formatted by user
Source code language	C and Microsoft BASIC 6
Hardware and operating system	IBM PS/2 or PC compatible; MS-DOS 3.2, 3.3 or 4.01; stand-alone or networked
Ability to input own algorithms	Yes
Relational database availability	All data approachable with report generator, Sculptor
Types of reports available	Daily transactions details and summary (sort user-defined) accounting accruals, average rate, for cap, swap or data range; future activity, cashflow for individual swap or overall; other reports user-defined as required
Number of swaps and currencies handled	999 currencies, 999 swap types, 999,999 swap transactions, depending on hardware
Speed with which portfolio can be valued	Depends on size of portfolio and hardware
Integration with mainframe	Interface with general ledger; user-defined export
Integration with other instruments	Fully integrated with complete FUTRAK risk management system
Hedging facilities	Can use any instrument input in a hedge with any other instrument or instruments
Integration with other databases	Data can be combined through report generator with data from other databases
Accounting capabilities	Comprehensive: mark to market, accrual, contingency entries, posting of journal entries to user-defined accounts
Frequency of P/L reporting	As required: real time, on line or end of day
Audit trails	System performs all calculations
Customisation policies	Flexible: any language, Bank of England and Basle requirements
Planned enhancements	Real time duration, convexity and hedge analysis

Login, 35 Cours Michelet, Cedex 57, 92060 Paris La Defense 10, France

System	M2S Micro Swaps Software
Types of swap handled	Currency, interest rate; delayed start, off-market coupon, up-front and final payment, amortising, fixing at beginning and end of period, compounding, broken periods, etc
User interface	Menu-driven, windowing, graphics, report generator, colour display, mouse, high performance laser printer interface, user access levels
Valuation method	Mark to market by zero coupon, pyramid, bond structure or yield methods; quarterly, semi-annual or annual aggregations; what-if capabilities
Interpolate intermediate swap points?	Linear
Sensitivity analysis	Gap, duration, parallel shift, tilt, user-defined
Automatic confirmations	Yes
Source code language	C
Hardware and operating system	386 PC with EMS expanded memory, math co-processor, colour display; MS-DOS 3xxx; network software (Novell or equivalent)386 PC with EMS expanded memory, math co-processor, colour display; MS-DOS 3xxx; network software (Novell or equivalent)
Ability to input own algorithms	Alogarithms can be modified by user
Relational database availability	Yes
Types of reports available	Contract print-outs, deals slips, contract telex, counterparty report, floating rates/maturity report, bond operations and positions, gap, duration, credit risk, payments, accrued interest, capital adequacy, portfolio P/L; customised reports on request
Number of swaps and currencies handled	No limit on currencies; 32,000 swaps
Speed with which portfolio can be valued	Depends on number and type of contracts
Integration with mainframe	Data feed in ASCII or user-defined formats
Integration with other instruments	Money market lending and borrowing, spot and forward foreign exchange, spot and forward payments, fixed and floating-rate bonds, FRAs, futures; options during 1991
Hedging facilities	Hedge prescriptions per contract or set of transactions; calculates cashflow parallel shift sensitivity, quantity of hedging bonds required to immunise cashflow and remaining risk
Integration with other databases	Via ASCII, Sylk, DIF and other user-defined formats
Accounting capabilities	Mark to market, accrual, payments, but no accounting-specific module included
Frequency of P/L reporting	On user request
Audit trails	Calculations and algorithms manual on request
Customisation policies	On request
Planned enhancements	On-line automatic market data feed; options

Lombard Risk Systems Ltd, 147 Strand, London WC2R IJD, UK

System	Oberon
Types of swap handled	All types of interest rate and currency swap; zero or low coupon, amortising, accreting, split coupon, fixed or variable floating rate offset, irregular cash-flow
User interface	Menus and function key selection
Valuation method	Zero coupon based on system-generated PV factors
Interpolate intermediate swap points?	Linear and splining, plus proprietary smoothing process; user's own yield curve can be used
Sensitivity analysis	Gap, non-parallel yield curve, convexity, volatility
Automatic confirmations	Yes
Source code language	C
Hardware and operating system	386 machine with hard disk and 4Mb of RAM; co-processor recommended
Ability to input own algorithms	No
Relational database availability	Records can be viewed and manipulated in ASCII format
Types of reports available	Risk reports in either futures, bonds, swaps or FRA equivalents; net equivalent position, cost of carry, gamma and volatility exposure, all broken down by user-defined time bucket; trades listing by book/group or counterparty, fixings diary, settlement diary, daily journal/audit trail
Number of swaps and currencies handled	Supplied with 17 currencies, others can be added by user; number of swaps limited only by hardware
Speed with which portfolio can be valued	Valuation of 1,000 5-year swaps takes 35 seconds on 20MHz 386 PC with co-processor
Integration with mainframe	Oberon file extractor allows full import/export with ASCII files which allows link-up with other systems
Integration with other instruments	FRAs, futures, swaptions, caps, floors, IRGs, bonds etc
Hedging facilities	All main hedging instruments supported; hedges can be reported either together with or separate from swaps
Integration with other databases	Interfaces discussed on case-by-case basis
Accounting capabilities	Mark to market: P/L and accounting control totals and accruals
Frequency of P/L reporting	At any time: since previous day, month to date, year to date, etc
Audit trails	Daily journal covers all events supplemented by detailed trade history
Customisation policies	For individual markets
Planned enhancements	Frequent improvements

Lor/Geske Bock Associates, 532 West 6th Street, Suite 220, Los Angeles, CA 90014, US

System	LOR/GB Advisory System
Types of swap handled	Interest rate and currency; any combination of payment frequency, notional and rate; non-averaging and averaging; swaps, caps and floors and American and European options on swaps, caps and floors
User interface	Menu-driven with batch processing option
Valuation method	Real time futures market data translated into term structures of forward rates and discount factors; valued by discounted cashflow; caps, floors and swaptions valued by conventional/proprietary models
Interpolate intermediate swap points?	Proprietary method based on no arbitrage of rates
Sensitivity analysis	Sensitivities to any type of term structure movements; single contract and portfolio analyses; what-if analyses of term structure movements on portfolios and hedges
Automatic confirmations	By customer interface to user's back office systems
Source code language	Fortran and C
Hardware and operating system	Dedicated PC; able to network with workstations or PCs in Unix or DOS
Ability to input own algorithms	Ability to specify term structures of interest rates and volatilities; others on request
Relational database availability	Via ASCII file
Types of reports available	Valuation and risk summary, sensitivity and risk profile maps, optimal hedge positions in futures, bonds and other instruments, pricing indications pages, aggregate portfolio and valuation risk summary, aggregate portfolio risk profile maps, graphical displays of inputs and outputs
Number of swaps and currencies handled	Unlimited
Speed with which portfolio can be valued	Depending on hardware, valuation, risk analysis and hedge advice, averages under 1 second/contract
Integration with mainframe	Interface through ASCII files
Integration with other instruments	Caps, floors, FRAs, bills, CDs, notes, bonds, futures, American and European options on above, mortgages, mortgage-backed securities, GICs, IOs, POs, options on other instruments
Hedging facilities	Optimal hedge advice in futures, bonds, FRAs and combinations
Integration with other databases	ASCII file interfacing
Accounting capabilities	Accounting of portfolio mark to market and hedge positions for front office valuation, hedging and risk assessment
Frequency of P/L reporting	Any time, automatic on rate change, integrated with real time feeds
Audit trails	Yes
Customisation policies	User-specified inputs and outputs, custom interfaces, custom models
Planned enhancements	Frequent enhancements

MYCA, One World Trade Center, Suite 1343, New York, NY 10048, US

System	Financial Engineering Workstation
Types of swap handled	Interest rate and cross-currency, coupon, basis, deferred, amortising, accreting, rollercoaster, zero coupon, irregular cash payment, IMM, arrears reset
User interface	Menu-driven with partial window capabilities
Valuation method	Zero coupon yield curve valuation with full display of par yield and zero coupon curve
Interpolate intermediate swap points?	Building zero coupon yield curve from bootstrapping or use of exponential spline
Sensitivity analysis	Delta, value of .01, gamma; scenario analysis based on incremental shift of yield curve on parallel and non-parallel basis
Automatic confirmations	Yes
Source code language	C and APL
Hardware and operating system	386 PC with DOS 3.3 or above; math co-processor recommended; CGA, EGA or VGA colour monitor
Ability to input own algorithms	Yes, based on importing zero coupon yield curve
Relational database availability	Yes
Types of reports available	Risk reports for Euro$ future equivalent, bond equivalent, FRA equivalent, or combination; counterparty and credit exposure reports
Number of swaps and currencies handled	25 currencies: 3,000–4,000 swaps
Speed with which portfolio can be valued	Average 10-year swap with 6-month reset will take 3 minutes per 100 swaps
Integration with mainframe	Based on ASCII files
Integration with other instruments	A complete interest rate risk management system, employing multiple synthetic and cash instruments for hedge management
Hedging facilities	FRAs, futures, fixed-income, caps, floors, swap options and debt options, incorporating a unified hedging methodology and multi-factor approach to model yield-curve behaviour
Integration with other databases	To any database via ASCII files
Accounting capabilities	Payment processing, general ledger accounting, accrued interest calculation, extensive management and regulatory reporting and related administrated functions
Frequency of P/L reporting	Mark to market can be generated as often as market data is updated
Audit trails	Details of cashflow and discount factors can be shown
Customisation policies	On request
Planned enhancements	Improvements to graphic displays; porting to DEC and Sun workstations

Quotient, 45 Broadway, 22nd Floor, New York, NY 10006, US

System	TMARK: Front-end pricing, hedging and portfolio analysis; CMARK: Full trade processing, accounting, reporting
Types of swap handled	Currency, interest rate, zero coupon, irregular cashflows, amortising, accreting, rollercoaster, reset in arrears, discounted swaps (FRA settlement), independent resetting/compounding/payment structures, forward and back-dated, IMM, swaps with day gaps, basis/generic/fixed swaps, money market and bond equivalent yields, IRR, deferred initial value
User interface	User-defined menu structure; swaps entered by specifying parameters of deal; cashflows calculated; TMARK has windowing capability
Valuation method	Zero coupon, par yield; will accept proprietary valuation methods
Interpolate intermediate swap points?	Linear and cubic splining
Sensitivity analysis	Yes; can be manipulated in any way, with analysis on customised and actual yield curve
Automatic confirmations	Yes; plus reset telexes and payment telexes
Source code language	C (TMARK), C and VAX Basic (CMARK)
Hardware and operating system	TMARK: 386 PC with EGA display, MS-DOS; Unix version runs on DECstation 3100 under Ultrix, minimal conversions required for other workstations CMARK: Any DEC VAX/VMS
Ability to input own algorithms	Yes; users may provide own models for both front office analytics and back office accounting
Relational database availability	No, but importing of cashflows, P/L and sensitivity analysis information is available
Types of reports available	Operational, accounting, audit trail; cross-instrument gap analysis, interest rate exposure, consolidated financial reporting, hedge analysis, customer exposure, ISDA report, capital adequacy etc; reports available in summary and detail formats
Number of swaps and currencies handled	100 currencies; unlimited number of swaps
Speed with which portfolio can be valued	8,000 swaps in 10 seconds
Integration with mainframe	Linked to back office VAX; file transmitted day-end
Integration with other instruments	Swaptions, caps, floors, futures, options (listed and OTC), FRAs bonds
Hedging facilities	User-defined hedge strategies, with analysis based on about 5 methods; gridded, pyramid, etc
Integration with other databases	Any
Accounting capabilities	Daily mark to market, accrual, settlement, fee accounting, net interest income, constant yield accruals, principal exchange, contingent
Frequency of P/L reporting	TMARK: Real time/CMARK: End of day
Audit trails	At every level
Customisation policies	Responsive to customer needs
Planned enhancements	New hedging and arbitrage models

Simuledge, 95 Avenue des Champs Elysees, 75008 Paris, France

System	ProDeal
Types of swap handled	Currency, interest rate; irregular cashflows and amortising to be implemented soon
User interface	Tailor-made user interface; access codes, pop-up menus, windows
Valuation method	Interest rate swaps: bond-like valuation, zero coupon, replacement cost, variable rate valuation. Currency swaps: zero coupon
Interpolate intermediate swap points?	Linear
Sensitivity analysis	Gap and duration analysis; delta and gamma calculations
Automatic confirmations	Yes; automatic contract production
Source code language	C
Hardware and operating system	PC; MS-DOS; Unix available second half 1990
Ability to input own algorithms	No
Relational database availability	PC: Btrieve, dBase; Unix: Oracle, Sybase; others can be studied if required by client
Types of reports available	Position by currency, maturity, counterparty; gap analysis; daily transaction report, regulatory reports, accounting; report generator
Number of swaps and currencies handled	Unlimited number of currencies
Speed with which portfolio can be valued	1,000 transactions in one minute with math co-processor
Integration with mainframe	File transfer: import and export
Integration with other instruments	Spot, forwards, deposits/borrowing, FRAs; money market instruments, caps, floors from second half 1990
Hedging facilities	Foreign exchange and treasury hedges
Integration with other databases	Multi-database integration; data can be extracted from Btrieve and dBase; others on request
Accounting capabilities	Mark to market or accrual, as defined by user
Frequency of P/L reporting	End of day; real time interface in development
Audit trails	No
Customisation policies	Very flexible: multi-language, multi-entity, report generator
Planned enhancements	–

Softbridge Capital Markets, 3 Crawford Place, London W1H 1JB, UK

System	Swaps Manager
Types of swap handled	Interest rate and currency; bullet, forward start, arrears reset, fixed/floating, fixed/fixed, IMM, asset swaps, amortising, accreting, roller-coaster with regular or irregular structures, with or without fees
User interface	Menu-driven
Valuation method	Bond equivalent or zero coupon
Interpolate intermediate swap points?	Linear
Sensitivity analysis	Gap, duration, sensitivity analysis: PVBP to linear and non-linear shifts
Automatic confirmations	Yes
Source code language	C
Hardware and operating system	640K PC; math co-processor recommended
Ability to input own algorithms	Download interface to spreadsheet enables user to perform own modelling
Relational database availability	No
Types of reports available	40 reports, including transaction details, transaction summary, diary reports, accruals, rate resets, counterparties, duration, mark to market exposure, revaluation, credit exposure, payment reports, principals; reportwriter module available for user-defined report generation
Number of swaps and currencies handled	Up to 30 currencies; number of transactions limited only by hardware
Speed with which portfolio can be valued	300 swaps marked to market on zero coupon basis in one minute (386 PC)
Integration with mainframe	ASCII interface allows data import/export
Integration with other instruments	Loans and deposits, securities, futures, FRAs, forward foreign exchange, swaptions
Hedging facilities	Portfolio analysis through structure of book/association/hedge scenario allows modelling and evaluation of hedge structures
Integration with other databases	ASCII interface
Accounting capabilities	Mark to market reports on either bond equivalent or zero coupon basis; accruals report; cash management module provides comprehensive management system for accruals, funding costs, etc
Frequency of P/L reporting	Any time
Audit trails	Yes
Customisation policies	On request
Planned enhancements	Interest rate options, caps, floors, collars, bond futures (third quarter 1991)

Software Options, 210 Sylvan Avenue, Englewood Cliffs, NJ 07632, US

System	COTS/DEALER: dealing support COTS/BOSS: back office system
Types of swap handled	Interest rate: fixed/floating, Fed funds, prime rate, commercial paper, amortising, irregular cashflows
User interface	Menu-driven with windows
Valuation method	Zero coupon, forward-forward prices
Interpolate intermediate swap points?	Linear
Sensitivity analysis	Parallel yield curve shift, duration/convexity
Automatic confirmations	In development
Source code language	C, BASIC
Hardware and operating system	PC, VAX/VMS, Unix
Ability to input own logarithms	No
Relational database availability	No
Types of reports available	Futures equivalent, bond equivalent, counterparty, currency, cashflow etc
Number of swaps and currencies handled	Limited only by hardware
Speed with which portfolio can be valued	—
Integration with mainframe	Extensive communications supported, including general ledger interface
Integration with other instruments	Futures, FRAs, bonds, options including swaptions
Hedging facilities	Best hedge, delta equivalents
Integration with other databases	Automatic interface between DEALER and BOSS, communications with branches, passing of books etc
Accounting databases	Mark to market, accrual, option premiums, dual P/L currencies, general ledger entries
Frequency of P/L reporting	Real time
Audit trails	For each payment date
Customisation policies	Available for regulatory reporting and communications interfaces
Planned enhancements	Currency and commodity swaps in development

Part V
Regulatory, legal and accounting developments

Chapter 35: BIS capital adequacy requirements

Stephen Mahony
San Paolo Bank

In July 1988, the Bank for International Settlements (BIS) and the Basle Committee on Banking Regulations and Supervisory Practices published a paper entitled "Proposals for international convergence of capital measures and capital standards". The Basle Committee, which is made up of representatives of the central banks and the supervisory authorities of the Group of Ten (G-10) countries plus Luxembourg, proposed a unified framework for determining the capital adequacy of banks, covering both minimum capital ratios and the treatment of instruments (both on and off the balance sheet) which expose banks to credit risk.

The method for determining the amount of capital required against a particular off-balance-sheet transaction is similar for all interest rate and exchange-related contracts including interest rate and currency swaps, interest rate options and currency options purchased by a bank (for example, caps, floors and swap options), and forward foreign exchange transactions.

The calculation of the capital required for swap transactions involves three steps. The notional amount of a swap is converted into a *credit risk equivalent* according to one of two methods. The credit risk equivalent is then weighted by a factor ranging from 0% to 50% according to the broad credit quality of the counterparty. This produces a risk-weighted asset, against which a capital ratio is then applied.

Calculation of the credit risk equivalent

The Basle Committee proposed two methods for the calculation of the credit equivalent amount of a swap.

Current exposure method

Under this method, which is likely to be applied in most countries, the credit risk equivalent of a swap transaction is equal to its current replacement cost plus an "add-on". The current replacement cost of a swap is measured by the contract's current mark-to-market value, if positive, or zero. The add-on factors are as follows:

Table 1: Current exposure method

Residual maturity	Interest rate contracts	Exchange rate contracts
Less than one year:	—	1.0%
One year and over:	0.5%	5.0%

The add-on factor for basis swaps in the same currency is taken as zero.

The Basle Committee did not specify any particular procedure for calculating mark-to-market values. However, since the authorities in some countries had doubts about relying on a mark-to-market mechanism, the Basle Committee proposed a second alternative, the original exposure method.

Original exposure method

Under this method the credit equivalent of a swap depends on the number of years until maturity of the contract. The credit equivalent of a swap is equal to:

Table 2: Original exposure method

Maturity	Interest rate contracts	Exchange rate contracts
Less than one year:	0.5%	2.0%
One year and less than two years:	1.0%	5.0% (ie, 2% + 3%)
For each additional year:	1.0%	3.0%

For interest rate contracts it is left to national discretion whether original or residual maturity is used. In the case of exchange rate contracts the original maturity must be used.

The Basle Committee proposed that a bank should have the option to select one of the two methods for converting swap notional amounts into credit equivalent amounts, although it should not be able to switch backwards and forwards between methods.

Calculation of the risk-weighted asset amount

The second step is to calculate a risk-weighted asset amount which varies according to the type of counterparty. There are four levels of risk weighting:

1. 0% Central governments of the OECD countries.

   Although all contracts with central governments which have a maturity of one year or less will attract the 0% risk weighting, national supervisory authorities may elect to assign contracts with a maturity of more than one year to the 10% risk category, to account for potential interest rate or currency risk associated with longer-term contracts.

2. 10% Certain public sector entities (other than the central government, such as state governments, local authorities and government agencies) located in the *same* country as the bank in question.

3. 20% Banks incorporated within OECD countries.

   All public sector entities located within the OECD (with the possible exception of those within the same country as the bank in question).

   Multilateral development banks (such as the World Bank and the European Investment Bank).

   Banks outside of the OECD provided that the maturity of the contract is one year or less.

4. 50% All other counterparties (including corporate users, non-bank financial institutions and banks incorporated outside of the OECD).

Calculation of the capital required

The capital required against a swap transaction is calculated with reference to the risk-weighted asset amount and the minimum capital ratio. The Basle Committee proposed a general minimum capital ratio of 8% (to be phased in by the end of 1992).

Examples

Consider a new Ecu20m five-year interest rate swap with a 50% weighted counterparty. The current exposure method produces a credit equivalent amount for the swap of Ecu100,000 (equal to 0.5% x Ecu20m). Assuming that a capital ratio of 4% (50% x 8%) would apply against this amount, the total capital requirement for this swap would be Ecu4,000.

Using the original exposure method, the credit equivalent amount would be Ecu800,000 for a five-year Ecu20m swap (Ecu800,000 = 4% x Ecu20m) which gives a capital requirement for the swap of Ecu32,000.

As time passes and the swap's mark-to-market value changes, the capital required will change. If, one year later, the mark-to-market value of the interest rate swap is Ecu200,000, the credit equivalent amount calculated by the current exposure method would increase to Ecu300,000 (Ecu200,000 plus 0.5% x Ecu20m), giving a capital requirement of Ecu12,000 (Ecu300,000 x 50% x 8%).

Using the original exposure method, the credit equivalent amount would not be related to the mark-to-market value of the contract. The credit equivalent amount would either remain unchanged (if the original maturity method is used) or (if the residual maturity method is used) would reduce with time; in this case falling to Ecu600,000 (3% x Ecu20m), giving a capital requirement of Ecu24,000 (Ecu24,000 = Ecu600,000 x 50% x 8%).

EC legislation

The Directive on Investment Services, proposed by the Commission of the European Communities, is intended to open the way for investment firms authorised in their home Member States to have access to all other Member States' financial markets. It is intended to establish a broadly level playing field between non-bank investment firms and credit institutions trading in the securities markets.

The framework employed requires capital to be allocated in respect of position risk, foreign exchange risk, settlement risk and the fixed overhead costs of a firm.

The directive goes on to set out a system for calculating the requirement for all OTC derivative instruments, including swaps, which coincide with the BIS proposals.

However, the directive provides that each Member State will appoint competent authorities to control the supervisory system in each state and these competent authorities may set alternative requirements for firms using swap models which provide, to the satisfaction of the competent authorities, a more accurate measure of the risks in swaps.

Netting

In 1988, the Basle Committee gave careful consideration to the arguments put forward for recognising netting. The criterion on which the decision was based was the status of netting contracts under national bankruptcy regulations. It is held that if a liquidator of a failed counterparty has (or may have) the right to unbundle the netted contracts, demanding performance on those contracts favourable to his client and defaulting on unfavourable contracts, there is no reduction in counterparty risk. At that time, the Basle Committee said that:

> banks may net contracts subject to novation, since it appears that counterparty risk is genuinely reduced by the substitution of a novated contract which legally extinguishes the previous obligation.

However, since the Committee considered that under some national bankruptcy laws liquidators might have the right to unbundle transactions undertaken within a given period under a charge of fraudulent preference, it was agreed that supervisory authorities would have national discretion to require a phase-in period before a novation agreement could be recognised in the weighting framework.

The Committee decided that banks might not net contracts subject to close-out clauses. However, the Committee did not wish to discourage market participants from employing clauses which might well afford protection in certain circumstances in some national jurisdictions; it would be prepared to reverse its conclusion if subsequent decisions in the courts support the integrity of close-out netting agreements.

Since the adoption of the Basle Accord, the enforceability of netting provisions under the insolvency laws of the G-10 countries has been substantially clarified. In August 1989, the Financial Institutions Reform, Recovery and Enforcement Act ("FIRREA") became law in the United States. FIRREA recognised the enforceability of such provisions during insolvency proceedings involving US domestic depository institutions. In June 1990, an amendment to the United States Bankruptcy Code clarified that such netting provisions would be enforceable against insolvent corporate end users of swaps and non-bank swap dealers. In addition, The International Swap Dealers Association (ISDA) has obtained legal opinions from counsel in Belgium, Canada, France, Germany, Italy, Japan, the Netherlands, Sweden and the United Kingdom indicating that netting provisions contained in bilateral master agreements will be upheld in each of those countries.

The Committee on Interbank Netting Schemes of the central banks of the Group of Ten reported in November 1990 (p 16, part B, section 2.24) that "bilateral master agreements...are likely to be enforceable in all 11 countries."

Industry bodies are now lobbying for the Basle Accord to be modified to permit parties to give effect for capital adequacy purposes to the netting provisions contained in swap master agreements.

However, in this context it is interesting to note that the 1991 ISDA member survey showed that a majority (62%) of members still assume their swap exposure to US counterparties is the gross amount and not the net. Outside the US, more than 80% assume gross and not net exposure.

It seems likely that domestic netting arrangements will be more easily accepted by the authorities than cross-border netting.

Capital adequacy standards for interest rate risk

It is likely that the BIS will propose position risk guidelines. Discussion of this subject has highlighted some uncertainties, particularly regarding the degree of netting within portfolios and across products. The calculation of portfolio sensitivities within one product area or across a range of products may require banks to install new computer systems. Progress in this area is likely to be gradual therefore.

Acknowledgement:
Part of this chapter is based on information published by ISDA and, in particular, on work carried out for ISDA by Cravach, Swaine and Moore. Neither is responsible for errors herein.

Chapter 36: Is a swap clearing house more likely now?

Michael S Rulle, Jr
Lehman Brothers

Three recent events have clearly provided the swap market with unprecedented challenges in the way of counterparty default. Coupled with the ongoing decline in credit quality throughout many industry sectors, these events have heightened the swap market's concern about credit exposure, particularly among dealers.

First, a British appeals court determined in the spring of 1990 that the Local Authority of Hammersmith and Fulham had entered into swaps and related products totalling several billions of pounds sterling for speculative rather than interest rate risk management purposes. Thus, the court ruled that the transactions were *ultra vires,* or unlawful, and the councils did not have to honour their obligations. The ruling, which was upheld by the House of Lords in November 1990, could generate losses for the professional swap counterparties to the transactions of up to £750m, by some estimates.

Secondly, a large number of swap dealers and end users, primarily thrifts, were exposed to default on their swaps with Drexel Burnham Lambert's swap subsidiary when the holding company filed for bankruptcy in February. Drexel was forced to dispose of its US$25–30bn portfolio of swaps and hedging instruments. The firm, after trying unsuccessfully to arrange for the wholesale assignment of its positions to another dealer, managed to terminate the majority of its transactions on a counterparty-by-counterparty basis during a relatively short period. Most counterparties were willing to pay Drexel termination amounts where due, although they were not contractually obliged to do so. To the extent possible, Drexel used these proceeds to make termination payments it owed. However, the consequences remain uncertain for those counterparties that have not yet received payments owed to them or had their collateral returned.[1]

Lastly, a leading dealer in New Zealand dollar swaps, DFC Limited, went bankrupt and was forced to seek a buyer for its swap portfolio. The New Zealand merchant bank successfully arranged for the complete sale of its portfolio to another swap dealer.

Given these significant occurrences, it may now be appropriate to readdress the feasibility of a swap clearing house, which theoretically would provide some type of protection or credit enhancement among dealers in the swap community. A clearing house would in no way provide a vehicle by which all swap risk could be divested — it would only insulate clearing house members, which would be comprised of dealers, from credit risk to each other. The clearing house would not alleviate BIS capital adequacy requirements either, since swaps with the clearing house would be subject to the same risk weight (50%) as swaps with the individual members of the clearing house. However, a clearing house could serve the purpose of reducing pressure on intra-dealer credit lines, and thereby promote more liquidity in the marketplace.

Several years ago, the clearing house concept received serious consideration by the International Swap Dealers Association (ISDA), but was eventually tabled while ISDA focused on other pertinent and imminent issues. Resolutions of many of these issues, such as netting, were in fact prerequisite to the establishment of a clearing house. Since that time, a number of important market developments and regulatory changes have transpired that would impact the development of a swap clearing house. Before reviewing them, however, it would be useful to outline how a swap clearing house might work.

The mechanics of a swap clearing house

The swap clearing house would be formed as a corporation owned by interested dealers meeting a specified credit criteria. Although non-dealer institutions could, in theory, be members, the primary purpose of the clearing house would be to reduce intra-dealer credit pressure. To avoid withholding tax problems, counterparties to an individual clearing house would have to be of the same nationality. Members would create their own governing body (ie, a board of directors) to run the clearing house, and select independent auditors. Obviously, confidentiality of information would be critical to the success of the clearing house.

In a manner similar to commodities clearing houses, each member would be required to post initial capital into the organisation to establish both a net worth and a fund to subsidise potential losses. Each swap entered into with the clearing house would require an initial margin and a variation margin for the duration of the transaction. Members of the clearing house would have to post collateral, based on a mark to market of each swap, in order to ensure that the clearing house is protected from default should interest rates move significantly. Counterparties would additionally be subject to a charge that would cover clearing house operating expenses.

Clearing houses in other financial markets are designed to "clear" contracts by matching trades submitted by buyers with those submitted by sellers. Once both sides can be matched, the clearing houses act as principals between the offsetting parties. Thus, these clearing houses perform two functions — they locate offsetting counterparties *and* they act as credit intermediaries. A swap clearing house, however, would perform only the role of credit intermediation after a swap has been agreed upon between two members. Although the clearing house could be designed to match offsetting counterparties, liquidity in the swap market is probably not yet deep enough to facilitate this function.

In order to ensure prompt execution of transactions, the clearing house would establish a single form of swap contract. Each member would enter into a standard master agreement with the clearing house that would provide for multiple swaps. Transactions could be in all currencies. Agreements would provide for the computation of required collateral and amounts due upon default. The methodology for computing the mark to market, and the mechanics for determining rates and spreads used in calculations would have to be determined by members. Bilateral (rather than multilateral) netting would apply, as master agreements would be between only two counterparties (the clearing house and the member dealer).

In the event of a member default, the clearing house would close out all of that member's positions, either transferring them to other members of the clearing house or liquidating them. If losses exceeded the initial capital and subsequent margin supplied to the corporation by the defaulting party, the clearing house would take a charge to its capital and assess members for a certain share of the losses. Most clearing houses have limits on the amount they can assess their individual members. If a major debacle occurs, a clearing house could go bankrupt if it does not have the authority to assess members over and above a predetermined maximum.

The capital for the clearing house could be assessed in a variety of ways, none of which would be universally popular. The first would be to assess members equally on a *pro rata* basis. Undoubtedly, this alternative would be viewed favourably by dealers that transact significant volume, but be less popular with smaller players. An alternative would be to assess members based upon their individual capitalisation. This method would be inequitable to highly-capitalised institutions with limited swap market exposure versus thinly-capitalised, high-volume members. The final, and seemingly the most logical, method would be to assess members based upon their swap volume. The inherent weakness of this alternative, however, is that the clearing house could just create a very complicated structure which essentially mirrors the credit exposures dealers already have as an ongoing part of their business.

Recent market developments

Several clearing houses for foreign exchange contracts, and one for French interest rate swaps, have recently been developed.

The foreign exchange clearing house

In recent years, International Clearing Systems Inc (ICSI) has been active in developing new netting and clearing systems in the international foreign exchange markets. As a result of its research, ICSI has proposed the creation of an international confederation of regional clearing houses to perform a multilateral netting of foreign exchange contracts. In a similar effort, a group of 13 European banks has recently developed a foreign exchange settlement system called ECHO Netting, which will allow a member bank to settle each transaction in a lump sum that will be apportioned to the correct recipient by a clearing house. The system is expected to reduce participants' financial risk significantly.

Proposed French interest rate swap clearing house

Earlier this year, the privately-owned French futures and options exchange, Optionsmarknad France (OMF), announced that it was finalising a system that would clear French franc interest rate swaps between members. The system is designed to net swaps with maturities up to 12 years against the French floating-rate bases Pibor, TAM and T4M. Members' positions would be marked to market each day, and the daily net position would be covered by a deposit and margin call.

However, as the need for member commitment approaches, the OMF is finding difficulty in gaining support from the major French banks. These banks are concerned that if the clearing house extends membership to weaker credits, they will relinquish their competitive advantage, and they are reluctant to commit to supporting the clearing house should one of the weaker credits default. Obviously, this would also be a major concern among US dealers as it relates to a swap clearing house.

Regulatory environment

Regulatory uncertainty has been a primary obstacle since the swap clearing house was first conceived. Although favourable advances were made in the US with the swap amendment to the United States Bankruptcy Code, the feasibility of a swap clearing house was severely diminished with the promulgation in 1989 of the CFTC's "safe harbour" criteria.

US Bankruptcy Code Amendment

The legal treatment pertaining to bankruptcy or default by a US counterparty to a swap transaction became significantly clearer with the recent passage of a swap amendment to the US Bankruptcy Code. This amendment expressly permits a swap participant to terminate its swaps upon the bankruptcy of its counterparty without being subject to the automatic stay provisions of the Code. In addition, it permits the non-defaulting party to net the market values of outstanding swaps without being subject to the risk that a bankruptcy trustee will "cherry pick" the most favourable contracts. The amendment also ensures that swaps will be exempt from the preference rules of the Code, under which a trustee can "claw back" cash payments made immediately prior to a bankruptcy. A similar measure pertaining to banks and thrifts was passed in 1989.

CFTC's safe harbour for swaps

In a policy statement published in July 1989, the US Commodity Futures Trading Commission (CFTC) set out the five criteria under which interest rate, currency and commodity swaps are free (or "safe harboured") from CFTC regulation. One of these criteria would virtually preclude the clearing house concept by stipulating that the safe harbour is applicable only to swap transactions that are *not* supported by the credit of a clearing organisation or by a mark-to-market and variation settlement system designed to eliminate individualised credit risk. However, legislation is being considered in Congress that would exclude swaps from CFTC regulation without regard to this requirement. The outcome of this legislative initiative could significantly alter the regulatory obstacle to establishing a swap clearing house.

SEC registration

Whether a swap clearing house would have to register as an exchange with the Securities and Exchange Commission or obtain exemptive relief, is unclear. In the past, an exemption from registration was granted to Security Pacific Bank to establish a government security options clearing house.

Withholding tax

If a clearing house were formed in the United States, withholding tax considerations may limit membership to US corporations and US subsidiaries of non-US entities that qualify as corporations.

Is a swap clearing house still feasible?

Several important regulatory, legal and operational issues would need to be resolved before a swap clearing house could be developed. Furthermore, a lack of consensus among swap dealers as to the benefits of a clearing house could present a major obstacle. Similar to the resistance the OMF proposal met with from the major French banks, swap dealers with strong credits are not likely to be willing to forego their competitive credit advantage and stand behind the clearing house in the event that a weaker member defaults. Whether most dealers would consent to the expense that would be required to make the clearing house operate effectively, is also questionable. In spite of these impediments, however, increasing credit concerns in the market may eventually force dealers to examine the clearing house concept more closely.

Note

1. The outcome of the Drexel bankruptcy case will also be germane to the "limited two-way payments" clause of the ISDA swap documentation, since neither the US Bankruptcy Code nor applicable bank and thrift insolvency law, which together cover the bankruptcy of virtually every US swap counterparty, deal with this issue. "Limited two-way payments" permits a non-defaulting counterparty to terminate its swaps without having to pay a mark-to-market value to the defaulting counterparty, thereby giving the non-defaulting party a windfall gain. The legal validity of limited two-way payments may ultimately depend on whether it constitutes an excessive penalty to the defaulting counterparty.

Chapter 37: The return of credit concern to the swap market — after Hammersmith and Fulham

Dr Eric Warner
NatWest Capital Markets Ltd

It is a truism that financial markets today are constantly evolving, aided by the rapid pace of technological change and the increasing linkage of distant financial centres into a "global market". Yet perhaps no change has been more sudden, surprising and complete than the reversal of fortunes within the international swap market. Between 1989 and 1990, the market which for much of the 1980s provided international banks with their most certain and rapidly-expanding profit centres suffered a dramatic downturn, handing many major players sizeable bottom-line losses. In the process the myth that the instrument, like the market, was credit insensitive has been rudely dispelled. Not surprisingly these events have radically altered the climate, re-focusing attention on fundamental credit concerns which for many years were obscured or slighted, and changing the shape of the marketplace itself.

Background to the market

The international swap market, now approaching its first decade of existence, is sufficiently mature to have developed its own mythology. Part of this myth is that the instrument and the market evolved as a means of circumventing credit constraints. The standard textbook accounts of the swap market inform us that the instrument began life as an inspired means of arbitraging different credit perceptions in distinct markets. The now classic account of the "first" swap — the IBM/World Bank exchange of debt obligations in dollars and Swiss francs — or the interest rate example of a AAA borrower tapping the Euromarket in order to exchange its interest obligations with a BBB corporate funding off the domestic bank market, make the same point: the two counterparties could share the arbitrage which came from differing credit perceptions in different marketplaces. Herein we can glimpse the beginning of the myth: weak credits could suddenly escape the constraints of their situation and achieve astonishing benefits in funding costs; and obscure companies long confined to domestic markets could effectively transcend the bounds of their anonymity and tap the fruits of the more name-sensitive international marketplace.

This trend took a quantum leap as the large money centre banks became involved in the developing market as intermediaries. It was these banks' international spread of business, and their expertise at credit analysis, which enabled them to assess the relative strengths of the two counterparties and stand in the middle of the swap. And, ironically enough, it was the credit standing of these banks which provided the necessary comfort level to the disparate counterparties (who probably would not have taken the risk on each other) to allow the market to develop as rapidly as it did. Not only were these institutions among the most tightly regulated and creditworthy in the world, but they developed sophisticated risk management systems and warehouse capacity which turned an immature "matching" exercise into a fully-functioning market of increasing liquidity and depth.

This was fine for the end users who were happy to use the banks' credit standing to access cheaper funding But what of the middle men themselves? As the market went on and the volume of swap transactions grew, they were assuming more and more credit risk. Indeed, in the very early days of the market, before standard documentation or ISDA-defined terms, swap contracts were entered into circumspectly, with a great deal of caution, and limited to investment-grade counterparties. Yet as the market became established and increasingly resembled a club whose players all knew each other, this aspect of the market diminished. With the fear of default receding at each profitable quarter, the market quickly became open to all comers. By the mid-1980s, the notion that the swap market was credit insensitive was firmly established in the minds of most participants.

Throughout this period a number of factors combined to enhance this myth of credit insensitivity. First, the 1980s was a period of continued stability and rising confidence in the major economies, with strong conservative governments in the US, Britain and Germany. This led to bull markets throughout the world, a prolonged boom when credit concerns were overshadowed by the large profits being made in financial markets. More importantly, in the early days of the swap market's development it remained firmly attached to the Euromarkets from where its origins lay. In this market the principal players were the large multinational corporations, whose credit was often better than the banks which ran the swap market.

Thus the perception grew that only top-tier credits played in the market, a perception reinforced by the simple, stunning fact that by the end of 1988, with total swap outstandings of some US$400bn, there had never been a major default.

This argument was deployed with telling effect by the banks in their response to the initial versions of the BIS capital adequacy proposals in 1987–88; as a result they achieved a 50% reduction in the capital weighting for all swap counterparties, a reduction which was meant to reflect the "superior" credits which played in this market. Finally, there was the impact of competitive pressure: increasing numbers of banks piled into the lucrative swap business with the result that spreads contracted and the transparency of the market increased. The market increasingly worked off clearly-defined rates and spreads which were available to anyone who possessed a Reuters or Telerate screen. Thus, as swap prices moved towards the status of a commodity, competitive pressures worked to iron out any residual credit concerns.

Present currents — sea changes

With such a background in mind, it is astonishing how radically the situation has changed in the last two years. Since the beginning of 1989 there have been two major shifts, or "sea changes" in the swap markets which have fundamentally altered the character of the marketplace and thrust credit concerns into prominence. These two changes are:

(1) the first major defaults in the market; and

(2) the erosion of banks' credit standing as the banking industry moves through a cyclical downturn.

As these two changes are conveniently sequential, we can treat each of them in turn.

Hammersmith and Fulham

The single greatest shock the swap market has suffered occurred in the spring of 1989, when the first major default occurred. This was a failure by the London Borough of Hammersmith and Fulham to honour its outstanding swap, option and derivative contracts. The Borough was one of the UK local authorities; these bodies had long been active in the sterling swap market (as they had been in the sterling money market) through their endless appetite for borrowing and investing funds.

As with any government agency, the scale of public expenditure meant heavy borrowing programmes, which in the UK came almost exclusively from the Public Works Loan Board. The opportunities for interest rate risk management through this avenue were limited, however; the result was that as the sterling swap market became established in the mid-1980s, the local authorities became increasingly active players, especially in the five to 10-year maturity spectrum, swapping fixed-rate debt into floating and *vice versa*. As they borrowed at rates close to that of the UK Government itself, there was often attractive arbitrage from a market which worked on a corporate spread above gilts. Indeed part of their standing in the sterling markets came from a presumed credit status approaching that of the UK Government itself. This encouraged the banking sector into large-scale trading with local authorities, most recently in swap and derivative products.

Hammersmith and Fulham had been one of the earliest participants in the market, completing its first swap in 1986. Events were to reveal that it had also been one of the most active, with total sterling swap and option contracts of some £6bn in 1988. This was subsequently revealed to be around a tenth of the entire sterling market, a staggering total for one counterparty. When set against the Council's underlying debt of some £300m, it became clear that the authority had been engaged in wholesale speculation, trading the instruments over and above any designs in debt management. Hammersmith and Fulham's district auditor ruled the Council's activity in these markets was *ultra vires* or beyond the powers conferred by statute on the authority — a ruling which meant that no further monies could be received or paid under the contracts.

This ruling triggered a remarkable sequence of events which at the time of writing is still ongoing. The implications of the suggestion that transactions entered into in good faith could simply be set aside by an auditor's ruling were simply too serious to be ignored. Some 35 London-based banks, of all nationalities, banded together to fight a protracted series of legal cases attempting to uphold the legitimacy of their contracts with the Council. In so doing they were also fighting for the wider principle that all such deals with UK local authorities were not invalid. After an initial High Court judgement and a second judgement in the Court of Appeal, the matter was resolved in a final legal decision at the House of Lords on 24 January 1991. Their Lordships took a strict and narrow interpretation of the Local Government Act 1972, which had made no mention of swaps; thus the instrument together with all its derivatives were held to be unlawful for local authorities.

The repercussions of this decision will reverberate through the financial community for many years. At present, a confusing morass of legal actions threaten to bog down the English courts as individual banks sue for restitution of their now invalid contracts. However, even before this decision the effects on the market have been the same as if the counterparty defaulted: most of the major banks exposed through their dealings with Hammersmith and Fulham have had to make provisions against doubtful debts. Some of these provisions have been large, for example, £76m at the Trustee Savings Bank, £31m at Midland Bank, £37m at Barclays Bank and £22m at British and Commonwealth merchant bank. Non-UK banks have also been affected, with all in all, some 40 banks believed to have approximately £480m exposed to the Council under derivative contracts. As the final judgement held that *no* local authority is entitled to enter such contracts, a further 70 authorities will be affected and the potential loss to major swap market banks will climb to a much greater figure, perhaps in the region of £750m. Such a significant sum has been enough to focus attention back to the issue of the underlying credit risk in swaps.

In one sense, of course, "credit" is not an issue in this affair: the councils concerned have always maintained their means and willingness to honour their obligations under the contracts. Rather, they have been legally banned from doing so. It is therefore a legal issue, a fact which has given rise to a new term, "legal risk". While true, this is something of a nice distinction which does not alter the fundamental point that a massive default has occurred in the swap market, impacting the bottom line of nearly every major market-maker.

The banking downturn

While the Hammersmith and Fulham case was undoubtedly the major shock to the market, it has been followed by a series of reinforcing disasters and disruptions. In the latter part of 1989, two spectacular failures — DFC in New Zealand and Drexel Burnham Lambert in the US — left many banks badly burned. Both entities had been active in swaps — indeed, Drexel had been an active market-maker in US dollars — and the year closed with yet more red ink being spilled in derivative dealings. At present the hope is that in the case of DFC the New Zealand central government will be persuaded to honour the obligations incurred by its former entity. Until such clarity emerges, however, the banks involved have had to write large provisions into their quarterly results. A related consequence of the Drexel failure in the US markets has been to drive a final wedge between the credit perception of investment banks *vis-à-vis* commercial banks. Whereas the US Federal Reserve came to the rescue of the ailing Continental Bank in 1984, no such succour was forthcoming for Drexel, and the confirmation that there is no lender of last resort for investment houses leads to a dramatic differentiation between the creditworthiness of the two classes of banks. As a result, most US investment houses have found their ability to write swap business of over three years maturity severely curtailed.

However, matters are scarcely better for the commercial banking community, particularly in the US. The second major sea-change to affect the swap market is the steadily-worsening credit position of the banks themselves. The large money centre banks, already weakened by successive years of provisioning against LDC debt, are now suffering set backs in their own back yard, with severe downturns in the property, retail and corporate markets. One of the boom areas of the 1980s, acquisition-led finance, has also suffered sharp contraction. As this business invariably demanded interest rate protection, its downturn has been bad news for the swap industry, particularly in the US. A succession of bank downgrades has followed, to the point where many of the once mighty names in the market are teetering on the edge of an investment-grade rating. More broadly still, it is clear that many of the world's major economies — the US, the UK, Japan and Germany — are on the brink of recession, with knock on effects for the banking sector.

Finally, one related development has had a major impact on the swaps industry. This was the agreement of the G10 countries to new minimum capital adequacy standards in 1988. Under the auspices of the Bank for International Settlements (BIS) in Basle, Switzerland, a new framework for minimum risk-weighted ratios of capital to assets were agreed for the world banking community. Under these provisions swaps and other off-balance-sheet instruments, which had previously been free from capital charges, were required to have capital held against them. This naturally increased the cost to the banks of providing such instruments, at the very time when their inherent profitability was declining. Many of the former giants of the swap market have been caught in this cruel vice, severely restricting their ability to write new business.

The 1990s have thus ushered in a particularly bad time for those banks which run the swap industry. At a point when their own credit position is worsening, with traditional forms of lending going sour, the swap market is handing out bitter medicine too in the form of substantial losses for some of the world's largest banks. Needless to say, all this has combined to bring into much sharper focus the underlying risks and credit implications of the swap business.

Reactions, responses and future developments

One of the first reactions to the altered circumstances in the swap market has been the same as in any credit crunch — a flight to quality. There has been a marked drop in liquidity in both longer-dated and cross-currency swaps where the credit risks are most severe. As mentioned above, US investment banks are currently finding it difficult to write this type of business on their own books, and are increasingly forced to use commercial banks as intermediaries in deals involving a swap. The situation has also affected some of the larger money centre banks such as Chase Manhattan, Chemical Bank and Manufacturers Hanover, which are reducing their once formidable swap teams, and confining their efforts to the shorter end of the market. In the UK, the well-publicised impact of the local authority crisis on several major UK banks has resulted in a reduction in liquidity for the sterling market and a similar concentration of business at the short end.

As the established houses contract their activities, the way is opened for new entrants. An interesting aspect of the downturn in the fortunes of American and English banks has been the corresponding rise in those from other countries. Continental banks such as Deutsche Bank and UBS Phillips & Drew, while still maintaining their AAA rating, have become far more prominent in the international swap market in the last two to three years. And the way is opening up for other newcomers with excellent credit: one of the most sparkling performers on the swap stage in recent years has been AIG Financial Products, the financing subsidiary of the US AAA-rated insurance company, AIG. This has led to copycat moves by the still larger General Re insurance company, which is currently setting up a global swap team using large-scale team defections from Manufacturers Hanover. Several other insurance companies are rumoured to be contemplating similar moves, attracted by the potential profits which will be available when trying to fill the vacuum in the market left by the retreating banks. More interesting still the large and successful Euromarket house, Credit Suisse First Boston, has managed to attract Allan Wheat and a large team from Bankers Trust to set up a separate derivatives subsidiary, CS Financial Products Ltd. Several Japanese banks, with clean balance sheets and strong ratings are moving in the same direction. All their moves will increase competition while at the same time directing the focus of and users on to counterparty risk, where the established players are most vulnerable.

Not the least significant outcome of the last two years in the swap market is the exposure of a new category of risk. This, as mentioned above, is the *legal* risk that the counterparty may not be legally empowered to enter into the transaction in the first place. Certainly this revelation has wrought profound change in the market. The question which must be asked by the banks is not simply one of credit, ie, does the counterparty have the credit standing to honour its commitment throughout the life of the transaction, but one of *power*, ie, does the counterparty have the legal right to enter into a swap? The fact that this question had not really been asked in the previous eight years of the markets' existence dawned on the international banking community shortly after the full extent of the problems with Hammersmith and Fulham became known. Many of the US banks, for example, began to revise their contracts with the public utilities, municipalities and university bodies, searching out the essential question of powers. On the international sphere, many major banks faced similar problems with the various EC agencies, supranationals and even sovereign credits. Underlying documentation has been reviewed and, where appropriate, new clauses spelling out the *vires* of the counterparty to enter into the contract have been inserted. This process is far from complete, and may be expected to continue as we approach 1992 and the Single European Market. Indeed, there already are suggestions that the BIS Capital Adequacy Agreement may be revised to take account of this development and the additional risks.

In the UK this process thas taken a particularly interesting twist, since it soon became apparent that everybody except those incorporated under the Companies Act of 1985 were at risk. Some banks hesitated before transacting swaps with such august quasi-governmental bodies at the ECGD, which had to incorporate a separate company merely to get around this provision.

Perhaps the largest and most spectacular demonstration of this concern, however, came with the building societies. Incorporated by statute under their own Act of Parliament, these societies were already major players in the sterling swap market. Though the largest were well known to many of the major swap houses, the haunting fear that swap and option exposures of a similar magnitude to those with the local authorities could suddenly become subject to an *ultra vires* ruling was impossible to ignore. As a result, some of the major UK clearing banks ceased doing business with the societies for some time. Others took the more pragmatic view that the commercial risk was worth taking to secure such an important sector of the market; but even these banks took elaborate steps to reinforce their documentation, putting the legal risk as to capacity as near as possible beyond doubt. Even here the process is far from over at the time of writing, and one suspects that the legal and documentation side of the business (which had evolved into more or less standard routine) will continue to be brought forward as new and more ingenious contractual forms are devised to get around this problem.

Finally, perhaps the major consequence of the last few years has been to re-establish and reinforce the credit component of the swap business. One form which this concern has taken has been the banks' attempt to quantify more precisely the actual degree of risk being assumed in a swap portfolio. The swap banks' risk management units have undertaken elaborate statistical studies of typical portfolios, quantifying maximum possible losses under various interest rate scenarios. Using these results the attempt is currently being made, admittedly in a sporadic and haphazard way, to buck the market and build in an intermediation charge to the "normal" swap spread now so clearly visible, a charge which varies depending on the credit standing of the counterparty. On the other hand, established participants now reaching saturation in terms of credit utilisation with counterparties, have become more energetic and efficient in managing their credit lines. Such banks are actively seeking to unwind deals and assign transactions on a regular basis, constantly attempting to keep credit lines clear and available.

Similarly, there has been renewed focus on the need to establish up-front credit reserves from ongoing swap business. In addition to building in a *capital* component to the swap spread in order to satisfy the new capital adequacy guidelines, a *credit* component will also be added in order to build reserves against such unwelcome shocks which can never again be regarded as theoretical. More significantly, there has undoubtedly been an increase in the bank's sensitivity to counterparty risk in transacting swap and options business, and a growing trend to quote differential pricing to counterparties of different credit standing.

Conclusion

It is clear that the last two years have brought a series of traumatic shocks to the $2trn swaps industry. These shocks have resulted in real losses, and taken the shine off of a business that for most of the 1980s had been the young darling of the commercial banking world. Perhaps this was a necessary part of the transition from adolescence to maturity. In any event, one thing is certain, though the overcapacity in the markets and competitive pressures work against this trend, it cannot be doubted that over the long term credit differentiation will become as established in the swap markets as it already is in the lending markets. The supposed credit insensitivity of the market will become a memory, a lost golden age for both users and operators which can never return.

Chapter 38: The capacity to enter into swaps

Heather Pilley and Christopher Style
Linklaters & Paines, London

Capacity is an important consideration in any financial transaction. What is meant by "capacity" is basically the legal ability of an entity to enter into a transaction. The term applies to swaps as it does to other financial transactions. In practice, it is most relevant to companies and other creatures of legislation (rather than human beings on their own). Capacity in this rather strict sense of legal ability is different from the notion of authority, although the two are related; authority involves the power of a person, board or committee to decide upon or enter into a transaction on behalf of the contracting entity.

The question of capacity has always been a consideration in modern financial dealings, but within the last year or two it has become very topical in relation to swaps. The interest has apparently been triggered by the events leading up to, and the progress of, the English legal case concerning the *London Borough of Hammersmith and Fulham* (see below). And it is from the English legal point of view that the authors write. Nevertheless, it should be noted that, although the details canvassed here are largely based on English law, the general principles and concerns may be relevant to a wider audience. The authors have therefore attempted to provide more of an overview than an exhaustive examination of the English position.

Jurisdiction

As mentioned already, this chapter concentrates on the position under English law. Even in English courts, though, other systems of law may be relevant. The whole subject of which law applies (and to what extent) is highly complex and, accordingly, the authors will stick to very general propositions.

Both the law of the place where an entity is established and the law of the country which governs the swap may be relevant to capacity. The issue turns on the legal positions in the jurisdiction involved. Therefore, a swap participant may need advice as to the law in those jurisdictions. So, for example, a company incorporated in Panama will have no capacity to enter into a swap contract governed by English law if under Panamanian law its constitution prohibits such contracts. Again, an English company whose constitution permits such contracts will have no capacity to enter into a swap expressed to be governed by a foreign system of law which characterises such contracts as illegal gaming transactions.

A brief note on different aspects of capacity should be made. The emphasis in this chapter is on capacity in the sense of the power belonging to an entity to enter into swaps, rather than on any legal prohibitions or limitations on the ability of anyone to contract a swap under a particular system of law. Those prohibitions or limitations, at least to the extent they exist in the countries whose laws govern swaps frequently — such as English law and New York law — seem not to be significant in practice.

Timing

The time to consider capacity is before dealing. There are three reasons for this. First, it is generally thought that a contract for a swap is made at the time of dealing. The requirements for a contract (and, in particular, a sufficient description of the swap's terms) would usually be met then. Of course, the parties could agree at the time of dealing that the transaction is subject to some sort of approval or other condition. If the contract is made at the time of dealing, the later parts of the process and, for example, sending confirmations, would largely be just that, confirmatory; although perhaps during the formalising process the parties would refine or change the terms already agreed.

Mention may be made of the London Code of Conduct which sets out principles for the London swap and other wholesale money markets. Theoretically, it applies to those institutions which are regulated by the Financial Services Act or authorised under the Banking Act; but, to the extent that it codified existing practice or developed new market standards, it could be thought of as having a broader relevance. It states that swap participants should consider themselves bound at the point where the commercial terms of the transactions are agreed and that making swap transactions subject to agreement on documentation is not best practice.

Secondly, a swap participant should be comfortable about its own capacity and that of its potential counterparty before it enters into a contract with that counterparty. From the start of the contract, that swap participant incurs liability (at least potential) to its counterparty. Further, both parties may at the same time make other arrangements on the basis of the first swap (such as transacting an equal but opposite swap to mirror the first one or going ahead with a financing for which the swap is intended as a hedge).

Thirdly, capacity is something, very generally, that does not change over time. If a party had sufficient capacity at the time the transaction was first entered into, it would probably continue to do so through the life of the transaction. Likewise, if there were not capacity at the start, the entity is unlikely to acquire it sometime during the course of the transaction. Unlike capacity, authority is something that can be given after the fact — for instance, a person can purport to contract on behalf of a company in England and the company can then later ratify his actions.

Documentation

A swap participant which anticipates entering into a swap with a new counterparty may try to provide itself with comfort and protection in the swap documentation on the question of that counterparty's capacity. Some types of contractual provisions which could be used for capacity issues are: closing documents, representations, agreements and events conferring a right to terminate. The next section gives examples of the swap capacity of some English entities. This demonstrates that the capacity of a swap participant to enter into a swap would usually be determined by the statute defining the powers of the participant and/or any constitutional document, rather than the documentation of the swap itself. Having said this, documentation can help, particularly in the ways described below.

In looking at documentation, an assumption will be made that the parties are working on the 1987 edition of the International Swap Dealers Association (ISDA) Interest Rate and Currency Exchange Agreement (the ISDA agreement). This assumption is not unrealistic as a large number of international swaps are now documented on the basis of the ISDA agreement.

The ISDA agreement can document one or more swaps transacted between the same two counterparties. The documentation comes in two parts. The first part is a master agreement containing the provisions that are not likely to change amongst swap transactions, largely the legal terms. The second part consists of the confirmations for the swap transactions (generally one confirmation for each swap) which contain the provisions which do change amongst transactions, basically their economic terms. Special legal terms which apply to one swap transaction, or are introduced in one swap transaction and are intended to apply from then on, can also be put into a confirmation. The master agreement and all the confirmations are together expressed to constitute a single agreement between the parties.

The most important part of swap documentation (in dealing with the capacity question) is the supplying of closing documents from one party to the other. The ISDA agreement provides for this — as an agreement to supply the documents detailed by the parties, not a condition precedent to further obligations. Closing documents can include internal approvals indicating capacity and a lawyer's opinion on capacity. An example of the use of the former (as described in more detail in the next section) is that a counterparty to a potential swap with an English building society can obtain good evidence of the society's capacity by obtaining a board minute reciting the purpose for the swap (so long as it is the requisite statutory purpose). With respect to the latter, there appears to be some divergence in practice about supplying legal opinions. But if a legal opinion is provided, its recipient can (depending, of course, on its source and contents) take some comfort from the knowledge that a lawyer will have looked at the capacity issue. And, on top of these more specific advantages of having closing documents, it is good practice in many different kinds of financial transactions (including swaps) to obtain and check documents from the other party as to capacity and authority.

The ISDA agreement contains an express representation as to the power of each party to enter into and perform the ISDA agreement. One purpose of having each party make this representation is for each party to address the point before execution; another is to try to give the responsibility for capacity of each party to that party itself. The trouble with the latter purpose is that if it later transpires that the party making the representation in an agreement did not have the capacity to enter into the agreement, the agreement may be void and of no effect, including the representation (which seems now to be a misrepresentation) contained in the agreement. Accordingly, it might not be possible to take action against the party lacking capacity by virtue of its taking responsibility for its own capacity (in giving the representation) and then being wrong.

Closing documents and representations are documentation features which can be dealt with before any swaps are transacted. This would fit in well with an investigation of a counterparty's capacity taking place before transacting (and, as discussed in the previous section, that is the time capacity should be considered).

Logistically, one way of proceeding would be to execute an ISDA master agreement, then exchange closing documents, and, assuming all looks well on the capacity issue, begin transacting swaps. Another way would be to exchange the closing documents before anything is executed and, if happy with capacity, execute the master and begin transacting.

The ISDA agreement, in the master agreement part, also provides an agreement by each party to supply to the other any documents which are specified in a confirmation. Then the parties can specify, after some swaps have already been transacted under an ISDA agreement, documents needed for just one new transaction or for all transactions after a certain time. An example would be documents showing the capacity of one of the parties to enter into a slightly new kind of transaction (let's say a swap option rather than a plain swap). Again, in terms of timing, the capacity issues for a particular transaction would best be sorted out before the transaction is actually done.

The remaining type of contractual provisions — events conferring a right to terminate the agreement early — applies to the transaction as it is ongoing. At that stage, each party will have acted within its capacity in entering into the swap — or not. If each has, there should not be a problem. If one of them has not, then it does not matter too much what was in the documents as whatever was executed was beyond the capacity of that party with whatever consequences may ensue. Also, if the parties were happy enough with one another to enter into the swap, an issue of capacity is unlikely to arise part way through the term unless there were some external impetus (and there were external developments in the case of English local authority swaps, as shown below). Accordingly, the usefulness of those contractual events to terminate would seemingly be limited.

If an issue about capacity does somehow arise, it may take some time, in practice, to decide whether a contract is void or not. And the party to the contract whose capacity is not being questioned could find itself in an uncertain and difficult situation. An applicable contractual right to terminate might be helpful in that situation. By relying on an event giving a right to terminate, the party whose capacity is not being questioned would have the option of treating the contract as having no ongoing future effect. It could terminate the agreement, assuming it were valid, and, assuming it were void as a result of the lack of capacity, it would be of no effect anyway. If the other party took this course and treated the contract as having no ongoing future effect, then some of its uncertainty would diminish and it would then rearrange its financial position accordingly. Whether that party might wish to do so could depend on many facts, including economic consequences.

One event conferring a right to terminate already in the ISDA agreement which could arise in connection with a capacity problem is a failure to pay. A party whose attention has been drawn to its possible lack of capacity in entering into the ISDA agreement may then decide it would be prudent not to make any further payments under the agreement. The other party may then be able to invoke a right to terminate to reduce its uncertainty.

Perhaps there may be some scope for additional provisions in a swap document dealing with capacity issues which may arise. But a search for standard wording could prove beset with problems. For example, by their nature, these types of issues are not usually foreseeable or predictable at the time of dealing (if they were, the contract might well not have been formed). And, as the purpose of such provisions would just be to limit uncertainty after a capacity issue had already arisen, their advantages are quite limited.

Therefore, in using documentation for capacity issues, participants should concentrate on checking the capacity of their counterparties, to the extent practicable in the circumstances.

Some specific entities

Before contracting with a specific entity a person should ask: What are the constraints on the capacity of this entity; and what will be the effect of a lack of capacity? The answers differ according to the entity concerned. Also, that person should ask those questions in relation to himself.

For present purposes, capacity issues will be discussed in relation to three kinds of incorporated associations in England. These associations all have a separate and distinct legal personality. They have been chosen because, in practice, they do enter into swaps and there have been some fairly recent developments in relation to their capacity to do so. They are:

(a) *Companies* incorporated by registration under the Companies Acts.

(b) *Building societies*, an example of entities which are incorporated under an Act of Parliament permitting incorporation by any body of persons which fulfils specified conditions.

(c) *Local authorities*, which are public corporations created by a special Act of Parliament which defines the corporations' powers.

(a) Companies

The recent change in the law on corporate capacity has been the bringing into force of the relevant provisions of the Companies Act 1989 on 4 February 1991. However, the old law may still be important, for example, in relation to a transaction which took place before those new provisions came into force. The traditional position will be considered first, followed by a description of the statutory changes and concluding with the practical implications.

The basic rule is that companies can only do that which they are empowered to do by their memorandum of association. The courts have generally taken a fairly liberal attitude in construing the express provisions in the memorandum. A company's powers may be implied from the objects specified in its memorandum — what might fairly be regarded as incidental to, or consequential upon, those objects should be within the company's powers, unless expressly prohibited. Effect will be given to a provision that all clauses are to be read separately and not limited by reference to any others. Also, effect will be given to a provision that the company can carry on any other business which can, in the directors' opinion, be advantageously carried on in connection with any of the businesses specified more particularly in the memorandum.

A finding that an agreement is *ultra vires*, that is beyond the capacity of a company, may have drastic consequences. Traditionally, it is void and cannot become valid or *intra vires* by reason of estoppel, lapse of time, ratification, acquiescence or delay. This has been modified somewhat by the Companies Act 1989 which provides that shareholders can ratify an act beyond a company's capacity.

A company entering into a swap should, obviously, have the corporate capacity to do so. It is possible for it to have as one of the express objects in its memorandum the entering into of swap transactions. This would, of course, give it capacity; however, such an object has rarely been seen in practice, except perhaps in the case of swap dealers. If there is no express specific object, the company's memorandum could be considered to see whether it, expressly or impliedly, gives the company capacity to enter into swaps.

There may be an express power "to enter into any financial transaction" or "to carry on the business of a banking or finance company". This should be sufficient to give it capacity to enter into ordinary swaps.

One line of analysis which might be helpful is to consider whether the power to enter into a swap could be implied from the company's objects as specified in its memorandum on the basis that the swap transaction is incidental to those objects. A straightforward swap, let's say a sterling interest rate swap, may be used in connection with a sterling borrowing. The result could be that the borrowing is effectively hedged by the swap and, commercially but not legally, the swap has converted the borrowing from a fixed rate of interest to a floating one (or *vice versa*). The swap can be viewed as one part of the company's whole borrowing exercise (although it must be borne in mind that the swap itself would not be a borrowing). In fact, a bank approaching the company with this kind of a proposal for raising funds may well present the borrowing and the swap as a single package and the bank may have suggested this option to decrease the overall costs of borrowing to the company. Assume also that the borrowing exercise is being undertaken for the purposes of the company's main business (described in its memorandum as an object) to allow the company to carry on that business. It would seem sensible to conclude that the company in this situation has the capacity to enter into the swap. In contrast, if that same company were to enter into numerous swap transactions with the same counterparty, at approximately the same time and in such a way that the company seemed to be trading in swaps for profit, the position may well be different.

The House of Lords judgement in the *Hammersmith and Fulham* case (see below) on local authority swaps may have cast a shadow of doubt over this type of analysis. It was decided there that a power to swap could not be implied as incidental to a local authority's express statutory power to borrow. That case is the only English case to consider an implied power to swap. However, the issue of corporate capacity was not before the Court. The authors consider that, although the position is not entirely clear, a power to swap should be able to be implied in the above situation.

The law on corporate capacity is closely related to the question of whether the person with whom you contract is properly authorised. However, an unauthorised transaction can be ratified by the company's shareholders, unlike (at least until February 1991) a transaction beyond corporate capacity. Furthermore, lack of authority to bind the company may be cured by the "indoor management" principle, that is, an outsider is entitled to assume that the internal procedures of a company have been properly conducted in the absence of notice to the contrary.

The question has been raised as to whether a company's exercise of a *power* (for instance, a power to swap) for a purpose outside its *objects* (for instance, the company has been trading in swaps for profit and does not have as an object the transacting of swaps) would be void. A transaction within the powers conferred by the memorandum but entered into for an improper purpose would be capable of binding the company on ordinary agency principles, that is, the directors would be held to have apparent authority, and the transaction would be binding if the other party contracted without notice of the excess or abuse of power.

These rules have now been somewhat superseded by statute. The original enactment in 1972 was replaced by Section 35 of the Companies Act 1985 which decreased the scope of the *ultra vires* rule. It provided, for the protection of a person dealing with a company, that the company was deemed to have the capacity to do a transaction if (a) the transaction was "decided on by the directors" and (b) that person was acting in good faith. Also, if conditions (a) and (b) were met, the power of the directors to bind the company was deemed to be free of any limits in the company's memorandum or articles.

The Companies Act 1989 introduces new rules to replace Section 35 of the 1985 Act. These came into effect on 4 February 1991. In relation to capacity in the strict sense, new Section 35(1) provides that "the validity of an act done by a company shall not be called into question on the ground of lack of capacity by reason of anything in the company's memorandum". For most practical purposes this should abolish the *ultra vires* rule for an independent party dealing on a swap with a commercial company (that is, not a charity). There are some residual elements of the rule: shareholders can restrain an *ultra vires* act of the company; and directors may incur personal liability to the company in respect of *ultra vires* contracts; but these are not likely to be of concern to a swap counterparty.

In relation to the issue of authority, a new Section 35A(1) provides that "in favour of a person dealing with a company in good faith, the power of the board of directors to bind the company, or authorise others to do so, shall be deemed to be free of any limitation under the company's constitution". As with the new Section 35(1), this Section 35A(1) would apply to an independent party dealing with a commercial company; also, a company still may be subject to internal consequences — for example, a shareholder may be able to restrain an act beyond the powers of the directors. It is not entirely clear what "good faith" will mean in this context — but it is expressly provided that mere knowledge that an act is beyond the directors' powers is not enough for there to be bad faith.

The practical implications are not, unfortunately, completely straightforward. The traditional approach would involve an inquiry to ensure that the company has capacity to enter into the transaction and has authorised the transaction. This would involve an examination of the memorandum and articles of the company, the board resolution (a certified copy) approving the transaction (and identifying people to act on its behalf) and documents obtained from the Registrar of Companies on a company search.

This approach should continue to be taken if, for some reason, the protection afforded by statute is not available or there is some uncertainty as to its availability. But, relying on the protection, if available, would be an easier option in practice.

The changes introduced by the Companies Act 1989 mean that, in most cases, a swap counterparty will not need to review the memorandum of a commercial company with which it is proposing to enter into a swap transaction — in order to check on corporate capacity. Nevertheless, a swap counterparty should make that review if it is connected to the company or where there is a real possibility that the shareholders of the company would try to restrain the company from entering into the transaction. Even if a party is relying on new Section 35A(1), at least some parts of the company's articles (for instance, the procedural part for executing documents) should be checked. In addition, to rely on the protection of the new Section 35A(1), a certified copy of a board resolution authorising the swap transaction and designating people to act on behalf of the company should be obtained. A company search (partly to check on the identity of the directors) would also still be advisable.

The statutory protection introduced by the 1989 Act is of little or no use to the company itself which is proposing to enter into a swap transaction — there may be internal consequences if a company's directors were proposing to enter into a swap transaction which was either beyond the company's capacity or within its capacity but beyond the powers of its directors.

(b) Building societies

Section 23 of the Building Societies Act 1986 constitutes a complete code governing the powers of building societies to hedge financial risk. It provides that a building society can enter into certain permitted contracts (see below) "for the purpose of reducing the risk of loss arising from changes in interest rates, currency rates or other factors of a prescribed description which affect its business".

The contracts which are permitted by this section are described by statutory instrument (subordinate legislation) and the current version covers most types of currency and/or interest rate swaps, swap option contracts (if the building society has the right to enter into the underlying swap) and sterling caps, collars and floors. That covers a good section of the swap market, but cannot be considered a complete coverage of every kind of present (and future) transaction.

Two other requirements need to be met for a building society to have the capacity to enter into swaps. First, at the time of the contract, it must satisfy the "qualifying asset holding", that is, currently, the aggregate value of its total commercial assets must be at least £100m. This can be checked by looking at the society's annual accounts; a society has a qualifying asset holding in a financial year if the aggregate value of its total commercial assets, as shown in its annual accounts for the most recent financial year, is at least £100m. Secondly, it must expressly adopt the powers conferred by Section 23 into its memorandum. A certified copy of the building society's memorandum should be checked.

The main problem facing counterparties dealing with building societies is that there is no practical method of achieving certainty as to the building society's purpose in entering into a swap. Its purpose is basically a question of fact and would be determined internally. A swap transaction could be within the description of permitted transactions in the statutory instrument but not effected for the Section 23 purpose. An outsider could consider doing one or more of the following to reduce the risks:

(1) It could conduct its own factual enquiry but this is likely to be commercially impractical, unacceptable to the building society and not economically viable. It also may not produce the correct answer in all cases.

(2) It could obtain a legal opinion, but a lawyer would probably not make an exhaustive determination on the point and would presumably need to rely, as would any counterparty, on some sort of evidence of purpose from the society.

(3) It can require of the building society one or more of the following:
   (i) A certified copy of a board minute approving the transaction and reciting a Section 23 purpose — this is the best protection because it will be evidence that is difficult to overturn.
   (ii) A representation given by the signatory on behalf of the building

society that he is authorised by the building society to enter into swaps and the transaction is for a Section 23 purpose — that would also be good evidence.

(iii) A representation given by the society itself, saying either that the society has the power to enter into the swap or that the society is acting with a Section 23 purpose.

But in all these cases, if the representation or other evidence turns out to be false, it may not be able to help the transaction.

None of these is a perfect solution. Until the law is clarified or changed, a contract with a building society is something of an act of faith. However, some counterparties may take the view that, given confidence in the management and regulation of building societies, coupled with one or more of the above procedures, the risk is small and can be accepted.

The effect of a building society having an improper purpose is likely to be that the transaction is *ultra vires* and void.

(c) Local authorities

Local authorities merit treatment as an object lesson. As a matter of English law there are no circumstances in which swaps can ever be within the capacity of a local authority. As the law stands, they are not therefore prospective counterparties. However, the establishment of this simple fact involved a long and painful process.

Local authorities have been active participants in the swap market since the early 1980s. This was known to the various regulatory bodies and they apparently approved. Swaps could be used to hedge an underlying debt or credit position to provide protection against adverse movements of interest rates, to the benefit of local ratepayers. In its Annual Report for the financial year 1986/87, the Audit Commission for Local Authorities in England and Wales (the body responsible for local authority audit arrangements) said that "it is right that local authorities should take advantage of the opportunities to reduce borrowing costs afforded by new types of financial instruments". In a press release in August 1987, the Commission stated that "interest rate swaps are a legitimate tool of debt management". *The Bank of England Quarterly Review* of February 1987 described swaps as "a valuable technique for managing financial flows — on both the liability and asset side. As such they are widely used by all kinds of institutions in the financial, corporate and government sectors".

The *cause célèbre* resulted from the activities of the London Borough of Hammersmith and Fulham. In 1988/89 Hammersmith had outstanding debt ranging between £308m and £461m and estimated net revenue expenditure of £85.7m. However, during the financial years of 1987/88 and 1988/89 they entered into 592 swaps, swap options, caps, floors, collars, gilt options, forward-rate agreements and cash options, with a total notional amount of some £6,052.5m. Far from using swaps for purposes of asset and liability management, they had been trading in swaps. They gambled on interest rates falling by assuming a predominantly floating-rate liability. In fact, rates rose, leaving Hammersmith's swap book with a negative mark-to-market value of several hundred million pounds. If the council had had to perform on current interest rates, it would have cost every ratepayer several thousand pounds.

It was against this background that Hammersmith's auditor, acting through the Audit Commission, applied to have the transactions declared unlawful. This public law proceeding involved the court in deciding on whether swaps were capable of being within the powers of local authorities. Predictably, Hammersmith saw a way of escaping from an extremely onerous liability and joined with the auditor. In order to enable the court to hear some opposing views, a number of representative banks intervened to argue that they were capable of lawful use.

Many banks had, of course, taken legal advice before entering into swaps. The advice had been that, although there was room for argument, the better view was that a swap entered into for the purpose of effectively hedging a borrowing was within the capacity of local authorities. The case of *Hazell v. London Borough of Hammersmith and Fulham and Others* provided the definitive answer, to contrary effect. The litigation was protracted. The proceedings began on 30 May 1989. After 15 and a half days of argument the Divisional Court decided, on 1 November 1989, that swaps were incapable of being within the powers of local authorities. After 10 and a half days the Court of Appeal, on 22 February 1990, allowed the banks' appeal: swaps were lawful if used for the purposes of interest rate risk management. The appeal to the House of Lords involved 14 days of argument. On 24 January 1991 they affirmed the order of the Divisional Court.

Local authorities are an example of a public corporation created by statute. They have the power to do only that which is expressly or impliedly authorised by Parliament. Not surprisingly, in 1972, Parliament did not include in the Local Government Act any express power to enter into interest rate swap agreements. The banks argued that there were nevertheless two bases on which swaps could be within the powers of local authorities:

(1) Under section 111 of the Local Government Act 1972:

> ...a local authority shall have power to do anything (whether or not involving the expenditure, borrowing or lending of money or the acquisition or disposal of any property or rights) which is calculated to facilitate, or is conducive or incidental to, the discharge of any of their functions

with swaps being calculated to facilitate, or conducive or incidental to, the discharge by a local authority of its function to borrow.

(2) Under an implied function of debt management.

Hammersmith and its auditor pointed to the very detailed statutory provisions which have, for many years, regulated the activity of local authorities in the field of financial management. Parliament had had many opportunities to introduce regulations governing swaps. The fact that it had not done so showed that swaps were outside the capacity of local authorities. They pointed to provisions which conferred a limited power of debt management. They were inconsistent with the existence of a broader, implied power. Finally, they argued that swaps were incapable of fitting within the existing statutory framework.

The House of Lords decided that statute provided a comprehensive code which defined and limited the powers of a local authority with regard to its borrowing. It would be inconsistent with the legislative structure to regard swaps as falling within Section 111. They rejected the notion that a function of debt management existed which could render lawful a transaction which was not otherwise lawful.

The effect was to declare void thousands of swap contracts between hundreds of counterparties. Those local authorities who had used swaps prudently, to manage interest rate risk, found themselves exposed to the very risk they thought they had protected themselves against. Banks were left nursing losses of hundreds of millions of pounds and had to look elsewhere for redress. The repercussions will continue for some time. There could not be a more clear illustration of the importance of capacity.

Remedies if the contract is unenforceable

A party may not be without remedy even if its contract is void and unenforceable. Here are some possibilities:

(1) *Recovery of payments.* The parties to an unenforceable contract may be able to make a claim for recovery of payments already made under that contract. But there are a number of uncertainties — such a claim should not result in the contract being indirectly enforced; and there is a suggestion that such a claim may be more successful for a local authority, say, acting beyond its capacity (the rules of capacity ultimately being for the benefit of ratepayers) than for its counterparty. The grounds for recovery include:

(i) *Total failure of consideration.* This could be invoked if the entity without capacity has paid nothing under the swap (for example, it has only received the premium on its sale of a swap option). It becomes more difficult where both parties have already made payments and more difficult still where all payments required by the contract have been made, making it a closed contract.

(ii) *Constructive trust.* That party may claim to be the beneficiary of a constructive trust for the payments it made.

(2) *Remedies against officers.* It may be possible to sue the officers or signatories of a party for breach of their implied warranty of authority or any express representation.

(3) *Others.* It may be possible to sue a broker of the swap, for example, if he were on notice of facts which indicated the other party's lack of capacity but failed to give a warning of these.

Therefore, if a contract is unenforceable due to a party's lack of capacity, there still may be some scope for recovery. But the legal position on those remedies and the way in which they would apply to an unenforceable swap are not clear.

There would still be one large commercial problem. Even if the claim were successful, a party would simply recover the amounts it paid in relation to the contract (and may need to repay the amounts it received). This recovery looks at what has already been paid. And it would not take into account the economic or market value of future payments set out under the contract. Accordingly, the claimant would not be able to recover what would have been its economic or market value in the contract had the contract been enforceable. If he has been running a balanced book, he will be left exposed.

It would, of course, be best to avoid contracts unenforceable for lack of capacity — to concentrate on prevention, not cures.

Conclusions

Capacity is an issue for any financial transaction, including a swap. A consideration of capacity should take place early. A swap participant should evaluate the capacity of its potential swap counterparty (and itself too). The participant should consider how, in practice, it is going to do so — appropriate procedures to be in place, internal and external checks to be available etc. The way in which it handles the capacity issue could ultimately impact upon profitability.

This is one area of the law where there may be further developments in the near future, and in particular on the consequences of the *Hammersmith and Fulham* swaps case.

Chapter 39: Developments in legal and documentary issues relating to swaps and swap derivatives

Schuyler K Henderson
Baker & McKenzie

Swaps evolved out of the back-to-back loan market of the mid-1970s as a creative response to documentation complexities, legal risks with respect to set-off and adverse accounting treatment. The first swap agreements were based on single bank lending agreements, though covenants, warranties and events of default were less onerous than similar clauses in loan transactions because of the security implicit in the conditionality of cross-payments. As the swap market evolved from one-off transactions to a more broadly-based dealing business and as the role of financial institutions shifted from being an intermediary to that of a dealer in swaps, repeat transactions between two dealers became commonplace. To facilitate completion of the transactions, dealers created master agreements which incorporated the substantive credit terms and provided for individual swap transactions to be completed by the exchange of relatively short confirmations setting forth the financial terms of individual swaps.

Early master agreements were of two basic forms. One expressed itself to be a set of standard terms and conditions which was then incorporated in subsequent confirmations, with the result that each swap transaction constituted a separate agreement incorporating terms agreed beforehand. While it was perceived that this form might facilitate assignment of swaps, concerns over netting of credit exposure (discussed below) led to widespread acceptance of the second approach, which was to treat the master agreement as the functional agreement, with individual confirmations acting as amendments or supplements.

Substantial delays were still, however, encountered in negotiating the terms of master agreements, and there was often disagreement as to fundamental definitions of rates, payment dates and other key financial terms and as to appropriate termination clauses. In order to promote the establishment of a dealing market, a number of financial institutions formed the International Swap Dealers Association, Inc ("ISDA"). ISDA's first major task was to prepare and publish in 1985 its Code of Standard Wording, Assumptions and Provisions for Swaps, which was revised and substantially expanded in 1986 ("Swaps Code"). While publication and utilisation of the Swaps Code laid the foundation for a dealing market with commonly agreed financial terms for US dollar swaps and eliminated a great deal of the negotiation involved in preparing master agreements, the substantial backlogs in documenting swaps remained and, in fact, grew as the volume of swap market participants continued to expand. In 1987, ISDA published two forms of standard master swap agreements: one for use with the Swaps Code and, accordingly, only effective for US dollar interest rate swaps ("the Rate Master"); and another, which did not incorporate the Swaps Code and which constituted a free-standing master agreement that could be used for any currencies (the "Rate and Currency Master"). ISDA also published a set of standard definitions for currencies, rates, and related calculation and payment definitions (the "1987 Definitions"), which can be incorporated into the Rate and Currency Master or confirmations thereunder. The 1987 Definitions are presently being expanded substantially, with the revised version to be published in the first quarter of 1991 and referred to as the "1990 Definitions". Although structurally different, the Rate Master and the Rate and Currency Master contain substantially the same terms. The Rate and Currency Master, for which the potential scope of available swap transactions is much greater, is used more widely than the Rate Master and is the one discussed in this chapter.

Description of the ISDA agreement

The ISDA agreement is presented on a standard, printed form. The body of the ISDA agreement recites that all swaps ("Swap Transactions") thereunder constitute part of a single unified agreement and contains provisions for:

- payments relating to individual Swap Transactions (including a condition that payment not be made to a party in default and a clause for payment of default interest);

- warranties as to the status, power and authorisation of the parties and absence of litigation affecting the ISDA agreement at the commencement of each Swap Transaction and the accuracy of certain specified information delivered by each party;

- treatment of withholding tax (including warranties with respect to the absence of such a tax and factual matters which would assure an exemption, covenants to deliver designated tax forms and the requirement to gross up if withholding is imposed);

- covenants of a very basic nature with which the parties must comply on an ongoing basis, including the delivery of specified documents;

- events ("Termination Events") relating to an adverse change in the tax or legal environment which would enable a party affected thereby ("Affected Party") to terminate;

- events of default ("Events of Default") which, if one were to occur with respect to a party ("Defaulting Party"), would enable the other party to terminate; and

- provisions for settlement of obligations on termination.

The body of the agreement also contains a number of definitions and other standard contractual provisions which are customarily found in financing documents, including those relating to: judgement currency, restrictions on transfer, submission to jurisdiction, and notices. In addition, there is a multibranch section for use if one or both parties is to act through more than one office.

Attached to the main body of the ISDA agreement is a Schedule, to be completed by the parties. In Part 1, the parties must choose whether or not to apply certain credit-related provisions and, if so, to what entities they apply. Part 2 of the Schedule provides for a menu from which can be selected tax representations to be given by each party as payer and payee. Part 3 provides for the designation of tax-related documents and other documents which one or both parties might require from the other and designation as to whether they are subject to the representation in the ISDA agreement as to accuracy. Part 4 provides for selection of governing law (English or New York), appointment of a process agent in the relevant jurisdiction, a definition for affiliate (if relevant and if different than the definition in the body of the ISDA agreement), specification of offices through which a multibranch party would act, details for notices, and details of any guarantee, security agreement or other credit support document ("Credit Support Document"). Finally, Part 5 may be used to amend provisions in the ISDA agreement or to add additional provisions.

Credit issues

As noted above, the warranties and covenants in the ISDA agreement generally relate to status, power, authorisation, legality and delivery of information rather than creditworthiness. Breach of these provisions constitutes an Event of Default.

Perhaps the only representations and covenants in the ISDA agreement which relate to credit are those which enable a party to monitor it: the warranty with respect to accuracy of information provided and the covenant to deliver specified information, made operative by completing the space provided in Part 3(2) of the Schedule. In this space the parties should designate information to be delivered under Section 4(d) and whether or not it is subject to the representation as to accuracy in Section 3(d). Information required by Part 3(2) is generally of two sorts. First, as prudence would require that a party monitor the creditworthiness of its counterparty, particularly in light of the fact that Swap Transactions may be entered into indefinitely in the future, parties generally would require the delivery of periodic financial statements. The required information is generally of a basic nature such as audited financial statements. Because of the operational difficulties in monitoring a dealer's obligations, it is often specified that this information is to be delivered only on request by the other party.

In addition, parties will use this section to provide for the delivery of any supporting documents which they require, such as resolutions of the directors of its counterparty, copies of constituent documents, incumbency and signature certificates, and legal opinions. These documents are generally obtained on execution of the ISDA agreement (which may be after a number of Swap Transactions have been entered into and confirmed). These documents are often not required in an ISDA agreement between dealers.

It should be noted that resolutions and opinions of counsel relating to the ISDA agreement alone may be of limited benefit for two reasons. First, the ISDA agreement is open-ended as to its duration and the number, aggregate notional amount and nature of Swap Transactions. Presumably, the supporting documents would provide comfort with respect to standard Swap Transactions entered into for a reasonable amount within a reasonable time after the dates of the supporting documents. Variation of one or more of these criteria could result in substantial questions as to the continued validity of the supporting documents and the authorisation of the party to enter into them. For instance, presumably a "plain vanilla" interest rate swap with a $20m notional amount entered into within six months of the resolutions and attorneys' opinion would be covered (assuming no revocation of the resolutions and no change in law). Whether or not a zero-coupon swap entered into 10 years later providing for notional fixed payments of $200m could be viewed as covered by these resolutions and attorneys' opinion is more questionable. Where the dividing line is may not be susceptible to clear analysis. Few if any dealers, however, update resolutions and attorneys' opinions and few dealers, if any, consider whether or not novel types of swaps are covered by the terms of the supporting documents.

Given the customary absence of substantive credit controls (such as financial ratios or a restriction on granting security to others) in swap agreements, parties are concerned that termination and enforcement based only on Events of Default such as non-payment by or insolvency of the counterparty would be too late. One of these defaults may be the culminating event in a long process of credit deterioration. By the time such a default occurs, the counterparty may either have already restructured its other debt and provided security to other creditors or may be so weakened that its assets are insufficient to satisfy its creditors.

Thus, attention is often focused on provisions which may provide early warning of credit difficulties: cross default to borrowed money, cross default to other swaps, the credit event on merger and the extent to which such clauses should relate to affiliates. Addressing these issues is the essence of Part 1 of the Schedule.

Application to affiliates

The term "Affiliate" is defined broadly in the definition section of the ISDA agreement, and space for amending the definition is included in Part 4. It is then only used twice in the printed form (Section 3(c), absence of litigation affecting the ISDA agreement, and Section 6(b)(ii), transfer to avoid a Termination Event). The primary significance of the term is determined by the parties' use of it in the Schedule.

A party may wish some or all of the credit-related provisions to apply to either all Affiliates or specified Affiliates of its counterparty for several reasons. First, the Affiliate rather than the counterparty may be the principal entity in the group. Even if the Affiliate is not providing credit support, a party may look to the overall creditworthiness of the Affiliate as a source of implied support for the counterparty. If the counterparty is a subsidiary of the main unit in the group, a party may wish to terminate the agreement if its parent company experienced difficulties.

Second, problems experienced by related companies may be an early sign of trouble within the group. Thus, a party would wish some credit provisions to extend to a broad range of its counterparty's Affiliates. On the other hand, because of the complexity of its corporate structure and the immateriality of many Affiliates in its overall credit context, a party may wish these provisions not to apply to a broad range of its own Affiliates.

Finally, the counterparty may be expressly acting under the guarantee or other support of a third party, which is usually an Affiliate. If so, and a Credit Support Document has been obtained, the provider is usually designated as a Specified Entity for purposes of certain provisions in the ISDA agreement which expressly relate to Credit Support Documents and the provider (if so designated as a Specified Entity for these purposes): Events of

Default in Section 5(a)(iii) (Credit Support Document) and 5(a)(iv) (Misrepresentation, including with respect to a Credit Support Document) and the Termination Event in Section 5(b)(i) (Illegality, including with respect to a Credit Support Document).

One, several or all Affiliates (or, if different, a provider of a Credit Support Document) can also be designated as a Specified Entity for other purposes. For instance, Part 1 of the Schedule contains space in which a Specified Entity of a party may be designated for purposes of the insolvency Event of Default. Designation of Affiliates as a Specified Entity for other purposes is discussed below under the relevant headings.

Cross Default to Specified Indebtedness

If a counterparty fails to pay indebtedness for borrowed money, it is unlikely to be able to perform under the Swap Transactions in the future. In addition, lenders generally obtain credit-related provisions in their loan agreements which are substantially more detailed than in swap agreements, and swap parties may, through an appropriate cross default clause, gain some protection from these provisions. Section 5(a)(vi) provides, if it is designated in Part 1 as applying to a party, that an Event of Default shall occur if payment of Specified Indebtedness of that party or any Specified Entity of that party in an amount in excess of a Threshold Amount becomes capable of being accelerated, is accelerated or is not paid when due. Thus, in Part 1 of the Schedule, the parties must agree:

- if the provision is to apply to one or both parties;
- if the parties wish Specified Indebtedness to be defined differently than the basic definition in the ISDA agreement (which relates to any obligation, contingent or otherwise, in respect of borrowed money);
- the definition of Threshold Amount; and
- any Specified Entity of a party to which the clause would apply.

Most parties wish Cross Default to Specified Indebtedness to apply to their counterparties and, since it is virtually impossible to obtain such a clause without giving it, are prepared to accept it as applicable to themselves. A few parties as a matter of policy refuse to give the provision and thus typically do not receive it as applicable to their counterparty. There are several reasons why a bank or financial institution would have concerns about the cross default clause being applicable to itself. First, indebtedness for borrowed money to a bank is analogous to trade debt for a commercial company. Trade debt is normally excluded from cross default provisions, the reference to borrowed money indicating indebtedness outside of the commercial company's normal course of business. Such a company may, in fact, not pay periodic trade debt when due for a variety of reasons, including commercial disputes, technical oversight as a result of volume of trade debt, or legal restrictions in different jurisdictions. Similarly, given the volume of a typical bank's financial obligations, it is common for deposits, for example, not to be paid when due and, when the oversight is discovered, to "backdate" the payment. Backdating satisfies the parties to the deposit, but cannot change the fact that, for a period, indebtedness was not paid when due. In addition, banks may have incurred contingent obligations in respect of third party debt (guarantees or standby letters of credit in the ordinary course of its business) payment of which could be restricted by judicial action or legal or regulatory changes. Finally, payment of deposits can be blocked by local governmental action.

Accordingly, banks often require (and are prepared to give) amendments to the definition of Specified Indebtedness. Some require blanket exceptions for deposits received; others require exceptions for payments not made solely by reason of technical error; and others also except non-payment caused by governmental or regulatory action.

Some parties also amend the definition of Specified Indebtedness to include indebtedness under swap agreements (other than Specified Swaps, discussed below). This may be particularly important if the counterparty is primarily a swap dealer for whom the bulk of its outstanding liabilities constitutes swap indebtedness. If this change is made, further consequential amendments are required. For instance, an acceleration of indebtedness does not necessarily cover termination of a swap agreement. In addition, Threshold Amount (discussed below) needs to be modified.

It should also be noted that some parties, particularly corporate parties with indebtedness outstanding under conventional loan agreements, propose the deletion in Cross-Default to Specified Indebtedness of the provision relating to debt becoming capable of being declared due. If the deletion is accepted, the clause would only be triggered by an actual non-payment or acceleration. The counterparty loses its ability to bring pressure on the potentially defaulting party during a period when other creditors may be doing so and obtaining additional protection. Of course, the party requiring the deletion is doing so in order that the counterparty not have the ability to upset restructuring negotiations, particularly in light of the possibility that, at that delicate stage, the party would lose any positive value in the ISDA agreement (see below).

If Cross Default to Specified Indebtedness is selected (as is customary, albeit sometimes with the above modifications), the parties must agree a

Threshold Amount. The number selected should thus be large enough to avoid the risk that non-payment or acceleration of minor amounts might result in triggering the cross-default clause but small enough to cover the minimum amount regarded as material in the context of the counterparty's financial position. Parties generally take one of two approaches. The first is to focus on a percentage of net worth or stockholders' equity. This approach is generally taken by larger institutions, particularly when dealing with smaller institutions. Selecting such a percentage has the advantage of appearing even-handed although the Threshold Amount will of course be significantly larger for a larger institution. The second approach, generally taken by smaller institutions, is to designate a specified amount such as, for example, $10,000,000. If Specified Indebtedness has been amended to include swap liabilities, Threshold Amount must be further amended to provide for translating such liabilities into an amount which can be used in calculating it. For instance, if no amendment is made, a default in respect of a swap which has a $20m notional principal amount could conceivably, under the terms of the clause as drafted, be included at that level. This clearly does not represent the economic exposure of either party and it is that economic exposure which should be included.

For the reasons set forth above, a party would wish Specified Entity to include, for purposes of the cross default clause, a broad range of Affiliates for its counterparty and to include no other entities for itself, and almost always should include the provider of a Credit Support Document. While it is unrealistic to define Specified Entity for this purpose too broadly, a party should analyse the debt structure of its counterparty's group to determine where significant debt is located

Cross Default to other swaps

Parties may have swaps between themselves under other agreements for a number of reasons. One or both may, as a matter of regulatory, credit or operational policy, enter into separate ISDA agreements for separate branches. Parties may have entered into swap agreements prior to publication of the ISDA agreement. A party may document US dollar swaps under the Rate Master and other currency swaps under the Rate and Currency Master. A holding company group may enter into swaps in different locations through different Affiliates. A party may enter into financial swaps under the ISDA agreement and other derivative transactions under separate agreements. Section 5(a)(v) provides for an Event of Default with respect to a party if an event of default occurs under a Specified Swap of that party and an Early Termination Date is established as a result.

Specified Swap means any rate swap or currency exchange agreement between one party or any applicable Specified Entity and the other party or any applicable Specified Entity. In Part 1 of the Schedule, there is a space provided to alter the definition of Specified Swap. Given the proliferation of derivative products, parties often amend this provision to include caps, collars and floors. Few parties expand it to include notional amount transactions and foreign exchange transactions in general.

If a swap between the first party and an Affiliate of the second party or a swap between an Affiliate of the first party and the second party or an Affiliate of the second is in default, the first party may wish to obtain leverage on the group as a whole by having the right to terminate all swaps. Whereas for most purposes a party may wish not to designate Specified Entities applicable to itself (for instance, with respect to bankruptcy or Cross Default to Specified Indebtedness), it may well be prepared to define Specified Entity with respect to itself for purposes of Section 5(a)(v) (Cross Default to Specified Swaps) to include any Affiliate, since this will broaden the scope of Specified Swaps to its advantage as well as its disadvantage. It would, of course, also wish Specified Entity for this purpose to be as broadly drafted for its counterparty.

Credit Event Upon Merger

Recent leveraged acquisitions, buy-outs and recapitalisations have drawn attention to the credit risk which such events can create, as bond issues with loose covenants have declined significantly in value following the downgrading which may result from such an event. While loan agreements typically have contained clauses restricting such events, bond issues and swaps generally have not. The ISDA agreement does contain a clause which specifies a "Credit Event Upon Merger", where the resulting entity is a materially weaker credit, as a Termination Event rather than an Event of Default. In this case, the Affected Party is the resulting entity. The parties must choose in Part 1 of the Schedule whether or not Credit Event Upon Merger will apply to either or both of the parties.

The definition of Credit Event Upon Merger has several gaps. First, the ISDA agreement includes as an Event of Default in Section 5(a)(viii) a provision relating to a relatively narrow and unlikely legal event: a party consolidating with, merging into or selling its assets to another entity and either the other entity not becoming liable under the ISDA agreement or the benefits of a Credit Support Document being lost ("Merger Without Assumption"). As the laws of most jurisdictions, and the terms of most guarantees and collateral documents, provide that either a surviving entity is liable for the obligations of its constituent parts or that the guarantee or security continues in effect regardless of such an event, it is highly unlikely that such an event would occur. Nonetheless, it is prudent to keep it in. However, in drafting Credit Event Upon Merger, the operative language of

"Merger Without Assumption" was imported verbatim. Credit Event Upon Merger thus only applies to a party merging *into,* consolidating *with* or selling its assets *to* another entity. It does not cover a situation where *another* party merges into or transfers substantially all of its assets to the counterparty. In addition, Credit Event Upon Merger does not cover a recapitalisation of the counterparty under circumstances where it has remained in existence and not merged or transferred assets to another but may have granted a security interest to another over a substantial portion of its assets.

Second, some object to the subjectivity inherent in determining whether an entity is materially weaker.

Third, the ISDA agreement does not provide a space for a Specified Entity to be designated for either party with respect to Credit Event Upon Merger such as may be desired for a provider of a Credit Support Document or, as noted above, the dominant credit in the group (if different from the counterparty). Because of the absence of a space for such designation, few parties apply Credit Event Upon Merger to issuers of Credit Support Documents or to significant Affiliates.

A few dealers seek to cut through these issues by amending "Credit Event Upon Merger" to mean a substantial downgrading by a rating agency of a party or a designated affiliate.

Finally, Credit Event Upon Merger does not cover the situation where the resultant entity may not be materially weaker but other concerns may arise. These may include a resulting increase in credit facilities to an imprudent level or the other (and surviving) entity being one with which the first party would prefer not to deal because of, for example, prior disputes or country limits. Some institutions accordingly provide for an additional Termination Event covering a merger which would result in a breach of a party's credit policies although, in this case, the Affected Party is generally the party whose credit policies are breached by the event.

Taxes

Withholding tax is a tax on a payee which is (usually) located outside the jurisdiction of the taxing authority. For purposes of collection, the taxing authority imposes the collection obligation on the payer, which is usually within the jurisdiction of the taxing authority. The payer either must withhold the tax and pay it to the relevant authority or be liable itself if it fails to do so. Because the payer presumably will be more familiar with the tax laws of its jurisdiction, financing documents generally place the risk of such a tax on the payer by requiring that it increase any payment so that, after deduction of tax, the amount paid equals that expressed to be paid under the document ("gross up"). Given the relatively narrow margins in Swap Transactions, the imposition of a withholding tax on a payment would substantially alter the profitability of the swap. (See Chapter 41 for discussion of taxes). The ISDA agreement contains a number of provisions intended to cover this situation, including the obligation to gross-up, representations as to status of the parties so that the parties can determine whether or not a withholding tax is payable and the ability to terminate if a withholding tax is imposed by reason of a change in law.

Description of tax provisions

The term "Tax" is broadly defined in the ISDA agreement. An "Indemnifiable Tax" is a Tax *other* than a Tax imposed as a result of a present or former connection between the jurisdiction of the taxing authority and the payee.

Section 2(d) of the ISDA agreement allocates the risk of Tax. If a Tax is imposed, the party obligated to withhold must notify the other party and pay it in full to the relevant authorities, promptly forwarding a receipt to the payee. If the Tax is an Indemnifiable Tax, the payer must gross the amount up, unless the Tax is imposed by reason of a failure of the payee to comply with or perform any agreement contained in Section 4(a)(i) or 4(d) or failure of a representation made by the payee in Section 3(f) (discussed below). If a party is required to withhold on account of a Tax for which it does not have to gross-up, but does not do so, and a liability is then imposed directly on it, it is entitled to reimbursement from the other party.

Since the parties would not wish to enter into the ISDA agreement if a Tax were to be imposed, Sections 3(e) and (f) of the ISDA agreement provide for representations to be made by each party as a potential payer and a potential payee under the ISDA agreement. Part 2 of the Schedule provides for the appropriate representations to be selected by each party.

As payer, each party would represent that it is not required to withhold any amount from a payment by it by reason of Tax imposed by any Relevant Jurisdiction ("Payer Tax Representation"). Relevant Jurisdiction is a jurisdiction:

- in which the payer is incorporated;
- where the branch or office through which it is acting is located;
- in which it executes the ISDA agreement; or
- through which a relevant payment by it is made.

Thus, the jurisdictions which a party must investigate in order to give the Payer Tax Representation are ascertainable and limited. Depending on the relevant tax law, in making the Payer Tax Representation the payer may need to obtain and rely upon the Payee Tax Representation made by the other party, the other party's delivery of any documents required under Section 4(a)(i) of the ISDA agreement (described below) and the satisfaction of the agreement of the other party in Section 4(d) of the ISDA agreement (which requires each party to advise the other if its tax representations cease to be true).

The "Payee Tax Representation" is made by each party to assure the other as payer of the basis on which the payer can make its Payer Tax Representation. Depending on the respective jurisdictions of the parties, each would therefore select the Payee Tax Representation it wishes its counterparty to make which will enable it to make its own Payer Tax Representation. First, if a Double Tax Treaty is to be relied upon by a party making its Payer Tax Representation, the counterparty would be requested to represent that it is eligible for the relevant treaty provision and that payments are not connected to a permanent establishment of the counterparty in the relevant jurisdiction (generally, but not always, that from which the payee is acting). There is also a space for the relevant treaty (Specified Treaty) and jurisdiction (Specified Jurisdiction) to be designated.

Second, the counterparty might be requested to make a representation that payments are received by it in connection with its regular business operations, thereby qualifying for exemption of payments to it from withholding tax under the laws of certain jurisdictions.

Third, if in fact a payment is connected with a trade or business of the payee in a Specified Jurisdiction, generally a tax would be imposed directly on the payee and there would be no withholding tax. Thus, a party that makes the Payee Tax Representation that such payments are so connected allows the payer to pay free and clear of withholding tax but becomes directly liable for income tax in the jurisdiction.

Fourth, special Payee Tax Representations are provided for in the United Kingdom. It is possible that a withholding tax might apply in the United Kingdom even if between two UK entities. However, swap payments to a bank recognised by the UK Inland Revenue as carrying on a *bona fide* banking business in the United Kingdom would not, under an Inland Revenue Tax concession, be subject to UK withholding tax. Thus, a UK corporate party dealing with such a bank would request that Payee Tax Representation from it. In addition, this concession was expanded following publication of the ISDA agreement to include recognised swap dealers, and if dealing with a non-bank swaps dealer, ISDA has approved a new Payee Tax Representation to be inserted in the space provided for "Other Representations".

If other representations are deemed appropriate, they can be inserted in this space.

Because certain of the exemptions referred to in the Payee Tax Representations require or are facilitated by the delivery of the payee to the payer of certain forms to enable the payer to pay free of withholding tax, Section 4 (a)(i) requires a party to deliver specified tax documents to the other. These forms and the party required to deliver them should be designated in the space provided in Part 3(1) of the Schedule.

If a party will be required to gross-up for a withholding tax as a result of a "Change in Tax Law" or there is a substantial likelihood that there will be such an obligation resulting from an action taken by a taxing authority or brought in a court of competent jurisdiction after the date on which a Swap Transaction was entered, a "Tax Event" occurs. Such a Tax Event constitutes a Termination Event permitting the party obligated to make the payment to terminate as an Affected Party.

In summary, both parties make representations as to tax status, in part relying on the payee's representation and delivery of documents. If an Indemnifiable Tax is imposed as a result of a change in law, the payer must gross up but may terminate. If a party's Payer Tax Representation is incorrect and withholding applies, it will generally have to gross-up but will not have the right to terminate. However, if it is incorrect because of a failure of a counterparty's Payee Tax Representation, breach by the counterparty of its obligation to notify the party of such failure or breach of the counterparty's obligation to deliver documents, the payer does not have to gross-up. Thus, breach of a tax representation or covenant as to delivery of a tax document does not constitute an Event of Default. The "punishment" lies elsewhere. If the Payer Tax Representation is breached and an Indemnifiable Tax must be paid by the breaching party, it would not be able to terminate (the Tax not being the result of a Change in Tax Law). If a payee breaches its Payee Tax Representation or obligation to deliver tax documents and a Tax is imposed, it does not receive a grossed-up payment and cannot terminate.

Revisions to ISDA agreement

A number of institutions, primarily German banks, opposed certain of the foregoing provisions. First, they often objected to the Payee Tax Representation based on the Double Tax Treaty on the theory that it required them to make a determination as to the interpretation of the treaty by the payer's jurisdiction.

Second, they objected to the definition of Indemnifiable Tax. Given the exclusion therefrom of Taxes imposed by reason of a connection with the taxing jurisdiction and the existence of their branch network, they were concerned that they would receive a payment net of Tax (ie, after deduction without grossing-up). Since the definition of Tax Event, which would permit termination, only refers to a party making a grossed-up payment, not to one receiving a payment net, they would not be able to terminate. A group of German banks made a proposal in February 1988 which would exclude from Indemnifiable Taxes only taxes (a) on income or turnover which (b) were imposed by the payee's jurisdiction. After discussions, they proposed another definition which would exclude any Tax imposed by the payee's jurisdiction or the jurisdiction where its payment account was located. The practical effect of their final proposal was to shift the burden of withholding tax from the payee, which otherwise would receive net payments, to the payer, which would now have to gross-up in more circumstances. If a payee has branches, this shift is favourable to it, since a Tax imposed on a payment to it by a jurisdiction because of a branch location would no longer necessarily be excluded from the definition of Indemnifiable Taxes. If a party has no branches, the shift is at best neutral but may be unfavourable, particularly if it is dealing with an entity which has branches in different locations.

The ISDA Board opposed this definition because shifting the initial incidence of the tax did not eliminate the tax risk and it believed that the definition in the ISDA agreement placed the initial burden on the right party, *ie*, the party whose connection to the taxing jurisdiction gave rise to the Tax and who should be aware of the tax consequences of its own operations. Furthermore, a party receiving payments net of withholding tax usually receives a tax credit in its home country for the tax withheld, thereby eliminating or reducing the economic burden of the Tax. However, ISDA found persuasive the argument that the ISDA agreement is asymmetrical because a payee receiving payments net of withholding tax after a Change in Tax Law (*ie*, a Tax, not being an Indemnifiable Tax, must be withheld) is unable to terminate the affected Swap Transactions.

The solution proposed by ISDA was to publish two provisions which the parties might elect to add to the ISDA agreement. The first is a new, ISDA-approved additional Tax Event which occurs if the withholding tax (even if resulting from a connection to the taxing jurisdiction) is due to a change in tax law and the party will, or is likely to, receive a payment net of withholding. Some parties which include this change amend it further so that it is clear that the failure to receive a grossed-up payment is not also a result of the payee's breach of its Payee Tax Representation or its obligation to deliver tax documents.

The second published change which may be elected is an addition to the definition of "Indemnifiable Tax" which includes therein a Tax (regardless of a connection of the payee to the taxing jurisdiction) if (i) the Tax is imposed by reason of a Change in Tax Law and (ii) the taxing jurisdiction is (A) the Relevant Jurisdiction of the payer and (B) is not the payee's home jurisdiction or that through which the payee is acting under the ISDA Master. This shifts the initial burden of the withholding tax to the payer in a limited number of circumstances: where a tax is imposed by reason of a peripheral connection of the payee to the taxing jurisdiction *and* a Change in Tax Law.

If the parties wish either or both of these changes, they would be included as amendments in Part 5 of the Schedule.

Termination and settlement

If an Event of Default or Credit Event Upon Merger occurs with respect to its counterparty or a Termination Event occurs with respect to itself, a party would wish to terminate the ISDA agreement and settle all liabilities. Section 6 of the ISDA agreement provides for termination and settlement.

Termination

A Swap Transaction can be terminated on a date (the "Early Termination Date") before its scheduled termination date by one party acting alone on either of two bases: an occurrence of a Termination Event with respect to itself or, in some cases, the other party; or the occurrence of an Event of Default with respect to the other party. If the Termination Event is a Tax Event or illegality, only the affected swaps may be terminated.

Because of the movement of rates since the trade dates, and also at times because of the mismatch of payments made prior to the Early Termination Date, a termination of the Swap Transactions and their future cash flows without a cash settlement will generally favour (often substantially) one party at the expense of the other party. If a Swap Transaction has become "out-of-the money" (ie, unfavourable) for a party, the Swap Transaction has a negative value for the party and termination results in a gain to it. If the Swap Transaction is "in-the-money" (ie, favourable) for a party, the Swap Transaction has a positive value for the party and termination results in a loss to it. The ISDA agreement provides for allocation of this gain and loss.

Calculation of cash settlement

Cash settlement under the ISDA agreement consists of two components: Unpaid Amounts and Settlement Amounts.

A party's Unpaid Amounts are payments (plus interest) which were initially scheduled to have been made to it before the Early Termination Date but which were never made. These payments may have not been made because of either a default by the payer or the deferral of payment as a result of, for instance, the payee being in default.

The Settlement Amount is the gain or loss to a party resulting from termination of the future cash flows of all terminated Swap Transactions, being the aggregate of Market Quotations for the individual terminated Swap Transactions. The ISDA agreement provides for the non-Defaulting Party or the non-Affected Party, as the case may be, to calculate a Market Quotation for each Terminated Swap. This is accomplished by going to the market and obtaining quotations from four leading dealers as to the amount each dealer would require from (a positive amount) — or would pay to (a negative amount) — the non-Defaulting or non-Affected Party for the market-maker to enter into a new replacement swap with that party on substantially the same economic terms as those of each terminated Swap Transaction. The highest and lowest quotations are disregarded and the Market Quotation for the Terminated Swap is the average of the remaining quotations. Under some circumstances, ie, where there are two Affected Parties, both parties go to the market and their respective Market Quotations are averaged. If Market Quotations are not available, the fall-back is to "Loss", which is the gain or loss determined by the relevant party to have been realised by itself on termination.

The Market Quotation for a given Swap Transaction will differ depending on which party obtains the Market Quotation for at least two reasons. First, due to the bid-offered spread, the party obtaining the quote will, other things being equal, always show a gain somewhat less than the other party's loss, or a loss somewhat greater than the other party's gain. Thus, the procedure is advantageous to the party obtaining the quote. Second, the quotes will differ depending on the creditworthiness of the parties. If the party obtaining the quote is a better credit than the other, it would have to pay less or would receive more from a market-maker than would the other party. If termination is a result of an Event of Default, the non-Defaulting Party will under most conceivable circumstances be the better credit and the replacement quote will be substantially better than that obtainable by the Defaulting Party. If termination is a result of a Termination Event, there is no structural, credit-related reason (unless the relevant event is Credit Event Upon Merger) why one party's quote would necessarily be more favourable than the other's, other than by reason of the bid-offered spread. Of course, the event constituting the Termination Event could be such that the Affected Party's attractiveness as a counterparty might be substantially reduced for reasons other than credit.

Settlement provisions

Having made these calculations, different settlement procedures are used depending on the nature of the event giving rise to termination.

The ISDA agreement provides that, where early termination is based on a Termination Event, a two-way payment obligation ("Two-Way Payments") applies. The non-Affected Party's Settlement Amount (positive or negative), being the aggregate of its Market Quotations, is aggregated with any Unpaid Amounts owing to the non-Affected Party and, from this sum (which may be positive or negative), any Unpaid Amounts owing to the Affected Party are subtracted. The resulting amount, if positive, is paid by the Affected Party to the non-Affected Party. If the amount is negative, the non-Affected Party would pay that amount to the Affected Party.

Where early termination is based on an Event of Default, the ISDA agreement provides for a one-way payment structure (termed Limited Two-Way Payments in the Rate Master but herein called "One-Way Payments"). The non-Defaulting Party would calculate the aggregate of its Settlement Amount and Unpaid Amounts owing it and subtract therefrom Unpaid Amounts owing to the Defaulting Party, as above. If the resulting amount is positive, the Defaulting Party is obligated to pay that amount to the non-Defaulting Party. If the resulting amount is negative, there is no obligation imposed on the non-Defaulting Party to make any payment to the Defaulting Party.

Concerns have been expressed that there may be a penalty aspect with respect to forfeiture of Unpaid Amounts otherwise owing to a Defaulting Party. If the Settlement Amount was zero and there were Unpaid Amounts owing to the Defaulting Party (for instance, as the result of deferral by reason of a Potential Event of Default with respect to the Defaulting Party at the time payment was due to it), no payment of those Unpaid Amounts would be made. Therefore, some dealers modify One-Way Payments so that the Settlement Amount, if it is a negative number, will be treated as equalling zero and the two Unpaid Amounts will be compared. If the Unpaid Amounts owing to the Defaulting Party exceed those owing to the non-Defaulting Party, the non-Defaulting Party would in this situation, and this situation alone, pay the excess to the Defaulting Party. This method of settlement is hereinafter referred to as "Modified One-Way Payments".

However, in Modified One-Way Payments a negative Settlement Amount cannot be used to reduce Unpaid Amounts owing to the non-Defaulting Party. For instance, assume the Settlement Amount were negative, Unpaid Amounts owing to the non-Defaulting Party were positive and Unpaid Amounts owing to the Defaulting Party were zero. Under One-Way Payments, the Defaulting Party would effectively be able to reduce Unpaid Amounts owing to the non-Defaulting Party by the amount of the negative Settlement Amount. Under Modified One-Way Payments, the Settlement Amount would be deemed to be zero and the Defaulting Party would not be able so to reduce its payment. Although it eliminates the forfeiture issue as to Unpaid Amounts, Modified One-Way Payments may create a greater risk of being regarded as an unenforceable penalty, since it may impose a payment obligation on the Defaulting Party in excess of the non-Defaulting Party's loss. For this reason, Modified One-Way Payments is rarely used.

Some end-users and a small but growing number of dealers modify the ISDA agreement so that Two-Way Payments is also used in default situations, where the non-Defaulting Party would make the above calculations and would be entitled to claim from the Defaulting Party any resulting positive amount or be obligated to pay to the Defaulting Party any resulting negative amount. Because of concerns that payments to a Defaulting Party might be made under circumstances where the non-Defaulting Party would be at further risk, it is advisable to include certain conditions to payment. The obligation to make any payment to the Defaulting Party would be subject to the conditions that (1) the non-Defaulting Party receive confirmation (including an unqualified opinion of counsel) that all Swap Transactions between the parties under their ISDA agreement and all other Swap Transactions between the parties or their Affiliates have been effectively terminated, (2) no other obligation (contingent or absolute, matured or unmatured) owed by either the Defaulting Party or any of its Affiliates to the non-Defaulting Party or any of its Affiliates is outstanding and (3) all costs of enforcement not otherwise paid are deducted from the payment. In addition, a party may wish to insert a set-off clause with respect to any amount owing by a non-Defaulting Party against amounts owing by the Defaulting Party or any of its Affiliates to the non-Defaulting Party or any of its Affiliates.

Enforcement issues

A number of legal issues arise in analysing the enforceability of the termination and settlement provisions of the ISDA agreement.

Enforcement of termination

Courts often refuse to uphold termination of agreements by reason of breaches deemed by the court to be immaterial or not central to the performance by the defaulting party of its primary obligations. In addition, general equitable considerations and questions of contract interpretation can result in termination being enjoined.

The most significant limitation on the right of termination, however, is found in jurisdictions with insolvency laws which are based on the principle of reorganisation rather than liquidation. Liquidation-oriented insolvency laws generally favour the termination of contracts and the distribution of the insolvent party's assets. Reorganisation-oriented insolvency laws are unsympathetic to termination and generally restrain termination and enforcement in order to permit the insolvent party to restructure its affairs in the hope it will emerge as a viable entity.

The bankruptcy laws of the United States, which apply to proceedings in the United States regardless of the governing law selected for the agreement, are primarily reorganisation-oriented. However, recent legislation in the United States (the Financial Institutions Reform, Recovery and Enforcement Act of 1989 with respect to banks and savings and loan associations and Public Law No 101–311, 1990, amending the US Bankruptcy Code, with respect to most other corporations) now permits termination of an insolvent party's swaps. The issue, however, remains in other reorganisation-oriented jurisdictions such as France.

Calculation of Settlement Amount

The provisions of the ISDA agreement for calculating Settlement Amount and Unpaid Amounts have not been tested in the courts. Even if termination were permitted, there are marginal concerns that a court might not uphold and apply the method of quantifying damages in the ISDA agreement.

Aggregation among swap transactions

In calculating the Settlement Amount, it is crucial that positive and negative values be aggregated because of the reduction of credit risk inherent in reducing losses by the amount of gains. This aggregation is often referred to as "netting" which can be misleading for several reasons.

Use of the term "netting" may result in confusion with use of that term in other contexts. First, the ISDA agreement provides in Section 2 that if, in respect of one Swap Transaction, each party is to make a payment in the same currency on the same date, the two payments will be compared and the party owing the larger will pay the difference. Second, the parties may (and generally do) select Net Payments — Corresponding Payment Dates in Part 4 (7) of the Schedule, the effect of which is that if payments under different Swap Transactions are being made to one another on the same date, in the same currency and by the parties acting through the same offices, those amounts will be netted. This type of netting, which is basically a settlement procedure avoiding delivery risk and multiplicity of payments, is generally referred to as "payment netting".

The aggregation of positive and negative values in all Terminated Swaps and the determination of a single Settlement Amount is referred to as "termination netting". Use of this term, however, may be misleading and could have adverse legal consequences. For instance, there is an implication in use of the term "netting" that separate obligations are involved. The ISDA agreement, in a self-serving manner which is nonetheless clearly consistent with the parties' intent, recites that all Swap Transactions constitute part of a unified agreement. Certain aspects of the ISDA agreement imply multiple transactions: provisions which differentiate among Swap Transactions, the fact that the ISDA agreement is open-ended as to amount and term, the further and inescapable fact that Swap Transactions are entered into separately by separate confirmations and the dealing practice of terminating or "transferring" individual Swap Transactions. In this sense, use of the term "netting" (which word does not appear in Section 6 of the ISDA agreement) in calculating Settlement Amount may further imply the existence of multiple contracts. In fact, the essence of determining Settlement Amount is calculating the gain or loss in termination of the ISDA agreement as a whole. Injudicious use of the term "netting" in this context may also focus attention on rules applicable to set-off (which may in some cases be unfavourable), conceding the existence of separate agreements and a perhaps restrictive set of legal rules before that issue is properly resolved.

In this connection, another misleading term has crept into the lexicon of swap financing: "netting by novation". This term was derived from a statement by the US banking authorities in the context of their determining, for the moment, not to permit netting out of exposure among Swap Transactions under a single ISDA agreement for purposes of applying capital adequacy requirements. They were apparently referring to contractual provisions which would obliterate the separate nature of Swap Transactions, from the Trade Date, by rolling all obligations into one single stream of payments. While this may be feasible with substantial restructuring of the ISDA agreement, the term itself is unfortunate. A novation is a three-party transaction in which a third party steps into the place of one party to a bilateral agreement, becomes directly liable on that agreement and obtains all rights with respect thereto as if it were the party it is replacing.

If termination netting is not allowed, several risks arise, primarily in the context of insolvency. In those jurisdictions where termination may be avoided, a receiver, trustee in bankruptcy or liquidator could "cherry-pick" among the Swap Transactions, continuing those which are favourable to it and rejecting the others. Second, if termination is allowed, termination netting might be permitted only to the extent consistent with the statutory scheme of set-off.

Market Quotations

Questions may also arise with respect to the use of Market Quotations as the basis for determining the value of each Swap Transaction.

Damages stipulated by an agreement will generally be treated as an impermissible penalty if (among other reasons) they are plainly disproportionate to the injury suffered by the non-Defaulting Party or result in an "unconscionable" recovery not related to actual damage. The ISDA agreement limits this risk by characterising the liquidated damage payments as a pre-estimate of loss. While perhaps helpful, if the results were found to be "grossly disproportionate", such characterisation would not stop a court from finding the payment to be a penalty or contrary to public policy, and therefore not enforceable. Nevertheless, because the Market Quotations are based on actual swap market replacement rates at the time of termination and because the act of replacement is generally regarded as reasonable, it is highly unlikely that a characterisation such as "grossly disproportionate" or "unconscionable" would apply. The widespread use of the ISDA agreement would further refute any claim of unconscionability.

Even if the resulting claim is not deemed grossly disproportionate, the expanding choice of hedging tools (eg, futures, long-dated foreign exchange contracts, caps, floors, and security purchases or sales) may make available to the non-Defaulting Party cheaper means of covering its exposure on early termination than use of a replacement swap, particularly if termination occurs a relatively short time before final maturity of the relevant Swap Transactions. Further, the definition of Market Quotation provides for an averaging of replacement quotations (to the extent obtainable) after disregarding the highest and lowest quotes. Thus, the method of calculating damages is not keyed into the cheapest form of replacement. Possibly a court would require proof of both actual loss and an attempt by the non-Defaulting Party to mitigate the loss.

Forfeiture

If One-Way Payments are used, its application might be challenged for causing a forfeiture. Forfeiture is considered a harsh remedy, and a court applying equitable principles often will not enforce a remedy for breach of contract if the forfeiture would cause hardship disproportionate to the injury caused by the breach or it is viewed as a penalty. An action for damages would provide adequate compensation for that injury and the party seeking the forfeiture is thereby attempting to gain an unjust advantage. While courts will enforce contractual provisions for forfeitures that have clearly been agreed to if these elements are not present, in many jurisdictions courts have the power to recover the amount forfeited.

A further risk is that termination under circumstances evidencing bad faith could render the terminating party liable for consequential damages incurred by the Defaulting Party. Termination by a party where it was not, as a practical matter, at risk or where it had not made efforts to buy out the swap or swaps could, in combination with other factors, result in a finding of bad faith.

Concerns over issues of forfeiture and bad faith become more visible (1) if viewed in conjunction with One-Way Payments and (2) if the value in the ISDA agreement represents in part a front-end or prior payment made by the other party or represents full prior performance by the Defaulting Party, as would be the case if the Defaulting Party held a cap or floor or was the fixed rate payer in an accelerated swap.

Ultra vires

If a swap transaction is beyond the powers of a party, it is possible that it would not be enforceable against the party. There are, of course, fall-back arguments that, even though beyond the power of a counterparty, a Swap Transaction, or damages in connection therewith, might be enforceable if the counterparty had the apparent authority to enter it. However, this is not always the case. The questions of powers, authorisation and enforceability have received prominent attention recently because of an English case involving a local authority's participation in the swap market (*Hazel v The Council of the London Borough of Hammersmith and Fulham, Midland Bank plc, Security Pacific National Bank, Chemical Bank, Barclays Bank plc and Mitsubishi Finance International plc*), discussed in detail in Chapters 37 and 38.

The key issues before the Court were: whether all or only selected classes of swaps were beyond the powers of the local authority; if the answer was that all or some of the swaps were beyond such powers, whether the bank counterparties could nonetheless enforce such swaps if they had not had proper notice of the defect; and whether, if all or some of the swaps were beyond the local authority's power, any of the local authority's prior payments to the counterparties must be restored to the former by the latter. The Court, taking a narrow interpretive approach which paid little attention to the reality of swap financing, held that all swaps were beyond the power of a local authority. The banks appealed the decision. In February 1990, the Court of Appeal took a substantially more commercial and realistic view of the economic factors underlying swaps and their relation to prudent management of risk within an institution. It held that, as part of its powers to borrow money and to manage debt and investments, a local authority could have the power to enter into swap instruments but that most of the local authority's swaps were unlawful because the local authority entered into them for an improper purpose.

The Auditor appealed to the House of Lords. In July 1990, a number of banks instituted suit against individual councillors.

In late 1990, the House of Lords handed down a provisional decision reversing the Court of Appeal and affirming the Lower Court's decision.

This case has drawn attention to the risks of enforcement which can arise by reason of a counterparty's ambiguous powers to enter swaps. For instance, a number of swap dealers are now hesitant to enter into swaps with UK building societies. These societies are established pursuant to specific legislation and their powers are limited to those conferred by statute. Included within their express powers are contracts for reducing risk, as described in an order of the Building Societies Commission. Implicit in the statute and order are that the swaps must have been entered into for that purpose, a determination as to which requires a finding as to an internal frame of mind. If that "purpose" is absent, the swap may be unenforceable. While a number of practical steps can be taken to reduce the possibility that the "purpose" was improper, the risk cannot be totally eliminated.

Derivative products

Swap financing techniques have evolved beyond the straightforward currency swap and interest rate swap to include a broader range of structures and a broader range of indices. Structural innovations include caps, collars, floors, swap options and forward-rate agreements. Product innovations (which can either use a standard swap structure or an innovative structure) include commodity-indexed transactions (where at least one of the payment flows is based on a commodity-index applied to an agreed volume of the commodity) and equity-indexed transactions (where at least one of the streams of income is based on a stock market or other equity index).

Documentation

The first choice in documentation is whether or not the particular transaction should be entered under a master agreement or on an agreement-by-agreement basis. Generally, because of credit enhancement achieved through termination netting, the master agreement form is used.

Use of the ISDA agreement or not

The next decision is whether or not to enter such transactions under an ISDA agreement, with modifications, or whether to use a separate master agreement. The advantage of using an ISDA agreement to document other types of transactions between two parties are, first, the basic one that fewer agreements will be required. Second, and perhaps more important, credit risk between the parties is reduced to the extent that termination netting among a broad range of products (including conventional swaps) would be more likely to result. Third, the swap market is probably (with the possible exception of the foreign exchange market) the single largest "over the counter" market for bilateral financial transactions and the ISDA agreement is widely accepted.

There are several counter-arguments. First, use of the ISDA agreement to cover a variety of types of transactions may in fact undercut the application of termination netting. As discussed above, there is in any case a marginal risk in some jurisdictions that a court would not treat all Swap Transactions under an ISDA agreement as part of an unified agreement. When the Rate Master and the Rate and Currency Master were first introduced, some institutions chose to use both forms (the first for only US dollar interest rate swaps and the second for currency swaps) because of the fear that inclusion of currency swaps with interest rate swaps would result in the transactions appearing less unified and more separate. To the extent that a broader range of transactions is brought in under the ISDA agreement, these fears might be intensified. It should be noted that these fears only have practical effect in jurisdictions where there is a risk that a trustee, a receiver or liquidator could "cherry-pick" among several transactions, where, even if all transactions were terminated, legal principles exist which would prevent the setting off of cross-liabilities or where the termination and settlement provisions of the ISDA agreement are inconsistent with the statutory insolvency set-off scheme.

Second, as an operational matter, institutions may prefer to keep the different types of dealing transaction separate in order to better monitor and manage rate exposure.

Third, conventions differ in different markets. For instance, as noted above, One-Way Payments is generally used on termination of the ISDA agreement. However, Two-Way Payments is generally used in FX netting agreements. In addition, many derivative products are of an option (or cap and floor) nature, such that one party may have fully performed. One-Way Payments may be viewed as inappropriate in this situation.

Finally the counterparties in one type of transaction are often not counterparties in other types of transaction. An overly complex agreement providing for multiple products may be unacceptable to a counterparty which intends only to participate in one type of product or is accustomed to shorter agreements.

Use of the ISDA agreement

If the ISDA agreement is to be used to cover a variety of transactions, certain changes are needed. It does not expressly provide for some swap products, such as swap options, caps, floors, collars or forward-rate agreements. However, with judicious selection of defined terms, an additional provision in the relevant Confirmation or both, the transactions can readily be effected. A cap or floor can be created by having only one fixed payment date (for the premium) and the regular payment dates for the cap or floor payments. A forward-rate agreement can be created by defining an effective date in the future and only one payment date, with an added provision to pay the present value of the single payment on the effective date. A swap option can be achieved through an additional clause in the confirmation setting forth the option, with the other specified standard terms dependent on its exercise. The 1990 Definitions will include some limited definitional changes to provide for price (as distinguished from accrual) transactions such as oil-based commodity swaps or equity-indexed swaps.

However, other changes, both structural and operational, are also advisable. ISDA has thus published an addendum for use with caps, collars and floors ("CCF Addendum") and an addendum for swap options ("Option

Addendum"). The Addenda, if desired, should be incorporated into the ISDA agreement by reference in Part 5 of the Schedule and may also be physically attached.

The CCF Addendum effects certain structural and operational changes. First, paragraphs 1 and 2 make certain necessary definitional and operational changes. "Rate Protection Transaction" is defined and the definition of Specified Swap is amended to include rate caps, rate floors, rate collars and forward-rate agreements or other exchange or rate protection transactions. Certain changes are also made to the calculation of floating amount so it works with the newly defined Cap Rate and Floor Rate.

Second, since in caps and floors (but not of course collars) one party will have fully performed its obligations, certain changes on termination are required. As noted above, a Market Quotation can be a positive or negative number, depending on whether or not the non-Affected Party or the non-Defaulting Party is in-the-money or out-of-the-money in the relevant transaction. However, a calculating party that has fully performed will always be in-the-money in the Rate Protection Transaction; if it has not fully performed (that is, it has written the cap or the floor), it will always be out-of-the-money. The economic value of the obligations being calculated will always be with the party which has fully performed, whether or not it is the Affected Party or Defaulting Party. Paragraph 3 of the CCF Addendum makes the change to the definitions of Market Quotation so that its determination is consistent with the structure of the Rate Protection Transaction.

The CCF Addendum also provides that if the only Swap Transactions outstanding are ones in which one party has fully performed, the other cannot terminate based on an Event of Default with respect to it. While this mitigates the most glaring excess of One-Way Payments as applied to fully performed transactions, it introduces into the ISDA agreement a basic conceptual flaw. For example, assume an ISDA agreement under which there are many fully performed transactions and, for example only one standard swap deeply in-the-money for the party which has performed on all the others (for example, a zero-coupon swap in which it is the fixed receiver, close to maturity but not in the final Calculation Period). The other party could still terminate and avail itself of the windfall, in this case massive, in One-Way Payments.

Because of such concerns, some dealers which use the CCF Addendum and One-Way Payments adopt the "Two-Pool Approach". Here, if a party has fully performed as to some transactions (for instance, purchased caps), the Market Quotations for these transactions are not included in the Settlement Amount, but rather are included as an Unpaid Amount owing to such party, and Modified One-Way Payments is applied. Again, this approach has flaws. It is subject to the same concerns regarding penalty as is Modified One-Way Payments. It also raises an inference that the various Swap Transactions are severable and not part of a single agreement, thereby increasing the risk of "cherry-picking" in some jurisdictions. It also has a basic conceptual flaw. It ignores the possibility that the transactions in the "fully-performed" pool could, for example, be split evenly among those in which one of the parties has fully performed and those in which the other party has fully performed. Thus, looking at the second pool as a whole, there may in fact be mutual performance as in a standard swap (which is simply an in-the-money cap and floor combined). The treatment of swaps differently than caps and floors mutually held is difficult to justify.

To avoid some of these problems some dealers document fully performed transactions on a separate ISDA agreement using the CCF Addendum. While this avoids the increased risk of severability among all Swap Transactions, it foregoes the possibility of netting between standard swaps on the one hand and fully performed swaps on the other. It also contains the basic flaw of the Two-Pool approach regarding mutual holding of caps and floors.

The Option Addendum also makes several useful definitional and operational changes to facilitate swap options under the ISDA agreement, including mandatory or optional cash settlement on the exercise date (if desired). It also includes changes with respect to Options for determination of Market Quotation and provisions for fully performed Options similar to those in the CCF Addendum.

Some dealers have prepared separate addenda for use with commodity swaps. A commodity swap addendum would define a number of new terms for use with the covered instruments in addition to required definitions by reason of the changed nature of the transaction (commodity, notional volume and unit). Because a commodity index transaction is not priced on the basis of accrual over time, certain definitions in the ISDA agreement must be modified to apply: Calculation Amount to mean the notional volume; and Floating and Fixed Rate Day Count Fraction to always equal one. In addition, Specified Swap would be amended to include a commodity price protection transaction. Because a number of banks require that exposure under commodity price protection transactions be limited, the new defined terms might include a floating-rate maximum and a floating-rate minimum which, if selected, establish a ceiling and floor on liability.

Finally, it should be noted that some participants in the commodity swap market feel that use of Market Quotation is inappropriate as there is not a liquid market for most transactions. Accordingly, some dealers prefer to use an alternate method set forth in the ISDA agreement when a Market Quotation is not available: defined in the ISDA agreement as "Loss". Basically, this provides for the non-Affected Party or the non-Defaulting Party to determine its gain or loss and for that, negative or positive, to be included in the Settlement Amount.

Use of other agreements

If a party chooses to use separate agreements for separate products, the practices in the marketplace differ on a product-to-product basis. For instance, forward-rate agreements in the London interbank market are generally effected through use of the British Bankers' Association recommended terms for forward-rate agreements ("FRABBA terms"). The FRABBA terms are a published set of standard terms and conditions which are incorporated into a given transaction by a telephone call followed by confirmation telex between the parties. Any benefits of termination netting are of course lost, but, given the short-term nature of most forward-rate agreements the simplicity and ease of execution obtained through use of the FRABBA terms is regarded as justification.

A number of financial institutions have entered into multilateral foreign exchange netting arrangements and bilateral foreign exchange agreements. These agreements are essentially cover agreements for the individual FX transactions entered into between the parties in the normal and ordinary course of their business. A number of these agreements use a contractual system of "netting by novation", which, as described above, is a misnomer but basically contemplates the merging of all payments due on a given date into one net obligation. The distinction between this and payment netting is that the single obligation is created as of each trade date, and is then adjusted by subsequent trades.

For commodity swaps or equity-indexed swaps (ie, those in which at least one stream of income is calculated by reference to a commodity price index applied to a volume or an equity index), parties tend to use swap agreement structures. Because of the length and complexity of the ISDA agreement, parties have tended to use the swap forms which were current in the market in 1984 and 1985, which are substantially shorter. As noted above, some participants prefer to use an indemnity rather than a swap replacement cost because of the thinness and illiquidity of the market. ISDA is currently working on a proposed draft form for a free-standing commodity swap master agreement.

Legal issues — commodity swaps

The most troublesome legal issues with respect to derivative products in the past four years have arisen under the commodity laws of the United States.

The purpose of US regulation of the commodities and futures market is protection of the investing public and preservation of the integrity of the relevant markets, and it is enforced by the Commodity Futures Trading Commission ("CFTC"). Under the US Commodity Exchange Act ("CEA"), futures contracts may lawfully be entered into in the US only on a regulated exchange. Forward contracts may lawfully be transacted off an exchange.

The CEA states clearly that not only physical commodities, but also intangible rights and interests, may be the subject of futures contracts. By extension, indices should also be subject to a forward contract. The CEA does not, however, clearly distinguish between futures and forward contracts. The category into which commodity swaps appropriately fit is thus not self-evident.

On most criteria, commodity swaps appear to be more like forward contracts. The key issue is whether or not delivery is anticipated. Since commodity swaps are netted in cash, it could be argued that delivery does not occur. However, actual delivery on futures contracts based on indices, such as stock index futures contracts, is by cash settlement rather than by delivery of the stocks underlying the index. The payment of cash on the payment dates for a swap could therefore be characterised as actual delivery of a commodity (the delivery of the rate index) under a forward contract.

The CFTC had approved the commodity swap activities of a US bank affiliate. Several organised exchanges in the United States strongly urged the CFTC to revoke this opinion. The exchanges' position was that such swaps violated the CEA as they were illegal off-exchange futures contracts which would undercut the exchanges' business.

Once the issue was raised with respect to commodity swaps, the attention of the CFTC was focused on off-exchange instruments in general. Indeed, in a parallel development, commodity-indexed instruments were being offered in the US, such as note issues by Standard Oil Company and USX in which interest rates rose and fell with oil prices. The spectre was raised of an explosion of products, some marketable to the public, which could provide an alternative to the organised futures exchanges. The financial swap market, perhaps to the regret of the CFTC staff, had developed to the point that it would be very difficult as a practical matter to impose regulation. Indeed, many CFTC staff members informally felt that financial swaps were illegal off-exchange futures contracts. The market for commodity swaps and hybrid securities was still small enough to control. In late 1986, the CFTC staff was prompted into action through the announcement by Wells Fargo that it was issuing gold-indexed certificates of deposit and publicity issued by Chase Manhattan that it was conducting commodity swaps. It threatened enforcement against both institutions and Wells Fargo promptly complied. Chase Manhattan, though resisting the CFTC's position, conducted no further commodity swaps in the United States pending clarification.

In February, 1987 the CFTC created a task force which proposed guidelines with respect to hybrid instruments and commodity swaps. On 5 January 1989, the CFTC issued new guidelines and proposals for hybrid securities, which would have permitted commodity swaps only between commercial counterparties (eg, only end users with no financial intermediaries). While the exchanges supported these proposals, industry and banking institutions, with banking and securities regulators, strongly opposed them.

Finally, in July 1989, the CFTC issued two separate releases, one of which dealt with hybrid securities and the other with swap transactions (including commodity swap transactions). The latter establishes a set of criteria, referred to as a "safe harbour", for swap transactions (including commodity swaps) and options on swaps. Transactions which satisfy these criteria may be transacted off-exchange, and will not be subjected to the CFTC's regulatory framework. If a transaction does not satisfy the safe harbour criteria, however, it will not necessarily be subject to CFTC regulation. Rather, the CFTC will, on request, review such transactions and will determine on a case-by-case basis whether they should be regulated or prohibited. To be eligible for the safe harbour a transaction:

- must be individually tailored in its material terms;
- must create performance obligations that are terminable, in the absence of default, only with the consent of the counterparty and that are entered into with the expectation of performance;
- must not be supported by the credit of a clearing organisation or primarily or routinely supported by a mark-to-market and variation settlement system designed to eliminate individualised credit risk;
- must be undertaken in conjunction with the parties' line of business (which may include financial intermediation); and
- must not be marketed to the public.

The release on swaps represented a vindication of the banks' position and effectively opened up the US market for commodity swaps using financial intermediaries subject to the restrictions imposed by their regulatory authorities. However, concerns remained. Implied in the CFTC release was their view that, absent the regulatory safe harbour, commodity swaps might be illegal. In addition, the need to refer to the CFTC for any swap which deviated from the safe harbour provisions was viewed as onerous. For instance, the restrictions against marking-to-market could be taken as a restriction against collateralised swaps (the CFTC concurred subsequently it was not). The applicability of the release to caps, floors and options on swaps is not clear. Finally, it is not entirely clear that the policy position taken by the CFTC would bind a court in applying the CEA in a judicial proceeding between private litigants.

These continuing concerns were highlighted by a decision of the US District Court for the Southern District of New York handed down in April 1990 (*Transnor (Bermuda) Limited v BP North America Petroleum et al*, 86 Civ 1493). In *Transnor* the plaintiff claimed, among other things, that the defendant oil companies had violated the CEA by engaging in manipulative transactions in Brent oil contracts. The Court found that, although the Brent market relates to oil produced outside of the United States, the bulk of trading in Brent oil contracts occurred in or was directed from the United States and had a significant impact on the US market. In addition, the Court determined that Brent oil contracts were futures contracts and not forward contracts. Although the contracts provided for actual delivery, the Court determined that they were in fact usually cash settled or settled by offset. The *Transnor* case was subsequently settled out of court and thus not appealed.

Because of the lingering concerns discussed above and the confusion caused by the *Transnor* case, ISDA has engaged in lobbying activities with the CFTC, in particular to obtain a statutory interpretation, rather than just a policy statement, that swaps are not subject to the CEA. In response to requests from ISDA and others, the CFTC in September 1990 issued a statutory interpretation stating that in its view Brent oil contracts were, for purposes of the CEA, forward contracts and not futures contracts.

Finally, with Bush-administration support, the proposed "Capital Markets Competition, Stability, and Fairness Act of 1990" was recently introduced in Congress. A primary feature of the bill would be to transfer to the Securities and Exchange Commission the authority to regulate stock index futures and options on stock index futures. Also, however, the bill would amend the CEA so as to exclude from the CEA and from CFTC jurisdiction any swap agreement (broadly defined and expressly including caps and floors) so long as, essentially, the swap agreement is "undertaken in conjunction with the business (including financial intermediation) or risk hedging activities of the parties." As of the date of writing, passage of this bill is uncertain.

Chapter 40a: Accounting guidelines for swaps in the United Kingdom

John I Tiner and Clive Bouch
Arthur Andersen & Co (London)

Interest rate, currency and cross-currency swaps are familiar tools to the corporate treasurer, providing flexible and effective mechanisms for asset and liability management. Financial institutions actively trade swap books, deriving income from making markets in the various swap instruments and regarding them as key products to serve their clients.

Historically, there has been no specific statutory or authoritative professional guidance on how to account for these instruments. This, however, is changing. The British Bankers' Association's (BBA) draft *Statement of Recommended Practice* (SORP) entitled "Commitments and Contingencies" considers the viewpoint of the banking industry. The Accounting Standards Board (ASB) is also reviewing an exposure draft (ED55) "Accounting for Investments" which may impact how the end user accounts for swaps in certain circumstances.

This chapter summarises current UK practice regarding the accounting for swaps by the corporate user and financial institutions.

Accounting framework

In the absence of specific guidance, accountants and the banking and securities industry have drawn on certain fundamental accounting principles to determine the appropriate accounting. Basically, the accounting treatment should reflect the underlying economics of the transaction subject to complying with the accruals and prudence concepts.

For end users, this means that the swap revenues and expenses are matched to the periods in which benefit is derived. For financial institutions making markets or actively trading in swaps the emerging practice is to mark the open swap positions to market. Marking-to-market causes a front-end loading of profit or loss which has to be balanced against the need to match revenues with the cost of capital required to support the swap positions, the ongoing costs of administration and adequate provision for credit exposure.

The corporate user

Table 1 demonstrates the application of the accruals and matching concept for a company with a calendar financial year which has used an interest rate swap to convert existing fixed-rate debt to floating rate. The value of the debt is £10m, drawn down on 1 January 19X1, maturing in two years and paying 15%. The fixed leg of a two-year swap is priced at 14% against six-month Libor. Settlement under the swap is assumed to be semi-annual and six-month Libor is assumed to be 14%, 13.5%, 13% and 12% in each period.

Table 1: Corporate user — cash flows

£000s

		19X1			19X2	
Year	**30/6**	**31/12**	**Total year 1**	**30/6**	**31/12**	**Total year 2**
Interest on debt	—	(1,500)	(1,500)	—	(1,500)	(1,500)
Swap cash flows:						
— fixed	700	700	1,400	700	700	1,400
— floating	(700)	(675)	(1,375)	(650)	(600)	(1,250)
	—	25	25	50	100	150
Interest expense			1,475			1,350
Effective cost of borrowing			14.75%			13.50%

The net income arising in each year under the swap is accounted for as an adjustment to the interest expense in each period. This properly reflects the economics that the borrowing has effectively been converted to floating-rate debt at Libor +1% and matches the cost over the life of the loan. The notes to the accounts should explain the broad terms of the swap and the fact that the swap income/expense is netted against interest expense. This latter point is important as legislation generally prohibits the netting of income and expenditure.

If the swap payments do not correspond with the company's financial year, then the income or expense due under the swap should be accrued with the corresponding debtor or creditor shown in the balance sheet under net current assets/liabilities. Fees incurred to establish the swap are usually amortised over the life of the swap, again as an adjustment to interest.

The accruals concept should also be applied where a company has transacted a swap to create a synthetic asset which it intends to hold to maturity.

Where swaps are transacted for speculative purposes (either outright or to create a speculative investment package), accruals accounting is inappropriate as it fails to reflect the economic substance of the transaction. In these circumstances, valuing the swap at the lower of cost and market (ie, providing for revaluation losses) is recognised as generally accepted accounting practice. Although this approach is prudent, it also fails to reflect the underlying economics and, in our view, does not provide an effective measure of performance.

ED55 recognises the benefits of full mark-to-market accounting for readily marketable investments held as current assets and this may become generally accepted accounting practice in the UK in due course. Although derivative products are outside the scope of ED55, we believe that the principle of marking-to-market should also be applied to speculative swaps provided there is sufficient liquidity in the market to close the position.

The financial institution

In response to the growth in off-balance-sheet business and the associated increase in the level of commitments and contingencies assumed by banks, the BBA has recently published a draft SORP which provides guidance on the related accounting issues. For swaps transacted for speculative purposes, or as part of a trading portfolio, the draft SORP recommends that the most appropriate accounting policy is marking-to-market. It also provides the following specific guidance:

(1) a proportion of the net present value of any expected future profit should be spread over the life of the swap portfolio to match the related costs, including the cost of maintaining capital and of any continuing credit and other risks;

(2) fees earned or paid as a result of the arranging or granting of swaps should generally be recognised immediately upon receipt or payment;

(3) swaps taken out to hedge existing income and expenditure (or to hedge assets and liabilities) should be accounted for on the same basis as the relevant income or expenditure (or assets and liabilities). Fees paid for the arrangement of such swaps should be treated in the same way as the swap itself.

As noted previously, the effect of marking a swap to market is to front-load the profit or loss. In applying the prudence concept care needs to be exercised in recognising up-front profit. Two instances, related to liquidity, may arise which may deem it inappropriate to recognise significant profit at the start of a transaction:

- The specific swap market is illiquid, and in normal trading conditions it would not always be possible to realise or lock-in the mark-to-market profit by executing offsetting swap transactions. Consideration could be given to recognising some element of front-loaded profit if, although the specific swap market is relatively illiquid, there is a liquid related derivative (futures or options) or cash market which could be used to hedge the swap position and hence to eliminate any outright position risk, subject only to basis risk. An element of the mark-to-market profit should, in this case, be deferred to cover basis risk.

- The institution has a sufficiently large book in the specific swap market that it could not match its swap position using offsetting swaps without adversely impacting the quoted market prices. In such a case, the institution would need to make a liquidity provision against the mark-to-market profit.

It is also common for swap traders to enter into security and derivative transactions to hedge prices and mismatch risks inherent in the swap portfolio. To properly reflect the economics and offsetting nature of hedge transactions, these positions should also be valued at market and any profit and loss recognised immediately.

The above recommendations are consistent with emerging industry practice. The mark-to-market policy accurately reflects the underlying economics and worth of the portfolio at the reporting date. However, given that the swap positions will utilise capital throughout the period to maturity, part of the mark-to-market profit should be deferred to allocate a return on capital over the period together with any provisions for credit risk and future administration costs. The remainder of this chapter considers the methods of swap revaluation and the approaches to income deferral.

Swap revaluation

For all swaps, whether interest rate, currency or cross-currency, the appropriate method of valuation is to determine the present value of the future cash flows.

The two most common methods used to revalue swaps are *replacement cost* and *bond simulation*. Both involve discounting future cash flow streams to express the swap in present value terms and assume a liquid market which enables the position to be closed easily.

In practice, the projected cash flows are discounted using zero-coupon yield rates. The use of these rates avoids assumptions regarding reinvestment

Figure 1: Zero-coupon rates

The coupon curve rate is as follows: one year, 14%; two years, 14.5%; three years, 15%.

The one-year zero-coupon rate is equal to the one-year coupon curve rate as there is only one cash flow at the end of the year.

The two and three-year zero-coupon rates are derived by discounting bond cash flows at the appropriate zero-coupon rates and solving to give a zero net present value.

The two-year zero-coupon rate

Period	Cash flow	Discount rate	Present value
t0	(100.00)	—	(100.00)
t1	14.50	14.00%	12.72
t2	114.50	X**	87.28*
			NIL

*Balancing figure to give NPV = 0

**Solved as follows: $(1 + X)^2 = 114.50/87.28$

$X = 14.54\%$

The three-year zero-coupon rate

Period	Cash flow	Discount rate	Present value
t0	(100.00)	—	(100.00)
t1	15.00	14.00%	13.16
t2	15.00	14.54%	11.43
t3	115.00	X**	75.41*
			NIL

*Balancing figure to give NPV = 0

**Solved as follows: $(1 + X)^3 = 115/75.41$

$X = 15.10\%$

returns. Zero-coupon rates are implicit in nominal par redemption yields and may be calculated through an iterative process termed bootstrapping. Figure 1 shows an example of the calculation.

A comparison of the two methods of revaluation, discounting at the zero-coupon rates derived in Figure 1, is set out in Table 2. The example assumes an interest rate swap with a notional principal of £100m, three years to maturity, receiving fixed rates at 12% and paying 12-month Libor. Assume the floating-rate leg has just reset at current rates.

Table 2: Replacement cost and bond simulation revaluation methods

£m

Replacement cost **Time period**	**t0**	**t1**	**t2**	**t3**	**Total**
Swap cash flows	—	12.00	12.00	12.00	
Replacement swap cash flows	—	15.00	15.00	15.00	
Cost to replace swap	—	(3.00)	(3.00)	(3.00)	
Discount rate		14.00%	14.54%	15.10%	
Present value	—	(2.63)	(2.28)	(1.96)	(6.87)

Bond simulation **Time period**	**t0**	**t1**	**t2**	**t3**	**Total**
Simulated bond cash flows	(100.00)	12.00	12.00	112.00	
Discount rate	—	14.00%	14.54%	15.10%	
Present value	(100.00)	10.53	9.15	73.45	(6.87)

The replacement cost method determines the present value of the incremental cash flows, assuming the swap is replaced immediately at current prices. In this example, the swap is out-of-the-money and assuming the three-year swap rate remains higher than the existing swap rate (ie, 15% compared to 12%) the institution has no replacement risk in the event of counterparty default. Accordingly, the existing swap has a negative value (ie, it shows a loss).

The bond simulation method is based on the analogy that a swap is equivalent to being long and short fixed and floating-rate securities, respectively. Simulated bond cash flows are determined from the swap coupon flows, plus the notional principal assumed to be invested today and returned at maturity of the swap.

In both examples the floating side of the swap has been ignored given the assumption that it has just reset at current rates. In practice this will not be the case and it should be revalued. The usual method is to compute the cost of replacement from revaluation date to the next reset date or simulate a bond assumed to redeem at the next reset date. The cash flows are again discounted at the zero-coupon rate, usually using simple rates as a close approximation for the appropriate discount factor.

Floating-rate cash flows beyond the next reset date are ignored on the grounds that, firstly, they can be easily hedged, and secondly, expectations regarding future variable rates are reflected in the fixed-rate quote.

Using the current swap rate also assumes that the swaps are generic (ie, fixed is quoted against the floating index). Where the swap is not generic, for example, where the floating-rate side is above or below the index or payment frequency is different to the index, then the fixed-rate coupon should be adjusted to reflect this. It is also important to reverse any swap coupon accruals to avoid double accounting of the future cash flows.

For a currency swap the revaluation simply involves discounting the future currency exchange, converting to the reporting currency at spot and subtracting the resulting value of the short position from that of the long position. For short-dated swaps the exposure may be marked at the forward foreign exchange rate. However, many swaps are long-dated and a liquid forward market does not exist. In these circumstances each currency cash flow is discounted at the zero-coupon rate applicable to that currency and the maturity of the swap.

For cross-currency swaps, which are simply a combination of interest rate and currency swaps and involve an exchange of both currency and interest, the same concepts apply. The swap position is analysed into interest and principal cash flows by currency and each component revalued separately.

Income deferral

The front-loading of swap profit must be balanced by prudent provisions to match revenue against ongoing credit exposure, administration costs and capital utilisation. Although a simple concept, this is perhaps more difficult to put into practice.

As referred to in the earlier example (Table 2), credit risk is a function of market risk and therefore of volatility. At any point in time the credit exposure is greater the deeper the swap is in-the-money. Out-of-the-money swaps are not exposed to credit risk other than in respect of the administration and legal costs involved in winding-up and replacing the position created when the counterparty defaults. All swaps carry some credit exposure because of the possibility that during the life of the swap it will be in-the-money. The longer the period to maturity and the greater the volatility, the greater the credit risk.

It is possible to develop sophisticated models which determine credit provisions as a function of volatility, period to maturity, the swap value and any mark-up inherent in the original swap price to reflect the counterparty's credit rating. However, many players in the market simplify the approach, for example, by applying a credit provision factor against the aggregate notional principal.

It is important to note that the above approaches are used to determine general provisions. The exposure to each counterparty should also be evaluated in order to determine whether a specific provision is required; for example, marking-to-market a swap that is profitable and recognising that profit would be imprudent if there were concerns regarding the ongoing viability of the counterparty. Whether the exposure to a counterparty is assessed on a swap-by-swap basis or in aggregate will depend upon whether a right of set-off exists in respect of all swaps transacted with that counterparty.

The problem of estimation also arises when determining the appropriate provision for future administration costs. Therefore it is important to determine a method based upon reasonable assumptions and apply it consistently.

Regarding the allocation of profits to future periods when capital is utilised, the approach should be based on the capital requirement rules set out by the banking supervisors and the UK securities regulators. Using these rules, the existing capital utilisation can be determined. On the assumption that the yield curve remains unchanged the capital utilisation can be calculated as at the end of each year throughout the life of the swap portfolio. Applying the desired return on capital (eg, based on the risk-free rate) to each period's capital utilisation and discounting gives the present value of the required future return on capital to be provided. The calculation can be updated at the end of each year or at shorter intervals if deemed necessary. This model can be modified to also provide for credit and ongoing administration costs by adding a premium to the "risk-free" rate.

Conclusion

Marking-to-market is the most appropriate accounting method for swaps unless the swap is used to hedge existing or anticipated assets, liabilities or cash flows which are carried at cost. Many financial institutions now account for swap positions using the mark-to-market basis. This properly reflects the underlying economics and also provides an essential management tool to monitor performance and credit risk.

For end users, the main treasury application is in liability management, whereby the swap cash flows are accrued over the life of the swap/underlying debt to properly match the cost of funds to the period when benefit is derived. Marking-to-market has therefore been of less importance. However, the use of swaps to create synthetic current asset investments — or indeed speculating in swaps as short-term investments — requires such positions to be marked-to-market in order to properly reflect economic performance. The eventual publication of ED55 may facilitate mark-to-market becoming acceptable UK accounting practice in these circumstances.

Chapter 40b: Accounting guidelines for swaps in the United States

Benjamin S Neuhausen
Arthur Andersen & Co (Chicago)

Due to the many different types of swap transactions, it is not possible to separately consider the accounting treatment for each type of swap. This chapter therefore aims to identify the accounting principles that are applied to currency swaps and interest rate swaps: those principles should provide guidance in accounting for transactions that aren't specifically covered.

Accounting framework

The Federal Accounting Standards Board (FASB) Statement No 52, *Foreign Currency Translation,* establishes the standards of accounting for currency swaps. No pronouncement covers the accounting for interest rate swaps. However, FASB Statement No 80, *Accounting for Futures Contracts*, which established the standards of accounting for futures contracts (other than foreign currency futures contracts), provides guidance that may be extended to interest rate swaps by analogy.

One aspect of accounting is common to both currency swaps and interest rate swaps — balance sheet treatment. A company that enters into a swap has a right to *receive* a stream of cash payments and is obligated to *make* a stream of cash payments. The right to receive payments could be recorded as a receivable at the discounted present value of the estimated payments to be received, and the obligation to make payments could be recorded as a liability at the discounted present value of the estimated payments to be made. This is not done, however, because executory contracts (contracts in which both parties have future performance obligations) generally are not recorded on balance sheets as assets and liabilities. For interest rate swaps, an additional reason is that the agreements typically provide for net cash settlements. Accordingly, under current practice, the gross contractual amounts or notional principal amounts of swaps are not recorded on balance sheets.

Accounting for currency swaps

For accounting purposes, a currency swap is viewed as a series of foreign currency forward contracts. Gains and losses on forward contracts are computed and accounted for differently depending on whether the contracts are hedges for accounting purposes.

If the contracts are hedges for accounting purposes, a discount or premium (ie, the foreign currency amount of the contract multiplied by the difference between the contracted forward rate and the spot rate at the date of the inception of the contract) is computed at contract inception and is accounted for separately over the life of the contract. Gain or loss on a forward contract that qualifies for hedge accounting is computed by multiplying the foreign currency amount of the contract by the difference between (1) the spot rate at the balance sheet date and (2) the spot rate at the date of the inception of the contract (or the spot rate last used to measure gain or loss on that contract).

If the contracts are considered speculative for accounting purposes, the discount or premium is not computed or separately accounted for. Gain or loss on a contract that is considered speculative for accounting purposes is computed by multiplying the foreign currency amount of the contract by the difference between (1) the forward rate available for the remaining maturity of the contract and (2) the contracted forward rate (or the forward rate last used to measure a gain or loss on that contract). Gains and losses on speculative forward contracts are included in income currently.[1]

The treatment of gains and losses and discount or premium on contracts that qualify as hedges for accounting purposes depends on what is being hedged. In all cases, a contract is a hedge for accounting purposes only if it is (1) designated as a hedge and (2) effective as a hedge. Three possibilities exist:

- If a contract is a hedge of a net investment in a foreign subsidiary or affiliate, the gain or loss is included with translation adjustments in the separate component of shareholders' equity. The discount or premium on such a contract may be either amortised to income over the life of the contract or included, along with the gain or loss on the contract, with translation adjustments in the separate component of shareholders' equity.

- If a contract is a hedge or an identifiable firm foreign currency commitment, the gain or loss is deferred and included in the measurement of the related foreign currency transaction. However, a loss may not be deferred if it is expected that deferral would lead to recognising a loss in a later period. The discount or premium on such a contract may be either amortised to income over the life of the contract, or the discount or premium applicable to the commitment period may be deferred and included, along with the gain or loss, in the measurement of the related foreign currency transaction. (A firm commitment is defined as an agreement, usually legally enforceable, under which performance is probable because of sufficiently large incentives for non-performance. Examples include interest on a loan or an investment, rent under a lease agreement, or non-cancellable purchase or sale commitments.)

- If a contract is a hedge of a foreign currency-denominated asset or liability, the gain or loss is included in income as it arises. The discount or premium is amortised to income over the life of the contract.

Statement 52 is relatively restrictive in its definitions of which forward contracts constitute hedges for accounting purposes. Contracts that represent hedges from an economic or treasury point of view may be classified as speculative for accounting purposes. For example, forward contracts intended to hedge anticipated and probable, but not firmly committed, foreign currency transactions are not considered hedges for accounting purposes. Statement 52 is explicit that the only future transactions that may be hedged from an accounting point of view are firm commitments.

Ordinarily a forward contract that is considered a hedge for accounting purposes should be denominated in the same currency as the exposure. If it is not practical or feasible to obtain a forward contract in the same currency, it is permissible to apply hedge accounting to a forward contract in another currency for which the exchange rate typically moves in tandem with the transaction currency. Thus, if it is practical to obtain a forward contract in the same currency, contracts in other currencies do not qualify as accounting hedges, regardless of how closely the changes in exchange rates correlate.

Hedge accounting is only appropriate where foreign currency risk is being eliminated, not where it is being increased. Thus, if a US company has dollar debt outstanding and wishes to create a "synthetic" Deutsche mark borrowing by entering into a dollar/Deutsche mark currency swap, the swap would be considered speculative for accounting purposes because it is creating rather than reducing foreign currency exposure. The accounting for a dollar debt with a speculative dollar/Deutsche mark swap differs from the accounting for a Deutsche mark borrowing, even though economically the transactions are quite similar.

Statement 52 also prescribes additional accounting for forward contracts that hedge firm commitments:

- A forward exchange contract that meets the criteria for a hedge of an identifiable foreign currency commitment might exceed the amount of the commitment. In such a case:

  - The gain or loss on the forward contract that is to be deferred and included in the measurement of the related foreign currency transaction is limited to the gain or loss on the portion of the forward contract that does not exceed the amount of the related commitment.
  - The gain or loss on that portion of the forward contract that (1) exceeds the amount of the related commitment and (2) is intended to provide a hedge on an after-tax basis must be deferred and included as an offset to the related tax effects in the period in which those tax effects are recognised.
  - A gain or loss on any portion of the forward contract that exceeds the amount that provides a hedge on an after-tax basis may not be deferred but must be included in net income as it arises. This portion of the forward contract is treated as speculative for accounting purposes.

- If a forward contract extends beyond the transaction date of the related foreign currency commitment, a gain or loss on the contract that arises after that date may not be deferred but must be included in net income as it arises.

- If a forward contract that had been treated as a hedge of an identifiable foreign currency commitment is terminated before the transaction date of the commitment, any deferred gain or loss continues to be deferred and accounted for as discussed above.

Accounting for interest rate swaps

Like currency swaps, the accounting for gains and losses on interest rate swaps depends on whether the swaps are considered hedges for accounting purposes. However, the criteria for what constitutes a hedge for accounting purposes are much less restrictive than Statement 52. Under Statement 80, which is the guidance considered most relevant, three criteria generally must be satisfied for an interest rate swap to be considered a hedge for accounting purposes:

- the underlying transaction that is being hedged exposes the company to interest rate risk;
- the company designates the interest rate swap as a hedge; and
- the interest rate swap is effective as a hedge.

In addition, to be considered a hedge of an anticipated transaction (such as the resetting of interest rates on variable-rate assets or debt or the rollover of short-term investments or debt), an additional two criteria must be satisfied:

- the significant characteristics and expected terms of the anticipated transaction are identified; and
- it is probable that the anticipated transaction will occur.

In practice, interest rate swaps sometimes are accounted for as hedges if the second and third criteria (designation and effectiveness) are satisfied: the first criterion is not necessarily applied. Often, of course, all of the criteria would be satisfied. For example, if a company issues long-term variable-rate debt and enters an interest rate swap to fix the rate, all three basic criteria are satisfied if the variable-rate side of the swap correlates well with the variable rate on the debt. In addition, the two additional criteria for hedges of anticipated transactions are satisfied. In other cases, however, such as the use of an interest rate swap to unfix the interest rate on a fixed-rate borrowing, the first criterion (underlying hedged item exposes the company to interest rate risk) may not be satisfied.

The criteria for applying hedge accounting to interest rate swaps are broader and more flexible than the criteria for hedge accounting for currency swaps:

- Interest rate swaps may be accounted for as hedges of probable, but not firmly committed, future transactions; currency swaps may not.
- Cross-hedging is permitted for accounting purposes with interest rate swaps, provided that (1) a clear economic relationship exists between the two interest rates and (2) high correlation is probable. Cross-hedging is permitted for accounting purposes with currency swaps only if it is not practical to hedge in the same currency.

- Interest rate swaps may be accounted for as hedges even though they create interest rate risk; currency swaps that create currency risk generally may not be accounted for as hedges.

Hedge accounting

The hedge accounting described in this section applies to companies that follow the usual practice of accounting for interest-bearing financial instruments at amortised cost (for assets) or amortised proceeds (for liabilities). The accounting for an interest rate swap that hedges an asset or liability accounted for on a market value basis would be the same as the accounting described below for speculative interest rate swaps.

If a swap is used to hedge an existing asset or liability, including fixing the interest rate on a variable-rate asset or liability, the accounting is quite simple. Any fee paid or received and any costs incurred to execute the swap should be deferred and amortised over the life of the swap. Settlement payments should be accrued each period as a net adjustment to interest income/expense for the underlying transaction. Under this approach, it is not necessary to determine the changing market value of the swap from period to period; as long as both the underlying transaction and the interest rate swap remain in effect, the income effect is solely a function of initial costs and fees and the settlement payments. This approach is sometimes described as "synthetic instrument" accounting, because it results in the accounting for the underlying asset/liability (instrument) as though its nature had been changed from variable to fixed rate or *vice versa*.

Sometimes an interest rate swap contract might be used to hedge a commitment to buy an interest bearing instrument or to issue debt. (A firm commitment is an agreement, usually legally enforceable, under which performance is probable because of sufficiently large disincentives for non-performance.) Any fee paid or received and any costs to execute a swap that hedges a firm commitment should be deferred and amortised by the interest method over the life of the resulting asset or liability to which the commitment relates. Settlement payments during the commitment period should be deferred and reported as an adjustment to interest income or expense over the life of the resulting asset or liability to which the commitment relates. If it is anticipated at any time that the firm commitment will not be fulfilled, the swap should be accounted for as a speculative position as described below, unless the swap can then be designated as a hedge of another transaction.

An interest rate swap also may be used to hedge a transaction that the company expects, but is not obligated, to enter, such as an anticipated issuance of debt. To follow hedge accounting in this particular situation, the swap should satisfy at least the second and third general criteria (designation and effectiveness) *and* the two special criteria for hedges of anticipated transactions (identification and probability). The accounting is identical to the accounting for a swap that hedges a firm commitment — defer fees, costs, and settlement payments during the period before the anticipated transaction is consummated and amortise them by the interest method over the life of the consummated transaction. If it is anticipated at any time that the anticipated transaction will be less than the amount originally hedged, a pro rata portion of the swap should be accounted for as a speculative position as described below, unless that portion can then be designated as a hedge of another transaction.

Speculative swaps

If a swap does not satisfy the conditions to be accounted for as a hedge or if a swap hedged a firm commitment or anticipated transaction that will not occur, the swap should be accounted for as a speculative position. In industries with specialised accounting principles that require market value accounting, these swaps should be accounted for on a market value basis, with gains and losses included in income currently. For other industries, speculative swap positions should be accounted for on a lower-of-cost-or-market/higher-of-proceeds-or-market basis (ie, defer gains but recognise losses currently).

Because prices of interest rate swaps are not quoted publicly, determining their fair value will require either mathematical models or quotations from knowledgeable third party intermediaries. Regardless of what means are used to estimate market value, it is important that the estimate considers the effect of credit considerations on the valuation. Significant factors include collateralisation of the transaction and the current credit standing of the swap counterparty.

Swap terminations

Sometimes a company will decide to terminate an interest rate swap before the expiration of its term. This may be accomplished in two ways. One is to directly terminate the swap and pay or receive the cash payment specified in the swap agreement for early termination. The other method is to enter into a reverse swap for a period equal to the remaining term of the original swap. For example, a company that issued 10-year variable-rate debt and entered a 10-year swap to receive variable rate and pay 12% fixed may wish to terminate that swap five years later to take advantage of lower interest rates. One method is to pay off the counterparty to terminate the swap. The other method is to enter a five-year reverse swap under which the company will pay variable rate and receive a fixed rate of, say 8%. No up-front cash payment is required in the latter case, but the company has locked in a 4% loss (12% minus 8%) for five years. The termination loss under the second method is the discounted present value of the locked-in 4% loss.

A gain or loss on early termination of an interest rate swap that qualified as a hedge generally should be deferred and amortised over the term of the original swap. However, if the underlying transaction being hedged also is closed out, the gain or loss from terminating the swap should be recognised currently in income. A gain or loss on early termination of a speculative interest rate swap should be included in income currently.

Swap extensions

In this transaction, a swap is extended beyond its original term and the fixed interest rate side of the swap is adjusted. For example, assume that the original swap calls for fixed payments at 12% for a remaining five-year term at a time when interest rates have dropped to 8%. The parties might agree to extend the swap to 10 years in exchange for a decrease in the fixed-rate side to 10%.

For accounting purposes, a swap extension should be viewed as a termination of the original interest rate swap and the acquisition of a replacement swap. These two elements are accounted for separately, using current market values and interest rates. In the example in the preceding paragraph, the loss on terminating the original swap is embedded in the above-market fixed rate on the replacement swap. The loss is equal to the discounted present value of the 2% above-market rate for the 10-year term of the replacement swap. The loss should be accounted for as described in the section on swap terminations above. The other side of the accounting journal entry recording the loss is to record a deferred income account that will be amortised back to income over the life of the replacement swap to reduce its fixed rate from 10% to the 8% market rate. Failing to follow the accounting specified in this paragraph would spread part of the loss on terminating the original swap over years six to 10.

Forward swaps

A forward interest rate swap is an agreement to enter into an interest rate swap with defined terms at an agreed date in the future. For example, a company may enter into a forward swap that calls for a seven-year swap beginning three years in the future under which the company will receive a variable rate and pay a fixed rate of 8%. A company might enter such an arrangement as a hedge of debt that it expects it issue three years in the future. Perhaps the company has existing high interest rate debt outstanding that can first be called three years from today. The company plans to call the existing debt and issue new seven-year notes. The forward swap "locks in" the cost of the refinancing notes. The forward swap clearly "locks in" a cost if the new notes are variable-rate notes matching the variable rate in the forward swap, but it also does so if the new seven-year notes are fixed-rate notes. If interest rates rise in the intervening three years, the forward swap can be terminated at a gain; the gain on the swap will economically offset the higher interest rate on the new notes and result in a financing cost based on today's interest rates. Conversely, if interest rates fall in the intervening three years, the forward swap can be terminated at a loss; the loss will effectively raise the financing cost on the new notes to today's interest rates.

Another form of the forward swap is a double swap. Rather than entering a forward seven-year swap beginning three years from today, the company in our example could enter two swaps:

- a 10-year swap beginning today under which it will receive a variable rate and pay 8% fixed; and
- a three-year swap beginning today under which it will pay the same variable rate and receive 7% fixed.

Effectively, this double swap creates a seven-year forward swap beginning three years from today. The company pays a 1% fee (8% rate paid less 7% rate received) for each of the next three years.

For a forward swap to qualify as a hedge for accounting purposes, it mush satisfy at least the second and third general criteria (designation and effectiveness) and the two criteria for hedges of anticipated transactions (identification and probability). If these conditions are satisfied, any fees paid for the forward swap (including the net amount paid or received during the double swap period) are deferred. Using our example above, if variable-rate debt is issued at the end of three years and the swap is left intact, the deferred fees would be amortised as an adjustment of interest on the debt. The settlement payments on the swap would be accounted for as adjustments of interest expense each period. If fixed-rate debt is issued at the end of three years, the swap will presumably be terminated. If the term of the fixed-rate debt is similar to the seven-year term of the swap, the gain or loss upon swap termination, including the deferred fees, would be recorded as premium or discount on the new debt and amortised as an adjustment of interest expense over the life of the debt.

Accounting by intermediaries

Recognition of income by intermediaries is an unsettled accounting issue in the US, and practice varies.

If the intermediary acts solely as an agent in arranging the swap and bringing the parties together, the intermediary's sole service is rendered at inception and the intermediary bears no risks. Therefore, the intermediary should recognise all fees in income immediately.

If the intermediary brings the two parties together, arranges the swap, and remains as a principal in the transaction, collecting from one party and paying the other party, then the intermediary assumes credit risk and services the swap throughout the life of the swap. Therefore, a portion of the intermediary's income should be recognised over the swap. Four accounting methods are used.

- Some intermediaries record all income over the life of the swap and record no income at inception.
- Some intermediaries recognise income at the inception of the swap to the extent of the direct costs of arranging the swap, and record the remainder of their income over the life of the swap.
- Some intermediaries calculate a fair price for assuming credit risk and servicing the swap and record that income over the life of the swap. The remainder of the income is recognised at inception. The amount recognised should not exceed the fee that would be charged for an agency-only role.
- Some intermediaries account for all swaps the same, whether they have located both counterparties or not. Accordingly, they use either lower-of-cost-or-market or mark-to-market accounting, as described in the next section.

If the intermediary enters a swap transaction with one party before locating a counterparty, the intermediary is exposed to interest rate risk unless otherwise hedged. No income should be recognised at inception because the retained risk is too great. Two methods may be used to account for unmatched swap positions:

- The aggregate lower-of-cost-or-market (higher-of-proceeds-or-market) method, under which the entire portfolio of unmatched swaps is revalued. Aggregate net losses are recognised immediately; aggregate net gains are deferred. Up-front fees are viewed as part of the original cost/proceeds of the swap. When a counterparty is located, income would be recognised using one of the methods described in the preceding section.
- The mark-to-market method under which each unmatched swap is revalued and gains and losses are included in income currently. When

a counterparty is located, income would be recognised using one of the methods described in the preceding section.

Disclosures

Statement 52 requires disclosure of the total exchange gain or loss included in income for each year and also requires an analysis of the activity in the separate foreign currency translation component of shareholders' equity. Gains and losses arising from currency swaps would be included in such disclosures but would not be separately identified.

For interest rate swaps, no specific disclosure requirements exist. Because practice varies, a company should disclose at a minimum the accounting policies it follows with respect to interest rate swaps. In addition, it is desirable to disclose how and why interest rate swaps are used and their effect on interest income and expense and interest rate risk. For example, a company might disclose that one-third of its short-term debt has effectively been changed to a weighted average fixed rate of 8% by the use of interest rate swaps.

All swaps are subject to the general US requirements to disclose material future commitments and contingent liabilities. Any contingent liabilities that are both probable and reasonably estimable must be recorded by accruing a loss and a liability.

FASB Statement No 105, *Disclosure of Information about Financial Instruments with Off-Balance-Sheet Risk and Financial Instruments with Concentrations of Credit Risk* requires certain additional disclosures about all financial instruments with off-balance-sheet risk, including currency and interest rate swaps:

- The face, contract, or notional principal amount.
- The nature and terms, including a discussion of (1) the credit, market, and liquidity risk of those instruments and (2) the related accounting policy.
- The accounting loss the company would incur if the counterparty failed to perform according to the terms of the swap contract and the collateral or other security, if any, for the amount due proved to be of no value.
- The company's policy of requiring collateral or other security, information about the company's access to that collateral or other security, and the nature and a brief description of the collateral or other security.

Future developments

The FASB has on its agenda a large, multi-part project on accounting for financial instruments. Certain phases of that project will address the accounting for financial instruments that transfer interest rate or currency risk. While those phases are not likely to be completed for several years, the conclusions could change the accounting described in this chapter.

Notes

1. For long-term speculative forward contracts, the gain or loss computed as described in this paragraph overstates the true unrealised gain or loss, because realisation of the spread between the contracted forward rate and available forward rate will not occur until the settlement of the forward contract. As a result, some entities in the US that engage in long-term speculative forward contracts compute gain or loss based on the discounted present value of the difference between the contracted forward rate and the available forward rate multiplied by the foreign currency amount of the contract.

Chapter 40c: Accounting and tax guidelines for swaps in Japan

Mark Rhys
Arthur Andersen & Co (Tokyo)

Summary

The following discussion is based on the status of accounting and tax rules at the time of writing (December 1990), but Japanese accounting practice for derivative instruments is in transition and the tax situation is correspondingly uncertain.

In the case of financial instruments such as swaps, where there is no specific guidance from Japanese GAAP (generally accepted accounting principles), the accounting will often follow general tax principles. Thus Japanese swap accounting emphasises recognition of the cash flows that are associated with the swap on the dates that they occur, with accruals between those dates.

Furthermore, there is generally no recognition in Japan of unrealised gains or losses. Earnings are only impacted on receipt or payment of net interest at the periodic settlement dates.

Swap derivatives are accounted for (where appropriate) by application of the Japanese option accounting rules. For accounting purposes, option premiums are generally capitalised in the balance sheet. With the exception of currency options held by banks, there is no recognition of unrealised gains or losses until exercise, sale or expiry. However, for tax purposes, option premiums are income when received and are expensed when paid (if the option term is less than one year).

The key differences from the swap accounting commonly used in the United States arise from Japan's tax driven emphasis on cash flows — in general, off-balance-sheet transactions are recorded on a settlement basis; and unrealised gains or losses are not recognised. The use of hedge accounting and the marking-to-market of traded financial assets and liabilities, often required by US GAAP, are thus not generally accepted practice in Japan.

Japanese GAAP

Japanese GAAP is a combination of the Commercial Code, Ministry of Finance (MoF) rules and regulations (including tax income recognition rules), pronouncements by the Japanese Institute of Certified Public Accountants (JICPA) and industry practice. However, there have been no official pronouncements on the accounting for, taxation of, or regulation of swaps in Japan.

In such areas, where there has been no GAAP pronouncement, financial accounting is often influenced by tax policy. In particular, tax positions which result in the deferral of income or in the acceleration of deductions must generally be consistent with a company's financial statements. Thus the accounting for derivative instruments used in the preparation of Japanese financial statements (and for MoF and Bank of Japan regulatory reporting by branches and subsidiaries of overseas companies in Japan) will, unless there is some other theoretical justification, usually be consistent with the accounting methods used to prepare the annual tax return.

Off-balance-sheet transactions (including futures, options, forward foreign exchange contracts and interest rate swaps) have usually been recorded on a settlement (cash) basis. For example, until very recently, option premiums paid (for short-term options) were immediately expensed and all premiums received were taken to income. This is still the tax accounting method (see discussion below).

This tax-related approach is also evident in the lack of mark-to-market accounting in Japan. Positions recorded in the balance sheet are generally carried at cost or, in certain cases, at the lower of cost and market value. Gains and losses on off-balance-sheet positions are not recorded until final settlement. The major exception to this is currency spot, forward and option positions held by banks — these must all be marked-to-market for financial reporting purposes.

Swap accounting in Japan

The assumption made in the accounting rules for swaps in Japan is that most interest rate swap transactions are entered into with the intention of adjusting the interest rates on long-term financing transactions. For such transactions, net payments and receipts are recognised as adjustments to the interest paid or received with respect to the underlying financial asset or liability.

It thus follows that income and expenses relating to interest rate swap transactions are recognised in accordance with each company's method of accounting for interest. All large and medium sized audited companies and all financial institutions are required to account for their interest income and expense on an accrual basis. Small companies are still permitted to use cash accounting.

For an interest rate swap, the periodic net settlements are accrued at each reporting date (usually 31 March for Japanese companies, but also at 30 September for financial institutions such as banks and securities houses).

Straight currency swaps are accounted for as series of forward foreign exchange contracts. Banks must mark these forward transactions to market, whilst non-banking companies will usually amortise the premium or discount over the period of each forward contract. (For speculative forward transactions, non-banks will not recognise any gain or loss until settlement date.)

Cross-currency interest rate swaps are split into their separate constituent parts — an exchange of principal at the start and the end of the contracted swap period; with periodic interest payments between these two dates. A cross-currency interest rate swap is thus accounted for as a forward foreign exchange contract (the exchange of principal), together with an interest rate swap (the periodic settlement of interest).

Any fees paid or received relating to a swap are amortised on a straight line basis over the life of the swap. However, if the swap contract covers a period of less than one year, any fees paid or received would usually be expensed.

Any gains or losses from early termination of a swap agreement will immediately impact income.

Corporate tax treatment

The tax treatment of swap transactions is generally the same as the accounting treatment outlined above. However, it is doubtful whether the estimated accrual of interest between settlement dates will result in a tax deductible expense prior to the actual payment date of the interest.

The treatment of swap fees received also differs. Swap fees paid are amortised over the life of the swap for tax purposes as they are for financial accounting. However, any fees received relating to a swap must be included in taxable income on receipt. Fees specifically and separately identified in the original swap agreement as being either (1) a payment for the continuing administration of the swap or (2) a payment related to the assumption of any credit risk, may be accrued over the life of the swap rather than recorded as income on receipt.

If a swap (or indeed any other financial) transaction is so structured that significant expenses are accelerated or income deferred, the tax authorities in a tax examination may possibly require a different accounting treatment from that outlined above in order to prevent any distortion of taxable income.

Other taxes

Periodic currency swap payments have been characterised by the Japanese tax authority as adjustments to interest for the purpose of determining the timing of interest and expense on an associated debt obligation. However, since the payments are not deemed to be with respect to any *specific* debt obligation, they are not treated as interest for withholding tax purposes. Thus, where a Japanese resident makes swap payments to a non-resident, there will be no withholding tax on the outbound payment.

Gross commissions paid on swap transactions within Japan between Japanese residents are subject to the 3% Japanese consumption tax. The interest payments themselves and any swap fees are not subject to consumption tax.

Option-based swap derivatives

It is often the case that use of derivative financial instruments, particularly "tailored" OTC instruments, will be innovative and consequently the tax (and hence often the accounting) treatment will depend on the interpretation of the particular case by the local tax office. As there has not yet been any specific pronouncements by the Ministry of Finance on swaps of any type, the accounting treatment for swap derivatives and related products is even less clear-cut.

The major swap-related derivative instruments (caps, collars, floors and swaptions) all involve some form of option feature. It is thus necessary to outline briefly some of the current issues in accounting for options in Japan.

Until very recently, the accounting treatment for options was identical to the tax treatment. Option premiums paid were immediately expensed (unless the option term was greater than one year, in which case the premium was deferred and amortised over the option term) and premiums received were taken to income. This treatment resulted from the tax principle that the receipt of an option premium is considered to be an incidence of taxation on the basis that the option writer is not obliged to return the value of the cash premium received. The fact that the writer assumes a liability on writing the option does not change this principle because the eventual liability may be indeterminate in amount and is contingent upon a future event.

Following concerns over recent abuse of these accounting rules — particularly by certain large Japanese city banks, who had been writing large volumes of options close to their year end, thus boosting earnings with the associated premium income — the MoF recently stated its intention to change the accounting rules for options so that such a distortion was no longer possible.

With the exception of currency options held by banks, option premiums paid or received should be capitalised and deferred until exercise, sale or expiry. On sale or expiry, any gain or loss should be immediately recognised. On exercise into a non-cash asset, the premium (together with the strike price) should be capitalised as the cost of that underlying asset. On exercise into cash, any gain or loss should immediately be recognised. Currency options held by banks are excluded from these new rules. Instead, the premiums related to currency options must be carried in the banks' balance sheets and marked-to-market at each reporting date.[1]

Swaptions (options to enter into a swap agreement) are an innovative product in the Japanese markets. As such the tax (and hence, in many cases, the financial accounting) treatment will depend on the tax authority's view of the nature of the swaption premium. If the cost of the swaption is viewed purely as an option premium, it should be capitalised in the balance sheet and any earnings impact deferred until exercise, sale or expiry of the swaption. On sale or expiry, there will be an immediate realised gain or loss. On exercise, the premium should be amortised over the life of the underlying swap. One possible alternative (depending on the wording of the swaption contract) would be to treat the payment for the swaption as a swap fee and account for it accordingly. Other more complex treatments could arise from different constructions of the swaption.

The treatment of caps, collars and floors will also depend on the tax office's view of their purpose and the structure of the individual instrument. In general the cap premium should be amortised over the period of the underlying notional loan contract. However, for tax purposes, if there is no loan being hedged, the cap premium must be accounted for as an option contract.

Swap-related hedging instruments

As hedges for open swap positions, the status of futures and FRA accounting should briefly be mentioned. Gains and losses on futures are recognised on a settlement date basis. If settled by physical delivery, any gain or loss on the future is included in the acquisition cost of the underlying asset. The related margin payments are carried in the balance sheet until settlement.

FRAs have been deemed by the MoF to be "gambling" (as defined in law) and are hence prohibited. With the establishment of TIFFE, off-balance-sheet transactions have increased in volume in Tokyo, and the MoF appears to ignore FRA transactions that are entered into by foreign banks in Japan. FRA trading by Japanese banks continues to be strictly controlled.

Industry differences

In comparing the tax and accounting rules for financial instruments in Japan, it is sometimes the case that different industries will use different accounting methods. For example, as noted above, banks must mark currency and currency derivatives to market. Insurance companies' income must be divided between net premium income and capital gains — the latter are not distributable to policy holders and shareholders (although this restriction on distribution policy is currently under MoF review). Thus further information should be sought before assuming that a particular accounting treatment is appropriate for any particular company.

The future

The Ministry of Finance and the various industry self-regulatory bodies continue to review accounting and reporting practices in Japan. Tax law and regulations are also undergoing review. It is not clear what changes will ultimately be made. However, it is expected that financial accounting will improve and will increasingly reflect the economic substance of financial derivative transactions.

Notes

1. At the time of writing this chapter (December1990) these new rules have not been finalised. Furthermore, the changes are intended to affect only *financial* reporting. The tax authorities have not yet decided whether they will modify their reporting requirements to reflect these changes or whether they will accept a divergence between the tax and accounting treatments for options. A final decision on the fiscal 1990/1 tax position will probably not be reached until close to the financial year end in March 1991.

Mark Rhys is a UK Chartered Accountant and is currently on assignment as a manager in Arthur Andersen's Tokyo office Capital Markets Consulting Group.

Chapter 40d: Accounting guidelines for swaps in Australia

Stuart J Robertson
Arthur Andersen & Co (Sydney)

Australia is in the early stages of developing a comprehensive framework of accounting policy for financial instruments. There have been a number of recent developments in accounting standards, exposure drafts and discussion papers which indirectly impact upon the treatment of swaps and swap derivatives. However, in the absence of specific provisions, general practice in Australia tends to follow that outlined for the United Kingdom.

Application of accounting standards in Australia

For most companies in Australia, compliance with Approved Accounting Standards issued by the Accounting Standards Review Board (ASRB) is compelled through the provisions of Section 298 of the Corporations Act.

The ASRB is a body established by legislation rather than by the major Australian accounting bodies. There are, however, certain types of entity which are exempt from the accounting requirements of the Corporations Act and which are significant users of financial instruments.

Both banking corporations and life insurance corporations are permitted to comply instead with the accounting requirements of their own relevant legislation. In neither case does this legislation require compliance with Approved Accounting Standards. The major Australian accounting bodies issue Australian Accounting Standards, which are now essentially parallel to Approved Accounting Standards. Auditors who are members of either accounting body are in theory required to qualify their audit reports in respect of any departures from Australian Accounting Standards. In practice, auditors will generally concur with departures from standards if those departures are consistent with industry practice.

The result of this situation is that banks and life insurers, unlike other companies, have an ability to depart from accounting standards. This situation is not immediately critical to the treatment of swaps due to the limited relevance of existing accounting standards. It will, however, need to be resolved in the near future as a more comprehensive body of relevant accounting standards emerges.

Significant current accounting issues

Balance sheet recognition

Internationally, the debate over swap accounting has generally focused on issues of valuation and income statement recognition. The off-balance-sheet treatment of "swap principal" obligations and entitlements has been broadly accepted.

This is not the case in Australia, where much debate has taken place over the past two years on the acceptability of off-balance-sheet treatment. The catalyst for this debate was the issuance in April 1988 of exposure draft ED44, "Extinguishment of Debt". ED44 contained a broadly-drawn prohibition on the setting-off of assets and liabilities in all except very limited circumstances. These circumstances would not have generally been applicable to swap transactions.

Both financial institutions and corporate users of financial instruments generally interpreted ED44 as requiring swaps, forward foreign exchange contracts and derivatives to be brought on balance sheet. At its most extreme, it was argued, ED44 could have resulted in, for example, a cross-currency swap between Australian dollars and a currency other than US dollars, which was entered into purely as a hedge, effectively tripling the balance sheet impact of the hedged exposure if the future obligations to exchange Australian dollars against US dollars and US dollars against the third currency were to be brought to account in the balance sheet.

When Approved Accounting Standard ASRB1014 "Set-off and Extinguishment of Debt" was issued subsequently, it contained a prohibition on set-off which was broadly consistent with ED44. The commentary to the current version of ASRB1014 does, however, note that:

> This Standard does not establish criteria for determining whether transactions or events should be accounted for as separate assets and liabilities. In relation to the set-off provisions, it is concerned only with preventing the omission of assets and liabilities from the face of the balance sheet by means of set-off where no right of set-off exists. The Standard does not therefore establish whether transactions such as cross-currency and interest-rate swaps, foreign currency forward exchange agreements and leveraged leases give rise to separate assets and liabilities.

Exposure Drafts ED42C and ED42D address the definition and recognition of assets and liabilities, describing forward exchange contracts and "hedge contracts" as "contracts equally proportionately unperformed". Such contracts are noted to be not generally brought to account, although balance sheet recognition may sometimes be appropriate. Most commentators have formed the view that commitments to re-exchange principal on cross-currency swaps, being analogous to forward foreign exchange contracts, are "contracts equally proportionately unperformed" which do not give rise to assets and liabilities as defined by ED42C and ED42D. Hence the set-off provisions of ASRB1014 are not considered to be relevant.

There is, however, some resistance to this view. The Australian Accounting Research Foundation recently issued Discussion Paper No 14, "Financial Reporting for Financial Institutions and Accounting for Financial Instruments". This paper has come down in favour of balance sheet recognition for all swap transactions — even interest rate swaps, where no exchanges of principal occur. The debate over balance sheet recognition should not be regarded as finalised.

In summary, current generally accepted practice in Australia is consistent with the rest of the world in treating swaps as off-balance-sheet instruments. However, it may not necessarily follow that this approach will remain unchallenged as a more comprehensive set of accounting standards develops.

Foreign currency translation

ASRB1012 "Foreign Currency Translation" has implications for swap accounting since it requires, with certain limited exceptions, that all foreign currency monetary items be translated at year-end spot rates, with gains and losses recorded in the profit and loss account.

ASRB1012 then requires that "hedge transactions" also be translated at year-end spot rates, with gains and losses also recorded in the profit and loss account. The forward exchange leg of a cross-currency swap would be recognised as a hedge transaction provided that the swap can be identified as:

> action taken with the object of avoiding or minimising possible adverse financial effects of movements in exchange rates.

ASRB1012 requires a "separate transaction" approach whereby the hedged exposure and the hedging transaction are revalued and accounted for separately. If the hedge is effective, the two revaluations will offset in the profit and loss account.

This is the only current Australian Standard which directly impacts upon swap accounting, except for the issues arising from ASRB1014 as discussed above.

Accelerated swaps

A number of Australian institutions have entered into accelerated swaps whereby all payments due on the fixed-rate leg of the swap are discharged by (usually) a single payment at commencement. Such transactions have generally been tax-driven.

In substance these transactions are financings, and should be accounted for as such. Nevertheless, it is believed that some institutions have treated the accelerated payment as, effectively, interest paid or received in advance.

Generally accepted accounting practice in Australia

Corporate users will have generally entered into swap transactions for hedging purposes. These users will accrue amounts payable or receivable as they arise, with the net effect being offset against the interest income or expense arising from the hedged transaction. If the swap is a hedge of an asset or liability that is marked to market, normal hedge accounting principals would require the swap to be also marked to market.

In the rare circumstances where a corporate uses swaps for speculative purposes those swaps should preferably be marked-to-market, although valuation at the lower of cost or market is probably still the more common treatment.

Financial institutions will generally account for hedging swaps on an accruals basis. Whilst the trend in respect of trading swap portfolios is clearly towards mark to market, it is understood that accrual accounting is still quite widely used. As with the rest of the world, Australian financial institutions which apply mark-to-market accounting are attempting to address the issues of provision for future administrative costs, credit risk, reinvestment risk and fee income.

Chapter 41: Principal tax issues arising from swap transactions

The rapid development of swap transactions and, indeed, other types of new financial instruments has meant that in virtually all countries many features of the transactions are not encompassed specifically by existing taxation laws. This has meant that general taxation laws not specifically designed to deal with swap transactions have often had to be adapted or interpreted in order to provide a tax regime for such transactions. A feature, therefore, of the taxation position in most countries is uncertainty as to the strict law and frequently an application of agreed practices to overcome this problem.

Perhaps the most important problem which has arisen in relation to the taxation treatment of swap transactions is the fact that although most swap transactions are closely related to debt obligations and, in particular, periodic payments under swap agreements are calculated on the basis of interest rates, the swap transaction does not itself create debt obligations and the periodic payments are not actually interest under most tax systems. Many countries have detailed taxation rules for dealing with actual debt obligations and interest payments, but under a proper interpretation of tax law, swap transactions fall outside of these provisions in most countries. This can often lead to inconsistencies in the taxation treatment of commercially similar transactions.

The main tax issues which have to be addressed in most countries when analysing the taxation treatment of swap transactions are as follows:

- whether tax relief is available for the periodic swap payments and the timing of any such relief (ie, whether on a payment or an accruals basis);
- whether tax has to be withheld at source from swap payments, especially where they are paid across national borders;
- on what basis should income from swap transactions be recognised (this may be especially important in relation to hybrid and other complex swap transactions);
- whether tax relief is available for up-front payment on swap transactions, such as arrangement fees;
- whether problems arise in relation to the taxation treatment of foreign exchange differences with respect to currency swaps.

Chapter 41a: Taxation of swaps in the United Kingdom and Continental Europe

Eric Tomsett
Touche Ross (London)

(1) The UK

Obtaining tax relief for periodic swap payments

Strict position under UK tax law

UK taxation law, with its rigid distinction between capital and revenue items and its uneven treatment of capital transactions whereby they may fall out of account entirely for taxation purposes (with respect to both taxability and tax deduction) unless covered by specific legislation, is particularly unsuitable to deal with new financial instruments such as swaps.

Where swap transactions are undertaken between banks or other financial traders which carry out such transactions as part of their normal trading operations, the periodic swap payments would represent normal trading expenses which would correspondingly be deductible on an accruals basis. In other circumstances, however, swap transactions would represent capital transactions such that the periodic swap payments would be non-deductible as capital items. This will be the case, for example, where a general trading company undertook a swap transaction to hedge a borrowing, even where the borrowing was for the purposes of its trade, except where the borrowing represented merely temporary financial accommodation such that it could be regarded as part of the company's circulating rather than fixed capital. This would also be the case where a bank or financial trader used a swap transaction in relation to a long-term borrowing which was part of the overall financing of the business rather than a current transaction with a client or customer. (It is often forgotten that interest itself or anything other than short-term borrowings was non-deductible for UK taxation purposes under general principles until specific legislation was introduced to allow relief.)

The position is even worse for a company which has the status of an investment company under UK tax law (this includes the parent companies of many groups). Such companies can only obtain a deduction for expenditure if it represents either an expense of managing the company's investments or a charge on income such as an annual payment. Periodic swap payments have not been regarded as being within the definition of management expenses, and would rarely represent annual payments under a proper interpretation of the definition of such payments as a fundamental condition for a payment to be treated as an "annual payment" for UK taxation purposes is that it must represent a pure income profit to the recipient, ie, be pure income to them rather than a receipt which represents an element of income against which deductions may be available.

Accordingly, under a strict application of UK tax law the periodic swap payments on many swap transactions are not deductible against the company's income.

Inland Revenue practice

As the treatment of periodic swap payments under a strict application of UK tax law was clearly out of line with commercial reality and would have prevented the development of swap transactions in the UK, the Inland Revenue sought to be helpful by stating to participants in the swap markets in 1977 that they were prepared to treat recurrent swap fees as if they were annual payments such that tax relief might be available as a charge on income in the period in which the swap fee is paid. Annual payments are, however, subject to deduction of basic rate income tax at source. As such withholding would have made many swap transactions uneconomic, in September 1979 the Inland Revenue further indicated that where periodic swap payments were made to or by banks carrying on business in the UK in the ordinary course of their business, the payment could be made without deduction of tax (this broadly mirrored the way in which interest payments are normally treated for taxation purposes).

The above statements by the Inland Revenue were not issued as formal Statements of Practice or concessions at that time and were subsequently criticised as favouring banks as compared to financial traders engaged in the swap markets who did not have banking status. In order to overcome this criticism the Inland Revenue practice was formalised into an extra-statutory concession dated 14 March 1989, which also extended the favoured treatment accorded to banks carrying on business in the UK to swap dealers recognised by the Bank of England or the Securities Association.

Under the concession, annual swap fees which are not deductible as trading expenses under strict law will be treated as if they were annual payments for UK corporation tax purposes. Where such fees are paid by or to a recognised UK bank or swap dealer in the ordinary course of its trade, deduction of the fees as a charge will not be conditional upon tax having been deducted and accounted for to the Inland Revenue. Where such swap fees are paid by a trading company for trading purposes they will be allowed as a trading expense rather than a charge on income.

Withholding of tax on swap payments

It is vital in practice that there is no withholding of tax at source on payments under a swap transaction as otherwise the transaction will often be rendered totally uneconomic.

Under a strict application of UK law there is no particular problem here as a swap payment will represent neither interest nor an annual payment where withholding of basic rate income tax from payments is normally required. Accordingly, there should be no requirement to withhold tax from swap payments, even when they are made to a non-resident counterparty located in a non-treaty country, eg, a tax haven. The treatment of periodic swap payments as annual payments in order to seek to obtain a deduction for UK corporation tax purposes, however, brings with it the potential requirement to withhold UK income tax at the basic rate (currently 25%) from each swap payment. The Inland Revenue practice formalised in the extra-statutory concession of 14 March 1989 (see above), however, allows periodic swap payments to be made to or by a recognised bank or swap dealer in the UK without any withholding of income tax, even if the swap payments are treated as annual payments in order to obtain a corporation tax deduction. These particular privileges of recognised banks and (since 14 March 1989) swap dealers has meant that most swap transactions in the UK involve such banks or swap dealers in order to ensure the favourable tax treatment.

Where a UK counterparty makes a swap payment to a foreign counterparty, the extra-statutory concession will often not apply (eg, where the UK counterparty is a general trading company or group rather than a bank or swap dealer) such that withholding of tax may potentially apply. Where, however, the other counterparty is resident in a country with which the UK has a double taxation treaty, exemption from UK withholding will often be available under either the "other income" or the "business profits" article of the double taxation treaty. It is necessary, however, to make a claim to the UK tax authorities for such relief before any payments are made gross.

Recognition of income

Banks and other swap traders will normally recognise income from swap transactions on an accruals basis as part of their trading profits. Other companies receiving income from swap transactions are generally required to treat such income as a source under Case III of Schedule D. Such income is taxed only in the period in which it is received, but suffers disadvantages in relation to the offset of losses as a company will not normally be able to offset a trading loss brought forward against such Case III income.

As it is a basic principle of UK tax law that profits should not be recognised until realised, the mark-to-market approach to accounting for swap transactions will not strictly be acceptable for UK taxation purposes as it would result in recognising unrealised profits.

Arrangement fees and other up-front payments

Where a swap transaction involves a one-off up-front payment, such as an arrangement fee, further taxation problems will arise. Except where such payments are made by banks or swap dealers in the ordinary course of their business, such payments will often represent capital items which are therefore not deductible against income for UK taxation purposes. The special tax relief available for the incidental costs of raising loan finance will not assist here as a swap transaction itself does not involve arranging loan finance.

The problem of the non-deductibility of such payments is sometimes overcome by building the fees into the periodic swap payment rather than charging them separately.

Other swap transactions

The complex types of swap transactions which are now being undertaken will themselves often create further taxation problems. For example, the buying and selling of swaps, the making of payments for the early termination of a swap agreement and swap options will all often involve one-off payments. Such payments will often represent capital items under a proper application of UK tax law with consequent problems of non-deductibility. Considerable taxation dangers can therefore arise in relation to such transactions.

Foreign exchange problems on currency swaps

Currency swaps can create additional taxation difficulties with surprising results if the swap is regarded as a capital rather than a trading transaction.

Currency swaps are often used to hedge a foreign currency exposure, but the application of UK tax law can result in a fragmentation of the transaction for taxation purposes which may destroy the commercial hedge.

For example, if a UK company borrowed $100m for 10 years and entered into a 10-year swap of the $100m for £60m, at the end of the 10 years it would receive back $100m in return for a payment of £60m. If the $100m is then used to repay the loan which was, for example, then equivalent to £150m because of exchange rate movements over the 10-year period, for tax purposes the company will be treated as having disposed at the end of the 10-year period of $100m for £150m (on repayment of the loan) and as having acquired the dollars not at the end of the 10-year period but at the commencement of the swap transaction such that their cost will only be £60m plus indexation allowance over the 10-year period. Hence a substantial capital gain will be realised on the currency swap transactions whilst a corresponding non-deductible capital loss will have arisen on the repayment of the matching loan as there is no tax relief in the UK for exchange losses on long-term foreign currency loans.

If, alternatively, the UK company borrowed £60m for a 10-year period and entered into a swap agreement whereby the £60m was swapped for $100m for a 10-year period, the re-exchange of the $100m for £60m in year 10 would be treated as a disposal for the purposes of tax on capital gains of $100m in year one. If the $100m required to meet the swap obligation in year 10 is acquired in year 10 at a cost of £150m, the company will incur a capital gains loss in year one of £90m, but it will not be possible to determine the result until year 10.

The above anomalies arise from the treatment of transactions for capital gains purposes as occurring at the time the contract is made rather than completed, provided that the contract is unconditional.

Proposal for a new tax regime for swap transactions

In order to try to overcome the current unsatisfactory position in relation to the taxation treatment of swap transactions, the Inland Revenue issued a consultative document entitled "Tax Treatment of Swap Fees" on 14 March 1989. This proposed the introduction of new legislation to deal specifically with swap transactions. The principal features of the proposals were as follows:

- Periodic swap payments would be deemed to be interest payments for most of the purposes of tax law, although deduction of tax at source would not be required from such payments, except where made to a non-resident by a person not undertaking swap transactions as part of a financial trade.

- Periodic swap payments would only be deductible if (i) the interest rates on which the swap fees were based were commercial rates and the fees payable were no more than would be paid in an arm's length transaction; (ii) the charging and payment dates for each party to the swap agreement were simultaneous; and (iii) swap fees were paid at least annually.

- Subject to rules (i), (ii) and (iii) above, periodic swap fees paid to UK residents wholly and exclusively for trade purposes or paid to non-residents in the course of financial trade would always be deductible, on an accruals basis, in computing trading profits. In such circumstances the corresponding swap fee received would be a trading receipt chargeable on an accruals basis. In other circumstances, swap payments would be allowed as charges on income and payments received taxed on the receipt as interest.

- Periodic swap fees that did not satisfy the criteria for deductibility to the paying company would nevertheless remain chargeable on the recipient.

- Where the periodic swap fees were deductible for taxation purposes, initial arrangement fees relating to the swap would also be deductible by being treated as if they were an incidental cost of obtaining loan finance.

Serious objections were raised to these proposals by the main participants in the swap market. As a result of this, the Inland Revenue agreed to look at the proposals again and it has yet to be announced how they may be revised.

(2) Continental Europe

Implications of accounting practice

In continental European countries the computation of taxable profits follows the normal accounting treatment of the transactions much more closely than is the case in the UK or, indeed, in other countries such as the US and Australia. Accordingly, the way in which a swap is accounted for in continental European countries will usually be of crucial significance in relation to the taxation treatment.

Most European countries follow accounting policies laid down by international accounting standards and, additionally, European Community countries are subject to the provisions of European harmonisation directives.

In continental European countries, however, the concept developed in the UK and the US of "mark-to-market" for accounting purposes in order to notionally close out all open positions at the year end is not generally followed. This is because it potentially recognises unrealised profits as well as unrealised losses which is considered to conflict with the prudence concept fundamental to accounting in most continental European countries.

There are some exceptions to the above general principles. In Denmark, financial institutions may adopt a mark-to-market policy and this will normally be followed for taxation purposes. In France, with respect to currency swaps, the taxation authorities may not, however, accept a situation where a loss may be recognised, but an expected profit on a matched swap is not. French tax law generally requires unrealised profits and losses from currency fluctuations to be recognised for tax purposes.

Obtaining tax relief for periodic swap payments

Generally there are few problems in European countries concerning the obtaining of tax relief for periodic swap payments. Normally they would be regarded as a business expense and the capital/revenue distinctions which are of such importance in the UK would not arise. In Germany, however, non-banks may have some difficulties concerning tax relief for the purposes of the trade tax (local municipal income tax) if the swap is related to a debt with a life of more than one year, as only 50% of the financing costs on such debt is normally deductible for trade tax purposes.

Withholding of tax on swap payments

In continental European countries periodic swap fee payments are not regarded as interest so that there is no question of interest withholding taxes applying. Normally such swap payments would not come within any other withholding tax provisions and, in practice, withholding tax problems have not normally been encountered.

Recognition of income

As indicated above, this normally follows accounting policy in continental European countries.

Arrangement fees and other up-front payments

Only in Denmark are such fees potentially disallowable. There, if a swap has a planned life of two years or more no deduction is available for an arrangement fee.

In other countries the issue normally is whether such arrangement fees can be deducted for tax purposes in full in the year of payment, or whether they should be amortised over the life of the swap.

Chapter 41b: Taxation of swaps in the United States

William G Dodge and Debra Davis
Deloitte & Touche (US)

Obtaining tax relief for periodic swap payments

For US tax purposes, periodic swap payments will normally represent ordinary expenses deductible against income in the period to which they relate.

There is some uncertainty as to whether the notional gross payments under a swap transaction should be treated as items of gross income and expense in situations where the computation of gross income is of importance for tax purposes, or alternatively, whether only the net payment due under the swap transaction should be taken into account. The general view is, however, that only the net payment should be taken into account as an item of gross income or expense.

Withholding of tax on swap payments

US income tax regulations under Section 863 provide source rules for income from an interest rate swap denominated in the taxpayer's functional currency (generally, the currency used by an entity for accounting purposes). For most purposes, interest rate swap income is sourced by reference to the taxpayer's residence. Therefore, although there are currently no rules which specifically address whether such payments are subject to US withholding tax, the regulations under Section 863 effectively eliminate the risk of a 30% withholding tax on payments to foreign parties because non-US parties have only foreign source income.

The regulations under Section 988 contain similar rules with respect to swap contracts which are not denominated in the taxpayer's functional currency (hereafter referred to as currency swaps). Income from periodic payments on currency swaps is generally sourced by reference to the residence of the taxpayer, thereby again essentially eliminating the risk that payments made to a foreign swap counterparty would be subject to US withholding tax since such counterparty would not have US source income.

Recognition of income

Periodic interim payments made pursuant to an interest rate swap will normally be recognised as ordinary income according to the taxpayer's method of accounting so long as that method of accounting clearly reflects income.

Periodic payments made pursuant to a currency swap contract must be segregated into an interest rate portion and a currency exchange portion. The portion relating to interest is computed by treating payments made under the swap as payments made pursuant to a hypothetical borrowing denominated in the currency in which payments are made.

Periodic payments received under the swap are treated as being received pursuant to a hypothetical loan that is denominated in the currency in which the payments are received. The interest expense and income is recognised under the interest amortisation principles of US tax law (including the original issue discount provisions). These principles must be independently applied to both receipts and payments. Exchange gain or loss is computed on the hypothetical interest amounts and recognised currently.

Under case law, the sale of an interest rate swap would result in gain or loss that would be capital in nature. The character of payments made or received to close out an interest rate contract is less clear. Absent specific guidance, it may be possible to take the position that if a payment is made or received to terminate an interest rate swap, the resulting gain or loss should be ordinary.

With respect to currency swaps, exchange differences arising on the final exchange of the principal amounts represent ordinary gain or loss for purposes of US taxation. Such gain or loss will generally only be recognised on the sale, exchange, repayment or redemption of the instrument. There will normally be no requirement to mark-to-market in respect of currency swaps or interest rate swaps.

Where a currency swap is used for hedging for US tax purposes, the underlying liability and the swap may be integrated and treated as a single transaction if the taxpayer complies with special documentation procedures prescribed by regulations under Section 988. No similar rules are provided with respect to integration of interest rate swaps.

Arrangement fees and other up-front payments

Where arrangement fees or other lump sum up-front payments are required under an interest rate swap agreement, such payments will normally be deductible by amortisation over the swap period by the payer. No specific guidance is given with respect to the method of amortisation to be used except that any such method must clearly reflect income.

In the case of a currency rate swap, any up-front payment must be broken down into two portions. The portion attributable to the difference in the values of the periodic interim payments (essentially, the interest element) and the portion attributable to the difference in the swap exchange rate and the spot rate on the date the contract is entered into. The amount of the premium attributable to interest is amortised under the principles of economic accrual. The portion attributable to the exchange rate difference is recognised as the principal amounts are taken into account.

Other swap transactions

Where swap transactions such as a zero-coupon swap involve the receipt or payment of lump sum amounts, they will normally be amortised over the life of the transaction. There are, however, no clear rules as to the precise basis of such amortisation.

Chapter 41c: Taxation of swaps in Japan

Katsushima & Co (Tokyo)[1]

Obtaining tax relief for periodic swap payments

Periodic swap fees will normally be fully deductible for Japanese taxation purposes. The deduction would be available on an accruals rather than a paid basis.

Withholding tax on swap payments

For Japanese tax purposes periodic swap fees are classified as service income. On this basis there is no requirement to withhold Japanese tax at source from such payments whether the payment is to another corporation within Japan or by a Japanese domestic corporation to a foreign corporation.

Actual interest payments made by parties to a swap transaction, are, however, subject to a 20% Japanese withholding tax, unless this is reduced by a double taxation treaty where the payment is to a non-resident of Japan located in a country with which Japan has an appropriate double taxation treaty. Usually the treaty reduction of interest withholding tax is to 10%.

Recognition of income

For Japanese tax purposes periodic swap fees receivable should be fully taken into income at the time the swap agreement is entered into as it is regarded as service income for a service which has already been provided.

Actual interest income received and paid by the parties to a swap transaction would be recognised on an accruals basis over the term of the swap agreement.

Arrangement fees and other up-front payments

Lump sum payments at the commencement of a swap transaction in relation to the arranging of the transaction should be amortised rateably over the term of the agreement and the amount amortised each year will be allowed as a deduction for Japanese tax purposes.

Payments for the early termination of a swap transaction would be fully deductible in the year of payment for Japanese tax purposes, provided that there was a *bona fide* business reason for the termination. Similarly, one-off payments on the purchase or sale of a swap agreement would be taxable or deductible in the year of receipt or payment.

Other swap transactions

Where swap transactions involve foreign currencies, income and expenditure realised in a foreign currency is taken into account at its yen equivalent using the exchange rate in effect at the time of receipt or payment. However, long-term receivables and payables which do not mature within one year from the end of the current fiscal period should be recorded at their historic exchange rate with any exchange gain or loss being recognised at the time the amount is received or the payment satisfied.

Short-term receivables and payables in a foreign currency are generally marked-to-market at the end of each tax year using the exchange rate in force on that date. It is possible, however, for a company to elect to use the historical exchange rate.

It should be noted that swap transactions have only been generally allowed in Japan for two to three years and no circulars have been issued indicating how Japanese tax law is to be interpreted in relation to swap transactions. Accordingly, great care is needed before any sophisticated swap agreements are entered into, especially if any motive of minimising Japanese taxation is involved.

Notes

1. Member firm of DRT International.

Chapter 41d: Taxation of swaps in Australia

Leonard Khaw and Glen Lawrence
Deloitte Ross Tohmatsu (Sydney)

Obtaining tax relief for periodic swap payments

For Australian tax purposes periodic swap fees received and paid on an interest rate swap are normally regarded as inherently of a revenue nature on the basis that the swap will effectively alter the interest rate exposure of the counterparties such that they have the characteristics of an interest hedge contract. Accordingly, such periodic swap fees will be deductible as revenue expenses. This approach has been confirmed by the Australian Tax Office on the basis that the periodic swap fees are attributable to existing interest expense, subject to the qualification that where the underlying interest obligations of the parties are significantly different a decision would need to be made as to whether the fees were really of a revenue nature. If they were not they may not be deductible from income.

Where, however, there is no underlying interest obligation a tax payer would need to be able to show that the periodic swap payments were incurred in carrying on a business or in producing assessable income, thus requiring a connection to be demonstrated with the underlying business if the periodic swap fees are to be deductible.

With regards to the timing of assessability and deductibility of periodic swap fees, the time at which such amounts are due and payable under the swap contract will be the time at which the income or expense is recognised for tax purposes.

The basis of the above analysis is that the payments between the swap counterparties should not be regarded as interest, but only amounts payable which arise from separate contractual obligations between the parties. Therefore, Australian tax law dealing with the deductiblility of interest expense on an accruals basis cannot necessarily be relied upon in the case of swap payments. Nevertheless, the Australian taxation authorities may be prepared to allow deductions for swap payments on an accruals basis where swap income is also brought into account on a similar accruals basis.

Withholding of tax on swap payments

Swap payments would not normally be regarded as amounts of interest or in the nature of interest and therefore should not give rise to an Australian withholding tax liability when paid by an Australian company to a non-resident of Australia. In general terms the Australian taxation authorities have accepted that such swap payments should not be subject to any withholding tax.

Recognition of income

As indicated above, swap receipts will generally be assessable when the amount is due and payable under the swap agreement. However, an accruals basis may be accepted if it is applied consistently to both income and expense.

Arrangement fees and other up-front payments

Arrangement fees paid at the commencement of the swap transaction would normally be regarded as being on revenue account and would be deductible when the payment is made, provided that the swap contract can be regarded as a hedge on revenue account.

Where the rights to receive swap payments under a swap contract are sold for a one-off receipt/payment or a one-off payment is made to terminate a swap agreement, the one-off amounts will normally be assessable or deductible when received or paid, again provided that the swap contract is regarded as being a hedge on revenue account.

Other provisions

Rights under swap contracts may constitute assets which are subject to Australian capital gains tax provisions. Any disposal of such rights will therefore need to be examined to determine the extent of any assessable capital gain that may arise as a result of such a disposal.

Index

B

G

O

PQ

R

S

Other titles available from IFR Publishing

Warrants, Options and Convertibles

Subjects treated in this book include: income valuation, present value, parity values, arbitrage, delta hedging, premiums, pricing theory, time value, premium expansion, and spread trading. Those who perceive derivatives to be mathematical and theoretical will be gratified by the use of non-technical analogies and examples to explain the subject. *Author: Quintin Price, James Capel Price: £75/US$135*

The Currency Hedging Debate

This title examines the arguments for total hedging, partial hedging or none at all. The book looks at the effects of hedging on foreign exchange-related investments. The main arguments are outlined in a clear, concise manner, with contributions from both academics and practitioners, and the evidence on the performance of various funds is examined in detail *Editor: Lee R Thomas III, Investcorp Ltd Price: £75/US$135*

The IFR Financial Glossary — 2nd Edition

The Glossary, in one practical volume, removes all confusion surrounding financial language and the profusion of terms in today's capital markets. Alphabetically sorted, the Glossary provides clear and concise contextual definitions of the terms used in the main international and domestic financial markets. *Author: IFR Price: £29.50/US$53*

Interest Rate Risk Management

The authors explain how to measure, approach and understand interest rate risk, how the various solutions have emerged and how to use them. Particular attention is paid to the rationale behind risk management, and the reader is helped to acquire an objective and reasoned understanding of markets and instruments. *Authors: Torben Andersen, SDS Securities, Copenhagen and Rikki Hasan, MTM Consulting Ltd, London Price: £75/US$135*

Swap Financing

The book covers complex swap structures including amortising swaps, forward swaps, basis swaps, swaptions, debt warrant swaps and interest rate and currency swaps. The economics and pricing of swaps and the relationships between the structures of the various instruments are also discussed. Hundreds of detailed examples associated with swap transactions are supplied. *Author: Satyajit Das, TNT International Price: £95/US$170*

Loans to China

The book offers expert advice on the role of the Chinese legal system in financial transactions, together with a unique insight into a very different negotiating process. The publication also covers issues relating to the recovery and enforcement of non-performing loans. *Author: Clifford Chance Price: £75/US$135*

For more information, or to place an order for any of the above titles, write to: Dept DMS, IFR Publishing Ltd, South Quay Plaza II, 183 Marsh Wall, London E14 9FU, UK. Tel: Intl +44 71 538 5959